VW Passat
Owners Workshop Manual

Martynn Randall

Models covered

(4888 - 288)

Saloon & Estate with 1.9 litre (1896cc) & 2.0 litre (1968cc) Turbo-Diesel engines

Does NOT cover 1.6 litre diesel engine, petrol models, 4-Motion or CC models
Does NOT cover new range introduced Oct 2010

© Haynes Publishing 2011

ABCDE
FGHIJ
KLMNO
P

A book in the **Haynes Owners Workshop Manual Series**

ISBN **978 1 84425 888 8**

British Library Cataloguing in Publication Data
A catalogue record for this book is available from the British Library.

Printed in the USA

Haynes Publishing
Sparkford, Yeovil, Somerset BA22 7JJ, England

Haynes North America, Inc
861 Lawrence Drive, Newbury Park, California 91320, USA

Haynes Publishing Nordiska AB
Box 1504, 751 45 UPPSALA, Sverige

Contents

Contents

REPAIRS AND OVERHAUL

REFERENCE

The VW Passat models covered by this manual were first introduced to the UK in May 2005. Saloon and Estate models are available, equipped with a variety of engine sizes. This manual covers the 4-cylinder turbocharged diesel engine models of 1.9 or 2.0 litre capacity, with SOHC 8v or DOHC 16v cylinder heads. Until February 2008, all diesel engines were equipped with unit injectors, utilising a rocker shaft and arm assembly with a second set of camshaft lobes to compress each unit injector in turn to provide higher injection pressures, and increased accuracy of injection timing. After this date, a 2.0 litre DOHC 16v engine was available with conventional common rail fuel injection.

Fully-independent front and rear suspension is fitted, with the components attached to a subframe assembly.

A five- or six-speed manual gearbox is fitted as standard to all models, with a six-speed DSG (Direct Shift Gearbox) automatic transmission available as an option on most 2.0 litre models.

A wide range of standard and optional equipment is available within the model range to suit most tastes, including an anti-lock braking system and air conditioning.

For the home mechanic, the Passat is quite straightforward to maintain, and most of the items requiring frequent attention are easily accessible.

Your VW Passat Manual

The aim of this manual is to help you get the best value from your vehicle. It can do so in several ways. It can help you decide what work must be done (even should you choose to get it done by a garage). It will also provide information on routine maintenance and servicing, and give a logical course of action and diagnosis when random faults occur. However, it is hoped that you will use the manual by tackling the work yourself. On simpler jobs it may even be quicker than booking the car into a garage and going there twice, to leave and collect it. Perhaps most important, a lot of money can be saved by avoiding the costs a garage must charge to cover its labour and overheads.

The manual has drawings and descriptions to show the function of the various components so that their layout can be understood. Tasks are described and photographed in a clear step-by-step sequence. The illustrations are numbered by the Section number and paragraph number to which they relate – if there is more than one illustration per paragraph, the sequence is denoted alphabetically.

References to the 'left' or 'right' of the vehicle are in the sense of a person in the driver's seat, facing forwards.

Acknowledgements

Thanks are due to Draper Tools, who provided some of the workshop tools, and to all those people at Sparkford who helped in the production of this manual.

This manual is not a direct reproduction of the vehicle manufacturer's data, and its publication should not be taken as implying any technical approval by the vehicle manufacturers or importers.

We take great pride in the accuracy of information given in this manual, but vehicle manufacturers make alterations and design changes during the production run of a particular vehicle of which they do not inform us. No liability can be accepted by the authors or publishers for loss, damage or injury caused by any errors in, or omissions from, the information given.

Project vehicles

The main vehicle used in the preparation of this manual, and which appears in many of the photographic sequences, was a 2008 VW Passat 2.0 litre diesel Estate with common rail injection. Also included was a 1.9 litre Saloon and a 2.0 litre DOHC automatic model.

Working on your car can be dangerous. This page shows just some of the potential risks and hazards, with the aim of creating a safety-conscious attitude.

General hazards

Scalding

• Don't remove the radiator or expansion tank cap while the engine is hot.
• Engine oil, transmission fluid or power steering fluid may also be dangerously hot if the engine has recently been running.

Burning

• Beware of burns from the exhaust system and from any part of the engine. Brake discs and drums can also be extremely hot immediately after use.

Crushing

• When working under or near a raised vehicle, always supplement the jack with axle stands, or use drive-on ramps. *Never venture under a car which is only supported by a jack*.
• Take care if loosening or tightening high-torque nuts when the vehicle is on stands. Initial loosening and final tightening should be done with the wheels on the ground.

Fire

• Fuel is highly flammable; fuel vapour is explosive.
• Don't let fuel spill onto a hot engine.
• Do not smoke or allow naked lights (including pilot lights) anywhere near a vehicle being worked on. Also beware of creating sparks (electrically or by use of tools).
• Fuel vapour is heavier than air, so don't work on the fuel system with the vehicle over an inspection pit.
• Another cause of fire is an electrical overload or short-circuit. Take care when repairing or modifying the vehicle wiring.
• Keep a fire extinguisher handy, of a type suitable for use on fuel and electrical fires.

Electric shock

• Ignition HT and Xenon headlight voltages can be dangerous, especially to people with heart problems or a pacemaker. Don't work on or near these systems with the engine running or the ignition switched on.

• Mains voltage is also dangerous. Make sure that any mains-operated equipment is correctly earthed. Mains power points should be protected by a residual current device (RCD) circuit breaker.

Fume or gas intoxication

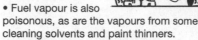

• Exhaust fumes are poisonous; they can contain carbon monoxide, which is rapidly fatal if inhaled. Never run the engine in a confined space such as a garage with the doors shut.
• Fuel vapour is also poisonous, as are the vapours from some cleaning solvents and paint thinners.

Poisonous or irritant substances

• Avoid skin contact with battery acid and with any fuel, fluid or lubricant, especially antifreeze, brake hydraulic fluid and Diesel fuel. Don't syphon them by mouth. If such a substance is swallowed or gets into the eyes, seek medical advice.
• Prolonged contact with used engine oil can cause skin cancer. Wear gloves or use a barrier cream if necessary. Change out of oil-soaked clothes and do not keep oily rags in your pocket.
• Air conditioning refrigerant forms a poisonous gas if exposed to a naked flame (including a cigarette). It can also cause skin burns on contact.

Asbestos

• Asbestos dust can cause cancer if inhaled or swallowed. Asbestos may be found in gaskets and in brake and clutch linings. When dealing with such components it is safest to assume that they contain asbestos.

Special hazards

Hydrofluoric acid

• This extremely corrosive acid is formed when certain types of synthetic rubber, found in some O-rings, oil seals, fuel hoses etc, are exposed to temperatures above 4000C. The rubber changes into a charred or sticky substance containing the acid. *Once formed, the acid remains dangerous for years. If it gets onto the skin, it may be necessary to amputate the limb concerned*.
• When dealing with a vehicle which has suffered a fire, or with components salvaged from such a vehicle, wear protective gloves and discard them after use.

The battery

• Batteries contain sulphuric acid, which attacks clothing, eyes and skin. Take care when topping-up or carrying the battery.
• The hydrogen gas given off by the battery is highly explosive. Never cause a spark or allow a naked light nearby. Be careful when connecting and disconnecting battery chargers or jump leads.

Air bags

• Air bags can cause injury if they go off accidentally. Take care when removing the steering wheel and trim panels. Special storage instructions may apply.

Diesel injection equipment

• Diesel injection pumps supply fuel at very high pressure. Take care when working on the fuel injectors and fuel pipes.

⚠ *Warning: Never expose the hands, face or any other part of the body to injector spray; the fuel can penetrate the skin with potentially fatal results.*

Remember...

DO

• Do use eye protection when using power tools, and when working under the vehicle.

• Do wear gloves or use barrier cream to protect your hands when necessary.

• Do get someone to check periodically that all is well when working alone on the vehicle.

• Do keep loose clothing and long hair well out of the way of moving mechanical parts.

• Do remove rings, wristwatch etc, before working on the vehicle – especially the electrical system.

• Do ensure that any lifting or jacking equipment has a safe working load rating adequate for the job.

DON'T

• Don't attempt to lift a heavy component which may be beyond your capability – get assistance.

• Don't rush to finish a job, or take unverified short cuts.

• Don't use ill-fitting tools which may slip and cause injury.

• Don't leave tools or parts lying around where someone can trip over them. Mop up oil and fuel spills at once.

• Don't allow children or pets to play in or near a vehicle being worked on.

The following pages are intended to help in dealing with common roadside emergencies and breakdowns. You will find more detailed fault finding information at the back of the manual, and repair information in the main chapters.

If your car won't start and the starter motor doesn't turn

- ☐ If it's a model with automatic transmission, make sure the selector is in the P or N position.
- ☐ Open the bonnet and make sure that the battery terminals are clean and tight.
- ☐ Switch on the headlights and try to start the engine. If the headlights go very dim when you're trying to start, the battery is probably flat. Get out of trouble by jump starting (see next page) using another car.

If your car won't start even though the starter motor turns as normal

- ☐ Is there fuel in the tank?
- ☐ Is there moisture on electrical components under the bonnet? Switch off the ignition, then wipe off any obvious dampness with a dry cloth. Spray a water-repellent aerosol product (WD-40 or equivalent) on fuel system electrical connectors like those shown in the photos.

A Check the condition and security of the battery connections

B Check the fuel injection system airflow meter wiring is secure

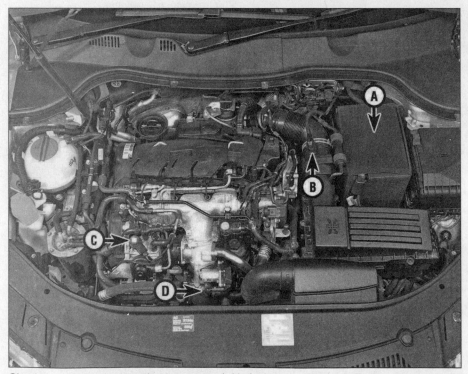

Check that electrical connections are secure (with the ignition switched off) and spray them with a water-dispersant spray like WD-40 if you suspect a problem due to damp.

C Check the fuel pump control valve sender wiring is secure

D Check the throttle valve motor wiring is secure

Jump starting

When jump-starting a car using a booster battery, observe the following precautions:

✔ Before connecting the booster battery, make sure that the ignition is switched off.

   Caution: Remove the key in case the central locking engages when the jump leads are connected

✔ Ensure that all electrical equipment (lights, heater, wipers, etc) is switched off.

✔ Take note of any special precautions printed on the battery case.

✔ Make sure that the booster battery is the same voltage as the discharged one in the vehicle.

✔ If the battery is being jump-started from the battery in another vehicle, the two vehicles MUST NOT TOUCH each other.

✔ Make sure that the transmission is in neutral (or PARK, in the case of automatic transmission).

HAYNES HINT Jump starting will get you out of trouble, but you must correct whatever made the battery go flat in the first place. There are three possibilities:

1 The battery has been drained by repeated attempts to start, or by leaving the lights on.

2 The charging system is not working properly (alternator drivebelt slack or broken, alternator wiring fault or alternator itself faulty).

3 The battery itself is at fault (electrolyte low, or battery worn out).

1 Connect one end of the red jump lead to the positive (+) terminal of the flat battery

2 Connect the other end of the red lead to the positive (+) terminal of the booster battery.

3 Connect one end of the black jump lead to the negative (-) terminal of the booster battery

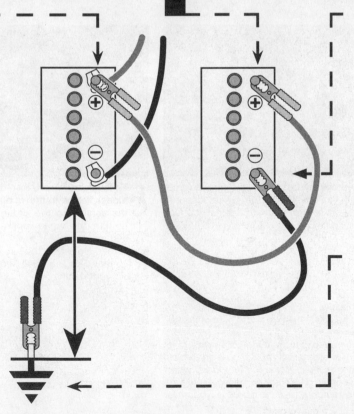

4 Connect the other end of the black jump lead to a bolt or bracket on the engine block, well away from the battery, on the vehicle to be started.

5 Make sure that the jump leads will not come into contact with the fan, drive-belts or other moving parts of the engine.

6 Start the engine using the booster battery and run it at idle speed. Switch on the lights, rear window demister and heater blower motor, then disconnect the jump leads in the reverse order of connection. Turn off the lights etc.

Wheel changing

Some of the details shown here will vary according to model. For instance, the location of the spare wheel and jack is not the same on all cars. However, the basic principles apply to all vehicles.

 Warning: Do not change a wheel in a situation where you risk being hit by other traffic. On busy roads, try to stop in a lay-by or a gateway. Be wary of passing traffic while changing the wheel – it is easy to become distracted by the job in hand.

Preparation

☐ When a puncture occurs, stop as soon as it is safe to do so.
☐ Park on firm level ground, if possible, and well out of the way of other traffic.
☐ Use hazard warning lights if necessary.

☐ If you have one, use a warning triangle to alert other drivers of your presence.
☐ Apply the handbrake and engage first or reverse gear (or Park on models with automatic transmission).

☐ Chock the wheel diagonally opposite the one being removed – a couple of large stones will do for this.
☐ If the ground is soft, use a flat piece of wood to spread the load under the jack.

Changing the wheel

1 The spare is stored beneath the luggage compartment floor covering. The jack and tool kit are located alongside the spare wheel. Unscrew the two fasteners and remove the lid from the tool kit. Undo the plastic nut and lift the spare wheel from the well in the floor.

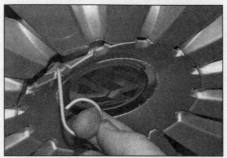

2 Where fitted, use the hook in the tool kit to pull the cover from the wheel. If caps are fitted to each bolt, use the tool to pull off the covers.

3 Loosen each wheel bolt by half a turn. Use the special adapter where a locking wheel bolt is fitted.

4 Locate the jack head below the reinforced jacking point nearest the wheel to be changed. The jacking point is indicated by a triangle pressed into the sill. Turn the handle to raise the wheel clear of the ground.

5 Remove the bolts and lift the wheel from the vehicle. Place the wheel beneath the sill as a precaution against the jack failing.

6 Fit the spare wheel, then tighten the bolts moderately with the wheel brace. Lower the vehicle to the ground, then finally tighten the wheel bolts in a diagonal sequence. Refit the wheel cover/cap as applicable. Note that the wheel bolts should be tightened to the specified torque at the earliest opportunity.

Finally . . .

☐ Remove the wheel chocks.
☐ Stow the jack and tools in the correct locations in the car.
☐ Check the tyre pressure on the wheel just fitted. If it is low, or if you don't have a pressure gauge with you, drive slowly to the nearest garage and inflate the tyre to the right pressure.
☐ Have the damaged tyre or wheel repaired as soon as possible.

Note: *If a temporary 'space-saver' spare wheel has been fitted, special conditions apply to its use. This type of spare wheel is only intended for use in an emergency, and should not remain fitted any longer than it takes to get the punctured wheel repaired. While the temporary wheel is in use, do not exceed 50 mph, and avoid harsh acceleration, braking or cornering. Note that, besides being narrower than a normal roadwheel, the temporary spare wheel is of smaller diameter; therefore, since ground clearance will be slightly reduced with the temporary spare in use, take care when travelling over rough ground.*

Identifying leaks

Puddles on the garage floor or drive, or obvious wetness under the bonnet or underneath the car, suggest a leak that needs investigating. It can sometimes be difficult to decide where the leak is coming from, especially if an engine undershield is fitted. Leaking oil or fluid can also be blown rearwards by the passage of air under the car, giving a false impression of where the problem lies.

 Warning: Most automotive oils and fluids are poisonous. Wash them off skin, and change out of contaminated clothing, without delay.

 The smell of a fluid leaking from the car may provide a clue to what's leaking. Some fluids are distinctively coloured. It may help to remove the engine undershield, clean the car carefully and to park it over some clean paper overnight as an aid to locating the source of the leak. Remember that some leaks may only occur while the engine is running.

Sump oil

Engine oil may leak from the drain plug...

Oil from filter

...or from the base of the oil filter.

Gearbox oil

Gearbox oil can leak from the seals at the inboard ends of the driveshafts.

Antifreeze

Leaking antifreeze often leaves a crystalline deposit like this.

Brake fluid

A leak occurring at a wheel is almost certainly brake fluid.

Power steering fluid

Power steering fluid may leak from the pipe connectors on the steering rack.

Towing

When all else fails, you may find yourself having to get a tow home – or of course you may be helping somebody else. Long-distance recovery should only be done by a garage or breakdown service. For shorter distances, DIY towing using another car is easy enough, but observe the following points:

☐ Use a proper tow-rope – they are not expensive. The vehicle being towed must display an ON TOW sign in its rear window.

☐ Always turn the ignition key to the 'On' position when the vehicle is being towed, so that the steering lock is released, and the direction indicator and brake lights work.

☐ A rear towing eye is provided below the right-hand side of the bumper. The front towing eye is provided behind the cover on the right-hand side of the front bumper – undo the bolt and pull the cover from the bumper.

☐ Before being towed, release the handbrake and select neutral on the transmission. On models with automatic transmission, do not exceed 30 mph or tow for more than 30 miles. If in doubt, do not tow, or transmission damage may result.

☐ Note that greater-than-usual pedal pressure will be required to operate the brakes, since the vacuum servo unit is only operational with the engine running. Similarly, greater-than-usual steering effort will also be required.

☐ The driver of the car being towed must keep the tow-rope taut at all times to avoid snatching.

☐ Make sure that both drivers know the route before setting off.

☐ Only drive at moderate speeds and keep the distance towed to a minimum. Drive smoothly and allow plenty of time for slowing down at junctions.

Introduction

There are some very simple checks which need only take a few minutes to carry out, but which could save you a lot of inconvenience and expense.

These *Weekly checks* require no great skill or special tools, and the small amount of time they take to perform could prove to be very well spent, for example:

☐ Keeping an eye on tyre condition and pressures, will not only help to stop them wearing out prematurely, but could also save your life.

☐ Many breakdowns are caused by electrical problems. Battery-related faults are particularly common, and a quick check on a regular basis will often prevent the majority of these.

☐ If your car develops a brake fluid leak, the first time you might know about it is when your brakes don't work properly. Checking the level regularly will give advance warning of this kind of problem.

☐ If the oil or coolant levels run low, the cost of repairing any engine damage will be far greater than fixing the leak, for example.

Underbonnet check points

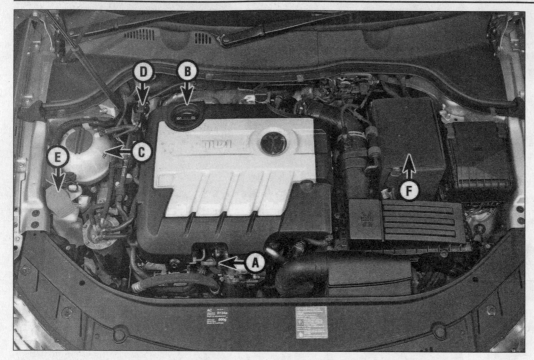

◀ **2.0 litre DOHC engine shown. Other models similar**

A *Engine oil level dipstick*

B *Engine oil filler cap*

C *Coolant expansion tank*

D *Brake fluid reservoir*

D *Washer fluid reservoir*

E *Washer fluid reservoir*

F *Battery*

Engine oil level

Before you start
✔ Make sure that the car is on level ground.
✔ Check the oil level before the car is driven, or at least 5 minutes after the engine has been switched off.

 HAYNES HiNT *If the oil is checked immediately after driving the vehicle, some of the oil will remain in the upper engine components, resulting in an inaccurate reading on the dipstick.*

The correct oil
Modern engines place great demands on their oil. It is very important that the correct oil for your car is used (see *Lubricants and fluids*).

Car care
● If you have to add oil frequently, you should check whether you have any oil leaks. Place some clean paper under the car overnight, and check for stains in the morning. If there are no leaks, then the engine may be burning oil.
● Always maintain the level between the upper and lower dipstick marks (see photo 3). If the level is too low, severe engine damage may occur. Oil seal failure may result if the engine is overfilled by adding too much oil.

1 The dipstick is located on the front of the engine (see *Underbonnet check points* for exact location). Withdraw the dipstick.

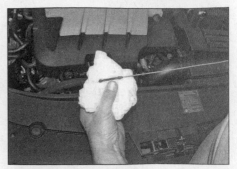

2 Using a clean rag or paper towel, wipe all oil from the dipstick. Insert the clean dipstick into the tube as far as it will go, then withdraw it again.

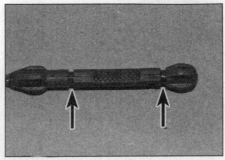

3 Note the oil level on the end of the dipstick, which should be between the upper and lower mark. Approximately 1.0 litre of oil will raise the level from the lower mark to the upper mark.

4 Oil is added through the filler cap on top of the engine. Turn the cap through a quarter-turn anti-clockwise and withdraw it. Top-up the level. A funnel may help to reduce spillage. Add the oil slowly, checking the level on the dipstick often. Do not overfill.

Coolant level

 Warning: Do not attempt to remove the expansion tank pressure cap when the engine is hot, as there is a very great risk of scalding. Do not leave open containers of coolant about, as it is poisonous.

Car care
● With a sealed-type cooling system, adding coolant should not be necessary on a regular basis. If frequent topping-up is required, it is likely there is a leak. Check the radiator, all hoses and joint faces for signs of staining or wetness, and rectify as necessary.

● It is important that antifreeze is used in the cooling system all year round, not just during the winter months. Don't top up with water alone, as the antifreeze will become diluted.

1 The coolant level varies with the temperature of the engine. When the engine is cold, the coolant level should be between the MIN and MAX marks.

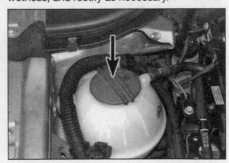

2 If topping-up is necessary, wait until the engine is cold. Slowly unscrew the cap to release any pressure present in the cooling system, and remove the cap.

3 Add a mixture of water and antifreeze to the expansion tank until the coolant level is on the MAX mark.

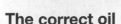

Brake (and clutch) fluid level

Warning:
• *Brake fluid can harm your eyes and damage painted surfaces, so use extreme caution when handling and pouring it.*
• *Do not use fluid that has been standing open for some time, as it absorbs moisture from the air, which can cause a dangerous loss of braking effectiveness.*

HAYNES HiNT
• *Make sure that your car is on level ground.*

• *The fluid level in the reservoir will drop slightly as the brake pads wear down, but the fluid level must never be allowed to drop below the MIN mark.*

Safety first!

● If the reservoir requires repeated topping-up this is an indication of a fluid leak somewhere in the system, which should be investigated immediately.
● If a leak is suspected, the car should not be driven until the braking system has been checked. Never take any risks where brakes are concerned

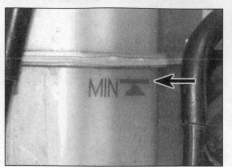

1 The MIN mark is indicated on the reservoir. The fluid level must be kept above this mark at all times.

2 If topping-up is necessary, first wipe clean the area around the filler cap to prevent dirt entering the hydraulic system. Unscrew the reservoir cap. Carefully add fluid, taking care not to spill it onto the surrounding components. Use only the specified fluid; mixing different types can cause damage to the system.

3 On completion, securely refit the cap and wipe away any spilt fluid. With the ignition switched on, check the operation of the brake fluid low level warning lamp by having an assistant depress the button on the top of the reservoir cap.

Battery

Caution: Before carrying out any work on the vehicle battery, read the precautions given in 'Safety first!' at the start of this manual.
✔ Make sure that the battery tray is in good condition, and that the clamp is tight. Corrosion on the tray, retaining clamp and the battery itself can be removed with a solution of water and baking soda. Thoroughly rinse all cleaned areas with water. Any metal parts damaged by corrosion should be covered with a zinc-based primer, then painted.
✔ Periodically (approximately every three months), check the charge condition of the battery as described in Chapter 5.
✔ If the battery is flat, and you need to jump start your vehicle, see *Roadside Repairs*.

HAYNES HiNT

Battery corrosion can be kept to a minimum by applying a layer of petroleum jelly to the clamps and terminals after they are reconnected.

1 Check the tightness of battery clamps to ensure good electrical connections. You should not be able to move them. Also check each cable for cracks and frayed conductors.

2 If corrosion (white, fluffy deposits) is evident, remove the cables from the battery terminals, clean them with a small wire brush, then refit them. Automotive stores sell a tool for cleaning the battery post . . .

3 . . . as well as the battery cable clamps

Electrical systems

✔ Check all external lights and the horn. Refer to the appropriate Sections of Chapter 12 for details if any of the circuits are found to be inoperative.

✔ Visually check all accessible wiring connectors, harnesses and retaining clips for security, and for signs of chafing or damage.

 If you need to check your brake lights and indicators unaided, back up to a wall or garage door and operate the lights. The reflected light should show if they are working properly.

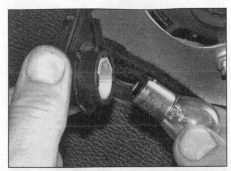

1 If a single indicator light, brake light or headlight has failed, it is likely that a bulb has blown and will need to be renewed. Refer to Chapter 12 for details. If both brake lights have failed, it is possible that the brake light switch operated by the brake pedal has failed. Refer to Chapter 9 for details.

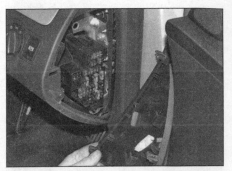

2 If more than one indicator light or headlight has failed, it is likely that either a fuse has blown or that there is a fault in the circuit (see Chapter 12). The main fusebox is located beneath a cover on the driver's end of the facia panel; further fuses are located in the engine compartment.

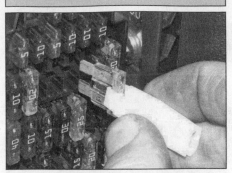

3 To renew a blown fuse, pull it from its location in the fusebox. Fit a new fuse of the same rating, available from car accessory shops.

Washer fluid level

● Screenwash additives not only keep the windscreen clean during bad weather, they also prevent the washer system freezing in cold weather – which is when you are likely to need it most. Don't top-up using plain water, as the screenwash will become diluted, and will freeze in cold weather.

 Warning: On no account use engine coolant antifreeze in the screen washer system – this may damage the paintwork.

1 The reservoir for the windscreen and headlight washer systems is on the right-hand side of the engine compartment.

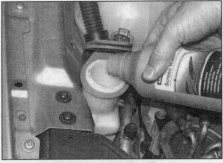

2 A screenwash additive should be added in the quantities recommended on the bottle.

Wiper blades

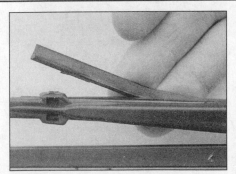

1 Check the condition of the wiper blades. If they are cracked or show any signs of deterioration, or if the glass swept area is smeared, renew them. For maximum clarity of vision, wiper blades should be renewed annually, as a matter of course.

2 To remove a windscreen wiper blade, depress the release button, and pull the blade from the arm.

Tyre condition and pressure

It is very important that tyres are in good condition, and at the correct pressure - having a tyre failure at any speed is highly dangerous. Tyre wear is influenced by driving style - harsh braking and acceleration, or fast cornering, will all produce more rapid tyre wear. As a general rule, the front tyres wear out faster than the rears. Interchanging the tyres from front to rear ("rotating" the tyres) may result in more even wear. However, if this is completely effective, you may have the expense of replacing all four tyres at once! Remove any nails or stones embedded in the tread before they penetrate the tyre to cause deflation. If removal of a nail does reveal that the tyre has been punctured, refit the nail so that its point of penetration is marked. Then immediately change the wheel, and have the tyre repaired by a tyre dealer.

Regularly check the tyres for damage in the form of cuts or bulges, especially in the sidewalls. Periodically remove the wheels, and clean any dirt or mud from the inside and outside surfaces. Examine the wheel rims for signs of rusting, corrosion or other damage. Light alloy wheels are easily damaged by "kerbing" whilst parking; steel wheels may also become dented or buckled. A new wheel is very often the only way to overcome severe damage.

New tyres should be balanced when they are fitted, but it may become necessary to re-balance them as they wear, or if the balance weights fitted to the wheel rim should fall off. Unbalanced tyres will wear more quickly, as will the steering and suspension components. Wheel imbalance is normally signified by vibration, particularly at a certain speed (typically around 50 mph). If this vibration is felt only through the steering, then it is likely that just the front wheels need balancing. If, however, the vibration is felt through the whole car, the rear wheels could be out of balance. Wheel balancing should be carried out by a tyre dealer or garage.

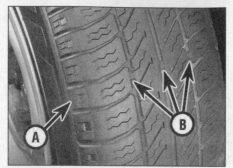

1 *Tread Depth - visual check*
The original tyres have tread wear safety bands (B), which will appear when the tread depth reaches approximately 1.6 mm. The band positions are indicated by a triangular mark on the tyre sidewall (A).

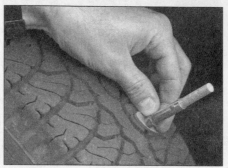

2 *Tread Depth - manual check*
Alternatively, tread wear can be monitored with a simple, inexpensive device known as a tread depth indicator gauge.

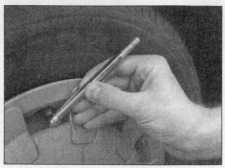

3 *Tyre Pressure Check*
Check the tyre pressures regularly with the tyres cold. Do not adjust the tyre pressures immediately after the vehicle has been used, or an inaccurate setting will result.

Tyre tread wear patterns

Shoulder Wear

Underinflation (wear on both sides)
Under-inflation will cause overheating of the tyre, because the tyre will flex too much, and the tread will not sit correctly on the road surface. This will cause a loss of grip and excessive wear, not to mention the danger of sudden tyre failure due to heat build-up.
Check and adjust pressures
Incorrect wheel camber (wear on one side)
Repair or renew suspension parts
Hard cornering
Reduce speed!

Centre Wear

Overinflation
Over-inflation will cause rapid wear of the centre part of the tyre tread, coupled with reduced grip, harsher ride, and the danger of shock damage occurring in the tyre casing.
Check and adjust pressures

If you sometimes have to inflate your car's tyres to the higher pressures specified for maximum load or sustained high speed, don't forget to reduce the pressures to normal afterwards.

Uneven Wear

Front tyres may wear unevenly as a result of wheel misalignment. Most tyre dealers and garages can check and adjust the wheel alignment (or "tracking") for a modest charge.
Incorrect camber or castor
Repair or renew suspension parts
Malfunctioning suspension
Repair or renew suspension parts
Unbalanced wheel
Balance tyres
Incorrect toe setting
Adjust front wheel alignment
Note: *The feathered edge of the tread which typifies toe wear is best checked by feel.*

Lubricants and fluids

Note: *Using lubricants and fluids which do not meet the VW standard may invalidate the warranty.*

Engine
Models fitted with a particulate filter. . . . .   LongLife oil
VW 507 00 **only**

Models without a particulate filter
    Standard (distance/time) service interval . . . .   Multigrade oil
VW 505 01 or better

    LongLife (variable) service interval . . . .   LongLife oil*
VW 506 01 or better

Cooling system
Models up to 2007 model year. . . . .   VW G12 Plus antifreeze
Models from 2008 model year . . . .   VW G12 Plus Plus antifreeze

Gearbox
Manual gearbox . . . .   Refer to dealer
Automatic gearbox G05 217 1A2

Braking system . . . .   Hydraulic fluid to DOT 4

Air conditioning system R134a

* A maximum of 0.5 litres of standard VW oil may be used for topping-up when LongLife oil is unobtainable.

Tyre pressures

Note: *The recommended tyre pressures for each vehicle are given on a sticker attached to the inside of the fuel filler flap. The pressures given are for the original equipment tyres – the recommended pressures may vary if any other make or type of tyre is fitted; check with the tyre manufacturer or supplier for latest recommendations.*

Chapter 1
Routine maintenance and servicing

Contents

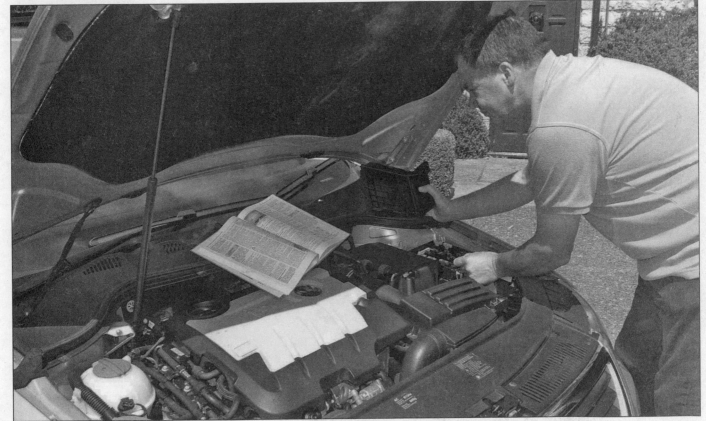

Degrees of difficulty

| Easy, suitable for novice with little experience | Fairly easy, suitable for beginner with some experience | Fairly difficult, suitable for competent DIY mechanic | Difficult, suitable for experienced DIY mechanic | Very difficult, suitable for expert DIY or professional |

Lubricants and fluids................................ Refer to the end of *Weekly checks* on page 0•15

Capacities – all approximate

Engine oil (including filter)
1.9 litre engines:
    Without particulate filter................................... 4.3 litres
    With particulate filter..................................... 3.8 litres
2.0 litre engines .... 4.0 litres

Cooling system
All models.. 8.0 litres

Transmission
Manual transmission:
    5-speed .... 1.9 litres
    6-speed .... 2.3 litres
Automatic (DSG) transmission fluid:
    Initial filling .... 7.0 litres
    Fluid change.. 5.2 litres

Fuel tank
All models.. 70 litres

Washer reservoirs
Without headlight washers................................. 2.5 litres
With headlight washers .... 6.0 litres

Engine codes
Manufacturer's engine codes*:
    PD unit injector engines:
      1.9 litre .... BKC, BLS and BXE
      2.0 litre .... BKP, BMA, BMR, BUZ, BVE and BWV
    Common rail engines .... CBAA, CBAB, CBAC and CBBB
* Note: *See 'Vehicle identification' at the end of this manual for the location of engine code markings.*

Cooling system
Antifreeze mixture:
    40% antifreeze .... Protection down to -25°C
    50% antifreeze .... Protection down to -35°C
Note: *Refer to antifreeze manufacturer for latest recommendations.*

Remote control battery
Type CR2032

Brakes
Brake pad minimum thickness (excluding backing plate) .... 2.0 mm

Torque wrench settings

	Nm	lbf ft
Engine sump drain plug	30	22
Manual transmission filler/level plug:		
6-speed:		
Hexagon socket head plug	30	22
Multipoint plug	45	33
Oil filter cap	25	18
Reversing light switch	20	15
Roadwheel bolts	120	89

Maintenance schedule

The maintenance intervals in this manual are provided with the assumption that you, not the dealer, will be carrying out the work. These are the minimum intervals recommended by us for vehicles driven daily. If you wish to keep your vehicle in peak condition at all times, you may wish to perform some of these procedures more often. We encourage frequent maintenance, since it enhances the efficiency, performance and resale value of your vehicle.

When the vehicle is new, it should be serviced by a dealer service department (or other workshop recognised by the vehicle manufacturer as providing the same standard of service) in order to preserve the warranty. The vehicle manufacturer may reject warranty claims if you are unable to prove that servicing has been carried out as and when specified, using only original equipment parts or parts certified to be of equivalent quality.

All models are equipped with a service interval display indicator in the instrument panel. Every time the engine is started the panel will illuminate for approximately 5 seconds with service information. With the standard non-variable display, the service intervals are in accordance with specific distances and time periods. With the LongLife display, the service interval is variable according to the number of starts, length of journeys, vehicle speeds, brake pad wear, bonnet opening frequency, fuel consumption, oil level and oil temperature, however the vehicle must be serviced at least every two years. At approximately 20 days before a service is due, 'Service in --- miles' or 'Service in --- days' or a spanner symbol will appear at the bottom of the odometer or in the display in the centre of the instrument cluster. Once the service interval has been reached, the display will flash 'Service'. Note that if the variable (LongLife) service

interval is being used, the engine must only be filled with the recommended LongLife engine oil (see *Lubricants and fluids*).

After completing a service, VW technicians use a special instrument to reset the service display to the next service interval, and a print-out is put in the vehicle service record. The display can be reset by the owner as

described in Section 5, but note that the procedure will automatically reset the display to the 10 000 miles 'distance' interval. To have the display reset to the 'variable' (LongLife) interval, it is necessary to take the vehicle to a VW dealer or suitably-equipped specialist who will use a special instrument to encode the on-board computer.

Every 250 miles or weekly
☐ Refer to *Weekly checks*

SERVICE on display or every 2 years, whichever comes first
☐ Renew the engine oil and filter (Section 3)
Note: *Frequent oil and filter changes are good for the engine. We recommend changing the oil at least once a year.*
☐ Check the front and rear brake pad thickness (Section 4)
☐ Reset the service interval display (Section 5)
☐ Check the condition of the exhaust system and its mountings (Section 6)
☐ Check all underbonnet components and hoses for fluid and oil leaks (Section 7)
☐ Check the condition of the auxiliary drivebelt (Section 8)
☐ Check the coolant antifreeze concentration (Section 9)
☐ Check the brake hydraulic circuit for leaks and damage (Section 10)
☐ Check the headlight beam adjustment (Section 11)
☐ Renew the pollen filter element (Section 12)
☐ Check the manual transmission oil level (Section 13)
☐ Check the underbody protection for damage (Section 14)
☐ Check the condition of the driveshaft gaiters (Section 15)
☐ Check the steering and suspension components for condition and security (Section 16)
☐ Check the battery condition, security and electrolyte level (Section 17)
☐ Lubricate all hinges and locks (Section 18)
☐ Check the condition of the airbag unit(s) (Section 19)
☐ Check the operation of the windscreen/tailgate/headlight washer system(s) (as applicable) (Section 20)
☐ Check the engine management self-diagnosis memory for faults (Section 21)
☐ Check the operation of the sunroof and lubricate the guide rails (Section 22)
☐ Carry out a road test and check exhaust emissions (Section 23)

Every 40 000 miles or 4 years, whichever comes first
Note: *Most dealers perform these tasks with the nearest SERVICE*
☐ Renew the fuel filter (Section 24)
☐ Renew the automatic (DSG) transmission fluid and filter (Section 25)

Every 60 000 miles
☐ Renew the air filter element (Section 26)

Every 76 000 miles
☐ Renew the timing belt and tensioning roller (PD unit injector engines up to 2006 model year) (Section 27)
Note: *VW recommend that the interval for timing belt renewal is 76 000 miles. However, if the vehicle is used mainly for short journeys or a lot of stop-start driving it is recommended that the renewal interval is shortened. The actual belt renewal interval is very much up to the individual owner but, bearing in mind that severe engine damage will result if the belt breaks in use, we recommend you err on the side of caution.*

After 95 000 miles then every 19 000 miles
☐ Check the particulate filter ash deposit mass (Section 28)

Every 95 000 miles
☐ Renew the timing belt and tensioning roller (PD unit injector engines from 2007 model year) (Section 29)
Note: *VW recommend that the interval for timing belt renewal is 95 000 miles. However, if the vehicle is used mainly for short journeys or a lot of stop-start driving it is recommended that the renewal interval is shortened. The actual belt renewal interval is very much up to the individual owner but, bearing in mind that severe engine damage will result if the belt breaks in use, we recommend you err on the side of caution.*

Every 120 000 miles
☐ Renew the timing belt and tensioning roller (common rail injection engines) (Section 30)
Note: *VW recommend that the interval for timing belt renewal is 120 000 miles. However, if the vehicle is used mainly for short journeys or a lot of stop-start driving it is recommended that the renewal interval is shortened. The actual belt renewal interval is very much up to the individual owner but, bearing in mind that severe engine damage will result if the belt breaks in use, we recommend you err on the side of caution.*

Every 2 years
☐ Renew the brake (and clutch) fluid (Section 31)
☐ Renew the coolant* (Section 32)
☐ Renew the remote control battery (Section 33)
* Note: *This work is not included in the VW schedule and should not be required if the recommended VW G12 Plus or G12 Plus Plus LongLife coolant antifreeze/inhibitor is used.*

Underbonnet view of a 2.0 litre common rail injection engine – other models are similar

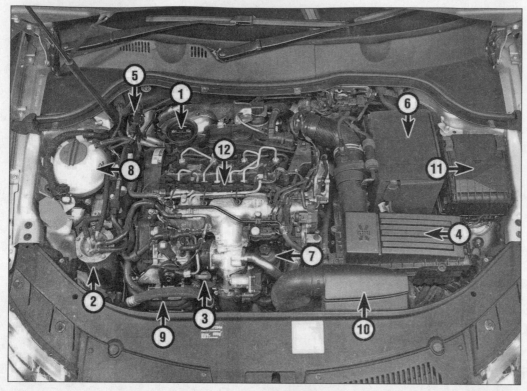

1 Engine oil filter cap
2 Fuel filter
3 Engine oil level dipstick
4 Air filter
5 Brake/clutch fluid reservoir
6 Battery
7 Oil filter
8 Coolant reservoir
9 Alternator
10 Air intake ducting
11 Fusebox
12 Common (fuel) rail

Front underbody view

1 Exhaust front downpipe
2 Brake caliper
3 Lower arm
4 Engine oil drain plug
5 Intercooler hoses
6 Anti-roll bar
7 Steering track rod
8 Driveshaft
9 Coolant circulation pump (common rail only)
10 Subframe
11 Air conditioning compressor
12 Auxiliary drivebelt

1 Track control rod
2 Trailing arm
3 Fuel tank
4 Rear silencer
5 Subframe
6 Anti-roll bar
7 Lower transverse link

Maintenance procedures

1 Introduction

This Chapter is designed to help the home mechanic maintain his/her vehicle for safety, economy, long life and peak performance.

The Chapter contains a master maintenance schedule, followed by Sections dealing specifically with each task in the schedule. Visual checks, adjustments, component renewal and other helpful items are included. Refer to the accompanying illustrations of the engine compartment and the underside of the vehicle for the locations of the various components.

Servicing your vehicle will provide a planned maintenance programme, which should result in a long and reliable service life. This is a comprehensive plan, so maintaining some items but not others will not produce the same results.

As you service your vehicle, you will discover that many of the procedures can – and should – be grouped together, because of the particular procedure being performed, or because of the proximity of two otherwise unrelated components to one another. For example, if the vehicle is raised for any reason, the exhaust can be inspected at the same time as the suspension and steering components.

The first step in this maintenance pro-gramme is to prepare yourself before the actual work begins. Read through all the Sections relevant to the work to be carried out, then make a list and gather all the parts and tools required. If a problem is encountered, seek advice from a parts specialist, or a dealer service department.

2 Regular maintenance

1 If, from the time the vehicle is new, the routine maintenance schedule is followed closely, and frequent checks are made of fluid levels and high-wear items, as suggested throughout this manual, the engine will be kept in relatively good running condition, and the need for additional work will be minimised.
2 It is possible that there will be times when the engine is running poorly due to the lack of regular maintenance. This is even more likely if a used vehicle, which has not received regular and frequent maintenance checks, is purchased. In such cases, additional work may need to be carried out, outside of the regular maintenance intervals.
3 If engine wear is suspected, a compression test (refer to the relevant Part of Chapter 2) will provide valuable information regarding the overall performance of the main internal components. Such a test can be used as a basis to decide on the extent of the work to be carried out. If, for example, a compression test indicates serious internal engine wear, conventional maintenance as described in this Chapter will not greatly improve the performance of the engine, and may prove a waste of time and money, unless extensive overhaul work is carried out first.
4 The following series of operations are those most often required to improve the performance of a generally poor-running engine:

Primary operations

a) Clean, inspect and test the battery (See 'Weekly checks).
b) Check all the engine-related fluids (See 'Weekly checks).
c) Check the condition and tension of the auxiliary drivebelt (Section 8).
d) Check the condition of the air filter, and renew if necessary (Section 26).
e) Check the condition of all hoses, and check for fluid leaks (Section 7).

5 If the above operations do not prove fully effective, carry out the following secondary operations:

Secondary operations

All items listed under Primary operations, plus the following:
a) Check the charging system (see Chapter 5).
b) Check the preheating system (see Chapter 5).
c) Renew the fuel filter (Section 24) and check the fuel system (see Chapter 4).

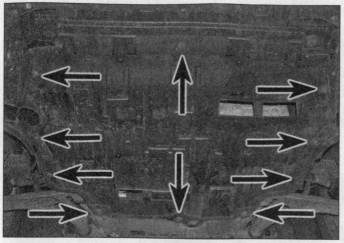

3.2a Undo the fasteners (arrowed) and remove the engine undershield

3.2b Pull up the front edge of the engine cover first

SERVICE on display or every 2 years

3 Engine oil and filter renewal

1 Frequent oil and filter changes are the most important preventative maintenance procedures which can be undertaken by the DIY owner. As engine oil ages, it becomes diluted and contaminated, which leads to premature engine wear.

3.3a Use a 32 mm socket to unscrew the filter cap

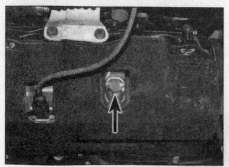

3.4 Unscrew the engine oil sump drain plug (arrowed)

2 Before starting this procedure, gather all the necessary tools and materials. Also make sure that you have plenty of clean rags and newspapers handy, to mop-up any spills. Ideally, the engine oil should be warm, as it will drain better, and more built-up sludge will be removed with it. Take care, however, not to touch the exhaust or any other hot parts of the engine when working under the vehicle. To avoid any possibility of scalding, and to protect yourself from possible skin irritants and other

3.3b On common rail engines, undo the bolt (arrowed) and move the vacuum valve to one side

HAYNES HiNT

Keep the drain plug pressed into the sump while unscrewing it by hand the last couple of turns. As the plug releases, move it away sharply so the stream of oil issuing from the sump runs into the container, not up your sleeve.

harmful contaminants in used engine oils, it is advisable to wear gloves when carrying out this work. Access to the underside of the vehicle will be greatly improved if it can be raised on a lift, driven onto ramps, or jacked up and supported on axle stands (see *Jacking and vehicle support*). Whichever method is chosen, make sure that the vehicle remains level, or if it is at an angle, that the drain plug is at the lowest point. Undo the retaining fasteners and remove the engine undershield, then remove the engine top cover. The cover simply pulls up from its rubber mountings **(see illustrations)**.

3 Slacken the oil filter housing cap (located to the front of the cylinder head) to allow the oil within to drain into the sump. Although there is a special VW tool to undo the cap, a 32 mm socket or a strap wrench is a suitable alternative **(see illustration)**. Place absorbent cloths around the filter housing to catch any spilt oil. **Note:** *On common rail injection engines, undo the Torx bolt and move the vacuum valve above the filter to one side* **(see illustration)**.

4 Working underneath the vehicle, slacken the sump drain plug about half a turn. Position the draining container under the drain plug, then remove the plug completely **(see illustration and Haynes Hint)**. Recover the sealing ring from the drain plug. **Note:** *On some engines the sealing ring is integral with the drain plug. On these engines the drain plug must be renewed.*

5 Allow some time for the old oil to drain, noting that it may be necessary to reposition the container as the oil flow slows to a trickle.

6 After all the oil has drained, wipe off the drain plug with a clean rag, and fit a new sealing washer. Clean the area around the drain plug opening, and refit the plug. Tighten the plug to the specified torque.

7 Completely unscrew the oil filter housing cap, and lift it with the filter element from the housing. Discard the O-ring(s).

3.8 Renew the filter cap O-ring seal

3.9a Fit the new element into the cap . . .

3.9b . . . and bolt the cap into the housing

8 Pull the old filter from the cap/housing. Wipe clean the inside of the oil filter housing and cap. Fit the new filter element to the housing/cap. Note that on 1.9 litre engines, the filter element is marked TOP on one end **(see illustration)**.

9 Fit the new O-ring(s) and lubricate it with a little clean engine oil, bolt the cap into the housing, and tighten it to the specified torque **(see illustrations)**.

10 Remove the old oil and all tools from under the car then refit the undershield and lower the car to the ground. Also refit the engine top cover.

11 Remove the dipstick, then unscrew the oil filler cap from the cylinder head cover. Fill the engine, using the correct grade and type of oil (see *Lubricants and fluids*). An oil can spout or funnel may help to reduce spillage. Pour in half the specified quantity of oil first, then wait a few minutes for the oil to run to the sump (see *Weekly checks*). Continue adding oil a small quantity at a time until the level is up to the maximum mark on the dipstick. Refit the filler cap.

12 Start the engine and run it for a few minutes; check for leaks around the oil filter cap and the sump drain plug. Note that there may be a few seconds delay before the oil pressure warning light goes out when the engine is started, as the oil circulates through the engine oil galleries and the new oil filter (where fitted) before the pressure builds-up.

⚠️ *Warning: Do not increase the engine speed above idling while the oil pressure light is illuminated, as considerable damage can be caused to the turbocharger.*

4.1 The outer brake pads can be observed through the holes in the wheels

13 Switch off the engine, and wait a few minutes for the oil to settle in the sump once more. With the new oil circulated and the filter completely full, recheck the level on the dipstick, and add more oil as necessary.

14 Dispose of the used engine oil safely, with reference to *General repair procedures* in the *Reference* section of this manual.

4 Brake pad check

1 On some models, the outer brake pads can be checked without removing the wheels, by observing the brake pads through the holes in the wheels **(see illustration)**. If necessary, remove the wheel trim. The thickness of the pad (including backing plate) must not be less than the dimension given in the Specifications.

2 If the outer pads are worn near their limits, it is worthwhile checking the inner pads as well. Apply the handbrake then jack up vehicle and support it on axle stands (see *Jacking and vehicle support*). Remove the roadwheels.

3 Use a steel rule to check the thickness of the brake pads friction material (excluding the backing plate), and compare with the minimum thickness given in the Specifications **(see illustration)**.

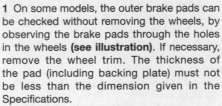

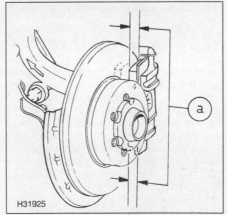

4.3 The thickness (a) of the brake pads friction material must not be less than the specified amount

4 For a comprehensive check, the brake pads should be removed and cleaned. The operation of the caliper can then also be checked, and the condition of the brake disc itself can be fully examined on both sides. Refer to Chapter 9.

5 If any pads are worn to the specified minimum thickness or less, *all four pads at the front or rear, as applicable, must be renewed as a set*.

6 On completion of the check, refit the road-wheels and lower the vehicle to the ground.

5 Resetting the service interval display

1 After all necessary maintenance work has been completed, the service interval display must be reset. VW technicians use a special dedicated instrument to do this, and a print-out is then put in the vehicle service record. It is possible for the owner to reset the display as described in the following paragraphs, but note that the procedure will automatically reset the display to a 10 000 mile interval. To continue with the 'variable' intervals which take into consideration the number of starts, length of journeys, vehicle speeds, brake pad wear, bonnet opening frequency, fuel consumption, oil level and oil temperature, the display must be reset by an VW dealership using the special dedicated instrument.

2 To reset the standard display manually, switch off the ignition, then press and hold down the service indicator call up button beneath the speedometer **(see illustration)**.

5.2 Service indicator call up button (arrowed)

6.2 Check the condition of the rubber exhaust mountings

3 Switch on the ignition, then release the service indicator call up button, and press the MIN (clock reset) button within 20 seconds.
4 The service interval display is now reset, and will return to the normal mode after a short delay. Switch off the ignition.

6 Exhaust system check

1 With the engine cold (at least an hour after the vehicle has been driven), check the complete exhaust system from the engine to the end of the tailpipe. The exhaust system is most easily checked with the vehicle raised on a hoist, or suitably supported on axle stands, so that the exhaust components are readily visible and accessible (see *Jacking and vehicle support*).
2 Check the exhaust pipes and connections for evidence of leaks, severe corrosion and damage. Make sure that all brackets and mountings are in good condition, and that all relevant nuts and bolts are tight **(see illustration)**. Leakage at any of the joints or in other parts of the system will usually show up as a black sooty stain in the vicinity of the leak.
3 Rattles and other noises can often be traced to the exhaust system, especially the brackets and mountings. Try to move the

A leak in the cooling system will usually show up as white- or antifreeze-coloured deposits in the area adjoining the leak.

pipes and silencers. If the components are able to come into contact with the body or suspension parts, secure the system with new mountings. Otherwise separate the joints (if possible) and twist the pipes as necessary to provide additional clearance.

7 Hose and fluid leak check

Note: *Also refer to Section 10.*
1 Visually inspect the engine joint faces, gaskets and seals for any signs of water or oil leaks. Pay particular attention to the areas around the camshaft cover, cylinder head, oil filter and sump joint faces. Bear in mind that, over a period of time, some very slight seepage from these areas is to be expected – what you are really looking for is any indication of a serious leak. Should a leak be found, renew the offending gasket or oil seal by referring to the appropriate Chapters in this manual.
2 Also check the security and condition of all the engine-related pipes and hoses. Ensure that all cable-ties or securing clips are in place and in good condition. Clips which are broken or missing can lead to chafing of the hoses, pipes or wiring, which could cause more serious problems in the future.
3 Carefully check the radiator hoses and heater hoses along their entire length. Renew any hose which is cracked, swollen or deteriorated. Cracks will show up better if the hose is squeezed. Pay close attention to the hose clips that secure the hoses to the cooling system components. Hose clips can pinch and puncture hoses, resulting in cooling system leaks.
4 Inspect all the cooling system components (hoses, joint faces, etc) for leaks **(see Haynes Hint)**. Where any problems of this nature are found on system components, renew the component or gasket with reference to Chapter 3.
5 Where applicable, inspect the automatic transmission fluid cooler hoses for leaks or deterioration.
6 With the vehicle raised, inspect the petrol tank and filler neck for punctures, cracks and other damage. The connection between the filler neck and tank is especially critical. Sometimes a rubber filler neck or connecting hose will leak due to loose retaining clamps or deteriorated rubber.
7 Carefully check all rubber hoses and metal fuel lines leading away from the petrol tank. Check for loose connections, deteriorated hoses, crimped lines, and other damage. Pay particular attention to the vent pipes and hoses, which often loop up around the filler neck and can become blocked or crimped. Follow the lines to the front of the vehicle, carefully inspecting them all the way. Renew damaged sections as necessary.
8 From within the engine compartment,

check the security of all fuel hose attachments and pipe unions, and inspect the fuel hoses and vacuum hoses for kinks, chafing and deterioration.
9 Where applicable, check the condition of the power steering fluid hoses and pipes.

8 Auxiliary drivebelt check and renewal

Check

1 The auxiliary drivebelt drives the alternator, and where applicable, the air conditioning compressor.
2 For access to the drivebelt, apply the handbrake, then jack up the front of the vehicle and support it on axle stands (see *Jacking and vehicle support*). Remove the engine undershield, and remove the engine top cover as well **(see illustrations 3.2a and 3.2b)**.
3 Examine the auxiliary drivebelt along its entire length for damage and wear in the form of cuts and abrasions, fraying and cracking. The use of a mirror and possibly an electric torch will help, and the engine may be turned with a spanner on the crankshaft pulley in order to observe all areas of the belt **(see illustration)**.
4 On most engines, the drivebelt tension is adjusted automatically by a spring-tensioned idler.
5 If a drivebelt requires renewal, proceed as follows:

Renewal

6 To remove the drivebelt first apply the handbrake, slacken the right-hand front roadwheel bolts, then jack up the front of the vehicle and support it on axle stands (see *Jacking and vehicle support*). Remove the roadwheel, then remove the undershield from under the engine compartment as described in Section 3.
7 If the drivebelt is to be re-used, mark it for clockwise direction to ensure it is refitted the same way round.
8 Undo the fasteners and remove the lower part of the lower front right-hand wheel arch liner **(see illustration)**.

8.3 Use a mirror to check the condition of the auxiliary drivebelt

PD unit injector engines

9 Unscrew the fuel filter and move it to one side with the hoses still attached **(see illustration)**. If improved access is required, disconnect the hoses and completely remove the filter. Plug the openings to prevent contamination.

10 Use an open-ended spanner to rotate the tensioner, and relieve the tension on the belt. Once the tensioner and bracket holes are aligned, use a suitable drill bit to lock the tensioner in place **(see illustration)**. Remove the belt from the pulleys.

Common rail injection engines with automatic tensioner and a/c

11 Using a spanner on the centre bolt, rotate the tensioner pulley clockwise.

12 As the holes in the tensioner hub and bracket align, insert a 4.0 mm drill bit/rod to lock them in place **(see illustration)**.

13 Remove the drivebelt.

Common rail injection engines with manual tensioner and a/c

14 Undo the tensioner adjusting bolt on the underside of the tensioner assembly to slacken the belt, and remove the tensioner pulley **(see illustration)**. Discard the bolt – a new one must be fitted. Remove the drivebelt.

Common rail injection engines without a/c

15 Using a sharp knife, cut through and remove the drivebelt.

Refitting

16 Locate the drivebelt on the alternator, crankshaft, air conditioning compressor (where applicable), making sure that each rib is correctly located in a groove **(see illustration)**.

PD unit injector engines

17 Locate the drivebelt on the tensioner pulley, then release the tensioner to tension the drivebelt.

Common rail injection engines with automatic tensioner and a/c

18 Locate the drivebelt on the tensioner pulley, then release the tensioner to tension the drivebelt.

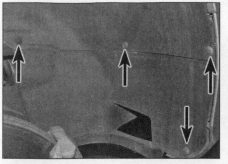

8.8 Undo the bolts (arrowed) and remove the lower section of the wheel arch liner

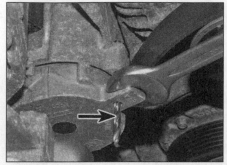

8.10 Rotate the tensioner and lock it in place with a suitable drill bit (arrowed)

Common rail injection engines with manual tensioner and a/c

19 Coat the guide surfaces of the tensioner roller with high-temperature anti-seize grease, then locate the roller in position against the belt, and insert the new adjusting bolt.

20 The adjusting bolt must be tightened in 5 stages:
1) *Hand-tighten the bolt.*
2) *Tighten the bolt with a spanner/socket until the bolt reaches its stop.*

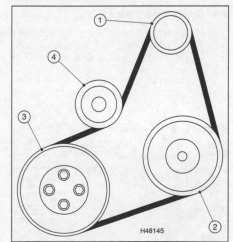

8.16 Auxiliary drivebelt routing – all models with air conditioning

1 Alternator pulley
2 Air conditioning compressor pulley
3 Crankshaft pulley
4 Tensioner pulley

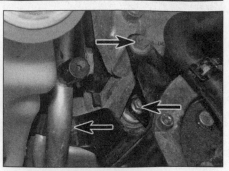

8.9 The fuel filter is secured by 2 bolts, and 1 nut (arrowed)

8.12 Insert a 4.0 mm drill bit (arrowed) to lock the tensioner in place

3) *Slacken the bolt ¼ of a turn.*
4) *Tighten the bolt to 30 Nm (22 lbf ft).*
5) *Tighten the bolt a further ¼ of a turn.*

21 Check that the end of the bolt protrudes approximately 2.5 mm above the circumference of the tensioner pulley **(see illustration)**.

Common rail injection engines without a/c

22 Models without air conditioning are fitted with a 'stretch' drivebelt. New drivebelts are supplied in a kit with a tool to slip the belt over the crankshaft pulley, and illustrated instructions. Follow the instructions supplied in the kit and fit the new belt.

All engines

23 The remainder of refitting is a reversal of removal.

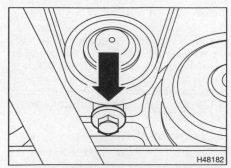

8.14 Undo the tensioner adjusting bolt (arrowed)

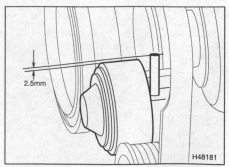

8.21 The end of the bolt must protrude approximately 2.5 mm above the pulley

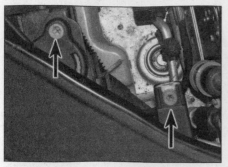

11.2 Headlight beam adjustment bolts (arrowed)

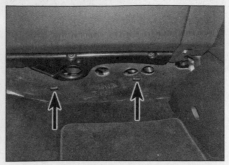

12.1 Undo the fasteners (arrowed) and remove the baffle plate

at the top of each light unit (**see illustration**).

3 Some models are equipped with an electrically-operated headlight beam adjustment system which is controlled through the switch in the facia. On these models, ensure that the switch is set to the basic 0 position before adjusting the headlight aim.

Gas discharge headlights

4 The headlamp range is controlled dynamically by an electronic control module which monitors the ride height of the vehicle by sensors fitted to the front and rear suspension. Beam adjustment can only be carried out using VW test equipment.

9 Antifreeze concentration check

1 The cooling system should be filled with the recommended antifreeze and corrosion protection fluid, which is designed to last the life of the vehicle. Vehicles up to 2007 model year are filled with G12 Plus, and vehicles from 2008 model year are filled with G12 Plus Plus. **Do not** mix this antifreeze with any other type. If it is mixed with other types, it loses its 'filled for life' quality. The only exception is that models filled with G12 Plus can be topped-up with G12 Plus Plus, but not *vice-versa*. Over a period of time, the concentration of fluid may be reduced due to topping-up (this can be avoided by topping-up with the correct antifreeze mixture – see Specifications) or fluid loss. If loss of coolant has been evident, it is important to make the necessary repair before adding fresh fluid.

2 With the engine **cold**, carefully remove the cap from the expansion tank. If the engine is not completely cold, place a cloth rag over the cap before removing it, and remove it slowly to allow any pressure to escape.

3 Antifreeze checkers (hydrometers) are available from car accessory shops. Draw some coolant from the expansion tank into the hydrometer and follow the manufacturer's instructions.

4 If the concentration is incorrect, it will be necessary to either withdraw some coolant and add antifreeze, or alternatively drain the old coolant and add fresh coolant of the correct concentration (see Section 32).

10 Brake hydraulic circuit check

1 Check the entire brake hydraulic circuit for leaks and damage. Start by checking the master cylinder in the engine compartment. At the same time, check the vacuum servo unit and ABS units for signs of fluid leakage.

2 Raise the front and rear of the vehicle and support it securely on axle stands (see *Jacking and vehicle support*). Check the rigid hydraulic brake lines for corrosion and damage.

3 At the front of the vehicle, check that the flexible hydraulic hoses to the calipers are not twisted or chafing on any of the surrounding suspension components. Turn the steering on full lock to make this check. Also check that the hoses are not brittle or cracked.

4 Lower the vehicle to the ground after making the checks.

11 Headlight beam adjustment

Halogen headlamps

1 Accurate adjustment of the headlight beam is only possible using optical beam setting equipment, and this work should therefore be carried out by a VW dealer or suitably-equipped workshop.

2 For reference, the headlights can be adjusted using the adjuster bolts, accessible

12 Pollen filter element renewal

1 Undo the 2 fasteners and remove the baffle plate under the passenger side of the heater unit (**see illustration**).

2 Slide the pollen filter cover to the left-hand side, and lower the filter from place (**see illustrations**). Note how the filter is fitted.

3 Insert the new filter into the heater housing, and slide the cover to the right to secure it in place.

4 Refit the baffle plate and tighten the fasteners securely.

13 Manual transmission oil level check

Note: *This operation is not included in the VW service schedule. However, if the vehicle is used mainly for short journeys, taxi work, or towing, we recommend the oil level is checked every 20 000 miles or 2 years.*

1 Apply the handbrake, then jack up the front and rear of the vehicle and support it on axle stands (see *Jacking and vehicle support*). To ensure an accurate check, make sure that the vehicle is level. Undo the fasteners and remove the engine/transmission undershield (**see illustration 3.2a**).

2 To improve access, remove the air cleaner assembly as described in Chapter 4A.

5-speed transmissions

3 There is no oil level plug. The only method of achieving the correct oil level is to drain the oil by removing the drain plug on the transmission underside, then unscrewing the reversing light switch on the top of the transmission casing, and adding the correct amount of oil through the reversing light aperture using a funnel and hose.

6-speed transmissions

4 The oil filler/level plug is located on the front side of the manual transmission. The plug may be either of Allen key type, or alternatively of multi-splined type (**see illustration**). Unscrew

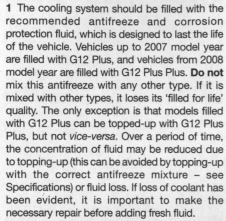

12.2a Slide the cover (arrowed) to the left . . .

12.2b . . . and lower the filter from place

the oil level plug. The fluid must be level with the bottom of the hole.

5 If necessary, add the specified oil through the filler/level hole. If the level requires constant topping-up, check for leaks and repair.

6 Refit the plug and tighten to the specified torque, then lower the vehicle to the ground.

14 Underbody protection check
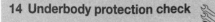

Raise and support the vehicle on axle stands (see *Jacking and vehicle support*). Using an electric torch or lead light, inspect the entire underside of the vehicle, paying particular attention to the wheel arches. Look for any damage to the flexible underbody coating, which may crack or flake off with age, leading to corrosion. Also check that the wheel arch liners are securely attached with any clips provided – if they come loose, dirt may get in behind the liners and defeat their purpose. If there is any damage to the underseal, or any corrosion, it should be repaired before the damage gets too serious.

15 Driveshaft gaiter check
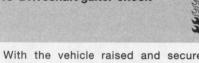

1 With the vehicle raised and securely supported on stands, slowly rotate the roadwheel. Inspect the condition of the outer constant velocity (CV) joint rubber gaiters, squeezing the gaiters to open out the folds. Check for signs of cracking, splits or deterioration of the rubber, which may allow the grease to escape, and lead to water and grit entry into the joint. Also check the security and condition of the retaining clips. Repeat these checks on the inner joints **(see illustration)**. If any damage or deterioration is found, the gaiters should be renewed (see Chapter 8).

2 At the same time, check the general condition of the CV joints themselves by first holding the driveshaft and attempting to rotate the wheel. Repeat this check by holding the inner joint and attempting to rotate the driveshaft. Any appreciable movement indicates wear in the joints, wear in the driveshaft splines, or a loose driveshaft retaining nut.

16 Steering and suspension check

1 Raise the front and rear of the vehicle, and securely support it on axle stands (see *Jacking and vehicle support*).

2 Visually inspect the track rod end balljoint dust cover, the lower front suspension balljoint dust cover, and the steering rack-and-pinion

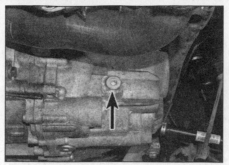

13.4 Oil level

gaiters for splits, chafing or deterioration. Any wear of these components will cause loss of lubricant, together with dirt and water entry, resulting in rapid deterioration of the balljoints or steering gear.

3 Check for signs of fluid leakage under pressure from the steering gear rubber gaiters, which would indicate failed fluid seals within the steering gear.

4 Grasp the roadwheel at the 12 o'clock and 6 o'clock positions, and try to rock it **(see illustration)**. Very slight free play may be felt, but if the movement is appreciable, further investigation is necessary to determine the source. Continue rocking the wheel while an assistant depresses the footbrake. If the movement is now eliminated or significantly reduced, it is likely that the hub bearings are at fault. If the free play is still evident with the footbrake depressed, then there is wear in the suspension joints or mountings.

5 Now grasp the wheel at the 9 o'clock and 3 o'clock positions, and try to rock it as before. Any movement felt now may again be caused by wear in the hub bearings or the steering track rod balljoints. If the inner or outer balljoint is worn, the visual movement will be obvious.

6 Using a large screwdriver or flat bar, check for wear in the suspension mounting bushes by levering between the relevant suspension component and its attachment point. Some movement is to be expected as the mountings are made of rubber, but excessive wear should be obvious. Also check the condition of any visible rubber bushes, looking for splits, cracks or contamination of the rubber.

16.4 Check for wear in the hub bearings by grasping the wheel and trying to rock it

15.1 Check the condition of the driveshaft gaiters

7 With the car standing on its wheels, have an assistant turn the steering wheel back-and-forth about an eighth of a turn each way. There should be very little, if any, lost movement between the steering wheel and roadwheels. If this is not the case, closely observe the joints and mountings previously described, but in addition, check the steering column universal joints for wear, and the rack-and-pinion steering gear itself.

8 Check for any signs of fluid leakage around the front suspension struts and rear shock absorber. Should any fluid be noticed, the suspension strut or shock absorber is defective internally, and should be renewed. **Note:** *Suspension struts/shock absorbers should always be renewed in pairs on the same axle to ensure correct vehicle handling.*

9 The efficiency of the suspension strut/shock absorber may be checked by bouncing the vehicle at each corner. Generally speaking, the body will return to its normal position and stop after being depressed. If it rises and returns on a rebound, the suspension strut/shock absorber is probably suspect. Examine also the suspension strut/shock absorber upper and lower mountings for any signs of wear.

17 Battery check
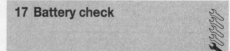

1 The battery is located on the left-hand side of the engine compartment. Release the catch and remove the cover from the top of the battery (where fitted) **(see illustration)**.

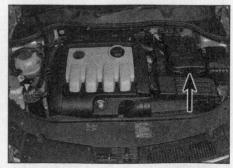

17.1 Release the clip (arrowed) and lift up the battery cover

2 Check that both battery terminals are securely attached and are free from corrosion.
3 Check the battery casing for signs of damage or cracking and check the battery retaining clamp bolt is securely tightened. If the battery casing is damaged in any way the battery must be renewed (see Chapter 5).
4 If the vehicle is not fitted with a sealed-for-life maintenance-free battery, check the electrolyte level is between the MAX and MIN level markings on the battery casing. If topping-up is necessary, remove the battery (see Chapter 5) from the vehicle then remove the cell caps/cover (as applicable). Using distilled water, top the electrolyte level of each cell up to the MAX level mark then securely refit the cell caps/cover. Ensure the battery has not been overfilled then refit the battery to the vehicle (see Chapter 5).
5 On completion of the check, refit the cover.

18 Hinge and lock lubrication

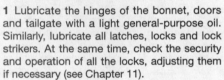

1 Lubricate the hinges of the bonnet, doors and tailgate with a light general-purpose oil. Similarly, lubricate all latches, locks and lock strikers. At the same time, check the security and operation of all the locks, adjusting them if necessary (see Chapter 11).
2 Lightly lubricate the bonnet release mechanism and cable with a suitable grease.

19 Airbag unit check

Inspect the exterior condition of the airbag(s) for signs of damage or deterioration. If an airbag shows signs of damage, it must be renewed (see Chapter 12). Note that it is not permissible to attach any stickers to the surface of the airbag, as this may affect the deployment of the unit.

20 Windscreen/tailgate/headlight washer system check

1 Check that each of the washer jet nozzles are clear and that each nozzle provides a strong jet of washer fluid.
2 The tailgate jet should be aimed to spray at the centre of the screen, using a pin.
3 The windscreen washer nozzles should be aimed slightly above the centre of the screen. Use a Torx bit to adjust the nozzle aim vertically only **(see illustration)**.
4 The aim of the headlight jets is set in the factory and there is no provision for adjustment.
5 Especially during the winter months, make sure that the washer fluid frost concentration is sufficient.

20.3 Use a Torx bit to adjust the washer jet aim (arrowed)

21 Engine management self-diagnosis memory fault check

This work should be carried out by a VW dealer or diagnostic specialist using special equipment. The diagnostic socket is located beneath the right-hand side of the facia on RHD models, and beneath the left-hand side on LHD models **(see illustration)**.

22 Sunroof check and lubrication

1 Check the operation of the sunroof, and leave it in the fully open position.
2 Wipe clean the guide rails on each side of the sunroof opening, then apply lubricant to them. VW recommend lubricant spray G 052 778 A2.

23 Road test and exhaust emissions check

Instruments and electrical equipment

1 Check the operation of all instruments and electrical equipment.
2 Make sure that all instruments read correctly, and switch on all electrical equipment in turn, to check that it functions properly.

21.1 EOBD diagnostic plug (arrowed)

Steering and suspension

3 Check for any abnormalities in the steering, suspension, handling or road feel.
4 Drive the vehicle, and check that there are no unusual vibrations or noises which may indicate wear in the driveshafts, wheel bearings, etc.
5 Check that the steering feels positive, with no excessive sloppiness, or roughness, and check for any suspension noises when cornering and driving over bumps.

Drivetrain

6 Check the performance of the engine, clutch (where applicable), gearbox/transmission and driveshafts.
7 Listen for any unusual noises from the engine, clutch and gearbox/transmission.
8 Make sure that the engine runs smoothly when idling, and that there is no hesitation when accelerating.
9 Check that, where applicable, the clutch action is smooth and progressive, that the drive is taken up smoothly, and that the pedal travel is not excessive. Also listen for any noises when the clutch pedal is depressed.
10 On manual gearbox models, check that all gears can be engaged smoothly without noise, and that the gear lever action is smooth and not abnormally vague or notchy.
11 On automatic transmission models, make sure that all gearchanges occur smoothly, without snatching, and without an increase in engine speed between changes. Check that all the gear positions can be selected with the vehicle at rest. If any problems are found, they should be referred to a VW dealer.
12 Listen for a metallic clicking sound from the front of the vehicle, as the vehicle is driven slowly in a circle with the steering on full-lock. Carry out this check in both directions. If a clicking noise is heard, this indicates wear in a driveshaft joint, in which case renew the joint if necessary.

Braking system

13 Make sure that the vehicle does not pull to one side when braking, and that the wheels do not lock when braking hard.
14 Check that there is no vibration through the steering when braking.
15 Check that the handbrake operates correctly without excessive movement of the lever, and that it holds the vehicle stationary on a slope.
16 Test the operation of the brake servo unit as follows. With the engine off, depress the footbrake four or five times to exhaust the vacuum. Hold the brake pedal depressed, then start the engine. As the engine starts, there should be a noticeable 'give' in the brake pedal as vacuum builds-up. Allow the engine to run for at least two minutes, and then switch it off. If the brake pedal is depressed now, it should be possible to detect a hiss from the servo as the pedal is depressed. After about four or five applications, no further hissing should be heard, and the pedal should feel considerably harder.
17 Under controlled emergency braking, the

pulsing of the ABS unit must be felt at the footbrake pedal.

Exhaust emissions check

18 Although not part of the manufacturer's maintenance schedule, this check will normally be carried out on a regular basis according to the country the vehicle is operated in. Currently in the UK, exhaust emissions testing is included as part of the annual MOT test after the vehicle is 3 years old. In Germany the test is made when the vehicle is 3 years old, then repeated every 2 years.

Every 40 000 miles or 4 years

24 Fuel filter renewal

1 The fuel filter is located on the right-hand side of the engine, or on some versions, on the engine compartment bulkhead at the rear of the engine. Pull the engine cover upwards to release the rubber mountings. Place cloth rags around the area beneath the filter unit.
2 Position a container underneath the filter unit and pad the surrounding area with rags to absorb any fuel that may be spilt.
3 At the top of the filter unit, undo the Torx bolts around the circumference and remove the upper part, leaving the fuel hoses attached to it. If necessary, use a flat-bladed screwdriver in the slot provided to prise the upper part from the lower part **(see illustrations)**.
Caution: Be prepared for an amount of fuel loss. Do not allow diesel fuel to contact any of the coolant hoses.
4 Lift the filter element from the housing, and remove the O-ring seal **(see illustration)**.
5 Use shop rags to remove any debris/residue/water from the filter housing.
6 Fit a new fuel filter into the housing, then moisten the new O-ring seal with clean fuel and fit it to the upper part of the filter housing **(see illustrations)**.
7 Fill the filter with clean diesel to aid restarting.
8 Refit the upper part to the lower part of the filter housing, ensuring its correctly seated, then refit the bolts and tighten them evenly **(see illustration)**.
9 Start and run the engine at idle, then check around the fuel filter for fuel leaks. **Note:** *It*

may take a few seconds of cranking before the engine starts.
10 Raise the engine speed to about 2000 rpm several times, then allow the engine to idle again.
11 Remove the collecting container and rags, then refit the engine top cover.

25 Automatic (DSG) transmission fluid and filter renewal

Renewal of the transmission fluid and filter requires access to VW diagnostic equipment to establish the correct temperature of the fluid, and special VW tools/adapters to replenish the fluid. Therefore we recommend this task is entrusted to a VW dealer or suitably-equipped specialist.

24.3a Undo the Torx bolts (arrowed) . . .

24.3b . . . then prise the upper part of the filter up using the slot provided

24.4 Lift the filter element from the lower housing

24.6a Renew the O-ring seal . . .

24.6b . . . and fit the new element to the upper housing

24.8 Lower the upper part, complete with filter element, into the housing

Every 60 000 miles

26 Air filter element renewal

1 Undo the bolts and lift away the upper part of the air cleaner housing (see illustration).
2 Remove the air filter element, noting which way round it is fitted (see illustration).
3 Wipe clean the main body, if necessary use a vacuum cleaner to remove any debris, then fit the new air filter, making sure it is the correct way round.
4 The remainder of refitting is a reversal of removal.

26.1 Undo the air filter cover bolts (arrowed)

26.2 Lift out the air filter element

Every 76 000 miles

27 Timing belt and tensioning roller renewal (PD unit injector engines up to 2006)

1 Refer to Chapter 2A for details of renewing the timing belt and tensioning roller. Note that VW recommend that the tensioning roller is renewed every second timing belt change.

After 95 000 miles then every 19 000 miles

28 Particulate filter ash deposit mass check

Eventually, the amount of ash deposited in the particulate filter by the filtration process will cause a blockage and engine running problems. VW state that the maximum amount of ash is 60g. At this point, the particulate filter must be renewed. Unfortunately, the mass of the ash can only be established using dedicated VW diagnostic equipment connected to the vehicle through the diagnostic plug under the driver's side of the facia. Consequently, we recommend this task is entrusted to a VW dealer or suitably-equipped specialist.

Particulate filters are fitted to the following engine codes (see Specifications): BLS, BMR, BUZ, CBAA, CBAB, CBAC and CBBB.

Every 95 000 miles

29 Timing belt and tensioning roller renewal (PD unit injector engines after 2007)

1 Refer to Chapter 2A for details of renewing the timing belt and tensioning roller. Note that VW recommend that the tensioning roller is renewed every second timing belt change.

Every 120 000 miles

30 Timing belt and tensioning roller renewal (common rail injection engines)

1 Refer to Chapter 2B for details of renewing the timing belt and tensioning roller. Note that VW recommend that the tensioning roller is renewed every second timing belt change.

Every 2 years

31 Brake (and clutch) fluid renewal

⚠ **Warning: Brake hydraulic fluid can harm your eyes and damage painted surfaces, so use extreme caution when handling and pouring it. Do not use fluid that has been standing open for some time, as it absorbs moisture from the air. Excess moisture can cause a dangerous loss of braking effectiveness.**

1 The procedure is similar to that for the bleeding of the hydraulic system as described in Chapter 9, except that the brake fluid reservoir should be emptied by siphoning, using a clean poultry baster or similar before starting, and allowance should be made for the old fluid to be expelled when bleeding a section of the circuit. Since the clutch hydraulic system on manual gearbox models also uses fluid from the brake system reservoir, it should also be bled at the same time by referring to Chapter 6, Section 2.
2 Working as described in Chapter 9, open the first bleed screw in the sequence, and pump the brake pedal gently until nearly all the old fluid has been emptied from the master cylinder reservoir.
3 Top-up to the MAX level with new fluid, and continue pumping until only the new fluid remains in the reservoir, and new fluid can be seen emerging from the bleed screw. Tighten the bolt, and top the reservoir level up to the MAX level line.
4 Work through all the remaining bleed screws in the sequence until new fluid can be seen at all of them. Be careful to keep the master

cylinder reservoir topped-up to above the MIN level at all times, or air may enter the system and greatly increase the length of the task.

5 When the operation is complete, check that all bleed screws are securely tightened, and that their dust caps are refitted. Wash off all traces of spilt fluid, and recheck the master cylinder reservoir fluid level.

6 On models with a manual transmission unit, once the brake fluid has been changed the clutch fluid should also be renewed. Referring to Chapter 6, bleed the clutch until new fluid is seen to be emerging from the slave cylinder bleed screw, keeping the master cylinder fluid level above the MIN level line at all times to prevent air entering the system. Once the new fluid emerges, securely tighten the bleed screw then disconnect and remove the bleeding equipment. Securely refit the dust cap then wash off all traces of spilt fluid.

7 On all models, ensure the master cylinder fluid level is correct (see *Weekly checks*) and thoroughly check the operation of the brakes and (where necessary) clutch before taking the car on the road.

32 Coolant renewal

Note: *The cooling system should be filled with the recommended antifreeze and corrosion protection fluid, which is designed to last the life of the vehicle. Vehicles up to 2007 model year are filled with G12 Plus, and vehicles from 2008 model year are filled with G12 Plus Plus. Do not mix this antifreeze with any other type. If it is mixed with other types, it loses its 'filled for life' quality. The only exception is that models filled with G12 Plus can be topped-up with G12 Plus Plus, but not vice-versa.*

Note: *This work is not included in the VW schedule and should not be required if the recommended VW G12 Plus or G12 Plus Plus LongLife coolant antifreeze/inhibitor is used. However, if standard antifreeze/inhibitor is used, the work should be carried out at the recommended interval.*

⚠️ *Warning: Wait until the engine is cold before starting this procedure. Do not allow antifreeze to come in contact with your skin, or with the painted surfaces of the vehicle. Rinse off spills immediately with plenty of water. Never leave antifreeze lying around in an open container, or in a puddle in the driveway or on the garage floor. Children and pets are attracted by its sweet smell, but antifreeze can be fatal if ingested.*

Cooling system draining

1 With the engine completely cold, cover the expansion tank cap with a wad of rag, and slowly turn the cap anti-clockwise to relieve the pressure in the cooling system (a hissing sound will normally be heard). Wait until any pressure remaining in the system is released,

then continue to turn the cap until it can be removed.

2 Release the fasteners and remove the engine undershield. Some models are equipped with a drain plug in the radiator bottom hose, whilst on others, it's necessary to disconnect the bottom hose from the radiator. Position a suitable container beneath the radiator bottom hose, then prise out the retaining clip a little, and pull the lower hose from the radiator hose, or undo the drain tap as applicable. Allow the coolant to drain into the container.

3 On common rail injection engines, release the clamps and disconnect the hoses from the coolant circulation pump located at the front side of the cylinder block, under the oil cooler **(see illustration)**.

4 If the coolant has been drained for a reason other than renewal, then provided it is clean, it can be re-used, but this is not recommended.

5 Once all the coolant has drained, refit the sensor ensuring the retaining clip is properly seated, or tighten the drain tap as applicable.

Cooling system flushing

6 If coolant renewal has been neglected, or if the antifreeze mixture has become diluted, then in time, the cooling system may gradually lose efficiency, as the coolant passages become restricted due to rust, scale deposits, and other sediment. Flushing the system clean can restore the cooling system efficiency.

7 The radiator should be flushed independently of the engine, to avoid unnecessary contamination.

Radiator flushing

8 To flush the radiator, disconnect the top and bottom hoses and any other relevant hoses from the radiator, with reference to Chapter 3.

9 Insert a garden hose into the radiator top inlet. Direct a flow of clean water through the radiator, and continue flushing until clean water emerges from the radiator bottom outlet.

10 If after a reasonable period, the water still does not run clear, the radiator can be flushed with a good proprietary cooling system cleaning agent. It is important that their manufacturer's instructions are followed carefully. If the contamination is particularly bad, insert the hose in the radiator bottom outlet, and reverse-flush the radiator.

Engine flushing

11 To flush the engine, remove the thermostat as described in Chapter 3, then temporarily refit the thermostat cover.

12 With the top and bottom hoses disconnected from the radiator, insert a garden hose into the radiator top hose. Direct a clean flow of water through the engine, and continue flushing until clean water emerges from the radiator bottom hose.

13 On completion of flushing, refit the thermostat and reconnect the hoses with reference to Chapter 3.

32.3 Disconnect the hoses from the circulation pump (arrowed) – common rail injection engines only

Cooling system filling

14 Before attempting to fill the cooling system, make sure that all hoses and clips are in good condition, and that the clips/connections are secure. Note that an antifreeze mixture must be used all year round, to prevent corrosion of the engine components (see following sub-Section).

15 Remove the expansion tank filler cap, and fill the system by slowly pouring the coolant into the expansion tank to prevent airlocks from forming.

16 If the coolant is being renewed, begin by pouring in a couple of litres of water, followed by the correct quantity of antifreeze, then top-up with more water.

17 Once the level in the expansion tank starts to rise, squeeze the radiator top and bottom hoses to help expel any trapped air in the system. Once all the air is expelled, top-up the coolant level to the MAX mark, refit the expansion tank cap, then refit the expansion tank to the bodywork.

18 Start the engine and run it at a fast idle for about three minutes. After this, allow the engine to idle normally until the bottom hose becomes hot.

19 Check for leaks, particularly around disturbed components. Check the coolant level in the expansion tank, and top-up if necessary. Note that the system must be cold before an accurate level is indicated in the expansion tank. If the expansion tank cap is removed while the engine is still warm, cover the cap with a thick cloth, and unscrew the cap slowly to gradually relieve the system pressure (a hissing sound will normally be heard). Wait until any pressure remaining in the system is released, then continue to turn the cap until it can be removed. Never remove the cap when the engine is still hot.

Antifreeze mixture

Caution: VW specify the use of G12 Plus or G12 Plus Plus (see Note) antifreeze (purple in colour). DO NOT mix this with any other type of antifreeze, as severe engine damage may result. If the coolant visible in the expansion tank is brown in colour, then the cooling system may have been topped-up with coolant containing the

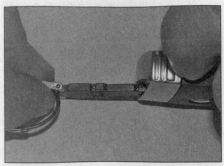

33.1 Depress the button and slide out the emergency key

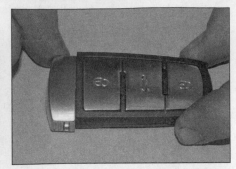

33.2 Slide the cap from the end of the remote control

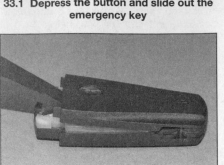

33.3 Prise up the cover . . .

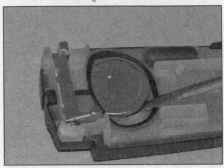

33.4 . . . and remove the battery (positive side up)

wrong type of antifreeze. If you are unsure of the type of antifreeze used, or if you suspect that mixing may have occurred, the best course of action is to drain, flush and refill the cooling system.

20 If the recommended VW coolant is not being used, the antifreeze should always be renewed at the specified intervals. This is necessary not only to maintain the antifreeze properties, but also to prevent corrosion which would otherwise occur as the corrosion inhibitors become progressively less effective.

21 The quantity of antifreeze and levels of protection are indicated in the Specifications.

22 Before adding antifreeze, the cooling system should be completely drained, preferably flushed, and all hoses checked for condition and security.

23 After filling with antifreeze, a label should be attached to the expansion tank, stating the type and concentration of antifreeze used, and the date installed. Any subsequent topping-up should be made with the same type and concentration of antifreeze.

Caution: Do not use engine antifreeze in the windscreen/tailgate/headlight washer system, as it will cause damage to the vehicle paintwork.

33 Remote control battery renewal

1 Depress the button and remove the emergency key from the remote control **(see illustration)**.

2 Slide the cap from the end of the remote control **(see illustration)**.

3 Carefully prise up the cover to expose the battery **(see illustration)**.

4 Remove the battery noting its orientation **(see illustration)**.

5 Before installing the new battery, press any button on the remote control once. This resets the transmitter unit so it can recognise a new battery.

6 Fit the new battery with the positive (+) side uppermost.

7 Refit the upper part of the remote control without disturbing the seal.

8 The remainder of refitting is a reversal of removal.

Chapter 2 Part A:
Engine in-car repair procedures – PD unit injector engines

Contents

Degrees of difficulty

Easy, suitable for novice with little experience 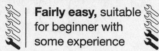	Fairly easy, suitable for beginner with some experience	Fairly difficult, suitable for competent DIY mechanic	Difficult, suitable for experienced DIY mechanic	Very difficult, suitable for expert DIY or professional

Specifications

General
Manufacturer's engine codes:*
1896 cc (1.9 litre), 8-valve, SOHC	BKC, BLS and BXE
1968 cc (2.0 litre), 16-valve, DOHC	BKP, BMA, BMR, BUZ, BVE and BWV

Maximum outputs:
	Power	Torque
Engine code BKC.	77 kW at 4000 rpm	250 Nm at 1900 rpm
Engine code BLS	77 kW at 4000 rpm	250 Nm at 1900 rpm
Engine code BXE	77 kW at 4000 rpm	250 Nm at 1900 rpm
Engine code BKP	103 kW at 4000 rpm	320 Nm at 1750 to 2500 rpm
Engine code BMA	100 kW at 4000 rpm	350 Nm at 1750 rpm
Engine code BMR.	125 kW at 4200 rpm	320 Nm at 1800 rpm
Engine code BUZ	120 kW at 4200 rpm	350 Nm at 1800 rpm
Engine code BVE	90 kW at 4000 rpm	320 Nm at 1750 rpm
Engine code BWV.	88 kW at 4000 rpm	300 Nm at 1750 rpm

Bore:
1896 cc engines	79.5 mm
1968 cc engines	81.0 mm
Stroke.	95.5 mm

Compression ratio:
Engine codes BKC and BLS.	19.0 : 1
All other codes	18.5 : 1

Compression pressures:
Minimum compression pressure	Approximately 19.0 bar
Maximum difference between cylinders.	Approximately 5.0 bar
Firing order	1 – 3 – 4 – 2
No 1 cylinder location.	Timing belt end

* Note: See 'Vehicle identification' at the end of this manual for the location of engine code markings.

Camshaft
Camshaft endfloat (maximum)	0.15 mm

Lubrication system
Oil pump type.	Gear type, chain-driven from crankshaft
Oil pressure (oil temperature 80°C, at 2000 rpm)	2.0 bar

Torque wrench settings

	Nm	lbf ft
Ancillary (alternator, etc) bracket mounting bolts.	45	33
Air conditioning compressor	45	33
Alternator and tensioner.	25	18
Auxiliary drivebelt tensioner securing bolt	25	18
Balance shaft assembly drive chain sprocket:*		
Stage 1.	10	7
Stage 2.	Angle-tighten a further 90°	
Balance shaft assembly to cylinder block:*		
M7 bolts:		
Stage 1.	13	10
Stage 2.	Angle-tighten a further 90°	
M8 bolts:		
Stage 1.	20	15
Stage 2.	Angle-tighten a further 90°	
Balance shaft drivegear:*		
Stage 1.	20	15
Stage 2.	Angle-tighten a further 90°	
Balance shaft idler gear:*		
Stage 1.	90	66
Stage 2.	Angle-tighten a further 90°	
Big-end bearing caps bolts:*		
Stage 1.	30	22
Stage 2.	Angle-tighten a further 90°	
Camshaft bearing cap bolts (SOHC engines):*		
Stage 1.	8	6
Stage 2.	Angle-tighten a further 90°	
Camshaft bearing frame bolts (DOHC engines)*	20	15
Camshaft cover nuts/bolts.	10	7
Camshaft sprocket hub centre bolt	100	74
Camshaft sprocket-to-hub bolts	25	18
Coolant pump bolts	15	11
Crankshaft oil seal housing bolts	15	11
Crankshaft pulley-to-sprocket bolts:*		
Stage 1.	10	7
Stage 2.	Angle-tighten a further 90°	
Crankshaft sprocket bolt:*		
Stage 1.	120	89
Stage 2.	Angle-tighten a further 90°	
Cylinder head bolts:*		
Stage 1.	35	26
Stage 2.	60	44
Stage 3.	Angle-tighten a further 90°	
Stage 4.	Angle-tighten a further 90°	
Engine mountings:*		
RH engine mounting:		
Mounting bracket to engine:		
Stage 1.	40	30
Stage 2.	Angle-tighten a further 180°	
Mounting to body:		
Stage 1.	40	30
Stage 2.	Angle-tighten a further 90°	
Mounting to bracket:		
Stage 1.	60	44
Stage 2.	Angle-tighten a further 90°	
LH engine mounting:		
Mounting to body:		
Stage 1.	40	30
Stage 2.	Angle-tighten a further 90°	
Mounting to bracket on transmission:		
Stage 1.	60	44
Stage 2.	Angle-tighten a further 90°	
Rear mounting link:		
To transmission:		
Stage 1.	40	30
Stage 2.	Angle-tighten a further 90°	
To subframe:		
Stage 1.	100	74
Stage 2.	Angle-tighten a further 90°	

Torque wrench settings (continued)

	Nm	lbf ft
Flywheel:*		
Stage 1	60	44
Stage 2	Angle-tighten a further 90°	
Injector rocker arm shafts:*		
Stage 1	20	15
Stage 2	Angle-tighten a further 90°	
Main bearing cap bolts:*		
Stage 1	65	48
Stage 2	Angle-tighten a further 90°	
Oil drain plug	30	22
Oil filter housing-to-cylinder block bolts:*		
Stage 1	15	11
Stage 2	Angle-tighten a further 90°	
Oil filter cover	25	18
Oil level/temperature sensor-to-sump bolts	10	7
Oil pick-up pipe securing bolts	10	7
Oil pressure relief valve plug	40	30
Oil pressure warning light switch	20	15
Oil pump chain tensioner bolt	15	11
Oil pump sprocket securing bolt:		
Stage 1	20	15
Stage 2	Angle-tighten a further 90°	
Oil pump to balance shaft assembly	10	7
Piston oil spray jet bolt	25	18
Sump:		
Sump-to-cylinder block bolts	15	11
Sump-to-transmission bolts	45	33
Tandem pump	20	15
Thermostat housing	15	11
Timing belt outer cover bolts	10	7
Timing belt rear cover-to-cylinder head bolt	10	7
Timing belt tensioner roller securing nut:		
Stage 1	20	30
Stage 2	Angle-tighten a further 45°	
Timing belt idler pulleys:*		
Right-hand idler roller (above coolant pump sprocket) bolt:		
Stage 1	40	30
Stage 2	Angle-tighten a further 90°	
Lower idler roller bolt/nut	20	15

Do not re-use fasteners

---

1 General information

How to use this Chapter

This Part of Chapter 2 describes those repair procedures that can reasonably be carried out on the engine while it remains in the vehicle. If the engine has been removed from the vehicle and is being dismantled as described in Part C, any preliminary dismantling procedures can be ignored.

Note that while it may be possible physically to overhaul certain items while the engine is in the vehicle, such tasks are not usually carried out as separate operations, and usually require the execution of several additional procedures (not to mention the cleaning of components and of oilways); for this reason, all such tasks are classed as major overhaul procedures, and are described in Part C of this Chapter.

Engine description

Throughout this Chapter, engines are referred to by type, and are identified and referred to by the manufacturer's code letters. A listing of all engines covered, together with their code letters, is given in the Specifications at the start of this Chapter.

The engines are water-cooled, single (1896 cc) or double (1968 cc) overhead camshaft(s), in-line four-cylinder units, with cast-iron cylinder blocks and aluminium-alloy cylinder heads. All are mounted transversely at the front of the vehicle, with the transmission bolted to the left-hand end of the engine.

The crankshaft is of five-bearing type, and thrustwashers are fitted to the centre main bearing to control crankshaft endfloat.

Drive for the camshafts is by a toothed timing belt from the crankshaft. Each camshaft is mounted at the top of the cylinder head, and is secured by bearing caps (1896 cc) or a bearing frame/ladder (1968 cc).

The valves are closed by coil springs, and run in guides pressed into the cylinder head.

On 1896 cc engines, the camshaft actuates the valves directly, through hydraulic tappets; on 1968 cc engines, the valves are operated by roller rocker arms incorporating hydraulic tappets.

The gear-type oil pump is driven by a chain from a sprocket on the crankshaft. Oil is drawn from the sump through a strainer, and then forced through an externally-mounted, renewable filter. From there, it is distributed to the cylinder head, where it lubricates the camshaft journals and hydraulic tappets, and also to the crankcase, where it lubricates the main bearings, connecting rod big-ends, gudgeon pins and cylinder bores. A coolant-fed oil cooler is fitted to the oil filter housing on all engines. Oil jets are fitted to the base of each cylinder – these spray oil onto the underside of the pistons, to improve cooling.

All engines are fitted with a combined brake servo vacuum pump and fuel lift pump (tandem pump), driven by the camshaft on the transmission end of the cylinder head.

2.3 Disconnect the injector solenoids wiring plug (arrowed)

On all engines, engine coolant is circulated by a pump, driven by the timing belt. For details of the cooling system, refer to Chapter 3.

Operations with engine in car

The following operations can be performed without removing the engine:

a) Compression pressure – testing.
b) Camshaft cover – removal and refitting.
c) Crankshaft pulley – removal and refitting.
d) Timing belt covers – removal and refitting.
e) Timing belt – removal, refitting and adjustment.
f) Timing belt tensioner and sprockets – removal and refitting.
g) Camshaft oil seals – renewal.
h) Camshaft(s) and hydraulic tappets – removal, inspection and refitting.
i) Cylinder head – removal and refitting.
j) Cylinder head and pistons – decarbonising.
k) Sump – removal and refitting.
l) Oil pump – removal, overhaul and refitting.
m) Crankshaft oil seals – renewal.
n) Engine/transmission mountings – inspection and renewal.
o) Flywheel – removal, inspection and refitting.

Note: *It is possible to remove the pistons and connecting rods (after removing the cylinder head and sump) without removing the engine. However, this is not recommended. Work of this nature is more easily and thoroughly completed with the engine on the bench, as described in Chapter 2C.*

2 Compression and leakdown tests – description and interpretation

Compression test

Note: *A compression tester suitable for use with diesel engines will be required for this test.*

1 When engine performance is down, or if misfiring occurs which cannot be attributed to the ignition or fuel systems, a compression test can provide diagnostic clues as to the engine's condition. If the test is performed regularly, it can give warning of trouble before any other symptoms become apparent.

2 The engine must be fully warmed-up to normal operating temperature, the battery must be fully-charged, and you will require the aid of an assistant.

3 Disconnect the injector solenoids by disconnecting the connector at the left-hand end of the cylinder head **(see illustration)**. **Note:** *As a result of the wiring being disconnected, faults may be stored in the ECM memory. These must be erased after the compression test.*

4 Remove the glow plugs as described in Chapter 5, then fit a compression tester to the No 1 cylinder glow plug hole. The type of tester which bolts into the plug thread is essential.

5 Have your assistant crank the engine for several seconds on the starter motor. After one or two revolutions, the compression pressure should build-up to a maximum figure and then stabilise. Record the highest reading obtained.

6 Repeat the test on the remaining cylinders, recording the pressure in each.

7 The cause of poor compression is less easy to establish on a diesel engine than on a petrol engine. The effect of introducing oil into the cylinders (wet testing) is not conclusive, because there is a risk that the oil will sit in the recess on the piston crown, instead of passing to the rings. However, the following can be used as a rough guide to diagnosis.

8 All cylinders should produce very similar pressures. Any difference greater than that specified indicates the existence of a fault. Note that the compression should build-up quickly in a healthy engine. Low compression on the first stroke, followed by gradually increasing pressure on successive strokes, indicates worn piston rings. A low compression reading on the first stroke, which does not build-up during successive strokes, indicates leaking valves or a blown head gasket (a cracked head could also be the cause).

9 A low reading from two adjacent cylinders is almost certainly due to the head gasket having blown between them and the presence of coolant in the engine oil will confirm this.

10 On completion, remove the compression tester, and refit the glow plugs, with reference to Chapter 5.

11 Reconnect the wiring to the injector solenoids. Finally, if necessary, have a VW dealer or suitably-equipped specialist erase the fault codes from the ECM memory.

Leakdown test

12 A leakdown test measures the rate at which compressed air fed into the cylinder is lost. It is an alternative to a compression test, and in many ways it is better, since the escaping air provides easy identification of where pressure loss is occurring (piston rings, valves or head gasket).

13 The equipment required for leakdown testing is unlikely to be available to the home mechanic. If poor compression is suspected, have the test performed by a suitably-equipped garage.

3 Engine assembly and valve timing marks – general information and usage

General information

1 TDC is the highest point in the cylinder that each piston reaches as it travels up-and-down when the crankshaft turns. Each piston reaches TDC at the end of the compression stroke and again at the end of the exhaust stroke, but TDC generally refers to piston position on the compression stroke. No 1 piston is at the timing belt end of the engine.

2 Positioning No 1 piston at TDC is an essential part of many procedures, such as timing belt removal and camshaft removal.

3 The design of the engines covered in this Chapter is such that piston-to-valve contact may occur if the camshaft or crankshaft is turned with the timing belt removed. For this reason, it is important to ensure that the camshaft and crankshaft do not move in relation to each other once the timing belt has been removed from the engine.

Setting TDC on No 1 cylinder

Note: *VAG special tool T10050 (round crankshaft sprocket) or T10100 (oval crankshaft sprocket) is required to lock the crankshaft sprocket in the TDC position. On the round sprocket the mark is on the tip of the tooth, and on the oval sprocket the mark is at the trough between the teeth.*

4 Remove the auxiliary drivebelt(s) as described in Chapter 1.

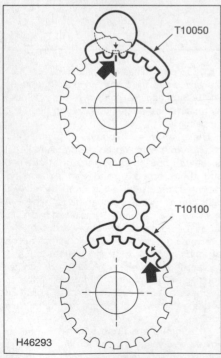

3.7a TDC setting tools

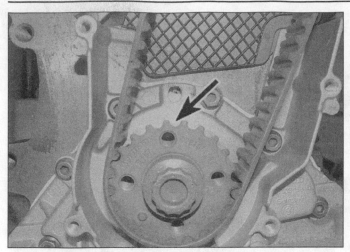

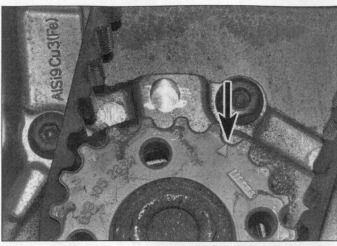

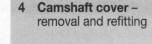

3.7b Position the crankshaft so that the mark on the sprocket (arrowed) is almost vertical . . .

3.7c . . . or at the 2 o'clock position (arrowed) depending on the sprocket type

5 Remove the crankshaft pulley/vibration damper as described in Section 5.

6 Remove the timing belt covers as described in Section 6.

7 Using a spanner or socket on the crankshaft sprocket bolt, turn the crankshaft in the normal direction of rotation (clockwise) until the alignment mark on the face of the sprocket is almost vertical for tool T10050, or at 2 o'clock for tool T10100 **(see illustrations)**.

8 The marking on the rear section of the upper timing belt upper cover aligns with the marking on the camshaft hub sender wheel **(see illustration)**.

9 While in this position it should be possible to insert the VAG tool to lock the crankshaft, and a 6 mm diameter rod/timing pin to lock the camshaft(s) **(see illustrations)**. **Note:** *The mark on the crankshaft sprocket and the mark on the VAG tool must align, whilst at the same time the shaft of tool must engage in the drilling in the crankshaft oil seal housing.*

10 The engine is now set to TDC on No 1 cylinder.

<table>
<tr><td>**4**</td><td>**Camshaft cover** – removal and refitting</td></tr>
</table>

Removal

1 Remove the dipstick and prise off and remove the engine top cover, then disconnect the breather hose from the camshaft cover **(see illustrations)**.

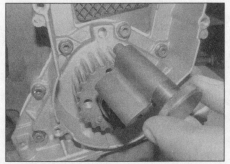

3.7d Then insert the locking tool . . .

3.7e . . . and align the marks (arrowed) on the tool and sprocket – round sprocket . . .

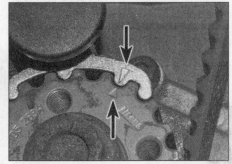

3.7f . . . and oval sprocket (arrowed)

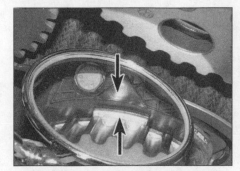

3.8 The triangular marking on the inner timing belt cover must align with the segment on the underside of the camshaft hub sender wheel (arrowed) – DOHC engine shown using a mirror

3.9a Insert a 6 mm drill bit/rod (arrowed) through the camshaft hub into the cylinder head to lock the camshaft – SOHC engines . . .

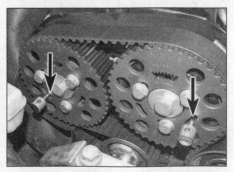

3.9b . . . and DOHC engines (arrowed)

4.1a Pull the engine cover upwards to release it

4.1b Disconnect the breather hose (arrowed)

4.4 Undo the bolts (arrowed) securing the pipes from the front of the cylinder head

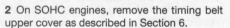

4.5 Ensure the retaining bolts are pushed fully through the gasket before refitting the camshaft cover

4.7a Apply sealant to the points (arrowed) on the cylinder head

Refitting

7 Refit the camshaft cover by following the removal procedure in reverse, noting the following points:

a) *On SOHC engines, apply suitable sealant to the points where the camshaft bearing cap contacts the cylinder head (see illustration).*

b) *Tighten the camshaft cover retaining nuts/bolts progressively to the specified torque in the sequence shown (see illustrations).*

5 Crankshaft pulley – removal and refitting

Removal

1 Switch off the ignition and all electrical consumers and remove the ignition key.

2 For improved access, raise the front right-hand side of the vehicle, and support securely on axle stands (see *Jacking and vehicle support*). Remove the roadwheel.

3 Remove the securing bolts and withdraw the engine undershield and the front lower section of the wheel arch liner.

2 On SOHC engines, remove the timing belt upper cover as described in Section 6.

3 On engine code BLS, undo the 2 bolts and detach the intake manifold flap from the intake manifold. Release the clamp and detach the intake hose from the ducting as the flap is removed.

4 Unscrew the camshaft cover retaining bolts and lift the cover away. If it sticks, do not attempt to lever it off – instead free it by working around the cover and tapping it lightly with a soft-faced mallet. Note that on DOHC engines, it will be necessary to unscrew the

air ducting from the rear of the cylinder head, and unscrew the fuel lines from the front of the cylinder head to provide additional clearance (see illustration).

5 Recover the camshaft cover gasket (see illustration). Inspect the gasket carefully, and renew it if damage or deterioration is evident – note that the retaining bolts must be pushed fully through the gasket before refitting the cover.

6 Clean the mating surfaces of the cylinder head and camshaft cover thoroughly, removing all traces of oil and old gasket – take care to avoid damaging the surfaces as you do this.

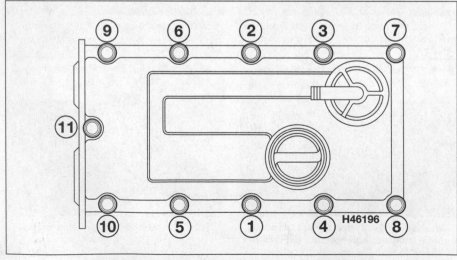

4.7b Camshaft cover tightening sequence (SOHC engines)

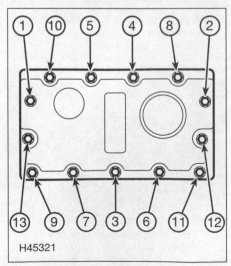

4.7c Camshaft cover tightening sequence (DOHC engines)

4 Where applicable, prise the cover from the centre of the pulley to expose the securing bolts.

5 Slacken the bolts securing the crankshaft pulley to the sprocket **(see illustration)**. If necessary, the pulley can be prevented from turning by counterholding with a spanner or socket on the crankshaft sprocket bolt.

6 Remove the auxiliary drivebelt, as described in Chapter 1.

7 Unscrew the bolts securing the pulley to the sprocket, and remove the pulley **(see illustration)**.

Refitting

8 Refit the pulley over the locating peg on the crankshaft sprocket, then refit the pulley securing bolts. Tighten them to the specified torque.

9 The remainder of refitting is a reversal of removal.

---

6 Timing belt covers – removal and refitting

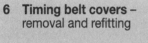
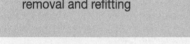

Upper outer cover

1 Pull the front edge of the plastic cover on the top of the engine upwards to release the rubber mountings.

2 On SOHC engines, release the clip and remove the charge air pipe between the intercooler and the intake manifold **(see illustration)**.

3 Release the uppermost part of the timing belt outer cover by prising open the metal spring clips, then withdraw the cover away from the engine. On DOHC engines there are three clips, two at the front and a single one at the rear of the cover **(see illustrations)**.

4 Refitting is a reversal of removal, noting that the lower edge of the upper cover engages with the centre cover.

Centre outer cover

5 Remove the auxiliary drivebelt as described in Chapter 1.

6 Remove the crankshaft pulley as described in Section 5. It is assumed that, if the centre cover is being removed, the lower cover will be also – if not, simply remove the components described in Section 5 for access

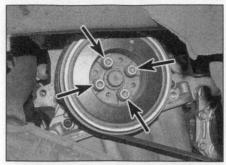

5.5 Crankshaft pulley retaining bolts (arrowed)

to the crankshaft pulley, and leave the pulley in position.

7 With the upper cover removed (paragraphs 1 to 3), unscrew and remove the retaining bolts from the centre cover. Withdraw the centre cover from the engine, noting how it fits over the lower cover **(see illustration)**.

8 Refitting is a reversal of the removal procedure.

Lower outer cover

9 Remove the upper and centre covers as described previously.

10 If not already done, remove the crankshaft pulley as described in Section 5, then unscrew the auxiliary drivebelt tensioner.

11 Unscrew the remaining bolt(s) securing the lower cover, and lift it out **(see illustration)**.

12 Refitting is a reversal of removal; locate the centre cover in place before fitting the top two bolts.

6.2 Prise up the clips (arrowed) and remove the air pipe

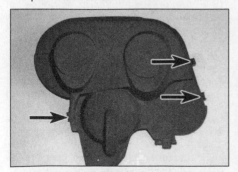

6.3b . . . and DOHC engines (arrowed)

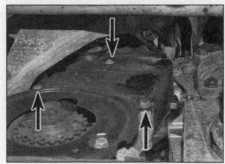

6.7 Centre cover retaining bolts (arrowed)

5.7 Note the hole in the pulley which locates over the peg on the sprocket (arrowed)

Rear cover

13 Remove the upper, centre and lower covers as described previously.

14 Remove the timing belt, tensioner and sprockets as described in Sections 7 and 8.

15 Slacken and withdraw the retaining bolts and lift the timing belt inner cover from the studs on the end of the engine, and remove it from the engine compartment.

16 Refitting is a reversal of removal.

---

7 Timing belt – removal, inspection and refitting

Removal

1 The primary function of the toothed timing belt is to drive the camshaft, but it also drives the coolant pump. Should the belt slip

6.3a Prise open the metal clips (arrowed) – SOHC engines . . .

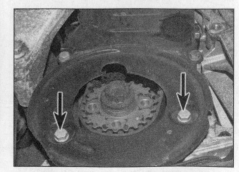

6.11 Lower cover bolts (arrowed)

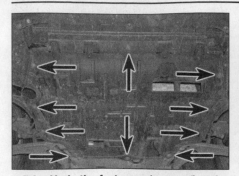

7.3a Undo the fasteners (arrowed) and remove the engine undershield

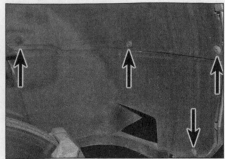

7.3b Undo the bolts (arrowed) and remove the lower section of the wheel arch liner

7.5 Unscrew the drivebelt tensioner (DOHC engine)

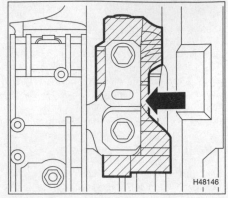

7.8a Engine mounting support close to the engine (Type A) . . .

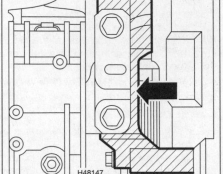

7.8b . . . and further from the engine (Type B)

or break in service, the valve timing will be disturbed and piston-to-valve contact may occur, resulting in serious engine damage. For this reason, it is important that the timing belt is tensioned correctly, and inspected regularly for signs of wear or deterioration.

2 Switch off the ignition and all electrical consumers and remove the ignition key. Apply the handbrake, then jack up the front of the vehicle and support securely on axle stands (see *Jacking and vehicle support*).

3 Remove the securing bolts and withdraw the engine undershield, and the front lower section of the right-hand wheel arch liner **(see illustrations)**. Also, remove the engine top cover by pulling it upwards from place.

4 On SOHC engines, release the clips and remove the charge air pipe from the intercooler

to the intake manifold **(see illustration 6.2)**.

5 Remove the auxiliary drivebelt as described in Chapter 1, then unscrew and remove the drivebelt tensioner **(see illustration)**.

6 Remove the crankshaft pulley/vibration damper as described in Section 5.

7 Remove the timing belt covers as described in Section 6.

8 On SOHC engines, a modified right-hand engine mounting was introduced gradually, making it unnecessary to remove the mounting for timing belt removal. The later mounting is identified by increased distance from the engine **(see illustrations)**. Even with the modified mounting, it is still necessary to remove the mounting to remove the tensioning roller.

9 On models with the Type A mounting (see

previous paragraph), support the engine and remove the right-hand engine mounting as described in Section 18.

10 On DOHC engines, support the engine from below, then remove the right-hand mounting and engine bracket.

11 On 06/2006-on DOHC engines, disconnect the fuel supply and return lines.

12 Unscrew the coolant expansion tank and position it to one side. **Note:** *Do not disconnect the hoses.*

13 Set the engine to TDC on No 1 cylinder as described in Section 3.

14 If the original timing belt is to be refitted, mark the running direction of the belt, to ensure correct refitting.

Caution: If the belt appears to be in good condition and can be re-used, it is essential that it is refitted the same way around, otherwise accelerated wear will result, leading to premature failure.

15 Loosen the bolts securing the sprocket(s) to the camshaft hub(s) while holding the sprockets with a suitable tool **(see illustration)**.

16 Loosen the timing belt tensioner securing nut, then use circlip pliers or an Allen key (as applicable) to turn the tensioner anti-clockwise until a suitable pin or drill bit can be inserted through the locking holes. Now, turn the tensioner clockwise to the stop and tighten the securing nut **(see illustration)**.

17 Slide the belt from the sprockets, taking care not to twist or kink the belt excessively if it is to be re-used.

Inspection

18 Examine the belt for evidence of contamination by coolant or lubricant. If this is the case, find the source of the contamination before progressing any further. Check the belt for signs of wear or damage, particularly around the leading edges of the belt teeth. Renew the belt if its condition is in doubt; the cost of belt renewal is negligible compared with potential cost of the engine repairs, should the belt fail in service. The belt must be renewed if it has covered the mileage given in Chapter 1, however, if it has covered less, it is prudent to renew it regardless of condition, as a precautionary measure.

19 If the timing belt is not going to be refitted for some time, it is a wise precaution to hang a

7.15 Prevent the sprocket from rotating with a suitable tool, and slacken the retaining bolts

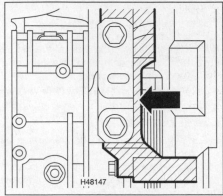

7.16 Tensioner securing nut, Allen key and locking pin (arrowed)

warning label on the steering wheel, to remind yourself (and others) not to attempt to start the engine.

Refitting

20 Ensure that the crankshaft and camshaft are still set to TDC on No 1 cylinder, as described in Section 3.

21 Position the camshaft sprocket(s) so that the securing bolts are in the centre part of the elongated holes **(see illustration)**. Note that the bolts should be slightly loose – it should be possible to rotate the sprocket independently of the hub.

22 Loop the timing belt loosely under the crankshaft sprocket. **Note:** *Observe any direction of rotation markings on the belt.*

23 Engage the timing belt teeth with the camshaft sprocket(s), then manoeuvre it into position around the tensioning roller, idler roller, crankshaft sprocket, and finally around the coolant pump sprocket. Make sure that the belt teeth seat correctly on the sprockets. **Note:** *Slight adjustment to the position of the camshaft sprocket may be necessary to achieve this.* Avoid bending the belt back on itself or twisting it excessively as you do this. Ensure that any slack in the belt is in the section of belt that passes over the tensioner roller.

24 Loosen the timing belt tensioner securing nut, and turn the tensioner anti-clockwise with the circlip pliers or an Allen key (as applicable) until the locking pin can be removed. Now, turn the tensioner clockwise until the pointer is in the middle of the gap in the tensioner backplate **(see illustration)**. With the tensioner held in this position, tighten the securing nut to the specified torque and angle.

25 Tighten the camshaft sprocket bolts to the specified torque. Prevent the sprocket from rotating using the same counterholding tool used during removal.

26 Remove the sprocket locking pin(s) and the crankshaft locking tool.

27 Using a spanner or wrench and socket on the crankshaft pulley centre bolt, rotate the crankshaft through two complete revolutions. Reset the engine to TDC on No 1 cylinder, with reference to Section 3 and check that the crankshaft and camshaft sprocket locking pins can still be inserted. If the camshaft sprocket locking pin(s) cannot be inserted, slacken the retaining bolts, turn the hub(s) until the pin(s) fit, and tighten the sprocket retaining bolts to the specified torque.

28 The remainder of refitting is a reversal of removal.

8 Timing belt tensioner and sprockets – removal and refitting

Timing belt tensioner

Removal

1 Remove the timing belt as described in Section 7.

7.21 Position the sprocket so that the securing bolts are in the centre part of the elongated holes

2 Remove the engine mounting bracket with reference to Section 18 (if not already done so).

3 Unscrew the timing belt tensioner nut, and remove the tensioner from the engine **(see illustration 7.16)**.

Refitting

4 When refitting the tensioner to the engine, ensure that the lug on the tensioner backplate engages with the corresponding cut-out in the rear timing belt cover, then refit the tensioner nut **(see illustration)**.

5 Refit and tension the timing belt as described in Section 7, making sure that the tensioner backplate is correctly engaged with the hole in the cylinder head.

Idler pulleys

Removal

6 Remove the timing belt as described in Section 7.

7 Unscrew the relevant idler pulley securing bolt/nut, then withdraw the pulley.

Refitting

8 Refit the pulley and tighten the securing bolt or nut to the specified torque. **Note:** *Renew the bolt/nut.*

9 Refit and tension the timing belt as described in Section 7.

Crankshaft sprocket

Note: *A new crankshaft sprocket securing bolt must be used on refitting.*

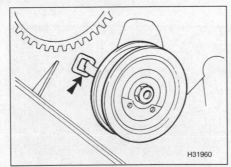

8.4 Ensure that the lug on the tensioner backplate engages with the cut-out in the rear timing belt cover

7.24 The pointer must be in the gap in the tensioner backplate (arrowed)

Removal

10 Remove the timing belt as described in Section 7.

11 The sprocket securing bolt must now be slackened, and the crankshaft must be prevented from turning as the sprocket bolt is unscrewed. To hold the sprocket, make up a suitable tool, and bolt it to the sprocket using a two bolts bolted into two of the crankshaft pulley bolt holes.

12 Hold the sprocket using the tool, then slacken the sprocket securing bolt. Take care, as the bolt is very tight. Do not allow the crankshaft to turn as the bolt is slackened.

13 Unscrew the bolt, and slide the sprocket from the end of the crankshaft, noting which way round the sprocket's raised boss is fitted.

Refitting

14 Commence refitting by positioning the sprocket on the end of the crankshaft, with the raised boss fitted as noted on removal.

15 Fit a new sprocket securing bolt, then counterhold the sprocket using the method employed on removal, and tighten the bolt to the specified torque in the two stages given in the Specifications **(see illustration)**.

16 Refit the timing belt as described in Section 7.

Camshaft sprocket

Removal

17 Remove the timing belt as described in Section 7.

18 Unscrew and remove the three retaining

8.15 Fit a new crankshaft sprocket bolt

8.23 Use a fabricated tool to counterhold the camshaft hub

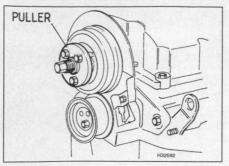

8.24 Attach a three-legged puller to the hub, and evenly tighten the puller until the hub is free of the camshaft taper

8.25 The integral key in the hub taper must align with the keyway in the camshaft taper (arrowed)

bolts and remove the camshaft sprocket from the camshaft hub.

Refitting

19 Refit the sprocket ensuring that it is fitted the correct way round, as noted before removal, then insert the sprocket bolts, and tighten by hand only at this stage.
20 If the crankshaft has been turned, turn the crankshaft clockwise 90° back to TDC.
21 Refit and tension the timing belt as described in Section 7.

Camshaft hub

Note: *VAG technicians use special tool T10051 to counterhold the hub, however it is possible to fabricate a suitable alternative – see below.*

Removal

22 Remove the camshaft sprocket as described previously in this Section.
23 Engage special tool T10051 with the three

locating holes in the face of the hub to prevent the hub from turning. If this tool is not available, fabricate a suitable alternative. Whilst holding the tool, undo the central hub retaining bolt about two turns **(see illustration)**.
24 Leaving the central hub retaining bolt in place, attach VW tool T10052 (or a similar three-legged puller) to the hub, and evenly tighten the puller until the hub is free of the camshaft taper **(see illustration)**.

Refitting

25 Ensure that the camshaft taper and the hub centre are clean and dry, locate the hub on the taper, noting that the built-in key in the hub taper must align with the keyway in the camshaft taper **(see illustration)**.
26 Hold the hub in this position with tool T10051 (or similar home-made tool), and tighten the central bolt to the specified torque.

27 Refit the camshaft sprocket as described previously in this Section.

Coolant pump sprocket

28 The coolant pump sprocket is integral with the coolant pump. Refer to Chapter 3 for details of coolant pump removal.

---

9 Pump injector rocker shaft assembly – removal and refitting

Removal

1 Remove the camshaft cover as described in Section 4. In order to ensure that the rocker arms are refitted to their original locations, use a marker pen or paint and number the arms 1 to 4, with No 1 nearest the timing belt end of the engine. If the arms are not fitted to their original locations the injector basic clearance setting procedure must be carried out as described in Chapter 4A.
2 Slacken the locknut of the adjustment bolt on the end of the rocker arm above the respective injector, and undo the adjustment bolt until the rocker arm lies against the plunger pin of the injector. Starting at the outside and working in, gradually and evenly slacken and remove the rocker shaft retaining bolts. Lift off the rocker shaft. Discard the rocker shaft bolts, new ones must be fitted **(see illustrations)**.

Refitting

3 Thoroughly check the rocker shaft, rocker arms and camshaft bearing cap seating surface for any signs of excessive wear or damage.
4 Smear some grease (VW No G000 100) onto the contact face of each rocker arm adjustment bolt, and refit the rocker shaft assembly, tightening the new retaining bolts as follows. Starting from the inside out, hand-tighten the bolts. Again, from the inside out, tighten the bolts to the Stage one torque setting. Finally, from the inside out, tighten the bolts to the Stage two angle tightening setting.
5 Attach a DTI (Dial Test Indicator) gauge to the cylinder head upper surface, and position the DTI probe against the top of the adjustment bolt **(see illustration)**. Turn the

9.2a Slacken the rocker shaft adjustment bolts

9.2b Start with the outer bolts first, carefully and evenly slacken the rocker shaft retaining bolts (SOHC engine)

9.2c Rocker shaft retaining bolts – 3 of 4 shown (DOHC engine)

9.5 Attach a DTI gauge to the cylinder head upper surface and position the DTI prove against the top of the adjustment bolt

10.4 Tandem fuel/vacuum pump (DOHC engine)

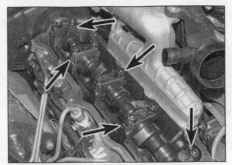

10.6 Check the camshaft bearing caps (arrowed) for markings

10.11 Remove the camshaft oil seal

crankshaft until the rocker arm roller is on the highest point of its corresponding camshaft lobe, and the adjustment bolt is at its lowest. Once this position has been established, remove the DTI gauge, bolt the adjustment bolt in until firm resistance is felt, and the injector spring cannot be compressed further. Turn the adjustment bolt **anti-clockwise** 180°, and tighten the locknut securely. Repeat this procedure for any other injectors that have been refitted.

6 Refit the camshaft cover and upper timing belt cover, as described in Section 4.

7 Start the engine and check that it runs correctly.

10 Camshaft and hydraulic tappets – removal, inspection and refitting

Note: *New camshaft oil seal(s) will be required on refitting. On DOHC engines, VW removal tool T10262 (or similar tool) will be required to remove the camshaft retaining frame – this is necessary to prevent distortion and damage to the frame as it is being removed.*

Removal

1 Turn the crankshaft to position No 1 piston at TDC on the firing stroke, and lock the camshaft in position, as described in Section 3.

2 Remove the timing belt as described in Section 7.

3 Remove the camshaft sprocket(s) and hubs as described in Section 8.

4 Remove the tandem fuel/brake vacuum

pump as described in Chapter 9 **(see illustration)**.

5 Remove the injector rocker arms and shaft as described in Section 9.

SOHC engines

6 Check the camshaft bearing caps for identification markings **(see illustration)**. The bearing caps are normally stamped with their respective cylinder numbers. If no marks are present, make suitable marks using a scriber or punch. The caps should be numbered from 1 to 5, with No 1 at the timing belt end of the engine. Note on which side of the bearing caps the marks are made to ensure that they are refitted the correct way round.

7 The camshaft rotates in shell bearings. As the camshaft bearing caps are removed, recover the shell bearing halves from the camshaft. Number the back of the bearings with a felt pen to ensure that, if re-used, the bearings are fitted to their original locations. **Note:** *Fitted into the cylinder head, under each camshaft bearing cap, is a washer for each cylinder head bolt.*

8 Unscrew the securing nuts, and remove Nos 1, 3 and 5 bearing caps.

9 Working progressively, in a diagonal sequence, slacken the nuts securing Nos 2 and 4 bearing caps. Note that as the nuts are slackened, the valve springs will push the camshaft up.

10 Once the nuts securing Nos 2 and 4 bearing caps have been fully slackened, lift off the bearing caps.

11 Carefully lift the camshaft from the cylinder head, keeping it level and supported at both

ends as it is removed so that the journals and lobes are not damaged. Remove the oil seal from the end of the camshaft and discard it – a new one will be required for refitting **(see illustration)**.

12 Lift the hydraulic tappets from their bores in the cylinder head, and store them with the valve contact surfaces facing downwards, to prevent the oil from draining out. It is recommended that the tappets are kept immersed in oil for the period they are removed from the cylinder head. Make a note of the position of each tappet, as they must be refitted in their original locations on reassembly – accelerated wear leading to early failure will result if the tappets are interchanged.

13 Recover the lower shell bearing halves from the cylinder head; number the back of the shells with a felt pen to ensure that, if re-used, the bearings are fitted to their original locations.

DOHC engines

14 Unscrew the upper bolt securing the EGR cooler bracket.

15 Disconnect the wiring from the unit injectors and glow plugs. To disconnect the wiring connector from the left-hand end of the cylinder head, use a screwdriver to pull out the plastic red lock, then unscrew the collar and pull the connector from the pins. To remove the wiring conduit, first undo the bolts retaining it to the cylinder head, then release the multipin plug by raising the clip and unscrewing the outer threaded collar, ideally using the special VW tool T10310 which engages the three slots **(see illustrations)**.

10.15a Disconnect the wiring from the unit injectors

10.15b Wiring loom connector, showing the 3 pins in the outer collar

10.15c Retaining clip on the inside of the wiring loom connector

10.24 Check the camshaft endfloat using a DTI gauge

16 Progressively unscrew the camshaft retaining frame bolts starting from the outside to inside.

17 The VW tool is now used to remove the retaining bearing frame. First, fully unscrew the *ejector* bolts, then fit the tool to the frame and tighten the bolts. Bolt in the *ejector* bolts until they contact the cylinder head bolt(s), then progressively tighten them so that the bearing frame is released from the cylinder head.

18 Carefully lift the camshafts from the cylinder head, keeping them identified for location. Remove the oil seals from the ends of the camshafts and discard them – new ones will be required for refitting.

19 To remove the exhaust roller rocker fingers and hydraulic tappets, carry out the following:

a) *Drain the coolant as described in Chapter 1.*
b) *Remove the connecting pipe between the EGR valve and bypass flap.*
c) *Remove the thermostat housing as described in Chapter 3.*
d) *Unscrew the plug from the end of the exhaust roller rocker shaft.* **Note:** *If the plug is very tight, the shaft may be deformed while unscrewing it, making the oil supply hole alignment incorrect. If this happens, renew the shaft.*
e) *Undo the bolt securing the roller rocker shaft to the cylinder head.*

20 To remove either exhaust or inlet roller

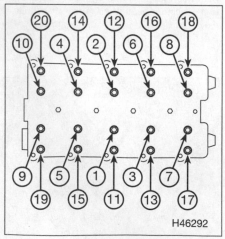

10.40 Camshaft bearing frame bolt tightening sequence

H46292

rocker fingers and hydraulic tappets, use VW slide hammer/puller tool T10055 to pull the shaft from the cylinder head while removing the roller rockers. Store the rockers in a container with numbered compartments to ensure they are refitted to their correct locations. It is recommended that the tappets are kept immersed in oil for the period they are removed from the cylinder head.

Inspection

21 With the camshaft(s) removed, examine the bearing caps/frame and the bearing locations in the cylinder head for signs of obvious wear or pitting. If evident, a new cylinder head will probably be required. Also check that the oil supply holes in the cylinder head are free from obstructions.

22 Visually inspect the camshaft for evidence of wear on the surfaces of the lobes and journals. Normally their surfaces should be smooth and have a dull shine; look for scoring, erosion or pitting and areas that appear highly polished, indicating excessive wear. Accelerated wear will occur once the hardened exterior of the camshaft has been damaged, so always renew worn items. **Note:** *If these symptoms are visible on the tips of the camshaft lobes, check the corresponding tappet, as it will probably be worn as well.*

23 If the machined surfaces of the camshaft appear discoloured or blued, it is likely that it has been overheated at some point, probably due to inadequate lubrication. This may have distorted the shaft, so check the run-out as follows: place the camshaft between two V-blocks and using a DTI gauge, measure the run-out at the centre journal. If it exceeds the figure quoted in the Specifications at the start of this Chapter, renew the camshaft.

24 To measure the camshaft endfloat, temporarily refit the camshaft to the cylinder head, then fit Nos 1 and 5 bearing caps and tighten the retaining nuts to the specified torque setting. Anchor a DTI gauge to the timing belt end of the cylinder head **(see illustration)**. Push the camshaft to one end of the cylinder head as far as it will travel, then rest the DTI gauge probe on the end face of the camshaft, and zero the gauge. Push the camshaft as far as it will go to the other end of the cylinder head, and record the gauge reading. Verify the reading by pushing the camshaft back to its original position and checking that the gauge indicates zero again. **Note:** *The hydraulic tappets must not be fitted whilst this measurement is being taken.*

25 Check that the camshaft endfloat measurement is within the limit listed in the Specifications. If the measurement is outside the specified limit, wear is unlikely to be confined to any one component, so renewal of the camshaft, cylinder head and bearing caps must be considered.

26 Inspect the hydraulic tappets for obvious signs of wear or damage, and renew if necessary. Check that the oil holes in the tappets are free from obstructions.

Refitting

SOHC engines

27 Smear some clean engine oil onto the sides of the hydraulic tappets, and offer them into position in their original bores in the cylinder head. Push them down until they contact the valves, then lubricate the camshaft lobe contact surfaces.

28 Lubricate the camshaft and cylinder head bearing journals and shell bearings with clean engine oil.

29 Carefully lower the camshaft into position in the cylinder head making sure that the cam lobes for No 1 cylinder are pointing upwards.

30 Refit a new camshaft oil seal on the end of the camshaft. Make sure that the closed end of the seal faces the camshaft sprocket end of the camshaft, and take care not to damage the seal lip. Locate the seal against the seat in the cylinder head.

31 Oil the upper surfaces of the camshaft bearing journals and shell bearings, then fit Nos 2 and 4 bearing caps. Ensure that they are fitted the right way round and in the correct locations, then progressively tighten the retaining nuts in a diagonal sequence to the specified torque. Note that as the nuts are tightened, the camshaft will be forced down against the pressure of the valve springs.

32 Fit bearing caps 1, 3 and 5 over the camshaft and progressively tighten the nuts to the specified torque. Note that it may be necessary to locate No 5 bearing cap by tapping lightly on the end of the camshaft.

33 Refit the injector rocker arms as described in Section 9.

DOHC engines

34 Oil the roller rocker fingers and hydraulic tappets together with the shafts, then insert each shaft into the cylinder head while at the same time fitting the roller rockers in their correct order. The inlet shaft must be inserted until flush with the cylinder head. The exhaust shaft must be correctly aligned with the retaining bolt hole. Insert and tighten the bolt securely.

35 Reverse the procedures listed in paragraph 19.

36 Lubricate the camshaft and cylinder head bearing journals with clean engine oil.

37 Carefully lower the camshafts into position in the cylinder head making sure that the cam lobes for No 1 cylinder are pointing upwards.

38 Fit new camshaft oil seals on the end of the camshafts. Make sure that the closed end of the seal faces the camshaft sprocket end of the camshaft, and take care not to damage the seal lip. Locate the seal against the seat in the cylinder head.

39 Oil the upper surfaces of the camshaft bearing frame journals, then apply sealant to the mating surfaces of the bearing frame and cylinder head.

40 Refit the bearing frame together with the rocker arms and shaft, using the VW tool, ensuring the frame is the correct way round.

Progressively tighten the retaining bolts to the specified torque in the order shown **(see illustration)**, then remove the tool. Note that as the bolts are tightened, the camshafts will be forced down against the pressure of the valve springs.

41 Tighten the rocker arm shaft bolts to the specified angle. Refit the wiring conduit and secure the connectors.

All engines

42 Renew the camshaft oil seal(s) as applicable with reference to Section 12.
43 Refit the tandem fuel/brake vacuum pump as described in Chapter 9.
44 Refit the camshaft sprocket(s) and hubs as described in Section 8.
45 Refit the timing belt as described in Section 7.

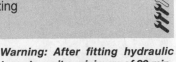

11 Hydraulic tappets – testing

⚠️ *Warning: After fitting hydraulic tappets, wait a minimum of 30 minutes (or preferably, leave overnight) before starting the engine, to allow the tappets time to settle, otherwise the valve heads will strike the pistons.*

1 The hydraulic tappets are self-adjusting, and require no attention whilst in service.
2 If the hydraulic tappets become excessively noisy, their operation can be checked as described below.
3 Start the engine, and run it until it reaches normal operating temperature, increase the engine speed to approximately 2500 rpm for 2 minutes.
4 If any hydraulic tappets are heard to be noisy, carry out the following checks.
5 Remove the camshaft cover as described in Section 4.
6 Using a socket or spanner on the crankshaft sprocket bolt, turn the crankshaft until the tip of the camshaft lobe above the tappet to be checked is pointing vertically upwards.
7 Using feeler blades, check the clearance between the top of the tappet, and the cam lobe. If the play is in excess of 0.1 mm, renew the relevant tappet. If the play is less than 0.1 mm, or there is no play, proceed as follows.

13.5 Undo the tandem pump retaining bolts (arrowed)

8 Press down on the tappet using a wooden or plastic instrument **(see illustration)**. If free play in excess of 1.0 mm is present before the tappet contacts the valve stem, renew the relevant tappet.
9 On completion, refit the camshaft cover as described in Section 4.

12 Camshaft oil seals – renewal

Right-hand oil seal(s)

1 Remove the timing belt as described in Section 7.
2 Remove the camshaft sprocket and hub, as described in Section 8.
3 Drill two small holes into the existing oil seal, diagonally opposite each other. Take great care to avoid drilling through into the seal housing or camshaft sealing surface. Thread two self-tapping screws into the holes, and using a pair of pliers, pull on the heads of the screws to extract the oil seal.
4 Clean out the seal housing and the sealing surface of the camshaft by wiping it with a lint-free cloth. Remove any swarf or burrs that may cause the seal to leak.
5 Do not lubricate the lip and outer edge of the new oil seal, push it over the camshaft until it is positioned in place above its housing. To prevent damage to the sealing lips, wrap some adhesive tape around the end of the camshaft.
6 Using a hammer and a socket of suitable diameter, drive the seal squarely into its housing. **Note:** *Select a socket that bears only on the hard outer surface of the seal, not the inner lip which can easily be damaged.*
7 Refit the camshaft sprocket and its hub, as described in Section 8.
8 Refit and tension the timing belt as described in Section 7.

Left-hand oil seal

9 The left-hand camshaft oil seal is formed by the brake vacuum pump seal. Refer to Chapter 9 for details of brake vacuum pump removal and refitting.

13 Cylinder head – removal, inspection and refitting

Note: *The cylinder head must be removed with the engine cold. New cylinder head bolts and a new cylinder head gasket will be required on refitting, and suitable studs will be required to guide the cylinder head into position – see text.*

Removal

1 Switch off the ignition and all electrical consumers, and remove the ignition key. For improved access on DOHC engines, remove the battery as described in Chapter 5.

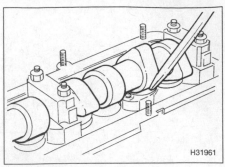

11.8 Press down on the tappet using a wooden or plastic tool

2 Drain the cooling system and engine oil as described in Chapter 1.
3 Remove the insulation from the top of the engine (where fitted).
4 Remove the air filter complete with the air mass meter and air ducts (see Chapter 4A). Also unscrew and remove the duct from the turbocharger.
5 Disconnect the fuel supply and return lines, and also the coolant hoses from the cylinder head. In the interests of safety, it is recommended that the fuel is siphoned from the tandem pump on the left-hand end of the cylinder head. If necessary, the pump may be unscrewed and removed **(see illustration)**.
6 Undo the bolts/nuts and move the fuel filter to one side.
7 Remove the front exhaust pipe/particulate filter as described in Chapter 4B.
8 Remove the turbocharger support and oil return line from the turbocharger. Also, remove the oil supply pipe and place to one side.
9 Remove the camshaft cover as described in Section 4.
10 Remove the timing belt as described in Section 7. Where the right-hand engine mounting has been removed, ensure the engine is supported adequately on a trolley jack and block of wood.
11 Remove the camshaft sprocket and timing belt tensioner as described in Section 8.
12 Where applicable, unscrew the bolt(s) securing the rear timing belt cover to the cylinder head **(see illustrations)**.
13 Remove the camshaft position sensor from the right-hand end of the cylinder head **(see illustration)**. Note that on DOHC engines,

13.12a Undo the bolt from the inner cover (arrowed) . . .

13.12b . . . and the one (arrowed) on the side of the cover

13.13 Unscrew the bolt and remove the camshaft position sensor

13.14 EGR connecting pipe at the flap housing

13.15 Disconnect the central connector for the injectors

13.16a Disconnect the coolant hose from the end of the cylinder head

13.16b Disconnect the vacuum pipes (arrowed)

the idler roller must be loosened to release the sensor wiring.

14 Remove the exhaust gas recirculation connecting pipe **(see illustration)**.

15 Note the locations of all the electrical wiring, then disconnect them methodically **(see illustration)**.

16 Disconnect all vacuum and coolant hoses **(see illustrations)**.

17 On DOHC engines, unscrew and remove the injector rocker arm shaft as follows. Slacken the locknut of the adjustment bolt on the end of the rocker arm above each of the injectors, and undo the adjustment bolt until the rocker arm lies against the plunger pin of the injector. Starting at the outside and working in, gradually and evenly slacken and remove the rocker shaft retaining bolts. Lift off the rocker shaft – this will allow access to the rear cylinder head bolts. Now unscrew the row

of inner bolts securing the camshaft retaining frame – the bolts bolt into the tops of the front cylinder head bolts, and are located behind the exhaust camshaft **(see illustration)**. As the bolts are removed, recover the large washers.

18 Using a multi-splined tool, undo the cylinder head bolts, working from the outside-in, evenly and gradually **(see illustration)**. Check that nothing remains connected, and lift the cylinder head from the engine block. Seek assistance if possible, as it is a heavy assembly, especially as it is being removed complete with the manifolds.

19 Remove the gasket from the top of the block, noting the locating dowels. If the dowels are a loose fit, remove them and store them with the head for safe-keeping. Do not discard the gasket yet – it will be needed for identification purposes. If desired, the manifolds can be removed from the cylinder

head with reference to Chapter 4A (inlet manifold) or 4B (exhaust manifold).

Inspection

20 Dismantling and inspection of the cylinder head is covered in Part Chapter 2C.

Cylinder head gasket selection

Note: *A dial test indicator (DTI) will be required for this operation.*

21 Examine the old cylinder head gasket for manufacturer's identification markings **(see illustration)**. These will be in the form of holes or notches, and a part number on the edge of the gasket. Unless new pistons have been fitted, the new cylinder head gasket must be of the same type as the old one.

22 If new piston assemblies have been fitted as part of an engine overhaul, or if a new short engine is to be fitted, the projection of

13.17 The camshaft retaining frame inner row bolts are tightened into the tops of the front cylinder head bolts

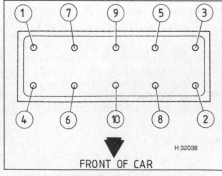

13.18 Cylinder head bolt slackening sequence

13.21 The thickness of the cylinder head gasket can be identified by notches or holes

13.24 Measure the piston projection at TDC using a DTI gauge

13.36 Two of the old head bolts (arrowed) can be used as cylinder head alignment guides

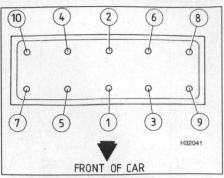

13.41a Cylinder head bolt tightening sequence

the piston crowns above the cylinder head mating face of the cylinder block at TDC must be measured. This measurement is used to determine the thickness of the new cylinder head gasket required.

23 Anchor a dial test indicator (DTI) to the top face (cylinder head gasket mating face) of the cylinder block, and zero the gauge on the gasket mating face.

24 Rest the gauge probe on No 1 piston crown, and turn the crankshaft slowly by hand until the piston reaches TDC. Measure and record the maximum piston projection at TDC **(see illustration)**.

25 Repeat the measurement for the remaining pistons, and record the results.

26 If the measurements differ from piston-to-piston, take the highest figure, and use this to determine the thickness of the head gasket required as follows.

Piston projection	(Gasket identification/ number of holes/notches)
0.91 to 1.00 mm	1
0.01 to 1.10 mm	2
1.11 to 1.20 mm	3

27 Purchase a new gasket according to the results of the measurements.

Refitting

Note: *If a VW exchange cylinder head, complete with camshaft(s), is to be fitted, the manufacturers recommend the following:*

a) Lubricate the contact surfaces between the tappets and the cam lobes before fitting the camshaft cover.

b) Do not remove the plastic protectors from the open valves until immediately before fitting the cylinder head.

c) Additionally, if a new cylinder head is fitted, VW recommend that the coolant is renewed.

28 The mating faces of the cylinder head and block must be perfectly clean before refitting the head. Use a scraper to remove all traces of gasket and carbon, also clean the tops of the pistons. Take particular care with the aluminium surfaces, as the soft metal is easily damaged.

29 Make sure that debris is not allowed to enter the oil and water passages – this is particularly important for the oil circuit, as carbon could block the oil supply to the

camshaft and crankshaft bearings. Using adhesive tape and paper, seal the water, oil and bolt holes in the cylinder block.

30 To prevent carbon entering the gap between the pistons and bores, smear a little grease in the gap. After cleaning a piston, rotate the crankshaft to that the piston moves down the bore, then wipe out the grease and carbon with a cloth rag. Clean the other piston crowns in the same way.

31 Check the head and block for nicks, deep scratches and other damage. If slight, they may be removed carefully with a file. More serious damage may be repaired by machining, but this is a specialist job.

32 If warpage of the cylinder head is suspected, use a straight-edge to check it for distortion, as described in Chapter 2C.

33 Ensure that the cylinder head bolt holes in the crankcase are clean and free of oil. Syringe or soak up any oil left in the bolt holes. This is most important in order that the correct bolt tightening torque can be applied, and to prevent the possibility of the block being cracked by hydraulic pressure when the bolts are tightened.

34 Turn the crankshaft anti-clockwise all the pistons at an equal height, approximately half-way down their bores from the TDC position (see Section 3). This will eliminate any risk of piston-to-valve contact as the cylinder head is refitted.

35 Where applicable, refit the manifolds with reference to Chapters 4A and/or 4B.

36 To guide the cylinder head into position, bolt two long studs (or old cylinder head bolts

with the heads cut off, and slots cut in the ends to enable the bolts to be unscrewed) into the cylinder block **(see illustration)**.

37 Ensure that the cylinder head locating dowels are in place in the cylinder block, then fit the new cylinder head gasket over the dowels, ensuring that the part number is uppermost. Where applicable, the OBEN/TOP marking should also be uppermost. Note that VW recommend that the gasket is only removed from its packaging immediately prior to fitting.

38 Lower the cylinder head into position on the gasket, ensuring that it engages correctly over the guide studs and dowels.

39 Fit the new cylinder head bolts to the eight remaining bolt locations, and bolt them in as far as possible by hand.

40 Unscrew the two guide studs from the exhaust side of the cylinder block, then bolt in the two remaining new cylinder head bolts as far as possible by hand.

41 Working progressively, in sequence, tighten all the cylinder head bolts to the specified Stage 1 torque **(see illustrations)**.

42 Again working progressively, in sequence, tighten all the cylinder head bolts to the specified Stage 2 torque.

43 Tighten all the cylinder head bolts, in sequence, through the specified Stage 3 angle **(see illustration)**.

44 Finally, tighten all the cylinder head bolts, in sequence, through the specified Stage 4 angle.

45 After finally tightening the cylinder head bolts, turn the camshaft so that the cam lobes for No 1 cylinder are pointing upwards.

13.41b Use a torque wrench to tighten the cylinder head bolts

13.43 Angle-tighten the cylinder head bolts

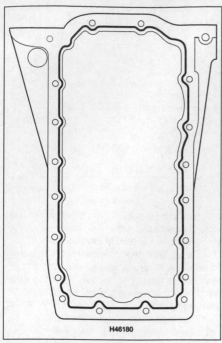

14.9 Apply sealant as shown by the black line

46 Where applicable, reconnect the lifting tackle to the engine lifting brackets on the cylinder head, then adjust the lifting tackle to support the engine. Once the engine is adequately supported using the cylinder head brackets, disconnect the lifting tackle from the bracket bolted to the cylinder block, and unscrew the improvised engine lifting bracket from the cylinder block. Alternatively, remove the trolley jack and block of wood from under the sump.

47 The remainder of the refitting procedure is a reversal of the removal procedure, bearing in mind the following points.

a) Refit the injector rocker shaft with reference to Section 9.

b) Refit the camshaft cover with reference to Section 4.

c) Use new sealing rings when reconnecting the turbocharger oil return pipe to the cylinder block.

d) Reconnect the exhaust front section/particulate filter to the turbocharger, with reference to Chapter 4B.

e) Refit the timing belt tensioner with reference to Section 8.

f) Refit the camshaft sprocket as described in Section 8, and refit the timing belt as described in Section 7.

g) Refill the cooling system and engine oil as described in Chapter 1.

14 Sump –
removal and refitting

Removal

1 Apply the handbrake, then jack up the front of the vehicle and support securely on axle stands (see *Jacking and vehicle support*).

2 Remove the securing bolts and withdraw the engine undershield(s).

3 Drain the engine oil as described in Chapter 1.

4 Where fitted, disconnect the wiring connector from the oil level/temperature sender in the sump.

5 Unscrew and remove the bolts securing the sump to the cylinder block, and the bolts securing the sump to the transmission casing, then withdraw the sump. If necessary, release the sump by tapping with a soft-faced hammer.

6 If desired, unscrew the oil baffle plate from the cylinder block.

Refitting

7 Begin refitting by thoroughly cleaning the mating faces of the sump and cylinder block. Ensure that all traces of old sealant are removed.

8 Where applicable, refit the oil baffle plate, and tighten the securing bolts.

9 Ensure that the cylinder block mating face of the sump is free from all traces of old sealant, oil and grease, and then apply a 2.0 to 3.0 mm thick bead of silicone sealant (VW D 176 404 A2 or equivalent) to the sump **(see illustration)**. Note that the sealant should be run around the inside of the bolt holes in the sump. The sump must be fitted within 5 minutes of applying the sealant.

10 Offer the sump up to the cylinder block, then refit the sump-to-cylinder block bolts, and lightly tighten them by hand, working progressively in a diagonal sequence. **Note:** *If the sump is being refitted with the engine and transmission separated, make sure that the sump is flush with the flywheel end of the cylinder block.*

11 Refit the sump-to-transmission casing bolts, and tighten them lightly, using a socket.

12 Again working in a diagonal sequence, lightly tighten the sump-to-cylinder block bolts, using a socket.

13 Tighten the sump-to-transmission casing bolts to the specified torque.

14 Working in a diagonal sequence, progressively tighten the sump-to-cylinder block bolts to the specified torque.

15 Refit the wiring connector to the oil level/temperature sender (where fitted), then refit the engine undershield(s), and lower the vehicle to the ground.

16 Allow at least 30 minutes from the time of refitting the sump for the sealant to dry, then refill the engine with oil, with reference to Chapter 1.

15 Oil pump, drive chain and balance shaft assembly –
removal, inspection and refitting

Note: *2 different oil pump arrangements may be encountered on these engines. The first has a chain-driven balance shaft assembly which also drives the oil pump. The second has a gear-driven balance shaft assembly which also drives the oil pump. Proceed under the appropriate heading.*

Chain-driven balance shaft and oil pump removal

1 Remove the sump as described in Section 14.

2 Lock the camshaft(s) and crankshaft at TDC on No 1 cylinder as described in Section 3.

3 Undo the bolts and remove the balance shaft sprocket cover.

4 Press the tensioner guide rail away from the chain, and lock it in place with a suitable drill bit **(see illustration)**.

5 Undo the 2 bolts and remove the chain tensioner assembly.

15.4 Compress the guide rail, and insert a drill bit to lock it in place. Undo the tensioner retaining bolts

6 Undo the 4 bolts and detach the sprocket from the balance shaft.

7 Working from the outside in, gradually unscrew the bolts securing the balance shaft assembly to the base of the cylinder block.

8 Remove the retaining circlip, then pull the oil pump shaft out using a M3 bolt.

9 Undo the retaining bolts and detach the pick-up pipe from the pump. Undo the 2 bolts and detach the oil pump from the balance shaft assembly.

Gear-driven balance shaft and oil pump removal

Oil pump

10 Remove the sump as described in Section 14.

11 Remove the retaining circlip, then pull the oil pump shaft out using an M3 bolt. Undo the retaining bolt and detach the pick-up pipe from the pump.

Balance shaft assembly

12 Remove the sump as described in Section 14.

13 Undo the 2 bolts and detach the oil pump from the balance shaft assembly.

14 Lock the camshaft(s) and crankshaft at TDC on No 1 cylinder as described in Section 3.

15 Working gradually from the outside in, undo the retaining bolts and detach the balance shaft assembly from the base of the cylinder block.

Inspection

16 At the time of writing, it would appear that no parts are available for the oil pump or balance shaft assembly. If defective, the oil pump or balance shaft assembly must be renewed. Consult a VW dealer or parts specialist.

Chain-driven balance shaft and oil pump refitting

17 Locate the pump on the dowels, and tighten the retaining bolts to the specified torque.

18 Refit the pick-up pipe with a new O-ring, and tighten the retaining bolts to the specified torque.

19 Push the driveshaft into the balance shaft housing and secure it with the circlip.

20 Ensure the engine is still locked at TDC on No 1 cylinder as described in Section 3, then position the balance shaft assembly over the locating dowels on the base of the cylinder block, and insert the new retaining bolts. Only finger-tighten the bolts at this stage.

21 The balance shafts must now be rotated until VW tool No T10255 can be fitted into the groove on the left-hand end of the rear shaft (see illustration).

22 Position the chain and sprocket on the shaft so the elongated holes of the sprocket align with the balance shaft holes. If they don't, move the sprocket around in the chain until they do. Fit the new sprocket retaining bolts, but only finger-tighten them at this stage.

23 Working from the centre outwards, tighten the balance shaft assembly retaining bolts to the specified torque.

24 Refit the chain tensioner, tighten the retaining bolts to the specified torque, then remove the locking rod/drill bit.

25 Check that the VW tool T10255 is still in place, locking the balance shaft assembly, then tighten the sprocket retaining bolts to the specified torque. Remove the VW tool.

26 Refit the cover over the sprocket, then apply a little thread locking compound, and tighten the retaining bolts securely.

27 The remainder of refitting is a reversal of removal.

Gear-driven balance shaft and oil pump refitting

Oil pump

28 Refit the pump to the balance shaft assembly and tighten the retaining bolts to the specified torque.

29 Refit the oil pick-up pipe using a new O-ring, then tighten the retaining bolt to the specified torque.

30 Push the driveshaft into place, and secure it with the circlip.

31 The remainder of refitting is a reversal of removal.

Balance shaft assembly

Note: *If the original balance shaft assembly is being refitted, it's essential that neither the drivegear on the crankshaft or the crankshaft itself has been renewed, or the idler gear bolt has been slackened. If they have, proceed under the heading for the installation of a new balance shaft assembly.*

Refitting the original assembly

32 Rotate the balance shaft until VW tool No T10255 can be fitted into the groove on the left-hand end of the rear shaft (see illustration 15.21).

33 Position the balance shaft assembly over the locating dowels on the base of the cylinder block. The idler gear must engage with the drive gear of the crankshaft, and there must be noticeable backlash.

34 Fit the new balance shaft assembly retaining bolts, and working from the centre outwards, tighten them to the specified torque. Remove the VW tool.

35 The remainder of refitting is a reversal of removal.

Fitting a new balance shaft assembly

36 New balance shaft assemblies are supplied with an idler gear with a special coating. Once fitted, the coating wears down to give the correct backlash between the gears.

37 Ensure the engine is still locked at TDC for No 1 cylinder as described in Section 3.

38 Slacken the idler gear retaining bolt 90°.

39 Position the balance shaft assembly over the locating dowels on the base of the cylinder block, ensuring the white mark on the idler gear is centrally aligned with the crankshaft drivegear. Idler gears not marked with a white mark can be installed in any position.

40 Fit the new balance shaft assembly retaining bolts, and working from the centre outwards, tighten them to the specified torque.

41 Rotate the balance shaft until VW tool No T10255 can be fitted into the groove on the left-hand end of the rear shaft (see illustration 15.21).

42 Fit the balance shaft drivegear onto the shaft so the holes in the gear align with the holes in the shaft. Tighten the retaining bolts to the specified torque.

43 Have an assistant push the idler gear between the two gears to remove any backlash. At the same time, rotate the balance shaft anti-clockwise slightly, and tighten the idler gear retaining bolt to the specified torque. Remove the balance shaft locking tool.

44 The remainder of refitting is a reversal of removal.

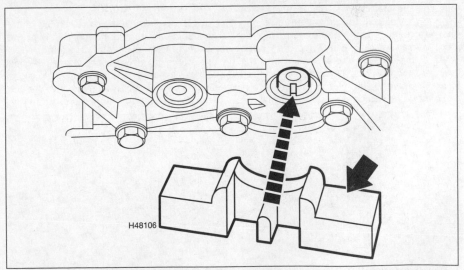

15.21 The tool T10255 must locate in the groove at the left-hand end of the rear balance shaft (arrowed)

16.4 Rotate the outside of the dual-mass flywheel to align the bolts with the holes

16.5 Use a locking tool (arrowed) to prevent the flywheel from rotating

16 Flywheel –
removal, inspection
and refitting

Removal

1 On manual gearbox models, remove the gearbox (see Chapter 7A) and clutch (see Chapter 6).
2 On automatic transmission models, remove the automatic transmission as described in Chapter 7B.
3 These models are fitted with a dual-mass flywheel. Begin by making alignment marks between the flywheel and the crankshaft.
4 Rotate the outside of the dual-mass flywheel so that the bolts align with the holes **(see illustration)**.
5 Unscrew the bolts and remove the flywheel. Use a locking tool to counterhold the flywheel **(see illustration)**. Discard the bolts, new ones must be fitted. **Note:** *In order not to damage the flywheel, do not allow the bolt heads to make contact with the flywheel during the unscrewing procedure.*

Inspection

6 Check the flywheel for wear and damage. Examine the starter ring gear for excessive wear to the teeth. If the driveplate or its ring gear are damaged, the complete driveplate must be renewed. The flywheel ring gear, however, may be renewed separately from the flywheel, but the work should be entrusted to a VW dealer. If the clutch friction face is discoloured or scored excessively, it may be

possible to regrind it, but this work should also be entrusted to a VW dealer.
7 With the flywheel removed, check the spigot needle bearing (where fitted) in the end of the crankshaft for wear by turning it with a finger. If there is any evidence of excessive wear or if the bearing has been running dry, it must be renewed. To do this, use a bearing removal puller which engages the rear end of the bearing. Drive the new bearing into position until its outer end is 1.5 mm below the end of the crankshaft.
8 The following are guidelines only, but should indicate whether professional inspection is necessary. The dual-mass flywheel should be checked as follows:
There should be no cracks in the drive surface of the flywheel. If cracks are evident, the flywheel may need renewing.

Warpage

Place a straight-edge across the face of the drive surface, and check by trying to insert a feeler gauge between the straight-edge and the drive surface **(see illustration)**. The flywheel will normally warp like a bowl – ie, higher on the outer edge. If the warpage is more than 0.40 mm, the flywheel may need renewing.

Free rotational movement

This is the distance the drive surface of the flywheel can be turned independently of the flywheel primary element, using finger effort alone. Move the drive surface in one direction and make a mark where the locating pin aligns with the flywheel edge. Move the drive surface in the other direction (finger pressure only)

and make another mark **(see illustration)**. The total of free movement should not exceed 10.0 mm. If it's more, the flywheel may need renewing.

Total rotational movement

This is the total distance the drive surface can be turned independently of the flywheel primary element. Insert two bolts into the clutch pressure plate/damper unit mounting holes, and with the crankshaft/flywheel held stationary, use a lever/pry bar between the bolts and use some effort to move the drive surface fully in one direction – make a mark where the locating pin aligns with the flywheel edge. Now force the drive surface fully in the opposite direction, and make another mark. The total rotational movement should not exceed 44.0 mm. If it does, have the flywheel professionally inspected.

Lateral movement

The lateral movement (up and down) of the drive surface in relation to the primary element of the flywheel, should not exceed 2.0 mm. If it does, the flywheel may need renewing. This can be checked by pressing the drive surface down on one side into the flywheel (flywheel horizontal) and making an alignment mark between the drive surface and the inner edge of the primary element. Now press down on the opposite side of the drive surface, and make another mark above the original one. The difference between the two marks is the lateral movement **(see illustration)**.

Refitting

9 Refitting is a reversal of removal. Use new bolts when refitting the flywheel, and coat the threads of the bolts with locking fluid before inserting them. Tighten them to the specified torque.

17 Crankshaft oil seals –
renewal

Note: *The oil seals are a PTFE (Teflon) type and are fitted dry, without using any grease or oil. These have a wider sealing lip and have been introduced instead of the coil spring type oil seal.*

16.8a Flywheel warpage check – see text

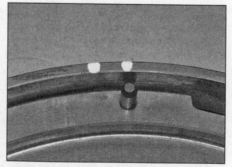

16.8b Flywheel free rotational movement check alignment marks – see text

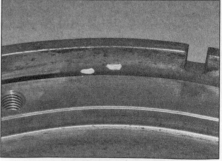

16.8c Flywheel lateral movement check marks – see text

Timing belt end oil seal

1 Remove the timing belt as described in Section 7, and the crankshaft sprocket with reference to Section 5.

2 To remove the seal without removing the housing, drill two small holes diagonally opposite each other, insert self-tapping screws, and pull on the heads of the screws with pliers **(see illustration)**.

3 Alternatively, to remove the oil seal complete with its housing, proceed as follows.

   a) *Remove the sump as described in Section 14. This is necessary to ensure a satisfactory seal between the sump and oil seal housing on refitting.*

   b) *Unscrew and remove the oil seal housing.*

   c) *Working on the bench, lever the oil seal from the housing using a suitable screwdriver. Take care not to damage the seal seating in the housing (see illustration).*

4 Thoroughly clean the oil seal seating in the housing.

5 Wind a length of tape around the end of the crankshaft to protect the oil seal lips as the seal (and housing, where applicable) is fitted.

6 Fit a new oil seal to the housing, pressing or driving it into position using a socket or tube of suitable diameter. Ensure that the socket or tube bears only on the hard outer ring of the seal, and take care not to damage the seal lips. Press or drive the seal into position until it is seated on the shoulder in the housing. Make sure that the closed end of the seal is facing outwards.

7 If the oil seal housing has been removed, proceed as follows, otherwise proceed to paragraph 11.

8 Clean all traces of old sealant from the crankshaft oil seal housing and the cylinder block, then coat the cylinder block mating faces of the oil seal housing with a 2.0 to 3.0 mm thick bead of silicone sealant (VW 176 404 A2, or equivalent). Note that the seal housing must be refitted within 5 minutes of applying the sealant. *Caution: DO NOT put excessive amounts of sealant onto the housing as it may get into the sump and block the oil pick-up pipe.*

9 Refit the oil seal housing, and tighten the bolts progressively to the specified torque **(see illustration)**.

10 Refit the sump as described in Section 14.

11 Refit the crankshaft sprocket with reference to Section 5, and the timing belt as described in Section 7.

Flywheel end oil seal

SOHC engines

12 Remove the flywheel as described in Section 16.

13 Remove the sump as described in Section 14. This is necessary to ensure a satisfactory seal between the sump and oil seal housing on refitting.

14 Unscrew and remove the oil seal housing, complete with the oil seal.

15 The new oil seal will be supplied ready-fitted to a new oil seal housing.

17.2 Pull the screw and seal from place using pliers

16 Thoroughly clean the oil seal housing mating face on the cylinder block.

17 New oil seal/housing assemblies are supplied with a fitting tool to prevent damage to the oil seal as it is being fitted. Locate the tool over the end of the crankshaft **(see illustration)**.

18 If the original oil seal housing was fitted using sealant, apply a thin bead of suitable silicone sealant (VW 176 404 A2, or equivalent) to the cylinder block mating face of the oil seal housing. Note that the seal housing must be refitted within 5 minutes of applying the sealant.
Caution: DO NOT put excessive amounts of sealant onto the housing as it may get into the sump and block the oil pick-up pipe.

19 Carefully fit the oil seal/housing assembly over the end of the crankshaft, then refit the securing bolts and tighten the bolts

17.9 Slide the oil seal housing over the end of the crankshaft

17.19a Fit the oil seal housing assembly over the end of the crankshaft . . .

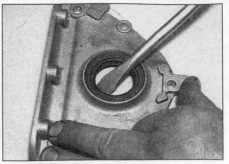

17.3 Prise the oil seal from the crankshaft oil seal housing

progressively, in a diagonal sequence, to the specified torque **(see illustrations)**.

20 Remove the oil seal protector tool from the end of the crankshaft.

21 Refit the sump as described in Section 14.

22 Refit the flywheel as described in Section 16.

DOHC engines

Note: *In these engines, the seal, sealing flange and TDC sender wheel are a complete unit. Special tools are required to refit the sealing flange, and press the sender wheel onto the end of the crankshaft. It is not possible to accurately fit these parts without the tools, which may be available from VW (part No T10134) and are available from aftermarket automotive tool specialists.*

23 Remove the flywheel as described in Section 16, then prise the intermediate plate from the locating dowels on the cylinder block.

17.17 Located the oil seal fitting tool over the end of the crankshaft

17.19b . . . then tighten the securing bolts

17.24 Sealing flange bolts (arrowed)

17.25 Screw in 6 x 35 mm bolts (arrowed) and draw the sealing flange and sender wheel from place

17.27a Rotate the nut until it's level with the end of the clamping surface (arrowed) . . .

17.27b . . . then clamp it in a vice

block is clean and free from debris. The new sealing flange/seal/sender wheel assembly is supplied with a sealing lip support ring, which serves as a fitting sleeve, and must not be removed prior to installation. Equally, the sender wheel must not be separated from the assembly.

27 If using the VW tool, proceed as follows. If using an aftermarket tool specialists product, follow the instructions supplied with the tool. Rotate the large spindle nut until it's level with the end of the clamping surface of the spindle, then clamp the spindle in a vice **(see illustration)**.

28 Press the tool housing downwards until it rests on the nut and washer. Rotate the nut until the inner part of the tool is at the same height as the housing **(see illustration)**.

29 Remove the seal securing clip. The hole on the sender wheel must align with the marking on the sealing flange **(see illustrations)**.

30 Place the flange outer side down on a clean, flat surface, then press the seal guide fitting sleeve (supplied ready fitted), housing, and sender wheel downwards until all the components are flat on the surface. In this position the upper edge of the sender wheel should be level with the edge of the sealing flange **(see illustrations)**.

31 Place the sealing flange on the assembly tool, so the pin locates in the hole in the sender wheel **(see illustration)**.

32 Push the sealing flange and guide fitting sleeve against the tool whilst tightening the 3 knurled bolts. Ensure the pin is still located in the sender wheel **(see illustration)**.

24 Undo the bolts securing the sealing flange to the cylinder block **(see illustration)**.

25 Insert three 6 x 35 mm bolts into the threaded holes in the sealing flange. Tighten the bolts gradually and evenly, and press the

sealing flange and sender wheel from the crankshaft/cylinder block **(see illustration)**. The seal, sender wheel and sealing flange are supplied as a complete unit.

26 Ensure the mating face of the cylinder

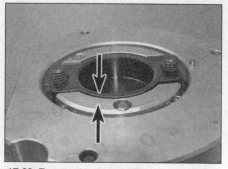

17.28 Rotate the nut until the inner part of the tool is flush with the housing (arrowed)

17.29a Remove the securing clip . . .

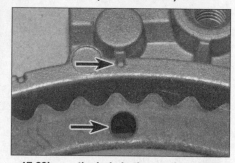

17.29b . . . the hole in the sender wheel should align with the marking on the flange (arrowed)

17.30a Press the assembly downwards on a clean, flat surface . . .

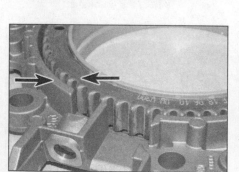

17.30b . . . so the upper edge of the sender wheel is level with the edge of the flange (arrowed)

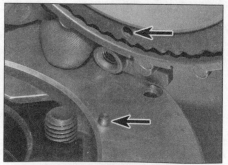

17.31 Fit the flange to the tool, ensuring the pin locates in the hole (arrowed)

33 Ensure the end of the crankshaft is clean, and is locked at TDC on No 1 cylinder as described in Section 3.
34 Unscrew the large nut to the end of the spindle threads, then press the spindle inwards as far as possible **(see illustration)**.
35 Align the flat side of the assembly with the sump flange, then secure the tool to the crankshaft using the integral Allen bolts **(see illustration)**. Only hand-tighten the bolts.
36 Insert two M7 x 35 mm bolts to guide the sealing flange to the cylinder block **(see illustration)**.
37 Using hand-pressure alone, push the tool assembly onto the crankshaft until the seal guide fitting sleeve contacts the crankshaft flange, then push the guide pin (black knob) into the hole in the crankshaft. This is to ensure the sender wheel reaches its correct installation position **(see illustration)**.
38 Rotate the large nut until it makes contact with the tool housing, then tighten it to 35 Nm (26 lbf ft). After tightening this nut, a small air gap must still be present between the sealing flange and cylinder block **(see illustration)**.
39 Unscrew the large nut, the two M7 x 35 mm bolts, the three knurled bolts and the Allen bolts securing the tool to the crankshaft. Remove the tool, and pull the seal guide fitting sleeve from place (if it didn't come out with the tool).
40 Use a vernier caliper or feeler gauge to measure the fitted depth of the sender wheel in relation to the crankshaft flange **(see illustration)**. The correct depth is 0.5 mm.
41 If the gap is correct, fit the sealing flange bolts and tighten them to the specified torque.
42 If the gap is too small, re-attach the tool to the sealing flange and crankshaft, then refit the two M7 x 35 mm guide bolts to the flange. Tighten the large spindle nut to 40 Nm (30 lbf ft), remove the tool and measure the air gap. If the gap is still too small, re-attach the tool and tighten the spindle nut to 45 Nm (33 lbf ft). Measure the gap again. When the gap is correct, refit the flange retaining bolts, and tighten them to the specified torque.
43 The remainder of refitting is a reversal of removal.

18 Engine/transmission mountings – inspection and renewal

Inspection

1 If improved access is required, jack up the front of the vehicle, and support it securely on axle stands (see *Jacking and vehicle support*). Remove the engine top cover which also incorporates the air filter, then remove the engine undershield(s).
2 Check the mounting rubbers to see if they are cracked, hardened or separated from the metal at any point; renew the mounting if any such damage or deterioration is evident.
3 Check that all the mountings are securely tightened; use a torque wrench to check if possible.

17.32 With the pin engaged in the hole, tighten the 3 knurled bolts to secure the flange to the tool

17.35 Hand-tighten the Allen bolts to secure the tool to the crankshaft (arrowed)

4 Using a large screwdriver or a crowbar, check for wear in the mounting by carefully levering against it to check for free play. Where this is not possible, enlist the aid of an assistant to move the engine/transmission back-and-forth, or from side-to-side, whilst you observe the mounting. While some free play is to be expected, even from new components, excessive wear should be obvious. If excessive free play is found, check first that the fasteners are correctly secured, then renew any worn components as described in the following paragraphs.

Renewal

Note: *New mounting securing bolts will be required on refitting.*

Right-hand mounting

5 Attach a hoist and lifting tackle to the engine

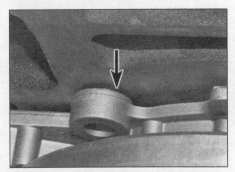
17.38 After tightening the spindle nut there should be an air gap between the sealing flange and the cylinder block (arrowed)

17.34 Unscrew the nut to the end of the thread, and push the spindle in as far as possible

17.36 Use 2 M7 x 35 mm bolts (arrowed) to guide the sealing flange

lifting brackets on the cylinder head, and raise the hoist to just take the weight of the engine. Alternatively the engine can be supported on a trolley jack under the engine. Use a block of

17.37 Push the black knob (arrowed) into the hole in the crankshaft

17.40 Measure the fitted depth of the sender wheel in relation to the end of the crankshaft

18.19 Rear mounting-to-transmission bolts (arrowed)

wood between the sump and the head of the jack, to prevent any damage to the sump.

6 For improved access, unscrew the coolant reservoir and move it to one side, leaving the coolant hoses connected.

7 Where applicable, move any wiring harnesses, pipes or hoses to one side to enable removal of the engine mounting.

8 Unscrew the bolts securing the mounting to the engine, then unscrew the bolts securing it to the body. Also, unscrew the movement limiter. Withdraw the mounting from the engine compartment.

9 Refitting is a reversal of removal, bearing in mind the following points.
 a) Use new securing bolts.
 b) Tighten all fixings to the specified torque.

Left-hand mounting

10 Remove the engine top cover.

11 Attach a hoist and lifting tackle to the engine lifting brackets on the cylinder head, and raise the hoist to just take the weight of the engine and transmission. Alternatively the engine can be supported on a trolley jack under the transmission. Use a block of wood between the transmission and the head of the jack, to prevent any damage to the transmission.

12 Remove the battery, as described in Chapter 5, then disconnect the main starter

motor feed cable from the positive battery terminal box.

13 Release any relevant wiring or hoses from the clips on the battery tray, then unscrew the 3 securing bolts and remove the battery tray.

14 Unscrew the bolts securing the mounting to the transmission, and the remaining bolts securing the mounting to the body, then lift the mounting from the engine compartment.

15 Refitting is a reversal of removal, bearing in mind the following points:
 a) Use new mounting bolts.
 b) Tighten all fixings to the specified torque.

Rear mounting (torque arm)

16 Apply the handbrake, then jack up the front of the vehicle and support securely on axle stands (see *Jacking and vehicle support*). Remove the engine undershhield(s) for access to the rear mounting (torque arm).

17 Support the rear of the transmission beneath the final drive housing. To do this, use a trolley jack and block of wood, or alternatively wedge a block of wood between the transmission and the subframe.

18 Working under the vehicle, unscrew and remove the bolt securing the mounting to the subframe.

19 Unscrew the two bolts securing the mounting to the transmission, then withdraw the mounting from under the vehicle **(see illustration)**.

20 Refitting is a reversal of removal, but use new mounting securing bolts, and tighten all fixings to the specified torque.

19 Engine oil cooler – removal and refitting

Removal

1 The oil cooler is mounted under the oil filter housing on the front of the cylinder block.

2 Position a container beneath the oil filter to catch escaping oil and coolant.

3 Clamp the oil cooler coolant hoses to minimise coolant spillage, then remove the clips, and disconnect the hoses from the oil cooler. Be prepared for coolant spillage.

4 Unscrew the oil cooler securing plate from the bottom of the oil filter housing, then slide off the oil cooler. Recover the O-rings from the top and bottom of the oil cooler.

Refitting

5 Refitting is a reversal of removal, bearing in mind the following points:
 a) Use new oil cooler O-rings.
 b) Tighten the oil cooler securing plate securely.
 c) On completion, check and if necessary top-up the oil and coolant levels.

20 Oil pressure warning light switch – removal and refitting

Removal

1 The oil pressure warning light switch is fitted to the oil filter housing. Remove the engine top cover to gain access to the switch (see Section 4).

2 Disconnect the wiring connector and wipe clean the area around the switch.

3 Unscrew the switch from the filter housing and remove it, along with its sealing washer. If the switch is to be left removed from the engine for any length of time, plug the oil filter housing aperture.

Refitting

4 Examine the sealing washer for signs of damage or deterioration and if necessary renew.

5 Refit the switch, complete with washer, and tighten it to the specified torque.

6 Securely reconnect the wiring connector then check and, if necessary, top-up the engine oil as described in Weekly checks. On completion, refit the engine top cover(s).

Chapter 2 Part B:
Engine in-car repair procedures – common rail injection engines

Contents

Degrees of difficulty

Easy, suitable for novice with little experience	**Fairly easy,** suitable for beginner with some experience	**Fairly difficult,** suitable for competent DIY mechanic	**Difficult,** suitable for experienced DIY mechanic	**Very difficult,** suitable for expert DIY or professional 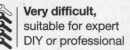

Specifications

General
Manufacturer's engine codes:*

1968 cc (2.0 litre), 16-valve, DOHC	CBAA, CBAB, CBAC and CBBB

Maximum outputs:

	Power	Torque
Engine code CBAA	100 kW at 4200 rpm	320 Nm at 1750 to 2500 rpm
Engine code CBAB	103 kW at 4200 rpm	320 Nm at 1750 to 2500 rpm
Engine code CBAC	105 kW at 4200 rpm	320 Nm at 1750 to 2500 rpm
Engine code CBBB	125 kW at 4200 rpm	350 Nm at 1750 to 2500 rpm

Bore	81.0 mm
Stroke	95.5 mm
Compression ratio	16.5 :1

Compression pressures:

Minimum compression pressure	Approximately 19.0 bar
Maximum difference between cylinders	Approximately 5.0 bar
Firing order	1 – 3 – 4 – 2
No 1 cylinder location	Timing belt end

* Note: See 'Vehicle identification' at the end of this manual for the location of engine code markings.

Lubrication system

Oil pump type	Gear type, chain-driven from crankshaft
Oil pressure (oil temperature 80°C, at 2000 rpm)	2.0 bar

Torque wrench settings

	Nm	lbf ft
Ancillary (alternator, etc) bracket mounting bolts:*		
Stage 1	40	30
Stage 2	Angle-tighten a further 45°	
Auxiliary drivebelt tensioner securing bolt:		
Stage 1	20	15
Stage 2	Angle-tighten a further 180°	
Balancer shaft drivegear bolts:*		
Stage 1	20	15
Stage 2	Angle-tighten a further 90°	

Torque wrench settings (continued)

	Nm	lbf ft
Balance shaft housing to cylinder block:*		
M7:		
Stage 1	13	10
Stage 2	Angle-tighten a further 90°	
M8:		
Stage 1	20	15
Stage 2	Angle-tighten a further 90°	
Balance shaft idler gear:*		
Stage 1	90	66
Stage 2	Angle-tighten a further 90°	
Big-end bearing caps bolts:*		
Stage 1	30	22
Stage 2	Angle-tighten a further 90°	
Camshaft bearing frame bolts/nut	10	7
Camshaft cover bolts	10	7
Camshaft sprocket hub centre bolt	100	74
Camshaft sprocket-to-hub bolts:*		
Stage 1	20	15
Stage 2	Angle-tighten a further 45°	
Common rail bolts	22	16
Coolant pump bolts	15	11
Crankshaft oil seal housing bolts	15	11
Crankshaft pulley-to-sprocket bolts:*		
Stage 1	10	7
Stage 2	Angle-tighten a further 90°	
Crankshaft sprocket bolt:*		
Stage 1	120	89
Stage 2	Angle-tighten a further 90°	
Cylinder head bolts:*		
Stage 1	30	22
Stage 2	50	37
Stage 3	Angle-tighten a further 90°	
Stage 4	Angle-tighten a further 90°	
Engine mountings:*		
RH engine mounting:		
Mounting bracket to engine:		
Stage 1	40	30
Stage 2	Angle-tighten a further 180°	
Mounting to body:		
Stage 1	40	30
Stage 2	Angle-tighten a further 90°	
Mounting to bracket:		
Stage 1	60	44
Stage 2	Angle-tighten a further 90°	
LH engine/transmission mounting:		
Mounting to body:		
Stage 1	40	30
Stage 2	Angle-tighten a further 90°	
Mounting to bracket on transmission:		
Stage 1	60	44
Stage 2	Angle-tighten a further 90°	
Rear mounting link:		
M10 strength class 8.8:		
Stage 1	40	30
Stage 2	Angle-tighten a further 90°	
M10 strength class 10.9:		
Stage 1	50	37
Stage 2	Angle-tighten a further 90°	
M12:		
Stage 1	60	44
Stage 2	Angle-tighten a further 90°	
Flywheel:*		
Stage 1	60	44
Stage 2	Angle-tighten a further 90°	
Fuel injector:		
Retaining nuts	22	16
Cover bolts	5	4

Torque wrench settings (continued)

	Nm	lbf ft
Fuel pump hub nut	95	70
Fuel pump sprocket bolts:*		
Stage 1	20	15
Stage 2	Angle-tighten a further 90°	
Intermediate gear bolt:*		
Stage 1	90	66
Stage 2	Angle-tighten a further 90°	
Main bearing cap bolts:*		
Stage 1	65	48
Stage 2	Angle-tighten a further 90°	
Oil cooler bolt	25	18
Oil drain plug*	30	22
Oil filter housing-to-cylinder block bolts:*		
Stage 1	15	11
Stage 2	Angle-tighten a further 90°	
Oil filter cover	25	18
Oil level/temperature sensor-to-sump bolts	10	7
Oil pick-up pipe securing bolts	10	7
Oil pressure warning light switch	22	16
Oil pump securing bolts:		
M6	10	7
M7:*		
Stage 1	13	10
Stage 2	Angle-tighten a further 90°	
Piston oil spray jet bolt	25	18
Sump:		
Sump-to-cylinder block bolts	15	11
Sump-to-transmission bolts	45	33
Thermostat housing	15	11
Timing belt outer cover bolts	10	7
Timing belt tensioner roller securing nut:		
Stage 1	20	30
Stage 2	Angle-tighten a further 45°	
Timing belt idler pulleys:		
Lower idler roller nut	20	15
Upper idler roller (small) bolt	20	15
Upper idler roller (large) bolt:*		
Stage 1	50	37
Stage 2	Angle-tighten a further 90°	

* Do not re-use fasteners

1 General information

How to use this Chapter

This Part of Chapter 2 describes those repair procedures that can reasonably be carried out on the engine while it remains in the vehicle. If the engine has been removed from the vehicle and is being dismantled as described in Part C, any preliminary dismantling procedures can be ignored.

Note that while it may be possible physically to overhaul certain items while the engine is in the vehicle, such tasks are not usually carried out as separate operations, and usually require the execution of several additional procedures (not to mention the cleaning of components and of oilways); for this reason, all such tasks are classed as major overhaul procedures, and are described in Part C of this Chapter.

Engine description

Throughout this Chapter, engines are referred to by type, and are identified and referred to by the manufacturer's code letters. A listing of all engines covered, together with their code letters, is given in the Specifications at the start of this Chapter.

The engines are water-cooled, double overhead camshafts (DOHC), in-line four-cylinder units, with cast-iron cylinder blocks and aluminium-silicon alloy cylinder heads. All are mounted transversely at the front of the vehicle, with the transmission bolted to the left-hand end of the engine.

The crankshaft is of five-bearing type, and thrustwashers are fitted to the centre main bearing to control crankshaft endfloat.

Drive for the exhaust camshaft is by a toothed timing belt from the crankshaft, with the intake camshaft driven by interlocking gears at the left-hand end of both camshafts. The gears incorporate a toothed backlash compensator element. Each camshaft is mounted at the top of the cylinder head, and is secured by a bearing frame/ladder.

The valves are closed by coil springs, and run in guides pressed into the cylinder head.

The valves are operated by roller rocker arms incorporating hydraulic tappets.

A twin, counter-rotating balance shaft assembly is fitted to the base of the cylinder block. The rearmost balance shaft is driven by a gear on the crankshaft, via an intermediate gear bolted to the balance shaft housing. The two balance shafts are geared together.

The gear-type oil pump is driven by the front balance shaft. Oil is drawn from the sump through a strainer, and then forced through an externally-mounted, renewable filter. From there, it is distributed to the cylinder head, where it lubricates the camshaft journals and hydraulic tappets, and also to the crankcase, where it lubricates the main bearings, connecting rod big-ends, gudgeon pins and cylinder bores. A coolant-fed oil cooler is fitted to the oil filter housing on all engines. Oil jets are fitted to the base of each cylinder – these spray oil onto the underside of the pistons, to improve cooling.

All engines are fitted with a brake servo vacuum pump driven by the camshaft on the transmission end of the cylinder head.

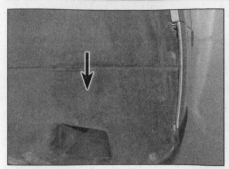

3.4 Remove the lower section of the wheel arch liner (arrowed)

On all engines, engine coolant is circulated by a pump, driven by the timing belt. For details of the cooling system, refer to Chapter 3.

Operations with engine in car

The following operations can be performed without removing the engine:
a) Compression pressure – testing.
b) Camshaft cover – removal and refitting.
c) Crankshaft pulley – removal and refitting.
d) Timing belt covers – removal and refitting.
e) Timing belt – removal, refitting and adjustment.
f) Timing belt tensioner and sprockets – removal and refitting.
g) Camshaft oil seals – renewal.
h) Camshafts and hydraulic tappets – removal, inspection and refitting.
i) Cylinder head – removal and refitting.
j) Cylinder head and pistons – decarbonising.
k) Sump – removal and refitting.
l) Oil pump – removal, overhaul and refitting.
m) Crankshaft oil seals – renewal.
n) Engine/transmission mountings – inspection and renewal.
o) Flywheel – removal, inspection and refitting.

Note: It is possible to remove the pistons and connecting rods (after removing the cylinder head and sump) without removing the engine. However, this is not recommended. Work of this nature is more easily and thoroughly completed with the engine on the bench, as described in Chapter 2C.

3.8 The alignment mark (arrowed) on the crankshaft sprocket should be almost vertical

2 Compression and leakdown tests – description and interpretation

Compression test

Note: A compression tester suitable for use with diesel engines will be required for this test.

1 When engine performance is down, or if misfiring occurs which cannot be attributed to the ignition or fuel systems, a compression test can provide diagnostic clues as to the engine's condition. If the test is performed regularly, it can give warning of trouble before any other symptoms become apparent.
2 The engine must be fully warmed-up to normal operating temperature, the battery must be fully-charged, and you will require the aid of an assistant.
3 Remove the glow plugs as described in Chapter 5, then fit a compression tester to the No 1 cylinder glow plug hole. The type of tester which bolts into the plug thread is preferred. **Note:** Part of the glow plug removal procedure is to disconnect the fuel injector wiring plugs. As a result of the plugs being disconnected and the engine cranked, faults will be stored in the ECM memory. These must be erased after the compression test.
4 Have your assistant crank the engine for several seconds on the starter motor. After one or two revolutions, the compression pressure should build-up to a maximum figure and then stabilise. Record the highest reading obtained.
5 Repeat the test on the remaining cylinders, recording the pressure in each.
6 The cause of poor compression is less easy to establish on a diesel engine than on a petrol engine. The effect of introducing oil into the cylinders (wet testing) is not conclusive, because there is a risk that the oil will sit in the recess on the piston crown, instead of passing to the rings. However, the following can be used as a rough guide to diagnosis.
7 All cylinders should produce very similar pressures. Any difference greater than that specified indicates the existence of a fault. Note that the compression should build-up quickly in a healthy engine. Low compression on the first stroke, followed by gradually increasing pressure on successive strokes, indicates worn piston rings. A low compression reading on the first stroke, which does not build-up during successive strokes, indicates leaking valves or a blown head gasket (a cracked head could also be the cause).
8 A low reading from two adjacent cylinders is almost certainly due to the head gasket having blown between them and the presence of coolant in the engine oil will confirm this.
9 On completion, remove the compression tester, and refit the glow plugs, with reference to Chapter 5.
10 Reconnect the wiring to the injector solenoids. Finally, have a VW dealer or suitably-equipped specialist erase the fault codes from the ECM memory.

Leakdown test

11 A leakdown test measures the rate at which compressed air fed into the cylinder is lost. It is an alternative to a compression test, and in many ways it is better, since the escaping air provides easy identification of where pressure loss is occurring (piston rings, valves or head gasket).
12 The equipment required for leakdown testing is unlikely to be available to the home mechanic. If poor compression is suspected, have the test performed by a suitably-equipped garage.

3 Engine assembly and valve timing marks – general information and usage

General information

1 TDC is the highest point in the cylinder that each piston reaches as it travels up-and-down when the crankshaft turns. Each piston reaches TDC at the end of the compression stroke and again at the end of the exhaust stroke, but TDC generally refers to piston position on the compression stroke. No 1 piston is at the timing belt end of the engine.
2 Positioning No 1 piston at TDC is an essential part of many procedures, such as timing belt removal and camshaft removal.
3 The design of the engines covered in this Chapter is such that piston-to-valve contact may occur if the camshaft or crankshaft is turned with the timing belt removed. For this reason, it is important to ensure that the camshaft and crankshaft do not move in relation to each other once the timing belt has been removed from the engine.

Setting TDC on No 1 cylinder

Note: VAG special tool T10050 is required to lock the crankshaft sprocket in the TDC position. Alternatively obtain a tool from automotive tool specialists.

4 Raise the front of the vehicle and support it securely on axle stands (see Jacking and vehicle support). Remove the front right-hand roadwheel, then release the fasteners and remove the lower section of the wheel arch liner **(see illustration)**.
5 Remove the auxiliary drivebelt as described in Chapter 1.
6 Remove the crankshaft pulley/vibration damper as described in Section 5.
7 Remove the timing belt outer covers as described in Section 6.
8 Using a spanner or socket on the crankshaft sprocket bolt, turn the crankshaft in the normal direction of rotation (clockwise) until the alignment mark on the face of the sprocket is almost vertical, and the hole in the camshaft sprocket hub aligns with the hole in the cylinder head **(see illustration)**.

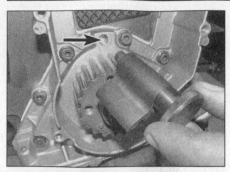

3.9a Fit the tool to the hole in the oil seal housing (arrowed) . . .

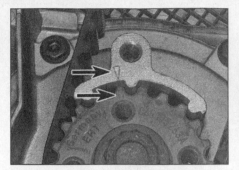

3.9b . . . so the marks on the tool and sprocket align (arrowed)

3.9c Insert a 6 mm drill bit/rod to lock the camshaft hub (arrowed)

9 While in this position it should be possible to insert the VAG tool T10050 to lock the crankshaft, and a 6 mm diameter rod/drill bit to lock the camshafts **(see illustrations)**. **Note:** *The mark on the crankshaft sprocket and the mark on the VAG tool must align, whilst at the same time the shaft of tool must engage in the drilling in the crankshaft oil seal housing.*
10 The engine is now set to TDC on No 1 cylinder.

4 Camshaft cover – removal and refitting

Removal

1 Remove the fuel injectors and common rail as described in Chapter 4A.
2 Remove the timing belt upper cover as described in Section 6.

3 Note their fitted positions, then disconnect the vacuum hoses from the camshaft cover, and release them and the wiring loom from the retaining clips at the left-hand end of the cover **(see illustration)**.
4 Squeeze together the sides of the collar, and disconnect the breather hose from the camshaft cover **(see illustration)**.
5 Release the wiring from the clips at the rear of the cover, then unscrew the camshaft cover retaining bolts and lift the cover away. If the cover sticks, do not attempt to lever it off – instead free it by working around the cover and tapping it lightly with a soft-faced mallet **(see illustration)**.
6 Recover the camshaft cover gasket. Inspect the gasket carefully, and renew it if damage or deterioration is evident – note that the retaining bolts and seals must be pushed fully through the cover **(see illustrations)**.

7 Clean the mating surfaces of the cylinder head and camshaft cover thoroughly, removing all traces of oil – take care to avoid damaging the surfaces as you do this.

Refitting

8 Refit the camshaft cover by following the removal procedure in reverse, tightening the cover retaining bolts to the specified torque in the sequence shown **(see illustration)**.

5 Crankshaft pulley – removal and refitting

Removal

1 Switch off the ignition and all electrical consumers and remove the ignition key.
2 Raise the front right-hand side of the vehicle, and support securely on axle stands

4.3 Disconnect the vacuum hoses from the camshaft cover (arrowed)

4.4 Squeeze together the sides of the collar (arrowed) and disconnect the breather hose

4.5 Undo the bolts and lift away the camshaft cover

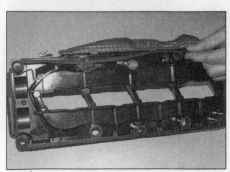

4.6a Renew the cover seal if necessary

4.6b The bolts and seals must be pushed fully through the cover before fitting the gasket

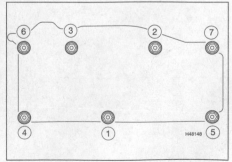

4.8 Cylinder head cover bolt tightening sequence

5.4 Undo the pulley bolts, counterholding it with a socket on the centre sprocket bolt

(see *Jacking and vehicle support*). Remove the roadwheel.

3 Remove the securing fasteners and withdraw the lower section of the front wheel arch liner.

4 Slacken the bolts securing the crankshaft pulley to the sprocket **(see illustration)**. If necessary, the pulley can be prevented from turning by counterholding with a spanner or socket on the crankshaft sprocket bolt.

5 Remove the auxiliary drivebelt, as described in Chapter 1.

6 Unscrew the bolts securing the pulley to the sprocket, and remove the pulley. Discard the bolts – new ones must be fitted.

Refitting

7 Refit the pulley over the locating peg on the crankshaft sprocket, then fit the new pulley securing bolts.

8 Refit and tension the auxiliary drivebelt as described in Chapter 1.

6.1 Pull the plastic cover upwards from the mountings

9 Prevent the crankshaft from turning as during removal, then fit the pulley securing bolts, and tighten to the specified torque.

10 Refit the wheel arch liner.

11 Refit the roadwheel and lower the vehicle to the ground.

6 Timing belt covers –
removal and refitting

Upper outer cover

1 Pull the engine top cover upwards to release the mountings **(see illustration)**.

2 Disconnect the wiring plug, undo the retaining bolt, and remove the exhaust gas pressure sensor bracket by pushing it forwards **(see illustration)**.

3 Disconnect the wiring plug, unclip the fuel hoses, then release the clamps and

6.2 Disconnect the wiring plug and undo the retaining bolt (arrowed)

disconnect the hoses from the filter **(see illustrations)**. Note the fitted locations of the hoses to aid refitting. Plug the openings to prevent contamination.

4 Undo the bolts/nut and remove the fuel filter assembly **(see illustration)**. Release the hose clamp as the filter assembly is withdrawn.

5 Disconnect the fuel temperature sensor wiring plug, then release the clamp and disconnect the fuel supply pipe from the high-pressure fuel pump **(see illustration)**. Plug the openings to prevent contamination, and place a rag above the alternator to prevent fuel ingress.

6 Slide up the hose retaining clips, then undo the 2 retaining bolts and remove the supplementary fuel pump **(see illustration)**.

7 Disconnect the radiator outlet temperature sensor wiring plug, then release the 3 clips and remove the timing belt upper cover **(see illustrations)**.

6.3a Note their positions, then disconnect the hoses from the fuel filter

6.3b Plug the openings to prevent contamination

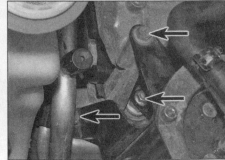

6.4 Undo the nut/bolts (arrowed) and remove the fuel filter

6.5 Disconnect the fuel supply hose and temperature sensor (arrowed)

6.6 Supplementary fuel pump retaining bolts (arrowed)

6.7a Disconnect the temperature sensor wiring plug (arrowed)

8 Refitting is a reversal of removal, noting that the lower edge of the upper cover engages with the centre cover.

Centre outer cover

9 Remove the crankshaft pulley as described in Section 5. It is assumed that, if the centre cover is being removed, the lower cover will be also – if not, simply remove the components described in Section 5 for access to the crankshaft pulley, and leave the pulley in position.

10 Undo the retaining nuts/bolts and move the coolant pipe that lies across the centre cover, away towards the inner wing.

11 With the upper cover removed (paragraphs 1 to 6), unscrew and remove the 3 retaining bolts from the centre cover. Withdraw the centre cover from the engine, noting how it fits over the lower cover (see illustration). Note if the auxiliary belt tensioner is in the 'locked' position as described in the belt removal procedure, the locking drill bit/rod must be removed for access to the cover retaining bolt.

12 Refitting is a reversal of the removal procedure, using a little thread-locking compound on the retaining bolts.

Lower outer cover

13 Remove the upper and centre covers as described previously.

14 If not already done, remove the crankshaft pulley as described in Section 5.

15 Unscrew the remaining bolts securing the lower cover, and remove it (see illustration).

16 Refitting is a reversal of removal; locate the centre cover in place before fitting the top two bolts.

Rear cover

17 Remove the timing belt, tensioner and sprockets as described in Sections 7 and 8.

18 Slacken and withdraw the retaining bolts and lift the timing belt inner cover from the studs on the end of the engine, and remove it from the engine compartment.

19 Refitting is a reversal of removal.

6.7b Release the clips (arrowed) . . .

6.7c . . . and manoeuvre the timing belt upper cover from place

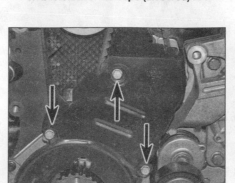

6.11 Centre timing belt cover bolts (arrowed)

6.15 Lower cover retaining bolts (arrowed)

7 Timing belt – removal, inspection and refitting

Removal

1 The primary function of the toothed timing belt is to drive the camshaft, but it also drives the coolant pump and high-pressure fuel pump. Should the belt slip or break in service, the valve timing will be disturbed and piston-to-valve contact may occur, resulting in serious engine damage. For this reason, it is important that the timing belt is tensioned correctly, and inspected regularly for signs of wear or deterioration.

2 Switch off the ignition and all electrical consumers and remove the ignition key.

3 Set the engine to TDC on No 1 cylinder as described in Section 3.

4 Slacken the 3 bolts securing the sprocket to the camshaft hub (see illustration).

5 Slacken the 3 bolts securing the sprocket to the high-pressure fuel pump (see illustration).

6 Insert a suitable Allen key into the tensioner hub, then slacken the retaining nut and rotate

7.4 Slacken the sprocket-to-hub bolts (arrowed)

7.5 Slacken the high-pressure fuel pump sprocket bolts (arrowed)

7.6 Insert and Allen key, slacken the nut, and rotate the hub anti-clockwise until a 2 mm rod/drill bit (arrowed) can be inserted to lock the hub to the pulley

7.14 Rotate the high-pressure fuel pump clockwise until a 6 mm drill bit/rod can be inserted into the housing and hub (arrowed)

the tensioner hub anti-clockwise until it can be locked in place using a 2.0 mm pin/drill bit **(see illustration)**.

7 Now rotate the tensioner hub clockwise to the stop, and hand-tighten the retaining nut.

8 If the original timing belt is to be refitted, mark the running direction of the belt, to ensure correct refitting.

Caution: If the belt appears to be in good condition and can be re-used, it is essential that it is refitted the same way around, otherwise accelerated wear will result, leading to premature failure.

9 Slide the belt from the sprockets, taking care not to twist or kink the belt excessively if it is to be re-used.

Inspection

10 Examine the belt for evidence of contamination by coolant or lubricant. If this is the case, find the source of the contamination before progressing any further. Check the belt for signs of wear or damage, particularly around the leading edges of the belt teeth.

Renew the belt if its condition is in doubt; the cost of belt renewal is negligible compared with potential cost of the engine repairs, should the belt fail in service. The belt must be renewed if it has covered the mileage given in Chapter 1, however, if it has covered less, it is prudent to renew it regardless of condition, as a precautionary measure.

11 If the timing belt is not going to be refitted for some time, it is a wise precaution to hang a warning label on the steering wheel, to remind yourself (and others) not to attempt to start the engine.

Refitting

12 Ensure that the crankshaft and camshaft are still set to TDC on No 1 cylinder, as described in Section 3. The camshaft sprocket bolts should be renewed, and slackened at this point.

13 Renew the high-pressure fuel pump sprocket bolts one at a time. They should be kept loose.

14 Using a screwdriver on the bolts heads,

rotate the high-pressure fuel pump clockwise until a 6.0 mm locking pin/drill bit can be inserted into the housing adjacent to the sprocket, locking the pump in place **(see illustration)**.

15 Rotate the camshaft sprocket and high-pressure fuel pump sprocket fully clockwise so that the securing bolts are at the end of the elongated holes **(see illustrations)**.

16 Loop the timing belt loosely under the crankshaft sprocket. **Note:** *Observe any direction of rotation markings on the belt.*

17 Fit the belt around the tensioner pulley, engage the timing belt teeth with the camshaft sprockets, then manoeuvre it into position around the coolant pump sprocket and the fuel pump sprocket. Make sure that the belt teeth seat correctly on the sprockets. **Note:** *Slight adjustment to the position of the camshaft sprocket may be necessary to achieve this. Avoid bending the belt back on itself or twisting it excessively as you do this.*

18 Finally, fit the belt around the idler roller

7.15a Rotate the sprockets fully clockwise until the fuel pump sprocket . . .

7.15b . . . and camshaft sprocket bolts are at the end of the elongated holes

7.18 Timing belt routing

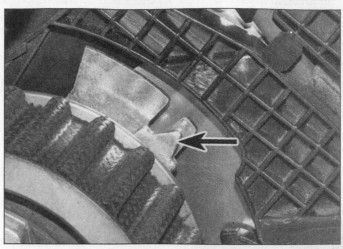

7.19 Rotate the tensioner clockwise until the pointer (arrowed) is just past the gap in the backplate

(see illustration). Ensure that any slack in the belt is in the section of belt that passes over the tensioner roller.

19 Loosen the timing belt tensioner securing nut, and pull out the tensioner locking pin. Turn the tensioner clockwise with an Allen key until the pointer is just past the middle of the gap in the tensioner backplate (see illustration). With the tensioner held in this position, tighten the securing nut to the specified torque and angle.

20 Counterhold the camshaft sprocket with a home-made tool to prevent any rotation, then tighten the camshaft sprocket and fuel pump sprocket bolts to 20 Nm (15 lbf ft). Remove the sprockets locking tools and the crankshaft locking tool.

21 Using a spanner or wrench and socket on the crankshaft pulley centre bolt, rotate the crankshaft clockwise through two complete revolutions. Reset the engine to TDC on No 1 cylinder, with reference to Section 3 and refit the crankshaft locking tool.

22 Check that the tensioner roller indicator arm is centred, or within a maximum of 5 mm to the right of the notch in the backplate (see illustration). If not, hold the tensioner hub stationary with an Allen key, slacken the retaining nut and position the arm in the centre of the notch. Tighten the retaining nut to the specified torque. Remove the Allen key.

23 Check that the camshaft sprocket locking pin can still be inserted. Note: It's very difficult to align the locking point of the fuel pump hub again. However, a misalignment of holes will not affect engine performance.

24 If the camshaft sprocket locking pin cannot be inserted, pull the crankshaft locking tool slight away from the engine, and rotate the crankshaft anti-clockwise slightly past TDC. Now slowly rotate the crankshaft clockwise until the camshaft sprocket locking tool can be inserted.

25 If the locating pin of the crankshaft locking tool is to the left of the corresponding hole, slacken the camshaft sprocket bolts, slowly rotate the crankshaft clockwise until the

locking tool can be fully inserted. Tighten the camshaft sprocket bolts to 20 Nm (15 lbf ft).

26 If the locating pin of the crankshaft locking tool is to the right of the corresponding hole, slacken the camshaft sprocket bolts, rotate the crankshaft anti-clockwise slightly until the pin is to the left of the hole, then slowly rotate it clockwise until the lock tool can be fully inserted. Tighten the camshaft sprocket bolts to 20 Nm (15 lbf ft).

27 Remove the crankshaft and camshaft locking tools, then rotate the crankshaft 2 complete revolutions clockwise and check the locking tools can be reinserted. If necessary, repeat the adjustment procedure described previously.

28 Tighten the camshaft and fuel pump sprocket bolts to the specified torque.

29 The remainder of refitting is a reversal of removal.

8 Timing belt tensioner and sprockets – removal and refitting

Timing belt tensioner

Removal

1 In order to remove the timing belt tensioner,

8.4 Coolant pipe upper mounting bolt and lower mounting nut (arrowed)

7.22 The pointer should be centred in, or within 5 mm to the right of, the gap in the backplate

then engine mounting bracket must first be removed. Either support the engine from above using a crossbeam or an engine hoist, or support if from underneath with a trolley jack and block of wood.

2 Remove the timing belt as described in Section 7.

3 Undo the bolts and remove the right-hand engine mounting.

4 Undo the bolt securing the coolant pipe to the mounting bracket (see illustration).

5 Working in the wheel arch area, undo the nut securing the lower end of the coolant pipe.

6 Undo the 3 retaining bolts and remove the engine mounting bracket (see illustration).

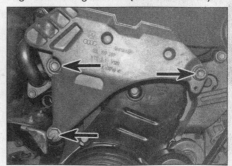

8.6 Engine mounting bracket bolts (arrowed)

8.8 Ensure the lug on the backplate engages with the cut-out in the timing belt cover (arrowed)

7 Unscrew the timing belt tensioner nut, and remove the tensioner from the engine.

Refitting

8 When refitting the tensioner to the engine, ensure that the lug on the tensioner backplate engages with the corresponding cut-out in the rear timing belt cover **(see illustration)**, then refit the tensioner nut **(see illustration)**.

9 The remainder of refitting is a reversal of removal.

Idler pulleys

Removal

10 Remove the timing belt as described in Section 7.

11 Unscrew the relevant idler pulley/roller securing bolt/nut, then withdraw the pulley.

Refitting

12 Refit the pulley and tighten the securing bolt or nut to the specified torque. **Note:** *Renew the large roller/pulley retaining bolt (where applicable).*

13 Refit and tension the timing belt as described in Section 7.

Crankshaft sprocket

Note: *A new crankshaft sprocket securing bolt must be used on refitting.*

Removal

14 Remove the timing belt as described in Section 7.

15 The sprocket securing bolt must now be slackened, and the crankshaft must be prevented from turning as the sprocket bolt is

unscrewed. To hold the sprocket, make up a suitable tool, and bolt it to the sprocket using a two bolts bolted into two of the crankshaft pulley bolt holes.

16 Hold the sprocket using the tool, then slacken the sprocket securing bolt. Take care, as the bolt is very tight. Do not allow the crankshaft to turn as the bolt is slackened.

17 Unscrew the bolt, and slide the sprocket from the end of the crankshaft, noting which way round the sprocket's raised boss is fitted.

Refitting

18 Commence refitting by positioning the sprocket on the end of the crankshaft.

19 Fit a new sprocket securing bolt, then counterhold the sprocket using the method employed on removal, and tighten the bolt to the specified torque in the two stages given in the Specifications.

20 Refit the timing belt as described in Section 7.

Camshaft sprocket

Removal

21 Remove the timing belt as described in Section 7, then rotate the crankshaft 90° anti-clockwise to prevent any accidental piston-to-valve contact.

22 Unscrew and remove the three retaining bolts and remove the camshaft sprocket from the camshaft hub.

Refitting

23 Refit the sprocket ensuring that it is fitted the correct way round, as noted before removal, then insert the new sprocket bolts, and tighten by hand only at this stage.

24 If the crankshaft has been turned, turn the crankshaft clockwise 90° back to TDC.

25 Refit and tension the timing belt as described in Section 7.

Camshaft hub

Note: *VAG technicians use special tool T10051 to counterhold the hub, however it is possible to fabricate a suitable alternative.*

Removal

26 Remove the camshaft sprocket as described previously in this Section.

27 Engage special tool T10051 with the three locating holes in the face of the hub to prevent

the hub from turning. If this tool is not available, fabricate a suitable alternative. Whilst holding the tool, undo the central hub retaining bolt about two turns **(see illustration)**.

28 Slide the hub from the camshaft. If necessary, attach VW tool T10052 (or a similar three-legged puller) to the hub, and evenly tighten the puller until the hub is free of the camshaft taper **(see illustration)**.

Refitting

29 Ensure that the camshaft taper and the hub centre are clean and dry, locate the hub on the taper, noting that the built-in key in the hub taper must align with the keyway in the camshaft taper **(see illustration)**.

30 Hold the hub in this position with tool T10051 (or similar home-made tool), and tighten the central bolt to the specified torque.

31 Refit the camshaft sprocket as described previously in this Section.

Coolant pump sprocket

32 The coolant pump sprocket is integral with the coolant pump. Refer to Chapter 3 for details of coolant pump removal.

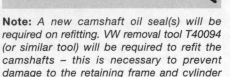

9 Camshaft and hydraulic tappets – removal, inspection and refitting

Note: *A new camshaft oil seal(s) will be required on refitting. VW removal tool T40094 (or similar tool) will be required to refit the camshafts – this is necessary to prevent damage to the retaining frame and cylinder head as the camshafts are refitted.*

Removal

1 Remove the camshaft hub as described in Section 8.

2 Remove the camshaft cover as described in Section 4.

3 Remove the brake vacuum pump as described in Chapter 9.

4 Progressively unscrew the camshaft retaining frame bolts in the **reverse** of the sequence shown in illustration 9.20, and carefully remove the retaining frame.

5 Carefully lift the camshafts from the cylinder head, keeping them identified for location.

8.27 Fabricate a home-made tool to counterhold the hub. Undo the bolt . . .

8.28 . . . and slide the hub from the camshaft

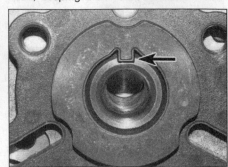

8.29 Ensure the integral key aligns with the keyway in the camshaft (arrowed)

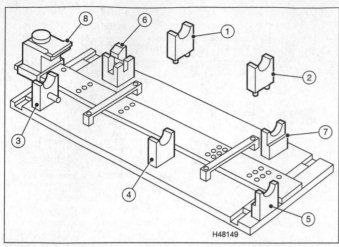

9.12a The different elements of tool No T40094

9.12b Position tools No 1, 2, 9 and 10 as shown

Remove the oil seal from the end of the camshaft and discard it – a new one will be required for refitting.

6 Lift the rocker arms and hydraulic tappets from place. Store the rockers and tappets in a container with numbered compartments to ensure they are refitted to their correct locations. It is recommended that the tappets are kept immersed in oil for the period they are removed from the cylinder head.

Inspection

7 With the camshafts removed, examine the retaining frame and the bearing locations in the cylinder head for signs of obvious wear or pitting. If evident, a new cylinder head will probably be required. Also check that the oil supply holes in the cylinder head are free from obstructions.

8 Visually inspect the camshafts for evidence of wear on the surfaces of the lobes and journals. Normally their surfaces should be smooth and have a dull shine; look for

scoring, erosion or pitting and areas that appear highly polished, indicating excessive wear. Accelerated wear will occur once the hardened exterior of the camshaft has been damaged, so always renew worn items. **Note:** *If these symptoms are visible on the tips of the camshaft lobes, check the corresponding rocker arm, as it will probably be worn as well.*
9 If the machined surfaces of the camshaft appear discoloured or blued, it is likely that it has been overheated at some point, probably due to inadequate lubrication. This may have distorted the shaft, so have the camshaft runout and endfloat checked by an automotive engine reconditioning specialist.
10 Inspect the hydraulic tappets for obvious signs of wear or damage, and renew if necessary. Check that the oil holes in the tappets are free from obstructions.

Refitting

11 Oil the rocker arms and hydraulic tappets, then refit them to their original positions.

⚠ *Warning: After fitting hydraulic tappets, wait a minimum of 30 minutes (or preferably, leave overnight) before starting the engine, to allow the tappets time to settle, otherwise the valve heads will strike the pistons.*

12 To set up the tool, remove the supports number 3, 4 and 5, then install the supports number 9 and 10 at the vacant outer places, support number 2 at position A and number 1 at position F **(see illustrations)**.
13 Position the inlet camshaft as shown with the cylinder head bolt indent facing outwards, then slide the support number 8 into the slot in the end of the camshaft and remove any free play with a 0.50 mm feeler gauge **(see illustration)**.
14 Position the exhaust camshaft on supports numbers 9 and 10, and fit the tool No 11 into the slot in the end of the camshaft **(see illustration)**.
15 Fit the clamping tool No T40096 to the gear on the exhaust camshaft, tightening the

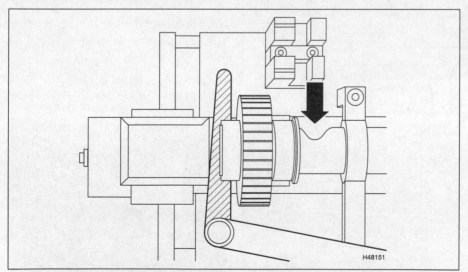

9.13 Position the inlet camshaft on the tool with the bolt indent (arrowed) facing outwards, then slide tool No 8 in to the slot in the end of the camshaft and use a 0.50 mm feeler gauge to remove any free play

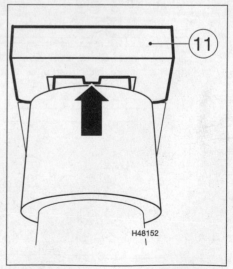

9.14 Fit tool No 11 into the slot (arrowed) in the end of the exhaust camshaft

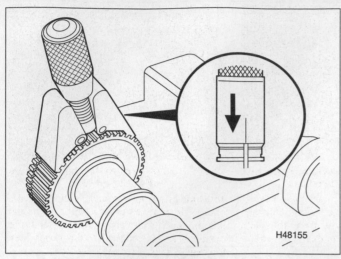

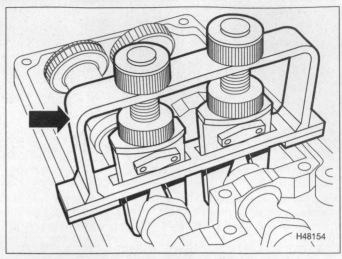

9.15 Tighten the thumbwheel to align the gear teeth. Ensure the clamping jaw with the arrow in seated on the wider gear

9.18 Secure the camshafts in place in the frame using tool No T40095 (arrowed)

knurled thumb wheel until the faces of the gear teeth are in alignment. If necessary, use a 13 mm spanner **(see illustration)**.
16 Slide the exhaust camshaft towards the inlet camshaft until the gear teeth engage.
17 Ensure the gasket faces of the retaining frame are clean, then apply a smear of clean engine oil to the bearing surfaces and lower the frame into position over the camshafts. Ensure the bearing surfaces locate correctly on the camshafts.

18 Fit the clamping tool No T40095 over the camshafts and frame, and tighten the thumbwheels to hold the camshafts in position in the frame **(see illustration)**.
19 Ensure the sealing surfaces of the cylinder head are clean, then apply a 2.0 mm wide bead of sealant (D 176 501 A1 or equivalent) as shown. Take care not to apply too much sealant, ensuring the oil holes supply holes are not blocked **(see illustration)**.
20 Slide out tool Nos 8 and 11, then lift the

camshafts, retaining frame and clamping tool from the tool No 40094. Place the camshafts, frame and tool in place on the cylinder head. Progressively and carefully, hand-tighten the frame retaining bolts in the sequence shown, until the retaining frame makes contact with the cylinder head over the complete surface, then tighten the bolts to the specified torque, again in the correct sequence **(see illustration)**.
21 Remove the gear aligning tool (T40096) and the clamping tool (T40095).
22 Renew the camshaft oil seal (Section 10), then drive in a new sealing cap.
23 The remainder of refitting is a reversal of removal.

10 Camshaft oil seals – renewal

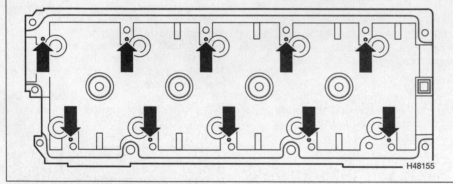

9.19 Apply a 2.0 mm thick bead of sealant to the area shown by the thick, black line. Take care not to block the oil holes (arrowed)

Right-hand oil seal

1 Remove the camshaft sprocket and hub, as described in Section 8.
2 Drill two small holes into the existing oil seal, diagonally opposite each other. Take great care to avoid drilling through into the seal housing or camshaft sealing surface.

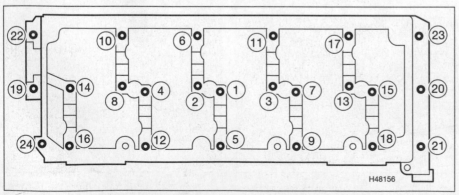

9.20 Camshaft retaining frame bolt tightening sequence

10.2 Bolt-in a self-tapping screw, then pull the bolt and seal from place

11.5 Battery tray bolts (arrowed)

11.11a Disconnect the pressure sensor wiring plug (arrowed) . . .

11.11b . . . then remove the charge air pipe and hose (arrowed)

Thread two self-tapping screws into the holes, and using a pair of pliers, pull on the heads of the screws to extract the oil seal **(see illustration)**.

3 Clean out the seal housing and the sealing surface of the camshaft by wiping it with a lint-free cloth. Remove any swarf or burrs that may cause the seal to leak.

4 Do not lubricate the lip and outer edge of the new oil seal, push it over the camshaft until it is positioned in place above its housing. To prevent damage to the sealing lips, wrap some adhesive tape around the end of the camshaft.

5 Using a hammer and a socket of suitable diameter, drive the seal squarely into its housing. **Note:** *Select a socket that bears only on the hard outer surface of the seal, not the inner lip which can easily be damaged.*

6 Refit the camshaft sprocket and its hub, as described in Section 8.

Left-hand oil seal

7 The left-hand camshaft oil seal is formed by the brake vacuum pump seal. Refer to Chapter 9 for details of brake vacuum pump removal and refitting.

---

11 Cylinder head – removal, inspection and refitting

Note: *The cylinder head must be removed with the engine cold. New cylinder head bolts and a new cylinder head gasket will be required on refitting, and suitable studs will be required to guide the cylinder head into position – see text.*

Removal

1 Remove the battery as described in Chapter 5.

2 Drain the cooling system and engine oil as described in Chapter 1.

3 Pull the plastic cover on the top of the engine upwards from its mountings.

4 Remove the air filter housing as described in Chapter 4A.

5 Undo the 3 bolts and remove the battery tray **(see illustration)**.

6 Remove the radiator cooling fan(s) and shroud as described in Chapter 3.

7 Undo the bolts and remove the air hose/duct from the intercooler to the turbocharger. Release the wiring looms from the clips as necessary to enable the duct to be manoeuvred from place.

8 Remove the camshaft cover as described in Section 4.

9 Remove the camshaft sprocket and hub as described in Section 8.

10 Disconnect the wiring plugs from the EGR valve and throttle body/intake manifold flap.

11 Disconnect the charge air pressure sensor wiring plug, then undo the 2 retaining bolts, release the clamps, and remove the charge air pipe and hose from the front of the engine **(see illustrations)**.

12 Undo the bolt securing the oil level dipstick guide tube to the throttle body/intake manifold flap **(see illustration)**.

13 Undo the 2 bolts securing the connecting pipe to the EGR valve **(see illustration)**.

14 Undo the front retaining bolt, twist the charge air pipe clockwise and disconnect it from the turbocharger. Note their fitted positions, and unclip the vacuum hoses from the charge air pipe **(see illustration)**.

15 Apply a little lubrication spray to the rubber sleeve, pull up the pipe from the vacuum pump, then undo the 4 retaining bolts and remove the vacuum pump from the left-hand end of the cylinder head **(see illustration)**. Renew the pump-to-cylinder head seal.

16 Disconnect the coolant temperature sensor wiring plug at the left-hand end of the cylinder head, and release the wiring loom from any retaining clips.

17 Disconnect the gearchange cables from the levers on the transmission as described in Chapter 7.

18 Undo the bolts/nut, securing the gearchange bracket to the top of the transmission. Move the bracket and cables to one side.

11.12 Oil level dipstick guide tube bolt (arrowed)

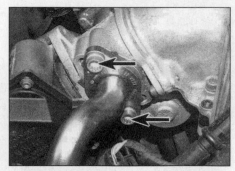

11.13 EGR pipe-to-valve bolts (arrowed)

11.14 Charge air pipe retaining bolt (arrowed). Note the position of the vacuum hoses

11.15 With some lubrication, the hose connection pulls up from the vacuum pump

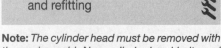

11.19 EGR pipe-to-cooler bolts (arrowed)

11.21 Remove the EGR pipe between the manifold and cooler

11.23a Undo the banjo bolt (arrowed) at the base of the turbocharger support bracket/oil return pipe and the bolt at the top (arrowed)

11.23b Note the 2 O-ring seals (arrowed) at the base of the oil return pipe

19 Undo the bolts securing the EGR pipe to the cooler at the left-hand end of the engine, and the nut securing the bracket to the cylinder head, then remove the pipe **(see illustration)**. Recover the gasket at each end.
20 Working underneath the vehicle, slacken the Allen bolt and release the clamp securing the diesel particulate filter/catalytic converter to the turbocharger, then undo the bolts/nuts securing the brackets to the cylinder block/head and lay the filter/converter to one side.
21 Undo the nuts and multi-spline bolts securing the EGR pipe to the right-hand end of the exhaust manifold and EGR cooler **(see illustration)**. Remove the pipe and recover the gaskets.
22 Trace the exhaust manifold gas temperature sensor wiring back, releasing it from any retaining clips, disconnect its wiring plug at the bulkhead, and slide it from the

retaining bracket. Unclip the wiring loom from the top of the turbocharger heatshield.
23 Undo the bolt securing the support bracket/oil return pipe to the underside of the turbocharger, then undo the bolt securing the top of the support bracket to the underside of the turbocharger. Now pull and twist the support bracket to disconnect it from the oil return pipe at the top. Remove the pipe/bracket **(see illustrations)**. Note the O-ring and copper sealing washer on the lower banjo bolt, and the 2 O-rings fitted to the base of the oil return pipe still fitted to the turbocharger.
24 Note their fitted locations, then release the clamps and disconnect the various coolant hoses from the cylinder head.
25 Undo the bolt securing the turbocharger oil supply pipe bracket at the left-hand end of the cylinder head, the nut securing the bracket

on the rear of the head, then undo the union bolts and remove the pipe. Renew any seals.
26 Undo the bolt securing the timing belt guard adjacent to the timing belt tensioner, and the bolt securing the camshaft position sensor, then remove the tensioner retaining nut **(see illustration)**.
27 Disconnect the turbocharger wastegate position sensor wiring plug, and the intake manifold changeover valve wiring plug. Note their fitted positions and disconnect the vacuum hoses from the EGR cooler (where the plastic pipe joins the metal pipe at the back of the cylinder head) and the turbocharger wastegate actuator. Undo the nuts securing the boost pressure solenoid valve to the bulkhead. Release the loom wiring plug, lay the wiring loom and vacuum hoses over the front of the engine, clear of the cylinder head **(see illustration)**. Make a final check to ensure all relevant wiring and vacuum hoses have been disconnected. Note the loom/hose routing to aid refitting.
28 Using an M12 multi-splined tool (12-pointed star), undo the cylinder head bolts, working from the outside-in, evenly and gradually **(see illustration)**. Remove the bolts and recover the washers. Check that nothing remains connected, and starting at the gearbox side, lift the cylinder head from the engine block, sliding the belt tensioner from the mounting stud as the cylinder head is removed. Seek assistance if possible, as it is a heavy assembly, especially as it is being removed complete with the manifolds.
29 Remove the gasket from the top of the block, noting the locating dowels. If the dowels are a loose fit, remove them and store them with the head for safe-keeping. Do not discard the gasket yet – it will be needed for identification purposes. If desired, the manifolds can be removed from the cylinder head with reference to Chapter 4A (inlet manifold) or 4B (exhaust manifold).

Inspection

30 Dismantling and inspection of the cylinder head is covered in Part Chapter 2C.

Cylinder head gasket selection

Note: A dial test indicator (DTI) will be required for this operation.

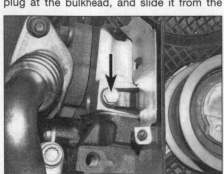

11.26 Undo the bolt (arrowed) securing the timing belt guard

11.27 Undo the boost pressure solenoid valve nuts (arrowed)

11.28 Undo the cylinder head bolts using a M12 multi-splined (12-pointed star) tool

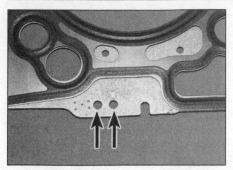

11.31 The holes (arrowed) identify the thickness of the cylinder head gasket

Piston projection	Gasket identification (number of holes)
0.91 to 1.00 mm	1
1.01 to 1.10 mm	2
1.11 to 1.20 mm	3

37 Purchase a new gasket according to the results of the measurements.

Refitting

38 The mating faces of the cylinder head and block must be perfectly clean before refitting the head. Use a scraper to remove all traces of gasket and carbon, also clean the tops of the pistons. Take particular care with the aluminium surfaces, as the soft metal is easily damaged.

39 Make sure that debris is not allowed to enter the oil and water passages – this is particularly important for the oil circuit, as carbon could block the oil supply to the camshaft and crankshaft bearings. Using adhesive tape and paper, seal the water, oil and bolt holes in the cylinder block.

40 To prevent carbon entering the gap between the pistons and bores, smear a little grease in the gap. After cleaning a piston, rotate the crankshaft to that the piston moves down the bore, then wipe out the grease and carbon with a cloth rag. Clean the other piston crowns in the same way.

41 Check the head and block for nicks, deep scratches and other damage. If slight, they may be removed carefully with a file. More serious damage may be repaired by machining, but this is a specialist job.

42 If warpage of the cylinder head is suspected, use a straight-edge to check it for distortion, as described in Chapter 2C.

43 Ensure that the cylinder head bolt holes in the crankcase are clean and free of oil. Syringe or soak up any oil left in the bolt holes. This is most important in order that the correct bolt tightening torque can be applied, and to prevent the possibility of the block being cracked by hydraulic pressure when the bolts are tightened.

31 Examine the old cylinder head gasket for manufacturer's identification markings **(see illustration)**. These will be in the form of holes, and a part number on the edge of the gasket. Unless new pistons have been fitted, the new cylinder head gasket must be of the same type as the old one.

32 If new piston assemblies have been fitted as part of an engine overhaul, or if a new short engine is to be fitted, the projection of the piston crowns above the cylinder head mating face of the cylinder block at TDC must be measured. This measurement is used to determine the thickness of the new cylinder head gasket required.

33 Anchor a dial test indicator (DTI) to the top face (cylinder head gasket mating face) of the cylinder block, and zero the gauge on the gasket mating face.

34 Rest the gauge probe on No 1 piston crown, and turn the crankshaft slowly by hand until the piston reaches TDC. Measure and record the maximum piston projection at TDC **(see illustration)**.

35 Repeat the measurement for the remaining pistons, and record the results.

36 If the measurements differ from piston-to-piston, take the highest figure, and use this to determine the thickness of the head gasket required as follows.

11.34 Measure the piston protrusion using a DTI guage

44 Turn the crankshaft anti-clockwise all the pistons at an equal height, approximately half-way down their bores from the TDC position (see Section 3). This will eliminate any risk of piston-to-valve contact as the cylinder head is refitted.

45 Where applicable, refit the manifolds with reference to Chapters 4A and/or 4B.

46 Ensure that the cylinder head locating dowels are in place in the cylinder block, then fit the new cylinder head gasket over the dowels, ensuring that the part number is uppermost **(see illustration)**. Note that VW recommend that the gasket is only removed from its packaging immediately prior to fitting.

47 Lower the cylinder head into position on the gasket, ensuring that it engages correctly over the dowels. Refit the timing belt tensioner as the cylinder head is refitted.

48 Fit the washers in place then fit the new cylinder head bolts to the locations, and bolt them in as far as possible by hand. Do not oil the bolt threads.

49 Working progressively, in sequence, tighten all the cylinder head bolts to the specified Stage 1 torque **(see illustrations)**.

50 Again working progressively, in sequence, tighten all the cylinder head bolts to the specified Stage 2 torque.

51 Tighten all the cylinder head bolts, in

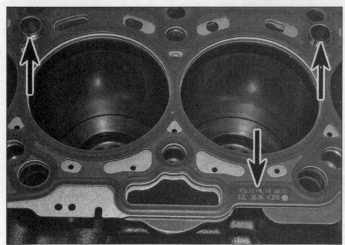

11.46 Ensure the dowels are in place, then fit the new gasket with the part number uppermost (arrowed)

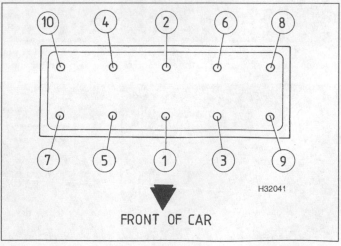

11.49a Cylinder head bolt tightening sequence

11.49b Tighten the cylinder head bolts to the Stage 1 torque

11.51 Use an angle-tightening gauge

sequence, through the specified Stage 3 angle **(see illustration)**.

52 Finally, tighten all the cylinder head bolts, in sequence, through the specified Stage 4 angle.

53 The remainder of the refitting procedure is a reversal of the removal procedure, noting the following points:

a) *Tighten all fasteners to their specified torque where given.*

b) *Renew all seals and gaskets.*

c) *Refill the cooling system as described in Chapter 1.*

d) *Ensure all wiring is correctly routed.*

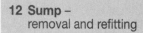

12 Sump –
removed and refitting

Removal

1 Apply the handbrake, then jack up the front

of the vehicle and support securely on axle stands (see *Jacking and vehicle support*).

2 Remove the securing bolts and withdraw the engine undershield(s).

3 Drain the engine oil as described in Chapter 1.

4 Release the clamp, raise the retaining clip and remove the air duct from the intercooler outlet **(see illustration)**.

5 Undo the retaining bolts, release the clamp and remove the charge air pipe from the front of the cylinder block **(see illustration 11.11a and 11.11b)**. Disconnect the charge air pressure sensor wiring plug as the pipe is withdrawn.

6 Undo the retaining bolt and move the electric coolant circulation pump to one side **(see illustration)**.

7 Undo the bolt securing the turbo-to-intercooler air pipe to the sump.

8 Disconnect the wiring connector from the oil level/temperature sender in the sump.

9 Pull the sump insulation cover downwards at the rear to release the retaining clips, then prise down the centre clip and pull the clip on the front side of the cover downwards (where fitted) **(see illustrations)**.

10 Unscrew and remove the bolts securing the sump to the cylinder block, and the bolts securing the sump to the transmission casing, then withdraw the sump. If necessary, release the sump by tapping with a soft-faced hammer.

Refitting

11 Begin refitting by thoroughly cleaning the mating faces of the sump and cylinder block. Ensure that all traces of old sealant are removed.

12 Ensure that the cylinder block mating face of the sump is free from all traces of old sealant, oil and grease, and then apply a 2.0 to 3.0 mm thick bead of silicone sealant (VW D 176 404 A2 or equivalent) to the sump **(see illustration)**. Note that the sealant should be run around the inside of the bolt holes in the sump. The sump must be fitted within 5 minutes of applying the sealant.

13 Offer the sump up to the cylinder block, then refit the sump-to-cylinder block bolts, and lightly tighten them by hand, working progressively in a diagonal sequence. **Note:** *If the sump is being refitted with the engine and transmission separated, make sure that the sump is flush with the flywheel end of the cylinder block.*

14 Refit the sump-to-transmission casing bolts, and tighten them lightly, using a socket.

12.4 Raise the clip (arrowed) and disconnect the air duct from the intercooler

12.6 Electric coolant circulation pump retaining bolt (arrowed)

12.9a Pull the insulation down at the rear to release the clips (arrowed)

12.9b At the front, prise down the centre pin and pull the clip downwards (arrowed)

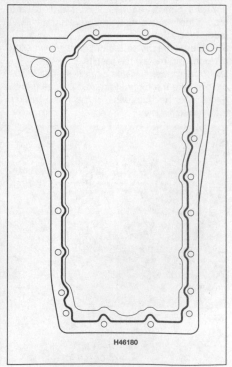

H46180

12.12 Apply a bead of sealant to the around the inside of the bolt holes

15 Again working in a diagonal sequence, lightly tighten the sump-to-cylinder block bolts, using a socket.
16 Tighten the sump-to-transmission casing bolts to the specified torque.
17 Working in a diagonal sequence, progressively tighten the sump-to-cylinder block bolts to the specified torque.
18 The remainder of refitting is a reversal of removal, noting to allow at least 30 minutes from the time of refitting the sump for the sealant to dry, then refill the engine with oil, with reference to Chapter 1.

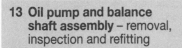

13 Oil pump and balance shaft assembly – removal, inspection and refitting

Removal

1 Remove the sump as described in Section 12.

Oil pump

2 Remove the retaining circlip, then pull the oil pump shaft out using an M3 bolt **(see illustrations)**.
3 Undo the retaining bolts and detach the pick-up pipe from the pump **(see illustration)**.
4 Undo the bolts and detach the oil pump from the balance shaft assembly **(see illustration)**.

Balance shaft assembly

5 Lock the camshafts and crankshaft at TDC on No 1 cylinder as described in Section 3.
6 Working gradually and evenly, undo the retaining bolts and detach the balance shaft assembly from the base of the cylinder block.

Inspection

7 At the time of writing, it would appear that no parts are available for the oil pump or balance shaft assembly. If defective, the oil pump or balance shaft assembly must be renewed. Consult a VW dealer or parts specialist.

Refitting

Oil pump

8 Refit the pump to the balance shaft assembly and tighten the retaining bolts to the specified torque.
9 Refit the oil pick-up pipe using a new O-ring, then tighten the retaining bolts to the specified torque **(see illustration)**.
10 Push the driveshaft into place, and secure it with the circlip.
11 The remainder of refitting is a reversal of removal.

Balance shaft assembly

Note: *If the original balance shaft assembly is being refitted, it's essential that neither the drivegear on the crankshaft or the crankshaft itself has been renewed, or the idler gear bolt has been slackened. If they have, proceed under the heading for the installation of a new balance shaft assembly.*

13.2a Remove the circlip . . .

13.2b . . . and pull out the oil pump shaft using an M3 bolt

13.3 Oil pump pick-up pipe bolts (arrowed)

13.4 Oil pump mounting bolts (arrowed)

Refitting the original assembly

12 Rotate the balance shaft until VW tool No T10255 can be fitted into the groove on the left-hand end of the rear shaft **(see illustrations)**.
13 Ensure the engine is still locked at TDC for

No 1 cylinder, then position the balance shaft assembly over the locating dowels on the base of the cylinder block. The idler gear must engage with the drivegear of the crankshaft, and there must be noticeable backlash.
14 Fit the new balance shaft assembly

13.9 Renew the pick-up pipe O-ring seal

13.12a Rotate the balance shaft until the groove (arrowed) on the end of the rear shaft is vertical . . .

13.12b . . . and tool No T10255 . . .

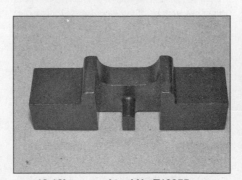

13.12c . . . can be fitted

14.5 Use a locking tool to counterhold the flywheel

14.7a Flywheel warpage check – see text

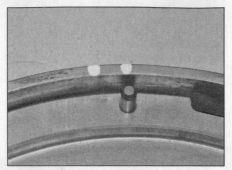

14.7b Flywheel free rotational movement check alignment marks – see text

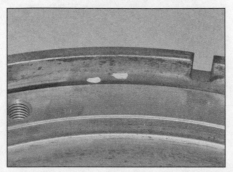

14.7c Flywheel lateral movement check marks – see text

retaining bolts, and working from the centre outwards, tighten them to the specified torque. Remove the VW tool.

15 The remainder of refitting is a reversal of removal.

Fitting a new balance shaft assembly

16 New balance shaft assemblies are supplied with an idler gear with a special coating. Once fitted, the coating wears down to give the correct backlash between the gears.

17 Ensure the engine is still locked at TDC for No 1 cylinder as described in Section 3.

18 Slacken the idler gear retaining bolt 90°.

19 Position the balance shaft assembly over the locating dowels on the base of the cylinder block, ensuring the white mark on the idler gear is centrally aligned with the crankshaft drivegear. Idler gears not marked with a white mark can be installed in any position.

20 Fit the new balance shaft assembly retaining bolts, and working from the centre outwards, tighten them to the specified torque.

21 Rotate the balance shaft until VW tool No T10255 can be fitted into the groove on the left-hand end of the rear shaft **(see illustration 13.12a, 13.12b and 13.12c)**.

22 Fit the balance shaft drivegear onto the shaft so the holes in the gear align with the holes in the shaft. Tighten the retaining bolts to the specified torque.

23 Have an assistant push the idler gear between the two gears to remove any backlash. At the same time, rotate the balance shaft anti-clockwise slightly, and tighten the

idler gear retaining bolt to the specified torque. Remove the balance shaft locking tool.

24 The remainder of refitting is a reversal of removal.

14 Flywheel – removal, inspection and refitting

Removal

1 On manual gearbox models, remove the gearbox (see Chapter 7A) and clutch (see Chapter 6).

2 On automatic transmission models, remove the automatic transmission as described in Chapter 7B.

3 These models are fitted with a dual-mass flywheel. The flywheel can only be fitted in one position due to the offset of the flywheel mounting holes in the end of the crankshaft.

4 Rotate the outside of the dual-mass flywheel so that the bolts align with the holes (if necessary).

5 Unscrew the bolts and remove the flywheel. Use a locking tool to counterhold the flywheel **(see illustration)**. Discard the bolts, new ones must be fitted. **Note:** *In order not to damage the flywheel, do not allow the bolt heads to make contact with the flywheel during the unscrewing procedure.*

Inspection

6 Check the flywheel for wear and damage. Examine the starter ring gear for excessive wear to the teeth. If the driveplate or its ring

gear are damaged, the complete driveplate must be renewed. The flywheel ring gear, however, may be renewed separately from the flywheel, but the work should be entrusted to a VW dealer. If the clutch friction face is discoloured or scored excessively, it may be possible to regrind it, but this work should also be entrusted to a VW dealer.

7 The following are *guidelines* only, but should indicate whether professional inspection is necessary. The dual-mass flywheel should be checked as follows:

There should be no cracks in the drive surface of the flywheel. If cracks are evident, the flywheel may need renewing.

Warpage

Place a straight-edge across the face of the drive surface, and check by trying to insert a feeler gauge between the straight-edge and the drive surface **(see illustration)**. The flywheel will normally warp like a bowl – ie, higher on the outer edge. If the warpage is more than 0.40 mm, the flywheel may need renewing.

Free rotational movement

This is the distance the drive surface of the flywheel can be turned independently of the flywheel primary element, using finger effort alone. Move the drive surface in one direction and make a mark where the locating pin aligns with the flywheel edge. Move the drive surface in the other direction (finger pressure only) and make another mark **(see illustration)**. The total of free movement should not exceed 20.0 mm. If it's more, the flywheel may need renewing.

Total rotational movement

This is the total distance the drive surface can be turned independently of the flywheel primary element. Insert two bolts into the clutch pressure plate/damper unit mounting holes, and with the crankshaft/flywheel held stationary, use a lever/pry bar between the bolts and use some effort to move the drive surface fully in one direction – make a mark where the locating pin aligns with the flywheel edge. Now force the drive surface fully in the opposite direction, and make another mark. The total rotational movement should not exceed 44.0 mm. If it does, have the flywheel professionally inspected.

Lateral movement

The lateral movement (up and down) of the drive surface in relation to the primary element of the flywheel, should not exceed 2.0 mm. If it does, the flywheel may need renewing. This can be checked by pressing the drive surface down on one side into the flywheel (flywheel horizontal) and making an alignment mark between the drive surface and the inner edge of the primary element. Now press down on the opposite side of the drive surface, and make another mark above the original one. The difference between the two marks is the lateral movement **(see illustration)**.

15.2 Pull the screw and seal from place using pliers

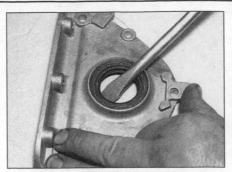

15.3 Prise the oil seal from the crankshaft oil seal housing

15.9 Slide the oil seal housing over the end of the crankshaft

Refitting

8 Refitting is a reversal of removal. Use new bolts when refitting the flywheel or driveplate, and coat the threads of the bolts with locking fluid before inserting them. Tighten them to the specified torque.

15 Crankshaft oil seals – renewal

Note: *The oil seals are a PTFE (Teflon) type and are fitted dry, without using any grease or oil. These have a wider sealing lip and have been introduced instead of the coil spring type oil seal.*

Timing belt end oil seal

1 Remove the timing belt as described in Section 7, and the crankshaft sprocket with reference to Section 8.

2 To remove the seal without removing the housing, drill two small holes diagonally opposite each other, insert self-tapping screws, and pull on the heads of the screws with pliers **(see illustration)**.

3 Alternatively, to remove the oil seal complete with its housing, proceed as follows.

a) *Remove the sump as described in Section 12. This is necessary to ensure a*

satisfactory seal between the sump and oil seal housing on refitting.

b) *Unscrew and remove the oil seal housing.*

c) *Working on the bench, lever the oil seal from the housing using a suitable screwdriver. Take care not to damage the seal seating in the housing (see illustration).*

4 Thoroughly clean the oil seal seating in the housing.

5 Wind a length of tape around the end of the crankshaft to protect the oil seal lips as the seal (and housing, where applicable) is fitted.

6 Fit a new oil seal to the housing, pressing or driving it into position using a socket or tube of suitable diameter. Ensure that the socket or tube bears only on the hard outer ring of the seal, and take care not to damage the seal lips. Press or drive the seal into position until it is seated on the shoulder in the housing. Make sure that the closed end of the seal is facing outwards.

7 If the oil seal housing has been removed, proceed as follows, otherwise proceed to paragraph 11.

8 Clean all traces of old sealant from the crankshaft oil seal housing and the cylinder block, then coat the cylinder block mating faces of the oil seal housing with a 2.0 to 3.0 mm thick bead of silicone sealant (VW D 176 404 A2, or equivalent). Note that the seal housing must be refitted within 5 minutes of applying the sealant.

Caution: DO NOT put excessive amounts of sealant onto the housing as it may get into the sump and block the oil pick-up pipe.

9 Refit the oil seal housing, and tighten the bolts progressively to the specified torque **(see illustration)**.

10 Refit the sump as described in Section 12.

11 Refit the crankshaft sprocket with reference to Section 8, and the timing belt as described in Section 7.

Flywheel end oil seal

Note: *In these engines, the seal, sealing flange and sender wheel are a complete unit. Special tools are required to refit the sealing flange, and press the sender wheel onto the end of the crankshaft. It is not possible to accurately fit these parts without the tools, which may be available from VW (part No T10134) and are available from aftermarket automotive tool specialists.*

12 Remove the flywheel as described in Section 14, then prise the intermediate plate from the locating dowels on the cylinder block.

13 Undo the bolts securing the sealing flange to the cylinder block **(see illustration)**.

14 Insert three 6 x 35 mm bolts into the threaded holes in the sealing flange. Tighten the bolts gradually and evenly, and press the sealing flange and sender wheel from the crankshaft/cylinder block **(see illustration)**.

15.13 Sealing flange bolts (arrowed)

15.14 Bolt in 6 x 35 mm bolts (arrowed) and draw the sealing flange and sender wheel from place

15.16a Rotate the nut until its level with the end of the clamping surface (arrowed) . . .

15.16b . . . then clamp it in a vice

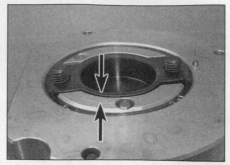

15.17 Rotate the nut until the inner part of the tool is flush with the housing (arrowed)

15.18a Remove the securing clip . . .

15.18b . . . the hole in the sender wheel should align with the marking on the flange (arrowed)

follow the instructions supplied with the tool. Rotate the large spindle nut until it's level with the end of the clamping surface of the spindle, then clamp the spindle in a vice **(see illustrations)**.

17 Press the tool housing downwards until it rests on the nut and washer. Rotate the nut until the inner part of the tool is at the same height as the housing **(see illustration)**.

18 Remove the seal securing clip. The hole on the sender wheel must align with the marking on the sealing flange **(see illustrations)**.

19 Place the flange outer side down on a clean, flat surface, then press the seal guide fitting sleeve (supplied ready fitted), housing, and sender wheel downwards until all the components are flat on the surface. In this position the upper edge of the sender wheel should be level with the edge of the sealing flange **(see illustrations)**.

20 Place the sealing flange on the assembly tool, so the pin locates in the hole in the sender wheel **(see illustration)**.

21 Push the sealing flange and guide fitting sleeve against the tool whilst tightening the 3 knurled bolts. Ensure the pin is still located in the sender wheel **(see illustration)**.

22 Ensure the end of the crankshaft is clean, and is locked at TDC on No 1 cylinder as described in Section 3.

23 Unscrew the large nut to the end of the spindle threads, then press the spindle inwards as far as possible **(see illustration)**.

24 Align the flat side of the assembly with the sump flange, then secure the tool to the crankshaft using the integral Allen bolts **(see illustration)**. Only hand-tighten the bolts.

The seal, sender wheel and sealing flange are supplied as a complete unit.

15 Ensure the mating face of the cylinder block is clean and free from debris. The new sealing flange/seal/sender wheel assembly is supplied with a sealing lip support ring,

which serves as a fitting sleeve, and must not be removed prior to installation. Equally, the sender wheel must not be separated from the assembly.

16 If using the VW tool, proceed as follows. If using an aftermarket tool specialists product,

15.19a Press the assembly downwards on a clean, flat surface . . .

15.19b . . . so the upper edge of the sender wheel is level with the edge of the flange (arrowed)

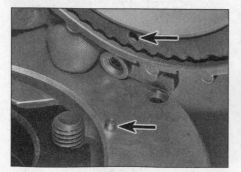

15.20 Fit the flange to the tool, ensuring the pin locates in the hole (arrowed)

15.21 With the pin engaged in the hole, tighten the 3 knurled bolts to secure the flange to the tool

15.23 Unscrew the nut to the end of the thread, and push the spindle in as far as possible

15.24 Hand-tighten the Allen bolts to secure the tool to the crankshaft (arrowed)

15.25 Use 2 M7 x 35 mm bolts (arrowed) to guide the sealing flange

15.26 Push the black knob (arrowed) into the hole in the crankshaft

25 Insert two M7 x 35 mm bolts to guide the sealing flange to the cylinder block **(see illustration)**.

26 Using hand-pressure alone, push the tool assembly onto the crankshaft until the seal guide fitting sleeve contacts the crankshaft flange, then push the guide pin (black knob) into the hole in the crankshaft. This is to ensure the sender wheel reaches its correct installation position **(see illustration)**.

27 Rotate the large nut until it makes contact with the tool housing, then tighten it to 35 Nm (26 lbf ft). After tightening this nut, a small air gap must still be present between the sealing flange and cylinder block **(see illustration)**.

28 Unscrew the large nut, the two M7 x 35 mm bolts, the three knurled bolts and the Allen bolts securing the tool to the crankshaft. Remove the tool, and pull the seal guide fitting sleeve from place (if it didn't come out with the tool).

29 Use a vernier caliper or feeler gauge to measure the fitted depth of the sender wheel in relation to the crankshaft flange **(see illustration)**. The correct depth is 0.5 mm.

30 If the gap is correct, fit the sealing flange bolts and tighten them to the specified torque.

31 If the gap is too small, re-attach the tool to the sealing flange and crankshaft, then refit the two M7 x 35 mm guide bolts to the flange. Tighten the large spindle nut to 40 Nm (30 lbf ft), remove the tool and measure the air gap. If the gap is still too small, re-attach the tool and tighten the spindle nut to 45 Nm (33 lbf ft). Measure the gap again. When the gap is correct, refit the flange retaining bolts, and tighten them to the specified torque.

32 The remainder of refitting is a reversal of removal.

---

16 Engine/transmission mountings – inspection and renewal

Inspection

1 If improved access is required, jack up the front of the vehicle, and support it securely on axle stands (see *Jacking and vehicle support*). Remove the engine top cover which also incorporates the air filter, then remove the engine undershield(s).

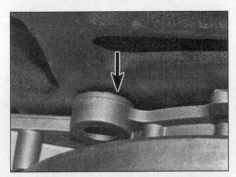

15.27 After tightening the spindle nut there should be an air gap between the sealing flange and the cylinder block (arrowed)

2 Check the mounting rubbers to see if they are cracked, hardened or separated from the metal at any point; renew the mounting if any such damage or deterioration is evident.

3 Check that all the mountings are securely tightened; use a torque wrench to check if possible.

4 Using a large screwdriver or a crowbar, check for wear in the mounting by carefully levering against it to check for free play. Where this is not possible, enlist the aid of an assistant to move the engine/transmission back-and-forth, or from side-to-side, whilst you observe the mounting. While some free play is to be expected, even from new components, excessive wear should be obvious. If excessive free play is found, check first that the fasteners are correctly secured, then renew any worn components as described in the following paragraphs.

Renewal

Note: *New mounting securing bolts will be required on refitting.*

Right-hand mounting

5 Attach a hoist and lifting tackle to the engine lifting brackets on the cylinder head, and raise the hoist to just take the weight of the engine. Alternatively the engine can be supported on a trolley jack under the engine. Use a block of wood between the sump and the head of the jack, to prevent any damage to the sump.

6 For improved access, unscrew the coolant reservoir and move it to one side, leaving the coolant hoses connected.

15.29 Measure the fitted depth of the sender wheel in relation to the end of the crankshaft

7 Where applicable, move any wiring harnesses, pipes or hoses to one side to enable removal of the engine mounting.

8 Unscrew the bolts securing the mounting to the engine bracket, then unscrew the bolts securing it to the body. Also, unscrew the movement limiter. Withdraw the mounting from the engine compartment.

9 Refitting is a reversal of removal, bearing in mind the following points.

a) Use new securing bolts.

b) There must be at least 10 mm between the engine mounting bracket and the right-hand side chassis member **(see illustration)**.

c) The side of the mounting support arm must be parallel to the side of the engine mounting bracket.

d) Tighten all fixings to the specified torque.

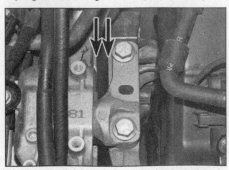

16.9 There must be at least 10 mm between the bracket and the chassis member (arrowed)

16.18 Rear mounting arm-to-transmission bolts (arrowed)

Left-hand mounting

10 Remove the engine top cover.

11 Attach a hoist and lifting tackle to the engine lifting brackets on the cylinder head, and raise the hoist to just take the weight of the engine and transmission. Alternatively the engine can be supported on a trolley jack under the transmission. Use a block of wood between the transmission and the head of the jack, to prevent any damage to the transmission.

12 Remove the battery and battery tray, as described in Chapter 5.

13 Unscrew the bolts securing the mounting to the transmission, and the remaining bolts securing the mounting to the body, then lift the mounting from the engine compartment.

14 Refitting is a reversal of removal, bearing in mind the following points:

a) *Use new mounting bolts.*

b) *The edges of the mounting support arm must be parallel to the edge of the mounting .*

c) *Tighten all fixings to the specified torque.*

Rear mounting (torque arm)

15 Apply the handbrake, then jack up the front of the vehicle and support securely on axle stands (see *Jacking and vehicle support*).

Remove the engine undershield(s) for access to the rear mounting (torque arm).

16 Support the rear of the transmission beneath the final drive housing. To do this, use a trolley jack and block of wood, or alternatively wedge a block of wood between the transmission and the subframe.

17 Working under the vehicle, unscrew and remove the bolt securing the mounting to the subframe.

18 Unscrew the two bolts securing the mounting to the transmission, then withdraw the mounting from under the vehicle **(see illustration).**

19 Refitting is a reversal of removal, but use new mounting securing bolts, and tighten all fixings to the specified torque.

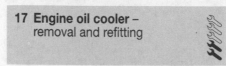

17 Engine oil cooler – removal and refitting

Removal

1 The oil cooler is mounted under the oil filter housing on the front of the cylinder block.

2 Position a container beneath the oil filter to catch escaping oil and coolant.

3 Clamp the oil cooler coolant hoses to minimise coolant spillage, then remove the clips, and disconnect the hoses from the oil cooler. Be prepared for coolant spillage.

4 Unscrew the oil cooler securing plate from the bottom of the oil filter housing, then slide off the oil cooler. Recover the O-rings from the top and bottom of the oil cooler.

Refitting

5 Refitting is a reversal of removal, bearing in mind the following points:

a) *Use new oil cooler O-rings.*

b) *Tighten the oil cooler securing plate securely.*

c) *On completion, check and if necessary top-up the oil and coolant levels.*

18.1 Oil pressure warning light switch

18 Oil pressure warning light switch – removal and refitting

Removal

1 The oil pressure warning light switch is fitted to the oil filter housing **(see illustration).** Remove the engine top cover to gain access to the switch (see Section 4).

2 Disconnect the wiring connector and wipe clean the area around the switch.

3 Unscrew the switch from the filter housing and remove it, along with its sealing washer. If the switch is to be left removed from the engine for any length of time, plug the oil filter housing aperture.

Refitting

4 Examine the sealing washer for signs of damage or deterioration and if necessary renew.

5 Refit the switch, complete with washer, and tighten it to the specified torque.

6 Securely reconnect the wiring connector then check and, if necessary, top-up the engine oil as described in Weekly checks. On completion, refit the engine top cover(s).

Chapter 2 Part C:
Engine removal and overhaul procedures

Contents

Degrees of difficulty

Easy, suitable for novice with little experience	**Fairly easy,** suitable for beginner with some experience	**Fairly difficult,** suitable for competent DIY mechanic	**Difficult,** suitable for experienced DIY mechanic	**Very difficult,** suitable for expert DIY or professional

Specifications

Engine codes

Manufacturer's engine codes:*
PD unit injector engines:

1.9 litre	BKC, BLS and BXE
2.0 litre	BKP, BMA, BMR, BUZ, BVE and BWV
Common rail injection engines	CBAA, CBAB, CBAC and CBBB

* Note: *See 'Vehicle identification' at the end of this manual for the location of engine code markings.*

Cylinder head

Cylinder head gasket surface, maximum distortion	0.1 mm
Minimum cylinder head height	Head resurfacing not possible
Cylinder head gasket selection:	
Piston projection 0.91 to 1.00 mm	1 hole/notch*
Piston projection 1.01 to 1.10 mm	2 holes/notches*
Piston projection 1.11 to 1.20 mm	3 holes/notches*

* Disregard single and double oval holes.

Valves

	Intake	Exhaust
Valve stem diameter:		
PD unit injector engine:		
1.9 litre	6.980 mm	6.956 mm
2.0 litre	5.980 mm	5.965 mm
Common rail injection engine	5.940 mm	5.940 mm
Maximum valve head deflection (end of stem flush with top of guide)	1.3 mm	1.3 mm

Pistons and piston rings

Piston diameter:	
1.9 litre	79.720 mm nominal
2.0 litre	80.960 mm nominal
Ring-to-groove clearance:	
Compression rings	0.25 mm maximum
Oil control ring	0.15 mm maximum
Piston ring end gap clearance (ring 15 mm from bottom of bore):	
New:	
Compression rings	0.20 to 0.40 mm
Oil scraper ring	0.25 to 0.50 mm
Wear limit	1.0 mm

Cylinder block

Bore diameter:
1.9 litre	79.51 mm nominal
2.0 litre	81.01 mm nominal

Crankshaft

Spigot needle bearing depth	1.5 mm
Endfloat:	
New	0.07 to 0.17 mm
Wear limit	0.37 mm
Main bearing journal diameter	54.00 mm nominal
Big-end bearing journal diameter	50.90 mm nominal

Torque wrench settings

Refer to Chapters 2A or 2B.

1 General information

Included in this Part of Chapter 2 are details of removing the engine from the car and general overhaul procedures for the cylinder head, cylinder block and all other engine internal components.

The information given ranges from advice concerning preparation for an overhaul and the purchase of parts, to detailed step-by-step procedures covering removal, inspection, renovation and refitting of engine internal components.

After Section 5, all instructions are based on the assumption that the engine has been removed from the car. For information concerning in-car engine repair, as well as the removal and refitting of those external components necessary for full overhaul, refer to the relevant in-car repair procedure section (Chapters 2A or 2B) and to Section 5 of this Chapter. Ignore any preliminary dismantling operations described in the relevant in-car repair sections that are no longer relevant once the engine has been removed from the car.

Apart from torque wrench settings, which are given at the beginning of the relevant in-car repair procedure in Chapters 2A or 2B, all specifications relating to engine overhaul are at the beginning of this Part of Chapter 2.

2 Engine overhaul – general information

It is not always easy to determine when, or if, an engine should be completely overhauled, as a number of factors must be considered.

High mileage is not necessarily an indication that an overhaul is needed, while low mileage does not preclude the need for an overhaul. Frequency of servicing is probably the most important consideration. An engine which has had regular and frequent oil and filter changes, as well as other required maintenance, should give many thousands of miles of reliable service. Conversely, a neglected engine may require an overhaul very early in its life.

Excessive oil consumption is an indication that piston rings, valve seals and/or valve guides are in need of attention. Make sure that oil leaks are not responsible before deciding that the rings and/or guides are worn. Perform a compression test, as described in the relevant Part A or B of this Chapter, to determine the likely cause of the problem.

Check the oil pressure with a gauge fitted in place of the oil pressure switch, and compare it with that specified (see Chapter 2A or 2B). If it is extremely low, the main and big-end bearings, and/or the oil pump, are probably worn out.

Loss of power, rough running, knocking or metallic engine noises, excessive valve gear noise, and high fuel consumption may also point to the need for an overhaul, especially if they are all present at the same time. If a complete service does not remedy the situation, major mechanical work is the only solution.

An engine overhaul involves restoring all internal parts to the specification of a new engine. During an overhaul, the pistons and the piston rings are renewed. New main and big-end bearings are generally fitted; if necessary, the crankshaft may be renewed, to restore the journals. The valves are also serviced as well, since they are usually in less-than-perfect condition at this point. While the engine is being overhauled, other components, such as the starter and alternator, can be overhauled as well. The end result should be an as-new engine that will give many trouble-free miles. **Note:** *Critical cooling system components such as the hoses, thermostat and coolant pump should be renewed when an engine is overhauled. The radiator should be checked carefully, to ensure that it is not clogged or leaking. Also, it is a good idea to renew the oil pump whenever the engine is overhauled.*

Before beginning the engine overhaul, read through the entire procedure, to familiarise yourself with the scope and requirements of the job. Overhauling an engine is not difficult if you follow carefully all of the instructions, have the necessary tools and equipment, and pay close attention to all specifications. It can, however, be time-consuming. Plan on the car being off the road for a minimum of two weeks, especially if parts must be taken to an engineering works for repair or reconditioning. Check on the availability of parts and make sure that any necessary special tools and equipment are obtained in advance. Most work can be done with typical hand tools, although a number of precision measuring tools are required for inspecting parts to determine if they must be renewed. Often the engineering works will handle the inspection of parts and offer advice concerning reconditioning and renewal. **Note:** *Always wait until the engine has been completely dismantled, and until all components (especially the cylinder block and the crankshaft) have been inspected before deciding what service and repair operations must be performed by an engineering works. The condition of these components will be the major factor to consider when determining whether to overhaul the original engine, or to buy a reconditioned unit. Do not, therefore, purchase parts or have overhaul work done on other components until they have been thoroughly inspected. As a general rule, time is the primary cost of an overhaul, so it does not pay to fit worn or sub-standard parts.*

As a final note, to ensure maximum life and minimum trouble from a reconditioned engine, everything must be assembled with care, in a spotlessly-clean environment.

3 Engine removal – preparation and precautions

If you have decided that the engine must be removed for overhaul or major repair work, several preliminary steps should be taken.

Locating a suitable place to work is extremely important. Adequate work space, along with storage space for the vehicle, will be needed. If a workshop or garage is not available, at the very least a solid, level, clean work surface is required.

If possible, clear some shelving close to the work area and use it to store the engine components and ancillaries as they are removed and dismantled. In this manner, the components stand a better chance of staying clean and undamaged during the overhaul. Laying out components in groups together

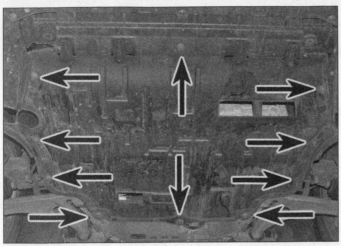

4.5 Undo the bolts and remove the engine undershield (arrowed)

4.6 Pull the front edge of the plastic cover upwards

with their fixings bolts, bolts, etc, will save time and avoid confusion when the engine is refitted.

Clean the engine compartment and engine before beginning the removal procedure; this will help visibility and help to keep tools clean.

The help of an assistant is essential; there are certain instances when one person cannot safely perform all of the operations required to remove the engine from the vehicle. Safety is of primary importance, considering the potential hazards involved in this kind of operation. A second person should always be in attendance to offer help in an emergency. If this is the first time you have removed an engine, advice and aid from someone more experienced would also be beneficial.

Plan the operation ahead of time. Before starting work, obtain (or arrange for the hire of) all of the tools and equipment you will need. Access to the following items will allow the task of removing and refitting the engine to be completed safely and with relative ease: a heavy-duty trolley jack – rated in excess of the weight of the engine, complete sets of spanners and sockets as described in the back of this manual, wooden blocks, and plenty of rags and cleaning solvent for mopping-up spilled oil, coolant and fuel. A selection of different sized plastic storage bins will also prove useful for keeping dismantled components grouped together. If any of the equipment must be hired, make sure that you arrange for it in advance, and perform all of the operations possible without it beforehand; this may save you time and money.

Plan on the vehicle being out of use for quite a while, especially if you intend to carry out an engine overhaul. Read through the whole of this Section and work out a strategy based on your own experience and the tools, time and workspace available to you. Some of the overhaul processes may have to be carried out by a VW dealer or an engineering works – these establishments often have busy

schedules, so it would be prudent to consult them before removing or dismantling the engine, to get an idea of the amount of time required to carry out the work.

When removing the engine from the vehicle, be methodical about the disconnection of external components. Labelling cables and hoses as they are removed will greatly assist the refitting process.

Always be extremely careful when lifting the engine from the engine bay. Serious injury can result from careless actions. If help is required, it is better to wait until it is available rather than risk personal injury and/or damage to components by continuing alone. By planning ahead and taking your time, a job of this nature, although major, can be accomplished successfully and without incident.

Note that the engine should ideally be removed with the vehicle standing on all four roadwheels, but access to the exhaust system downpipe and lower bolts will be improved if the vehicle can be temporarily raised onto axle stands.

4 Engine – removal and refitting

Removal

1 On common rail injection models with air conditioning, have the refrigerant discharged by a suitably-equipped specialist.
2 Select a solid, level surface to park the vehicle on. Give yourself enough space to move around it easily.
3 Remove the battery and battery tray as described in Chapter 5.
4 Apply the handbrake, then jack up the front of the vehicle and support it on axle stands (see *Jacking and vehicle support*). Remove both front roadwheels.
5 Remove the retaining bolts, and remove engine compartment undershield (see illustration).

6 Remove the cover from the top of the engine (see illustration).
7 Move the lock carrier to the 'Service position' as described in Chapter 11. If improved access is required, remove the lock carrier assembly as described in Chapter 11.
8 Remove the air cleaner assembly as described in Chapter 4A.

PD unit injector engines

9 Note their fitted positions, and disconnect the coolant, fuel supply and return hoses at the right-hand end of the cylinder head. Plug the openings to prevent contamination.
10 Remove the auxiliary drivebelt as described in Chapter 1.
11 On models with air conditioning, unscrew the compressor and secure it to the lock carrier without disconnecting, or kinking, the refrigerant pipes.

Common rail injection engines

12 Disconnect the wiring plug, undo the retaining bolt, and remove the exhaust gas pressure sensor bracket by pushing it forwards (see illustration).
13 Disconnect the wiring plug, unclip the fuel hoses from the clips, then release the clamps and disconnect the hoses from the filter (see illustrations).
14 Disconnect the fuel temperature sensor

4.12 Disconnect the pressure sensor wiring plug and undo the bracket retaining bolt (arrowed)

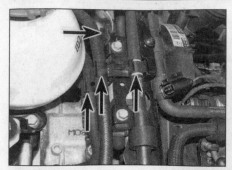

4.13a Disconnect the wiring plug and unclip the hoses (arrowed)

4.13b Note their positions and disconnect the hoses from the filter

4.14 Disconnect the fuel temperature sensor and the supply hose (arrowed)

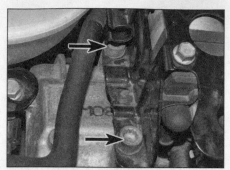

4.15 Undo the supplementary fuel pump retaining bolts (arrowed) at the right-hand end of the cylinder head

4.17 The coolant circulation pump bracket retaining bolt (arrowed – shown with the charge air pipe removed)

4.18 Charge pressure regulating valve (arrowed)

4.20 Disconnect the wiring plug beneath the left-hand headlight (arrowed – headlight removed for clarity)

4.21 Disconnect the wiring plug and the earth strap (arrowed)

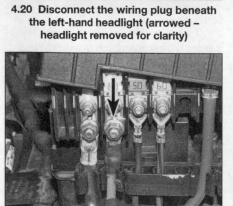

4.22 Alternator positive lead (arrowed) at the central electrics box

4.23 Disconnect the Mechatronic connector (arrowed) from the DSG transmission

wiring plug, release the clamp and disconnect the fuel supply hose from the high-pressure pump **(see illustration)**.

15 Undo the 2 retaining bolts and remove the supplementary fuel pump **(see illustration)**.

16 Undo the retaining bolts and disconnect the refrigerant pipes from the air conditioning compressor. Plug the pipe openings to prevent contamination.

17 Undo the bolt securing the electric coolant circulation pump to the front of the cylinder block **(see illustration)**.

18 Detach the charge pressure regulating valve from the plenum chamber bulkhead and lay it on the engine together with the vacuum hoses **(see illustration)**.

All engines

19 Remove the engine control module as described in Chapter 4A.

20 Open the wiring guide catches of the left-hand chassis member, then disconnect the engine wiring harness connector beneath the left-hand headlight, and lift the wiring harness from the guide **(see illustration)**. Lay the harness to one side.

21 Disconnect the wiring plug adjacent to the left-hand end of the radiator, and undo the bolt securing the earth strap to the chassis member **(see illustration)**.

22 Disconnect the alternator positive lead from the central electrics box, and the wiring from the starter motor **(see illustration)**.

23 On models with the DSG automatic gearbox, disconnect the selector cable from the transmission as described in Chapter 7B, then disconnect the Mechatronic connector from the gearbox by rotating the catch and pulling the connector from place **(see illustration)**.

24 On models with the manual gearbox, disconnect the gearchange cables from the transmission as described in Chapter 7A, then disconnect the hydraulic hose from the clutch slave cylinder as described in Chapter 6 (plug the openings to prevent contamination), and the wiring plug from the reversing light switch.

25 Slacken the clamp and detach the air pipe from the throttle body **(see illustration)**.

26 Disconnect the hose from the vacuum pump at the left-hand end of the cylinder head.

27 Remove both driveshafts as described in Chapter 8.

28 Remove the steering rack as described in Chapter 10. Note that there is no need to detach the steering gear or anti-roll bar from the front subframe.

29 Remove the particulate filter/catalytic converter (as applicable) as described in Chapter 4B.

30 Remove any remaining charge air pipes.

31 Disconnect the heater pipes at the quick-release couplings on the plenum chamber bulkhead **(see illustration)**.

32 Note their fitted positions and disconnect any remaining coolant/vacuum hoses from the engine/transmission assembly.

33 Attach a suitable hoist to the engine, and lift the engine and transmission slightly. Make sure that the engine is adequately supported. Alternatively, support the engine/transmission from underneath with trolley jacks, etc. Take the weight of the engine/transmission.

34 Unscrew the rear engine support/torque arm from the transmission **(see illustration)**. Note that the black steel bracket should not be separated from the aluminium arm.

35 Unscrew the right- and left-hand engine mountings with reference to Chapter 2A or 2B.

36 Make a final check to ensure that all relevant wiring, hoses and pipes have been disconnected, then carefully lower the engine and transmission from the engine compartment, and withdraw forwards from the front of the car.

Separation

37 Remove the starter motor (Chapter 5).

38 Where applicable, unscrew the bolt securing the small engine-to-transmission plate to the transmission adjacent to the right-hand driveshaft flange **(see illustration)**.

39 Ensure that both engine and transmission are adequately supported, then unscrew the remaining engine-to-transmission bolts, noting the location of each bolt, and the locations of any brackets secured by the bolts.

40 Carefully withdraw the transmission from the engine, ensuring that the weight of the transmission is not allowed to hang on the input shaft while it is engaged with the clutch friction disc. Recover the engine-to-transmission plate.

Reconnection and refitting

41 Reconnection and refitting are a reversal of removal, bearing in mind the following points:

a) Smear the splines of the transmission input shaft with a little high melting-point grease: VW G 052 133 A2 – auto models, or G 000 100 – manual models.

b) Ensure that any brackets noted before removal are in place on the engine-to-transmission bolts.

4.25 Remove the air pipe (arrowed) – common rail engine shown

c) Tighten all fixings to the specified torque, where given.

d) Where applicable, have the air conditioning system recharged with refrigerant by a suitably-qualified professional.

e) Ensure that all wiring, hoses and pipes are correctly reconnected and routed as noted before removal.

f) Ensure that the fuel lines are correctly reconnected.

g) On completion, refill the cooling system as described in Chapter 1.

5 Engine overhaul – preliminary information

It is much easier to dismantle and work on the engine if it is mounted on a portable engine stand. These stands can often be hired from a tool hire shop. Before the engine is mounted on a stand, the flywheel should be removed, so that the stand bolts can be tightened into the end of the cylinder block/crankcase. **Note:** Do not measure cylinder bore dimensions with the engine mounted on this type of stand.

If a stand is not available, it is possible to dismantle the engine with it blocked up on a sturdy workbench, or on the floor. Be very careful not to tip or drop the engine when working without a stand.

If you intend to obtain a reconditioned engine, all ancillaries must be removed first, to be transferred to the new engine (just as

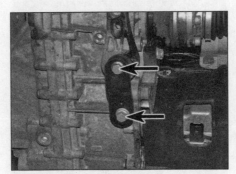

4.34 Rear engine support retaining bolts (arrowed)

4.31 Prise out the clips, and disconnect the heater hoses at the bulkhead

they will if you are doing a complete engine overhaul yourself). These components include the following:

a) Alternator (including mounting brackets) and starter motor (Chapter 5).

b) The glow plug/preheating system components (Chapter 5)

c) All fuel system components, including all sensors and actuators (Chapter 4A)

d) The tandem/vacuum pump (Chapter 4A or 9)

e) All electrical switches, actuators and sensors, and the engine wiring harness (Chapters 4 and 5).

f) Intake and exhaust manifolds, and turbocharger (Chapter 4).

g) The engine oil level dipstick and its tube.

h) Flywheel (Chapter 2A or 2B).

i) Clutch components (Chapter 6).

Note: When removing the external components from the engine, pay close attention to details that may be helpful or important during refitting. Note the fitted position of gaskets, seals, spacers, pins, washers, bolts, and other small components.

If you are obtaining a short engine (the engine cylinder block/crankcase, crankshaft, pistons and connecting rods, all fully assembled), then the cylinder head, sump, oil pump, timing belt (together with its tensioner and covers), auxiliary belt (together with its tensioner), coolant pump, thermostat housing, coolant outlet elbows, oil filter housing and where applicable oil cooler will also have to be removed.

4.38 Remove the bolt (arrowed) securing the engine-to-transmission plate

6.4 Keep groups of components together in labelled bags or boxes

6.5 Compress the valve springs with a compressor tool

6.6a Remove the upper spring seat . . .

6.6b . . . and valve spring

If you are planning a full overhaul, the engine can be dismantled in the order given below:

a) Intake and exhaust manifolds (see the relevant part of Chapter 4).
b) Timing belt, sprockets and tensioner (see Chapter 2A or 2B).
c) Cylinder head (see Chapter 2A or 2B).
d) Flywheel (see Chapter 2A or 2B).
e) Sump (see Chapter 2A or 2B).
f) Oil pump and balancer shaft assembly (see Chapter 2A or 2B).
g) Piston/connecting rod assemblies (see Section 7).
h) Crankshaft (see Section 8).

6 Cylinder head –
dismantling, cleaning, inspection and reassembly

Note: New and reconditioned cylinder heads

are available from VW, and from engine specialists. Specialist tools are required for the dismantling and inspection procedures, and new components may not be readily available. It may, therefore, be more practical for the home mechanic to buy a reconditioned head, rather than to dismantle, inspect and recondition the original head.

Dismantling

1 Remove the cylinder head from the engine block as described in Part A or B of this Chapter. Also remove the camshafts, rockers and hydraulic tappets as described in Part A or B of this Chapter.

2 Remove the injectors (if not already done so) and glow plugs (see Chapters 4 and 5).

3 Where applicable, remove the rear coolant outlet elbow together with its gasket/O-ring.

4 It is important that groups of components are kept together when they are removed and,

if still serviceable, refitted in the same groups. If they are refitted randomly, accelerated wear leading to early failure will occur. Stowing groups of components in plastic bags or storage bins will help to keep everything in the right order – label them according to their fitted location, eg, No 1 exhaust, No 2 intake, etc **(see illustration)**. Note that No 1 cylinder is nearest the timing belt end of the engine.

5 Turn the cylinder head over, and rest it on one side. Using a valve spring compressor, compress each valve spring in turn, extracting the split collets when the upper valve spring seat has been pushed far enough down the valve stem to free them. If the spring seat sticks, tap the upper jaw of the compressor with a hammer to free it **(see illustration)**.

6 Release the valve spring compressor and remove the upper spring seat, and single valve spring (2.0 litre engines) or double valve springs (1.9 litre engines) **(see illustrations)**.

7 Use a pair of pliers or a special removal tool to extract the valve stem oil seal, then remove the lower spring seat from the valve guide. Withdraw the valve itself from the head gasket side of the cylinder head. Repeat this process for the remaining valves **(see illustrations)**.

Cleaning

8 Using a suitable degreasing agent, remove all traces of oil deposits from the cylinder head, paying particular attention to the journal bearings, hydraulic tappet bores, valve guides and oilways. Scrape off any traces of old gasket from the mating surfaces, taking care not to score or gouge them. If using emery paper, do not use a grade of less than 100. Turn the head over and using a blunt blade, scrape any carbon deposits from the combustion chambers and ports. Finally, wash the entire head casting with a suitable solvent to remove the remaining debris.

9 Clean the valve heads and stems using a fine wire brush. If the valve is heavily coked, scrape off the majority of the deposits with a blunt blade first, then use the wire brush.

10 Thoroughly clean the remainder of the components using solvent and allow them to dry completely. Discard the oil seals, as new ones must be fitted when the cylinder head is reassembled.

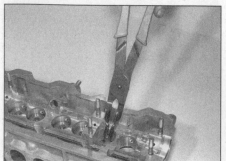

6.7a Use a removal tool . . .

6.7b . . . to pull the valve stem oil seal from place

6.7c Remove the valves from the gasket side of the cylinder head

6.13 Measure the gasket surface distortion with a straight-edge and feeler gauges

6.17 Measure the maximum deflection of the valve in its guide using a DTI

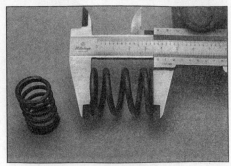

6.19 Measure the free length of each valve spring

Inspection

Cylinder head

11 Examine the head casting closely to identify any damage or cracks that may have developed. Pay particular attention to the areas around the valve seats and spark plug holes. If cracking is discovered in this area, VW state that the cylinder head may be re-used, provided the cracks are no larger than 0.5 mm wide. More serious damage will mean the renewal of the cylinder head.

12 Moderately pitted and scorched valve seats can be repaired by grinding in the valves in during reassembly, as described later in this Section. The valve seats must not be recut.

13 Measure any distortion of the gasket surfaces using a straight-edge and a set of feeler blades. Take one measurement longitudinally on both the intake and exhaust manifold mating surfaces. Take several measurements across the head gasket surface, to assess the level of distortion in all planes **(see illustration)**. Compare the measurements with the figures in the Specifications. If the distortion exceeds the specification, the cylinder head may need to be renewed – no machining is recommended. Consult an engine reconditioning specialist.

Valves and associated components

Note: *On all engines, the valve heads cannot be recut, although they may be ground in..*

14 Examine each valve closely for signs of wear. Inspect the valve stems for wear ridges, scoring or variations in diameter; measure their diameters at several points along their lengths with a micrometer.

15 The valve heads should not be cracked, badly pitted or charred. Note that light pitting of the valve head can be rectified by grinding in the valves during reassembly, as described later in this Section.

16 Check that the valve stem end face is free from excessive pitting or indentation; this would be caused by defective hydraulic tappets.

17 Insert each valve into its respective guide in the cylinder head and set up a DTI gauge against the edge of the valve head. With the valve end face flush with the top of the valve guide, measure the maximum side-to-side

deflection of the valve in its guide **(see illustration)**.

18 If the measurement exceeds that given in the Specifications, the valve and valve guide should be renewed as a pair. **Note:** *Valve guides are an interference fit in the cylinder head and their removal requires access to a hydraulic press. For this reason, it would be wise to entrust the job to an engine reconditioning specialist.*

19 Using vernier calipers, measure the free length of each of the valve springs. As a manufacturer's figure is not quoted, the only way to check the length of the springs is by comparison with a new component. Note that valve springs are usually renewed during a major engine overhaul **(see illustration)**.

20 Stand each spring on its end on a flat surface, against an engineer's square **(see illustration)**. Check the squareness of the spring visually, and renew it if it appears distorted.

Reassembly

21 To achieve a gas-tight seal between the valves and their seats, it will be necessary to grind in (or lap in) the valves. To complete this process you will need a quantity of fine/coarse grinding paste and a grinding tool – this can either be of the rubber sucker type, or the automatic type which is driven by a rotary power tool.

22 Smear a small quantity of *fine* grinding paste on the sealing face of the valve head. Turn the cylinder head over so that the combustion chambers are facing upwards

and insert the valve into the correct guide. Attach the grinding tool to the valve head and using a backward/forward rotary action, grind the valve head into its seat. Periodically lift the valve and rotate it to redistribute the grinding paste **(see illustration)**.

23 Continue this process until the contact between valve and seat produces an unbroken, matt grey ring of uniform width, on both faces. Repeat the operation on the remaining valves.

24 If the valves and seats are so badly pitted that coarse grinding paste must be used, bear in mind that there is a maximum protrusion of the end of the valve stem from the valve guide. Refer to a VW dealer or engine reconditioning specialist. If this dimension is outside the limit due to excessive grinding-in, the hydraulic tappets may not operate correctly.

25 Assuming the repair is feasible, work as described previously but use coarse grinding paste initially, to achieve a dull finish on the valve face and seat. Wash off the coarse paste with solvent and repeat the process using fine grinding paste to obtain the correct finish.

26 When all the valves have been ground in, remove all traces of grinding paste from the cylinder head and valves with solvent, and allow them to dry completely.

27 Working on one valve at a time, lubricate the valve stem with clean engine oil, and insert it into the guide. Fit one of the protective plastic sleeves supplied with the new valve stem oil seals over the valve end face – this will protect the oil seal whilst it is being fitted **(see illustrations)**.

6.20 Check the squareness of the valve springs

6.22 Grind in the valves with a reciprocating rotary motion

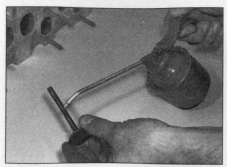

6.27a Lubricate the valve stem with clean engine oil

6.27b Fit a protective sleeve over the valve stem before fitting the oil seal

6.28a Fit a new stem seal over the valve

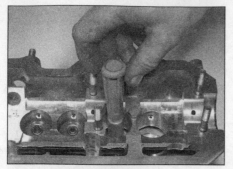

6.28b Use a special installer or long reach socket to fit the valve stem oil seals

6.29 Fit the valve spring(s)

28 Dip a new valve stem seal in clean engine oil, and carefully push it over the valve and onto the top of the valve guide – take care not to damage the stem seal as it passes over the valve end face. Use a suitable long reach socket or special installer to press it firmly

into position **(see illustrations)**. Remove the protective sleeve.
29 Locate the valve spring(s) over the valve stem **(see illustration)**.
30 Fit the upper seat over the top of the springs, then using a valve spring compressor,

compress the springs until the upper seat is pushed beyond the collet grooves in the valve stem. Refit the split collet, using a dab of grease to hold the two halves in the grooves **(see illustrations)**. Gradually release the spring compressor, checking that the collet remains correctly seated as the spring extends. When correctly seated, the upper seat should force the two halves of the collet together, and hold them securely in the grooves in the end of the valve.
31 Repeat this process for the remaining sets of valve components. To settle the components after installation, strike the end of each valve stem with a mallet, using a block of wood to protect the stem from damage. Check before progressing any further that the spilt collets remain firmly held in the end of the valve stem by the upper spring seat.
32 The remainder of refitting is a reversal of removal.

6.30a Fit the upper seat over the top of the valve spring

6.30b Use grease to hold the two halves of the spring collets in the groove

7 Piston/connecting rod assemblies – removal and inspection

Removal

1 Refer to Part A or B of this Chapter (as applicable) and remove the cylinder head, flywheel, sump and oil pump/balance shaft assembly.
2 Inspect the tops of the cylinder bores for ridges at the point where the pistons reach top dead centre. These must be removed otherwise the pistons may be damaged when they are pushed out of their bores. Use a scraper or ridge reamer to remove the ridges.
3 Rotate the crankshaft until piston No 1 is at bottom dead centre; piston No 4 will also be at bottom dead centre. Unless they are already identified, mark the big-end bearing caps and connecting rods with their respective piston numbers, using a centre-punch or a scribe **(see illustration)**. Note the orientation of the bearing caps in relation to the connecting rod; it may be difficult to see the manufacturer's markings at this stage, so scribe alignment arrows on them both to ensure correct reassembly.
4 Unscrew the bearing cap bolts/nuts, half a turn at a time, until they can be removed and the cap withdrawn **(see illustrations)**.

7.3 Mark the big-end caps and connecting rods with their cylinder numbers

7.4a Unscrew the big-end cap bolts . . .

Recover the bottom shell bearing, and tape it to the cap for safe-keeping. Note that if the shell bearings are to be re-used, they must be refitted to the same connecting rod.

5 Drive the piston out of the top of the bore using a piece of wooden dowel or a hammer handle. As the piston and connecting rod emerge, recover the top shell bearing and tape it to the connecting rod for safe-keeping. On engines fitted with piston cooling jets at the bottom of the cylinders, take care not to allow the connecting rod to damage the jet as the piston is being removed.

6 Remove No 4 piston and connecting rod in the same manner, then turn the crankshaft through half a turn and remove No 2 and 3 pistons and connecting rods. Remember to maintain the components in their cylinder groups, whilst they are in a dismantled state.

7 If applicable, remove the retaining bolts and withdraw the piston cooling jets from the bottom of the cylinder (**see illustrations**).

Inspection

8 Insert a small flat-bladed screwdriver into the removal slot and prise the gudgeon pin circlips from each piston. Push out the gudgeon pin, and separate the piston and connecting rod (**see illustrations**). Discard the circlips as new items must be fitted on reassembly. If the pin proves difficult to remove, heat the piston to 60°C with hot water – the resulting expansion will then allow the two components to be separated.

9 Before an inspection of the pistons can be carried out, the existing piston rings must be removed, using a removal/installation tool, or an old feeler blade if such a tool is not available. Always remove the upper piston rings first, expanding them to clear the piston crown. The rings are very brittle and will snap if they are stretched too much – sharp edges are produced when this happens, so protect your eyes and hands. Discard the rings on removal, as new items must be fitted when the engine is reassembled (**see illustration**).

10 Use a section of old piston ring to scrape the carbon deposits out of the ring grooves, taking care not to score or gouge the edges of the groove.

11 Carefully scrape away all traces of carbon from the tops of the pistons (**see illustration**). A hand-held wire brush (or a piece of fine emery cloth) can be used, once the majority of the deposits have been scraped away. Be careful not to remove any metal from the piston, as it is relatively soft. **Note:** *Make sure each piston is kept identified for position during cleaning.*

12 Once the deposits have been removed, clean the pistons and connecting rods with paraffin or a suitable solvent, and dry thoroughly. Make sure that the oil return holes in the ring grooves are clear.

13 Examine the pistons for signs of excessive wear or damage. Some normal wear will be apparent, in the form of a vertical 'grain' on the piston thrust surfaces and a slight

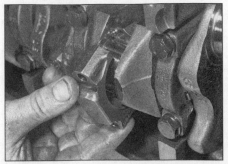

7.4b . . . and remove the cap

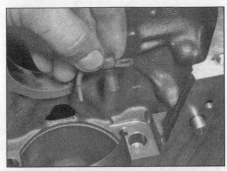

7.7b . . . and withdraw the jets from their mounting holes

looseness of the top compression ring in its groove. Abnormal wear should be carefully examined, to assess whether the component is still serviceable and what the cause of the wear might be.

14 Scuffing or scoring of the piston skirt may

7.8a Insert a small screwdriver into the slot and prise out the circlips

7.9 Piston rings can be removed using an old feeler gauge

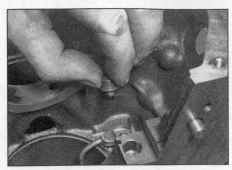

7.7a Remove the piston cooling jet retaining bolts . . .

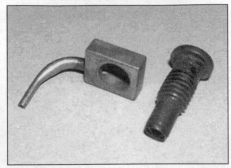

7.7c Piston cooling jet and retaining bolt

indicate that the engine has been overheating, through inadequate cooling or lubrication. Scorch marks on the skirt indicate that gas blow-by has occurred, perhaps caused by worn bores or piston rings. Burnt areas on the piston crown are usually an indication of

7.8b Push out the gudgeon pin to separate the piston and connecting rod

7.11 The piston crown on a diesel engine

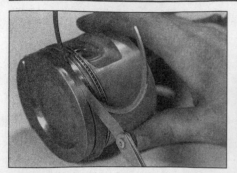

7.17 Measure the piston ring-to-groove clearance using a feeler gauge

7.19a The piston crown is marked with an arrow which must point towards the timing belt end of the engine

pre-ignition, pinking or detonation. In extreme cases, the piston crown may be melted by operating under these conditions. Corrosion pit marks in the piston crown indicate that coolant has seeped into the combustion chamber. The faults causing these symptoms must be corrected before the engine is brought back into service, or the same damage will recur.

15 Check the pistons, connecting rods, gudgeon pins and bearing caps for cracks. Lay the connecting rods on a flat surface, and look along the length to see if it appears bent or twisted. If you have doubts about their condition, get them measured at an engineering workshop. Inspect the small-end bush bearing in the connecting rod for signs of wear or cracking.

16 Have the diameter of the pistons checked

by an engine reconditioning specialist at the same time as the cylinder block is inspected.

17 Locate a new piston ring in the appropriate groove and measure the ring-to-groove clearance using a feeler blade (see illustration). Note that the rings are of different widths, so use the correct ring for the groove. Compare the measurements with those listed; if the clearances are outside of the tolerance band, then the piston must be renewed. Confirm this by checking the width of the piston ring with a micrometer.

18 Examine the small-end bearing and gudgeon pin for wear and damage. If excessive, the gudgeon pin will have to be renewed and a new bush fitted to the connecting rod. This work must be entrusted to an engine reconditioning specialist.

19 The orientation of the piston with respect

to the connecting rod must be correct when the two are reassembled. The piston crown is marked with an arrow (which may be obscured by carbon deposits); this must point towards the timing belt end of the engine when the piston is installed. On some engines, the connecting rod and its bearing cap both have recesses/lugs machined into them, close to their mating surfaces – these recesses/lugs must both face the same way as the arrow on the piston crown (ie, towards the timing belt end of the engine) when correctly installed (see illustrations). Reassemble the two components to satisfy this requirement. Other engines are fitted with 'fractured' split connecting rods. On these engines, the bearing caps are split from the connecting rod during the manufacturing process. The resultant mating surfaces are unique, and consequently, will only fit properly to their original positions. Any attempt to fit them in an alternative position with ruin both connecting rod and bearing cap.

20 Lubricate the gudgeon pin and small-end bush with clean engine oil. Slide the pin into the piston, engaging the connecting rod small-end. Fit two new circlips to the piston at either end of the gudgeon pin. Repeat this operation for the remaining pistons.

8 Crankshaft – removal and inspection

Note: *If no work is to be done on the pistons and connecting rods, then removal of the cylinder head and pistons will not be necessary. Instead, the pistons need only be pushed far enough up the bores so that the connecting rods are positioned clear of the crankpins. The use of an engine stand is strongly recommended.*

Removal

1 With reference to Chapter 2A or 2B as applicable, carry out the following:
  a) *Remove the timing belt and crankshaft sprocket.*
  b) *Remove the flywheel.*
  c) *Remove the sump, oil pump and balancer shaft assembly.*
  d) *Remove the crankshaft oil seals and housings.*

2 Remove the pistons and connecting rods or disconnect them from the crankshaft as described in Section 7 (see Note above).

3 With the cylinder block upside down on the bench, carry out a check of the crankshaft endfloat as follows. **Note:** *This can only be accomplished when the crankshaft is still installed in the cylinder block/crankcase, but is free to move.* Set up a DTI gauge so that the probe is in line with the crankshaft axis and is in contact with a fixed point on the end of the crankshaft. Push the crankshaft along its axis to the end of its travel, and then zero the gauge. Push the crankshaft fully the other way,

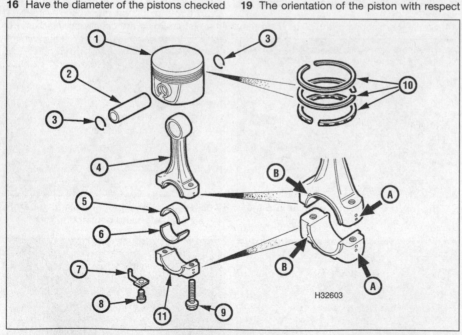

H32603

7.19b Piston assembly

1 Piston	5 Bearing shell	9 Big-end bearing cap
2 Gudgeon pin	6 Bearing shell	bolts
3 Circlips	7 Oil jet for piston cooling	10 Piston rings
4 Connecting rod	8 Oil jet retaining bolt	11 Bearing cap

A Connecting rod/bearing cap identification marks
B Connecting rod/bearing cap orientation marks

and record the endfloat indicated on the dial **(see illustration)**. Compare the result with the figure given in the Specifications and establish whether new thrustwashers are required.

4 If a dial gauge is not available, feeler blades can be used. First push the crankshaft fully towards the flywheel end of the engine, then use a feeler blade to measure the gap between cylinder No 3 crankpin web and the main bearing thrustwasher **(see illustration)**. Compare the results with the Specifications.

5 Observe the manufacturer's identification marks on the main bearing caps. The number indicates the cap position in the crankcase, as counted from the timing belt end of the engine **(see illustration)**.

6 Loosen the main bearing cap bolts half a turn at a time, until they can be removed. Using a soft-faced mallet, strike the caps lightly to free them from the crankcase. Recover the lower main bearing shells, using tape to attach them to the cap for safe-keeping. Mark them to aid identification, but do not score or scratch them in any way. Remove the thrustwashers from each side of the No 3 main bearing cap where applicable.

7 Carefully lift the crankshaft out, taking care not to dislodge the upper main bearing shells **(see illustration)**.

8 Extract the upper main bearing shells from the crankcase, and tape them to their respective bearing caps. Remove the two thrustwasher bearings from either side of No 3 bearing saddle (where applicable).

9 With the shell bearings removed, observe the recesses machined into the bearing caps and crankcase – these provide location for the lugs which protrude from the shell bearings and so prevent them from being fitted incorrectly.

Inspection

10 Wash the crankshaft in a suitable solvent and allow it to dry. Flush the oil holes thoroughly, to ensure they are not blocked.

11 Inspect the main bearing and crankpin journals carefully. If uneven wear, cracking, scoring or pitting are evident then the crankshaft should be reground by an engineering workshop, and refitted to the engine with undersize bearings.

12 Have the crankshaft measured and inspected by an engine reconditioning specialist. If the crankshaft is worn and can be reground, they will be able to carry out the work and supply suitable undersize bearing shells.

9 Cylinder block/crankcase – cleaning and inspection

Cleaning

1 Remove all external components as applicable including lifting eyes, mounting brackets, the coolant pump, oil cooler and filter mounting housing and electrical switches/

8.3 Measure the crankshaft endfloat using a DTI gauge . . .

8.5 Manufacturers identification markings on the main bearing caps (arrowed)

sensors from the block. For complete cleaning, the core plugs should ideally be removed. Drill a small hole in the plugs, then insert a self-tapping screw into the hole. Extract the plugs by pulling on the screw with a pair of grips, or by using a slide hammer.

2 Scrape all traces of gasket and sealant from the cylinder block/crankcase, taking care not to damage the sealing surfaces.

3 Remove all oil gallery plugs (where fitted). The plugs are usually very tight – they may have to be drilled out, and the holes re-tapped. Use new plugs when the engine is reassembled.

4 If the casting is extremely dirty, it should be steam-cleaned. After this, clean all oil holes and galleries one more time. Flush all internal passages with warm water until the water runs clear. Dry thoroughly, and apply a light film of oil to all mating surfaces and cylinder bores, to prevent rusting. If you have access to compressed air, use it to speed up the drying process, and to blow out all the oil holes and galleries.

⚠️ *Warning: Wear eye protection when using compressed air.*

5 If the castings are not very dirty, you can do an adequate cleaning job with hot, soapy water and a stiff brush. Take plenty of time, and do a thorough job. Regardless of the cleaning method used, be sure to clean all oil holes and galleries very thoroughly, and to dry all components well. Protect the cylinder bores as described above, to prevent rusting.

6 All threaded holes must be clean, to ensure accurate torque readings during reassembly.

8.4 . . . or feeler gauges

8.7 Lift the crankshaft from the crankcase

To clean the threads, run the correct-size tap into each of the holes to remove rust, corrosion, thread sealant or sludge, and to restore damaged threads **(see illustration)**. If possible, use compressed air to clear the holes of debris produced by this operation.

Note: *Take extra care to exclude all cleaning liquid from blind tapped holes, as the casting may be cracked by hydraulic action if a bolt is threaded into a hole containing liquid.*

7 Apply suitable sealant to the new oil gallery plugs, and insert them into the holes in the block. Tighten them securely. Similarly, apply sealant to the core plugs and tap them into the cylinder block using a close-fitting tube or socket.

8 If the engine is not going to be reassembled immediately, cover it with a large plastic bag to keep it clean; protect all mating surfaces and the cylinder bores as described above, to prevent rusting.

9.6 Use a correct-sized tap to clean the cylinder block threads

Inspection

9 Visually check the casting for cracks and corrosion. Look for stripped threads in the threaded holes. If there has been any history of internal water leakage, it may be worthwhile having an engine overhaul specialist check the cylinder block/crankcase with professional equipment. If defects are found, have them renewed or if possible, repaired.

10 Check the cylinder bores for scuffing or scoring. Any evidence of this kind of damage should be cross-checked with an inspection of the pistons (see Section 7 of this Chapter). If the damage is in its early stages, it may be possible to repair the block by reboring it. Seek the advice of an engineering workshop.

11 Have the cylinder bores measured and inspected by an engine reconditioning specialist. If the bores are worn/damaged, they will be able to carry out any remedial work (reboring) and supply suitable oversize pistons, etc.

12 Apply a light coating of engine oil to the mating surfaces and cylinder bores to prevent rust forming.

13 Refit all the components removed in paragraph 1.

10 Main and big-end bearings – inspection and selection

Inspection

1 Even though the main and big-end bearings should be renewed during the engine overhaul, the old bearings should be retained for close examination, as they may reveal valuable information about the condition of the engine **(see illustration)**.

2 Bearing failure can occur due to lack of lubrication, the presence of dirt or other foreign particles, overloading the engine, or corrosion. Regardless of the cause of bearing failure, the cause must be corrected before the engine is reassembled, to prevent it from happening again.

3 When examining the bearing shells, remove them from the cylinder block/crankcase, the main bearing caps, the connecting rods and the connecting rod big-end bearing caps. Lay them out on a clean surface in the same general position as their location in the engine. This will enable you to match any bearing problems with the corresponding crankshaft journal. *Do not* touch any shell's internal bearing surface with your fingers while checking it, or the delicate surface may be scratched.

4 Dirt and other foreign matter gets into the engine in a variety of ways. It may be left in the engine during assembly, or it may pass through filters or the crankcase ventilation system. It may get into the oil, and from there into the bearings. Metal chips from machining operations and normal engine wear are often present. Abrasives are sometimes left in engine components after reconditioning, especially when parts are not thoroughly cleaned using the proper cleaning methods. Whatever the source, these foreign objects often end up embedded in the soft bearing material, and are easily recognised. Large particles will not embed in the bearing, but will score or gouge the bearing and journal. The best prevention for this cause of bearing failure is to clean all parts thoroughly, and keep everything spotlessly-clean during engine assembly. Frequent and regular engine oil and filter changes are also recommended.

5 Lack of lubrication (or lubrication breakdown) has a number of interrelated causes. Excessive heat (which thins the oil), overloading (which squeezes the oil from the bearing face) and oil leakage (from excessive bearing clearances, worn oil pump or high engine speeds) all contribute to lubrication breakdown. Blocked oil passages, which usually are the result of misaligned oil holes in a bearing shell, will also oil-starve a bearing, and destroy it. When lack of lubrication is the cause of bearing failure, the bearing material is wiped or extruded from the steel backing of the bearing. Temperatures may increase to the point where the steel backing turns blue from overheating.

6 Driving habits can have a definite effect on bearing life. Full-throttle, low-speed operation (labouring the engine) puts very high loads on bearings, tending to squeeze out the oil film. These loads cause the bearings to flex, which produces fine cracks in the bearing face (fatigue failure). Eventually, the bearing material will loosen in pieces, and tear away from the steel backing.

7 Short-distance driving leads to corrosion of bearings, because insufficient engine heat is produced to drive off the condensed water and corrosive gases. These products collect in the engine oil, forming acid and sludge. As the oil is carried to the engine bearings, the acid attacks and corrodes the bearing material.

8 Incorrect bearing installation during engine assembly will lead to bearing failure as well. Tight-fitting bearings leave insufficient bearing running clearance, and will result in oil starvation. Dirt or foreign particles trapped behind a bearing shell result in high spots on the bearing, which lead to failure.

9 *Do not* touch any shell's internal bearing surface with your fingers during reassembly as there is a risk of scratching the delicate surface, or of depositing particles of dirt on it.

10 As mentioned at the beginning of this Section, the bearing shells should be renewed as a matter of course during engine overhaul. To do otherwise is false economy.

Bearing selection

11 Main and big-end bearings for the engines described in this Chapter are available in standard sizes and a range of undersizes to suit reground crankshafts. Refer to an engine reconditioning specialist for details.

11 Engine overhaul – reassembly sequence

1 Before reassembly begins, ensure that all new parts have been obtained, and that all necessary tools are available. Read through the entire procedure to familiarise yourself with the work involved, and to ensure that all items necessary for reassembly of the engine are at hand. In addition to all normal tools and materials, thread-locking compound will be needed. A suitable tube of liquid sealant will also be required for the joint faces that are without gaskets. It is recommended that the manufacturer's own products are used, which are specially formulated for this purpose; the relevant product names are quoted in the text of each Section where they are required.

2 In order to save time and avoid problems, engine reassembly should ideally be carried out in the following order:

a) *Crankshaft (see Section 12).*
b) *Piston/connecting rod assemblies (see Sections 13 and 14).*
c) *Oil pump and balancer shaft assembly (see Chapter 2A or 2B).*
d) *Sump (see Chapter 2A or 2B).*
e) *Flywheel (see Chapter 2A or 2B).*
f) *Cylinder head (see Chapter 2A or 2B).*
g) *Timing belt tensioner, sprockets and timing belt (see Chapter 2A or 2B).*
h) *Intake and exhaust manifolds (see the relevant part of Chapter 4).*
i) *Engine external components and ancillaries (see list in Section 5 of this Chapter).*

3 At this stage, all engine components should be absolutely clean and dry, with all faults repaired. The components should be laid out (or in individual containers) on a completely clean work surface.

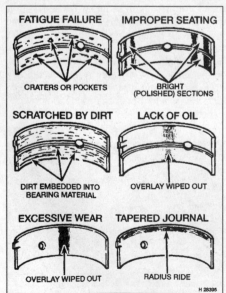

FATIGUE FAILURE **IMPROPER SEATING**

CRATERS OR POCKETS   BRIGHT (POLISHED) SECTIONS

SCRATCHED BY DIRT **LACK OF OIL**

DIRT EMBEDDED INTO BEARING MATERIAL   OVERLAY WIPED OUT

EXCESSIVE WEAR **TAPERED JOURNAL**

OVERLAY WIPED OUT   RADIUS RIDE

H 28395

10.1 Typical bearing failures

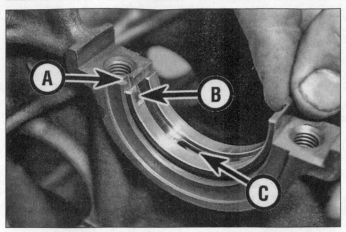

12.4 Upper main bearing shells correctly fitted

A Recess in the bearing   B Lug on the bearing shell
   saddle   C Oil hole

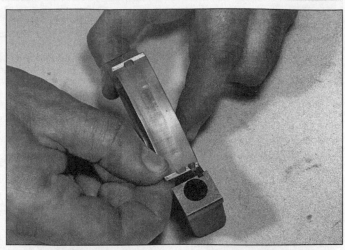

12.5 Fit the new lower half main bearing shells into the main
bearing caps

12 Crankshaft – refitting

1 Where removed, the oil jets must be refitted at this stage and their mounting bolts tightened to the specified torque.

2 If new shells are being fitted, ensure that all traces of the protective grease are cleaned off using paraffin.

3 Clean the backs of the bearing shells, and the bearing locations in both the cylinder block/crankcase and the main bearing caps.

4 With the cylinder block positioned on a clean work surface, with the crankcase opening uppermost, press the bearing shells into their locations, ensuring that the tab on each shell engages in the notch in the cylinder block or bearing cap, and that the oil holes in the cylinder block and bearing shell are aligned (see illustration). Note that the shells with the oil groove are fitted to the cylinder block, whilst the ones without the groove are fitted to the bearing caps. Take care not to touch any shell's bearing surface with your fingers.

5 Wipe off the rear surfaces of the new lower half main bearing shells and fit them to the main bearing caps, ensuring the locating lugs engage correctly (see illustration).

6 At this point, it is assumed that the crankshaft, cylinder block/crankcase and bearings have been cleaned, inspected and reconditioned or renewed.

7 Give the newly-fitted main bearing shells and the crankshaft journals a final clean with a cloth. Check that the oil holes in the crankshaft are free from dirt, as any left here will become embedded in the new bearings when the engine is first started.

8 Liberally coat the bearing shells in the crankcase with clean engine oil of the appropriate grade (see illustration). Install the new thrustwashers each side of the No 3 bearing position in the cylinder block. Use a small quantity of grease to hold them in place.

Ensure that they are seated correctly in the machined recesses, with the oil grooves facing outwards.

9 Lower the crankshaft into position so that No 1 cylinder crankpin is at BDC, ready for fitting No 1 piston.

10 Lubricate the lower bearing shells in the main bearing caps with clean engine oil, then fit the thrustwashers to each side of No 3 bearing cap. Use a small quantity of grease to hold them in place. Ensure that they are seated correctly in the machined recesses, with the oil grooves facing outwards (see illustrations).

11 Fit the main bearing caps in the correct order and orientation – No 1 bearing cap must be at the timing belt end of the engine and the bearing shell locating recesses in the bearing saddles and caps must be adjacent to each other (see illustrations). Insert the new bearing cap bolts and hand-tighten them only.

12 Working from the centre bearing cap outwards, tighten the new retaining bolts to their specified torques and angles in the stages given (see illustrations).

13 Check that the crankshaft rotates freely by turning it manually.

12.8 Lubricate the upper main bearing shells . . .

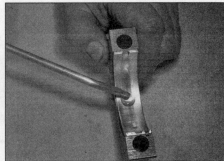

12.10a . . . and lower main bearing shells with clean engine oil . . .

12.10b . . . then fit the thrustwashers each side of the bearing cap . . .

12.10c . . . and/or bearing saddle (see text)

12.11a Fit the No 3 main bearing cap

12.11b Fit the No 1 main bearing cap

12.11c No 1 main bearing cap

12.12a Tighten the main bearing cap bolts
to the specified torque . . .

12.12b . . . and angle

14 Carry out a check of the crankshaft endfloat as described at the beginning of Section 8. If the thrust surfaces of the crankshaft have been checked and new thrustwashers have been fitted, then the endfloat should be within specification.

15 Refit the pistons and connecting rods or reconnect them to the crankshaft as described in Section 14.

16 With reference to Chapter 2A or 2B as applicable, carry out the following:
a) Refit the crankshaft oil seal housings, together with new oil seals.
b) Refit the oil pump and balancer shaft assembly, baffle plate and sump.
c) Refit the flywheel.
d) Refit the crankshaft sprocket and timing belt.

13 Pistons and piston rings – assembly

1 At this point it is assumed that the pistons have been correctly assembled to their respective connecting rods and that the piston ring-to-groove clearances have been checked. If not, refer to the end of Section 7.

2 Before the rings can be fitted to the pistons, the end gaps must be checked with the rings fitted into the cylinder bores.

3 Lay out the piston assemblies and the new ring sets on a clean work surface so that the components are kept together in their groups during and after end gap checking. Place the crankcase on the work surface on its side, allowing access to the top and bottom of the bores.

4 Take the No 1 piston top ring and insert it into the top of the bore. Using the No 1 piston, push the ring close to the bottom of the bore, at the lowest point of the piston travel. Ensure that it is perfectly square in the bore.

5 Use a set of feeler blades to measure the gap between the ends of the piston ring. The correct blade will just pass through the gap with a minimal amount of resistance **(see illustration)**. Compare this measurement with that listed in Specifications. Check that you have the correct ring before deciding that a gap is incorrect. Repeat the operation for the remaining rings.

6 If new rings are being fitted, it is unlikely that the end gaps will be too small. If a measurement is found to be undersize, it must be corrected or there is the risk that the ends of the ring may contact each other during operation, possibly resulting in engine damage. This is achieved by gradually filing down the ends of the ring, using a file clamped in a vice. Fit the ring over the file such that both its ends contact opposite faces of the file. Move the ring along the file, removing small amounts of material at a time. Take great care as the rings are brittle and form sharp edges if they fracture. Remember to keep the rings and piston assemblies in the correct order.

7 When all the piston ring end gaps have been verified, they can be fitted to the pistons. Work from the lowest ring groove (oil control ring) upwards. Note that the oil control ring may be two side rails separated by a expander ring, or a one-piece oil control ring with a internal expander spring. Note also that the two compression rings are different in cross-section, and so must be fitted in the correct groove and the right way up, using a piston ring fitting tool. Both of the compression rings may have marks stamped on one side to indicate the top facing surface. Ensure that these marks face up when the rings are fitted **(see illustration)**.

8 Distribute the end gaps around the piston, spaced at 120° intervals to the each other.
Note: *If the piston ring manufacturer supplies specific fitting instructions with the rings, follow these exclusively.*

13.5 Check the piston ring end gap using feeler gauges

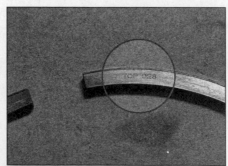

13.7 Piston ring top marking

14.2 Ensure the shells are fitted squarely into place

14.3a Lubricate the pistons . . .

14.3b . . . and the big-end upper bearing shells

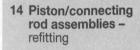

14 Piston/connecting rod assemblies – refitting

Note: *At this point, it is assumed that the crankshaft has been fitted to the engine, as described in Section 12. A piston ring compressor tool will be required for this operation.*

1 Clean the backs of the bearing shells, and the bearing locations in both the connecting rods and the big-end bearing caps.
2 Press the bearing shells into their locations in the connecting rods and caps. The shells are not positively located by lugs and recesses – simply ensure the shells are fitted squarely and centrally into place **(see illustration)**. On PD unit injector engines, the upper bearing shell is more wear-resistant than the lower, and is identified by a black line on the bearing surface in the area of the bearing joint. On common rail injection engines, the upper bearing shell has an oil hole, which must align with the corresponding oil hole in the connecting rod. Take care not to touch any shell's bearing surface with your fingers.

3 Lubricate the cylinder bores, the pistons, piston rings and upper bearing shells with clean engine oil **(see illustrations)**. Lay out each piston/connecting rod assembly in order on a work surface. Where the bearing caps are secured with nuts, pad the threaded ends of the bolts with insulating tape to prevent them scratching the crankpins and bores when the pistons are refitted.
4 Start with piston/connecting rod assembly No 1. Make sure that the piston rings are still spaced as described in Section 13, then clamp them in position with a piston ring compressor.
5 Insert the piston/connecting rod assembly into the top of cylinder No 1. Lower the big-end in first, guiding it to protect the cylinder bores. Where oil jets are located at the bottoms of the bores, take particular care not to break them off when guiding the connecting rods onto the crankpins.
6 Ensure that the orientation of the piston in its cylinder is correct – the piston crown, connecting rods and big-end bearing caps have markings, which must point towards the timing belt end of the engine when the piston

is installed in the bore – refer to Section 7 for details.
7 The piston crowns are specially shaped to improve the engine's combustion characteristics. Because of this, on SOHC engines, pistons 1 and 2 are different to pistons 3 and 4. When correctly fitted, the larger intake valve chambers on pistons 1 and 2 must face the flywheel end of the engine, and the larger intake valve chambers on the remaining pistons must face the timing belt end of the engine. New pistons have number markings on their crowns to indicate their type – 1/2 denotes piston 1 or 2, 3/4 indicates piston 3 or 4 **(see illustration)**.
8 Using a block of wood or hammer handle against the piston crown, tap the assembly into the cylinder until the piston crown is flush with the top of the cylinder **(see illustration)**.
9 Ensure that the bearing shell is still correctly installed. Liberally lubricate the crankpin and both bearing shells with clean engine oil. Taking care not to mark the cylinder bores, tap the piston/connecting rod assembly down the bore and onto the crankpin. Fit the big-end bearing cap, tightening its new retaining bolts finger-tight at first. Note that the orientation of the bearing cap with respect to the connecting rod must be correct when the two components are reassembled. These engines are fitted, with 'fractured' split connecting rods. The bearing caps are split from the connecting rod during the manufacturing process. The resultant mating surfaces are unique, and consequently will only fit properly to their original positions. Any attempt to fit

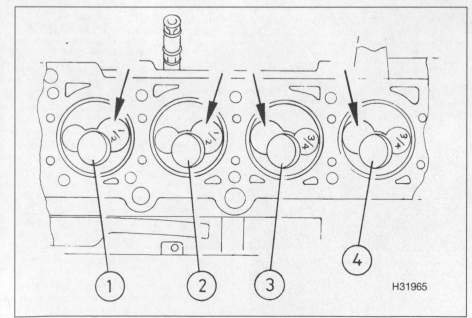

14.7 Piston orientation and coding

14.8 Use a hammer handle to tap the piston into its bore

14.10 Tighten the big-end bearing cap bolts to the Stage 1 setting . . .

14.11 . . . and then angle-tighten them to the Stage 2 setting

them in an alternative position will ruin both connecting rod and bearing cap.

10 Tighten the retaining bolts to the specified Stage 1 torque **(see illustration)**.

11 Angle-tighten the retaining bolts to the specified Stage 2 angle **(see illustration)**.

12 Refit the remaining three piston/connecting rod assemblies in the same way.

13 Rotate the crankshaft by hand. Check that it turns freely; some stiffness is to be expected if new parts have been fitted, but there should be no binding or tight spots.

14 If new pistons are fitted or if a new short engine is installed, the projection of the piston crowns above the cylinder head at TDC must be measured, to determine the type of head gasket that should be fitted. Follow the procedure description given in Chapter 2A or 2B as applicable.

15 Note that if the original pistons have been refitted, then a new head gasket of the same type as the original item must be fitted.

16 Refer to Part A or B of this Chapter (as applicable) and refit the oil pump and balancer shaft assembly, sump and baffle plate, flywheel and cylinder head.

15 Engine – initial start-up after overhaul and reassembly

1 Refit the remainder of the engine components in the order listed in Section 11 of this Chapter. Refit the engine to the vehicle as described in Section 4 of this Chapter. Double-check the engine oil and coolant levels and make a final check that everything has been reconnected. Make sure that there are no tools or rags left in the engine compartment.

2 Disconnect the injector harness wiring plug.

3 Turn the engine using the starter motor until the oil pressure warning lamp goes out.

4 If the lamp fails to extinguish after several seconds of cranking, check the engine oil level and oil filter security. Assuming these are correct, check the security of the oil pressure switch cabling – do not progress any further until you are satisfied that oil is being pumped around the engine at sufficient pressure.

5 Reconnect the injector wiring plug. Note that disconnecting the injector harness may result in fault codes being stored by the engine management ECM. Have these codes erased by a VW dealer or suitably-equipped specialist.

6 Start the engine, but be aware that as fuel system components have been disturbed, the cranking time may be a little longer than usual.

7 While the engine is idling, check for fuel, water and oil leaks. Don't be alarmed if there are some odd smells and the occasional plume of smoke as components heat up and burn off oil deposits.

8 Assuming all is well, keep the engine idling until hot water is felt circulating through the top hose.

9 After a few minutes, recheck the oil and coolant levels, and top-up as necessary.

10 There is no need to retighten the cylinder head bolts once the engine has been run following reassembly.

11 If new pistons, rings or crankshaft bearings have been fitted, the engine must be treated as new, and run-in for the first 600 miles. *Do not* operate the engine at full-throttle, or allow it to labour at low engine speeds in any gear. It is recommended that the engine oil and filter are changed at the end of this period.

Chapter 3
Cooling, heating and ventilation systems

Contents

Degrees of difficulty

Easy, suitable for novice with little experience	Fairly easy, suitable for beginner with some experience	Fairly difficult, suitable for competent DIY mechanic	Difficult, suitable for experienced DIY mechanic	Very difficult, suitable for expert DIY or professional

Specifications

Engine codes
Manufacturer's engine codes:*
PD unit injector engines:
1.9 litre .... BKC, BLS and BXE
2.0 litre .... BKP, BMA, BMR, BUZ, BVE and BWV
Common rail injection engines.......................... CBAA, CBAB, CBAC and CBBB
* **Note:** See 'Vehicle identification' at the end of this manual for the location of engine code markings.

General
Maximum system pressure .... 1.4 to 1.6 bar

Thermostat
Opening temperature....................................... 85° C (approx)

Air conditioning
Refrigerant capacity....................................... 600 ± 25 g

Torque wrench settings	Nm	lbf ft
Air conditioning compressor	25	18
Coolant pump	15	11
Thermostat housing-to-cylinder block bolts	15	11

1 General information and precautions

The cooling system is of the pressurised type, comprising a coolant pump, an aluminium radiator, cooling fan(s), a thermostat, heater matrix, and all associated hoses and switches. The coolant pump is driven by the camshaft timing belt. All models are fitted with an electrically operated fan. Common rail engines are also fitted with an electrically driven coolant circulation pump. The system functions as follows.

When the engine is cold, the coolant in the engine is pumped around the cylinder block and head passages, and through an engine oil cooler. After cooling the cylinder bores, combustion surfaces and valve seats, the coolant passes through the heater, and is returned via the cylinder block to the coolant pump. The thermostat is initially closed, preventing the cold coolant from the radiator entering the engine **(see illustrations)**.

When the coolant in the engine reaches a predetermined temperature, the thermostat opens. The cold coolant from the radiator is then allowed to enter the engine through the bottom hose and the hot coolant from the engine flows through the top hose to the radiator. As the coolant circulates through the radiator, it is cooled by the inrush of air when the car is in forward motion. The airflow is supplemented by the action of the cooling fan(s) when necessary. As the coolant reduces in temperature, it passes to the bottom of the radiator and the cycle is repeated.

On all models, the cooling fan(s) are electrically powered, and are controlled by the engine management ECM, which receives data from the engine coolant temperature sensor and radiator outlet temperature sensor (where fitted). At a predetermined coolant temperature, the sensor actuates the fan. The switch then cuts the power supply to the fan when the coolant temperature has reduced sufficiently.

On models with an automatic transmission unit, a transmission fluid cooler is built into the radiator. The transmission unit is linked to the radiator by two pipes and the fluid is circulated around the cooler to keep its temperature stable under arduous operating conditions.

⚠️ *Warning: Do not attempt to remove the expansion tank filler cap, or to disturb any part of the cooling system, while the engine is hot, as there is a high risk of scalding. If the expansion tank filler cap must be removed before the engine and radiator have fully cooled (even though this is not recommended), the pressure in the cooling system must first be relieved. Cover the cap with a thick layer of cloth to avoid scalding, and slowly unscrew the filler cap until a hissing sound is heard. When the hissing has stopped, indicating that the pressure has reduced, slowly unscrew the filler cap until it can*

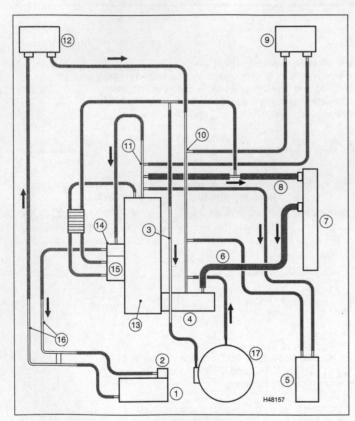

1.2a Cooling system details – 1.9 litre engines

1 Auxiliary heater (optional)	6 Lower coolant hose	11 Connection
2 Auxiliary heater circulation pump	7 Radiator	12 Heater matrix
3 Upper coolant pipe	8 Upper coolant hose	13 Cylinder head/block
4 Coolant pump and thermostat	9 Transmission oil cooler (auto models only)	14 EGR cooler
5 Oil cooler	10 Front coolant pipe	15 Bypass flap
		16 Rear coolant pipe
		17 Expansion tank

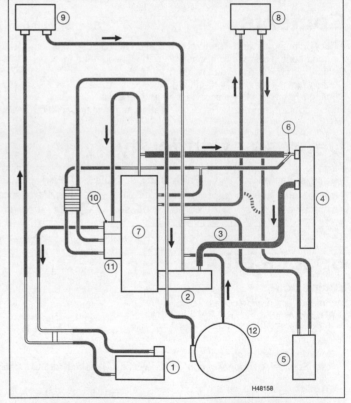

1.2b Cooling system details – 2.0 litre PD unit injector engines

1 Auxiliary heater (optional)	5 Engine oil cooler	8 Transmission oil cooler (auto models only)
2 Coolant pump and thermostat	6 Upper coolant hose	9 Heater matrix
3 Lower coolant hose	7 Cylinder head/block	10 EGR cooler
4 Radiator		11 Bypass flap
		12 Expansion tank

be removed; *if more hissing sounds are heard, wait until they have stopped before unscrewing the cap completely. At all times, keep well away from the filler cap opening, and protect your hands.*

• *Do not allow antifreeze to come into contact with your skin, or with the painted surfaces of the vehicle. Rinse off spills immediately, with plenty of water. Never leave antifreeze lying around in an open container, or in a puddle in the driveway or on the garage floor. Children and pets are attracted by its sweet smell, but antifreeze can be fatal if ingested.*

• *If the engine is hot, the electric cooling fan may start rotating even if the engine is not running. Be careful to keep your hands, hair, and any loose clothing well clear when working in the engine compartment.*

• *Refer to Section 10 for precautions to be observed when working on models equipped with air conditioning.*

2 Cooling system hoses – disconnection and renewal

Note: *Refer to the warnings given in Section 1 of this Chapter before proceeding. Hoses should only be disconnected once the engine has cooled sufficiently to avoid scalding.*

1 If the checks described in Chapter 1 reveal a faulty hose, it must be renewed as follows.

2 First drain the cooling system (see Chapter 1). If the coolant is not due for renewal, it may be re-used, providing it is collected in a clean container.

3 To disconnect a hose, release the retaining clips, then move them along the hose, clear of the relevant inlet/outlet. Carefully work the hose free. The hoses can be removed with relative ease when new – on an older car, they may have stuck.

4 In order to disconnect the radiator inlet and outlet hoses, and the heater hoses fitted to some models, apply pressure to hold the hose on to the relevant union, pull out the spring clip and pull the hose from the union **(see illustration)**. Note that the radiator inlet and outlet unions are fragile; do not use excessive force when attempting to remove the hoses. If a hose proves to be difficult to remove, try to release it by rotating the hose ends before attempting to free it.

5 If a hose proves to be difficult to remove, try to release it by rotating its ends before attempting to free it. Gently prise the end of the hose with a blunt instrument (such as a flat-bladed screwdriver), but do not apply too much force, and take care not to damage the pipe stubs or hoses. Note in particular that the radiator inlet stub is fragile; do not use excessive force when attempting to remove the hose. If all else fails, cut the hose with a sharp knife, then slit it so that it can be peeled off in two pieces. Although this may prove expensive if the hose is otherwise

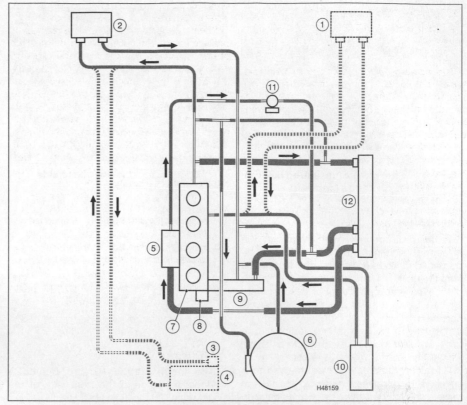

1.2c Cooling system details – common rail engines

1 *Transmission oil cooler (auto models only)*	4 *Auxiliary heater (optional)*	9 *Thermostat and 4/2-way valve*
2 *Heater matrix*	5 *EGR cooler*	10 *Engine oil cooler*
3 *Auxiliary heater circulation pump (optional)*	6 *Expansion tank*	11 *Electric coolant circulation pump*
	7 *Cylinder head/block*	12 *Radiator*
	8 *Coolant pump*	

undamaged, it is preferable to buying a new radiator. Check first, however, that a new hose is readily available.

6 When fitting a hose, first slide the clips onto the hose, then work the hose into position. On some hose connections alignment marks are provided on the hose and union; if marks are present, ensure they are correctly aligned.

7 Ensure the hose is correctly routed, then slide each clip back along the hose until it passes over the flared end of the relevant inlet/outlet, before tightening the clip securely.

2.4 Prise out the clip and little, and pull the radiator hose from the union

Prior to refitting a radiator inlet or outlet hose, renew the connection O-ring regardless of condition. The connections are a push-fit over the radiator unions.

8 Refill the cooling system with reference to the relevant part of Chapter 1.

9 Check thoroughly for leaks as soon as possible after disturbing any part of the cooling system.

3 Radiator – removal, inspection and refitting

Removal

1 Remove the cooling fan and shroud assembly as described in Section 5.

2 Drain the cooling system as described in Chapter 1.

3 Disconnect the radiator top and bottom coolant hoses (see Section 2), noting the correct fitted locations **(see illustration 2.4)**. **Note:** *On some models, quick-release couplings are fitted to the hoses.*

4 Undo the radiator mounting bolts, and lift it from place **(see illustrations)**.

3.4a Undo the radiator mounting bolt on the left-hand side (arrowed) . . .

3.4b . . . and the right-hand side (arrowed) . . .

3.4c . . . then lift the radiator from place

Inspection

5 If the radiator has been removed due to suspected blockage, reverse-flush it as described in Chapter 1. Clean dirt and debris from the radiator fins, using an airline (in which case, wear eye protection) or a soft brush. Be careful, as the fins are sharp, and easily damaged.
6 If necessary, a radiator specialist can perform a flow test on the radiator, to establish whether an internal blockage exists.
7 A leaking radiator must be referred to a specialist for permanent repair. Do not attempt to weld or solder a leaking radiator, as damage to the plastic components may result.
8 If the radiator is to be sent for repair or renewed, remove all hoses and switches (where fitted).
9 Inspect the condition of the radiator mounting rubbers, and renew them if necessary.

Refitting

10 Refitting is a reversal of removal, bearing in mind the following points.
a) Ensure that the radiator is correctly engaged with its mounting rubbers.
b) On models with automatic transmission, fit new sealing rings to the fluid pipe end fittings, lubricating them with fresh transmission fluid to ease installation. Ease both pipes fully into position before refitting the retaining bolts and tighten them securely.
c) Make sure all coolant hoses are correctly

reconnected and securely retained by their clips.
d) Refill the cooling system with new antifreeze as described in Chapter 1.

4 Thermostat – removal, testing and refitting

Removal

1 The thermostat is located behind a connection flange in the front side of the engine block, at the timing belt end.
2 Drain the cooling system as described in Chapter 1.
3 Remove the plastic cover on the top of the engine by pulling it upwards from its mountings.
4 Remove the alternator as described in Chapter 5.
5 Release the securing clip and disconnect the coolant hose from the thermostat cover/connection flange.
6 Unscrew the two securing bolts, and remove the thermostat cover/connection flange complete with the thermostat. Note the locations of any brackets secured by the bolts. Recover the O-ring if it is loose (see illustrations).
7 To remove the thermostat from the cover, twist the thermostat 90° clockwise, and pull it from the cover (see illustration).

Testing

Note: If there is any question about the

operation of the thermostat, it's best to renew it – they are not usually expensive items. Testing involves heating in, or over, an open pan of boiling water, which carries with it the risk of scalding. A thermostat which has seen more than five years' service may well be past its best already.
8 A rough test of the thermostat may be made by suspending it with a piece of string in a container full of water, but not touching the container. Heat the water to bring it to the boil – the thermostat must open by the time the water boils. If not, renew it.
9 If a thermometer is available, the precise opening temperature of the thermostat may be determined, and compared with the figure given in the Specifications. The opening temperature is also marked on the thermostat.
10 A thermostat which fails to close as the water cools must also be renewed.

Refitting

11 Refitting is a reversal of removal, bearing in mind the following points.
a) Refit the thermostat using a new O-ring.
b) Insert the thermostat into the cover and twist 90° anti-clockwise.
c) The thermostat should be fitted with the brace almost vertical.
d) Ensure that any brackets are in place on the thermostat cover bolts as noted before removal.
e) Refill the cooling system with the correct type and quantity of coolant as described in Chapter 1.

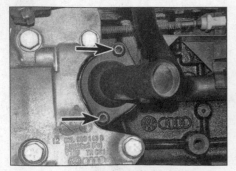

4.6a Thermostat cover bolts (arrowed)

4.6b Renew the thermostat cover O-ring seal

4.7 Twist the thermostat 90° clockwise and withdraw it from the cover

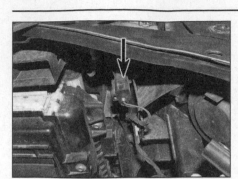

5.2a Disconnect the bonnet lock wiring plug (arrowed) . . .

5.2b . . . and the fan motor wiring plug (arrowed) at the base of the fan assembly

5.3 Remove the intake hood from the lock carrier (right-hand bolt arrowed)

5.4a The fan shroud is secured by 2 bolts on the right-hand side (upper bolt arrowed) . . .

5.4b . . . and 2 bolts on the left-hand side (upper bolt arrowed)

Refitting

6 Fit the motor assembly to the shroud and securely tighten its retaining nuts. Ensure the motor wiring is correctly routed and clipped securely in position.

7 Refit the shroud assembly to the radiator and securely tighten its retaining bolts.

8 Reconnect the wiring plugs and refit the lock carrier.

6 Engine coolant temperature sensor – testing, removal and refitting

Testing

1 On all models, an engine coolant temperature sensor is located at the left-hand end of the cylinder head, whilst on some engines, a second sensor is fitted to the radiator outlet pipe **(see illustrations)**.

2 The sensor is a thermistor. A thermistor is an electronic component whose electrical resistance changes at a predetermined rate as the temperature changes. The engine management electronic control module (ECM) supplies the sensor with a set voltage and then, by measuring the current flowing in the sensor circuit, determines the engine's temperature.

5 Cooling fan(s) – removal and refitting

Removal

1 Place the lock carrier assembly in the 'Service position' as described in Chapter 11.

2 Unplug the fan motor and bonnet lock wiring plugs, then on models with automatic climate control, remove the bolt securing the fan control unit to the radiator shroud **(see illustrations)**. Move the wiring to one side.

3 Undo the 2 bolts and remove the air intake hood from the lock carrier **(see illustration)**.

4 Slacken and remove the retaining bolts (2 each side) and remove the fan shroud assembly upwards from the rear of the radiator **(see illustrations)**.

5 Unclip the motor wiring from the rear of the shroud then undo the fasteners and pull the motor assembly away from the shroud **(see illustration)**. If the motor is faulty, the complete unit may have to be renewed – consult your VW dealer or parts specialist.

5.4c Lift the fan and shroud assembly upwards from the engine compartment

5.5 Undo the fasteners (arrowed) and separate the fan motor(s) from the shroud

6.1a Coolant temperature sensor (arrowed) – PD unit injector engines

6.1b Coolant temperature sensor (arrowed) – common rail injection engines

6.1c Radiator outlet coolant temperature sensor (arrowed) is at the left-hand side of the radiator – PD unit injector engines

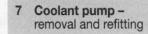

6.1d The radiator outlet coolant temperature sensor (arrowed) is at the right-hand end of the cylinder head – common rail injection engines

This information is then used, in conjunction with other inputs, to control the injector timing, the temperature gauge/warning light, the idle speed, etc. It is also used to determine the glow plug preheating and post-heating times.

3 If the sensor circuit should fail to provide adequate information, the ECM's back-up facility will override the sensor signal. In this event, the ECM assumes a predetermined setting which will allow the engine management system to run, albeit at reduced efficiency. When this occurs, the warning light on the instrument panel will come on, and a fault code will be stored by the systems self-diagnosis facility – the advice of a

VW dealer or specialist should be sought. The sensor itself can only be tested using special diagnostic equipment. *Do not* attempt to test the circuit using any other equipment, as there is a high risk of damaging the ECM.

Removal

Engine-mounted sensor

4 Either partially drain the cooling system to just below the level of the sensor (as described in Chapter 1), or have a suitable plug which can be used to plug the sensor aperture whilst it is removed. If a plug is used, take great care

not to damage the sensor unit aperture, and do not use anything which would allow foreign matter to enter the cooling system.

5 Pull the plastic cover on the top of the engine upwards from its mountings.

6 Disconnect the sensor wiring plug.

7 Press the sensor unit in, and slide out the retaining clip. Withdraw the sensor from the engine and recover the sealing ring **(see illustration 6.1a or 6.1b)**.

Radiator outlet pipe sensor

8 Drain the cooling system as described in Chapter 1.

9 Disconnect the sensor wiring plug **(see illustration 6.1c or 6.1d)**.

10 Prise out the retaining clip and pull the sensor from the pipe.

Refitting

11 Fit a new sealing ring, then push the sensor fully into the aperture and slide in the retaining clip.

12 Reconnect the wiring plug, and refill the cooling system (Chapter 1). Refit the cover to the top of the engine.

---

7 Coolant pump – removal and refitting

Primary coolant pump

Removal

1 Drain the cooling system as described in Chapter 1.

2 Place the lock carrier in the 'Service position', as described in Chapter 11.

3 Remove the auxiliary drivebelt as described in Chapter 1.

4 With reference to Chapter 2A or 2B, remove the timing belt.

5 Unscrew and remove the coolant pump securing bolts. Carefully withdraw the pump from the cylinder block and recover the sealing O-ring **(see illustrations)**.

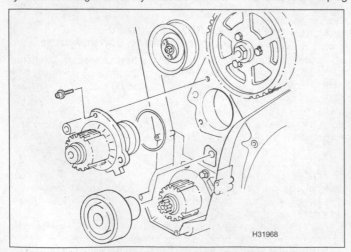

H31968

7.5a Coolant pump – PD unit injector engines . . .

7.5b . . . and common rail injection engines

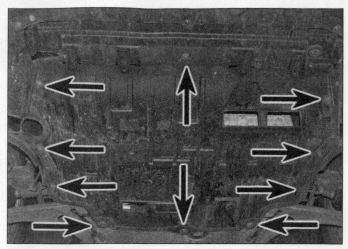

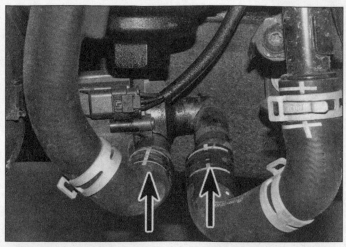

7.14 Undo the fasteners (arrowed) and remove the engine undershield

7.15 Disconnect the hoses from the circulation pump (arrowed)

Refitting

6 Ensure that the pump and housing mating surfaces are clean and free from all traces of corrosion.

7 Obtain a new sealing O-ring and moisten it with undiluted antifreeze of the specified type (see *Lubricants and fluids*). Position the sealing ring on the pump.

8 Fit the coolant pump to the cylinder block

9 Insert the mounting bolts and tighten them evenly and progressively to the specified torque.

10 Refit the timing belt as described in Chapter 2A or 2B.

11 Refit the lock carrier and tighten the securing bolts to the specified torque (see Chapter 11).

12 On completion refill the cooling system as described in Chapter 1.

Electric circulation pump

Note: *This pump is only fitted to common rail engines.*

Removal

13 Raise the front of the vehicle and support is securely on axle stands (see *Jacking and vehicle support*).

14 Undo the fasteners and remove the engine undershield **(see illustration)**.

7.17 Circulation pump bracket retaining bolt (arrowed – shown with the charge air pipe removed for clarity)

15 Fit hose clamps to the coolant hoses connected to the pump, and release the clips and disconnect the hoses from the pump **(see illustration)**.

16 Disconnect the pump wiring plug.

17 Undo the retaining bolt and remove the pump **(see illustration)**.

Refitting

18 Refitting is a reversal of removal. Top-up the coolant as described in Chapter 1.

---

8   Heating and ventilation system – general information

1 The heating/ventilation system consists of a fully-adjustable blower motor (housed behind the facia), face level vents in the centre and at each end of the facia, and air ducts to the front and rear footwells.

2 The heater control unit is located in the facia, and the controls operate flap valves to deflect and mix the air flowing through the various parts of the heating/ventilation system. The flap valves are contained in the air distribution housing, which acts as a central distribution unit, passing air to the various ducts and vents.

3 Cold air enters the system through the grille at the rear of the engine compartment. If required, the airflow is boosted by the blower, and then flows through the various ducts, according to the settings of the controls. Stale air is expelled through ducts at the rear of the vehicle. If warm air is required, the cold air is passed over the heater matrix, which is heated by the engine coolant.

4 The outside air supply to the vehicle can be closed off which is useful to prevent unpleasant odours entering from outside the vehicle. This is achieved either by setting the blower motor switch to position 0 or by operating the recirculation switch (depending on model). This facility should only be used briefly, as the recirculated air inside the vehicle will soon become stale.

5 The heating and air conditioning systems fitted to the VW Passat are equipped with a sophisticated self-diagnosis facility. Should a fault occur, before attempting a repair procedure, have the facility interrogated using VW's diagnosis equipment (VAS 5051 or VAG 1551/2). This may reveal any stored fault codes, and pin-point the problem area. Consult a VW dealer or suitably-equipped specialist. Note that the control unit communicates with the rest of the vehicle's electrical system by means of databus network. Traditional 'back-probing' of connectors should not be attempted without first identifying the databus connections.

---

9   Heater/ventilation components – removal and refitting

General information

1 The information in this Section is applicable to heating/ventilation element of the vehicle. The air conditioning elements are described in Section 11.

Heater/ventilation/ air conditioning control panel

2 On models with manual heating/air conditioning controls, set the heater control knob to 'cold', the blower motor to '0' and the vent direction to 'facia' (3 o'clock position), then remove the infotainment control panel as described in Chapter 12. This enables the cable for the vent directional control to be reconnected.

3 Disconnect the battery negative lead (see Chapter 5).

4 Use a blunt, flat-bladed tool to prise away the control panel surround trim **(see illustration)**.

5 Undo the retaining bolts and pull the control panel from place **(see illustration)**.

6 Note their fitted positions, then prise up the locking catches, squeeze together the

9.4 Carefully prise the control panel trim from place

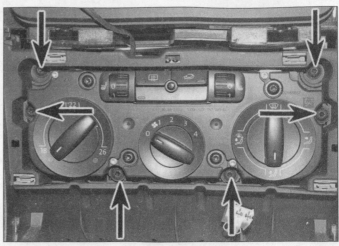

9.5 Heater control panel retaining bolts (arrowed)

retaining tabs and disconnect the wiring plugs from the rear of the panel **(see illustration)**.

7 Refitting is a reversal of removal. Note that if a new fully automatic Climatronic control panel has been fitted, it will be necessary to carry out the basic setting procedure. This procedure necessitates the use of VW diagnostic equipment VAS5051/1. Consequently, this task should be entrusted to a VW dealer, or suitably-equipped specialist.

Blower motor

Note: *On models equipped with fully automatic Climatronic air conditioning systems, the* blower motor is integral with its control unit, and cannot be renewed separately. No resistor is fitted.

8 Remove the passenger's glovebox as described in Chapter 11.

9 Undo the 2 bolts and remove the baffle plate beneath the blower motor **(see illustration)**.

10 Disconnect the wiring plug from the blower motor, then remove the bolt at the lower corner of the facia panel **(see illustration)**.

11 Undo the retaining bolt (where fitted), release the catch, rotate the blower motor clockwise and lower it from the housing **(see illustrations)**.

12 Refitting is a reversal of removal.

Blower motor resistor

13 Remove the passenger's glovebox as described in Chapter 11.

14 Undo the 2 bolts and remove the baffle plate beneath the blower motor **(see illustration 9.9)**.

15 Disconnect the resistor wiring plug, depress the clip and pull the resistor from the housing **(see illustration)**.

16 Refitting is a reversal of removal.

Heater matrix

17 Remove the battery as described in Chapter 5.

9.6 Prise up the wiring plug locking catches, and squeeze together the tabs (arrowed)

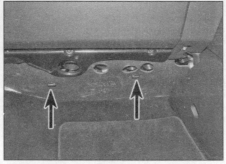

9.9 Baffle plate bolts (arrowed)

9.10 Remove the bolt (arrowed) at the corner of the facia

9.11a Undo the bolt (where fitted) and release the catch (arrowed) . . .

9.11b . . . then rotate the motor clockwise and remove it (shown with the heater housing removed for clarity)

9.15 Heater blower motor resistor wiring plug (arrowed)

9.18 Prise out the clips and disconnect the heater hoses

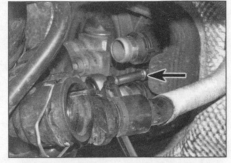

9.20 Slacken the bolt (arrowed) between the matrix tubes

9.22 Release the wiring loom from the bracket, and disconnect the control unit wiring plug (arrowed)

9.23 Convenience system control unit nuts (arrowed)

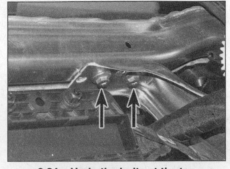

9.24a Undo the bolts at the top (arrowed) . . .

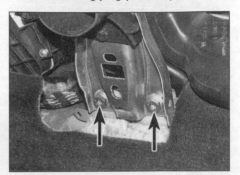

9.24b . . . and base of the support bracket (arrowed)

18 Using hose clamps, clamp the heater matrix inlet and return hoses located on the bulkhead at the rear of the engine compartment. Place a container beneath the hoses, then prise out the clips and disconnect them (see illustration). Note the location of the hoses for correct refitting.
19 With the hoses disconnected, remove the coolant from the matrix by blowing air into the upper tube, preferably using a compressed air line.
20 Using a 6 mm socket, loosen (but do not remove) the bolt located between the matrix upper and lower tubes (see illustration). This will make removal of the matrix easier.
21 Remove the facia as described in Chapter 11.
22 Note its routing, then unclip the wiring loom from the left-hand facia crossmember support brackets, and disconnect the plug from the control unit on the heater housing (see illustration).
23 Undo the 2 plastic nuts and move the convenience system control unit to one side (see illustration).
24 Unscrew the left-hand crossmember support bracket (see illustrations).
25 Unscrew and remove the footwell vent, followed by the glovebox cooling hose (where fitted) (see illustration).
26 Unclip the wiring loom, and disconnect the wiring plug from the servo motor at the top of the matrix cover.
27 Undo the retaining bolt, unclip the linkage, and remove the servo motor from the matrix cover (see illustrations).

28 Undo the bolts and remove the cover from the heater matrix (see illustration).
29 Place cloth rags or similar on the floor beneath the heater matrix, then release the pipe clamps and pull the coolant pipes from

the matrix (see illustration). Discard the pipes-to-matrix seals – new ones must be fitted.
30 Slide the heater matrix from the heater unit.

9.25 Footwell vent bolt (arrowed)

9.27a Undo the servo motor bolt (arrowed) . . .

9.27b . . . and unclip the linkage (arrowed)

9.28 Heater matrix cover bolts (arrowed)

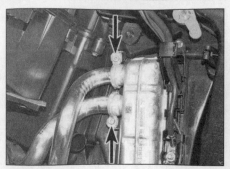

9.29 Undo the pipe clamps (arrowed)

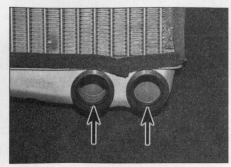

9.31 Moisten the new seals with coolant (arrowed)

31 Refitting is a reversal of removal, noting the following.

a) *Make sure the seal is fitted correctly around the perimeter of the matrix.*

b) *When reconnecting the coolant pipes, moisten the seals with coolant and fit them to the matrix, not the pipes **(see illustration)**. After reconnecting the pipes, the clamps must turn easily before tightening them securely.*

c) *Check that the rubber grommet around the pipes in the bulkhead is correctly located in its hole.*

d) *Top-up the coolant level with reference to 'Weekly checks' at the beginning of this Manual.*

Fresh air/recirculating air flaps motor

Note: *The motor can only be removed when the flap is set to the 'Fresh air' position.*

9.54 Right-hand side air vent temperature sensor (arrowed)

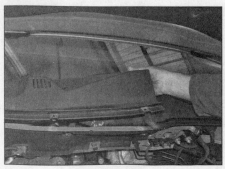

9.57b Pull the plenum chamber cover up from the windscreen

32 Remove the glovebox assembly as described in Chapter 11.
33 Release the catches and remove the retainer.
34 Unplug the wiring connector from the side, and pull the motor from place.
35 Refitting is a reversal of removal.

Defroster flap control motor

36 Remove the facia as described in Chapter 11.
37 Undo the bolt and remove the left-hand footwell vent.
38 Undo the bolts and remove the bracket over the distribution motor.
39 Disconnect the motor wiring plug.
40 Remove the plastic cover, then undo the retaining bolts, and detach the motor from the mounting. Detach the connecting rod from the motor lever as the motor is withdrawn.
41 Refitting is a reversal of removal.

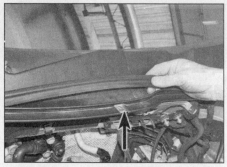

9.57a Pull up the sealing strip, and slide the clips forwards (arrowed)

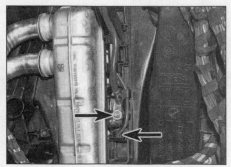

9.62 Disconnect the auxiliary heater element wiring plugs (arrowed)

Temperature flap control motors

42 Remove the facia as described in Chapter 11.
43 Disconnect the motor wiring plug.
44 Undo the retaining bolts, and detach the motor from the mounting. Detach the connecting rod from the motor lever as the motor is withdrawn.
45 Refitting is a reversal of removal.

Central flap control motor

46 Remove the facia as described in Chapter 11.
47 Disconnect the motor wiring plug.
48 Undo the retaining bolts, and detach the motor from the mounting.
49 Refitting is a reversal of removal.

Air vent temperature sensors

Left-hand side

50 Remove the glovebox as described in Chapter 11.
51 Disconnect the sensor wiring plug, then rotate the sensor 90° and remove it from the air duct.
52 Refitting is a reversal of removal.

Right-hand side

53 Remove the instrument panel as described in Chapter 12.
54 Rotate the sensor 90° and remove it from the air duct. Disconnect the wiring plug as the sensor is withdrawn **(see illustration)**.
55 Refitting is a reversal of removal.

Air quality sensor

56 Remove the wipers arms as described in Chapter 12.
57 Pull up the rubber sealing strip, slide the clips forwards, then starting in the middle, pull the plenum chamber cover upwards from the base of the windscreen **(see illustrations)**.
58 Remove the cover over the air intake, and rotate the sensor 90°. Disconnect the wiring plug as the sensor is withdrawn.
59 Refitting is a reversal of removal.

Auxiliary heater element

60 Diesel models may be equipped with an electrically-operated heating element, fitted into the heater housing alongside the heater matrix. To remove the element, first disconnect

9.63a Undo the retaining bolt (arrowed) ...

9.63b ... and pull the auxiliary heating element from place

the battery negative lead as described in Chapter 5.

61 Remove the heater matrix cover as described earlier in this Section.

62 Note their fitted positions, and disconnect the wiring plugs from the element **(see illustration)**.

63 Undo the retaining bolt and pull the element from the heater housing **(see illustrations)**.

64 Refitting is a reversal of removal.

10 Air conditioning system – general information and precautions

1 Air conditioning is fitted as standard equipment to all models. It combines a conventional air heating system with an air cooling and dehumidifying system. This allows greater control over the temperature and humidity of the air inside the car, giving increased comfort and rapid window demisting.

2 The cooling side of the system works in the same way as a domestic refrigerator. Refrigerant gas, contained in a sealed network of alloy pipes, is drawn into a belt-driven compressor, and is forced through a condenser mounted on the front of the radiator. On entering the condenser, the refrigerant changes state from gas to liquid and releases heat, which is absorbed by the air flowing into the front of the engine compartment through the condenser. The liquid refrigerant passes through an expansion valve to an evaporator, where it changes from liquid under high pressure to gas under low pressure. This change in state is accompanied by a drop in temperature, which cools the evaporator. Air passing through the evaporator is cooled before flowing into the air distribution unit. The refrigerant then returns to the compressor, and the cycle begins again.

3 The cooled air passes to the air distribution unit/heater housing, where it is blended with hot air blown through the heater matrix to achieve the desired temperature in the passenger compartment. When the air conditioning system is operating in Automatic mode, a series of air valves controlled by servo motors automatically regulate the cabin temperature by blending hot and cold air.

4 The heating side of the system operates as described in Section 8.

5 The operation of the air conditioning system is managed by an electronic control module, which controls the electric cooling fan, the compressor, and the facia-mounted warning light. The heating and air conditioning systems fitted to the VW Passat are equipped with a sophisticated self-diagnosis facility. Should a fault occur, before attempting a repair procedure, have the facility interrogated using VW's diagnosis equipment (VAS 5051 or VAG 1551/2). This may reveal any stored fault codes, and pin-point the problem area. Consult an VW dealer or suitably-equipped specialist. Note that the control unit communicates with the rest of the vehicle's electrical system by means of databus network. Traditional 'back-probing' of connectors should not be attempted without first identifying the databus connections.

6 When working on the air conditioning system, it is necessary to observe special precautions. If for any reason the refrigerant lines must be disconnected, you must entrust this task to a VW dealer or an air conditioning specialist. Similarly, the system can only be evacuated and recharged by a dealer or air conditioning specialist. The refrigerant circuit service ports are located in the right-hand front corner of the engine compartment **(see illustration)**.

⚠ *Warning: The air conditioning system contains a pressurised liquid refrigerant. If the system is discharged in an uncontrolled manner without the aid of specialist equipment, the refrigerant will boil as soon as it is exposed to the atmosphere, causing severe frostbite if it comes into contact with unprotected skin. In addition, certain refrigerants, in the presence of a naked flame (including a lit cigarette), will oxidise to form a highly poisonous gas. It is therefore extremely dangerous to disconnect any part of the air conditioning system without specialised knowledge and equipment.*

7 Uncontrolled discharging of the refrigerant can also be damaging to the environment, as certain refrigerants contain CFCs.

8 As no clutch is fitted to the air conditioning compressor (the compressor operates

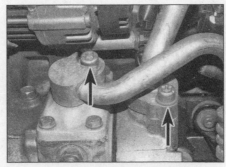

11.4 Undo the bolts (arrowed) and disconnect the refrigerant pipes

10.6 Refrigerant circuit service ports (arrowed)

continuously), do not operate the engine if it is known to be short of refrigerant, as this will damage the compressor.

11 Air conditioning system components – removal and refitting

⚠ *Warning: Do not attempt to discharge the refrigerant circuit yourself (refer to the precautions given in Section 10). Have the air conditioning system discharged by a suitably-equipped specialist. On completion, have the engineer fit new O-rings to the line connections and evacuate and recharge the system.*

Compressor

Removal

1 Have the air conditioning system discharged by a suitably-equipped specialist.

2 Place the lock carrier in the 'Service position' (see Chapter 11).

3 Remove the auxiliary drivebelt as described in Chapter 1.

4 Unscrew the retaining bolts and disconnect the refrigerant lines from the compressor **(see illustration)**. Remove the O-ring seals and renew them if necessary. Plug the open pipes and ports to prevent the ingress of moisture.

5 Disconnect the wiring plug, then unscrew the retaining bolts from the compressor, then remove the compressor from its mounting bracket **(see illustration)**.

11.5 Compressor mounting bolts (arrowed)

11.15 Undo the Torx bolts (arrowed) securing the refrigerant pipes at the bulkhead

11.17 Unclip the rear footwell air ducts each side

11.18 Front right-hand side footwell duct bolt (arrowed)

11.19 Disconnect the drain tube (arrowed) at the front of the heater housing

11.20 Right-hand side crossmember support bracket bolts (arrowed)

Refitting

6 Refitting is a reversal of the removal procedure; ensure that all fixings are tightened to the specified torque, where given. On completion, have the refrigerant engineer fit new O-rings to the line connections and then evacuate and recharge the refrigerant circuit.

Evaporator/heater matrix housing

Removal

7 Have the air conditioning system discharged by a suitably-equipped specialist.
8 Ensure that engine has cooled completely before starting work.
9 Remove both front seats as described in Chapter 11.
10 Locate the heater matrix hoses and trace them back to the point where they connect

to bulkhead stub pipes. Where fitted, release the fasteners and remove the protective plate over the pipes.
11 Place a draining container underneath the hoses, to catch the coolant that will escape when they are disconnected.
12 Apply proprietary hose clamps to both heater hoses, then prise out the wire clips and disconnect the hoses from the bulkhead stubs **(see illustration 9.18)**. Allow the coolant from the heater circuit to collect in the draining container.
13 If you have access to a source of compressed air, apply it carefully at low pressure to the upper bulkhead stub and blow the remainder of the coolant from the heater matrix.

⚠ *Warning: Always wear eye protection when working with compressed air.*

14 If you do not have access to compressed

air, bear in mind that a larger volume of coolant will remain in the heater circuit and that this may escape as the heater unit is removed from the inside of the car.
15 Undo the bolts and disconnect the refrigerant pipes from the engine compartment bulkhead. Plug the openings to prevent contamination **(see illustration)**. Discard the O-ring seals – new ones must be fitted.
16 Remove the entire facia panel as described in Chapter 11.
17 Pull the up the sill trims, remove the driver's side footwell bulkhead panel/footrest, remove the accelerator pedal assembly (Chapter 4A), then raise the carpet, then unclip the rear footwell air ducts each side **(see illustration)**. Alternatively, use a sharp knife to cut through the carpet in front of the gear/selector lever, then disconnect the vents.
18 Undo the bolts and remove the left- and right-hand side footwell vents **(see illustration)**.
19 Detach the drain tube from the base of the heater housing at the front **(see illustration)**.
20 Undo the bolts and remove the crossmember support brackets each side of the heater housing. Release the wiring loom from any retaining clips and disconnect the wiring plug from the control unit **(see illustration)**.
21 Undo the retaining bolt, unclip the linkage and remove the servo motor from the top of the matrix cover **(see illustrations 9.27a and 9.27b)**.
22 Undo the retaining bolts and remove the heater matrix cover **(see illustration 9.28)**.
23 Note their fitted positions, then disconnect the auxiliary heating element wiring plugs (where fitted) **(see illustration 9.62)**.
24 Undo the nut/bolts and remove the support bracket at the left-hand end of the housing **(see illustration)**.
25 Undo the 2 bolts securing the bracket at the right-hand end of the housing **(see illustration)**. Note that the upper bolt stays in the bracket.
26 Undo the 2 bolts, release the clips at each end, and remove the facia demister vent from the heater housing **(see illustration)**.
27 Remove the 2 nuts and move the convenience system control unit to one side **(see illustration 9.23)**.

11.24 Remove the support bracket (arrowed) at the end of the housing

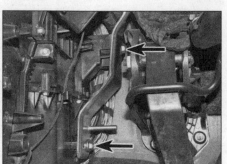

11.25 Undo the bolts (arrowed) securing the right-hand bracket

11.26 Facia demister vent bolts (arrowed)

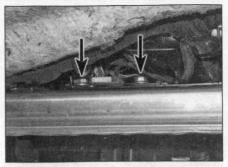
11.28a Undo the 2 bolts (arrowed) on the front face of the crossmember . . .

11.28b . . . and the 2 underneath (arrowed), then remove the bracket

28 Undo the 4 bolts securing the support bracket at the left-hand side of the crossmember, securing the top of the heater housing **(see illustrations)**.
29 Undo the 2 bolts securing the wiring support bracket to the front of the left-hand end of the crossmember, and the bolt securing it to the front of the blower housing.
29 Pull the heater housing assembly rearwards.
30 With the help of an assistant, remove the unit from the vehicle, keeping it upright to avoid spilling the residual coolant.

Refitting

31 Refitting is the reverse of removal, noting the following points.
 a) Ensure the ducts, elbows and gaiter are all securely joined to the housing and the wiring/cables are correctly routed before securing the housing in position.

 b) Ensure the coolant hoses are securely reconnected to the matrix; the feed hose from the cylinder head must be connected to the lower union and the return hose to the coolant pump to the upper union.
 c) Ensure that the rubber grommet is securely seated over the bulkhead stub pipes.
 d) Reconnect the refrigerant pipes using new O-ring seals.
 e) On completion, top-up the cooling system as described in Chapter 1.

Evaporator

Removal

32 Remove the evaporator/heater matrix housing as described in this Section.
33 Completely remove the bolt securing the matrix pipe to the heater housing, then

remove the rubber grommet and foam seal **(see illustration)**.
34 Slacken the clamps and pull the two coolant pipes from the heater matrix **(see illustration 9.29)**. Be prepared for coolant spillage.
35 Undo the bolt and remove the servo motor over the top of the matrix cover **(see illustration 9.27a and 9.27b)**.
36 Undo the retaining bolts, remove the cover then slide the heater matrix from the housing **(see illustration 9.28)**.
37 Disconnect the wiring plugs from the temperature sensors on the right-hand side of the housing.
38 Undo the 4 retaining bolts, release the 2 catches, and separate the matrix housing from the distributor housing **(see illustrations)**.
39 Undo the retaining bolt (where fitted), slide the cover across and remove the pollen filter **(see illustration)**.

11.33 Remove the rubber and foam seals

11.38a Undo the bolt (arrowed) under the vent outlet on the left-hand side . . .

11.38b . . . the one (arrowed) on the right-hand side . . .

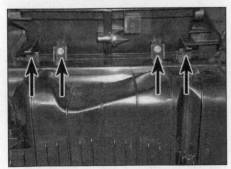
11.38c . . . then remove the bolts in the centre and release the clips (arrowed) . . .

11.38d . . . and separate the matrix housing from the distributor housing

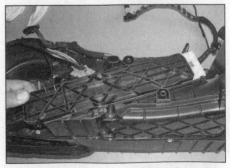
11.39 Slide off the cover and remove the pollen filter

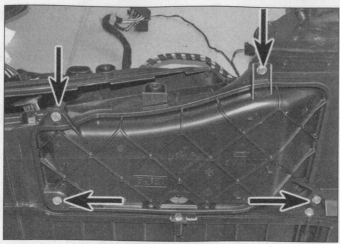

11.40 Undo the bolts (arrowed) and remove the cover

11.42a Remove the various bolts securing the halves of the housing (left-hand bolts arrowed) ...

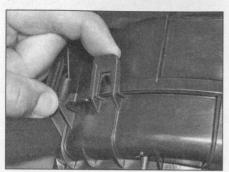

11.42b ... and release the catches ...

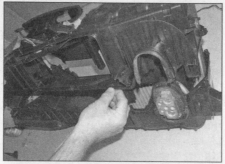

11.42c ... then separate the halves of the housing

40 Undo the bolts and remove the plastic cover from the front side of the housing **(see illustration)**.
41 Disconnect the recirculation flap servo motor wiring plug.
42 Remove the 14 retaining bolts around the circumference of the evaporator/blower motor housing, release the catches, and separate the halves of the housing **(see illustrations)**.
43 Lift the evaporator from position **(see illustration)**.
44 If required, remove the rubber seal, undo the retaining bolts and detach the expansion valve from the evaporator pipes **(see illus-**

tration)**. Recover the seals between the pipes and valve.

Refitting

45 Refitting is the reverse of removal, noting the following points.
  a) Check the condition of the evaporator seal and renew it if necessary.
  b) Reconnect the coolant pipes to the heater matrix using new seals.
  c) Top-up the cooling system as described in Chapter 1.
  d) On completion, have the refrigerant engineer fit new O-rings to the line connections and then evacuate and recharge the refrigerant circuit.

Evaporator outflow temperature sensor

Removal

46 Remove the driver's side footwell trim panel as described in Chapter 11.
47 Disconnect the wiring plug, then rotate the sensor 90° and pull it from the housing **(see illustration)**.

Refitting

48 Refitting is a reversal of removal.

Sunlight photo-sensor

Removal

49 Carefully prise up the rear edge of the facia panel around the sensor a maximum of 15 mm. If the panel is lifted more than this, there is a risk of damage. Use a piece of cardboard on the facia to prevent damage.
50 Insert a long, flat-bladed screwdriver beneath the panel, position a small block of wood as a pad, then push the screwdriver handle downwards, release the clip and prise the sensor upwards from position. Disconnect the sensor wiring plug as it is withdrawn, and tie the connector back to prevent it from disappearing down inside the facia.

Refitting

51 Refitting is a reversal of removal.

11.43 Lift the evaporator from place

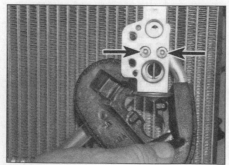

11.44 Remove the rubber seal and undo the expansion valve bolts (arrowed)

11.47 Evaporator outflow temperature sensor (arrowed)

Receiver/drier

Removal

52 Have the air conditioning refrigerant discharged by a suitably-equipped specialist.
53 Place the lock carrier in the 'Service position' as described in Chapter 11.
54 Unclip/unscrew and remove the air deflector panels each side, and above the intercooler/condenser **(see illustrations)**.
55 Undo the intercooler mounting bolts each side **(see illustration)**.
56 Gently push the intercooler/radiator/condenser rearwards slightly, then using a T55 Torx bit, unscrew the cap from the receiver/drier **(see illustration)**.
57 Insert a 5 mm bolt into the receiver/drier sealing cover, push the downwards slightly and extract the retaining circlip. Pull the receiver/drier element from place **(see illustrations)**.

Refitting

58 Refitting is a reversal of removal. Have the refrigerant recharged by a suitably-equipped specialist.

Condenser

Removal

59 Have the air conditioning refrigerant discharged by a suitably-equipped specialist.
60 Remove the intercooler as described in Chapter 4A.
61 Undo the bolts and detach the refrigerant pipes from the condenser. Renew the O-ring seals on the connections where necessary

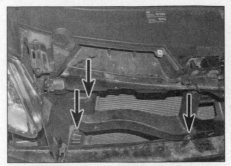

11.54a Release the clips and undo the bolt each side (arrowed) . . .

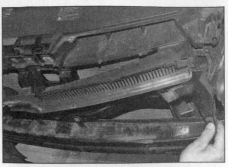

11.54b . . . then remove the air deflector panels

11.55 Undo the intercooler mounting bolt each side (left-hand side bolt arrowed)

(see illustrations). Plug/seal the openings to prevent contamination.
62 Lift the condenser from place **(see illustration)**.

11.56 Use T55 Torx bit to unscrew the cap

Refitting

63 Refitting is a reversal of removal. Have the refrigerant recharged by a suitably-equipped specialist.

11.57a Insert a 5 mm bolt, push down and extract the circlip (arrowed) . . .

11.57b . . . pull out the cap . . .

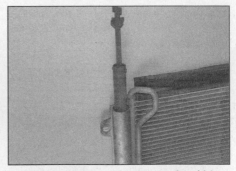

11.57c . . . followed by the receiver/drier

11.61a The refrigerant pipes are secured by Torx bolts (arrowed)

11.61b Refrigerant pipe O-ring seals (arrowed)

11.62 Lift the condenser from place

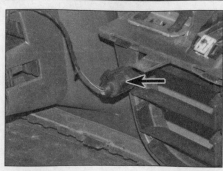

11.66 Ambient temperature sensor wiring plug (arrowed)

Ambient temperature sensor

Removal

64 Raise the front of the vehicle and support it securely on axle stands (see *Jacking and vehicle support*).

65 Undo the fasteners and remove the engine undershield **(see illustration 7.14)**.

66 The sensor is fitted behind the front bumper. Unclip the sensor and disconnect the wiring plug **(see illustration)**.

Refitting

67 Refitting is a reversal of removal.

Expansion valve

Removal

68 Have the air conditioning refrigerant discharged by a suitably-equipped specialist.

69 Remove the battery as described in Chapter 5.

70 Undo the bolts and disconnect the refrigerant pipes from the engine compartment bulkhead. Plug the openings to prevent contamination **(see illustration 11.15)**. Renew the O-ring seals if necessary.

71 Undo the 2 bolts and remove the expansion valve **(see illustration 11.44)**. Recover the seals between the expansion valve and refrigerant pipes.

Refitting

72 Refitting is a reversal of removal, remembering to renew the valve to pipe seals where necessary.

Chapter 4 Part A:
Fuel systems

Contents

Degrees of difficulty

| Easy, suitable for novice with little experience | | Fairly easy, suitable for beginner with some experience | | Fairly difficult, suitable for competent DIY mechanic | | Difficult, suitable for experienced DIY mechanic | | Very difficult, suitable for expert DIY or professional | |

Specifications

Engine codes
Manufacturer's engine codes:*
PD unit injector engines:
  1.9 litre . . . . BKC, BLS and BXE
  2.0 litre . . . . BKP, BMA, BMR, BUZ, BVE and BWV
  Common rail injection engines . . . . CBAA, CBAB, CBAC and CBBB
* Note: *See 'Vehicle identification' at the end of this manual for the location of engine code markings.*

General
Fuel injection system . . . . Electronic, direct injection
Firing order 1-3-4-2
Maximum engine speed . . . . N/A (ECM controlled)
Engine fast idle speed . . . . N/A (ECM controlled)

Tandem pump (PD unit injector engines only)
Fuel pressure at 4000 rpm:
  SOHC engines . . . . 7.5 bar minimum
  DOHC engines . . . . 10.5 bar minimum

Turbocharger
Type . . . . Garrett or KKK

Torque wrench settings

	Nm	lbf ft
Camshaft position sensor	10	7
Common fuel rail	15	11
EGR pipe flange bolts	20	15
EGR valve mounting bolt	10	7
Engine speed/TDC sender	5	4
Exhaust gas temperature sensor	45	33
Exhaust manifold nuts*	20	15
Flap motor housing	10	7
Fuel pressure regulating valve	80	59
Fuel pressure sensor	100	74
High-pressure fuel pipe unions	28	21
High-pressure fuel pump bolts	20	15
Injector clamp/mounting:		
1.9 litre PD unit injector engines:*		
Stage 1	12	9
Stage 2	Angle-tighten a further 270°	
2.0 litre PD unit injector engines:*		
Stage 1	3	2
Stage 2	Angle-tighten a further 90°	
Stage 3	Angle-tighten a further 180°	
Common rail injector engines:		
Clamp nut	10	7
Cover bolt	5	4
Intake manifold to cylinder head:		
PD unit injector engines*	22	16
Common rail injection engines*	10	7
Pump injector rocker shaft bolts:*		
Stage 1	20	15
Stage 2	Angle-tighten a further 90°	
Rear axle bolts:*		
Stage 1	90	66
Stage 2	Angle-tighten a further 90°	
Tandem pump bolts:		
SOHC engines:		
Upper	20	15
Lower	10	7
DOHC engines	20	15
Throttle valve module	10	7
Turbocharger support bracket:		
To engine block*	60	44
To turbocharger	20	15
Turbocharger oil return pipe to turbo	15	11

* Do not re-use

1 General information and precautions

All engines covered by this Manual are fitted with a direct-injection fuelling system, incorporating a fuel tank, an engine-bay mounted fuel filter with an integral water separator, fuel supply and return lines and four fuel injectors. Models with the 1.9 or 2.0 litre PD unit injector engines also have a fuel cooler mounted beneath the right-hand side of the car, on the underbody. All engines are fitted with a turbocharger.

Two different types of fuel injection system are fitted to the Passat model. The first is first is known as the PD (Pumpe Duese) or unit injector system, where fuel is delivered by a camshaft-driven 'tandem pump' at low pressure to the injectors (known as unit injectors). A 'roller rocker' assembly, mounted above the camshaft bearing caps, uses an extra set of camshaft lobes to compress the top of each injector once per firing cycle. This arrangement creates high injection pressures. The precise timing of the pre-injection and main injection is controlled by the engine management ECM and a solenoid on each injector.

The second type is the familiar common rail system, where fuel is supplied from a timing belt-driven high-pressure pump to a common fuel rail (or reservoir). The four injectors are fitted into the cylinder head and are connected to the fuel rail by rigid metal pipes. The precise timing of the pre-, main, and post-injections are controlled by the engine management ECM and an electrically-operated Piezo crystal incorporated into the injector design.

The direct-injection fuelling system is controlled electronically by a diesel engine management system, comprising an Electronic Control Module (ECM) and its associated sensors, actuators and wiring. In addition, the ECM manages the operation of the Exhaust Gas Recirculation (EGR) emission control system (Chapter 4B), the turbocharger boost pressure control system and the glow plug control system (Chapter 5).

A flap valve/throttle valve module fitted to the intake manifold is closed by the ECM for 3 seconds as the engine is switched off, to minimise the air intake as the engine shuts down. This minimises the vibration felt as the pistons come up against the volume of highly compressed air present in the combustion chambers.

It should be noted that fault diagnosis of the diesel engine management system is only possible with dedicated electronic test equipment. Problems with the system's operation should therefore be referred to a VW dealer or suitably-equipped specialist for assessment. Once the fault has been identified, the removal/refitting sequences detailed in the following Sections will then allow the appropriate component(s) to be renewed as required.

The EOBD diagnostic connector is located under the driver's side of the facia (see illustration).

Precautions

Many of the operations described in this Chapter involve the disconnection of fuel lines, which may cause an amount of fuel spillage. Before commencing work, refer to the warnings below and the information in *Safety first!* at the beginning of this manual.

⚠️ *Warning: When working on any part of the fuel system, avoid direct contact skin contact with diesel fuel – wear protective clothing and gloves when handling fuel system components. Ensure that the work area is well-ventilated to prevent the build-up of diesel fuel vapour.*

• *Fuel injectors operate at extremely high pressures and the jet of fuel produced at the nozzle is capable of piercing skin, with potentially fatal results. When working with pressurised injectors, take care to avoid exposing any part of the body to the fuel spray. It is recommended that a diesel fuel systems specialist should carry out any pressure testing of the fuel system components.*

• *Under no circumstances should diesel fuel be allowed to come into contact with coolant hoses – wipe off accidental spillage immediately. Hoses that have been contaminated with fuel for an extended period should be renewed.*

• *Diesel fuel systems are particularly sensitive to contamination from dirt, air*

and water. Pay particular attention to cleanliness when working on any part of the fuel system, to prevent the ingress of dirt. Thoroughly clean the area around fuel unions before disconnecting them. Only use lint-free cloths and clean fuel for component cleansing.

• *Store dismantled components in sealed containers to prevent contamination and the formation of condensation.*

2 Air cleaner assembly – removal and refitting

Removal

1 Disconnect the wiring from the air mass meter. Also disconnect the vacuum hose from the air filter cover (see illustration).
2 Loosen the clip and disconnect the air duct from the air mass meter.
3 Undo the bolts securing the intake hood/ducting to the lock carrier (see illustration), then pull the ducting from the base of the air cleaner assembly. On some models, the clips each side of the ducting must be depressed.
4 Undo the bolts, remove the air filter cover, lift out the filter element and the grating in the base of the lower housing (see illustration).
5 Undo the retaining bolt at the rear of the air cleaner housing (see illustration).
6 Use a small screwdriver to ease the rubber grommet in the base of the housing over the locating pin, pulling up the lower housing at the same time (see illustration).

1.1 EOBD diagnostic plug (arrowed)

7 Release the remaining rubber mounting and manoeuvre the air cleaner assembly from the engine compartment.

Refitting

8 Refit the air cleaner by following the removal procedure in reverse.

3 Engine management system – component removal and refitting

Throttle pedal/position sensor

Removal

1 Undo the bolts and remove the panel under the steering column in the driver's footwell.
2 Prise out the plastic cap, and undo the retaining bolt at the top of the pedal assembly (see illustration).

2.1 Disconnect the airflow meter wiring plug and the vacuum hose (arrowed)

2.3 Intake hood retaining bolts (arrowed)

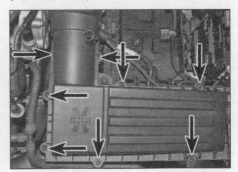

2.4 Air filter cover bolts (arrowed)

2.5 Air cleaner assembly retaining bolt (arrowed)

2.6 Use a screwdriver to ease the rubber grommet over the locating pin

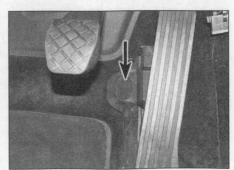

3.2 Prise out the cap (arrowed) at the top of the pedal

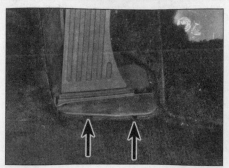

3.3a Insert the VW tool/screwdrivers into the slots (arrowed) . . .

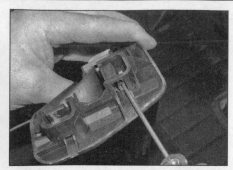

3.3b . . . and release the clips (pedal/ sensor removed for clarity)

3.12a Fuel temp sensor (arrowed) – PD unit injector engines

3.12b Release the clamps (arrowed) and remove the fuel temperature sensor assembly – common rail injection engines

3 Insert VW tool into the base of the assembly to release the clips and lift it from place. In the absence of the special tool, insert a small screwdriver into the slots at the base

of the pedal, and release the clips. Push the right-hand clip rewards to release it, and the left-hand clip to the right **(see illustrations)**.
4 Disconnect the sensor wiring plug.

5 No further dismantling of the assembly is recommended – no component parts are available. If the assembly if faulty, a new one must be fitted.

Refitting

6 Position the assembly, ensuring that the two pins on the floor and the centring pin on the bulkhead locate correctly.
7 The remainder of refitting is a reversal of removal.

Coolant temperature sensor

8 Refer to Chapter 3.

Fuel temperature sensor

9 The fuel temperature sensor is located in the fuel line at the front of the cylinder head (PD unit injector engines) or on the top of the high-pressure fuel pump (common rail injection engines).
10 Pull the plastic cover on the top of the engine upwards from the rubber mountings.
11 Disconnect the wiring from the sensor.
12 On PD unit injector engines, release the clips and pull the sensor from the hoses. On common rail injection engines, release the clamps and disconnect the hoses from the sensor assembly **(see illustrations)**.
13 Refit the fuel temperature sensor by reversing the removal procedure.

Intake air temperature/ charge pressure sensor

14 The intake air temperature/charge pressure sensor is located on the air duct leading from the intercooler to the intake manifold, at the front of the engine compartment **(see illustrations)**. First disconnect the wiring.
15 Undo the bolts and remove the sensor from the air duct.
16 Refitting is a reversal of removal.

Engine speed sensor

17 The engine speed sensor is mounted on the front left-hand side of the cylinder block, adjacent to the mating surface of the block and transmission bellhousing. Raise the front of the vehicle, and support is securely on axle stands (see *Jacking and vehicle support*).
18 Undo the fasteners and remove the engine undershield **(see illustration)**.
19 Drain the cooling system as described in Chapter 1.
20 Undo the bolts securing the coolant pipe under the intake manifold, release the clamps and disconnect the hoses from the pipe.
21 Disconnect the wiring plug, then unscrew the oil pressure switch from the oil filter housing. Be prepared for oil spillage.
22 Undo the turbocharger oil supply pipe union at the oil filter housing.
23 Remove the bolt securing the pipe bracket at the rear of the cylinder head.
24 Lift the retaining clip and disconnect the air intake hose from the intake manifold/flap motor housing.
25 Release the clamps and disconnect the coolant hose from the oil cooler.

3.14a Charge pressure sensor (arrowed) – 1.9 litre PD unit injector engines

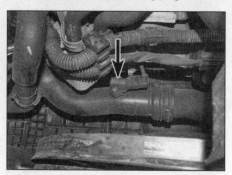

3.14b Charge pressure sensor (arrowed) – 2.0 litre PD unit injector engines

3.14c Charge pressure sensor (arrowed) – common rail injection engines

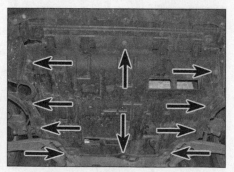

3.18 Undo the fasteners (arrowed) and remove the engine undershield

26 Undo the 2 retaining bolts and pull the oil level dipstick guide tube upwards from place.

27 Undo the 4 bolts and remove the oil filter housing **(see illustration)**. Renew the gasket/seals. Be prepared for oil spillage.

28 Disconnect the wiring plug, unscrew the retaining bolt and pull the engine speed sensor from place **(see illustration)**.

29 Refit the sensor by reversing the removal procedure. Top-up the coolant as described in Chapter 1.

Airflow meter

30 Disconnect the airflow meter wiring plug **(see illustration)**.

31 Loosen the clip and disconnect the air intake hose from the airflow meter.

32 Undo the two bolts and pull the air flow meter from the guide on the air cleaner housing. Handle the airflow meter carefully, as it is a delicate component.

33 Refitting is a reversal of removal.

Intake manifold flap housing

34 As diesel engines have a very high compression ratio, when the engine is turned off, the pistons still compress a large quantity of air for a few revolutions and cause the engine unit to shudder. The intake manifold change-over flap is located in the intake flange housing bolted to the intake manifold. When the ignition switch is turned to the 'off' position, the engine management ECM-controlled valve actuates the flap, which shuts off the air supply to the cylinders. This allows the pistons to compress very little air, and the engine runs softly to a halt. The flap must open again approximately 3 seconds after switching off the ignition switch.

35 Remove the plastic cover from the top of the engine.

36 Release the retaining clips, and disconnect the air intake trucking from the intake manifold flap housing **(see illustration)**.

37 Disconnect the wiring plug from the intake manifold flap motor. Where applicable, undo the bolts and disconnect the EGR pipe from the housing.

38 Undo the bolts, and remove the flap motor from the manifold. Discard the O-ring seal, a new one must be fitted.

39 Refitting is a reversal of removal. Tighten the intake manifold flap motor housing bolts to the specified torque.

Clutch position sensor

40 Remove the plastic cover from the top of the engine by pulling it up from the mountings.

41 Undo the nuts and remove the heat shield over the particulate filter, and the heat shield over the clutch master cylinder at the engine compartment bulkhead (where fitted).

42 Apply a hose clamp to the fluid supply hose to the clutch master cylinder.

43 Prise out the retaining clip a little, then pull the pressure hose from the master cylinder at the engine compartment bulkhead.

3.27 Oil cooler/filter housing bolts (arrowed)

3.28 Engine speed sensor bolt (arrowed) – shown with the flywheel removed for clarity

44 Unclip the position sensor and slide it from the master cylinder **(see illustrations)**. Disconnect the wiring plug as the sensor is withdrawn.

45 Refitting is a reversal of removal. If necessary, bleed the clutch hydraulic system as described in Chapter 6.

Electronic control module (ECM)

Caution: The ECM is programmed and identified specifically for the vehicle it is fitted to, and the identity coding must be transferred to any new module. This process requires the use of dedicated VW diagnostic equipment VAS 5051/2. For this reason, it is recommended that ECM renewal is carried out by a VW dealer or suitably-equipped specialist, however removal and refitting of the original ECM is possible by the home mechanic. Note also that if the ECM is renewed, the

identification of the new ECM must be transferred to the immobiliser control module by a VW dealer or specialist.

Caution: Always wait at least 30 seconds after switching off the ignition before disconnecting the wiring from the ECM. When the wiring is disconnected, all the learned values may be erased, although any contents of the fault memory are retained. After reconnecting the wiring, the vehicle must be driven for several miles so that the ECM can learn its basic settings. If the engine still runs erratically, the basic settings may be reinstated by a VW dealer or specialist using a special test instrument.

46 The electronic control module is located on the bulkhead at the rear of the engine compartment. Disconnect the battery negative (earth) lead (see Chapter 5).

47 Remove the wiper arms as described in Chapter 12.

3.30 Disconnect the airflow meter wiring plug (arrowed)

3.36 Disconnect the air intake trunking (arrowed)

3.44a Press the clip (arrowed) across . . .

3.44b . . . and slide the clutch position sensor downwards

3.48 Pull up the rubber sealing strip, and slide forwards the clips (arrowed)

3.49 Starting at the middle, pull up the plenum chamber covers

3.51 Undo the cover retaining bolts (arrowed)

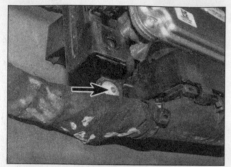

3.52a The security plate is retained by a shear bolt each side (right-hand bolt arrowed)

3.52b We used a chisel to undo the shear bolts. Take care not to damage the wiring loom

3.52c Remove the security plate

48 Pull up the rubber sealing strip, then slide forwards the clips securing the plenum chamber cover (see illustration).

49 Starting in the middle, pull the plenum chamber cover upwards from the base of the windscreen (see illustration). Unclip the bonnet wiring/hoses from the cover as it's withdrawn.

50 Disconnect the wiring plug from the heater windscreen control unit (where fitted).

51 Undo the 2 bolts and remove the cover from the ECM (see illustration).

52 Drill out the shear bolts securing the security plate over the ECM wiring plugs, and remove the plate (see illustrations). We managed to undo the bolt heads using a sharp chisel. If using this method, take great care not to damage the wiring looms.

53 Slide the locking catches outwards and disconnect the both wiring plugs from the ECM (see illustration).

54 Slide and lift the control unit and retainer frame from place. If required, press the locking device each side outwards and slide the ECM from the frame (see illustrations).

55 Refitting is a reversal of removal. Reconnect the battery as described in Chapter 5.

Camshaft position sensor

1.9 litre engines

56 With reference to Chapter 2A, remove the timing belt upper cover.

57 Undo the retaining bolt, and remove the sensor from the cylinder head. Trace the sensor wiring back to the connector on the engine bulkhead and unplug.

58 Prise out the grommet in the timing belt rear cover and manoeuvre the sensor out through the hole.

59 Refitting is a reversal of removal, noting

that the sensor has a locating peg which must be fitted into the hole in the cylinder head (see illustration 3.74). Tighten the sensor retaining bolt to the specified torque.

2.0 litre PD unit injector engines

60 Remove the timing belt from the camshaft pulleys and idler roller as described in Chapter 2A. Trace the wiring to the connecting plug, then undo the retaining bolt and remove the sensor.

61 Refitting is a reversal of removal, noting that the sensor has a locating peg which must be fitted into the hole in the cylinder head (see illustration 3.74). Tighten the sensor retaining bolt to the specified torque.

Common rail engines up to 12.2007

62 Remove the camshaft pulley hub, idler rollers and tensioner roller as described in Chapter 2B.

3.53 Slide out the catches and disconnect the ECM wiring plugs

3.54a Remove the ECM and retainer frame

3.54b Press out the clips and separate the ECM from the frame

63 Remove the coolant pump as described in Chapter 3.

64 Remove the high-pressure fuel pump upper retaining bolt.

65 Undo the bolt securing the timing belt inner cover above the high-pressure pump.

66 Undo the bolt securing the timing belt guard at the rear of the engine. Unclip the timing belt inner cover at the top.

67 Disconnect the camshaft position sensor wiring plug and release it from the retaining bracket.

68 Undo the sensor retaining bolt, pull the timing belt inner cover away from the engine slightly, and remove the sensor **(see illustration)**.

69 Refitting is a reversal of removal, noting that the sensor has a locating peg which must be fitted into the hole in the cylinder head **(see illustration 3.74)**. Tighten the sensor retaining bolt to the specified torque.

Common rail engines from 01.2008

70 Remove the timing belt as described in Chapter 2B.

71 Disconnect the camshaft position sensor wiring plug and release it from the retaining bracket.

72 Use a screwdriver to remove the repair aperture webs from the timing belt inner cover.

73 Unscrew the retaining bolt and manoeuvre the camshaft position sensor and wiring plug through the repair aperture in the timing belt cover **(see illustration 3.68)**.

74 Refitting is a reversal of removal, noting that the sensor has a locating peg which must be fitted into the hole in the cylinder head **(see illustration)**. Tighten the sensor retaining bolt to the specified torque.

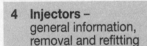

4 Injectors – general information, removal and refitting

⚠️ *Warning: Exercise extreme caution when working on the fuel injectors. Never expose the hands or any part of the body to injector spray, as the high working pressure can cause the fuel to penetrate the skin, with possibly fatal results. You are strongly advised to have any work which involves testing the injectors under pressure carried out by a dealer or fuel injection specialist. Refer to the precautions in Section 1 of this Chapter before proceeding.*

General information

1 Injectors deteriorate with prolonged use, and it is reasonable to expect them to need reconditioning or renewal after 60 000 miles or so. Accurate testing, overhaul and calibration of the injectors must be left to a specialist.

Removal

Note: *Take care not to allow dirt into the injectors or fuel pipes during this procedure. Do not drop the injectors or allow the needles at their tips to become damaged. The injectors are precision-made to fine limits, and must*

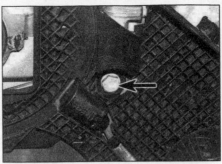

3.68 Camshaft position sensor bolt (arrowed)

4.4 Undo the adjustment bolt until the rocker arm lies against the plunger pin of the injector

not be handled roughly. Keep the injectors identified for position to ensure correct refitting.

1.9 litre engines

2 With reference to Chapter 2A, remove the upper timing belt cover and camshaft cover.

3 Using a spanner or socket, turn the crankshaft pulley until the rocker arm for the injector which is to be removed, is at its highest, ie, the injector plunger spring is under the least amount of tension.

4 Slacken the locknut of the adjustment bolt on the end of the rocker arm above the injector, and undo the adjustment bolt until the rocker arm lies against the plunger pin of the injector **(see illustration)**.

5 Starting at the outside and working in, gradually and evenly slacken and remove the rocker shaft

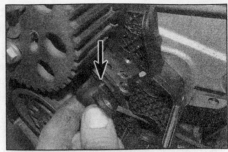

3.74 The camshaft position sensor has a locating peg which must locate into the hole in the cylinder head

4.6 Remove the clamping block securing bolt (arrowed)

retaining bolts. Lift off the rocker shaft. Check the contact face of each adjustment bolt, and renew any that show signs of wear.

6 Undo the clamping block securing bolt and remove the block from the side of the injector **(see illustration)**.

7 Using a small screwdriver, carefully prise the wiring connector from the injector.

8 VW technicians use a slide hammer (tool T10055) to pull the injector from the cylinder head. This is a slide hammer which engages in the side of the injector. If this tool is not available, it is possible to fabricate an equivalent using a short section of angle-iron, a length of threaded rod, a cylindrical weight, and two locknuts. Weld/braze the rod to the angle-iron, slide the weight over the rod, and lock the two nuts together at the end of the rod to provide the stop for the weight **(see illustration)**. *Seat*

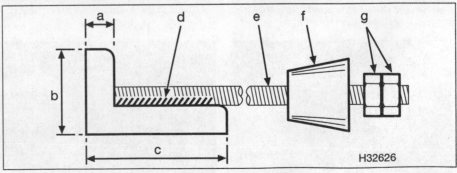

4.8a Unit injector removal tool

a = 5 mm
b = 15 mm
c = 25 mm

d   Weld/braze the rod to the angle iron
e   Threaded rod

f   Cylindrical weight
g   Locknuts

H32626

4.8b Seat the slide hammer/tool in the slot on the side of the injector, and pull the injector out

the slide hammer/tool in the slot on the side on the injector, and pull the injector out using a few gently taps. Recover circlip, the heat shield and O-rings and discard. New ones must be used for refitting (see illustration).

9 If required, the injector wiring loom/rail can be removed from the cylinder head by undoing the two retaining nuts/bolts at the left-hand end of the head. To prevent the wiring connectors fouling the cylinder head casting as the assembly is withdrawn, insert the connectors into the storage slots in the plastic wiring rail. Carefully push the assembly to the rear, and out of the casting (see illustrations).

2.0 litre PD unit injector engines

10 With reference to Chapter 2A, remove the upper timing belt cover and camshaft cover.
11 Slacken the locknut of the adjustment bolt on the end of the rocker arm above the

4.16a Pull the plastic cover upwards to release the mountings

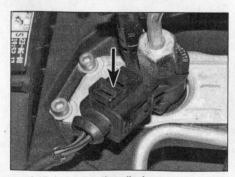

4.17 Lever up the clip (arrowed) and disconnect the injector wiring plugs

4.9a Undo the two nuts at the left-hand end of the head and slide the injector loom/rail out

respective injector, and undo the adjustment bolt until the rocker arm lies against the plunger pin of the injector.
12 Starting at the outside and working in, gradually and evenly slacken and remove the rocker shaft retaining bolts. Lift off the rocker shaft. Check the contact face of each adjustment bolt, and renew any that show signs of wear.
13 Using a pair of pliers, carefully pull the wiring connector from the injector.
14 The unit injectors have two mounting bolts each. Unscrew and remove the two bolts.
15 VW technicians use a slide hammer (tool T10133) to pull the injector from the cylinder head. This is a slide hammer which engages in the injector bolt holes. If this tool is not available, it is possible to fabricate an equivalent using a short section of angle-iron, a length of threaded rod, a cylindrical weight,

4.16b Lift the foam insulation (arrowed) from place

4.18a Hold down the outer tabs, and prise up the centre piece (arrowed) . . .

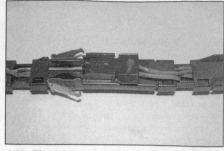

4.9b The injector connectors will slide into the loom/rail to prevent them from being damaged as the assembly is withdrawn/ inserted into the cylinder head

and two locknuts. Weld/braze the rod to the angle-iron, slide the weight over the rod, and lock the two nuts together at the end of the rod to provide the stop for the weight (see illustration 4.8a). Pull the injector out of the cylinder head. Recover the heat shield and O-rings and discard. New ones must be used for refitting.

Common rail engines

16 Pull the plastic cover over the engine upwards from its mountings. Where fitted, remove the foam insulation over the injectors (see illustrations).
17 Disconnect the injector wiring plugs (see illustration).
18 Ensure the area around the injectors and the pipes/return hoses is clean and free from debris. The use of a vacuum cleaner is recommended. Push the return hose connector downwards at its tabs, then pull up the centre piece and disconnect them from the injectors (see illustrations). Plug the openings to prevent contamination.
19 Undo the unions remove the high-pressure pipes between the common fuel rail and the injectors (see illustration). Plug the openings to prevent contamination.
20 Undo the bolts securing the injector clamp cover, the slightly lift the cover and rotate it 90° for access to the injector retaining nuts (see illustrations).
21 Unscrew the injector retaining nuts.
22 VW technicians use a slide hammer (tool T10055) and adapter (T10055/1) to pull the injector from the cylinder head. This is a slide

4.18b . . . then pull the return hose connector upwards from the injector

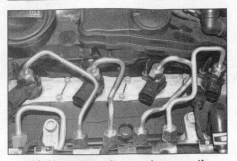

4.19 Undo the unions and remove the high-pressure pipes between the common rail and the injectors

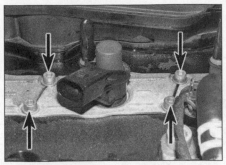

4.20a Undo the injector clamp cover bolts (arrowed) . . .

4.20b . . . then lift and rotate it 90°

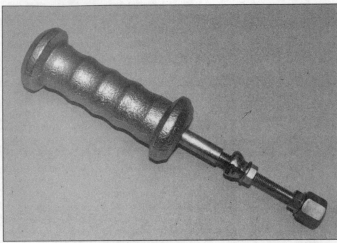

4.22a We affixed an old injector pipe union onto the end of the slide hammer . . .

4.22b . . . screwed it onto the top of the injector . . .

hammer with an adapter which bolts onto the top of the. If this tool is not available, it is possible to fabricate an equivalent using slide hammer with the union from an old injector pipe brazed/welded onto the end. Screw the tool onto the top of the injector, and pull the injector out using a few gently taps. Recover the clamping piece, copper seal and O-rings and discard. New ones must be used for refitting (see illustrations). Note: *The injectors*

can only be refitted to their original positions. Make the injectors to avoid confusion if refitting the original injectors.

Refitting

1.9 litre engines

23 Prior to refitting the injectors, the three O-rings, heat insulation washer and clip must be renewed. Due to the high injection

pressures, it is essential that the O-rings are fitted without being twisted. VW recommend the use of three special assembly sleeves to install the O-rings squarely, although suitably-equivalent tools are available from automotive tool manufacturers. It may be prudent to entrust O-ring renewal to a VW dealer or suitably-equipped injection specialist, rather than risk subsequent leaks (see illustration).
24 After renewing the O-rings, fit the heat

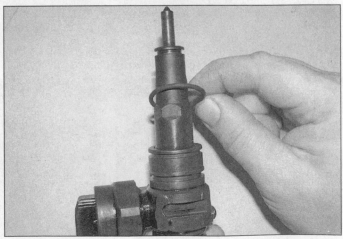

4.22c . . . and pulled it from the cylinder head

4.23 Great care must be used to ensure that the injector O-rings are fitted without being twisted

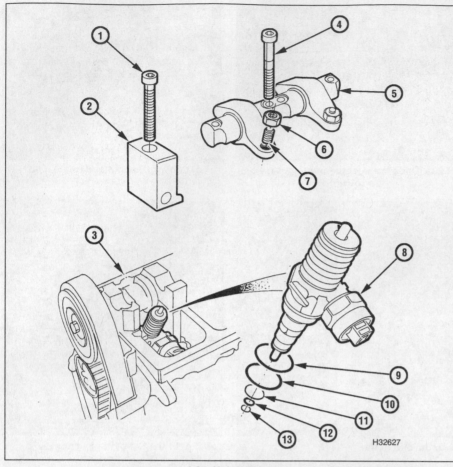

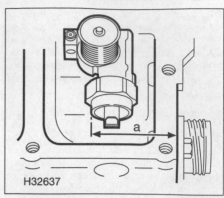

4.27a Measure the distance (a) from the end of the cylinder head to the rounded section of the injector

4.24 Unit injector

1 Bolt	3 Cylinder head	7 Adjuster	11 O-ring
2 Clamping	4 Bolt	8 Unit injector	12 Heat shield
block	5 Rocker arm	9 O-ring	13 Circlip
	6 Nut	10 O-ring	

shield and secure it in place with the circlip **(see illustration)**.

25 Smear clean engine oil onto the O-rings, and push the injector evenly down into the cylinder head onto its stop.

26 Fit the clamping block alongside the injector, but only hand-tighten the new retaining bolt at this stage.

27 It is essential that the injectors are fitted at right-angles to the clamping block. In order

to achieve this, measure the distance from the end of the cylinder head to the rounded section of the injector **(see illustrations)**. The dimensions (a) are as follows:

Cylinder 1 = 333.0 ± 0.8 mm
Cylinder 2 = 245.0 ± 0.8 mm
Cylinder 3 = 153.6 ± 0.8 mm
Cylinder 4 = 65.6 ± 0.8 mm

28 Once the injector(s) are aligned correctly, tighten the clamping bolt to the specified

Stage 1 torque setting, and the Stage 2 angle tightening setting. **Note:** *If an injector has been renewed, it is essential that the adjustment bolt, locknut of the corresponding rocker and ball-pin are renewed at the same time. The ball-pins simply pull out of the injector spring cap. There is an O-ring in each spring cap to stop the ball-pins from falling out.*

29 Smear some grease (VW No G000 100) onto the contact face of each rocker arm adjustment bolt, and refit the rocker shaft assembly to the camshaft bearing caps, tightening the retaining bolts as follows. Starting from the inside out, hand-tighten the bolts. Again, from the inside out, tighten the bolts to the Stage 1 torque setting. Finally, from the inside out, tighten the bolts to the Stage 2 angle tightening setting.

30 The following procedure is only necessary if an injector has been removed. Attach a DTI (Dial Test Indicator) gauge to the cylinder head upper surface, and position the DTI probe against the top of the adjustment bolt **(see illustration)**. Turn the crankshaft until the rocker arm roller is on the highest point of its corresponding camshaft lobe, and the adjustment bolt is at its lowest. Once this position has been established, remove the DTI gauge, screw the adjustment bolt in until firm resistance is felt, and the injector spring cannot be compressed further. Turn the adjustment bolt **anti-clockwise** 180°, and tighten the locknut securely. Repeat this procedure for any other injectors that have been removed.

4.27b Use a set square against the rounded edge of the injector . . .

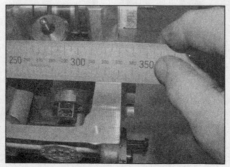

4.27c . . . and measure the distance to the end of the cylinder head

4.30 Attach a DTI (Dial Test Indicator) gauge to the cylinder head upper surface

31 Reconnect the wiring plug to the injector.
32 Refit the camshaft cover and upper timing belt cover, as described in Chapter 2A.
33 Start the engine and check that it runs correctly.

2.0 litre PD unit injector engines

34 Prior to refitting the injectors, the O-ring and heat insulation washer must be renewed. Due to the high injection pressures, it is essential that the O-ring is fitted without being twisted. VW recommend the use of a special assembly sleeve to install the O-ring squarely. It may be prudent to entrust O-ring renewal to a VW dealer or suitably-equipped injection specialist, rather than risk subsequent leaks. In addition, VW recommend that the adjustment bolts and the ball-pins (located on the tops of the injectors) are renewed.
35 Smear clean engine oil onto the O-ring, and push the injector together with the heat shield evenly down into the cylinder head onto its stop. It is absolutely important that the injector is inserted fully at this stage, as subsequent tightening of the mounting bolts may otherwise cause damage. VW technicians use a special lever to press the injectors fully into the head.
36 Insert the mounting bolts and tighten in the three stages given in the Specifications.
37 Smear some grease (VW No G000 100) onto the contact face of each rocker arm adjustment bolt, and refit the rocker shaft assembly, tightening the retaining bolts as follows. Starting from the inside out, hand-tighten the bolts. Again, from the inside out, tighten the bolts to the Stage 1 torque setting. Finally, from the inside out, tighten the bolts to the Stage 2 angle tightening setting.
38 The following procedure is only necessary if an injector has been removed. Attach a DTI (Dial Test Indicator) gauge to the cylinder head upper surface, and position the DTI probe against the top of the adjustment bolt **(see illustration 4.30)**. Turn the crankshaft until the rocker arm roller is on the highest point of its corresponding camshaft lobe, and the adjustment bolt is at its lowest. Once this position has been established, remove the DTI gauge, bolt the adjustment bolt in until firm resistance is felt, and the injector spring cannot be compressed further. Turn the adjustment bolt **anti-clockwise** 180°,

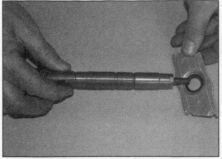

4.43 Slide the new cover plate onto the injector

and tighten the locknut securely. Repeat this procedure for any other injectors that have been refitted.
39 Reconnect the wiring plug to the injector.
40 Refit the camshaft cover and upper timing belt cover, as described in Chapter 2A.
41 Start the engine and check that it runs correctly.

Common rail engines

42 Ensure the area around the injector locations in the cylinder head are clean and free from debris. Use a vacuum cleaner if available. Clean any carbon deposits from the injector and sealing surfaces with a cloth soaked in clean engine oil or rust-releasing spray.
43 If new cover plates are to be fitted, slide them on now **(see illustration)**.
44 To remove the copper seal, spray rust-releasing spray around the injector nozzle, then clamp the seal in a vice, and use a twisting motion to pull the injector from the seal. Push the new copper seal into place **(see illustration)**.
45 Apply a little clean engine oil to the return pipe connection on the injector, and fit the new O-ring **(see illustration)**.
46 To renew the main injector O-ring seal, VW specify the use of tool No T10377. This tool allows the O-ring to slide over the end of the injector without twisting. With care, the seals can be fitted without the tool **(see illustration)**.
47 Slide the new clamping piece onto injector as shown **(see illustration)**.
48 Apply a smear of clean engine oil to the

4.44 Push the new copper seal (arrowed) into place

main O-ring seal, and insert the injector into place in the cylinder head. Note that if the original injectors are being refitted, they must go into their original positions. Tighten the injector clamping piece retaining nuts to the specified torque.
49 Rotate the cover back to position and tighten the retaining bolt to the specified torque.
50 Refit the high-pressure fuel pipes and tighten the unions to the specified torque. Note that the pipes may be re-used providing the tapered seats are undamaged, and the pipes are not deformed, constricted or corroded.
51 The remainder of refitting is a reversal of removal, noting the following:
a) If one or more injectors have been renewed, the injector delivery and injector voltage calibration values must be entered into the ECM using VW diagnostic equipment (VAS 5051). Entrust this task to a VW dealer or suitably-equipped specialist.
b) After completion of the work, the fuel system must be bled as described in Section 13.

5 Intake manifold – removal and refitting

Removal

1 Remove the intake manifold flap housing and motor as described in Section 3 of this Chapter.

4.45 Fit the new return pipe O-ring (arrowed) to the top of the injector

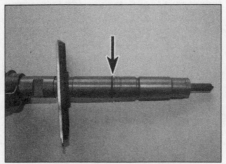

4.46 Fit a new main O-ring (arrowed) without twisting it

4.47 Slide the new clamping piece (arrowed) onto the injector

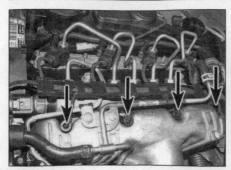

5.2 Pull the wiring plugs (arrowed) from the glow plugs

Common rail engines

2 Using thin, long-nosed pliers, carefully pull the wiring plugs from the top of the glow plugs **(see illustration)**.

3 With reference to Section 4, disconnect the fuel return pipes from the injectors, fuel rail, and high-pressure pump.

4 Undo the retaining nut and remove the fuel return pipe **(see illustration)**.

5 Undo the unions and disconnect the high-pressure fuel pipe between the pump and fuel rail.

6 Disconnect the wiring plug from the manifold change-over motor.

All engines

7 Where applicable, undo the 2 retaining bolts and pull the engine oil level dipstick guide tube upwards from place.

8 Undo the retaining bolts and manoeuvre the manifold from position.

6.6 Remove the high-pressure pipe between the pump and common rail (arrowed)

6.7b Unscrew the pressure sensor . . .

5.4 Fuel return pipe nut (arrowed)

Refitting

9 Refitting is a reversal of removal, using new manifold bolts, seals, EGR pipe and manifold flap assembly gaskets. Remember to renew any self-locking nuts.

---

6 Common fuel rail – removal and refitting

Note: *Observe the precautions in Section 1 before working on any component in the fuel system.*

Removal

1 Pull the plastic cover on the top of the engine upwards from its mountings and remove the foam insulation (where fitted) **(see illustrations 4.16a and 4.16b)**. Ensure the area around the fuel rail and pipes is clean and

6.7a Undo the bolts (arrowed) securing the common rail

6.7c . . . and pressure regulator

---

free from debris. If available, use a vacuum cleaner.

2 Disconnect the wiring plugs from the fuel pressure regulating valve, and the fuel pressure sensor at each end of the fuel rail.

3 Undo the retaining bolts, disconnect the coolant return hose from the expansion tank, and move the coolant pipe/hose to one side.

4 Unplug the centre 2 glow plugs, disconnect the fuel return hoses from the high-pressure pump and common fuel rail, then undo the retaining nuts and remove the fuel return pipe from the intake manifold **(see illustrations 5.2 and 5.4)**. Plug the openings to prevent contamination.

5 Unclip the wiring loom guide from the common fuel rail, pull the wiring plugs from the top of the remaining glow plugs, and move the wiring guide to one.

6 Undo the unions and remove the high-pressure pipes from the common fuel rail to the injectors and the high-pressure pump **(see illustration)**. Release the pipe from the retaining clips. Plug the openings to prevent contamination.

7 Undo the multi-spline retaining bolts and remove the common rail **(see illustration)**. If required, note their fitted positions, then unscrew the fuel pressure sensor and pressure regulating valve from the common rail **(see illustrations)**. Plug the openings to prevent contamination. **Note:** *VW insist that once removed, the pressure regulating valve cannot be re-used.*

Refitting

8 Where applicable, refit the fuel pressure sensor and the new regulating valve to the common rail, and tighten them to the specified torque. Note that the threads of the sensors must be clean and free from oil and grease.

9 The remainder of refitting is a reversal of removal, noting the following points:

a) *Refit the high-pressure fuel pipes and tighten the unions to the specified torque. Note that the high-pressure fuel pipes may be re-used providing the tapered seats are undamaged, and the pipes are not deformed, constricted or corroded.*

b) *After completion of the work, the fuel system must be bled as described in Section 13.*

---

7 Fuel gauge sender unit – removal and refitting

Note: *Observe the precautions in Section 1 before working on any component in the fuel system.*

⚠ **Warning: Avoid direct skin contact with fuel – wear protective clothing and gloves when handling fuel system components. Ensure that the work area is well-ventilated to prevent the build-up of fuel vapour.**

Removal

1 The fuel gauge sender unit is mounted in

7.4 Prise the access hatch from the floor

7.5 Depress the retaining tabs (arrowed) and disconnect the fuel hoses

7.6 Undoing the metal securing ring with 2 strips of steel and a tyre lever

the top of the fuel tank. The access cover is beneath the rear seat cushion. The unit protrudes into the fuel tank, and its removal involves exposing the contents of the tank to the atmosphere.

2 Ensure that the vehicle is parked on a level surface, then disconnect the battery negative (earth) lead (see Chapter 5).

3 Refer to Chapter 11, and remove the rear seat cushion, then undo the nut securing the side padding, and fold back the carpet from the right-hand side of the vehicle floor.

4 Lift the carpet, and prise the access hatch away from the floorpan **(see illustration)**, then unplug the wiring connector from the pump/sender unit.

5 Place rags beneath the fuel hoses to catch spilt fuel. Depress the retaining tabs and disconnect the fuel supply and return hoses **(see illustration)**. Mark/identify each hose for position – the blue hose is fuel return, and the black hose is fuel supply.

6 Unscrew the metal ring securing the pump/sender unit in the tank. VW technicians use a special tool (T10202) to unscrew the ring, however a home-made equivalent will suffice. Alternatively use a pair of large water pump pliers **(see illustration)**.

7 Remove the fuel pump/sender unit from the tank **(see illustration)**. Take great care not to bend or damage the sender unit float and arm as they are removed from the tank.

8 Inspect the float on the sender unit swinging arm for punctures and fuel ingress, and renew it if it appears damaged. Inspect the rubber seal from the fuel tank aperture and renew it if necessary. Inspect the sender unit wiper and

7.7 Manoeuvre the fuel pump/sender unit from the tank

track; clean off any dirt and debris that may have accumulated and look for breaks in the track.

9 Connect a hand-held multimeter to the blue and black wires terminals in the sender/pump unit socket. With the float arm at its lower stop position (empty tank) the resistance should be approximately 290 ohms. With the float arm at its upper stop position (full tank) the resistance should be approximately 50 ohms **(see illustration)**.

Refitting

10 Refitting is a reversal of removal, noting the following points:
a) Renew the fuel tank aperture seal if necessary, and refit it dry **(see illustration)**.
b) Do not bend the float arm during refitting.
c) Ensure all hoses are securely reconnected to their original positions.

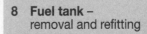

7.9 Connect a multimeter to the sender unit terminals (see text) and measure the resistance

d) The flange will only fit in one position – extended lug at the rear **(see illustration)**.
e) Reconnect the battery as described in Chapter 5.

8 Fuel tank – removal and refitting

Note: *Observe the precautions in Section 1 before working on any component in the fuel system.*

Removal

1 As no drain plug is provided, it is preferable to carry out this operation with the tank almost empty.

2 Open the fuel filler flap, and unscrew the fuel filler cap – leave the cap loosely in place. Undo the retaining bolt and remove the tank flap unit with the rubber cap **(see illustration)**.

7.10a Fit the new seal dry

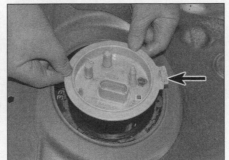

7.10b The flange will only fit with the extended lug (arrowed) at the rear

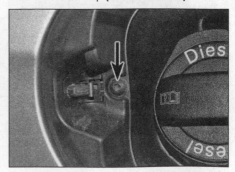

8.2 Fuel filler flap bolt (arrowed)

8.7 Fuel filler pipe retaining bolt (arrowed)

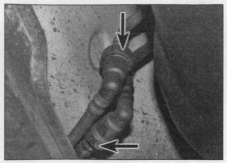

8.8 Depress the release buttons (arrowed) and pull the connections apart

8.11 Fuel tank rearmost strap retaining bolts (arrowed)

3 Disconnect the battery negative lead and position it away from the terminal as described in Chapter 5. Using a hand pump or siphon, remove any remaining fuel from the bottom of the tank.

4 Gain access to the top of the fuel pump/sender unit as described in Section 7, and disconnect the wiring harness from the top of the pump/sender unit at the multiway connector.

5 Loosen the rear wheel bolts, then jack up the rear of the car and support it securely on axle stands (see *Jacking and vehicle support*). Remove the rear roadwheels.

6 Remove the right-hand rear wheel arch liner as described in Chapter 11.

7 Unscrew the filler pipe from the body, and unclip the wiring harness from the pipe **(see illustration)**.

8 Depress the release buttons and disconnect the fuel supply and return pipes located at the front of the tank **(see illustration)**.

9 Place a trolley jack beneath the rear axle. The rear axle must be lowered to remove the fuel tank. Make alignment marks between the axle and body, then undo the 4 retaining bolts and lower the rear axle. Take care not to strain any hoses, wires or cables. Note that new axle retaining bolts must be fitted.

10 Position a trolley jack under the centre of the tank. Insert a block of wood between the jack head and the tank to prevent damage to the tank surface. Raise the jack until it just takes the weight of the tank.

11 Unscrew the mounting bolts and detach the tank straps **(see illustration)**.

12 Lower the jack and tank away from the underside of the vehicle. Guide the filer neck between the rear axle and body.

13 If the tank is contaminated with sediment or water, remove the fuel pump/sender unit (see Section 7) and swill the tank out with clean fuel. The tank is injection-moulded from a synthetic material, and if damaged, it should be renewed. However, in certain cases it may be possible to have small leaks or minor damage repaired. Seek the advice of a suitable specialist before attempting to repair the fuel tank.

Refitting

14 Refitting is the reverse of the removal procedure, noting the following points:
  a) *When lifting the tank back into position, make sure the mounting rubbers are correctly positioned, and take care to ensure none of the hoses get trapped between the tank and vehicle body.*
  b) *Ensure that all pipes and hoses are correctly routed, are not kinked, and are securely held in position with their retaining clips.*
  c) *Align the previously-made marks when refitting the rear axle.*
  d) *Tighten all fasteners to their specified torque where given.*
  e) *On completion, refill the tank with fuel, and exhaustively check for signs of leakage prior to taking the vehicle out on the road.*

9.4 Fuel supply hose (A) and return (B) – DOHC engine shown

9.6 Ensure the tandem pump pinion engages correctly with the drive slot in the camshaft

9 Tandem fuel pump – removal and refitting

Note: *A tandem fuel pump is only fitted to PD unit injection engines.*

Removal

1 Remove the air cleaner housing as described in Section 2.

2 Pull the plastic cover on the top of the engine upwards to release the mountings.

3 Release the retaining clip (where fitted) and disconnect the brake servo pipe from the tandem pump.

4 Disconnect the fuel supply hose (marked white) from the tandem pump **(see illustration)**. Be prepared for fuel spillage.

5 Unscrew the four retaining bolts and move the tandem pump away from the cylinder head. As the pump is lifted up, disconnect the fuel return hose (marked blue). Be prepared for fuel spillage. There are no serviceable parts within the tandem pump. If the pump is faulty, it must be renewed.

Refitting

6 Reconnect the fuel return hose to the pump and refit the pump to the cylinder head, using new rubber seals, and ensuring that the pump pinion engages correctly with the drive slot in the camshaft **(see illustration)**.

7 Refit the pump retaining bolts, and tighten them to the specified torque.

8 Re-attach the fuel supply hose and brake servo hose to the pump.

9 The remainder of refitting is a reversal of removal. Upon completion, attach a hand-held vacuum pump to the return outlet from the pump, and operate the pump until a steady stream of fuel appears from the outlet. Start the engine and check for leaks.

10 Turbocharger – general information, removal and refitting

General information

1 A turbocharger is fitted to all engines in

10.9 Turbocharger oil supply pipe union (arrowed)

10.10 Undo the bolts (arrowed) and remove the turbocharger support bracket

10.11 Return pipe bolts (arrowed). Note the O-ring seals where the pipe slides into the support bracket (arrowed)

this Manual, and it is integral with the exhaust manifold. Lubrication is provided by an oil supply pipe that runs from the engine oil filter mounting. Oil is returned to the sump by a return pipe that connects to the side of the cylinder block. The turbocharger unit has an integral wastegate valve and vacuum actuator diaphragm or electric servo motor, which is used to control the boost pressure applied to the intake manifold.

2 The turbocharger's internal components rotate at a very high speed, and as such are very sensitive to contamination; a great deal of damage can be caused by small particles of dirt, particularly if they strike the delicate turbine blades.

Caution: Thoroughly clean the area around all oil pipe unions before disconnecting them, to prevent the ingress of dirt. Store dismantled components in a sealed container to prevent contamination. Cover the turbocharger air intake ducts to prevent debris entering, and clean using lint-free cloths only.

Removal

3 Apply the handbrake, then jack up the front of the vehicle and support it on axle stands (see *Jacking and vehicle support*). Remove the engine compartment undershield **(see illustration 3.18)**.

4 Remove the air cleaner housing as described in Section 2.

5 Remove the right-hand driveshaft as described in Chapter 8.

6 Remove the front subframe/steering rack as described in Chapter 10.

7 Undo the nuts/bolts and remove the heat shields form the turbocharger (as applicable).

8 Remove the particulate filter/catalytic converter (as applicable) as described in Chapter 4B.

9 Unscrew the union nut and disconnect the oil supply pipe from the turbocharger **(see illustration)**. Release the oil supply pipe supporting bracket from its mounting point.

10 Undo the bolts/nuts, and remove the support bracket from the underside of the turbocharger **(see illustration)**. Note that on some models the oil return pipe fits inside the support bracket. If necessary, twist and pull the bracket from the pipe.

11 Disconnect the oil return pipe from the

turbocharger. Note that the return pipe fits inside the support bracket on some models **(see illustration)**.

12 Undo the bolts/clamp and remove the EGR pipe from the manifold and cooler **(see illustration)**.

13 Release the fasteners and detach the charge air pipe and intake pipe from the turbocharger.

14 Note their fitted positions, then disconnect the vacuum hose/wiring plug from the turbocharger wastegate control.

15 Undo the bolts/nuts securing the exhaust manifold to the cylinder head, then tilt the engine forwards a little, and lower the manifold and turbocharger assembly from place **(see illustration)**.

16 Where fitted, unscrew the exhaust gas temperature sensor from the exhaust manifold/turbocharger **(see illustration)**.

17 The turbocharger is integral with the

exhaust manifold. If defective, the complete assembly must be renewed.

Refitting

18 Refit the turbocharger by following the removal procedure in reverse, noting the following points:
a) Renew the gasket/seals **(see illustration)**.
b) Renew all self-locking nuts.
c) Before reconnecting the oil supply pipe, fill the turbocharger with fresh oil using an oil can.
d) Apply high-temperature grease to the turbocharger/exhaust pipe mounting studs.
e) Tighten all nuts and bolts to the specified torque where given.
f) When the engine is started after refitting, allow it to idle for approximately one minute to give the oil time to circulate around the turbine shaft bearings.

10.12 EGR cooler-to-manifold pipe (arrowed)

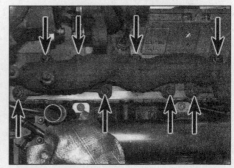

10.15 Exhaust manifold/turbocharger nuts (arrowed)

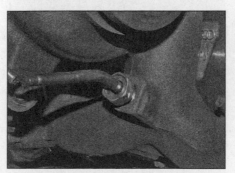

10.16 Unscrew the exhaust gas temperature sensor

10.18 Remove the banjo bolt, copper washer and O-ring (arrowed)

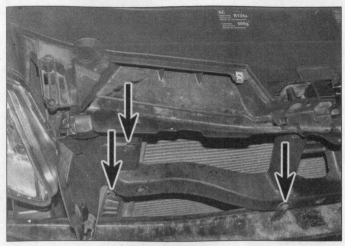

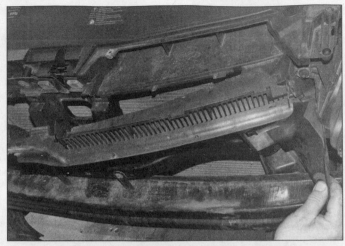

11.4a Release the clips and bolt each side (arrowed) . . .

11.4b . . . then remove the air deflector panels

11.6 Remove the intercooler mounting bolt each side (left-hand side bolt arrowed)

11.7a Undo the condenser-to-intercooler Torx bolts (upper left-hand side bolt arrowed) . . .

11.7b . . . and lift the intercooler from place

11 Intercooler – removal and refitting

Removal

1 Apply the handbrake, then jack up the front of the vehicle and support it on axle stands (see *Jacking and vehicle support*). Remove the engine compartment undershield.

2 Place the lock carrier in the 'Service position' as described in Chapter 11.

3 Remove the radiator as described in Chapter 3.

4 Release the fasteners and remove the air deflector panels above, and each side of the condenser/intercooler **(see illustrations)**.

5 On engine code BLS, disconnect the charge air pressure sensor wiring plug at the top of the intercooler.

6 Undo the intercooler mounting bolts **(see illustration)**.

7 Tip the assembly rearwards a little, then undo the 4 condenser mounting bolts and remove the intercooler upwards from its mountings **(see illustrations)**.

Refitting

8 Refitting is a reversal of removal. Note that

the hoses for the intercooler must be free from oil and grease before assembly.

12 High-pressure fuel pump – removal and refitting

Note: *A high-pressure fuel pump is only fitted to common rail injection engines.*

Removal

1 Remove the timing belt and pump sprocket as described in Chapter 2B.

2 Disconnect the fuel supply hose from the pump **(see illustration)**. Plug all openings to prevent contamination.

3 Disconnect the wiring plug from the sensor on the pump.

4 Undo the bolts securing the pump-to-common rail high-pressure pipe support brackets **(see illustration)**.

5 Pulling only under the ridge at the top of the connectors, disconnect the glow plug wiring connectors **(see illustration 5.2)**. **Note:** *Take care not to damage the connectors or wiring, as the glow plug wiring loom/connectors are only available as a complete assembly.*

6 Undo the bolts securing the coolant pipe to the intake manifold, and position the pipe to one side.

12.2 Release the clip (arrowed) and disconnect the fuel supply hose

12.4 High-pressure pipe support bracket bolts (arrowed)

12.7 Fuel pump return hose (arrowed)

12.9 Counterhold the pump hub with a C-spanner, and undo the nut

12.10a Use a two-legged puller and 8 mm bolts to pull the hub from the pump shaft

12.10b Note the locating peg (arrowed) in the pump shaft

12.12 The triangles adjacent to the pump apertures indicate fuel flow (arrowed)

7 Disconnect the fuel return pipes from the pump and the common fuel rail (see illustration).

8 Undo the unions and disconnect the high-pressure fuel pipe between the pump and common fuel rail.

9 Counterhold the pump hub using VW tool No T10051, and undo the pump hub nut. In the absence of this special tool, counterhold the hub using a suitable C-spanner (see illustration).

10 Using a suitable two-legged puller and two 8 mm bolts, remove the hub from the pump shaft (see illustrations).

11 Undo the 3 retaining bolts and remove the pump.

Refitting

12 Refitting is a reversal of removal, noting the following points:
a) Ensure all fuel pipes/hose connections are clean and free from debris.
b) The high-pressure fuel pipe from the pump to the common rail maybe re-used providing it's not been damaged.
c) Tighten all fasteners to their specified torque where given.
d) Fill the pump with clean fuel through the fuel supply pipe aperture prior to starting (see illustration).
e) Bleed the fuel system as described in Section 13.

13 Fuel system bleeding

PD unit injector engines

1 Attach a hand-held vacuum pump to the return outlet (coloured blue) from the tandem fuel pump, and operate the pump until a steady stream of fuel appears from the outlet. Start the engine and check for leaks.

Common rail engines

2 Prime the high-pressure fuel pump by

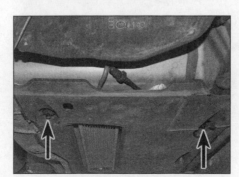

14.2 Undo the rearmost underbody panel fasteners (arrowed)

filling it with clean diesel through the fuel supply aperture (see illustration 12.12), then operate the starter for shorts bursts (no more than 10 seconds at a time) until the engine starts. Operate the engine at a fast idle (approx 2000 rpm) for several minutes before allowing it to return to its normal idle speed.

3 If the engine fails to start, it must be filled/bled using VW diagnostic equipment. Using this equipment operates the electric fuel pumps for 3 minutes.

4 Once the engine has been started, test drive the vehicle over a distance of at least 15 miles with at least one period of full acceleration. If there is any air left in the fuel system, the engine management ECM may switch to 'limp home' mode, and store a fault code. Have the fault code cleared and road test the vehicle again.

14 Fuel cooler – removal and refitting

Removal

1 Raise the right-hand side of the vehicle and support is securely on axle stands (see Jacking and vehicle support).

2 Undo the 2 rearmost fasteners and lower the underbody panelling around the fuel cooler (see illustration).

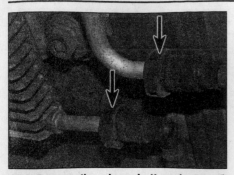

14.3 Depress the release buttons (arrowed) and pull the hoses from the cooler

3 Note their fitted positions, then depress the release buttons and disconnect the fuel feed and return hoses from the cooler **(see illustration)**. Plug the openings to prevent contamination.

4 Undo the retaining nuts and lower the cooler from place.

Refitting

5 Refitting is a reversal of removal. Check the system for leaks before refitting the underbody panelling.

Chapter 4 Part B:
Emission control and exhaust systems

Contents

Degrees of difficulty

Easy, suitable for novice with little experience	**Fairly easy,** suitable for beginner with some experience	**Fairly difficult,** suitable for competent DIY mechanic	**Difficult,** suitable for experienced DIY mechanic	**Very difficult,** suitable for expert DIY or professional

Specifications

Engine codes
Manufacturer's engine codes:*
PD unit injector engines:
   1.9 litre . . . . BKC, BLS and BXE
   2.0 litre . . . . BKP, BMA, BMR, BUZ, BVE and BWV
  Common rail injection engines . . . . CBAA, CBAB, CBAC and CBBB
* Note: *See 'Vehicle identification' at the end of this manual for the location of engine code markings.*

Emissions equipment
Exhaust Gas Recirculation system. . . . . All engines
Catalytic converter . . . . All engines
Particulate filter. . . . . PD unit injector engine codes BLS, BMR and BUZ, and all common
  rail injection engines

Torque wrench settings

	Nm	lbf ft
EGR valve to intake manifold.	10	7
Exhaust gas temperature sensor	45	33
Exhaust mounting brackets to underbody.	25	18
Front pipe to bracket	25	18
Oxygen sensor	50	37

1 General information

Emission control systems

All models have a crankcase emission control system, and in addition are fitted with a catalytic converter, and an Exhaust Gas Recirculation (EGR) system to reduce exhaust emissions. Some models are also fitted with a particulate filter in the exhaust system to further reduce harmful emissions from the exhaust (see *Specifications*).

Crankcase emission control

To reduce the emission of unburned hydrocarbons from the crankcase into the atmosphere, the engine is sealed and the blow-by gases and oil vapour are drawn from inside the crankcase, through a wire mesh oil separator, into the intake tract to be burned by the engine during normal combustion.

Under all conditions the gases are forced out of the crankcase by the (relatively) higher crank- case pressure. All engines have a pressure- regulating valve on the camshaft cover to control the flow of gases from the crankcase.

Exhaust emission control

An oxidation catalyst is fitted in the exhaust system of all models. This has the effect of removing a large proportion of the gaseous hydrocarbons, carbon monoxide and particulates present in the exhaust gas. On other models, a particulate filter is fitted. This device is designed to trap carbon particulates produced by the combustion process

An Exhaust Gas Recirculation (EGR) system is also fitted to all models. This reduces the level of nitrogen oxides produced during combustion by introducing a proportion of the exhaust gas back into the intake manifold under certain engine operating conditions, via a plunger valve. The system is controlled electronically by the engine management ECM.

Exhaust systems

On all models, the exhaust system comprises the exhaust manifold/turbocharger, front pipe and integral catalytic converter/ particulate filter, a short connecting pipe, intermediate pipe and silencer, and tailpipe and silencer. The system is supported by rubber bushes and/or rubber mounting rings.

Initially, the exhaust intermediate and rear sections are manufactured as one unit, but they are available separately as service items.

2 Crankcase emission system – general information

1 The crankcase emission control system consists of hoses connecting the crankcase to the air cleaner or intake manifold. A pressure regulating valve is fitted to all engines.
2 The system requires no attention other than to check at regular intervals that the hoses, valve and oil separator are free of blockages and in good condition.

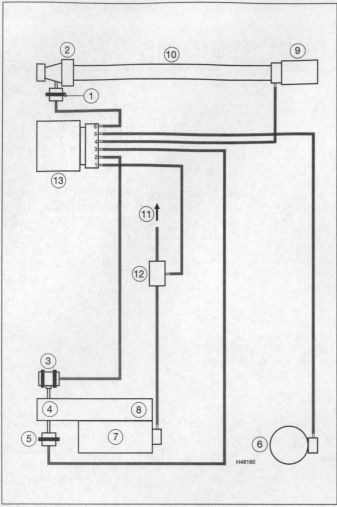

3.1a Vacuum hose layout for 1.9 litre models with no particulate filter

1	Non-return valve	6	Vacuum reservoir	10	Air filter-to-turbocharger pipe
2	Turbocharger	7	Cylinder head/block	11	To brake servo
3	EGR valve	8	Intake manifold	12	Non-return valve
4	EGR cooler	9	Air filter	13	Solenoid valve block
5	Bypass valve				

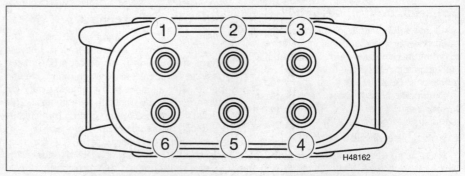

3.1b Vacuum hose layout for 1.9 litre models with a particulate filter

1	Vacuum unit	6	Bypass flap	11	To brake servo
2	Non-return valve	7	Intake manifold	12	Non-return valve
3	EGR cooler changeover valve	8	Cylinder head/block	13	Air filter-to-turbocharger pipe
4	EGR valve	9	Air filter	14	Turbocharger
5	EGR cooler	10	Charge pressure control solenoid valve		

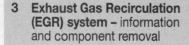

3 Exhaust Gas Recirculation (EGR) system – information and component removal

Information

1 An Exhaust Gas Recirculation (EGR) system is fitted to all engines; it consists of an EGR valve, modulator valve, delivery pipe(s), and a series of connecting vacuum hoses **(see illustrations)**.

2 The EGR valve is controlled by the engine management control unit (ECM), and is separate from the intake flap housing. On some models a cooler is fitted to the EGR pipe, with a vacuum-operated bypass valve to allow the gases to avoid being cooled when not necessary.

3.1c Solenoid valve block vacuum hose connections – PD unit injector engines (except engine codes BMR and BUZ)

1	EGR valve	5	Bypass valve
2	Air filter	6	Vacuum connection on non-return valve for the brake servo
3	Vacuum unit on turbocharger		
4	Vacuum reservoir		

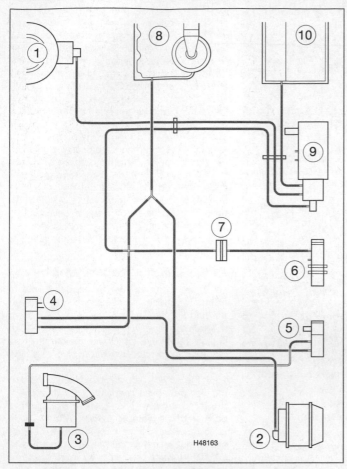

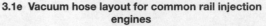

3.1d Vacuum hose layout for PD unit injector engines codes BMR and BUZ

1 Vacuum unit on turbocharger
2 Intake manifold changeover unit
3 EGR cooler changeover unit
4 Intake manifold flap air control valve
5 EGR cooler changeover valve
6 Vacuum pipe to brake servo
7 Non-return valve
8 Cylinder head cover
9 Charge pressure control solenoid valve
10 Air filter

3.1e Vacuum hose layout for common rail injection engines

1 EGR cooler changeover vacuum unit
2 Cylinder head cover
3 EGR cooler changeover valve
4 Non-return valve
5 Vacuum pump connection
6 To brake servo
7 Air filter
8 Silencer
9 Charge pressure control solenoid valve
10 Vacuum unit on turbocharger (with position sensor)

EGR valve

Removal

3 Remove the plastic cover from the top of the engine.

4 Remove the intake manifold flap housing as described in Chapter 4A.

5 Undo the bolts securing the pipe to the EGR valve (see illustration).

6 Disconnect the EGR valve vacuum hose or wiring plug as applicable.

7 Undo the bolts and detach the valve from the intake manifold. Discard the O-ring seal, a new one must be fitted.

Refitting

8 Refitting is a reversal of removal, using a new EGR valve O-ring seal, and tightening the retaining bolts to the specified torque.

EGR control valve

Removal

9 The valve controls the vacuum supply to the EGR valve. The EGR control valve is in turn controlled by the engine management ECM. The EGR control valve is located on the engine compartment bulkhead to the left of the engine.

10 Note their fitted locations, and disconnect the vacuum pipes from the control valve (see illustration).

11 Disconnect the wiring plug from the control valve.

12 Undo the two retaining bolts and remove the control valve.

Refitting

13 Refitting is a reversal of removal.

3.5 EGR pipe-to-valve bolts (arrowed)

3.10 Note their fitted locations, and disconnect the vacuum pipes from the control valve (arrowed)

5.5 The temperature and oxygen sensors connectors are located on the engine compartment bulkhead

5.6 Exhaust gas pressure sensor (arrowed)

5.7a Particulate filter/catalytic converter upper bracket (arrowed) . . .

5.7b . . . and lower bracket (arrowed)

4 Exhaust manifold – removal and refitting

The exhaust manifold is integral with the turbocharger and cannot be renewed separately. Refer to Chapter 4A for the turbocharger removal and refitting procedure details.

5 Exhaust system – component renewal

⚠️ **Warning: Allow ample time for the exhaust system to cool before starting work. In particular, note that the catalytic converter runs at very high temperatures. If there is any chance that the system may still be hot, wear suitable gloves.**

1 Each exhaust section can be removed individually, however because the system is located above the rear axle, the system cannot be removed complete.
2 To remove part of the system, first jack up the front or rear of the car and support it on axle stands (see *Jacking and vehicle support*). Alternatively, position the car over an inspection pit or on car ramps.

Catalytic converter/ particulate filter removal

3 Remove the steering rack as described in Chapter 10. Note there is no need to detach the steering gear or anti-roll bar from the subframe.
4 Slacken the clamp securing the catalytic converter/particulate filter to the turbocharger.

Models with a particulate filter

5 Trace the exhaust gas temperature sensors and oxygen sensor wiring looms back to their connectors, releasing them from any retaining clips. Note their fitted positions, then unplug the connectors **(see illustration)**.
6 Disconnect the pressure take-off pipes from the sensor at the right-hand end of the cylinder head **(see illustration)**.

All models

7 Undo the bolts/nuts and remove the upper and lower support brackets **(see illustrations)**.
8 Slacken the clamp bolts and slide the connecting sleeve between the catalytic converter/particulate filter and exhaust pipe rearwards. Remove the catalytic converter/particulate filter. Renew the seal between the filter/catalytic converter and the turbocharger.

Intermediate pipe and silencer removal

9 Working under the car, support the front pipe on an axle stand or trolley jack.

10 If the original intermediate/tail pipe is fitted, it will be necessary to cut through the middle pipe in order to separate it from the tailpipe and silencer. The pipe should have an indentation to indicate where the cut must be made before the rear silencer. Using a hacksaw, cut through the pipe at right-angles.
11 If the service pipe has been fitted, unscrew the clamp bolts and separate the intermediate pipe from the tailpipe.
12 Note the fitted position of the clamp attaching the intermediate pipe to the catalytic converter or short pipe (the bolts should be on the left-hand side of the clamp, and the lower ends of the bolts should not be below the bottom of the pipe), then unscrew the clamp bolts and separate the catalytic converter.
13 Disconnect the rubber mounting and withdraw the intermediate pipe and silencer from under the car.

Tailpipe and silencer removal

14 If the original intermediate/tail pipe is fitted, it will be necessary to cut through the middle pipe in order to separate it from the tailpipe and silencer. The pipe has an indentation to indicate where the cut must be made. Using a hacksaw, cut through the pipe at right-angles.
15 If the service pipe has been fitted, unscrew the clamp bolts and separate the tailpipe from the intermediate pipe. Note that the fitted position of the clamp should be with the bolts facing the rear of the car, and the bolt ends should not be below the bottom of the pipe.
16 Disconnect the rubber mountings and withdraw the tailpipe and silencer from under the car.

Refitting

17 Each section is refitted by a reversal of the removal sequence, noting the following points.
   a) Ensure that all traces of corrosion have been removed from the flanges or pipe ends and renew all necessary gaskets.
   b) Inspect the rubber mountings for signs of damage or deterioration and renew as necessary.
   c) Prior to tightening the exhaust system mounting, ensure that all rubber mountings are correctly located and that there is adequate clearance between the exhaust system and vehicle underbody.
   d) Renew all self-locking nuts.
   e) Apply high-temperature grease to all mounting studs.
   f) If the particulate filter or temperature sensors have been renewed, the values stored in the engine management ECM must be adapted using VW diagnostic equipment. Entrust this task to a VW dealer or suitably-equipped specialist.

Chapter 5
Starting and charging systems

Contents

Degrees of difficulty

Easy, suitable for novice with little experience	Fairly easy, suitable for beginner with some experience	Fairly difficult, suitable for competent DIY mechanic	Difficult, suitable for experienced DIY mechanic	Very difficult, suitable for expert DIY or professional

Specifications

General
System type . . . . 12 volt, negative earth

Starter motor
Type . . . . Pre-engaged

Battery
Rating . . . . 44 to 80 Ah (depending on model and market)

Alternator
Type . . . . Bosch or Valeo
Rating . . . . 90 or 120 amp
Minimum brush length . . . . 5.0 mm

Torque wrench settings

	Nm	lbf ft
Alternator connections	15	11
Alternator mounting bolt	20	15
Battery clamp bolt	15	11
Glow plug:		
PD unit injector engines	15	11
Common rail injection engines	18	13
Oil level/temperature sensor bolts	10	7
Starter motor:		
M10	40	30
M12	80	59

1 General information and precautions

The engine electrical system consists mainly of the charging, starting, and preheating systems. Because of their engine-related functions, these are covered separately from the body electrical devices such as the lights, instruments, etc, which are covered in Chapter 12.

The electrical system is of the 12 volt negative earth type.

The battery, which may be of the low maintenance or maintenance-free (sealed for life) type, is charged by the alternator, which is belt-driven from the crankshaft pulley.

The starter motor is of the pre-engaged type, with an integral solenoid. On starting, the solenoid moves the drive pinion into engagement with the flywheel ring gear before the starter motor is energised. Once the engine has started, a one-way clutch prevents the motor armature being driven by the engine until the pinion disengages from the flywheel.

Two primary earth straps are fitted; one from the battery negative terminal to the body, and

one from the engine to the body (see Chapter 12).

To assist cold starting, a preheating system is fitted which comprises four glow plugs, a glow plug control unit (incorporated in the ECM), a facia-mounted warning lamp and the associated electrical wiring.

The glow plugs are miniature electric heating elements, encapsulated in a metal or ceramic case with a probe at one end and electrical connection at the other. Each combustion chamber has a glow plug threaded into it, which is positioned directly in line with the incoming spray of fuel. When the glow plug is energised, the air in the combustion chamber is heated, allowing optimum combustion temperature to be achieved more quickly.

The duration of the preheating period is governed by the ECM, which monitors the temperature of the engine via the coolant temperature sensor and alters the preheating time to suit the conditions. Preheating only takes place at coolant temperatures below 9ºC.

A facia-mounted warning light informs the driver that preheating is taking place. The light extinguishes when sufficient preheating has taken place to allow the engine to be started, but power will still be supplied to the glow plugs for a further period until the engine is started. If no attempt is made to start the engine, the power supply to the glow plugs is switched off to prevent battery drain and glow plug burn-out. After the engine is started, there is a period of post-heating which takes place irrespective of whether it is preceded by preheating or not. This period lasts for a maximum of 4 minutes after the engine has been started, at engine speeds of under 2500 rpm. The heating is switched off after this period, or if the engine speed exceeds 2500 rpm. Post-heating reduces combustion noise and improves idling quality, and additionally reduces hydrocarbon emissions.

The warning light comes on when the ignition is initially switched on with a cold engine, and indicates that the glow plugs are being energised. If the light does not come on in these conditions, there is a defect in the glow plug system which should be investigated. When the engine is warm, the light may not come on, and the engine can be started straight away, and any post-heating will take place automatically.

Further details of the various systems are given in the relevant Sections of this Chapter. While some repair procedures are given, the usual course of action is to renew the component concerned.

⚠️ *Warning: It is necessary to take extra care when working on the electrical system to avoid damage to semi-conductor devices (diodes and transistors), and to avoid the risk of personal injury. In addition to the precautions given in 'Safety first!', observe the following when working on the system:*

• *Always remove rings, watches, etc, before working on the electrical system*. Even with the battery disconnected, capacitive discharge could occur if a component's live terminal is earthed through a metal object. This could cause a shock or nasty burn.
• *Do not reverse the battery connections*. Components such as the alternator, electronic control modules, or any other components having semi-conductor circuitry could be irreparably damaged.
• Never disconnect the battery terminals, the alternator, any electrical wiring or any test instruments when the engine is running.

• Do not allow the engine to turn the alternator when the alternator is not connected.
• Never test for alternator output by 'flashing' the output lead to earth.
• Always ensure that the battery negative lead is disconnected when working on the electrical system.
• If the engine is being started using jump leads and a slave battery, connect the batteries *negative-to-negative* and *positive-to-positive* (see *Jump starting* at the beginning of the manual). This also applies when connecting a battery charger.
• Before using electric-arc welding equipment on the car, *disconnect the battery, alternator and components such as electronic control modules* to protect them from the risk of damage.
Caution: The audio unit fitted as standard equipment has a built-in security code to deter thieves. If the power source to the unit is cut, the anti-theft system will activate. Even if the power source is immediately reconnected, the audio unit will not function until the correct security code has been entered. Therefore, if you do not know the correct security code for the radio, do not disconnect the battery negative terminal or remove the radio from the vehicle.

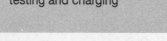

2 Battery – testing and charging

Testing

Standard and low-maintenance battery

1 If the vehicle covers a small annual mileage, it is worthwhile checking the specific gravity of the electrolyte every three months to determine the state of charge of the battery. Use a hydrometer to make the check, and compare the results with the following table. Note that the specific gravity readings assume an electrolyte temperature of 15°C; for every 10°C below 15°C subtract 0.007. For every 10°C above 15°C add 0.007.

	Ambient temperature	
	Above 25°C	Below 25°C
Fully-charged	1.210 to 1.230	1.270 to 1.290
70% charged	1.170 to 1.190	1.230 to 1.250
Discharged	1.050 to 1.070	1.110 to 1.130

2 If the battery condition is suspect, first check the specific gravity of electrolyte in each cell. A variation of 0.040 or more between any cells indicates loss of electrolyte or deterioration of the internal plates.
3 If the specific gravity variation is 0.040 or more, the battery should be renewed. If the cell variation is satisfactory but the battery is discharged, it should be charged as described later in this Section.

Maintenance-free battery

4 In cases where a sealed for life maintenance-free battery is fitted, topping-up and testing of the electrolyte in each cell is not possible. The

condition of the battery can therefore only be tested using a battery condition indicator or a voltmeter.
5 Certain models may be fitted with a maintenance-free battery with a built-in charge condition indicator. The indicator is located in the top of the battery casing and indicates the condition of the battery from its colour. If the indicator shows green, then the battery is in a good state of charge. If the indicator turns darker, eventually to black, then the battery requires charging, as described later in this Section. If the indicator shows clear/yellow, then the electrolyte level in the battery is too low to allow further use, and the battery should be renewed. **Do not** attempt to charge, load or jump start a battery when the indicator shows clear/yellow.

All battery types

6 If testing the battery using a voltmeter, connect the voltmeter across the battery and note the voltage. The test is only accurate if the battery has not been subjected to any kind of charge for the previous six hours. If this is not the case, switch on the headlights for 30 seconds, then wait four to five minutes before testing the battery after switching off the headlights. All other electrical circuits must be switched off, so check that the doors and tailgate are fully shut when making the test.
7 If the voltage reading is less than 12.2 volts, then the battery is discharged, whilst a reading of 12.2 to 12.4 volts indicates a partially-discharged condition.
8 If the battery is to be charged, remove it from the vehicle and charge it as described later in this Section.

Charging

Note: *The following is intended as a guide only. Always refer to the manufacturer's recommendations (often printed on a label attached to the battery) before charging a battery.*

Standard and low-maintenance battery

9 Charge the battery at a rate equivalent to 10% of the battery capacity (eg, for a 45 Ah battery charge at 4.5 A) and continue to charge the battery at this rate until no further rise in specific gravity is noted over a four-hour period.
10 Alternatively, a trickle charger charging at the rate of 1.5 amps can safely be used overnight.
11 Specially rapid boost charges which are claimed to restore the power of the battery in 1 to 2 hours are not recommended, as they can cause serious damage to the battery plates through overheating.
12 While charging the battery, note that the temperature of the electrolyte should never exceed 38°C.

Maintenance-free battery

13 This battery type takes considerably longer to fully recharge than the standard type, the time taken being dependent on the extent of

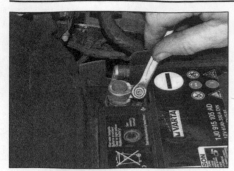

3.3 Slacken the clamp nut and disconnect the battery negative (-) lead

3.4 Slacken the clamp nut and disconnect the battery positive (+) lead

3.9 Lift the fabric type box from around the battery

discharge, but it can take anything up to three days.

14 A constant voltage type charger is required, to be set, when connected, to 13.9 to 14.9 volts with a charger current below 25 amps. Using this method, the battery should be useable within three hours, giving a voltage reading of 12.5 volts, but this is for a partially-discharged battery and, as mentioned, full charging can take far longer.

15 If the battery is to be charged from a fully-discharged state (condition reading less than 12.2 volts), have it recharged by your local automotive electrician, as the charge rate is higher and constant supervision during charging is necessary.

3 Battery –
disconnection, reconnection, removal and refitting

Note: *If the vehicle has a security-coded audio unit, check that you have a copy of the code number before disconnecting the battery cable; refer to the caution in Section 1.*

Disconnection and reconnection

1 The battery is located on the left-hand side of the engine compartment. Ensure the ignition switch is switched OFF before disconnecting the battery. **Note:** *If the battery is to be disconnected prior to airbag removal, then it must be disconnected with the ignition switch in the ON position, then wait at least 5 minutes for any residual electrical energy to dissipate before proceeding.*

2 Release the catch and remove the battery cover (where fitted).

3 Loosen the clamp nut and disconnect the battery negative (-) lead from the terminal **(see illustration)**.

4 Loosen the clamp nut and disconnect the battery positive (+) lead from the terminal **(see illustration)**.

5 Reconnection is a reversal of disconnection, ensuring the battery positive (+) lead is reconnected first. **Note:** *If the battery has been disconnected prior to airbag removal, ensure that no-one is in the passenger cabin, and the ignition is switched ON before reconnecting the battery.*

6 After both leads have been reconnected, note the following:
  a) Re-activate the audio unit by inserting the security code (where applicable).
  b) The ESP and TCS warning lights on the instrument panel may illuminate until the vehicle has been driven at 15 to 20 km/h in a straight line.
  c) Fully open and close all electric windows to the limit stops, then hold the switch until the relay audibly switches.
  d) To restore the electric window automatic opening/closing function, ensure all windows and doors are closed, then lock the vehicle via the driver's door. Now unlock the driver's door, and then lock it again –hold the key in the locking position for at least one second.

Removal

7 Disconnect the battery terminals as previously described.

8 Where fitted, disconnect the vent pipe from the battery. Note on some models the vent incorporates a flashback arrester.

9 Lift the front section of the battery surround/box from place, or lift the fabric-type box from around the battery **(see illustration)**.

10 Undo the clamp bolt **(see illustration)**.

11 Lift out the battery and withdraw it from the engine compartment.

12 If required, remove the air cleaner assembly as described in Chapter 4A, then undo the 3 bolts and remove the battery tray **(see illustration)**.

Refitting

13 Clean the battery mounting, then refit the battery in position and refit the clamp. Tighten the bolt to the specified torque.

14 Where fitted, refit the vent pipe.

15 Reconnect the battery terminals as previously described in this Section.

4 Alternator/charging system –
testing in vehicle

Note: *Refer to Section 1 of this Chapter before starting work.*

1 If the charge warning light fails to illuminate when the ignition is switched on, first check the alternator wiring connections for security. Check the condition of the auxiliary drivebelt. If all is satisfactory, the alternator maybe at fault and should be renewed or taken to an auto-electrician for testing and repair.

2 Similarly, if the charge warning light comes on with the ignition, but is then slow to go out when the engine is started, this may indicate an impending alternator problem. Check all the items listed in the preceding paragraph, and refer to an auto-electrical specialist if no obvious faults are found.

3 If the charge warning light illuminates when the engine is running, stop the engine and check that the drivebelt is correctly tensioned (see Chapter 1) and that the alternator connections are secure. If the fault persists, the alternator should be renewed, or taken to an auto-electrician for testing and repair.

3.10 Undo the battery clamp bolt (arrowed)

3.12 Undo the bolts (arrowed) and remove the battery tray

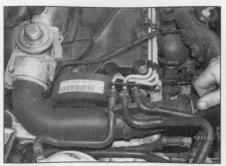

5.2a Prise out the clip and disconnect the rubber intake hose from the plastic hose

5.2b Undo the bolts (arrowed) and move the hose to one side

5.3 Undo the bolts/nut (arrowed) and move the fuel filter to one side

4 If the alternator output is suspect even though the warning light functions correctly, the regulated voltage may be checked as follows.

5 Connect a voltmeter across the battery terminals, and start the engine.

6 Increase the engine speed until the voltmeter reading remains steady; the reading should be approximately 12 to 13 volts, and no more than 14 volts.

7 Switch on as many electrical accessories as possible (eg, the headlights, heated rear window and heater blower), and check that the alternator maintains the regulated voltage at around 13 to 14 volts.

8 If the regulated voltage is not as stated, this may be due to worn brushes, weak brush springs, a faulty voltage regulator, a faulty diode, a severed phase winding or worn or damaged slip-rings. Have the alternator checked and tested by an auto-electrician.

5 Alternator – removal and refitting

Removal

1 The alternator is fitted to the right-hand front of the engine. First, disconnect the battery negative lead and position it away from the terminal – refer to Section 3. Remove the plastic cover from the top of the engine.

1.9 litre engines

2 Release the clip and disconnect the charge air rubber hose from the plastic hose above the alternator, then undo the bolts securing the plastic hose to the bracket above the alternator **(see illustrations)**.

3 Undo the bolts/nut and lift the fuel filter from place **(see illustration)**. There's no need

to disconnect the fuel hoses – place the filter to one side.

4 Remove the auxiliary drivebelt as described in Chapter 1.

2.0 litre PD unit injector engines

5 Note their fitted positions, disconnect the vacuum pipes, undo the retaining bolt and detach the vacuum reservoir, then undo the bolts and remove the bracket from the front of the engine **(see illustrations)**. Unscrew the oil level dipstick guide tube bracket at the same time.

6 On engine codes BMR and BUZ, disconnect the wiring plug and the vacuum hose and unclip the valve from above the alternator. Unclip the hose from the retaining clips, then undo the bolts securing the bracket.

7 Remove the auxiliary drivebelt as described in Chapter 1.

8 Undo the bolts/nut and lift the fuel filter from place **(see illustration 5.3)**. There's no need to disconnect the fuel hoses.

Common rail injection engines

9 Place the lock carrier in the 'Service position' as described in Chapter 11.

10 Remove the auxiliary drivebelt as described in Chapter 1.

11 Disconnect the wiring plug, undo the bolts and move the air conditioning compressor to one side. Suspend the compressor from a suitable position using wire, etc. There is no need to disconnect the refrigerant pipes.

12 Undo the nut securing the wiring loom retainer to the rear of the alternator.

13 Undo the bolts/nut and lift the fuel filter to one side **(see illustration 5.3)**. There is no need to disconnect the fuel hoses.

All engines

14 Note their fitted positions, then disconnect the wiring from the rear of the alternator **(see illustration)**. Where necessary, release the wiring loom from any clips on the rear of the alternator.

15 Support the alternator, then unscrew and remove the mounting bolts **(see illustration)**.

Refitting

16 Refitting is a reversal of removal. Refer to Chapter 1 for details of refitting the drivebelt. Tighten the alternator mounting bolts, and the wiring connections to the specified torque.

5.5a Undo the bolt (arrowed) and detach the vacuum reservoir from the bracket . . .

5.5b . . . then undo the bolt (arrowed) and remove the bracket

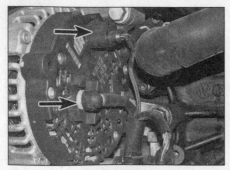

5.14 Disconnect the wiring (arrowed) from the rear of the alternator

5.15 Alternator mounting bolts (arrowed)

6.3 On the Bosch type, remove the outer cover . . .

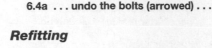

6.4a . . . undo the bolts (arrowed) . . .

6.4b . . . and remove the brush holder/regulator

6 Alternator – brush holder/voltage regulator module renewal

Removal

1 Remove the alternator, as described in Section 5.
2 Place the alternator on a clean work surface, with the pulley facing down.

Bosch

3 Undo the bolt and the two retaining nuts, and lift away the outer plastic cover (see illustration).
4 Unscrew the three securing bolts, and remove the voltage regulator (see illustrations).

Valeo

5 Prise off the spring clips, and remove the outer plastic cover (see illustration).
6 Undo the two bolts and single nut, and remove the voltage regulator (see illustrations).
7 Slide off the brush cover by depressing the lugs on each side.

Inspection

8 Measure the free length of the brush contacts (see illustration). Check the measurement with the Specifications; renew the module if the brushes are worn below the minimum limit.
9 Clean and inspect the surfaces of the slip-rings at the end of the alternator shaft (see illustration). If they are excessively worn, or damaged, the alternator must be renewed.

6.6b . . . and remove the voltage regulator

Refitting

Bosch

10 Refit the voltage regulator using a reversal of the removal procedure, tightening the bolts securely. On completion, refer to Section 5 and refit the alternator.

Valeo

11 Depress the carbon brushes into the housing, then refit the voltage regulator and tighten the bolts and nut securely. Slide on the brush cover until it is heard to engage. On completion, refer to Section 5 and refit the alternator.

7 Starting system – testing

Note: Refer to Section 1 of this Chapter before starting work.

6.5 On the Valeo type, remove the outer plastic cover . . .

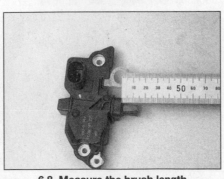

6.8 Measure the brush length

1 If the starter motor fails to operate when the ignition key is turned to the appropriate position, the following possible causes may be to blame:
a) The battery is faulty.
b) The electrical connections between the switch, solenoid, battery and starter motor are somewhere failing to pass the necessary current from the battery through the starter to earth.
c) The solenoid is faulty.
d) The starter motor is mechanically or electrically defective.

2 To check the battery, switch on the headlights. If they dim after a few seconds, this indicates that the battery is discharged – recharge (see Section 2) or renew the battery. If the headlights glow brightly, operate the ignition switch and observe the lights. If they dim, then this indicates that current is reaching the starter motor, therefore the fault must lie in

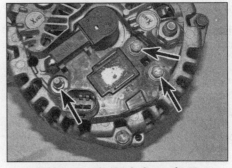

6.6a . . . undo the bolts and nut (arrowed) . . .

6.9 Clean and inspect the surfaces of the slip-rings

8.3 Disconnect the wiring plug and power lead from the starter motor

8.4 Disconnect the earth lead from the upper starter motor mounting bolt

8.6 Detach the wiring loom support bracket from the lower starter motor mounting bolt (arrowed)

the starter motor. If the lights continue to glow brightly (and no clicking sound can be heard from the starter motor solenoid), this indicates that there is a fault in the circuit or solenoid – see following paragraphs. If the starter motor turns slowly when operated, but the battery is in good condition, then this indicates that either the starter motor is faulty, or there is considerable resistance somewhere in the circuit.

3 If a fault in the circuit is suspected, disconnect the battery leads (including the earth connection to the body), the starter/ solenoid wiring and the engine/transmission earth strap. Thoroughly clean the connections, and reconnect the leads and wiring, then use a voltmeter or test light to check that full battery voltage is available at the battery positive lead connection to the solenoid, and that the earth is sound.

4 If the battery and all connections are in good condition, check the circuit by disconnecting the wire from the solenoid blade terminal. Connect a voltmeter or test light between the wire end and a good earth (such as the battery negative terminal), and check that the wire is live when the ignition switch is turned to the start position. If it is, then the circuit is sound – if not the circuit wiring can be checked as described in Chapter 12.

5 The solenoid contacts can be checked by connecting a voltmeter or test light between the battery positive feed connection on the starter side of the solenoid, and earth. When the ignition switch is turned to the start position, there should be a reading or lighted

bulb, as applicable. If there is no reading or lighted bulb, the solenoid is faulty and should be renewed.

6 If the circuit and solenoid are proved sound, the fault must lie in the starter motor. Remove the starter motor, and have it inspected by an auto-electrician.

8 Starter motor – removal and refitting

Removal

1 Disconnect the battery negative lead as described in Section 3.

2 Remove the air cleaner housing as described in Chapter 4A.

3 Slide off the protective cap, then note their fitted positions and disconnect the wiring from the starter **(see illustration)**.

4 Undo the nut and detach the earth strap from the starter mounting bolt **(see illustration)**.

5 Raise the front of the vehicle and support it securely on axle stands (see *Jacking and vehicle support*). Undo the fasteners and remove the engine undershield.

6 Undo the retaining bolts and remove the starter. Note the wiring loom support bracket shares a starter mounting bolt **(see illustration)**.

Refitting

7 Refit the starter motor by following the removal procedure in reverse. Tighten the mounting bolts to the specified torque.

10.4 Oil level/temperature sensor retaining bolts (arrowed)

9 Starter motor – testing and overhaul

If the starter motor is thought to be defective, it should be removed from the vehicle and taken to an auto-electrician for assessment. In the majority of cases, new starter motor brushes can be fitted at a reasonable cost. However, check the cost of repairs first as it may prove more economical to purchase a new or exchange motor.

10 Oil level/temperature sensor – removal and refitting

Removal

1 Where fitted, the engine oil level/ temperature sensor is located in the base of the oil sump. Apply the handbrake, then jack up the front of the vehicle and support it on axle stands (see *Jacking and vehicle support*). Undo the fasteners, and remove the engine undershield.

2 Position a container beneath the sump, then unscrew the drain plug (refer to Chapter 1) and drain the engine oil. Clean, refit, and tighten the plug after all the oil has drained.

3 Disconnect the oil level/temperature sensor wiring plug.

4 Undo the securing bolts, and lower the sensor from the sump. Discard the O-ring seal, a new one must be fitted **(see illustration)**.

Refitting

5 Clean the mating surfaces of the sensor and the sump. Smear the new O-ring seal with clean engine oil, and position it on the sensor.

6 Fit the sensor to the sump, insert the securing bolts and tighten them to the specified torque.

7 Reconnect the sensor wiring plug

8 Refit the engine undershield, lower the vehicle to the ground.

9 Refill the engine with new oil as described in the relevant part of Chapter 1. Start the engine and check for leaks.

11 Glow plugs – testing, removal and refitting

Testing

1 If the system malfunctions, testing is ultimately by substitution of known good units, but some preliminary checks may be made as described in the following paragraphs.

2 Before testing the system, check that the battery voltage is at least 11.5 volts using a voltmeter. Switch off the ignition.

3 Where necessary for access, remove the engine top cover(s). Removal details vary

11.19 Pull the connector (arrowed) from the top of the glow plug

11.23 Disconnect the wiring plugs from the injectors (arrowed)

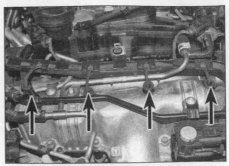

11.25 Pull the connectors (arrowed) from the top of the glow plugs

according to model, but the cover retaining nuts are concealed under circular covers, which are prised out of the main cover. Remove the nuts, and lift the cover from the engine, releasing any wiring or hoses attached.

4 Disconnect the wiring plug from the coolant temperature sender at the rear of the engine. Disconnecting the sender in this way simulates a cold engine, which is a requirement for the glow plug system to activate.

5 Disconnect the wiring connector from the most convenient glow plug, and connect a suitable voltmeter between the wiring connector and a good earth.

6 Have an assistant switch on the ignition. Battery voltage should be displayed for approximately 20 seconds – note that the voltage will drop to zero when the pre- and post-heating periods end.

7 If no supply voltage can be detected at the glow plug, then either the glow plug relay (where applicable) or the supply wiring must be faulty. Also check that the glow plug fuse or fusible link (usually located on top of the battery) has not blown – if it has, this may indicate a serious wiring fault; consult a VW dealer or specialist for advice.

8 To locate a faulty glow plug, first disconnect the battery negative cable and position it away from the terminal (see Chapter 5A).

9 Disconnect the wiring plug from the glow plug terminal. Measure the electrical resistance between the glow plug terminal and the engine earth. Ceramic glow plugs should have a resistance of no more than 1 ohm, and as a guide on metal glow plugs, more than a few ohms indicates that the plug is defective. Ceramic glow plugs are identified by a white- or silver-seal around the top of the plug. Metal plugs have a red seal around the top of the plug.

10 If a suitable ammeter is available, connect it between the glow plug and its wiring connector, and measure the steady-state current consumption (ignore the initial current surge, which will be about 50% higher). As a guide, high current consumption (or no current draw at all) indicates a faulty glow plug.

11 As a final check, remove the glow plugs and inspect their stems for signs of damage. A badly burned or charred stem may be an indication of a faulty fuel injector.

Removal – PD unit injector engines

Ceramic glow plugs

12 Ceramic glow plugs are identified by a white- or silver-seal at the top of the plug. Due to the materials used in their construction, special rules must be followed regarding their handling:

a) *Do not remove the plugs from the packaging until you are ready to fit them.*

b) *Ceramic plugs are very delicate. Protect them from knocks. VW claim that plugs which have been dropped (even from 2.0 cm) must not be fitted.*

c) *Damaged glow plugs may cause engine damage. Remove any fragments of damaged ceramic heater tips from the combustion chamber.*

d) *The software within the ECM is specific to ceramic plugs. Therefore, these type of plugs are not interchangeable with metal plugs.*

13 Remove the plastic cover on the top of the engine.

14 On the 2.0 litre engines, remove the cylinder head cover as described in Chapter 2A.

15 Carefully pull the connector(s) from the top of the glow plug(s).

16 Using a universal joint, extension and a deep 10 mm socket, unscrew and remove the glow plug(s) from the cylinder head. Note that the plug must be kept 'straight' when being removed – if the ceramic heater tip touches the cylinder head, etc, it may easily be damaged.

Metal glow plugs

17 Remove the plastic cover on the top of the engine.

18 On the DOHC engines, remove the cylinder head cover as described in Chapter 2A

19 Carefully pull the connector(s) from the top of the glow plug(s) **(see illustration)**.

20 Using a universal joint, extension and a deep 10 mm socket, unscrew and remove the glow plug(s) from the cylinder head.

Removal – common rail injection engines

21 Pull the plastic cover on the top of the engine upwards from its mountings.

22 Remove the noise insulation from above the injectors.

23 Disconnect the wiring plugs from the injectors, exhaust gas pressure sensor, and fuel rail pressure sensor **(see illustration)**.

24 Undo the retaining bolts and detach the coolant pipe from the intake manifold. Move the pipe to the front of the manifold.

25 Pull the connectors from the top of the glow plugs. Be sure to only pull on the underside of the ridge at the top of the connectors **(see illustration)**.

26 Release the clamp and disconnect the fuel return hose from the fuel rail. Be prepared for fuel spillage.

27 Push down the tabs, pull up the centre piece and disconnect the fuel return connectors from the top of the injectors **(see illustrations)**. Plug the openings to prevent contamination.

28 Move the entire fuel return pipe assembly to the front of the manifold.

11.27a Hold down the tabs (arrowed) . . .

11.27b . . . and pull up the centre piece of the fuel return connectors (arrowed)

29 Lay the glow plug wiring harness to one side.

30 Clean the area around the glow plugs. Use a vacuum cleaner if possible.

31 Using a universal joint, extension and a deep 10 mm socket, unscrew and remove the glow plug(s) from the cylinder head. Note that the plug must be kept 'straight' when being removed – if the ceramic heater tip touches the cylinder head, etc, it may easily be damaged.

Refitting

Ceramic glow plugs

32 Ensure the threads in the cylinder head and on the glow plugs are clean and dry, and free of oil or grease. Clean any combustion deposits from the area around the glow plug apertures in the cylinder head.

33 Fit the glow plugs finger-tight only, taking great care not to allow the ceramic heater tips to contact any part of the cylinder head, etc.

34 Tighten the plugs to the specified torque.

35 Using a hand-held multimeter, check the resistance of the plugs. If the resistance of any of the plugs exceeds 1 ohm, remove it and check the ceramic heater tip is not damaged. If any of the tips are damaged, the ceramic fragments must be removed from the combustion chamber before the engine is started, otherwise extensive engine damage may result.

36 Reconnect the glow plug wiring plugs.

37 VW insist that the engine management ECM self-diagnosis system must be interrogated for any stored faults relating to the glow plugs before the engine is started. If any glow plug related faults are stored, do not start the engine. Remove the plugs and inspect them for damage.

38 The remainder of refitting is a reversal of removal.

Metal glow plugs

39 Ensure the threads in the cylinder head and glow plugs are clean, then refit the plugs to the cylinder head.

40 Tighten the plugs to the specified torque.

41 Reconnect the glow plug wiring plugs.

42 The remainder of refitting is a reversal of removal.

Chapter 6
Clutch

Contents

Degrees of difficulty

Easy, suitable for novice with little experience	Fairly easy, suitable for beginner with some experience	Fairly difficult, suitable for competent DIY mechanic	Difficult, suitable for experienced DIY mechanic	Very difficult, suitable for expert DIY or professional

Specifications

General

Type:
Luk clutch .... Single dry friction disc, diaphragm spring with spring-loaded hub, self-adjusting pressure plate (SAC)
Sachs .... Single dry friction disc, diaphragm spring with spring-loaded hub
Operation .... Hydraulic with slave and master cylinders

Torque wrench settings

	Nm	lbf ft
Clutch pedal bracket mounting nuts*	25	18
Clutch pedal pivot nut*	25	18
Clutch slave cylinder mounting bolt:		
5-speed gearbox	20	15
6-speed gearbox:*		
Metal slave cylinder	12	8
Non-metallic slave cylinder	15	10
Hydraulic pipe unions	15	11
Pressure plate-to-flywheel bolt:		
M6	13	10
M7	20	15

* Use new fasteners

1 General information

The clutch is of single dry plate type, incorporating a diaphragm spring pressure plate, and is hydraulically-operated.

The clutch cover (pressure plate) is bolted to the rear face of the flywheel, and the friction disc is located between the pressure plate and the flywheel friction surface. The disc hub is splined to the transmission input shaft and is free to slide along the splines. Friction lining material is riveted to each side of the disc and the disc hub incorporates cushioning springs to absorb transmission shocks and ensure a smooth take-up of drive. The flywheel is manufactured in two parts instead of the conventional single unit; the friction surface has a limited buffered movement in relation to the main flywheel mass bolted to the rear of the crankshaft. This has the effect of absorbing the initial clutch engagement shock and makes for a smoother gearchange.

When the clutch pedal is depressed, the slave cylinder pushrod moves the release lever forwards (on 5-speed gearboxes) or the concentric slave cylinder acts directly upon the release bearing (6-speed gearboxes), and the release bearing is forced onto the diaphragm spring fingers. As the centre of the spring is pushed in, the outer part of the spring moves out and releases the pressure plate from the friction disc. Drive then ceases to be transmitted to the transmission.

When the clutch pedal is released, the diaphragm spring forces the pressure plate into contact with the linings on the friction disc, and at the same time pushes the disc slightly forward along the input shaft splines into engagement with the flywheel. The friction disc is now firmly sandwiched between the pressure plate and flywheel. This causes drive to be taken up.

An over-centre spring is fitted to the clutch pedal to equalise the operating effort over the full pedal stroke.

As the linings wear on the friction disc, the pressure plate rest position moves closer to the flywheel resulting in the 'rest' position of the diaphragm spring fingers being raised. Some vehicles may have a self-adjusting clutch (SAC) fitted. On these units, as the friction disc wears, an adjustment ring of varied thickness within the pressure plate assembly rotates slightly to compensate. This should ensure a more consistent feel to the clutch pedal. The hydraulic system requires no adjustment since the quantity of hydraulic fluid in the circuit automatically compensates for wear every time the clutch pedal is operated.

2.10a Clutch slave cylinder bleed screw (arrowed) – 5-speed transmission . . .

2 Hydraulic system – bleeding

Warning: Hydraulic fluid is poisonous; thoroughly wash off spills from bare skin without delay. Seek immediate medical advice if any fluid is swallowed or gets into the eyes. Certain types of hydraulic fluid are inflammable and may ignite when brought into contact with hot components. Hydraulic fluid is also an effective paint stripper. If spillage occurs onto painted bodywork or fittings, it should be washed off immediately, using copious quantities of cold water. It is also hygroscopic (it absorbs moisture from the air) therefore old fluid should never be re-used.

1 The correct operation of any hydraulic system is only possible after removing all air from the components and circuit; this is achieved by bleeding the system.

2 During the bleeding procedure, add only clean, unused hydraulic fluid of the recommended type; never re-use fluid that has already been bled from the system. Ensure that sufficient fluid is available before starting work.

3 If there is any possibility of incorrect fluid being already in the system, the hydraulic circuit must be flushed completely with uncontaminated, correct fluid.

4 If hydraulic fluid has been lost from the system, or air has entered because of a leak, ensure that the fault is cured before continuing further.

2.10b . . . and 6-speed transmission (arrowed)

5 The bleed screw is located on the slave cylinder located on the left-hand upper side of the transmission. As access to the bleed screw is limited it will be necessary to remove the air cleaner assembly as described in Chapter 4A.

6 Check that all pipes and hoses are secure, unions tight and the bleed screw is closed. Clean any dirt from around the bleed screw.

7 Unscrew the master cylinder fluid reservoir cap (the clutch shares the same fluid reservoir as the braking system), and top the master cylinder reservoir up to the upper (MAX) level line. Refit the cap loosely, and remember to maintain the fluid level at least above the lower (MIN) level line throughout the procedure, or there is a risk of further air entering the system.

8 There are a number of one-man, do-it-yourself bleeding kits currently available from motor accessory shops. It is recommended that one of these kits is used whenever possible, as they greatly simplify the bleeding operation, and reduce the risk of expelled air and fluid being drawn back into the system. If such a kit is not available, the basic (two-man) method must be used, which is described in detail below.

9 If a kit is to be used, prepare the vehicle as described previously, and follow the kit manufacturer's instructions, as the procedure may vary slightly according to the type being used; generally, they are as outlined below in the relevant sub-section.

Bleeding

Basic (two-man) method

10 Collect a clean glass jar, a suitable length of plastic or rubber tubing which is a tight fit over the bleed screw (see illustrations), and a ring spanner to fit the screw. The help of an assistant will also be required.

11 Remove the dust cap from the bleed screw. Fit the spanner and tube to the screw, place the other end of the tube in the jar, and pour in sufficient fluid to cover the end of the tube.

12 Ensure that the fluid level is maintained at least above the lower level line in the reservoir throughout the procedure.

13 Have the assistant fully depress the clutch pedal several times to build-up pressure, then maintain it on the final downstroke.

14 While pedal pressure is maintained, unscrew the bleed screw (approximately one turn) and allow the compressed fluid and air to flow into the jar. The assistant should maintain pedal pressure and should not release it until instructed to do so. When the flow stops, tighten the bleed screw again, have the assistant release the pedal slowly, and recheck the reservoir fluid level.

15 Repeat the steps given in paragraphs 13 and 14 until the fluid emerging from the bleed screw is free from air bubbles. If the master cylinder has been drained and refilled allow approximately five seconds between cycles for the master cylinder passages to refill.

16 When no more air bubbles appear, tighten the bleed screw securely, remove the tube

and spanner, and refit the dust cap. Do not overtighten the bleed screw.

Using a one-way valve kit

17 As their name implies, these kits consist of a length of tubing with a one-way valve fitted, to prevent expelled air and fluid being drawn back into the system; some kits include a translucent container, which can be positioned so that the air bubbles can be more easily seen flowing from the end of the tube.

18 The kit is connected to the bleed screw, which is then opened. The user returns to the driver's seat, depresses the clutch pedal with a smooth, steady stroke, and slowly releases it; this is repeated until the expelled fluid is clear of air bubbles.

19 Note that these kits simplify work so much that it is easy to forget the fluid reservoir level; ensure that this is maintained at least above the lower level line at all times.

Using a pressure-bleeding kit

20 These kits are usually operated by the reservoir of pressurised air contained in the spare tyre. However, note that it will probably be necessary to reduce the pressure to a lower level than normal; refer to the instructions supplied with the kit.

21 By connecting a pressurised, fluid-filled container to the fluid reservoir, bleeding can be carried out simply by opening the bleed screw and allowing the fluid to flow out until no more air bubbles can be seen in the expelled fluid.

22 This method has the advantage that the large reservoir of fluid provides an additional safeguard against air being drawn into the system during bleeding.

All methods

23 When bleeding is complete, and correct pedal feel is restored, tighten the bleed screw securely and wash off any spilt fluid. Refit the dust cap to the bleed screw.

24 Check the hydraulic fluid level in the master cylinder reservoir, and top-up if necessary (see *Weekly checks*).

25 Discard any hydraulic fluid that has been bled from the system; it will not be fit for re-use.

26 Check the operation of the clutch pedal. If the clutch is still not operating correctly, air must still be present in the system, and further bleeding is required. Failure to bleed satisfactorily after a reasonable repetition of the bleeding procedure may be due to worn master cylinder/release cylinder seals.

3 Clutch pedal – removal and refitting

Removal

1 Remove the facia as described in Chapter 11. Note that in theory, it's possible to remove the pedal bracket after having removed the panel above the pedals, but in practice, access is so restricted as to make

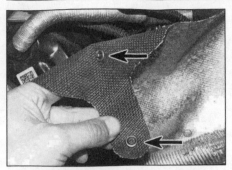

3.3 The heat shield fasteners 'pop' apart

3.4 Disconnect the fluid supply pipe from the brake master cylinder (arrowed)

3.5 Prise out the clip (arrowed) a little and disconnect the pressure pipe

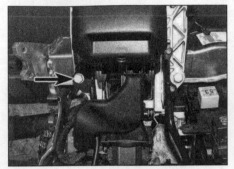

3.7 Undo the bolt (arrowed) and remove the crash bar

3.8 Pedal assembly retaining nuts (arrowed)

3.10 Depress the clip (arrowed) on each side of the pedal

the task virtually impossible. Therefore we recommend the removal of the facia.

2 Remove the battery as described in Chapter 5. This is to allow access to the clutch master cylinder pipes at the engine compartment bulkhead.

3 Release the fastener and pull the heat shield away from the engine compartment bulkhead to access the clutch master cylinder (see illustration).

4 Disconnect the fluid supply pipe for the clutch master cylinder at the brake master cylinder fluid reservoir (see illustration).

5 Prise out the clip and pull the fluid pressure pipe from the clutch master cylinder. Plug the openings to prevent contamination (see illustration).

6 Disconnect the wiring plug from the clutch position sensor on the cylinder.

7 Undo the bolt and remove the crash bar from under the facia (see illustration).

8 Undo the 3 nuts and remove the pedal assembly, complete with master cylinder (see illustration).

9 Holding the pedal bracket in a vice, undo the retaining nut and slide the pedal pivot bolt from place. Ease the pedal from the bracket and remove the over-centre spring. Note the bush at the pedal end of the over-centre spring.

10 Lower the clutch pedal, depress the clip each side, and disconnect the master cylinder pushrod from the pedal (see illustration).

Refitting

11 Refitting is a reversal of removal. Renew any self-locking nuts, and bleed the hydraulic system as described in Section 2.

4 Master cylinder – removal, overhaul and refitting

Note: Refer to the warning at the beginning of Section 2 regarding the hazards of working with hydraulic fluid.

Removal

1 Remove the clutch pedal mounting bracket as described in Section 3.

2 Compress the clips each side and separate the clutch master cylinder pushrod from the pedal (see illustration 3.10).

3 Insert a 40 mm spacer (eg, a socket) between the clutch pedal and the stop.

4 Release the clip, rotate the master cylinder anti-clockwise and pull it from the bracket.

Overhaul

5 At the time of writing, it would appear repair kits are not available. Check with your local VW dealer or parts specialist.

Refitting

6 Refitting is a reversal of removal, but tighten all nuts and bolts to the specified torques where given. When repositioning the pedal bracket onto the bulkhead, have an assistant guide the clutch master cylinder through the location hole from the engine compartment side. When reconnecting the fluid pressure line, the clip must engage audibly. Bleed the clutch hydraulic system as described in Section 2.

5 Slave cylinder – removal, overhaul and refitting

Note: Refer to the warning at the beginning of Section 2 regarding the hazards of working with hydraulic fluid.

Note: A new slave cylinder mounting bolt will be required.

Removal

5-speed gearbox

1 The slave cylinder is located on top of the transmission on the left-hand side.

2 Remove the battery and battery tray as described in Chapter 5.

3 Remove the retaining clips and disconnect the gear selector cables from the pins on the levers (see illustration).

5.3 Slide off the retaining clips (arrowed)

5.4 Undo the bolts (arrowed) securing the gearchange cable bracket

5.6 Remove the support bracket above the slave cylinder

5.9 Undo the slave cylinder retaining bolts (arrowed)

5.11 Prise up the clip (arrowed) and pull the bleed screw connection assembly from place

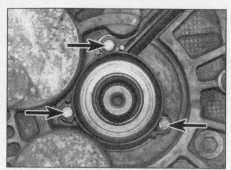

5.12 Slave cylinder/release bearing retaining bolts (arrowed)

4 Undo the 3 bolts and move the gearchange cable support bracket (complete with cables) to one side, to access the slave cylinder **(see illustration)**.
5 Remove the slave cylinder pressure pipe support bracket from the transmission casing.
6 Undo the bolts and remove the transmission support bracket above the slave cylinder **(see illustration)**.
7 Clamp the rubber section of the hydraulic hose leading from the master cylinder to the slave cylinder using a brake hose clamp to prevent loss of hydraulic fluid.
8 Using a screwdriver, prise out the spring clip and disconnect the hydraulic line from the slave cylinder. Tape over or plug the end of the line and the slave cylinder aperture.
9 Unscrew the mounting bolts and withdraw the slave cylinder **(see illustration)**.

Caution: Do not depress the clutch pedal with the slave cylinder removed.

6-speed gearbox

10 Remove the transmission as described in Chapter 7A.
11 Prise out the retaining clip and pull the bleed screw connection assembly from the slave cylinder **(see illustration)**.
12 Undo the 3 retaining bolts and remove the slave cylinder along with the release bearing **(see illustration)**. Note that the cylinder is integral with the release bearing. Renew the retaining bolts.

Overhaul

13 At the time of writing, it would appear that slave cylinder overhaul kits are not available. Check with your local VW dealer or spare parts specialist.

Refitting

14 Refitting is a reversal of removal, noting the following points:
a) *Tighten all fasteners to their specified torque where given.*
b) *Adjust the gearchange cables as described in Chapter 7A (where applicable).*
c) *Bleed the clutch hydraulic system as described in Section 2.*

| 6 | Clutch friction disc and pressure plate – removal, inspection and refitting | |

> ⚠ *Warning: Dust created by clutch wear and deposited on the clutch components may contain asbestos, which is a health hazard. DO NOT blow it out with compressed air or inhale any of it. DO NOT use petrol or petroleum-based solvents to clean off the dust. Brake system cleaner or methylated spirit should be used to flush the dust into a suitable receptacle. After the clutch components are wiped clean with clean rags, dispose of the contaminated rags and cleaner in a sealed container.*

Removal

1 Access to the clutch is obtained by removing the transmission as described in Chapter 7A.
2 Mark the clutch pressure plate and flywheel in relation to each other.
3 Hold the flywheel stationary, then unscrew the clutch pressure plate bolts ¼ of a turn at a time **(see illustration)**. With the bolts unscrewed two or three turns, check that the pressure plate is not binding on the dowel pins. If necessary, use a screwdriver to release the pressure plate. On models with the Sachs clutch, as the bolts are removed the stop-pin must slacken. If it doesn't, press the pin towards the flywheel **(see illustration)**.
4 Remove all the bolts, then lift the clutch pressure plate and friction disc from the flywheel.

Inspection

Note: *Due to the amount of work necessary*

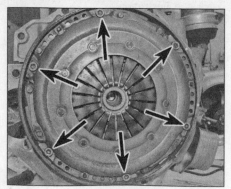

6.3a Undo the pressure plate retaining bolts (arrowed)

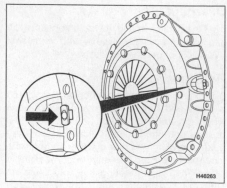

6.3b Ensure the stop-pin is free to move

to remove and refit clutch components, it is usually considered good practice to renew the clutch friction disc, pressure plate assembly and release bearing as a matched set, even if only one of these is actually worn enough to require renewal. It is also worth considering the renewal of the clutch components on a preventative basis if the engine and/or transmission have been removed for some other reason.

5 Clean the pressure plate friction surface, clutch friction disc and flywheel. Do not inhale the dust, as it may contain asbestos which is dangerous to health.

6 Examine the fingers of the diaphragm spring for wear or scoring. If the depth of wear exceeds half the thickness of the fingers, a new pressure plate assembly must be fitted.

7 Examine the pressure plate for scoring, cracking, distortion and discoloration. Light scoring is acceptable, but if excessive, a new pressure plate assembly must be fitted. If the distortion of the friction surface exceeds 1.0 mm, renew it.

8 Examine the friction disc linings for wear and cracking, and for contamination with oil or grease. The linings are worn excessively if they are worn down to, or near, the rivets. Check the disc hub and splines for wear by temporarily fitting it on the transmission input shaft. Renew the friction disc as necessary.

9 Examine the flywheel friction surface for scoring, cracking and discoloration (caused by overheating). If excessive, it may be possible to have the flywheel machined by an engineering works, otherwise it should be renewed.

10 Ensure that all parts are clean, and free of oil or grease, before reassembling. Apply just a small amount of lithium-based grease (VW No G000100) to the splines of the friction disc hub. **Do not** use copper-based grease. Note that new pressure plates and clutch covers may be coated with protective grease. It is only permissible to clean the grease away from the friction disc lining contact area. Removal of the grease from other areas will shorten the service life of the clutch.

Refitting

11 Commence reassembly by locating the friction disc on the flywheel, with the raised side of the hub facing outwards (normally marked 'Getriebeseite' or 'Gearbox side'). If possible, the centralising tool (see paragraph 19) should be used to hold the disc on the flywheel at this stage **(see illustration)**.

Self-adjusting clutch (SAC)

12 On models with a self-adjusting clutch (SAC), where a new friction disc is fitted, but the pressure plate is to be re-used, it is necessary to reset the pressure plate adjusting ring prior to assembly as follows.

13 Insert three 8 mm bolts into the pressure plate mounting holes at intervals of 120°. The bolts should be inserted from the flywheel side, and retained by nuts **(see illustration)**.

14 Place the pressure plate face down on the bed of an hydraulic press so that only

6.11 The friction disc should be marked 'Getriebeseite' or 'Gearbox side'

the heads of the bolts make contact with the press bed, then place a circular spacer over the ends of the diaphragm springs fingers.

15 Use 2 screwdrivers to attempt to rotate the adjuster ring anti-clockwise. Apply just enough pressure with the hydraulic press until it's just possible to move the adjuster ring **(see illustration)**.

16 Once the adjuster ring edges are between the notches, relieve the pressure. The ring is now reset. **Note:** *New pressure plates are supplied in this reset position.*

All models

17 Locate the clutch pressure plate on the disc, and fit it onto the location dowels **(see illustration)**. If refitting the original pressure plate, make sure that the previously-made marks are aligned.

18 Insert the bolts finger-tight to hold the pressure plate in position.

19 The friction disc must now be centralised,

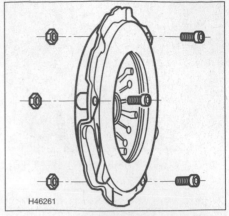

6.13 Insert three 8 mm bolts from the flywheel side, and secure with nuts

to ensure correct alignment of the transmission input shaft with the disc centre. To do this, a proprietary tool may be used, or alternatively, use a wooden mandrel made to fit inside the friction disc and the hole in the centre of the crankshaft. Insert the tool through the friction disc into the crankshaft, and make sure that it is central.

20 Tighten the pressure plate bolts progressively and in diagonal sequence, until the specified torque setting is achieved, then remove the centralising tool **(see illustration)**.

21 Check the release bearing in the transmission bellhousing for smooth operation, and if necessary renew it with reference to Section 7.

22 Refit the transmission with reference to Chapter 7A.

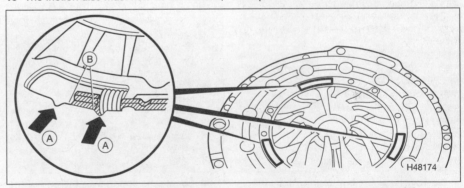

6.15 The edges of the adjuster ring (B) must be between the notches (A)

6.17 Fit the pressure plate over the locating dowel pins (arrowed)

6.20 With the pressure plate bolts tightened, remove the centralising tool

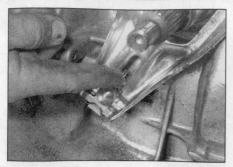

7.2a Push the spring clip to release the arm from the ball-stud

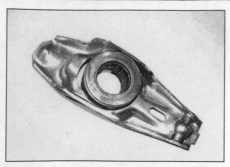

7.2b Release lever and bearing removed from the transmission

7.3a Depress the retaining tabs . . .

7.3b . . . and remove the release bearing from the arm

7 Release bearing and lever – removal, inspection and refitting

Note: *The following only applies to models with a 5-speed transmission.*

7.5 Lubricate the ball-stud with a little grease

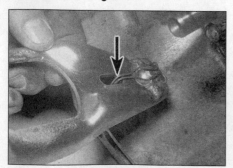

7.6b . . . and press the spring into the hole . . .

Removal

1 Remove the transmission (See Chapter 7A).
2 Use a screwdriver to prise the release lever from the ball-stud inside the transmission bell-housing. If this proves difficult, push the spring clip from the pivot end of the release lever by pushing it through the hole. This will release the

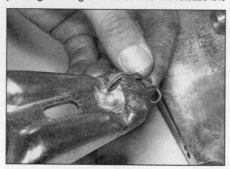

7.6a Locate the spring over the end of the release lever . . .

7.6c . . . then press the release lever onto the ball-stud until the spring clip holds it in position

pivot end of the lever from the ball-stud. Now withdraw the lever together with the release bearing from the guide sleeve **(see illustrations)**.
3 Use a screwdriver to depress the plastic tabs and separate the bearing from the lever **(see illustrations)**.

Inspection

4 Spin the release bearing by hand, and check it for smooth running. Any tendency to seize or run rough will necessitate renewal of the bearing. If it is to be re-used, wipe it clean with a dry cloth; on no account should the bearing be washed in a liquid solvent, otherwise the internal grease will be removed.

Refitting

5 Commence refitting by lubricating the ball-stud and plastic pivot with a little lithium-based grease (VW No G000100) **(see illustration)**. Smear a little grease on the release bearing surface which contacts the diaphragm spring fingers and the release lever, and also on the guide sleeve. Wipe off any excess grease.
6 Fit the spring onto the release lever, and make sure the plastic pivot is in place on the ball-stud. Refit the lever together with the bearing and press the release lever onto the ball-stud until the spring holds it in position **(see illustrations)**.

8 Clutch pedal position sensor – removal and refitting

Removal

1 Pull the plastic cover on the top of the engine upwards from its mountings.
2 On models with a particulate filter, undo the nuts and remove the heat shield from the filter. Remove the insulation mat (where fitted).
3 Undo the fasteners and remove the heat shield over the clutch master cylinder pipes/hoses **(see illustration 3.3)**.
4 Disconnect the wiring plug from the clutch position sensor on the cylinder.
5 Push the clip to the side, and slide the sensor downwards from the master cylinder **(see illustration)**.

Refitting

6 Refitting is a reversal of removal.

8.5 Press the clip (arrowed) to the side and lower the sensor from the master cylinder

Chapter 7 Part A:
Manual transmission

Contents

Degrees of difficulty

Easy, suitable for novice with little experience	**Fairly easy,** suitable for beginner with some experience	**Fairly difficult,** suitable for competent DIY mechanic	**Difficult,** suitable for experienced DIY mechanic	**Very difficult,** suitable for expert DIY or professional

Specifications

General

Type	Transversely-mounted, front-wheel-drive layout with integral transaxle differential/final drive, 5 or 6 forward speeds and 1 reverse
Application:	
1.9 litre models	5-speed transmission (0A4)
2.0 litre models	6-speed transmission (02Q)

Torque wrench settings

	Nm	lbf ft
Gearchange bracket	20	15
Reversing light switch	20	15
Selector lever	23	17
Transmission to engine:		
M12 bolts	80	59
M10 bolt	40	30

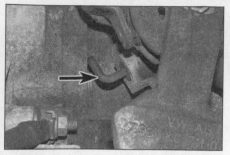

2.2 Pull the collar down and lock in position

2.3 Push down the selector shaft, then push the locking pin (arrowed) inwards whilst turning it clockwise

2.4 Lock the gear lever in position using a drill bit (arrowed)

1 General information

The manual transmission is bolted directly to the left-hand end of the engine. This layout has the advantage of providing the shortest possible drive path to the front wheels, as well as locating the transmission in the airflow through engine bay, optimising cooling. The unit is cased in aluminium alloy.

Drive from the crankshaft is transmitted through the clutch to the gearbox input shaft, which is splined to accept the clutch friction disc.

All forward gears are fitted with synchromesh. The floor-mounted gear lever is connected to the gearbox by shift cable. Levers on the transmission actuate internal selector forks which are connected to the synchromesh sleeves. The sleeves are locked to the gearbox shafts but can slide axially by means of splined hubs, and they press baulk rings into contact with the respective gear/pinion. The coned surfaces between the baulk rings and the pinion/gear act as a friction clutch, that progressively matches the speed of the synchromesh sleeve (and hence the gearbox shaft) with that of the gear/pinion. This allows gearchanges to be carried out smoothly.

Drive is transmitted to the differential crownwheel, which rotates the differential case and planetary gears, thus driving the sun gears and driveshafts. The rotation of the differential planetary gears on their shaft allows the inner roadwheel to rotate at a slower speed than the outer roadwheel during cornering.

2 Gearchange linkage – adjustment

1 Remove the air cleaner housing as described in Chapter 4A.
2 With the gearchange set in the neutral position, push the two locking collars (one on each cable) forwards to compress the springs, turn them clockwise (looking from the driver's seat) to lock into position **(see illustration)**.
3 Press down on the selector shaft on the top of the transmission, and push the locking pin into the transmission while turning it clockwise until it engages and the selector shaft cannot move **(see illustration)**.
4 Working inside the vehicle, unclip the gear lever gaiter from the centre console. Still in the neutral position, insert the locking pin (or drill bit) through the hole in the base of the gear lever and into the hole in the housing **(see illustration)**.
5 Working back in the engine bay, turn the two locking collars on the cables anti-clockwise so that the springs will release them back into position and lock the cables.
6 With the cable adjustment set, the locking pin can now be turned anti-clockwise to its original position.
7 Inside the vehicle, remove the locking pin from the gear lever, then check the operation of the selector mechanism. When the gear lever is at rest in neutral, it should be central, ready to select 3rd or 4th. The gear lever gaiter can now be refitted to the centre console.
8 Refit the air cleaner housing as described in Chapter 4A.

3 Manual transmission – removal and refitting

Removal

1 Select a solid, level surface to park the vehicle upon. Give yourself enough space to move around it easily. Apply the handbrake and chock the rear wheels.
2 Raise the front of the vehicle and support it securely on axle stands (see *Jacking and vehicle support*). Where fitted, remove the engine/transmission undershield **(see illustration)**. Position a suitable container beneath the transmission, then unscrew the drain plug and drain the transmission oil.
3 Remove the air cleaner assemble as described in Chapter 4A.
4 Remove the battery and battery tray with reference to Chapter 5.
5 Prise off the clips and disconnect the gear selector cables from the gear selector levers. Note that on some models, the left-hand cable is not retained by a clip, and must be prised from place. Extract the clip and remove the relay lever, then unscrew the nut and remove the selector lever from the top of the transmission. Unscrew and remove the gearchange cables bracket **(see illustrations)**.

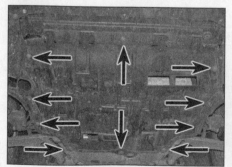

3.2 Release the fasteners (arrowed) and remove the engine undershield

3.5a Prise up the edge (arrowed) and slide the retaining clip to one side

3.5b Gearchange cables bracket bolts/nut (arrowed)

6 On 5-speed transmissions, undo the gearbox support bracket, then unscrew the clutch slave cylinder from the transmission and place to one side.

7 On 6-speed transmissions, seal the slave cylinder flexible hose using a hose clamp, then prise out the clip and pull the fluid pipe from the bleeder connection on the slave cylinder **(see illustration)**.

8 Unscrew the earth cable from the transmission or vehicle body **(see illustration)**.

9 Disconnect the wiring from the reversing light switch, and the neutral position sensor (vehicles with Stop-Start system only).

10 Unscrew and remove the upper bolts securing the transmission to the engine.

11 With reference to Chapter 5, remove the starter motor.

12 Remove the lower left-hand wheel arch liner.

13 Unscrew the driveshaft protective cover.

14 Remove both driveshafts as described in Chapter 8.

15 With reference to Chapter 4B, loosen the clamp and slide the connecting tube between the front and rear sections of the exhaust pipe. This will allow the engine to be moved forwards and backwards during the transmission removal and alignment procedures.

16 Remove the steering gear as described in Chapter 10. Note there is no need to detach the steering gear or anti-roll bar from the subframe.

17 Where applicable, unscrew the cover plate from the transmission bellhousing **(see illustration)**.

18 Using a suitable hoist, support the weight of the engine.

19 Unscrew the bolts securing the transmission mounting to the bracket on the transmission, then unscrew the mounting bracket from the transmission **(see illustration)**.

20 Lower the engine/transmission assembly slightly and, using a trolley jack, support the transmission. Position the jack so that it can be withdrawn from the left-hand side of the car.

21 Unscrew and remove the remaining lower transmission-to-engine mounting bolts, including the bolt located on the left-hand rear of the engine.

22 Carefully pull the transmission directly away from the engine, taking care not to allow its weight to rest on the clutch friction disc hub. A second person is helpful to pull the engine as far forwards as possible.

⚠️ **Warning: Support the transmission to ensure that it remains steady on the jack head. Keep the transmission level until the input shaft is fully withdrawn from the clutch friction disc.**

23 When the transmission is clear of the locating dowels and clutch components, lower the transmission to the ground and withdraw from under the car.

3.7 Prise up the clip a little and pull the hose from the bleeder connection

3.8 Earth cable (arrowed)

Refitting

24 Refitting the transmission is essentially a reversal of the removal procedure, but note the following points:

a) Apply a smear of high melting-point grease (VW No G000100) to the clutch friction disc hub splines; take care to avoid contaminating the friction surfaces.

b) In order to align the transmission with the flywheel, gently pull the engine forward as the transmission is manoeuvred into place.

c) Tighten the transmission-to-engine bolts to the specified torque.

d) Refer to the relevant part of Chapter 2 and tighten the engine mounting bolts to the correct torque.

e) Refer to Chapter 8 and tighten the driveshaft bolts to the specified torque.

f) On completion, refer to Section 2 and check the gearchange linkage/cable adjustment.

g) Refill the transmission with the correct grade and quantity of oil. Refer to 'Lubricants and fluids' and Chapter 1.

4 Manual transmission overhaul – general information

The overhaul of a manual transmission is a complex (and often expensive) task for the DIY home mechanic to undertake, which requires access to specialist equipment. It involves dismantling and reassembly of many small components, measuring clearances precisely and if necessary adjusting them by selecting shims and spacers. Internal transmission components are also often difficult to obtain and in many instances, extremely expensive. Because of this, if the transmission develops a fault or becomes noisy, the best course of action is to have the unit overhauled by a specialist repairer or to obtain an exchange reconditioned unit.

Nevertheless, it is not impossible for the more experienced mechanic to overhaul the transmission if the special tools are available and the job is carried out in a deliberate step-by-step manner, to ensure nothing is overlooked.

The tools necessary for an overhaul include internal and external circlip pliers, bearing pullers, a slide hammer, a set of pin punches, a dial test indicator and possibly a hydraulic press. In addition, a large, sturdy workbench and a vice will be required.

During dismantling of the transmission, make careful notes of how each component is fitted to make reassembly easier and accurate.

Before dismantling the transmission, it will help if you have some idea of where the problem lies. Certain problems can be closely related to specific areas in the transmission, which can make component examination and renewal easier. Refer to the *Fault finding* Section in this manual for more information.

3.17 Undo the bolt (arrowed) and remove the cover plate

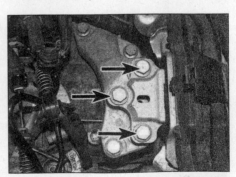

3.19 Mounting-to-bracket bolts (arrowed)

5 Reversing light switch –
testing, removal and refitting

Testing

1 Ensure that the ignition switch is turned to the OFF position.
2 Unplug the wiring harness from the reversing light switch at the connector. The switch is located on the front/top of the casing.
3 Connect the probes of a continuity tester, or multimeter set to the resistance measurement function, across the terminals of the reversing light switch.
4 The switch contacts are normally open, so with any gear other than reverse selected, the tester/meter should indicate an open circuit or infinite resistance. When reverse gear is selected, the switch contacts should close, causing the tester/meter to indicate continuity or zero resistance.

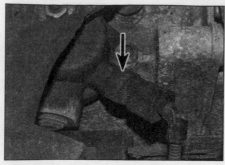

5.7a Reversing light switch (arrowed) – 5-speed transmission . . .

5 If the switch does not operate correctly, it should be renewed.

Removal

6 Ensure that the ignition switch is turned to the OFF position.
7 Unplug the wiring harness from the

5.7b . . . and 6-speed transmission (arrowed)

reversing light switch at the connector **(see illustrations)**.
8 Unscrew the switch from the transmission casing, and recover the sealing ring.

Refitting

9 Refitting is a reversal of removal.

Chapter 7 Part B:
Automatic transmission

Contents

Degrees of difficulty

| Easy, suitable for novice with little experience | Fairly easy, suitable for beginner with some experience | Fairly difficult, suitable for competent DIY mechanic | Difficult, suitable for experienced DIY mechanic | Very difficult, suitable for expert DIY or professional |

Specifications

General
Description . . . . DSG (Direct Shift Gearbox) semi-automatic 6-speed transmission with dual multi-plate clutch, and differential

Transmission type number 02E

Torque wrench settings

	Nm	lbf ft
Transmission-to-engine bolts:		
M10 bolts	40	30
M12 bolts	80	59
Transmission mounting spacer-to-bracket bolts:*		
Stage 1	60	44
Stage 2	Angle-tighten a further 90°	
Transmission mounting spacer-to-casing bolts:*		
Stage 1	40	30
Stage 2	Angle-tighten a further 90°	

* Do not re-use

1 General information

The VW type 02E semi-automatic DSG (Direct Shift Gearbox) has six forward speeds (and one reverse). In contrast to traditional automatic transmissions where a fluid flywheel (torque converter) transmits the power from the engine to the gearbox, the DSG has two multiplate clutches. The twin-clutch transmission is essentially two separate gearboxes with a pair of clutches between them. One gearbox provides odd-numbered speeds (first, third and fifth gear), the other provides even-numbered speeds (second, fourth and sixth). Initially, the 'odd' gearbox is in first gear and the 'even' gearbox is in second gear. The clutch engages the odd gearbox and the car proceeds in first gear. To change to second gear, the transmission uses the clutches to switch from the odd gearbox to the even gearbox. The odd gearbox immediately pre-selects third gear. At the next change the transmission swaps gearboxes again, engaging third gear, and the even gearbox pre-selects fourth gear. The transmission ECM (Electronic Control Module) calculates the next likely gearchange based on vehicle speed and driver behaviour and has the 'idle' gearbox pre-select that gear. The main advantages of the DSG is near-instant gearchanges, with seamless, highly efficient drive, resulting in less exhaust emissions and fuel consumption.

A fault diagnosis system is integrated into the control unit, but analysis can only be undertaken with specialised equipment. It is important that any transmission fault be identified and rectified at the earliest possible opportunity. A VW dealer or suitably-equipped specialist can 'interrogate' the ECM fault memory for stored fault codes, enabling him to pin-point the fault quickly. Once the fault has been corrected and any fault codes have been cleared, normal transmission operation is restored.

Because of the need for special test equipment, the complexity of some of the parts, and the need for scrupulous cleanliness when these transmissions, the work which the owner can do is limited. Most major repairs and overhaul operations should be left to a VW dealer or specialist, who will be equipped with the necessary equipment for fault diagnosis and repair. The information in this Chapter is therefore limited to a description of the removal and refitting of the transmission as a complete unit. The removal, refitting and adjustment of the selector cable is also described.

In the event of a transmission problem occurring, consult a VW dealer or transmission specialist before removing the transmission from the vehicle, since the majority of fault diagnosis is carried out with the transmission in situ.

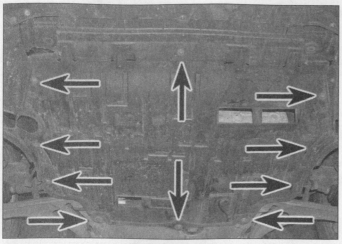

2.2 Undo the fasteners (arrowed) and remove the engine undershield

2.7 Selector cable clip and outer cable circlip (arrowed)

2 Transmission – removal and refitting

Removal

1 The automatic transmission is removed downwards from the engine compartment. First, select a solid, level surface to park the vehicle upon. Give yourself enough space to move around it easily. Select P, apply the handbrake, and chock the rear wheels.

2 Loosen the front wheel bolts, and the driveshaft hub bolts, then raise the front of the vehicle and rest it securely on axle stands (see *Jacking and vehicle support*). Remove the front wheels. Allow a suitable working clearance underneath for the eventual withdrawal of the transmission. Undo the fasteners and remove the engine/transmission undershield **(see illustration)**.

3 Remove the air cleaner housing as described in Chapter 4A.

4 Remove the turbocharger intake hose.

5 Remove the battery and battery tray as described in Chapter 5.

6 Remove the starter motor as described in Chapter 5.

7 Remove the retaining clip, lever off the end of the selector cable from the selector shaft

lever, then prise up the circlip and remove the outer cable from the support bracket. Position the cable to one side. Note that both the retaining clip and circlip must be renewed **(see illustration)**.

8 Clamp off the automatic transmission fluid cooler hoses with brake hose type clamps. Release the retaining clips and detach the hoses from the cooler (located on the top of the transmission) **(see illustration)**.

9 Rotate the collar anti-clockwise and disconnect the transmission wiring plug **(see illustration)**. Undo the nuts and detach the wiring loom retainer from the gearbox cover.

10 Remove the upper engine-to-transmission mounting bolts.

11 Release the clips and remove the air hose between the intercooler and the charge air pipe.

12 Remove the radiator cooling fan assembly as described in Chapter 3.

13 Disconnect the wiring plug from the engine oil level/temperature sensor on the sump.

14 Undo the bolts securing the exhaust pipe front mounting bracket to the subframe.

15 Undo the bolts and slide rearwards the tubular exhaust pipe connecting piece between the front and rear sections of the exhaust system.

16 Remove both driveshafts as described in Chapter 8.

17 Undo the bolts and remove the engine rear mounting (torque arm). Position a block of wood between the sump and the subframe to prevent the engine from swinging rearwards.

18 Support the engine with a hoist or support bar located on the front wing inner channels. Depending on the engine, temporarily remove components as necessary to attach the hoist.

19 Position a trolley jack underneath the transmission, and raise it to just take the weight of the unit.

20 Undo and remove the bolts securing the left-hand gearbox mounting to the mounting spacer, and the bolts securing the spacer to the transmission casing. By controlling both the engine hoist/support bar and the trolley jack, lower the transmission approximately 60 mm. Remove the transmission mounting spacer.

21 Remove the transmission-to-engine bolt located in the starter motor aperture.

22 Undo the retaining bolt and remove the small cover plate located above the right-hand driveshaft flange.

23 Lower the engine/transmission until there is sufficient clearance between the upper edge of the transmission and the left-hand chassis member.

24 Unscrew and remove the lower bolts securing the transmission to the engine, noting the bolt locations, as they are of different sizes and lengths.

25 Check that all the fixings and attachments are clear of the transmission. Enlist the aid of an assistant to help in guiding and supporting the transmission during its removal.

26 The transmission is located on engine alignment dowels, and if stuck on them, it may be necessary to carefully tap and prise the transmission free of the dowels to allow separation. Once the transmission is disconnected from the location dowels, swivel the unit out and lower it out of the vehicle.

2.8 Clamp the transmission cooler hoses (arrowed)

2.9 Transmission wiring plug and earth cable (arrowed)

 Warning: Support the transmission to ensure that it remains steady on the jack head.

4.2 Slacken the cable adjustment bolt (arrowed)

5.2 Prise up the selector lever gaiter surround trim

5.3 Press down the yellow plastic wedge (arrowed)

Refitting

27 Refitting is a reversal of the removal procedure, but note the following special points:

a) *Apply a little high-temperature grease (VW No G052133A2) to the needle bearing in the crankshaft.*

b) *When reconnecting the transmission to the engine, ensure that the location dowels are in position, and that the transmission is correctly aligned with them before pushing it fully into engagement with the engine.*

c) *Tighten all retaining bolts to their specified torque wrench settings.*

d) *Be sure to guide the selector cable into the support bracket as the transmission is refitted – renew the retaining clips.*

e) *Adjust the selector cable, as described in Section 4.*

f) *On completion, check the transmission fluid level and coolant level (see Chapter 1).*

g) *If a new transmission unit has been fitted, it may be necessary to have the transmission ECM 'matched' to the engine management ECM electronically, to ensure correct operation – seek the advice of your VW dealer or suitably-equipped specialist.*

3 Transmission overhaul – general information

In the event of a fault occurring, it will be necessary to establish whether the fault is electrical, mechanical or hydraulic in nature, before repair work can be contemplated. Diagnosis requires detailed knowledge of the transmission's operation and construction, as well as access to specialised test equipment, and so is deemed to be beyond the scope of this manual. It is therefore essential that problems with the automatic transmission are referred to a VW dealer or specialist for assessment.

Note that a faulty transmission should not be removed before the vehicle has been assessed by a dealer or specialist, as fault diagnosis is carried out with the transmission in situ.

4 Selector cable – removal, refitting and adjustment

Removal

1 Move the selector lever to the S position, and remove the battery and battery tray as described in Chapter 5.

2 Slacken the adjustment bolt on the cable end fitting at the transmission end **(see illustration)**.

3 Prise out the clips securing the cable to the lever on the transmission, and the outer cable to the support bracket. Discard the clips – new ones must be fitted.

4 Pull the cable from the lever and support bracket on the transmission.

5 Raise the front of the vehicle and support it securely on axle stands (see *Jacking and vehicle support*).

6 Separate the exhaust downpipe from the intermediate pipe with reference to Chapter 4B.

7 Remove the centre tunnel heat shield from the underside of the vehicle to gain access to the selector lever housing.

8 Undo the securing nuts and remove the cover from the selector lever housing.

9 Remove the clip securing the outer cable to the selector lever housing.

10 Push the retaining tab forwards, then using a screwdriver from beneath, push out the pin from the selector cable end fitting. Remove the cable.

Refitting

11 Refit the selector cable by reversing the removal procedure, noting the following points:

a) **Do not** grease the cable end fittings. This is stated by VW.

b) *Ensure that the cable is correctly routed, as noted on removal, and that it is securely held by its retaining clips.*

c) *Take care not to bend or kink the cable.*

d) *Carry out the cable adjustment procedure described below before reconnecting the cable at the transmission end.*

e) *When refitting the outer cable to the selector lever housing and the support bracket, use new clips.*

Adjustment

12 Inside the car, move the selector lever to the P position.

13 At the transmission, slacken the cable adjusting bolt at the ball socket. Check that both the selector lever inside the car and the lever on the transmission are in their P positions by gently rocking them backwards and forwards to settle the cable. Do not move either lever out of the P position.

14 Tighten the cable locking bolt.

15 Verify the operation of the selector lever by shifting through all gear positions and checking that every gear can be selected smoothly and without delay.

5 Emergency release of selector lever

1 If the vehicle's battery is disconnected or discharged, it is possible to release the selector lever from its locked position. First, ensure the handbrake is fully applied.

2 Carefully prise up the selector lever gaiter surround trim from the console and move it to the left-hand side **(see illustration)**.

3 Press the yellow plastic wedge downwards **(see illustration)**. It should now be possible to move the selector lever to the desired position.

Notes

Chapter 8
Driveshafts

Contents

Degrees of difficulty

| **Easy,** suitable for novice with little experience | | **Fairly easy,** suitable for beginner with some experience | | **Fairly difficult,** suitable for competent DIY mechanic | | **Difficult,** suitable for experienced DIY mechanic | | **Very difficult,** suitable for expert DIY or professional | |

Specifications

General

Driveshaft type	Steel shafts with outer constant velocity joints and inner tripod or constant velocity joints (according to type)
Type code differences:	
VL 100	CV joints each end, inner joint diameter 100 mm bolted to transmission drive flanges on each side
VL 107	CV joints each end, inner joint diameter 107 mm bolted to drive flange on transmission
AAR 2600i	CV outer joint, tripod inner joint located in housing splined to sun gear
AAR 3300i	CV outer joint, tripod inner joint housing bolted to transmission drive flange or splined to sun gear

Lubrication

Overhaul and repair	Use only special grease supplied in sachets with gaiter/overhaul kits; joints are otherwise pre-packed with grease and sealed
Joint grease quantity:	
Outer joint	80 g
Inner joint	130 g

Torque wrench settings

	Nm	lbf ft
Driveshaft-to-transmission flange bolts:*		
Stage 1	10	7
Stage 2:		
M8	40	30
M10	70	52
Hub bolt:*		
Hexagon (6-sided) bolt:		
Stage 1	200	148
Stage 2	Angle-tighten a further 180°	
12-sided bolt:		
Stage 1	70	52
Stage 2	Angle-tighten a further 90°	
Lower arm-to-balljoint nuts:*		
Cast steel lower arm	60	44
Sheet steel or aluminium lower arm	100	74
Wheel bolts	120	89

Use new bolt/nuts

1 General information

Drive is transmitted from the differential to the front wheels by means of two steel driveshafts of either solid or hollow construction (depending on model). Both driveshafts are splined at their outer ends, to accept the wheel hubs, and are secured to the hub by a large bolt. The inner end of each driveshaft is either bolted to a transmission drive flange or splined directly into the differential sun gear.

Ball-bearing type constant velocity (CV) joints are fitted to the outer ends of each driveshaft, to ensure the smooth and efficient transmission of drive at all the angles possible as the roadwheels move up-and-down with the suspension, and as they turn from side-to-side under steering.

Plastic gaiters are fitted over both CV joints with steel clips. The gaiters contain the grease which lubricates the joints, and also protect the joints from the entry of dirt and debris.

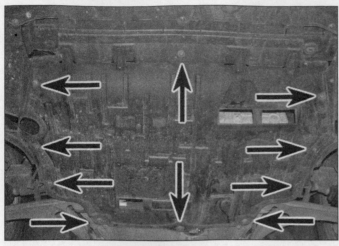

2.3a Undo the fasteners and remove the undershield (arrowed)

2.3b Remove the heat shield (arrowed)

2 Driveshafts – removal and refitting

Removal

1 Remove the wheel trim/hub cap (as applicable) then apply the handbrake, and partially unscrew, by a maximum of 90°, the relevant hub bolt with the vehicle resting on its wheels – note that the bolt is very tight, and a suitable extension bar will probably be required to aid unscrewing. Also unscrew the roadwheel securing bolts. **Note:** *Do not loosen the bolt more than 90° with the vehicle standing on the ground, as the wheel bearings may be damaged.*

2 Apply the handbrake, then jack up the front of the vehicle and support it on axle stands (see *Jacking and vehicle support*). Remove the appropriate front roadwheel.

3 Remove the fasteners, and remove the undertray from beneath the engine/transmission unit to gain access to the driveshafts. Where necessary, also unscrew the heat shield above the right-hand inner joint to improve access **(see illustrations)**.

4 Unscrew and remove the hub bolt **(see illustration)**. **Note:** *Discard the bolt and obtain a new one.*

5 Unscrew the three nuts securing the front suspension lower arm balljoint to the lower arm. Discard the nuts as new ones must be used on refitting.

6 Lever the lower arm downwards to release it from the balljoint studs, then pull the hub carrier outwards, and at the same time withdraw the driveshaft outer constant velocity joint from the hub. If the joint splines are a tight fit in the hub, tap the joint out of the hub using a soft-faced mallet and drift. If this fails to free the driveshaft from the hub, the joint will have to be pressed out using a suitable tool bolted to the hub.

7 Proceed as follows according to type.

Caution: Support the driveshaft by suspending it with wire or string – do not allow it to hang under its own weight, or the joint may be damaged.

Inner joint with drive flange

8 Using a multi-splined tool, unscrew and remove the bolts securing the inner driveshaft joint to the transmission flange and, where applicable, recover the retaining plates from underneath the bolts **(see illustration)**. Discard the bolts – new ones must be fitted.

Inner joint splined to sun gear

9 Position a container beneath the transmission to catch spilt oil, then pull out the driveshaft. The internal driveshaft circlip may be tight in the transmission side gear, in which case careful use of a lever against the transmission casing will be required. Lever against a block of wood to prevent damage to the casing, and take care not to damage the oil seal as the driveshaft is being removed. **Note:** *Pull only on the inner joint housing, not the driveshaft itself, otherwise the gaiter/joint may be damaged.*

All types

10 Manoeuvre the driveshaft out from underneath the vehicle and (where fitted) recover the gasket from the end of the inner constant velocity joint. **Note:** *Discard the gasket and obtain a new one.*

Caution: Do not allow the vehicle to rest on its wheels with one or both driveshaft(s) removed, as damage to the wheel bearings may result.

11 If moving the vehicle is unavoidable, temporarily insert the outer end of the driveshaft(s) in the hub(s), and tighten the driveshaft retaining bolt(s); in this case, the inner end(s) of the driveshaft(s) must be supported, for example by suspending with string from the vehicle underbody.

Refitting

12 Where applicable, check the condition of the circlip on the inner end of the driveshaft, and if necessary, renew it.

13 As applicable, clean the splines on each

2.4 Undo the driveshaft/hub bolt

2.8 Driveshaft inner joint and flange bolts (arrowed)

2.14 Locate a new gasket on the inner joint

end of the driveshaft and in the hub and apply a little oil, and where applicable wipe clean the oil seal in the transmission casing. Check the oil seal and if necessary renew it. Smear a little oil on the lips of the oil seal before fitting the driveshaft.

Inner joint with drive flange

14 Ensure that the transmission flange and inner joint mating surfaces are clean and dry. Where necessary, fit a new gasket to the joint by peeling off its backing foil and sticking it in position **(see illustration)**.
15 Manoeuvre the driveshaft into position, and align the inner joint holes with those on the transmission flange. Fit the new retaining bolts and where necessary, the plates. Tighten the retaining bolts in a diagonal pattern to the specified torque.

Inner joint splined to sun gear

16 Locate the inner end of the driveshaft into the transmission – turn the driveshaft as necessary to engage the splines. Press in the

driveshaft until the internal circlip engages the groove. Check that the circlip is engaged by attempting to pull out the driveshaft with only moderate force.

All types

17 With the lower arm levered downwards, engage the outer joint with the hub. Fit the new hub bolt and use it to draw the joint fully into position.
18 Align the balljoint studs with the holes in the lower arm, then release the arm and fit the three new nuts. Tighten the nuts to the specified torque.
19 Tighten the driveshaft bolt to the Stage 1 torque (see *Specifications*). **Note:** *The bolt must be tightened with the wheel clear of the ground.*
20 Refit the roadwheel and lower the vehicle to the ground, then angle-tighten the driveshaft bolt through the Stage 2 angle (see *Specifications*).
21 Once the driveshaft bolt is correctly tightened, tighten the wheel bolts to the specified torque and refit the wheel trim/hub cap.

3 Driveshaft rubber gaiters – renewal

1 Remove the driveshaft from the car, as described in Section 2. Continue as described under the relevant sub-heading. Driveshafts with a tripod type inner joint can be identified by the shape of the inner CV joint; the driveshaft retaining bolt holes are in extensions from the joint, giving it a six-pointed star-shaped exterior, in contrast to the smooth, circular shape of the ball-and-cage joint **(see illustrations)**.

Outer CV joint gaiter

2 Secure the driveshaft in a vice equipped with soft jaws, and release the two outer joint gaiter retaining clips **(see illustration)**. If necessary, the retaining clips can be cut to release them.
3 Slide the rubber gaiter down the shaft to

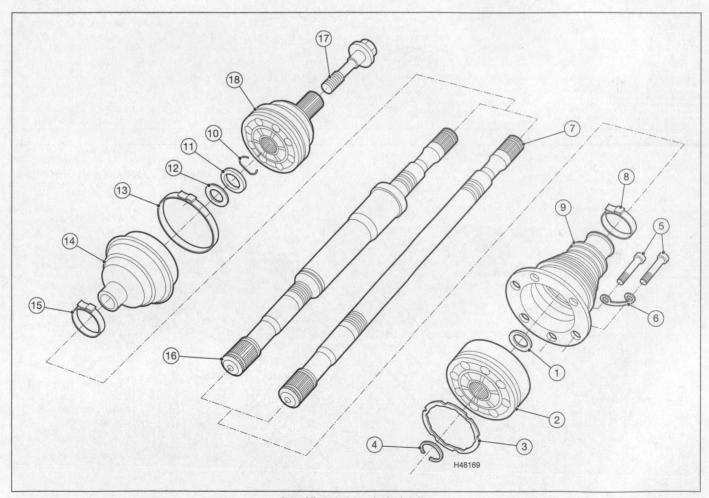

3.1a VL 100 driveshaft details

1 Dished spring	4 Circlip	7 Left-hand driveshaft	10 Circlip	14 Gaiter	17 Bolt
2 Inner constant velocity joint	5 Bolts	8 Clamp	11 Thrustwasher	15 Clamp	18 Outer constant velocity joint
3 Seal	6 Retaining plate	9 Gaiter	12 Dished spring 13 Clamp	16 Right-hand driveshaft	

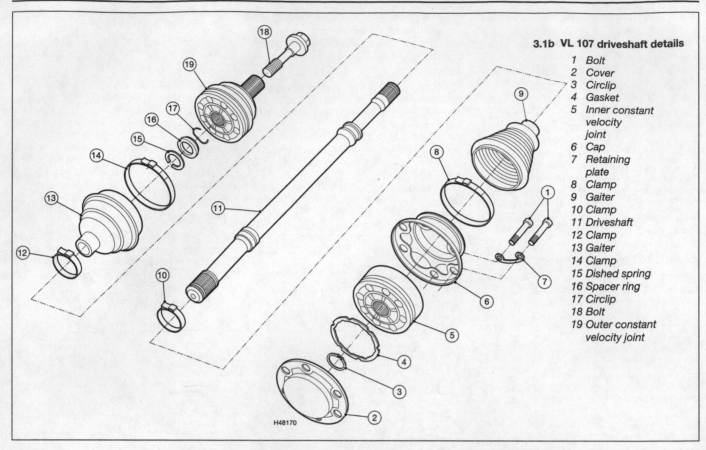

3.1b VL 107 driveshaft details

1 Bolt
2 Cover
3 Circlip
4 Gasket
5 Inner constant velocity joint
6 Cap
7 Retaining plate
8 Clamp
9 Gaiter
10 Clamp
11 Driveshaft
12 Clamp
13 Gaiter
14 Clamp
15 Dished spring
16 Spacer ring
17 Circlip
18 Bolt
19 Outer constant velocity joint

H48170

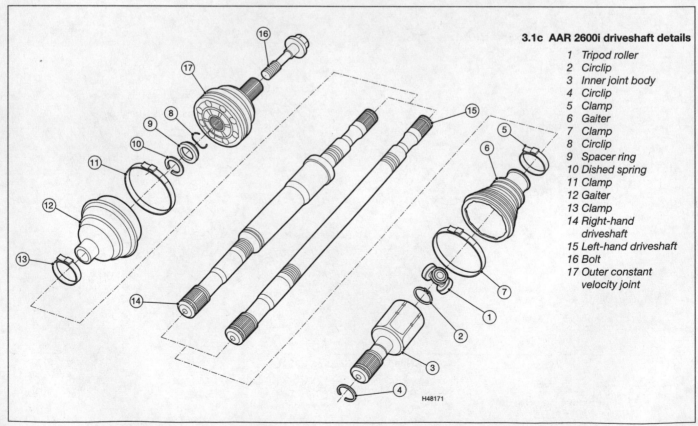

3.1c AAR 2600i driveshaft details

1 Tripod roller
2 Circlip
3 Inner joint body
4 Circlip
5 Clamp
6 Gaiter
7 Clamp
8 Circlip
9 Spacer ring
10 Dished spring
11 Clamp
12 Gaiter
13 Clamp
14 Right-hand driveshaft
15 Left-hand driveshaft
16 Bolt
17 Outer constant velocity joint

H48171

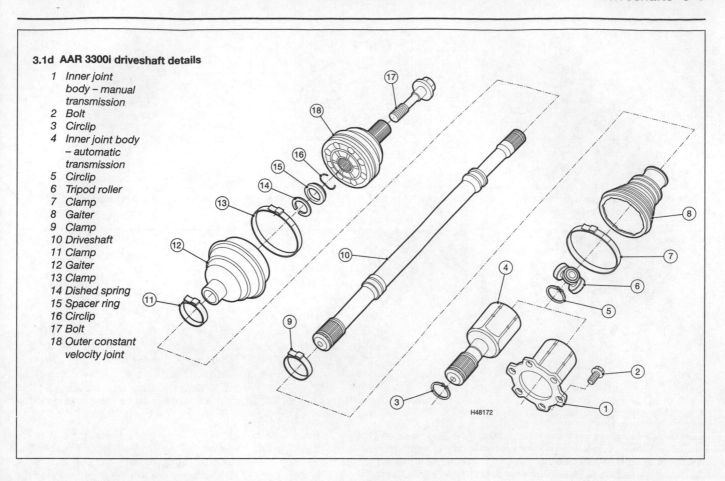

3.1d AAR 3300i driveshaft details

1 Inner joint body – manual transmission
2 Bolt
3 Circlip
4 Inner joint body – automatic transmission
5 Circlip
6 Tripod roller
7 Clamp
8 Gaiter
9 Clamp
10 Driveshaft
11 Clamp
12 Gaiter
13 Clamp
14 Dished spring
15 Spacer ring
16 Circlip
17 Bolt
18 Outer constant velocity joint

H48172

expose the constant velocity joint, and scoop out excess grease **(see illustration)**.

4 Using a soft-faced mallet, tap the joint off the end of the driveshaft **(see illustration)**.

5 Remove the circlip from the driveshaft groove, and slide off the thrustwasher/spacer ring and dished washer, noting which way around it is fitted **(see illustration)**.

6 Slide the rubber gaiter off the driveshaft and discard it **(see illustration)**.

7 Thoroughly clean the constant velocity joint(s) using paraffin, or a suitable solvent, and dry thoroughly. Carry out a visual inspection as follows.

8 Move the inner splined driving member from

3.2 Release the outer joint gaiter clips . . .

3.3 . . . and slide the gaiter away from the joint

3.4 Use a mallet to drive the outer joint from the driveshaft

3.5 Remove the circlip, thrustwasher and dished washer

3.6 Remove the outer gaiter

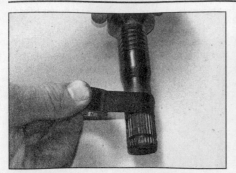

3.11 Temporarily tape over the splines to protect the new gaiter

3.14a Pack half of the grease in the joint . . .

3.14b . . . and the remaining half in the gaiter

3.15a Fit a new circlip . . .

3.15b . . . then refit the outer joint

3.16 Seat the gaiter on the outer joint and driveshaft, then lift its inner lip to equalise the air pressure

side-to-side to expose each ball in turn at the top of its track. Examine the balls for cracks, flat spots or signs of surface pitting.

9 Inspect the ball tracks on the inner and outer members. If the tracks have widened, the balls will no longer be a tight fit. At the same time, check the ball cage windows for wear or cracking between the windows.

10 If on inspection any of the constant velocity joint components are found to be worn or damaged, it will be necessary to renew the complete joint assembly. If the joint is in satisfactory condition, obtain a new gaiter and retaining clips, a constant velocity joint circlip and the correct type of grease. Grease is usually supplied with the joint repair kit – if not, use a good-quality molybdenum disulphide grease.

11 Tape over the splines on the end of the driveshaft to protect the new gaiter as it is slid into place (see illustration).

12 Slide the new gaiter onto the end of the driveshaft, then remove the protective tape from the driveshaft splines.

13 Slide on the dished washer, making sure its convex side is innermost, followed by the thrustwasher.

14 Pack the joint with half the quantity of grease. Work the grease well into the bearing tracks whilst twisting the joint, and fill the rubber gaiter with the remaining half (see illustrations).

15 Fit a new circlip to the driveshaft, then tap the joint onto the driveshaft until the circlip engages in its groove (see illustrations). Make sure that the joint is securely retained by the circlip.

16 Ease the gaiter over the joint, and ensure that the gaiter lips are correctly located on both the driveshaft and constant velocity joint. Lift the outer sealing lip of the gaiter to equalise air pressure within the gaiter (see illustration).

17 Fit the large metal retaining clip to the gaiter. Pull the clip as tight as possible, and locate the hooks on the clip in their slots. Remove any slack in the gaiter retaining clip by carefully compressing the raised section of the clip. In the absence of the special tool, a pair of side-cutters may be used, taking care not to cut the clip (see illustrations). Secure the small retaining clip using the same procedure.

18 Check the constant velocity joint moves freely in all directions, then refit the driveshaft to the vehicle, as described in Section 2.

Tripod inner CV joint gaiter

19 Release the two outer joint gaiter retaining clips. If necessary, the retaining clips can be cut to release them. Slide the rubber gaiter down the shaft, away from the joint outer member.

20 Carefully secure the joint outer member in a vice equipped with soft jaws.

21 Scoop out excess grease from the joint, then on models with a splined inner joint, remove the circlip from the groove in the end of the joint splined member.

22 Using a suitable marker pen or a scriber, make alignment marks between the end of the driveshaft, the tripod roller assembly, and the outer member.

23 Support the driveshaft and the joint, and withdraw the outer member from the vice. As the assembly is removed from the vice, make sure that the rollers do not fall off the tripod.

24 Slowly slide the joint outer member down

3.17a Fit the large metal retaining clip . . .

3.17b . . . and use a suitable tool to tighten it

the driveshaft, away from the joint, making sure that the rollers stay on the tripod.

25 Mark the rollers and the arms of the tripod, so that the rollers can be refitted in their original positions, then lift off the rollers and place them to one side on a dry, clean surface.

26 Remove the circlip from the end of the driveshaft.

27 Press or drive the driveshaft from the tripod, taking great care not to damage the surfaces of the roller locating arms.

28 Slide the outer member and the rubber gaiter from the end of the driveshaft.

29 Thoroughly clean the joint components using paraffin, or a suitable solvent, and dry thoroughly. Carry out a visual inspection as follows.

30 Inspect the tripod rollers and the joint outer member for signs of wear, pitting or scuffing on their mating surfaces. Check that the joint rollers rotate smoothly, with no traces of roughness **(see illustration)**.

31 If the rollers or outer member shown signs of wear or damage, it will be necessary to renew the complete driveshaft, since the joint is not available separately. If the joint is in satisfactory condition, obtain a repair kit, consisting of a new gaiter, retaining clips, circlip, and the correct type and quantity of grease.

32 Tape over the splines on the end of the driveshaft, to protect the new gaiter as it is slid into place, then slide the new gaiter and securing clips, and the joint outer member over the end of the driveshaft **(see illustrations)**. Remove the protective tape from the driveshaft splines.

33 Press or drive the tripod onto the end of the driveshaft until it contacts the stop, ensuring that the marks made on the end of the driveshaft and the tripod before dismantling are aligned. Note that the chamfered edge of the internal splines on the tripod should face towards the driveshaft.

34 Fit the new circlip to retain the tripod on the end of the driveshaft.

35 Refit the rollers to the tripod, ensuring that they are refitted in their original locations, as noted before removal.

36 Work half of the grease supplied with the repair kit into the inner end of the joint outer

3.39 Lift the gaiter outer end to equalise the air pressure

3.30 Check the tripod rollers and outer member for signs of wear

3.32b . . . then lever the gaiter carefully over the ridge on the driveshaft

member, then slide the outer member over the tripod, ensuring that the marks made during dismantling are aligned, and clamp the outer member in the vice.

37 Work the rest of the grease supplied with the repair kit into the rear of the joint outer member **(see illustration)**.

38 Slide the rubber gaiter up the driveshaft onto the joint outer member, and secure with the large clip, as described in paragraph 17.

39 Lift the gaiter outer end to equalise the air pressure in the gaiter, then secure the outer gaiter securing clip in position using the same method used previously **(see illustration)**.

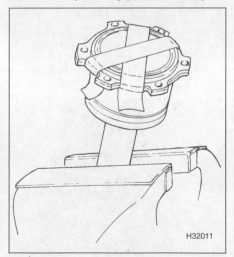

3.41 Tape over the end of the driveshaft joint

H32011

3.32a Tape over the driveshaft splines to protect the new gaiter . . .

3.37 Work the grease into the joint outer member

40 Check that the grease in the joint outer member is evenly distributed around the tripod rollers.

41 Check the driveshaft joint moves freely in all directions, then refit the driveshaft to the vehicle, as described in Section 2. To prevent the tripod joint from being pushed back down the driveshaft during refitting, temporarily stick adhesive tape over the open end of the joint outer member **(see illustration)**. Remove the tape just before reconnecting the inner end of the driveshaft to the transmission.

Ball-and-cage type inner CV joint

42 Secure the driveshaft in a vice equipped with soft jaws, then release the gaiter clamp(s), securing the gaiter to the driveshaft **(see illustration)**.

43 Using a hammer and a small drift, carefully drive the gaiter metal ring from the joint outer member **(see illustration)**.

3.42 Release the gaiter small securing clip . . .

3.43 . . . and drive the metal ring from the joint outer member

3.46 Remove the circlip . . .

3.47a . . . followed by the joint . . .

3.47b . . . dished washer . . .

3.48 . . . and gaiter

3.49a Tilt the splined hub and cage to remove the ball-bearings . . .

44 Slide the gaiter down the driveshaft to expose the constant velocity joint, and scoop out excess grease.
45 Where fitted, prise the metal cover from the end of the driveshaft.

46 Remove the circlip from the end of the driveshaft using circlip pliers **(see illustration)**.
47 Press or drive the driveshaft from the joint, taking great care not to damage the

joint. Recover the dished washer (where fitted) between the constant velocity joint and the shaft **(see illustrations)**.
48 Slide the gaiter from the end of the driveshaft **(see illustration)**.
49 Proceed as described previously in paragraphs 7 to 12 **(see illustrations)**.
50 Slide the dished washer (where fitted) onto the driveshaft, making sure its convex side is innermost.
51 Fit the joint to the end of the driveshaft, noting that the chamfered edge of the internal splines on the joint should face towards the driveshaft. Drive or press the joint into position until it contacts the shoulder on the driveshaft.
52 Fit a new circlip to retain the joint on the end of the driveshaft.
53 Pack the joint with the half the recommended quantity of grease (see *Specifications*), then pack the gaiter with the remaining half **(see illustrations)**.

3.49b . . . then separate the hub from the cage

3.49c Inner CV joint gaiter repair kit

3.53a Pack the inner joint with half of the grease . . .

3.53b . . . then pack the gaiter with the remaining grease

3.54a Temporarily fit one of the flange bolts to ensure the bolt holes are correctly aligned . . .

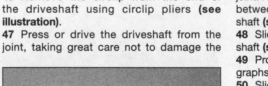

3.54b ... then drive the metal ring onto the joint outer member

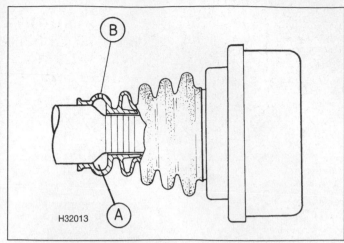

H32013

3.55 Installation position of inner joint gaiter

A Vent chamber in gaiter   B Vent hole

54 Slide the gaiter up the driveshaft, and press or drive the gaiter metal ring onto the joint outer member. To ensure the bolt holes are correctly positioned, temporarily fit one of the flange bolts **(see illustrations)**.
55 Slide the outboard end of the gaiter into position on the driveshaft, then secure the gaiter securing clamps in position as described in paragraph 17 **(see illustration)**.
56 Position the new gasket in place on the inner joint body, then (where applicable) press on the new metal cover.
57 Check the driveshaft joint moves freely in all directions, then refit the driveshaft to the vehicle, as described in Section 2.

4 Driveshaft overhaul – general information

If any of the checks described in Chapter 1 reveal wear in any driveshaft joint, first remove the roadwheel trim or centre cap (as applicable) and check that the hub bolt is tight. If the bolt is loose, obtain a new one, and tighten it to the specified torque (see Section 2). If the bolt is tight, refit the centre cap/trim, and repeat the check on the other hub bolt.

Road test the vehicle, and listen for a metallic clicking from the front of the vehicle as the vehicle is driven slowly in a circle on full-lock. If a clicking noise is heard, this indicates wear in the outer constant velocity joint; this means that the joint must be renewed.

If vibration consistent with roadspeed is felt through the car when accelerating, there is a possibility of wear in the inner constant velocity joints.

To check the joints for wear, remove the driveshafts, then dismantle them as described in Section 3. If any wear or free play is found, the affected joint must be renewed. Refer to a VW dealer for information on the availability of driveshaft components.

Notes

Chapter 9
Braking system

Contents

Degrees of difficulty

Easy, suitable for novice with little experience	Fairly easy, suitable for beginner with some experience	Fairly difficult, suitable for competent DIY mechanic	Difficult, suitable for experienced DIY mechanic	Very difficult, suitable for expert DIY or professional

Specifications

Front brakes

Type	Disc, with single-piston sliding FN3 (ATE) calipers
Disc diameter	312 mm
Disc (ventilated) thickness:	
New	25 mm
Minimum	22 mm
Maximum disc run-out	0.05 mm
Brake pad wear limit (friction material only – not including backing plate)	2 mm

Rear brakes

Type	Disc, with single-piston sliding CII38 caliper
Disc diameter	286 mm
Disc thickness:	
New	12 mm
Minimum thickness	10 mm
Maximum disc run-out	0.05 mm
Brake pad wear limit (friction material only – not including backing plate)	2 mm

Torque wrench settings

	Nm	lbf ft
ABS hydraulic unit mounting bolts	10	7
Brake pedal pivot bolt nut*	25	18
Front brake caliper:		
Guide pins	30	22
Mounting bracket bolts*	200	148
Wiring/brake hose bracket bolt	10	7
Handbrake motor-to-caliper bolts	12	9
Hydraulic pipe union nuts:		
8.5 mm diameter pipes	17	13
6.0 mm diameter pipes	14	10
Master cylinder retaining nuts*	25	18
Rear brake caliper:		
Guide pin bolts*	35	26
Mounting bracket bolts:*		
Stage 1	90	66
Stage 2	Angle-tighten a further 90°	
Roadwheel bolts	120	89
Vacuum pump bolts (common rail injection engines)	10	7
Vacuum servo-to-bulkhead/pedal bracket through-bolts*	25	18
Wheel speed sensor bolt	8	6

Use new fasteners

1 General information

All models have disc brakes fitted at the front and rear wheels as standard. ABS (Anti-lock Braking System) is also fitted as standard on all models (refer to Section 18 for further information on ABS operation).

The front and rear disc brakes are actuated by single-piston sliding type calipers, which ensure that equal pressure is applied to each disc pad. An electro-mechanical handbrake mechanism is built into the rear calipers, where instead of the cable forcing the caliper pistons to act upon the brake pads, an electric motor acts upon the pads.

Because the diesel engines have no throttle valve, there is insufficient vacuum in the inlet manifold to operate the braking system servo effectively at all times. To overcome this problem, a vacuum pump is fitted to these models, to provide sufficient vacuum to operate the servo unit. The vacuum pump is mounted on the rear of the cylinder head and driven by the camshaft.

ESP (Electronic Stability Program) is fitted to all models. The ESP (Electronic Stability Program) incorporates the ABS, EBS (Electronic Brake Assist) system and TCS (Traction Control System). It stabilises the vehicle when oversteering or understeering by applying the brake, or applying increased power to the relevant roadwheel, to increase the driver's control of the vehicle. In order for the ESP system to function, it utilises sensors which provide data concerning the speed of the vehicle around a vertical axis, the lateral movement of the vehicle, the brake pressure and the angle of the front wheels.

Note: *When servicing any part of the system, work carefully and methodically; also observe scrupulous cleanliness when overhauling any part of the hydraulic system. Always renew components (in axle sets, where applicable) if in doubt about their condition, and use only genuine VW parts, or at least those of known good quality. Note the warnings given in 'Safety first!' and at relevant points in this Chapter concerning the dangers of asbestos dust and hydraulic fluid.*

2 Hydraulic system – bleeding

⚠ **Warning: Hydraulic fluid is poisonous; wash off immediately and thoroughly in the case of skin contact, and seek immediate medical advice if any fluid is swallowed or gets into the eyes. Certain types of hydraulic fluid are inflammable, and may ignite when allowed into contact with hot components; when servicing any hydraulic system, it is safest to assume that the fluid is** *inflammable, and to take precautions against the risk of fire as though it is petrol that is being handled. Hydraulic fluid is also an effective paint stripper, and will attack plastics; if any is spilt, it should be washed off immediately, using copious quantities of fresh water. Finally, it is hygroscopic (it absorbs moisture from the air) – old fluid may be contaminated and unfit for further use. When topping-up or renewing the fluid, always use the recommended type, and ensure that it comes from a freshly-opened sealed container.*

Note: *If the hydraulic circuit upstream of the ABS modulator has been disturbed, the system may need to be bled using VW diagnostic equipment. Entrust this task to a VW dealer or suitably-equipped specialist.*

General

1 The correct operation of any hydraulic system is only possible after removing all air from the components and circuit; this is achieved by bleeding the system.
2 During the bleeding procedure, add only clean, unused hydraulic fluid of the recommended type; *never* re-use fluid that has already been bled from the system. Ensure that a sufficient quantity of new fluid is available before starting work.
3 If there is any possibility of incorrect fluid being already in the system, the brake components and circuit must be flushed completely with uncontaminated, correct fluid, and new seals should be fitted to the various components.
4 If hydraulic fluid has been lost from the system, or air has entered because of a leak, ensure that the fault is cured before proceeding further.
5 Park the vehicle on level ground, securely chock the wheel then release the handbrake.
6 Check that all pipes and hoses are secure, unions tight and bleed screws closed. Clean any dirt from around the bleed screws.
7 Unscrew the master cylinder reservoir cap, and top the master cylinder reservoir up to the MAX level line; refit the cap loosely, and remember to maintain the fluid level at least above the MIN level line throughout the procedure, or there is a risk of further air entering the system.
8 There is a number of one-man, do-it-yourself brake bleeding kits currently available from motor accessory shops. It is recommended that one of these kits is used whenever possible, as they greatly simplify the bleeding operation, and also reduce the risk of expelled air and fluid being drawn back into the system. If such a kit is not available, the basic (two-man) method must be used, which is described in detail below.
9 If a kit is to be used, prepare the vehicle as described previously, and follow the kit manufacturer's instructions, as the procedure may vary slightly according to the type being used; generally, they are as outlined below in the relevant sub-section.

10 Whichever method is used, the same sequence must be followed (see paragraphs 11 and 12) to ensure the removal of all air from the system.

Bleeding

Sequence

11 If the system has been only partially disconnected, and suitable precautions were taken to minimise fluid loss, it should be necessary only to bleed that part of the system (ie, the primary or secondary circuit).
12 If the complete system is to be bled, then it should be done working in the following sequence:
  a) *Left-hand front brake.*
  b) *Right-hand front brake.*
  c) *Left-hand rear brake.*
  d) *Right-hand rear brake.*

Basic (two-man) method

13 Collect a clean glass jar, a suitable length of plastic or rubber tubing which is a tight fit over the bleed screw, and a ring spanner to fit the screw. The help of an assistant will also be required.
14 Remove the dust cap from the first bolt in the sequence. Fit the spanner and tube to the bolt, place the other end of the tube in the jar, and pour in sufficient fluid to cover the end of the tube.
15 Ensure that the master cylinder reservoir fluid level is maintained at least above the MIN level line throughout the procedure.
16 Have the assistant fully depress the brake pedal several times to build-up pressure, then maintain it on the final downstroke.
17 While pedal pressure is maintained, unscrew the bleed screw (approximately one turn) and allow the compressed fluid and air to flow into the jar.
18 The assistant should maintain pedal pressure, following it down to the floor if necessary, and should not release it until instructed to do so. When the flow stops, tighten the bleed screw again, have the assistant release the pedal slowly, and recheck the reservoir fluid level.
19 Repeat the steps given in paragraphs 16 to 18 inclusive until the fluid emerging from the bleed screw is free from air bubbles. If the master cylinder has been drained and refilled, and air is being bled from the first screw in the sequence, allow approximately five seconds between cycles for the master cylinder passages to refill.
20 When no more air bubbles appear, tighten the bleed screw securely, remove the tube and spanner, and refit the dust cap. Do not overtighten the bleed screw.
21 Repeat the procedure on the remaining screws in the sequence, until all air is removed from the system and the brake pedal feels firm again. On completion, lower the vehicle to the ground (where necessary).

Using a one-way valve kit

22 As their name implies, these kits consist of

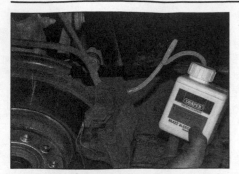

2.23 Attach the bleeding kit to the bleed screw on the caliper

a length of tubing with a one-way valve fitted, to prevent expelled air and fluid being drawn back into the system; some kits include a translucent container, which can be positioned so that the air bubbles can be more easily seen flowing from the end of the tube.

23 The kit is connected to the bleed screw, which is then opened **(see illustration)**. The user returns to the driver's seat, depresses the brake pedal with a smooth, steady stroke, and slowly releases it; this is repeated until the expelled fluid is clear of air bubbles.

24 Note that these kits simplify work so much that it is easy to forget to watch the master cylinder reservoir fluid level; ensure that this is maintained at least above the MIN level line at all times, otherwise air will be reintroduced into the system.

Using a pressure-bleeding kit

25 These kits are usually operated by the reservoir of pressurised air contained in the spare tyre. However, note that it will probably be necessary to reduce the pressure to a lower level than normal; refer to the instructions supplied with the kit.

26 By connecting a pressurised, fluid-filled container to the master cylinder reservoir, bleeding can be carried out simply by opening each screw in turn (in the specified sequence), and allowing the fluid to flow out until no more air bubbles can be seen in the expelled fluid.

27 This method has the advantage that the large reservoir of fluid provides an additional safeguard against air being drawn into the system during bleeding.

28 Pressure-bleeding is particularly effective when bleeding difficult systems, or when bleeding the complete system at the time of routine fluid renewal.

All methods

29 When bleeding is complete, and firm pedal feel is restored, wash off any spilt fluid, tighten the bleed screws securely, and refit their dust caps.

30 Check the hydraulic fluid level in the master cylinder reservoir, and top-up if necessary (see *Weekly checks*).

31 Discard any hydraulic fluid that has been bled from the system; it will not be fit for re-use.

32 Check the feel of the brake pedal. If it

feels at all spongy, air must still be present in the system, and further bleeding is required. Failure to bleed satisfactorily after a reasonable repetition of the bleeding procedure may be due to worn master cylinder seals.

33 Because the clutch hydraulic system shares the same fluid reservoir, we recommend that the clutch is bled at the same time (see Chapter 6).

3 Hydraulic pipes and hoses – renewal

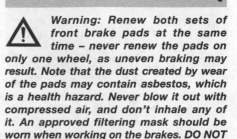

Note: *Before starting work, refer to the note at the beginning of Section 2 concerning the dangers of hydraulic fluid.*

1 If any pipe or hose is to be renewed, minimise fluid loss by first removing the master cylinder reservoir cap, then tightening it down onto a piece of polythene to obtain an airtight seal. Alternatively, flexible hoses can be sealed, if required, using a proprietary brake hose clamp; metal brake pipe unions can be plugged (if care is taken not to allow dirt into the system) or capped immediately they are disconnected. Place a wad of rag under any union that is to be disconnected, to catch any spilt fluid.

2 If a flexible hose is to be disconnected, unscrew the brake pipe union nut and remove the spring clip which secures the hose to its mounting bracket.

3 To unscrew the union nuts, it is preferable to obtain a brake pipe spanner of the correct size; these are available from most large motor accessory shops. Failing this, a close-fitting open-ended spanner will be required, though if the nuts are tight or corroded, their flats may be rounded-off if the spanner slips. In such a case, a self-locking wrench is often the only way to unscrew a stubborn union, but it follows that the pipe and the damaged nuts must be renewed on reassembly. Always clean a union and surrounding area before disconnecting it. If disconnecting a component with more than one union, make a careful note of the connections before disturbing any of them.

4 If a brake pipe is to be renewed, it can be obtained, cut to length with the union nuts and end flares in place, from VW dealers. All

that is then necessary is to bend it to shape, following the line of the original, before fitting it to the car. Alternatively, most motor accessory shops can make up brake pipes from kits, but this requires very careful measurement of the original, to ensure that the new one is of the correct length. The safest answer is usually to take the original to the shop as a pattern.

5 On refitting, do not overtighten the union nuts. It is not necessary to exercise brute force to obtain a sound joint.

6 Ensure that the pipes and hoses are correctly routed, with no kinks, and that they are secured in the clips or brackets provided. After fitting, remove the polythene from the reservoir, and bleed the hydraulic system as described in Section 2. Wash off any spilt fluid, and check carefully for fluid leaks.

4 Front brake pads – renewal

⚠️ *Warning: Renew both sets of front brake pads at the same time – never renew the pads on only one wheel, as uneven braking may result. Note that the dust created by wear of the pads may contain asbestos, which is a health hazard. Never blow it out with compressed air, and don't inhale any of it. An approved filtering mask should be worn when working on the brakes. DO NOT use petrol or petroleum-based solvents to clean brake parts; use brake cleaner or methylated spirit only.*

1 Apply the handbrake, then loosen the front roadwheel nuts. Jack up the front of the vehicle and support it on axle stands. Remove both front roadwheels.

2 Follow the accompanying photos **(illustrations 4.2a to 4.2t)** for the actual pad renewal procedure. Be sure to stay in order and read the caption under each illustration, and note the following points:

a) *The inner pad (with a spring) may be marked with an arrow. The arrow must point in the direction of brake disc rotation.*

b) *New pads may have an adhesive foil on the backplates. Remove this foil prior to installation.*

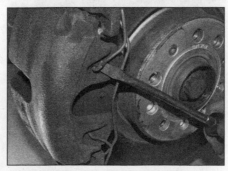

4.2a Prise off the retaining spring clip

4.2b Pull the pad wear sensor wiring plug upwards from the bracket, depress the clip and disconnect it

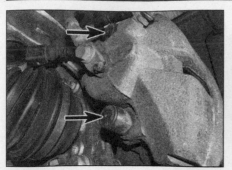

4.2c Prise out the guide pins rubber caps (arrowed) . . .

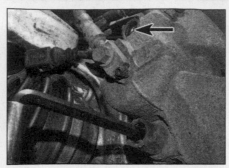

4.2d . . . and use an Allen key to unscrew the guide pins

4.2e If there's a wear/rust lip around the disc, use a screwdriver to force the inner pad away from the disc a little

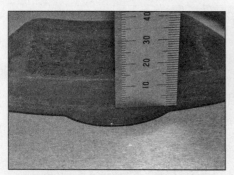

4.2f Slide the caliper from place and rest it on top of the brake disc/hub bearing housing

4.2g Remove the outer brake pad from the caliper mounting bracket . . .

4.2h . . . and pull the inner pad from the caliper piston

4.2i Measure the thickness of the pad's friction material – the minimum is 2 mm

4.2j Use a wire brush to clean the pad mounting surfaces on the caliper bracket

4.2k If new pads are to be fitted, push the piston back into the caliper body using a pad retraction tool. Keep an eye on the fluid level in the master cylinder reservoir

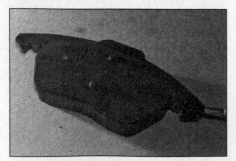

4.2l Apply a thin smear of high-temperature anti-seize grease to the areas on the pad backing plate that contacts the caliper mounting bracket. Take great care not to get any on the friction material of the pad

4.2m Fit the outer pad to the caliper mounting bracket. Ensure the friction material is against the disc . . .

4.2n . . . the clip the inner pad into the caliper piston

4.2o Slide the caliper into place . . .

4.2p . . . and screw in the guide pins

4.2q Tighten the guide pins to the specified torque . . .

4.2r . . . and refit the rubber caps

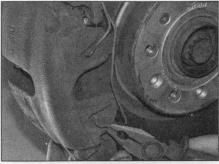

4.2s Refit the retaining spring clip

4.2t Reconnect the wear sensor wiring plug and slide it into the bracket

c) *Thoroughly clean the caliper guide surfaces, and apply a little brake assembly grease (polycarbamide).*

d) *When pushing the caliper piston back to accommodate new pads, keep a close eye on the fluid level in the reservoir.*

Caution: Pushing back the piston causes a reverse-flow of brake fluid, which has been known to 'flip' the master cylinder rubber seals, resulting in a total loss of braking. To avoid this, clamp the caliper flexible hose and open the bleed screw – as the piston is pushed back, the fluid can be directed into a suitable container using a hose attached to the bleed screw. Close the screw just before the piston is pushed fully back, to ensure no air enters the system.

3 Depress the brake pedal repeatedly, until the pads are pressed into firm contact with the brake disc, and normal (non-assisted) pedal pressure is restored.

4 Repeat the above procedure on the remaining front brake caliper.

5 Refit the roadwheels, then lower the vehicle to the ground and tighten the roadwheel bolts to the specified torque.

6 Check the hydraulic fluid level as described in *Weekly checks*.

Caution: New pads will not give full braking efficiency until they have bedded-in. Be prepared for this, and avoid hard braking as far as possible for the first hundred miles or so after pad renewal.

5 Rear brake pads – renewal

⚠️ *Warning: Renew both sets of rear brake pads at the same time – never renew the pads on only one wheel, as uneven braking may result. Note that the dust created by wear of the pads may contain asbestos, which is a health hazard. Never blow it out with compressed air, and don't inhale any of it. An approved filtering mask should be worn when working on the brakes. DO NOT use petrol or petroleum-based solvents to clean brake parts; use brake cleaner or methylated spirit only.*

Note: *In order to accommodate the increased thickness of new brake pads, the caliper piston must be retracted and the brake system basic setting performed using VW diagnostic equipment VAS5051. Equivalent equipment is available at reasonable cost from automotive tool and parts suppliers. In the absence of these tools, have the pads renewed by a VW dealer or suitably-equipped specialist.*

1 Chock the front wheels, then jack up the rear of the vehicle and support it on axle stands (see *Jacking and vehicle support*). Remove the rear wheels. Whilst the wheels are removed, refit at least one wheel bolt to each hub to ensure the brake discs remain correctly positioned on the hubs.

2 With the handbrake released, follow the accompanying photos **(see illustrations 5.2a to 5.2s)** for the actual pad renewal procedure. Be sure to stay in order and read the caption under each illustration, and note the following points:

a) *If re-installing the original pads, ensure they are fitted to their original positions.*

b) *Renewal guide pin bolts and fitting shims are available as a repair kit.*

c) *If new pads are to be fitted, extract some of the brake fluid from the reservoir prior to retracting the caliper piston – keep an eye on the fluid level in the reservoir whilst retracting the piston.*

5.2a Plug the scanner/tool into the vehicle's diagnostic socket (beneath the driver's side of the facia) and follow the instructions to 'release' the handbrake. This actually winds the electric motor back away from the caliper piston

5.2b Using an open-ended spanner to counterhold the guide pin, undo the upper and lower guide pin bolts (arrowed)

5.2c If necessary, use a screwdriver to lever the piston (arrowed) back into the caliper body a little . . .

5.2d . . . so the caliper can be slid from the bracket. Suspend the caliper from the coil spring to prevent straining the hose

5.2e Remove the outer pad . . .

5.2f . . . and inner pad

5.2g Remove the lower fitting shim . . .

5.2h . . . and upper fitting shim

5.2i Clean the shim mounting surfaces with a wire brush

5.2j Fit the new lower shim (new shims are supplied with genuine pads) . . .

5.2k . . . and upper shim

5.2l Slide the new inner pad into place . . .

5.2m . . . followed by the outer pad

5.2n Use a retraction tool to force the piston back into the caliper body. Keep an eye on the fluid level in the master cylinder reservoir

5.2o Slide the caliper over the pads and into place on the bracket

5.2p Fit the new guide pin bolts (supplied with genuine pads) . . .

5.2q . . . and tighten them to the specified torque

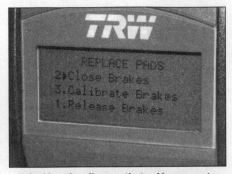

5.2r Use the diagnostic tool/scanner to close the brakes (wind the electric motor against the piston, forcing the piston against the pads) . . .

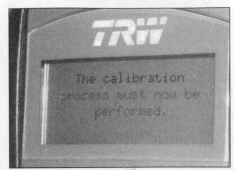

5.2s . . . and carry out the basic setting calibration

d) Fit new caliper guide pin bolts and fitting shims – included in the VW repair kit.

e) After fitting new pads, move the pistons towards the discs (using the diagnostic tool) then perform the system basic setting procedure as explained in the note above.

3 Depress the brake pedal repeatedly, until the pads are pressed into firm contact with the brake disc, and normal (non-assisted) pedal pressure is restored.

4 Repeat the above procedure on the remaining brake caliper.

5 Refit the roadwheels, then lower the vehicle to the ground and tighten the roadwheel bolts to the specified torque.

6 Check the hydraulic fluid level as described in *Weekly checks*.

Caution: New pads will not give full braking efficiency until they have bedded-in. Be prepared for this, and avoid hard braking as far as possible for the first hundred miles or so after pad renewal.

6 Front brake disc – inspection, removal and refitting

Note: *Before starting work, refer to the note at the beginning of Section 4 concerning the dangers of asbestos dust.*

Inspection

Note: *If either disc requires renewal, BOTH should be renewed at the same time, to ensure even and consistent braking. New brake pads should also be fitted.*

1 Apply the handbrake, then jack up the front of the car and support it on axle stands (see *Jacking and vehicle support*). Remove the appropriate front roadwheel. Whilst the wheel is removed, refit at least one of the wheel bolts to ensure the brake disc remains correctly positioned on the hub; if necessary fit spacers to the wheel bolts to clamp the disc firmly in position **(see illustration)**.

2 Slowly rotate the brake disc so that the full area of both sides can be checked; remove

the brake pads if better access is required to the inboard surface. Light scoring is normal in the area swept by the brake pads, but if heavy scoring or cracks are found, the disc must be renewed.

3 It is normal to find a lip of rust and brake dust around the disc's perimeter; this can be scraped off if required. If, however, a lip has formed due to excessive wear of the brake pad swept area, then the disc's thickness must be measured using a micrometer. Take measurements at several places around the disc, at the inside and outside of the pad swept area; if the disc has worn at any point to the specified minimum thickness or less, the disc must be renewed **(see illustration)**.

6.1 Refit at least one of the wheel bolts to retain the disc

6.3 Use a micrometer to measure the thickness of the disc

6.5 Use a DTI gauge to measure the disc run-out

4 If the disc is thought to be warped, it can be checked for run-out. Secure the disc firmly to the hub by refitting at least two roadwheel bolts – fit plain washers to the bolts to ensure that the disc is properly seated on the hub.
5 Either use a dial gauge mounted on any convenient fixed point, while the disc is slowly rotated, or use feeler blades to measure (at several points all around the disc) the clearance between the disc and a fixed point, such as the caliper mounting bracket **(see illustration)**. If the measurements obtained are at the specified maximum or beyond, the disc is excessively warped, and must be renewed, however, it is worth checking first that the hub bearing is in good condition (Chapter 10).
6 Check the disc for cracks, especially around the wheel bolt holes, and any other wear or damage, and renew if necessary.

Removal

7 Unscrew and remove the two bolts securing the brake caliper mounting bracket to the hub carrier. Slide the whole caliper assembly off the hub and away from the disc and tie the assembly to the front coil spring, using a piece of wire or string, to avoid placing any strain on the hydraulic brake hose **(see illustration)**. The caliper mounting bracket can be unscrewed and removed separately if required (see Section 8).
8 Use chalk or paint to mark the relationship of the disc to the hub, then remove all the wheel bolts and washers used to secure the disc in position and remove the disc. If it is tight, lightly tap its rear face with a hide or plastic mallet to free it from the hub.

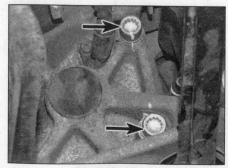

7.3 Rear caliper mounting bracket bolts (arrowed)

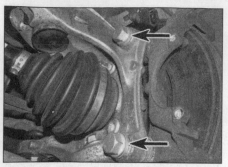

6.7 Caliper mounting bracket bolts (arrowed)

Refitting

9 Refitting is the reverse of the removal procedure, noting the following points:
 a) Ensure that the mating surfaces of the disc and hub are clean and flat.
 b) On refitting, align (if applicable) the marks made on removal.
 c) If a new disc has been fitted, use a suitable solvent to wipe any preservative coating from the disc, before refitting the caliper. Note that new brake pads should always be fitted when the disc is renewed.
 d) Prior to installation, renew the caliper mounting bracket bolts. Slide the caliper into position, making sure the pads pass either side of the disc, and tighten the caliper bracket bolts to the specified torque setting.
 e) Refit the roadwheel then lower the vehicle to the ground and tighten the wheel bolts to the specified torque. Apply the footbrake several times to force the pads back into contact with the disc before driving the vehicle.

7 Rear brake disc – inspection, removal and refitting

Note: Before starting work, refer to the note at the beginning of Section 5 concerning the dangers of asbestos dust.

Inspection

Note: If either disc requires renewal, BOTH should be renewed at the same time, to ensure even and consistent braking. New brake pads should be fitted also.
1 Firmly chock the front wheels, engage 1st gear (or P), then jack up the rear of the car and support it on axle stands (see Jacking and vehicle support). Remove the appropriate rear roadwheel.
2 Inspect the disc as described in Section 6.

Removal

3 Unscrew the two bolts (12-point star socket head M14) securing the brake caliper mounting bracket in position, then slide the whole caliper, bracket and pads off the disc **(see illustration)**. The bolts should be discarded

and new ones fitted. If preferred, the caliper and pads can be removed separately before unscrewing the mounting bracket. Using a piece of wire or string, tie the caliper to the exhaust hanger/vehicle body, to avoid placing any strain on the hydraulic brake hose.
4 Use chalk or paint to mark the relationship of the disc to the hub, then remove the disc. If it is tight, lightly tap its rear face with a hide or plastic mallet to free it from the hub.

Refitting

5 Refitting is the reverse of the removal procedure, noting the following points:
 a) Ensure that the mating surfaces of the disc and hub are clean and flat.
 b) On refitting, align (if applicable) the marks made on removal.
 c) If a new disc has been fitted, use a suitable solvent to wipe any preservative coating from the disc, before refitting the caliper. Note that new brake pads should always be fitted when the disc is renewed.
 d) Prior to installation, renew the caliper bracket mounting bolts. Slide the caliper into position, making sure the pads pass either side of the disc, and tighten the caliper bracket bolts to the specified torque setting.
 e) Refit the roadwheel then lower the vehicle to the ground and tighten the wheel bolts to the specified torque. Apply the footbrake several times to force the pads back into contact with the disc before driving the vehicle.

8 Front brake caliper – removal, overhaul and refitting

Note: Before starting work, refer to the note at the beginning of Section 2 concerning the dangers of hydraulic fluid, and to the warning at the beginning of Section 4 concerning the dangers of asbestos dust.

Removal

1 Apply the handbrake, then jack up the front of the vehicle and support it on axle stands (see Jacking and vehicle support). Remove the front roadwheels. Whilst the wheels are removed, refit at least one wheel bolt to the hub to ensure the brake disc remains correctly positioned on the hub.
2 Minimise fluid loss by first removing the master cylinder reservoir cap, and then tightening it down onto a piece of polythene, to obtain an airtight seal. Alternatively, use a brake hose clamp to clamp the flexible hose.
3 Where applicable, disconnect the wiring connector from the brake pad wear sensor connector. Unclip the connector from the caliper bracket.
4 Clean the area around the caliper brake pipe union then unscrew the union nut. Unscrew the mounting bracket from the caliper and

position the pipe clear. Plug/cover the pipe end and caliper union to minimise fluid loss and prevent the entry of dirt into the hydraulic system. Wash off any spilt fluid immediately with cold water.

5 Carefully lever the pad retaining spring out position and remove it from the brake caliper using a flat-bladed screwdriver.

6 Remove the end caps from the guide bushes then unscrew and remove the caliper guide pins.

7 Lift the caliper out of position, freeing it from the pad wear sensor wiring (where applicable). Remove the inner and outer brake pads with reference to Section 4, then if required, unscrew and remove the caliper mounting bracket.

Overhaul

Note: *At the time of writing, it would appear that caliper overhaul kits are available. However, it would be prudent to check with a VW dealer or parts specialist prior to commencing work.*

8 With the caliper on the bench, wipe away all traces of dust and dirt, but *avoid inhaling the dust, as it is injurious to health.*

9 Withdraw the partially-ejected piston from the caliper body, and remove the dust seal. If the caliper piston is reluctant to move, apply low air pressure (eg, from a foot pump) to the fluid inlet, but note that the piston may be ejected with some force.

10 Using a soft flat-bladed instrument, such as a plastic spatula, extract the piston hydraulic seal, taking great care not to damage the caliper bore.

11 Thoroughly clean all components, using only methylated spirit, isopropyl alcohol or clean brake fluid as a cleaning medium. Never use mineral-based solvents such as petrol or paraffin, as they will attack the hydraulic system's rubber components. Dry the components immediately, using compressed air or a clean, lint-free cloth. Use compressed air to blow clear the fluid passages.

12 Check all components, and renew any that are worn or damaged. Check particularly the cylinder bore and piston; these should be renewed if they are scratched, worn or corroded in any way (note that this means the renewal of the complete body assembly). Similarly check the condition of the guide pins and the bushes in the caliper body; both pins should be undamaged and (when cleaned) a reasonably tight sliding fit in the bushes. If there is any doubt about the condition of any component, renew it.

13 If the caliper is fit for further use, obtain the appropriate repair kit. All rubber seals should be renewed as a matter of course; these should never be re-used.

14 On commencement of re-assembly, ensure that all components are clean and dry **(see illustrations)**.

15 Soak the seals in the special fluid provided in the overhaul kit for at least 45 minutes – check with the instructions provided in the

kit. Smear some of the special fluid on the cylinder bore surface.

16 Fit the new piston (fluid) seal, using only your fingers (no tools) to manipulate it into the cylinder bore groove.

17 Fit the new dust seal to the rear of the piston and seat the outer lip of the seal in the caliper body groove. Carefully ease the piston squarely into the cylinder bore using a twisting motion. Press the piston fully into position and seat the inner lip of the dust seal in the piston groove.

18 If the guide bushes are being renewed, push the old bushes out from the body and press the new ones into position, making sure they are correctly seated.

19 Prior to refitting, fill the caliper with fresh hydraulic fluid by unscrewing the bleed screw and pumping the fluid through the caliper until bubble-free fluid is expelled from the union hole.

Refitting

20 Refit the caliper mounting bracket to the hub carrier using new bolts, and tighten them to the specified torque **(see illustration 6.7)**. Refit the brake pads with reference to Section 4, then manoeuvre the caliper into position over the brake pads.

21 Fit the caliper guide pins, tightening them to the specified torque setting, and refit the end caps to the guide bushes.

22 Reconnect the brake pipe to the caliper and refit the mounting bracket to the caliper. Tighten the bracket retaining bolt and the brake pipe union nut to their specified torque settings.

23 Refit the pad retaining spring, ensuring its ends are correctly located in the caliper body holes.

24 Ensure the wiring is correctly routed through the loop on the lower cap then clip the pad wear sensor wiring connector onto its bracket on the caliper. Securely reconnect the wiring connector.

25 Remove the brake hose clamp or polythene (where fitted) and bleed the hydraulic system as described in Section 2. Note that, providing the precautions described were taken to minimise brake fluid loss, it should only be necessary to bleed the relevant front brake.

26 Refit the roadwheel, then lower the vehicle to the ground and tighten the roadwheel bolts to the specified torque.

9 Rear brake caliper – removal, overhaul and refitting

Note: *Before starting work, refer to the note at the beginning of Section 2 concerning the dangers of hydraulic fluid, and to the warning at the beginning of Section 5 concerning the dangers of asbestos dust.*
Note: *New guide pin bolts must be used on refitting.*

Removal

1 Chock the front wheels, release the handbrake, then jack up the rear of the vehicle and support it on axle stands (see *Jacking and vehicle support*). Remove the relevant rear wheel. Whilst the wheel is removed, refit at

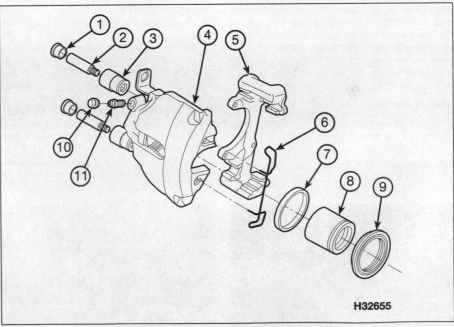

H32655

8.14 Exploded view of the front brake caliper

1 Dust cap	5 Caliper mounting	8 Piston
2 Guide pins	bracket	9 Dust seal
3 Guide sleeves	6 Pad retaining spring	10 Dust cap
4 Caliper	7 Piston seal	11 Bleed screw

9.3 Use a brake hose clamp to clamp the flexible hose

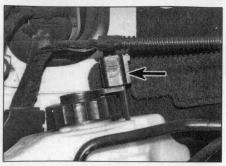

10.2 Disconnect the level sensor wiring plug (arrowed)

least one wheel bolt to the hub to ensure the brake disc remains in position.

2 With the handbrake released, switch off the ignition, wait at least 30 seconds, then disconnect the wiring plug from the electric handbrake motor from the rear brake caliper.

3 Minimise fluid loss by first removing the master cylinder reservoir cap, and then tightening it down onto a piece of polythene, to obtain an airtight seal. Alternatively, use a brake hose clamp, a G-clamp or a similar tool to clamp the flexible hose **(see illustration)**.

4 Clean the area around the caliper brake pipe then slacken the union, and undo the bolt securing the pipe bracket to the caliper.

5 Unscrew and remove the caliper guide pin bolts, using a slim open-ended spanner to prevent the guide pins from rotating. Discard the guide pin bolts – new bolts must be used on refitting.

6 Lift the brake caliper away from the its mounting bracket and unscrew the brake pipe union completely. Plug/cover the pipe end and caliper port to minimise fluid loss and prevent the entry of dirt into the hydraulic system. Wash off any spilt fluid immediately with cold water. Remove the inner and outer brake pads from the caliper mounting bracket. If required, unscrew and remove the caliper mounting bracket.

Overhaul

7 At the time of writing, no renewal parts were available for the rear caliper. Check with a VW dealer or parts specialist.

Refitting

8 Where applicable, refit the caliper mounting

bracket to the rear hub carrier using new bolts, and tighten them to the specified torque. Refit the brake pads to the caliper mounting bracket with reference to Section 5.

9 Before fitting the caliper, it must be pre-bled as follows. Attach a hose from a brake fluid dispenser to the bleed screw on the caliper. Hold the caliper with the brake hose port uppermost, then open the bleed screw and allow fluid to flow into the caliper. Once bubble-free fluid emerges from the port, close the bleed screw and disconnect the hose.

10 Engage the brake fluid pipe with the caliper, bolt the union into the caliper thread, then manoeuvre the caliper into position over the pads then fit the new guide pin bolts, tightening them to the specified torque setting.

11 Remove the brake hose clamp or polythene (where used) and securely tighten the brake pipe union, and secure the pipe bracket to the caliper.

12 Reconnect the handbrake motor wiring plug.

13 Bleed the hydraulic system as described in Section 2. Note that, providing the precautions described were taken to minimise brake fluid loss, it should only be necessary to bleed the relevant rear brake.

14 Note that the brake system basic setting procedure must be carried out using dedicated VW diagnostic equipment or an aftermarket equivalent – refer to Section 5.

15 Refit the roadwheel, then lower the vehicle to the ground and tighten the roadwheel bolts to the specified torque.

Removal

1 On LHD models, remove the battery and battery tray as described in Chapter 5.

2 On all models, disconnect brake fluid level sensor wiring plug, unscrew the reservoir cap, and siphon the hydraulic fluid from the reservoir **(see illustration)**. **Note:** *Do not siphon the fluid by mouth as it is poisonous; use a syringe or an old poultry baster.*

3 Disconnect the wiring plug from the brake light switch located on the master cylinder body.

4 On manual transmission models, disconnect and plug the clutch master cylinder supply hose from the brake fluid reservoir **(see illustration)**.

5 Remove the hydraulic fluid reservoir from the top of the master cylinder. To do this, undo the retaining bolt and pull the reservoir upwards from the rubber grommets **(see illustration)**.

6 Wipe clean the area around the brake pipe unions on the side of the master cylinder, and place absorbent rags beneath the pipe unions to catch any leaking fluid. Make a note of the correct fitted positions of the unions, then unscrew the union nuts and carefully withdraw the pipes. Plug or tape over the pipe ends and master cylinder orifices to minimise the loss of brake fluid, and to prevent the entry of dirt into the system. Wash off any spilt fluid immediately with cold water.

7 Unscrew and remove the two nuts and washers securing the master cylinder to the vacuum servo unit, remove the heat shield (where fitted), then withdraw the unit from the engine compartment **(see illustration)**. Remove the O-ring from the rear of the master cylinder, and discard it. Discard the nuts, new ones must be fitted.

Overhaul

8 If the master cylinder is faulty, it must be renewed. Repair kits are not available from VW dealer, so the cylinder must be treated as a sealed unit.

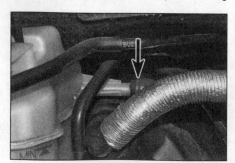

10.4 Disconnect the clutch master cylinder supply hose (arrowed) from the brake fluid reservoir

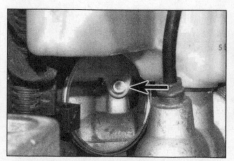

10.5 Undo the bolt (arrowed in the mirror) and pull the reservoir upwards from the grommets

10.7 Master cylinder retaining nuts (arrowed)

11.2 Remove the brake pedal pivot bolt (arrowed)

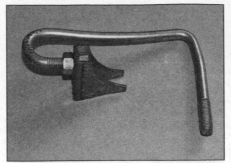

11.3a Improvised special tool constructed from a modified exhaust clamp, used to release the brake pedal from the servo pushrod

11.3b Use the tool to release the brake pedal from the servo pushrod

9 The only items which can be renewed are the mounting seals for the fluid reservoir; if these show signs of deterioration, prise them out with a screwdriver. Lubricate the new seals with clean brake fluid, and press them into the master cylinder ports.

Refitting

10 Remove all traces of dirt from the master cylinder and servo unit mating surfaces, and fit a new O-ring to the groove on the master cylinder body.

11 Fit the master cylinder to the servo unit, ensuring that the servo unit pushrod enters the master cylinder bore centrally. Refit the heat shield (where applicable), and the new master cylinder mounting nuts and washers, and tighten them to the specified torque.

12 Wipe clean the brake pipe unions, then refit them to the master cylinder ports and tighten them securely.

13 Refit the hydraulic fluid reservoir, making sure it is entered correctly in the rubber grommets.

14 On manual transmission models, reconnect the clutch master cylinder supply hose to the reservoir.

15 Refill the master cylinder reservoir with new fluid, and bleed the complete hydraulic system as described in Section 2.

16 Reconnect the wiring to the brake level sender unit and brake light switch.

17 On LHD models, refit the battery and tray.

18 Refit the air cleaner housing where necessary.

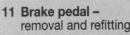

11 Brake pedal – removal and refitting

Removal

1 Remove the steering column as described in Chapter 10.

2 Unscrew the brake pedal pivot bolt (see illustration).

3 The end of the servo pushrod is shaped as a ball, and engages with a retaining clip in the back of the lever/pedal. To release the clip a special VW tool is available, but a suitable alternative can be improvised as shown. Note that the plastic lugs are very stiff, and it will

not be possible to release them by hand. Using the tool, release the securing lugs and pull the pedal from the servo pushrod (see illustrations).

4 Examine all components for signs of wear or damage, renewing them as necessary.

Refitting

5 Apply a smear of multipurpose grease to the pedal pivot bore and the pushrod ball.

6 The remainder of the refitting procedure is a reversal of the removal procedure, noting the following points:

a) *Apply locking fluid to the threads of the brake pedal pivot bolt before tightening it to the specified torque.*

b) *Tighten all fixings to the correct torque, where specified.*

12 Vacuum servo unit – testing, removal and refitting

Testing

1 To test the operation of the servo unit, depress the footbrake several times to exhaust the vacuum, then start the engine whilst keeping the pedal firmly depressed. As the engine starts, there should be a noticeable give in the brake pedal as the vacuum builds-up. Allow the engine to run for at least two minutes, then switch it off. If the brake pedal is now depressed it should feel normal, but further applications should result in the

pedal feeling firmer, with the pedal stroke decreasing with each application.

2 If the servo does not operate as described, first inspect the servo unit check valve as described in Section 13. Also check the vacuum pump as described in Section 20.

3 If the servo unit still fails to operate satisfactorily, the fault may lie within the unit itself. Repairs to the unit are not possible – if faulty, the servo unit must be renewed.

Removal

4 Remove the master cylinder as described in Section 10.

5 Carefully ease the vacuum hose connection out from the servo unit, taking care not to damage the grommet.

6 Remove the driver's side footwell cover (see illustration). Unclip the diagnostic plug as the cover is withdrawn.

7 Working underneath the facia, locate the servo unit pushrod. The end of the servo pushrod is shaped as a ball, and engages with a retaining clip in the back of the lever/pedal. To release the clip a special VW tool is available, but a suitable alternative can be improvised as shown. Note that the plastic lugs are very stiff, and it will not be possible to release them by hand. Using the tool, release the securing lugs and pull the pedal from the servo pushrod (see illustrations 11.3a and 11.3b).

8 Undo the bolts/nuts securing the brake pedal bracket to the bulkhead and manoeuvre the servo from place (see illustration). Recover the gasket which is fitted between the servo and bulkhead. Examine the gasket for signs of wear or damage and renew if

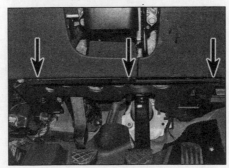

12.6 Undo the bolts (arrowed) and remove the footwell cover

12.8 Undo the bolts/nuts (arrowed) securing the pedal bracket to the bulkhead

13.1 Vacuum check valve (arrowed)

necessary. Recover the sealing ring fitted to the rear of the master cylinder and discard it; a new one must be used on refitting.

Overhaul

9 If the servo is faulty, it must be renewed. Repair kits are not available from VW dealers, so the servo must be treated as a sealed unit.

Refitting

10 Ensure the servo unit and bulkhead mating surfaces are clean, fit the gasket to the rear of the servo unit, and then sealing ring between the master cylinder and servo. Position the master cylinder on the servo and manoeuvre the assembly into position.

11 From inside the vehicle, make sure the pushrod is correctly engaged with the rear of the pedal then press the pushrod firmly into position until the balljoint can be felt to

engage. Lift the brake pedal by hand to check that the pushrod is securely reconnected.

12 Refit the bracket bolts/nut and tighten them to the specified torque.

13 The remainder of refitting is a reversal of removal.

13 Vacuum servo unit check valve – removal, testing and refitting

Removal

1 Carefully ease the vacuum hose connections from the check valve located at the rear of the vacuum pump at the left-hand end of the cylinder head (see illustration).

2 Slacken the retaining clip then disconnect the vacuum hose from the vacuum pump and remove it from the vehicle.

Testing

3 Examine the vacuum hose for signs of damage, and renew if necessary. The valve may be tested by blowing through it in both directions. Air should flow through the valve in one direction only – when blown through from the servo unit end of the valve. Renew the valve if this is not the case.

Refitting

4 Refitting is a reversal of removal. On completion, start the engine and check the check valve-to-servo unit connection for signs of air leaks.

15.4 Handbrake motor retaining bolts (arrowed)

15.5 Lubricate the new seal with clean brake fluid

15.6a Align the piston spindle with the motor spindle . . .

15.6b . . . then refit the motor without twisting the seal

14 Brake servo pressure sensor – removal and refitting

Removal

1 Pull the plastic cover on the top of the engine upwards to release it from its mountings.

2 Pull the vacuum hose, complete with pressure sensor (where fitted), from the servo.

3 Using a pair of pliers, release the two clips and pull the sensor from place.

Refitting

4 Refitting is a reversal of removal.

15 Handbrake motor – removal and refitting

Removal

1 Chock the front wheels, release the hand brake, turn off the ignition then wait at least 30 seconds before commencing work.

2 Raise the rear of the vehicle and support it securely on axle stands (see *Jacking and vehicle support*).

3 Release the clip and disconnect the motor wiring plug.

4 Undo the 2 Torx bolts and pull the motor from the caliper (see illustration). Recover the seal.

Refitting

5 Unsure the area around the seal groove is clean, then lubricate the seal with clean brake fluid and fit it into the groove (see illustration).

6 Using a 12-pointed star M8 bit, rotate the piston spindle until it aligns with the motor spindle, then carefully fit the motor, aligning the bolt holes, without allowing the seal to rotate (see illustrations). Once the motor is fully inserted, refit the retaining bolts and tighten them to the specified torque. Don't use the bolts to 'draw' the motor into position.

7 Reconnect the wiring plug, and lower the vehicle to the ground.

8 The brake system basic setting must now be carried out using VW diagnostic equipment (VAS 5051) or equivalent (available from automotive tool/parts suppliers). In the absence of this equipment, entrust this task to a VW dealer or suitably-equipped specialist.

16 Electromechanical handbrake control unit – removal and refitting

Removal

1 Disconnect the battery negative lead as described in Chapter 5.

2 Remove the centre console as described in Chapter 11.

3 Undo the 3 retaining nuts and remove the control unit (see illustration). Slide out the locking element and disconnect the wiring plug as the unit is withdrawn. Note: *Several ESP sensors (lateral acceleration, yaw rate and longitudinal acceleration) are incorporated into the control unit. Handle the unit with great care as the sensors are easily damaged by shocks/knocks.*

Refitting

4 Refitting is a reversal of the removal procedure. If a new unit has been fitted, the basic settings of the brake system and ESP systems must be carried out using dedicated diagnostic equipment (VAS 5051 or equivalent). In the absence of this equipment, entrust the task to a VW dealer or suitably-equipped specialist.

17 Stop-light switch – removal and refitting

Removal

1 Disconnect the battery negative lead as described in Chapter 5. On LHD models, remove the battery and battery tray (Chapter 5), then remove the air cleaner housing as described in Chapter 4A.
2 Pull the plastic cover on the top of the engine upwards to release it from its mountings.
3 Disconnect the wiring connector from the switch body located on the underside of the master cylinder.
4 Undo the retaining bolt, then lower the switch from place. Note the locating lug at the top of the switch (see illustrations).

Refitting

5 Refitting is a reversal of removal.

18 Anti-lock braking system (ABS) – general information

1 ABS is fitted as standard to all models in the range. The system comprises a hydraulic unit, an electronic control unit (ECM) and four roadwheel sensors. The hydraulic unit contains the eight hydraulic solenoid valves (two for each brake – one inlet and one outlet) and the electrically-driven return pump. The purpose of the system is to prevent the roadwheels locking during heavy braking. This is achieved by automatic release of the brake on the relevant wheel, followed by re-application of the brake. In the case of the rear wheels, both rear brakes are released and applied at the same time.
2 The solenoid valves are controlled by the ECM, which itself receives signals from the four wheel sensors (front sensors are fitted to the hubs and the rear sensors are fitted to the rear axle), which monitor the speed of rotation of each wheel. By comparing these

16.3 Electromechanical handbrake control unit nuts (arrowed)

signals, the ECM can determine the speed at which the vehicle is travelling. It can then use this speed to determine when a wheel is decelerating at an abnormal rate, compared to the speed of the vehicle, and therefore predicts when a wheel is about to lock. During normal operation, the system functions in the same way as a non-ABS braking system.
3 If the ECM senses that a wheel is about to lock, it closes the relevant outlet solenoid valves in the hydraulic unit, which then isolates the relevant brake on the wheel which is about to lock from the master cylinder, effectively sealing-in the hydraulic pressure.
4 If the speed of rotation of the wheel continues to decrease at an abnormal rate, the ECM opens the inlet solenoid valves on the relevant brake and operates the electrically-driven return pump which pumps the hydraulic fluid back into the master cylinder, releasing the brake. Once the speed of rotation of the wheel returns to an acceptable rate, the pump stops; the solenoid valves switch again, allowing the hydraulic master cylinder pressure to return to the caliper, which then re-applies the brake. This cycle can be carried out many times a second.
5 The action of the solenoid valves and return pump creates pulses in the hydraulic circuit. When the ABS system is functioning, these pulses can be felt through the brake pedal.
6 The operation of the ABS system is entirely dependent on electrical signals. To prevent the system responding to any inaccurate signals, a built-in safety circuit monitors all signals received by the ECM. If an inaccurate signal or low battery voltage is detected, the

17.4a Stop-light switch retaining bolt (arrowed)

ABS system is automatically shut down, and the warning light on the instrument panel is illuminated to inform the driver that the ABS system is not operational. Normal braking should still be available, however.
7 On all models, the ABS system also includes Electronic Differential Lock (EDL) and Traction Control (TCS) functions. If under acceleration the ECM senses that a wheel is spinning, it uses the hydraulic unit to gradually apply the brake on that wheel until traction is regained. Once the wheel regains traction, the brake is released.
8 The ESP (Electronic Stability Program) function is a further expansion of the ABS system which takes into consideration the angle of the steering wheel, using a steering angle sender and a combined lateral acceleration, yaw rate, and longitudinal acceleration sensor built into the electromechanical handbrake control unit under the centre console.
9 The ABS/ESP/TCS ECM and hydraulic unit are combined into one unit, and must not be separated.
10 If a fault does develop in the system, the vehicle must be taken to a VW dealer or suitably-equipped specialist for fault diagnosis and repair.

19 Anti-lock braking system (ABS) components – removal and refitting

Hydraulic unit

Note: *VW state that the operation of the hydraulic unit should be checked using special test equipment after refitting. Bearing this in mind, it is recommended that removal and refitting of the unit is entrusted to a VW dealer or specialist. If you decide to remove/refit the unit yourself, ensure that the operation of the braking system is checked at the earliest opportunity by a VW dealer or specialist.*

Removal

1 Disconnect the battery negative terminal (see Chapter 5). Where necessary, remove the engine plastic cover.
2 Remove the intake manifold flap motor as described in Chapter 4A.
3 On 2.0 litre models, remove the particulate filter (where fitted) as described in Chapter 4B.

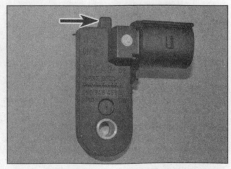

17.4b Note the lug (arrowed) at the top of the switch

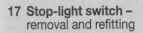

19.15 Front ABS sensor retaining bolt (arrowed)

19.22 Rear wheel speed sensor retaining bolt (arrowed)

4 Remove the heat shield (where fitted), then release the locking bar and disconnect the main wiring connector from the hydraulic unit.
5 Connect a length of hose to the left-hand front brake caliper bleed screw, then direct the other end of the hose into a suitable receptacle, as described in Section 2. Open the bleed screw and then depress the brake pedal through one full stroke and hold it in this position, using a suitable weight, or a wedge such as a block of wood. When the expelled brake fluid has collected into the receptacle, close the bleed screw. **Note:** *The brake pedal must be held in the depressed position until the brake pipes have been reconnected to the hydraulic unit, at the end of this procedure.*
6 Wipe clean the area around all the pipes unions and mark the locations of the hydraulic fluid pipes to ensure correct refitting. Unscrew the union nuts and disconnect the pipes from the regulator assembly. Be prepared for fluid spillage, and plug the open ends of the pipes and the hydraulic unit unions to prevent dirt ingress and further fluid loss.
7 Pull the unit upwards to release the rubber mountings. **Note:** *Keep the hydraulic unit upright to minimise the risk of fluid loss, and to prevent air locks inside the unit.*

Refitting

Note: *New hydraulic units are supplied prefilled with brake fluid and fully bled; it is vitally important that the union plugs are not removed until the brake pipes are reconnected as loss of fluid will introduce air into the unit.*
8 Manoeuvre the hydraulic unit into position, and push it downwards into the rubber mountings.

20.3 Pull the vacuum hose from the pump

9 Remove the plugs and reconnect the hydraulic pipes to the correct unions on the hydraulic unit and tighten the union nuts to the specified torque.
10 Securely reconnect the wiring connector to the hydraulic unit.
11 The remainder of refitting is a reversal of removal.
12 Remove the weight/wedge from the brake pedal and then bleed the entire braking hydraulic system as described in Section 2. Thoroughly check the operation of the braking system before using the vehicle on the road. Have the operation of the ABS system checked by a VW dealer or specialist at the earliest possible opportunity.

Front wheel sensor

Removal

13 Apply the handbrake, then jack up the front of the vehicle and support securely on axle stands (see *Jacking and vehicle support*). To improve access, remove the roadwheel.
14 Disconnect the sensor wiring plug.
15 Undo the retaining bolt, then carefully pull the sensor out from the hub carrier assembly and remove it from the vehicle **(see illustration)**.

Refitting

16 Ensure that the mating faces of the sensor and hub carrier are clean and dry then lubricate the wheel sensor surfaces with a small quantity of copper-based grease.
17 Ensure the sensor wiring is correctly positioned then push the sensor firmly into

20.5 Vacuum pump retaining bolts (arrowed)

position until it is fully home in the hub carrier, and tighten the retaining bolt to the specified torque.
18 Ensure the sensor is securely retained then work along the sensor wiring, making sure it is correctly routed, securing it in position with all the relevant clips and ties. Reconnect the wiring connector.
19 Refit the wheel then lower the vehicle and tighten the wheel bolts to the specified torque.

Rear wheel sensor

Removal

20 Chock the front wheels, then jack up the rear of the vehicle and support it on axle stands (see *Jacking and vehicle support*). To improve access, remove the appropriate roadwheel.
21 Working underneath the vehicle, disconnect the wiring plug from the sensor.
22 Note the fitted position of the speed sensor, then undo the retaining bolt and carefully prise the sensor from the hub carrier **(see illustration)**.

Refitting

23 Ensure that the mating faces of the sensor and axle are clean and dry, then lubricate the wheel sensor surfaces with a little copper-based grease.
24 Ensure the sensor wiring is correctly positioned then push the sensor firmly into position until it is fully home in the hub carrier, and tighten the retaining bolt to the specified torque.
25 Reconnect the sensor wiring plug.
26 Refit the roadwheel then lower the vehicle to the ground and tighten the wheel bolts to the specified torque.

20 Vacuum pump – removal and refitting

PD unit injector engines

1 Refer to Chapter 4A, Section 9.

Common rail injection engines

Removal

2 Remove the air cleaner housing as described in Chapter 4A.
3 Disconnect the vacuum hose from the top of the pump **(see illustration)**.
4 Undo the charge air pipe retaining bolts, then push the pipe down a little to access the rearmost pump retaining bolt.
5 Undo the 4 bolts and remove the pump **(see illustration)**. Recover the seal.

Refitting

6 Renew the pump seal, then fit the pump, ensuring it seats properly in the camshaft.
7 Tighten the pump retaining bolts to the specified torque.
8 The remainder of refitting is a reversal of removal.

21 ESP system components – removal and refitting

1 The ESP system comprises of the ABS, TCS and EDL system. The ESP, TCS and EDL systems rely on the ABS system components for measuring and reducing wheel speed. In addition to the wheel speed sensors and brake pressure sensors, the ESP receives information concerning the steering wheel angle, lateral acceleration, vehicle rotational speed (yaw rate), and longitudinal acceleration. Testing of the various system components should be entrusted to a VW dealer or specialist.

Lateral acceleration/yaw rate/longitudinal acceleration sensor

⚠️ *Warning: Handle the sensor with great care. Severe shakes/jolts can destroy the sensors.*

2 This sensor assembly is incorporated into the electromechanical handbrake control unit, located under the centre console. The removal and refitting procedure is described in Section 16 of this Chapter.

Brake pressure sensor

3 The brake pressure sensor is fitted to the ABS hydraulic control unit. VW state that the sensor should not be detached from the control unit.

Steering angle sensor

4 The steering angle sensor is incorporated into the airbag contact unit between the steering wheel and column switch. To remove the sensor, refer to Chapter 12, and remove the contact unit. Note that if the contact unit has been renewed, specialist equipment is required to perform a 'zero comparison'. This must be entrusted to a VW dealer or specialist.

Notes

Chapter 10
Suspension and steering systems

Contents

Degrees of difficulty

Easy, suitable for novice with little experience | **Fairly easy,** suitable for beginner with some experience | **Fairly difficult,** suitable for competent DIY mechanic | **Difficult,** suitable for experienced DIY mechanic | **Very difficult,** suitable for expert DIY or professional

Specifications

Front suspension
Type . . . . Independent, with MacPherson struts incorporating coil springs, telescopic shock absorbers and anti-roll bar

Rear suspension
Type . . . . Trailing arm with Multi-link transverse arms, separate gas-filled telescopic shock absorbers, coil springs and anti-roll bar

Steering
Type . . . . Rack-and-pinion. Electro-mechanical power assistance standard

Wheel alignment and steering angles*

Front wheel:
Camber angle:
Standard and self-levelling suspension . . . .   -30' ± 30'
Sports and Blue Motion suspension . . . .   -41' ± 30'
Heavy duty suspension . . . .   -14' ± 30'
Maximum difference between sides (all models) . . . .   30'
Castor angle:
Standard and self-levelling suspension . . . .   7° 32' ± 30'
Sports and Blue motion suspension. . . . .   7° 44' ± 30'
Heavy duty suspension . . . .   7° 16' ± 30'
Maximum difference between sides (all models) . . . .   30'
Toe setting . . . .   10' ± 10'
Toe-out on turns (20° left or right):
Standard and self-levelling suspension . . . .   1° 19' ± 20'
Sports and Blue motion suspension. . . . .   1° 21' ± 20'
Heavy duty suspension . . . .   1° 18' ± 20'
Ride height:
Standard and self-levelling suspension . . . .   383 ± 10 mm
Sports and Blue motion suspension. . . . .   368 ± 10 mm
Heavy duty suspension . . . .   403 ± 10 mm
Rear wheel:
Camber angle:
Standard and Blue motion suspension . . . .   -1°20' ± 30'
Self-levelling (Nivomat) suspension . . . .   -1°45' ± 30'
Sports suspension:
Except 18" wheels . . . .   -1°20' ± 30'
18" wheels . . . .   -1°45' ± 30'
Heavy duty suspension . . . .   -1°20' ± 30'
Maximum difference between sides. . . . .   30'
Toe setting . . . .   +10' ± 10'
Ride height:
Standard suspension . . . .   383 ± 10 mm
Self-levelling (Nivomat) suspension . . . .   373 ± 10 mm
Sports suspension . . . .   368 ± 10 mm
Blue motion suspension . . . .   373 ± 10 mm
Heavy duty suspension . . . .   393 ± 10 mm
* Refer to a VW dealer for the latest recommendations.

Torque wrench settings

	Nm	lbf ft
Front suspension		
Anti-roll bar link nut*	65	48
Anti-roll bar to subframe:*		
Stage 1	20	15
Stage 2	Angle-tighten a further 90°	
Balljoint to wheel bearing housing:*		
Stage 1	20	15
Stage 2	Angle-tighten a further 90°	
Hub bolt*	See Chapter 8	
Hub to wheel bearing housing:		
Stage 1	70	52
Stage 2	Angle-tighten a further 90°	
Lower arm:		
Mounting bracket to subframe:		
M10:		
Stage 1	50	37
Stage 2	Angle-tighten a further 90°	
M12:		
Stage 1	70	52
Stage 2	Angle-tighten a further 180°	
To front lower balljoint:*		
Cast steel arm	60	44
Sheet steel or aluminium arm	100	74
To subframe:*		
Stage 1	70	52
Stage 2	Angle-tighten a further 180°	

Torque wrench settings (continued)	Nm	lbf ft
Rear engine mounting:		
To subframe:*		
Stage 1	100	74
Stage 2	Angle-tighten a further 90°	
To transmission:*		
Class 8.8:		
Stage 1	40	30
Stage 2	Angle-tighten a further 90°	
Class 10.9:		
Stage 1	50	37
Stage 2	Angle-tighten a further 90°	
Splash plate to wheel bearing housing	10	7
Subframe-to-underbody bolts:*		
Stage 1	70	52
Stage 2:		
100 mm length (under head)...........................	Angle-tighten a further 180°	
110 mm length (under head)...........................	Angle-tighten a further 90°	
Suspension strut:		
Bottom clamp:*		
Stage 1	70	52
Stage 2	Angle-tighten a further 90°	
Upper mounting:*		
Stage 1	15	11
Stage 2	Angle-tighten a further 90°	
Upper piston rod*	60	44
Vehicle level sender to subframe and lower arm	9	7
Rear suspension		
ABS speed sensor	8	6
Anti-roll bar:		
To subframe:*		
Stage 1	25	18
Stage 2	Angle-tighten a further 45°	
Anti-roll bar link*	45	33
Hub to wheel bearing housing:*		
Stage 1	200	148
Stage 2	Angle-tighten a further 180°	
Lower transverse link to wheel bearing housing:*		
Stage 1	90	66
Stage 2	Angle-tighten a further 90°	
Shock absorber:		
To body:*		
Stage 1	50	37
Stage 2	Angle-tighten a further 45°	
To shock absorber mounting bracket........................	25	18
To wheel bearing housing*	180	133
Splash plate to wheel bearing housing	12	9
Stone deflector to transverse link.............................	8	6
Subframe to body:*		
Stage 1	90	66
Stage 2	Angle-tighten a further 90°	
Track control rod to subframe:*		
Stage 1	90	66
Stage 2	Angle-tighten a further 90°	
Track control rod to wheel bearing housing:*		
Stage 1	130	96
Stage 2	Angle-tighten a further 90°	
Trailing arm:		
Mounting bracket to underbody:*		
Stage 1	50	37
Stage 2	Angle-tighten a further 45°	
To mounting bracket:*		
Stage 1	90	66
Stage 2	Angle-tighten a further 90°	
To wheel bearing housing:*		
Stage 1	90	66
Stage 2	Angle-tighten a further 45°	

Torque wrench settings (continued)

	Nm	lbf ft
Rear suspension (continued)		
Transverse links to subframe*	95	70
Upper transverse link to wheel bearing housing:*		
Stage 1	130	96
Stage 2	Angle-tighten a further 90°	
Vehicle level sender	5	4
Steering		
Steering column:		
Mounting bracket to body	20	15
Strut to mounting bracket/body	20	15
To mounting bracket*	20	15
Universal joint to steering gear:*		
Stage 1	20	15
Stage 2	Angle-tighten a further 90°	
Combination switch bolts	10	7
Steering gear:		
Shield*	6	4
To subframe:*		
Stage 1	50	37
Stage 2	Angle-tighten a further 90°	
Steering wheel to column:*		
Stage 1	30	22
Stage 2	Angle-tighten a further 90°	
Track rod end to track rod	70	52
Track rod end to wheel bearing housing:*		
Stage 1	100	74
Stage 2	Slacken 180°	
Stage 3	100	74
Track rod to steering gear	100	74
Roadwheels		
Roadwheel bolts	120	89

Do not re-use

1 General information

The independent front suspension is of the MacPherson strut type, incorporating coil springs and integral telescopic shock absorbers. The struts are located by transverse lower suspension arms, which use rubber inner mounting bushes, and incorporate a balljoint at the outer ends. The front wheel bearing housings, which carry the wheel bearings, brake calipers and the hub/disc assemblies, are attached to the MacPherson struts by clamp bolts, and connected to the lower arms through the balljoints. A front anti-roll bar is fitted to all models. The anti-roll bar is rubber-mounted, and is connected to both lower suspension arms by short links.

The rear suspension consists of a trailing arm, rubber-mounted at its front end to the underbody, a wheel bearing housing, lower main transverse link and coil spring, track control rod, upper transverse link, and separate shock absorber. A rear anti-roll bar is fitted to all models. The anti-roll bar is rubber-mounted on the rear subframe, and is connected to the wheel bearing housings on each side by a short connecting link.

The safety steering column incorporates an intermediate shaft at its lower end. The intermediate shaft is connected to both the steering column and steering gear by universal joints, although the shaft is supplied as part of the column assembly and cannot be separated. Both the inner steering column and intermediate shaft have splined sections which collapse during a major frontal impact. The outer column is also telescopic with two sections, to facilitate reach adjustment.

The steering gear is mounted onto the front subframe, and is connected by two track rods, with balljoints at their inner and outer ends, to the steering arms projecting rearwards from the wheel bearing housings. The track rod ends are threaded to the track rods in order to allow adjustment of the front wheel toe setting. The steering gear has electro-mechanical assistance, and incorporates an integral control unit. It is only functional when the engine is running. There are no hydraulic components, and steering assistance is automatically matched to the vehicle speed, steering wheel torque and steering wheel angle.

All models are fitted with an Anti-lock Brake System (ABS), and can also be fitted with a Traction Control System (TCS), an Electronic Differential Lock (EDL) system and an Electronic Stability Program (ESP). The ABS may also be referred to as including EBD (Electronic Brake Distribution) which means it adjusts the front and rear braking forces according to the weight being carried. The TCS may also be referred to as ASR (Anti Slip Regulation).

The TCS system prevents the front wheels from losing traction during acceleration by reducing the engine output. The system is switched on automatically when the engine is started, and it utilises the ABS system sensors to monitor the rotational speeds of the front wheels.

The ESP system extends the ABS, TCS and EDL functions to reduce wheel spin in difficult driving conditions. It does this by using highly-sensitive sensors which monitor the speed of the vehicle, lateral movement of the vehicle, the brake pressure, and the steering angle of the front wheels. If, for example, the vehicle is tending to oversteer, the brake will be applied to the front outer wheel to correct the situation. If the vehicle is tending to understeer, the brake will be applied to the rear inside wheel. The steering angle of the front wheels is monitored by an angle sensor on the top of the steering column.

The TCS/ESP systems should always be switched on, except when driving with snow chains, driving in snow or driving on loose surfaces, when some wheel spin may be advantageous. The ESP switch is located in the centre of the facia.

Some models are also fitted with an Electronic Differential Lock (EDL) which

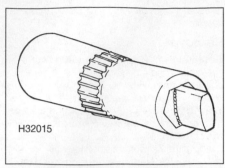

2.10a Tool used by VW technicians to open the split in the wheel bearing housing

2.10b Use a cold chisel to carefully open up the split in the wheel bearing housing and release the strut

2.10c Withdraw the wheel bearing housing from the bottom of the suspension strut

reduces unequal traction from the front wheels. If one front wheel spins 100 rpm or more faster than the other, the faster wheel is slowed down by applying the brake to that wheel. The system is not the same as the traditional differential lock, where the actual differential gears are locked. Because the system applies a front brake, in the event of a brake disc overheating the system will shut down until the disc has cooled. No warning light is displayed if the system shuts down. As is the case with the TCS system, the EDL system uses the ABS sensors to monitor front wheel speeds.

2 Front wheel bearing housing – removal and refitting

Note: *Renewal of the hub bearings does not require removal of the wheel bearing housing (see Section 3). This Section describes removal of the wheel bearing housing leaving the suspension strut in situ, however, if necessary it can be removed together with the suspension strut, then separated on the bench. All self-locking nuts and bolts disturbed on removal must be renewed as a matter of course.*

Removal

1 Remove the wheel trim/hub cap (as applicable) and loosen the driveshaft retaining bolt (hub bolt) by 90° with the vehicle resting on its wheels. Also loosen the wheel bolts. **Note:** *Do not loosen the hub bolt more than 90° at this stage, or the wheel bearing may be damaged.*

2 Apply the handbrake, then jack up the front of the vehicle and support it on axle stands (see *Jacking and vehicle support*). Remove the front roadwheel.

3 Unscrew and remove the driveshaft retaining bolt.

4 Remove the ABS wheel sensor as described in Chapter 9.

5 Remove the brake disc as described in Chapter 9. This procedure includes removing the brake caliper, however do not disconnect the hydraulic brake hose from the caliper. Using a piece of wire or string, tie the caliper to the front suspension coil spring, to avoid

placing any strain on the hydraulic brake hose.

6 Unscrew the splash plate from the wheel bearing housing.

7 Loosen the nut securing the steering track rod balljoint to the wheel bearing housing. To do this, fit a ring spanner to the nut, then hold the balljoint pin stationary using an Allen key. With the nut removed, it may be possible to release the balljoint from the wheel bearing housing by turning the balljoint pin with an Allen key. If not, leave the nut on by a few turns to protect the threads, then use a universal balljoint separator to release the balljoint. Remove the nut completely once the taper has been released.

8 Unscrew the front suspension lower balljoint-to-lower arm retaining nuts **(see illustration 4.5a)**, then lever the lower arm down to release the balljoint studs from the arm. Now use a soft-faced mallet to tap the driveshaft from the hub splines while pulling out the bottom end of the wheel bearing housing. If the driveshaft is tight on the splines, it may be necessary to use a puller bolted to the hub to remove it. Tie the driveshaft to one side.

9 Note which way round it is fitted, then unscrew the nut and remove the clamp bolt securing the wheel bearing housing to the bottom of the strut.

10 The wheel bearing housing must now be released from the strut. To do this, VW technicians insert a special tool into the split wheel bearing housing, and turn it through 90° to open up the clamp. A similar tool can be made out of an old screwdriver, or alternatively a suitable cold chisel can be driven into the split as a wedge. Slightly press the top of the wheel bearing housing inwards, then push it downwards from the bottom of the strut **(see illustrations)**.

Refitting

11 Ensure that the driveshaft outer joint and hub splines are clean and dry, then lubricate the splines with fresh engine oil. Also lubricate the threads and contact surface of the hub nut/bolt with oil.

12 Lift the wheel bearing assembly into position, and engage the hub with the splines on the outer end of the driveshaft. Fit the new hub bolt, tightening it by hand only at this stage.

13 Engage the wheel bearing housing with the bottom of the suspension strut, making sure that the hole in the side plate aligns with the holes in the split housing. Remove the tool used to open the split.

14 Insert the strut-to-wheel bearing housing clamp bolt from the rear, and fit the new retaining nut. Tighten the nut to the specified torque.

15 Refit the lower arm balljoint to the lower arm, and tighten the new nuts to the specified torque.

16 Refit the track rod balljoint to the wheel bearing housing, then fit a new retaining nut and tighten it to the specified torque. If necessary, hold the balljoint pin with an Allen key while tightening the nut.

17 Refit the splash plate and tighten the bolts.

18 Refit the brake disc and caliper with reference to Chapter 9.

19 Refit the ABS wheel sensor as described in Chapter 9.

20 Ensure that the outer joint is drawn fully into the hub, then refit the roadwheel.

21 Have an assistant depress the brake pedal, then tighten the driveshaft retaining bolt in the stages given in the Specifications. It is recommended that an angle gauge is used to ensure the correct tightening angle. **Note:** *The car must not be standing on its wheels when tightening the bolt, or the wheel bearing may be damaged.*

22 Lower the vehicle to the ground, tighten the roadwheel bolts, and refit the wheel trim/hub cap.

3 Front hub bearings – renewal

Note: *The bearing is a sealed, pre-adjusted and pre-lubricated, double-row roller type, and requires no maintenance. It is bolted to the wheel bearing housing.*

1 Remove the wheel trim/hub cap (as applicable) and loosen the driveshaft retaining bolt (hub bolt) with the vehicle resting on its wheels. **Note:** *Do not loosen the hub bolt more than 90° at this stage, or the wheel bearing may be damaged. Also loosen the wheel bolts.*

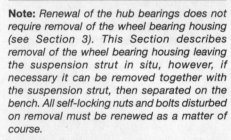

3.6 Front wheel bearing retaining bolts (arrowed)

2 Apply the handbrake, then jack up the front of the vehicle and support it on axle stands (see *Jacking and vehicle support*). Remove the front roadwheel.

3 Unscrew and remove the driveshaft retaining bolt.

4 Remove the ABS wheel sensor as described in Chapter 9.

5 Remove the brake disc as described in Chapter 9. This procedure includes removing the brake caliper, however do not disconnect the hydraulic brake hose from the caliper. Using a piece of wire or string, tie the caliper to the front suspension coil spring, to avoid placing any strain on the hydraulic brake hose.

6 Press the driveshaft outer stub towards the transmission as far as possible, then unscrew and remove the wheel bearing retaining bolts from the rear of the housing **(see illustration)**.

7 Remove the hub/wheel bearing complete

with hub from the outside of the housing while sliding it from the driveshaft splines.

8 Fit the new wheel bearing to the housing and engage the hub splines with the driveshaft outer stub. Fit the new bolts and tighten them to the specified torque.

9 Refit the brake disc and caliper with reference to Chapter 9.

10 Refit the ABS wheel sensor as described in Chapter 9.

11 Pull the driveshaft outer stub fully into the hub and fit a new hub bolt, hand-tight at this stage.

12 Ensure that the outer joint is drawn fully into the hub, then refit the roadwheel.

13 Tighten the new driveshaft retaining bolt in the stages given in the Specifications. It is recommended that an angle gauge is used to ensure the correct tightening angle. **Note:** *The car must not be standing on its wheels when tightening the bolt, or the wheel bearing will be damaged.*

14 Lower the vehicle to the ground, tighten the roadwheel bolts, and refit the wheel trim/hub cap.

4 Front suspension strut – removal, overhaul and refitting

Note: *This section describes removal of the suspension strut leaving the wheel bearing housing in situ, however, if necessary it can be removed together with the wheel bearing housing, then separated on the bench. All self-locking nuts and bolts disturbed on*

removal must be renewed as a matter of course.

Removal

1 Remove the wheel trim/hub cap (as applicable) and loosen the driveshaft retaining bolt (hub bolt) with the vehicle resting on its wheels. **Note:** *Do not loosen the hub bolt more than 90° at this stage, or the wheel bearing may be damaged. Also loosen the wheel bolts.*

2 Apply the handbrake, then jack up the front of the vehicle and support it on axle stands (see *Jacking and vehicle support*). Remove the appropriate roadwheel.

3 Unscrew the nut and disconnect the anti-roll bar link from the strut **(see illustration)**.

4 Unscrew and remove the driveshaft retaining bolt **(see illustration)**. Refit 2 of the roadwheel bolts, then have an assistant apply the brakes to prevent the disc/hub from rotating whist slackening the bolt.

5 Unscrew the front suspension lower balljoint-to-lower arm retaining nuts, then lever the lower arm down to release the balljoint studs. Now use a soft-faced mallet to tap the driveshaft from the hub splines while pulling out the bottom end of the wheel bearing housing **(see illustrations)**. If the driveshaft is tight on the splines, it may be necessary to use a puller bolted to the hub to remove it. Tie the driveshaft to one side, then refit the lower balljoint to the lower arm and secure with the nuts, hand-tightened.

6 Note which way round it is fitted, then unscrew the nut and remove the clamp bolt securing the wheel bearing housing to the bottom of the strut **(see illustration)**.

7 The wheel bearing housing must now be released from the strut. To do this, VW technicians insert a special tool into the split wheel bearing housing, and turn it through 90° to open up the clamp. A similar tool such as an Allen key can be used, or alternatively a suitable cold chisel can be driven into the split as a wedge. Slightly press the top of the wheel bearing housing inwards, then push it downwards from the bottom of the strut **(see illustration 2.10a, 2.10b and 2.10c)**. Support the wheel bearing housing to one side without straining the hydraulic brake hose.

8 Remove the wiper arms (Chapter 12) then

4.3 Use an Allen key to counterhold the anti-roll bar link balljoint whilst slackening the nut

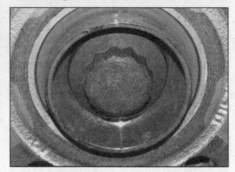

4.4 Undo the driveshaft bolt

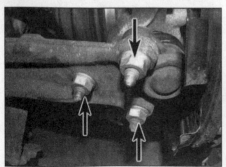

4.5a Undo the balljoint-to-lower arm nuts (arrowed)

4.5b Pull the driveshaft from the hub splines

4.6 Undo the nut (arrowed) and pull the strut lower clamp bolt from place

pull up the rubber seal, slide forwards the clips, and starting in the middle, pull the plenum chamber cover upwards from the base of the windscreen (see illustrations).

9 To ensure correct refitting, mark the strut upper mounting in relation to the body. If the reason for removing the strut is overhaul, loosen the upper mounting centre nut one turn, while holding the piston rod with an Allen key.

10 Support the strut, then unscrew the upper mounting bolts and lower the strut from under the wheel arch (see illustration).

Overhaul

⚠️ **Warning: Before attempting to dismantle the suspension strut, a suitable tool to hold the coil spring in compression must be obtained. Adjustable coil spring compressors are readily available, and are recommended for this operation. Any attempt to dismantle the strut without such a tool is likely to result in damage or personal injury.**

11 With the strut removed from the car, clean away all external dirt. If necessary, mount it upright in a vice during the dismantling procedure.

12 Fit the spring compressor, and compress the coil spring until all tension is relieved from the upper spring seat (see illustration).

13 Unscrew and remove the upper centre retaining nut, whilst retaining the strut piston with a suitable Allen key, then remove the mounting/thrust bearing, and coil spring (see illustrations).

4.8a Lift the rubber seal and slide the clips forwards (arrowed)

4.10 Undo the strut upper mounting bolts (arrowed)

14 Remove the gaiter, bump stop and protective sleeve (see illustrations).

15 With the strut assembly now completely dismantled, examine all the components for wear, damage or deformation, and check the

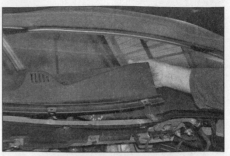
4.8b Starting at the middle, lift the plenum chamber cover from the base of the windscreen

4.12 Compress the coil spring evenly and progressively until all tension is relieved from the spring seats

bearing for smoothness of operation. Renew any of the components as necessary.

16 Examine the strut for signs of fluid leakage. Check the strut piston for signs of pitting along its entire length, and check the

4.13a Hold the piston with an Allen key and undo the centre nut

4.13b Remove the upper mounting/thrust bearing . . .

4.13c . . . and coil spring

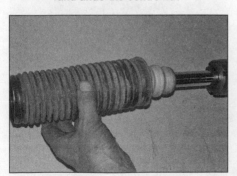
4.14a Remove the gaiter . . .

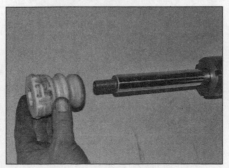
4.14b . . . bump stop . . .

4.14c . . . and protective sleeve

4.22 One of the two arrows must point forwards

strut body for signs of damage. While holding it in an upright position, test the operation of the strut by moving the piston through a full stroke, and then through short strokes of 50 to 100 mm. In both cases, the resistance felt should be smooth and continuous. If the resistance is jerky, or uneven, or if there is any visible sign of wear or damage to the strut, renewal is necessary.

17 If any doubt exists about the condition of the coil spring, carefully remove the spring compressors, and check the spring for distortion and signs of cracking. Renew the spring if it is damaged or distorted, or if there is any doubt as to its condition.

18 Inspect all other components for signs of damage or deterioration, and renew as necessary.

19 Fit the protective sleeve to the strut, then assemble the bump stop to the upper mounting, and refit the gaiter to the mounting. The larger diameter of the bump stop must be against the upper mounting, and the lower edge of the gaiter must be pulled down around the protective sleeve.

20 Fit the coil spring (together with the compressor tool) onto the strut, making sure its lower (larger diameter) end is correctly located against the spring seat stop.

21 Refit the thrust bearing and upper mounting, then screw on a new retaining nut. Tighten the nut to the specified torque while holding the piston rod with an Allen key.

Refitting

22 Manoeuvre the strut into position under the wheel arch, and locate in the suspension strut turret in the previously-noted position. If a new strut is being fitted, locate it so that one of the two arrows marked on the upper mounting points forwards, and the bolt holes are aligned **(see illustration)**. Insert the new bolts and tighten to the specified torque.

23 Refit the plenum chamber cover and wiper arms.

24 Engage the wheel bearing housing with the bottom of the suspension strut, making sure that the hole in the side plate aligns with the holes in the split housing. Raise the housing, while pressing it inwards to assist entry. Use a trolley jack if necessary. When fully entered, remove the tool used to open the split.

25 Insert the new strut-to-wheel bearing housing bolt from the rear, and fit the new retaining nut. Tighten the nut to the specified torque.

26 Unscrew the nuts from the lower balljoint and lever down the lower arm to release it from the wheel bearing housing. Insert the outer end of the driveshaft through the hub and engage it with the splines. Fit the new hub bolt, tightening it by hand only at this stage.

27 Refit the lower arm balljoint to the lower arm, and tighten the new nuts to the specified torque. Where applicable, refit the headlight range control sensor arm to the lower arm and tighten the nut.

28 Refit the ABS wheel sensor as described in Chapter 9.

29 Ensure that the outer joint is drawn fully into the hub, then refit the roadwheel.

30 Have an assistant depress the brake pedal, then tighten the driveshaft retaining bolt in the stages given in the Specifications. It is recommended that an angle gauge is used to ensure the correct tightening angle. **Note:** *The car must not be standing on its wheels when tightening the bolt, or the wheel bearing may be damaged.*

31 Lower the vehicle to the ground, tighten the roadwheel bolts, and refit the wheel trim/hub cap. We recommend the front wheel alignment is checked at the earliest opportunity.

---

5 Front suspension lower arm – removal, overhaul and refitting

Note: *The lower arm is available in either cast steel, sheet steel or aluminium – when renewing the arm, make sure the correct type is fitted according to model. VW subframe locating pins (T10096) or similar are required for the work in this Section, to ensure correct front wheel alignment. All self-locking nuts and bolts disturbed on removal must be renewed as a matter of course.*

Removal

1 Apply the handbrake, then jack up the front of the vehicle and support it on axle stands (see *Jacking and vehicle support*). Remove the appropriate front roadwheel and the engine compartment undershield.

2 On models with automatic transmission, if removing the left-hand side lower arm, the subframe must be lowered as described in Section 22, to enable the removal of the front mounting bolt.

3 Unscrew the front suspension lower balljoint-to-lower arm retaining nuts, then lever down the lower arm to release the arm from the balljoint studs.

4 At this stage, VW technicians use locating pins T10096 in place of the rear outer subframe mounting bolts to ensure correct front wheel alignment. If these pins are not available, only remove and refit one lower arm at a time, and

mark the position of the subframe accurately with dabs of paint.

5 Unscrew and remove the rear outer mounting bolt and, where available, substitute it with a locating pin tightened to 20 Nm (15 lbf ft).

6 Unscrew and remove the front mounting bolt, then support the lower arm and unscrew the two rear inner mounting bolts. Remove the lower arm from beneath the car.

Overhaul

7 Thoroughly clean the lower arm, then check carefully for cracks or any other signs of wear or damage, paying particular attention to the rubber mounting bushes. If either bush requires renewal, take the lower arm to a VW dealer or suitably-equipped garage. Alternatively, a hydraulic press and suitable spacers may be used to press the bushes out of the arm and rear bracket, and to install the new ones. Dip the bushes in a mild solution of washing-up liquid and water. Note the following:

a) *When fitting a new front mounting bush, it must be initially tilted with one lip in the bore. As the bush is inserted, it will straighten up. Make sure the bush is centred in its bore.*

b) *After pressing a new rear mounting bush into the rear mounting bracket, press the bracket and bush fully onto the lower arm rear pivot.*

Refitting

8 Locate the lower arm on the subframe and insert the front mounting bolt loosely.

9 Insert the two rear outer mounting bolts loosely, then position the inner bolt hole in the exact position noted during removal. If a VW location pin was used on removal, the bracket will be correctly positioned on the pin. Tighten the two outer bolts to the specified torque, then remove the pin and refit the inner bolt, and tighten to the specified torque.

10 Tighten the front mounting bolt to the specified torque.

11 Lever down the lower arm and locate the balljoint studs in their holes. Fit the new nuts and tighten to the specified torque.

12 Refit the roadwheel and undershield, and lower the car to the ground.

---

6 Front suspension lower arm balljoint – removal, inspection and refitting

Note: *All self-locking nuts and bolts disturbed on removal must be renewed as a matter of course.*

Removal

Method 1

1 Remove the wheel bearing housing as described in Section 2.

2 Unscrew and remove the balljoint retaining nut **(see illustration)**, then release the balljoint from the wheel bearing housing using a

universal balljoint separator. Withdraw the balljoint.

Method 2

3 Remove the wheel trim/hub cap (as applicable) and loosen the driveshaft retaining bolt (hub bolt) with the vehicle resting on its wheels. **Note:** *Do not loosen the hub bolt more than 90° at this stage, or the wheel bearing may be damaged. Also loosen the wheel bolts.*

4 Apply the handbrake, then jack up the front of the vehicle and support it on axle stands (see *Jacking and vehicle support*). Remove the appropriate roadwheel.

5 Unscrew and remove the driveshaft retaining bolt.

6 Unscrew the front suspension lower balljoint-to-lower arm retaining nuts, then lever the lower arm down to release the balljoint studs **(see illustration 4.5a)**. Now use a soft-faced mallet to tap the driveshaft from the hub splines while pulling out the bottom end of the wheel bearing housing. If the driveshaft is tight on the splines, it may be necessary to use a puller bolted to the hub to remove it. It is not necessary to remove the driveshaft completely from the hub. Retain the wheel bearing housing away from the lower arm by inserting a block of wood between the strut and the inner body panel.

7 Unscrew and remove the balljoint retaining nut, then release the balljoint from the wheel bearing housing using a universal balljoint separator. Withdraw the balljoint.

Inspection

8 With the balljoint removed, check that it moves freely, without any sign of roughness. Check also that the balljoint rubber gaiter shows no sign of deterioration, and is free from cracks and splits. Renew as necessary.

Refitting

Method 1

9 Fit the balljoint to the wheel bearing housing and fit the new retaining nut. Tighten the nut to the specified torque setting, noting that the balljoint shank can be retained with an Allen key if necessary to prevent it from rotating.

10 Refit the wheel bearing housing with reference to Section 2.

Method 2

11 Fit the balljoint to the wheel bearing housing and fit the new retaining nut. Tighten the nut to the specified torque setting, noting that the balljoint shank can be retained with an Allen key if necessary to prevent it from rotating.

12 Remove the wooden block and move the strut inwards, then refit the balljoint to the lower arm using new nuts, and tighten them to the specified torque.

13 Refit the driveshaft retaining bolt and tighten it sufficiently to draw the driveshaft fully into the hub, then refit the roadwheel.

14 Have an assistant depress the brake pedal, then tighten the driveshaft retaining bolt in the stages given in the Specifications. It is

6.2 Undo the nut and use a balljoint splitter to separate the balljoint from the bearing housing

recommended that an angle gauge is used to ensure the correct tightening angle. **Note:** *The car must not be standing on its wheels when tightening the bolt, or the wheel bearing may be damaged.*

15 Lower the vehicle to the ground, tighten the roadwheel bolts, and refit the wheel trim/hub cap.

7 Front anti-roll bar – removal and refitting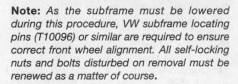

Note: *As the subframe must be lowered during this procedure, VW subframe locating pins (T10096) or similar are required to ensure correct front wheel alignment. All self-locking nuts and bolts disturbed on removal must be renewed as a matter of course.*

Removal

1 Apply the handbrake, then jack up the front of the vehicle and support it on axle stands (see *Jacking and vehicle support*). Remove both front roadwheels and the engine compartment undershield.

2 Inside the car, undo the nuts and remove the trim beneath the foot pedals for access to the steering column universal joint. Unscrew the clamp bolt and pull the universal joint from the steering gear pinion.

3 The anti-roll bar may be removed with or without the side links. Unscrew the nuts securing the links to the struts or anti-roll bar as required **(see illustration 4.3)**.

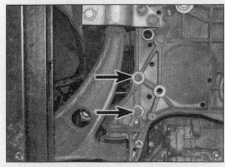

7.5a Anti-roll bar clamp bolts on the left-hand side (arrowed) . . .

4 Working on each side in turn, unscrew the front suspension lower balljoint-to-lower arm retaining nuts, then disconnect the track rod ends with reference to Section 24.

5 Unscrew the bolts securing the anti-roll bar clamps to the subframe **(see illustrations)**. Mark the anti-roll bar to indicate which way round it is fitted, and the position of the rubber mounting bushes; this will aid refitting.

6 Unscrew and remove the engine/transmission rear mounting bolts from the transmission.

7 Support the subframe with a trolley jack and block of wood. If not using the special VW locating pins T10096, accurately mark the position of the subframe to ensure correct wheel alignment.

8 Unscrew the mounting bolts and slightly lower the subframe, taking care not to damage the electrical wiring. Where available, fit the VW locating pins to facilitate refitting.

9 Lift the anti-roll bar forwards over the bracket, and lower it to the floor.

10 Carefully examine the anti-roll bar components for signs of wear, damage or deterioration, paying particular attention to the rubber mounting bushes. Renew worn components as necessary.

Refitting

11 Refitting is a reversal of removal but tighten all nuts and bolts to the specified torque where given. When refitting the subframe, align it with the marks made on removal, or use the special VW location pins before tightening the mounting bolts. To assist entry of the steering gear gaiter through the bulkhead, apply a soapy solution to it. Have the front wheel alignment checked at the earliest opportunity.

8 Front anti-roll bar connecting link – removal and refitting

Note: *All self-locking nuts and bolts disturbed on removal must be renewed as a matter of course.*

Removal

1 Apply the handbrake, then jack up the front of the vehicle and support it on axle stands

7.5b . . . and on the right-hand side (arrowed)

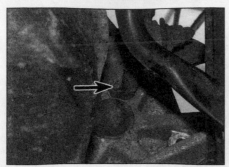

9.5 Rear ABS sensor retaining bolt (arrowed)

(see *Jacking and vehicle support*). Remove the relevant front roadwheel.

2 Unscrew and remove the nuts securing the link to the strut and anti-roll bar **(see illustration 4.3).**

3 Inspect the link rubbers for signs of damage or deterioration. If evident, renew the link complete.

Refitting

4 Refitting is a reversal of removal, but tighten the nuts to the specified torque.

9 Rear wheel bearing housing – removal and refitting

Removal

1 Chock the front wheels, then jack up the rear of the vehicle and support it on axle stands (see *Jacking and vehicle support*).

2 Remove the rear coil spring as described in Section 14.

3 Remove the rear hub as described in Section 10.

4 Unscrew the splash plate from the rear wheel bearing housing.

5 Disconnect the wiring, then unscrew the mounting bolt and remove the ABS sensor from the rear wheel bearing housing **(see illustration).**

6 Unscrew the bolt securing the rear shock absorber to the rear wheel bearing housing.

7 Unscrew the bolts securing the upper

10.3 Prise the dust cap from the hub

9.17 Measure from the centre of the wheel arch to the centre of the hub

transverse link and lower transverse links to the rear wheel bearing housing.

8 Unscrew the bolt securing the rear track control rod to the rear wheel bearing housing.

9 Support the rear wheel bearing housing, then unscrew the mounting bolts from the trailing arm. Also, undo the nut and disconnect the anti-roll bar link from the trailing arm.

10 Withdraw the rear wheel bearing housing from the car.

Refitting

11 Attach the rear wheel bearing housing to the rear track control rod, and the upper and lower transverse links, and hand-tighten the bolts.

12 Fit the wheel bearing housing to the trailing arm and hand-tighten the bolts.

13 Attach the anti-roll bar link rod to the housing/trailing arm and hand-tighten the nut.

14 Refit the shock absorber lower mounting bolt and tighten to the specified torque.

15 Refit the splash plate and tighten the bolts to the specified torque.

16 Refit the rear hub with reference to Section 10.

17 Position the centre of the rear hub the ride-height distance (see *Specifications*) from the centre of the wheel arch, according to model **(see illustration).** Use the trolley jack to adjust the position.

18 Tighten the wheel bearing housing-to-trailing arm bolts to the specified torque.

19 Tighten the following bolts to their specified torque, in the order given:
  a) *Track control rod.*
  b) *Upper transverse link. Position the washer so that it clears the splash plate.*
  c) *Lower transverse link.*

20 Tighten the anti-roll bar link nut to the specified torque.

21 Remove the trolley jack, then refit the rear coil spring with reference to Section 14.

22 Refit the ABS sensor and tighten the mounting bolt. Reconnect the wiring.

23 Refit the roadwheel, then lower the vehicle to the ground, tighten the roadwheel bolts, and refit the wheel trim/hub cap. Have the rear wheel alignment checked and if necessary adjusted by a VW dealer or specialist.

10 Rear hub/wheel bearings – checking and renewal

Note: *The rear wheel bearings cannot be renewed independently of the rear hub, because the outer races are formed in the hub itself. If excessive wear is evident, the rear hub must be renewed complete. The rear hub nut must always be renewed after removal.*

Removal

1 Chock the front roadwheels, then jack up the rear of the vehicle and support on axle stands (see *Jacking and vehicle support*). Release the handbrake and remove the relevant rear roadwheel.

2 Remove the rear disc as described in Chapter 9.

3 Remove the dust cap from the centre of the hub using a screwdriver or cold chisel **(see illustration).**

4 Unscrew and remove the hub bolt, using a multi-spline key. Note that it is tightened to a high torque and a socket extension bar may be required to loosen it. The bolt must be renewed whenever removed.

5 Using a suitable puller, pull the hub and bearings from the stub axle. The bearing inner race will remain on the stub axle, and a puller will be required to remove it; use a sharp cold chisel to move the race away from the stub axle base so that the puller legs can fully engage the race.

6 Examine the hub and bearings for wear, pitting and damage. If any damage is evident, renew the hub complete.

Refitting

7 Wipe clean the stub axle, then check that the bearing races are adequately lubricated with suitable grease. Check that the inner bearing race is located correctly in the hub. Also make sure that the ABS rotor is pressed firmly onto the inner end of the hub.

8 Locate the hub as far as possible on the stub axle.

9 Screw on the new bolt and tighten it to the specified torque.

10 Check the dust cap for damage and renew it if necessary. Use a hammer to carefully tap the cap into the hub. **Note:** *A badly fitting dust cap will allow moisture to enter the bearing, reducing its service life.*

11 Refit the brake disc as described in Chapter 9.

12 Refit the roadwheel and lower the vehicle to the ground.

11 Rear track control rod – removal and refitting

Removal

1 Chock the front roadwheels, then jack up

the rear of the vehicle and support on axle stands (see *Jacking and vehicle support*). Remove the relevant rear roadwheel.

2 Remove the rear anti-roll bar as described in Section 16. This is to allow removal of the control rod inner bolt.

3 Note the fitted position of the rear track control rod, with the 'closed' side facing forwards. Also, note which way round the mounting bolts are fitted.

4 Unscrew the inner bolt retaining nut, then use a large adjustable spanner to counteract the 'twist' loading on the control rod to allow the inner bolt to be removed **(see illustrations)**.

5 Unscrew and remove the outer mounting bolt and nut, and withdraw the track control rod from under the vehicle. Note the location of the special 'star' washer beneath the head of the bolt securing the outer end of the rod to the wheel bearing housing **(see illustration)**.

Refitting

6 Refitting is a reversal of removal, but tighten the bolts to the specified torque only when the weight of the vehicle is back on its wheels. Check that a clearance exists between the special 'star' washer and the track control rod. Have the rear wheel alignment checked and if necessary adjusted by a VW dealer or specialist.

---

12 Rear transverse links – removal and refitting

Upper link

Removal

1 Chock the front roadwheels, then jack up the rear of the vehicle and support on axle stands (see *Jacking and vehicle support*). Remove the roadwheel.

2 Remove the rear coil spring as described in Section 14.

3 Release the ABS speed sensor wiring from the upper link, then unscrew the bolt securing the link to the wheel bearing housing **(see illustration)**.

4 At the inner end of the upper link, mark the position of the eccentric bolt and subframe

11.4a Undo the track control rod inner bolt and nut . . .

in relation to each other. This alignment determines the camber setting of the rear wheels **(see illustration)**.

5 Note which way round the eccentric bolt is fitted, then unscrew and remove it, and withdraw the upper link.

Refitting

6 Refitting is a reversal of removal, but delay fully-tightening the mounting bolts until the rear suspension is set to the correct ride-height as described in Section 9. Make sure the eccentric bolt is correctly aligned as previously-noted, and also position the 'star' washer to provide a clearance between one of its points and the splash plate. Have the rear wheel alignment checked and if necessary adjusted by a VW dealer or specialist.

Lower link

Removal

7 Chock the front roadwheels, then jack up the rear of the vehicle and support on axle stands (see *Jacking and vehicle support*). Remove the roadwheel.

8 Remove the rear coil spring as described in Section 14.

9 Unscrew the bolt securing the lower transverse link to the wheel bearing housing.

10 On models with headlight range control, unscrew the nut and disconnect the sensor arm from the link.

11 At the inner end of the upper link, mark the position of the eccentric bolt and subframe in relation to each other **(see illustration)**. This

11.4b . . . then 'twist' the control rod and remove the bolt

11.5 Undo the track control rod outer mounting bolt

alignment determines the camber setting of the rear wheels.

12 Refer to Chapter 4B and lower the rear section of the exhaust system for improved access. Support the exhaust on an axle stand.

13 Unscrew and remove the inner bolt and withdraw the lower transverse link from under the car.

Refitting

14 Refitting is a reversal of removal, but delay fully-tightening the mounting bolts until the rear suspension is set to the correct ride-height as described in Section 9. Make sure the eccentric bolt is correctly aligned as previously-noted, and also position the 'star' washer to provide a clearance between one of its points and the splash plate. Have the rear wheel alignment checked and if necessary adjusted by a VW dealer or specialist.

12.3 Rear upper link outer bolt (arrowed)

12.4 Mark the position of the eccentric washer (arrowed) – upper transverse link

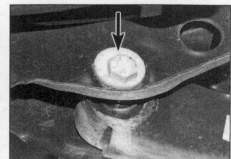

12.11 Lower transverse link inner bolt eccentric washer (arrowed)

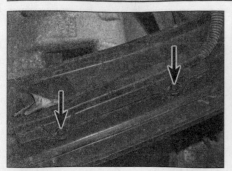

13.3 Prise out the pins (arrowed) and remove the wiring loom guide

13.6 Mark the position of the trailing arm front bracket in relation to the underbody

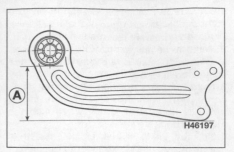

13.9a Make a vertical line on the arm as shown . . .

A = 114.0 mm

13 Rear trailing arm and bracket – removal, overhaul and refitting

Removal

1 Chock the front roadwheels, then jack up the rear of the vehicle and support on axle stands (see *Jacking and vehicle support*). Remove the roadwheel.
2 Remove the rear coil spring as described in Section 14.
3 Prise out the centre pins of the plastic expansion rivets, then remove the retainer guide for the ABS wiring loom attached to the trailing arm **(see illustration)**.
4 Unscrew the nut and detach the anti-roll bar link.
5 Unscrew the bolts securing the trailing arm to the rear wheel bearing housing.
6 Mark the position of the trailing arm front mounting bracket in relation to the underbody **(see illustration)**.
7 Support the front mounting bracket on a trolley jack, then unscrew the bolts, lower the assembly and withdraw the rear trailing arm and bracket from under the vehicle.

Overhaul

8 Thoroughly clean the trailing arm and bracket, then unscrew the front pivot bolt and separate the arm from the bracket. Check carefully for cracks or any other signs of wear or damage, paying particular attention to the rubber mounting bush.
9 If the bush requires renewal, take the arm to a VW dealer or suitably-equipped garage. Alternatively, a hydraulic press and suitable spacers may be used to press the bush out of the arm, and to install the new one. Dip the bush in a mild solution of washing-up liquid and water. When fitting the new bush to the front of the trailing arm, it is important to position it correctly. Make a vertical line on the arm as shown in the accompanying illustration, then press in the new bush so that the line is between the two projections shown **(see illustrations)**.
10 With the new bush in position, locate the front of the arm in the bracket, and insert the bolt. Position the arm in relation to the bracket as shown **(see illustration)** then tighten the bolt/nut to the specified torque. There may be two types of bush.

Refitting

11 Fit the trailing arm to the wheel bearing housing and insert the bolts loosely.
12 Fit the anti-roll bar link and bolt on the nut loosely.
13 Raise the front mounting bracket and locate it on the underbody in its previously-noted position. Insert the new bolts and tighten to the specified torque.

14 Lower the jack then tighten the arm-to-housing bolts to the specified torque.
15 Tighten the anti-roll bar link nut.
16 Refit the wiring loom retainer guide.
17 Refit the rear coil spring with reference to Section 14.
18 Refit the roadwheel and lower the vehicle to the ground. Have the rear wheel alignment checked and if necessary adjusted by a VW dealer or specialist.

14 Rear coil spring – removal and refitting

 Warning: Adjustable coil spring compressors are readily available, and are recommended for this operation. Any attempt to remove the coil spring without such a tool is likely to result in damage or personal injury.

Removal

1 Chock the front roadwheels, then jack up the rear of the vehicle and support on axle stands (see *Jacking and vehicle support*). Remove the relevant rear roadwheel.
2 Fit the tool to the coil spring and compress it until it can be removed from the transverse arm and underbody **(see illustration)**. With the coil spring on the bench, carefully release the tension of the tool and remove it.

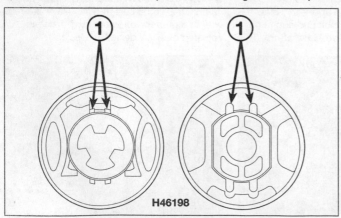

13.9b . . . then press in the new bush so that the line is between the two projections (1)

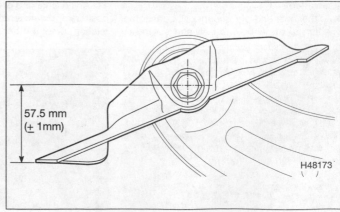

13.10 Bracket position on the rear trailing arm

57.5 mm (± 1mm)

3 With the coil spring removed, recover the upper and lower spring seats and check them for damage. Obtain new ones if necessary, but note that they are different, the lower one having a location pin which enters a hole in the lower transverse link. Also clean the spring locations on the underbody and trailing arm thoroughly.

Refitting

4 Refitting is a reversal of removal, but make sure that the lower spring seat engages the hole in the lower transverse link, the lower end of the coil spring abuts the stop on the seat, and the upper seat is correctly engaged with the lug on the underbody **(see illustrations)**.

15 Rear shock absorber – removal and refitting

Note: *All self-locking nuts and bolts disturbed on removal must be renewed as a matter of course.*

Removal

1 Before removing the shock absorber, an idea of how effective it is can be gained by depressing the rear corner of the car. If the shock absorber is in good condition, the body should rise then settle in its normal position. If the body oscillates more than this, the shock absorber is probably defective. **Note:** *To ensure even rear suspension, both rear shock absorbers should be renewed at the same time.*

2 Chock the front roadwheels, then jack up the rear of the vehicle and support on axle stands (see *Jacking and vehicle support*). Remove the relevant rear roadwheel.

3 Undo the Torx bolts and remove the wheel arch liner.

4 Position a trolley jack and block of wood beneath the coil spring position on the trailing arm, and raise the arm so that the shock absorber is slightly compressed. Note on some models, it may be necessary to remove the stone protection guard first. If preferred, the rear coil spring may be removed completely at this stage as described in Section 14.

5 Unscrew the lower mounting bolt, then unscrew the upper mounting bolts and withdraw the shock absorber **(see illustrations)**.

6 With the shock absorber on the bench, remove the cap, then unscrew the nut from the top of the piston rod and remove the upper mounting bracket, followed by the bump stop, and where fitted the support ring, protective tube, and protective cap **(see illustrations)**. **Note:** *Two types of bump stop are supplied; a short version with a support ring, and a long version without a support ring.*

7 If necessary, the action of the shock absorber can be checked by mounting it upright in a vice. Fully depress the rod, then pull it up fully. The piston rod must move smoothly over its complete length.

Refitting

8 Locate the components removed from the

14.2 Compress the coil spring with a special tool

14.4a The lug on the underside of the spring seat (arrowed) . . .

14.4b . . . must locate in the hole (arrowed)

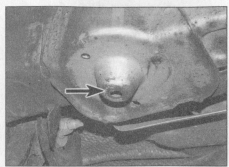

14.4c The upper end of the coil spring must locate around the lug (arrowed) on the underbody

top of the shock absorber in their correct order, and bolt on a new nut. Tighten the nut and fit the cap.

9 Locate the shock absorber in the rear wheel

arch, then insert the upper mounting bolts and tighten to the specified torque.

10 Extend the shock absorber if necessary, and insert the lower mounting bolt loosely.

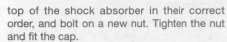

15.5a Rear shock absorber lower mounting bolt (arrowed) . . .

15.5b . . . and upper mounting bolts (arrowed)

15.6a Prise off the cap and undo the nut (arrowed) . . .

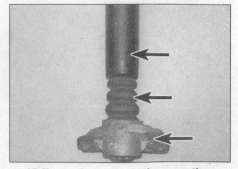

15.6b . . . then remove the mounting, bump stop and sleeve (arrowed)

16.2 Use a multi-spline bit in the end of the anti-roll bar link balljoint shank (arrowed) to counterhold the nut

16.4 Anti-roll bar clamp bolts (arrowed)

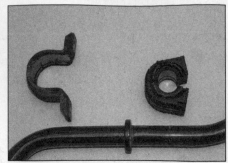

16.5 Prise off the clamps and remove the split rubber bushes

Note the washer between the shock absorber and wheel bearing housing.

11 Raise the trailing arm until the rear suspension is set to the correct ride-height given as described in Section 9, then fully tighten the shock absorber lower mounting bolt.

12 Refit the rear coil spring with reference to Section 14.

13 Refit the wheel arch liner.

14 Refit the roadwheel and lower the vehicle to the ground.

16 Rear anti-roll bar – removal and refitting

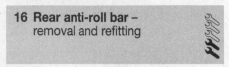

Removal

1 Chock the front roadwheels, then jack up the rear of the vehicle and support on axle stands (see *Jacking and vehicle support*). Remove both rear roadwheels.

2 Working on each side in turn, unscrew the nut and detach the side links from the anti-roll bar. Discard the nuts – new ones must be fitted. Use a multi-spline bit to counterhold the nut (see illustration).

3 Mark the anti-roll bar to indicate which way round it is fitted, and the position of the rubber mounting bushes; this will aid refitting.

4 Unscrew the multi-spline bolts securing the anti-roll bar clamps to the rear subframe, and recover the clamps (see illustration).

19.3 Unscrew the steering wheel bolt using a multi-spline bit

5 If required, prise off the clamps and remove the split bushes from the bar (see illustration)

Refitting

6 Refitting is a reversal of removal but tighten all nuts and bolts to the specified torque only when the weight of the vehicle is back on the wheels.

17 Rear anti-roll bar connecting link – removal and refitting

Removal

1 Chock the front roadwheels, then jack up the rear of the vehicle and support on axle stands (see *Jacking and vehicle support*). Remove the relevant rear roadwheel.

2 Unscrew the nuts securing the link to the anti-roll bar and trailing arm, and withdraw it from under the vehicle (see illustration 16.2). Discard the nuts – new ones must be fitted. Use a multi-spline bit to counterhold the nuts.

3 Inspect the link rubbers/balljoints for signs of damage or deterioration. If evident, renew the link complete.

Refitting

4 Refitting is a reversal of removal, but tighten the nuts to the specified torque only when the weight of the vehicle is back on the wheels.

18 Vehicle level sender – removal and refitting

Removal

1 The front sender for the headlight range control system is located on the left-hand side of the front subframe, and incorporates an arm and link attached to the left-hand front lower suspension arm. The rear sender is bolted to the rear subframe, and an arm and link is attached to a bracket on the lower transverse link. The system is controlled by an ECM located behind a cover on the passenger's side of the instrument panel.

2 To remove the front sender, apply the handbrake then jack up the front of the vehicle and support it on axle stands (see *Jacking and vehicle support*). Remove the front roadwheel, then note the position of the sender on the lower arm. Unscrew the nut and disconnect the link and bracket from the lower arm. Disconnect the wiring then unscrew the bolt and remove the sender from the front subframe.

3 To remove the rear sender, chock the front roadwheels then jack up the rear of the vehicle and support on axle stands (see *Jacking and vehicle support*). Disconnect the wiring from the sender. Unscrew the bolts securing the link and bracket to the lower transverse link, then unscrew the bolts and remove the sender from the rear subframe.

Refitting

4 Refitting is a reversal of removal, but tighten the mounting bolts to the specified torque. If a sender has been renewed, the basic setting of the system needs to be performed using dedicated diagnostic equipment. Entrust this task to a VW dealer or suitably-equipped specialist.

19 Steering wheel – removal and refitting

Removal

1 Remove the driver's airbag as described in Chapter 12.

2 Adjust the steering column to its highest position, then extend it into the passenger compartment as far as possible, and lock it in this position.

3 Using a multi-spline bit, unscrew and remove the retaining bolt, while holding the steering wheel stationary (see illustration). Discard the bolt – a new one must be fitted.

4 Check if the steering wheel is marked in relation to the column. If not, use a dab of paint to mark them, then ease the steering wheel from the column splines by firmly rocking it side-to-side (see illustration).

Refitting

5 Locate the steering wheel on the column splines making sure that the previously-made marks are correctly aligned.

6 Fit the new retaining bolt and tighten to the specified torque while holding the steering wheel stationary.

7 Refit the driver's airbag with reference to Chapter 12.

20 Steering column –
removal, inspection and refitting

Removal

1 Adjust the steering column to its lowest position and extend it into the passenger compartment as far as possible, then lock it in this position.

2 Remove the steering wheel as described in Section 19.

3 Release the gap cover, then unclip and remove the upper shroud from the steering column (**see illustrations**).

4 Undo the two upper bolts and single lower bolt and remove the lower shroud from the steering column (**see illustrations**). As the shroud is being removed, release it from the height and reach adjustment handle.

5 Undo the 2 retaining bolts and remove the trim panel above the driver's pedals. Unclip the diagnostic connector from the panel as it's withdrawn (**see illustration**).

6 Unclip the cover (where fitted), undo the bolt in the recess, then pull the driver's side footwell trim downwards to release it from the centre console, then rearwards to release the front 'hook' (**see illustration**).

7 Undo the bolt and remove the footwell vent from under the steering column.

8 Remove the combination switch assembly from the top of the steering column as described in Section 21. **Note:** *If it is not imperative to remove the assembly, leave it in position on the steering column, and disconnect the wiring plugs.*

9 Unscrew the nut and disconnect the earth cable, then disconnect all relevant wiring plugs and remove the wiring harness from the steering column (**see illustration**).

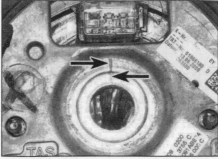

19.4 Make alignment marks between the wheel and column shaft (arrowed)

20.3b . . . then prise the upper shroud from the lower shroud

20.4a Undo the upper bolts (arrowed) . . .

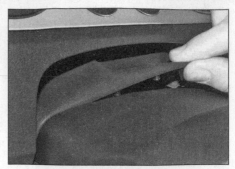

20.3a Unclip the gap cover . . .

20.3c Note how the lug (arrowed) at the front of the shroud, engages with the slot (arrowed)

10 Remove the cable guide from below the steering column. To do this, carefully prise up the lugs from the retaining clips (**see illustration**).

11 Undo the nuts and remove the trim beneath the foot pedals for access to the steering column universal joint. Unscrew the clamp bolt and pull the universal joint from the

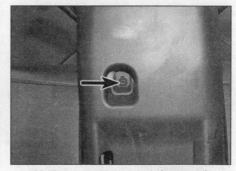

20.4b . . . and lower bolt (arrowed)

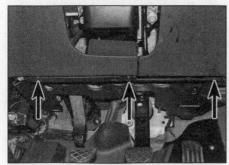

20.5 Undo the bolts (arrowed) and remove the panel above the pedals

20.6 Undo the bolt (arrowed) securing the panel in the footwell

20.9 Undo the nut (arrowed) and disconnect the earth cable

20.10 Prise up the lugs from the retaining clips (arrowed)

20.11a Undo the nuts (arrowed) and remove the trim panel

20.11b Universal joint pinch-bolt (arrowed)

steering gear pinion (see illustrations). Note that the pinion shaft has a cut-out to enable fitting of the clamp bolt, and the splined pinion shaft incorporates a flat making it impossible to assemble the joint to the shaft in the wrong position. Discard the clamp bolt; a new one should be used on refitting.

12 Note that the inner and outer columns, and the intermediate shaft, are telescopic, to facilitate the reach adjustment. It is important to keep the splined sections of the inner steering column engaged with each other while the steering column is removed. If they become detached due to the outer column sections being separated, especially on a vehicle which has completed a high mileage, it is possible that rattling noises may occur.

13 Unscrew and remove two diagonally-opposite mounting bolts, then support the steering column and unscrew the two remaining bolts (see illustration). Withdraw the steering column from inside the car. Discard the bolts as new ones must be used on refitting. Note that the mounting bracket on the bulkhead has location pins which align the steering column.

Caution: Do not carry the steering column by suspending it from the universal joint or intermediate shaft, as this will damage the universal joint and steering column bushes. Also, do not bend the joints by more than 90°.

Inspection

14 The steering column is designed to collapse in the event of a front-end crash, to

prevent the steering wheel injuring the driver. Before refitting the steering column, examine the column and mountings for signs of damage and deformation.

15 Check the inner column sections for signs of free play in the column bushes. If any damage or wear is found on the steering column bushes, the column must be renewed as an assembly.

16 The intermediate shaft is permanently attached to the inner column and cannot be renewed separately. Inspect the universal joints for excessive wear. If evident, the complete steering column must be renewed.

Refitting

17 Refit the steering column to the bulkhead bracket, insert the new mounting bolts, and tighten to the specified torque.

18 Reconnect the earth cable and tighten the bolt. Refit the wiring harness.

19 Attach the universal joint on the steering gear pinion splines, insert the new clamp bolt, and tighten to the specified torque.

20 The remainder of refitting is a reversal of removal. Note that the steering angle sensor basic settings may need to be set using dedicated diagnostic equipment. Entrust this task to a VW dealer or suitably-equipped specialist.

21 Steering column switch assembly – removal and refitting

Removal of the switch/control unit/sensor/contact assembly is described in Section 5 of Chapter 12.

22 Steering gear assembly – removal, overhaul and refitting

Note: Two different steering gear assemblies may be fitted. Vehicles up to model year 2008 are fitted with a '2nd Generation' assembly, and vehicles from model year 2009 are fitted with a '3rd Generation' assembly. If the 2nd Generation steering gear is to be renewed, only 3rd Generation assemblies are available, and the electrical wiring harness from the

engine electrical box to the steering gear will also have to be renewed.

Removal

1 Disconnect the battery negative lead and remove the battery tray as described in Chapter 5.

2 Disconnect the steering gear loom wiring from the engine compartment fusebox, earth connection and wiring plug. Release the loom retaining clip, then release the loom from the from the plastic cable guide.

3 Apply the handbrake, then jack up the front of the vehicle and support it on axle stands positioned on the underbody, leaving the subframe free (see Jacking and vehicle support). Position the steering straight-ahead, then remove both front roadwheels. Also remove the engine compartment undershield.

4 Inside the vehicle, undo the bolts and remove the plastic cover for access to the universal joint connecting the steering inner column to the steering gear pinion. Unscrew and remove the clamp bolt, and pull the universal joint from the pinion splines. Note: The steering gear pinion incorporates a cut-out for the clamp bolt, and therefore the joint can only be fitted in one position. Discard the clamp bolt, a new one should be used on refitting.

5 Working on each side in turn, unscrew the nuts from the track rod ends, then use a balljoint separator tool to release the ends from the steering arms on the front wheel bearing housings.

6 Working on each side in turn, unscrew the nuts securing the anti-roll bar links to the struts. Use an Allen key to counterhold the link balljoint shanks (see illustration 4.3).

7 Working on each side in turn, unscrew the front suspension lower balljoint-to-lower arm retaining nuts, then lever the lower arms down to release the balljoint studs. Discard the nuts – new ones must be fitted.

8 Unscrew and remove the engine/transmission rear mounting bolts from the transmission.

9 Unscrew the exhaust system mounting from the subframe (see illustration).

10 Undo the 3 Torx bolts and detach the heat shield from the steering gear. Unclip any wiring loom from the heat shield.

20.13 Steering column mounting bolts (arrowed)

22.9 Exhaust mounting bolts (arrowed)

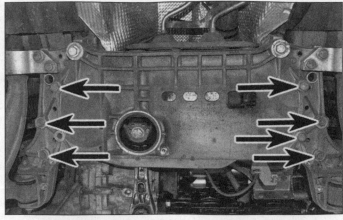

22.11 Steering gear and anti-roll bar bolts (arrowed)

11 Undo the bolts securing the steering gear and anti-roll bar to the subframe (see illustration).

12 Support the subframe with a trolley jack and block of wood. If not using the special VW locating pins T10096, accurately mark the position of the subframe to ensure correct wheel alignment.

13 Unscrew the mounting bolts and slightly lower the subframe, taking care not to damage the electrical wiring. Where available, fit the VW locating pins to facilitate refitting.

14 Remove the heat shield from over the steering gear.

15 Lower the subframe together with the steering gear to the floor.

16 Remove the cable guide and disconnect the wiring plugs from the steering gear. Release the wiring from all clips.

Caution: Do not touch the wiring terminals on the electronic control unit, as a static electricity discharge may damage the internal components.

17 Manoeuvre the steering gear from place, and carefully place it on the floor taking care not to damage the electronic control unit.

Overhaul

18 Examine the steering gear assembly for signs of wear or damage, and check that the rack moves freely throughout the full length of its travel, with no signs of roughness or excessive free play between the steering gear pinion and rack.

19 It is not possible to overhaul the steering gear assembly housing components, and if it is faulty, the assembly must be renewed. The only components which can be renewed individually are the steering gear gaiters, the track rod end balljoints and the track rods, as described later in this Chapter.

Refitting

20 Locate the steering gear on the subframe, and reconnect the wiring loom. Ensure the loom is clipped into place in its original locations.

21 Insert and tighten the new bolts for the gear and anti-roll bar.

22 Refit the heat shield, then raise the subframe onto the underbody and align it with the marks made on removal, or use the special VW location pins before tightening the new mounting bolts. To assist entry of the steering gear gaiter through the bulkhead, apply a soapy solution to it.

23 Refit the exhaust mounting, then refit the engine/transmission rear mounting bolts to the transmission and tighten to the specified torque.

24 Locate the front suspension lower balljoints in the lower arms, screw on the new nuts and tighten to the specified torque.

25 Refit the track rod ends with new nuts, and tighten to the specified torque.

26 Inside the car, attach the universal joint on the steering gear pinion splines, insert the new clamp bolt, and tighten to the specified torque.

27 The remainder of refitting is a reversal of removal. Have the front wheel alignment checked at the earliest opportunity. If a new steering gear has been fitted, the steering angle sensor basic settings must be set using dedicated diagnostic equipment, and it must also be adapted to the vehicle by a VW dealer or specialist.

23 Steering gear rubber gaiters and track rods – renewal

Steering gear rubber gaiters

1 Remove the track rod end balljoint as described in Section 24. Also, unscrew the locking nut after noting its position.

2 Wipe clean the rubber gaiter to prevent entry of dirt or moisture. Note the fitted position of the gaiter on the track rod, then release the retaining clips and slide the gaiter off the steering gear housing and track rod (see illustration).

3 Carefully slide the new gaiter onto the track rod, and locate it on the steering gear housing. Position the gaiter as noted on removal, making sure that it is not twisted, then lift the

outer sealing lip of the gaiter to equalise air pressure within the gaiter.

4 Secure the gaiter in position with new retaining clips. Where crimped-type clips are used, pull the clip as tight as possible, and locate the hooks in their slots. Remove any slack in the clip by carefully compressing the raised section. In the absence of the special crimping tool, a pair of side-cutters may be used, taking care not to cut the clip.

5 Screw on the locking nut, then refit the track rod end balljoint as described in Section 24.

Track rods

6 Remove the relevant steering gear rubber gaiter as described earlier. If there is insufficient working room with the steering gear mounted in the car, remove it as described in Section 22 and hold it in a vice while renewing the track rod.

7 Hold the steering rack stationary with one spanner on the flats provided, then loosen the balljoint nut with another spanner. Fully unscrew the nut and remove the track rod from the rack.

8 Locate the new track rod on the end of the steering rack and bolt on the nut. Hold the rack stationary with one spanner and tighten the balljoint nut to the specified torque. A crow's foot adapter may be required since the track rod prevents access with a socket, and care must be taken to apply the correct torque in this situation.

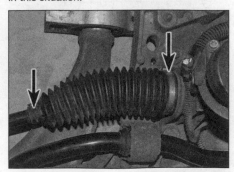

23.2 Steering gear gaiter clips (arrowed)

24.4 Use a balljoint splitter to separate the track rod end balljoint from the bearing housing

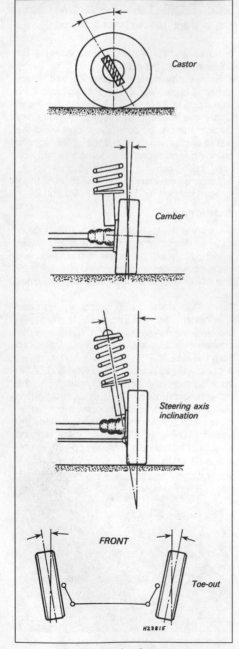

25.1 Front wheel geometry

9 Refit the steering gear or rubber gaiter with reference to the earlier paragraphs or Section 22. On completion check and, if necessary, adjust the front wheel alignment as described in Section 25.

24 Track rod end – removal and refitting

Removal

1 Apply the handbrake, then jack up the front of the vehicle and support it on axle stands (see *Jacking and vehicle support*). Remove the relevant roadwheel.
2 If the track rod end is to be re-used, mark its position in relation to the track rod to facilitate refitting.
3 Unscrew the track rod end locknut by a quarter of a turn. Do not move the locknut from this position, as it will serve as a handy reference mark on refitting.
4 Loosen and remove the nut securing the track rod end balljoint to the wheel bearing housing, and release the balljoint tapered shank using a universal balljoint separator. Note that the balljoint shank has a hexagon hole – hold the shank with an Allen key while loosening the nut **(see illustration)**.
5 Counting the exact number of turns necessary to do so, unscrew the track rod end from the track rod.
6 Carefully clean the balljoint and the threads. Renew the balljoint if its movement is sloppy or too stiff, if excessively worn, or if damaged in any way; carefully check the stud taper and threads. If the balljoint gaiter is damaged, the complete balljoint assembly must be renewed; it is not possible to obtain the gaiter separately.

Refitting

7 Screw the track rod end onto the track rod by the number of turns noted on removal. This should bring the track rod end to within a quarter of a turn of the locknut, with the alignment marks that were made on removal (if applicable) lined up. Tighten the locknut.
8 Refit the balljoint shank to the steering arm on the wheel bearing housing, then fit a new retaining nut and tighten it to the specified torque. Hold the shank with an Allen key if necessary.
9 Refit the roadwheel, then lower the car to the ground and tighten the roadwheel bolts to the specified torque.
10 Check and, if necessary, adjust the front wheel toe setting as described in Section 25.

25 Wheel alignment and steering angles – general information

Definitions

1 A car's steering and suspension geometry is defined in three basic settings – all angles are expressed in degrees; the steering axis is defined as an imaginary line drawn through the axis of the suspension strut, extended where necessary to contact the ground **(see illustration)**.
2 **Camber** is the angle between each roadwheel and a vertical line drawn through its centre and tyre contact patch, when viewed from the front or rear of the car. Positive camber is when the roadwheels are tilted outwards from the vertical at the top; negative camber is when they are tilted inwards.
3 Camber angle is only adjustable by loosening the front suspension subframe mounting bolts and moving it slightly to one side. This also alters the Castor angle. The camber angle can be checked using a camber checking gauge.
4 **Castor** is the angle between the steering axis and a vertical line drawn through each roadwheel's centre and tyre contact patch, when viewed from the side of the car. Positive castor is when the steering axis is tilted so that it contacts the ground ahead of the vertical; negative castor is when it contacts the ground behind the vertical. Slight castor angle adjustment is possible by loosening the front suspension subframe bolts and moving it slightly to one side. This also alters the Camber angle.
5 Castor is not easily adjustable, and is given for reference only; while it can be checked using a castor checking gauge, if the figure obtained is significantly different from that specified, the car must be taken for careful checking by a professional, as the fault can only be caused by wear or damage to the body or suspension components.
6 **Toe** is the difference, viewed from above, between lines drawn through the roadwheel centres and the car's centre-line. Toe-in is when the roadwheels point inwards, towards each other at the front, while toe-out is when they splay outwards from each other at the front.
7 The front wheel toe setting is adjusted by bolting the track rod(s) in/out of the outer balljoint(s) to alter the effective length of the track rod assembly.
8 Rear wheel toe setting is not adjustable, and is given for reference only. While it can be checked, if the figure obtained is significantly different from that specified, the car must be taken for careful checking by a professional, as the fault can only be caused by wear or damage to the body or suspension components.

Checking and adjustment

9 Due to the special measuring equipment necessary to check the wheel alignment, and the skill required to use it properly, the checking and adjustment of these settings is best left to a VW dealer or similar expert. Note that most tyre-fitting centres now possess sophisticated checking equipment.

Chapter 11
Bodywork and fittings

Contents

Degrees of difficulty

Easy, suitable for novice with little experience	Fairly easy, suitable for beginner with some experience	Fairly difficult, suitable for competent DIY mechanic	Difficult, suitable for experienced DIY mechanic	Very difficult, suitable for expert DIY or professional

Specifications

Torque wrench settings	Nm	lbf ft
Bonnet hinge bolts	21	15
Bonnet lock bolts	12	9
Boot lid (Saloon) mounting bolts	22	16
Door hinge bolts	28	21
Door lock bolts	20	15
Door mirror bolt	10	7
Front bumper mounting tube (lock carrier)-to-bodywork bolts	60	44
Seat belt anchor bolts*	40	30
Seat belt front stalk mounting bolt	20	15
Seat belt inertia reel bolt	40	30
Tailgate (Estate) mounting bolts/nuts	10	7

* Do not re-use

1 General description

Two body types are covered by this manual – the four-door Saloon and the five-door Estate. The body is of all-steel construction, and incorporates calculated impact crumple zones at the front and rear, with a central safety cell passenger compartment.

During manufacture, the underbody is treated with underseal and, as a further anti-rust aid, some of the more exposed body panels are galvanised. The bumpers and wheel arch liners are plastic mouldings, for durability and strength.

2 Maintenance – bodywork and underframe

The general condition of a vehicle's bodywork is the one thing that significantly affects its value. Maintenance is easy, but needs to be regular. Neglect, particularly after minor damage, can lead quickly to further deterioration and costly repair bills. It is important also to keep watch on those parts of the vehicle not immediately visible, for instance the underside, inside all the wheel arches, and the lower part of the engine compartment.

The basic maintenance routine for the bodywork is washing – preferably with a lot of water, from a hose. This will remove all the loose solids which may have stuck to the vehicle. It is important to flush these off in such a way as to prevent grit from scratching the finish. The wheel arches and underframe need washing in the same way, to remove any accumulated mud which will retain moisture and tend to encourage rust. Paradoxically enough, the best time to clean the underframe and wheel arches is in wet weather, when the mud is thoroughly wet and soft. In very wet weather, the underframe is usually cleaned of large accumulations automatically, and this is a good time for inspection.

Periodically, except on vehicles with a wax-based underbody protective coating, it is a good idea to have the whole of the underframe of the vehicle steam-cleaned, engine compartment included, so that a thorough inspection can be carried out to see what minor repairs and renovations are necessary. Steam cleaning is available at many garages, and is necessary for the removal of the accumulation of oily grime, which sometimes is allowed to become thick in certain areas. If steam-cleaning facilities are not available, there are some excellent grease solvents available which can be brush-applied; the dirt can then be simply hosed off. Note that these methods should not be used on vehicles with wax-based underbody protective coating, or the coating will be removed. Such vehicles should be inspected annually, preferably just before Winter, when the underbody should be washed down, and any damage to the wax coating repaired. Ideally, a completely fresh coat should be applied. It would also be worth considering the use of wax-based protection for injection into door panels, sills, box sections, etc, as an additional safeguard against rust damage, where such protection is not provided by the vehicle manufacturer.

After washing paintwork, wipe off with a chamois leather to give an unspotted clear finish. A coat of clear protective wax polish will give added protection against chemical pollutants in the air. If the paintwork sheen has dulled or oxidised, use a cleaner/polisher combination to restore the brilliance of the shine. This requires a little effort, but such dulling is usually caused because regular washing has been neglected. Care needs to be taken with metallic paintwork, as special non-abrasive cleaner/polisher is required to avoid damage to the finish. Always check that the door and ventilator opening drain holes and pipes are completely clear, so that water can be drained out. Brightwork should be treated in the same way as paintwork. Windscreens and windows can be kept clear of the smeary film which often appears, by proprietary glass cleaner. Never use any form of wax or other body or chromium polish on glass.

3 Maintenance – upholstery and carpets

Mats and carpets should be brushed or vacuum-cleaned regularly, to keep them free of grit. If they are badly stained, remove them from the vehicle for scrubbing or sponging, and make quite sure they are dry before refitting. Seats and interior trim panels can be kept clean by wiping with a damp cloth. If they do become stained (which can be more apparent on light-coloured upholstery), use a little liquid detergent and a soft nail brush to scour the grime out of the grain of the material. Do not forget to keep the headlining clean in the same way as the upholstery. When using liquid cleaners inside the vehicle, do not over-wet the surfaces being cleaned. Excessive damp could get into the seams and padded interior, causing stains, offensive odours or even rot. If the inside of the vehicle gets wet accidentally, it is worthwhile taking some trouble to dry it out properly, particularly where carpets are involved. *Do not leave oil or electric heaters inside the vehicle for this purpose.*

4 Minor body damage – repair

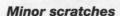

Minor scratches

If the scratch is very superficial, and does not penetrate to the metal of the bodywork, repair is very simple. Lightly rub the area of the scratch with a paintwork renovator or a very fine cutting paste to remove loose paint from the scratch, and to clear the surrounding bodywork of wax polish. Rinse the area with clean water.

Apply touch-up paint to the scratch using a fine paint brush; continue to apply fine layers of paint until the surface of the paint in the scratch is level with the surrounding paintwork. Allow the new paint at least two weeks to harden, then blend it into the surrounding paintwork by rubbing the scratch area with a paintwork renovator or a very fine cutting paste. Finally, apply wax polish.

Where the scratch has penetrated right through to the metal of the bodywork, causing the metal to rust, a different repair technique is required. Remove any loose rust from the bottom of the scratch with a penknife, then apply rust-inhibiting paint to prevent the formation of rust in the future. Using a rubber or nylon applicator, fill the scratch with bodystopper paste. If required, this paste can be mixed with cellulose thinners to provide a very thin paste which is ideal for filling narrow scratches. Before the stopper-paste in the scratch hardens, wrap a piece of smooth cotton rag around the top of a finger. Dip the finger in cellulose thinners, and quickly sweep it across the surface of the stopper-paste in the scratch; this will ensure that the surface of the stopper-paste is slightly hollowed. The scratch can now be painted over as described earlier in this Section.

Dents

When deep denting of the vehicle's bodywork has taken place, the first task is to pull the dent out, until the affected bodywork almost attains its original shape. There is little point in trying to restore the original shape completely, as the metal in the damaged area will have stretched on impact, and cannot be reshaped fully to its original contour. It is better to bring the level of the dent up to a point which is about 3 mm below the level of the surrounding bodywork. In cases where the dent is very shallow anyway, it is not worth trying to pull it out at all. If the underside of the dent is accessible, it can be hammered out gently from behind, using a mallet with a wooden or plastic head. Whilst doing this, hold a suitable block of wood firmly against the outside of the panel, to absorb the impact from the hammer blows and thus prevent a large area of the bodywork from being 'belled-out'.

Should the dent be in a section of the bodywork which has a double skin, or some other factor making it inaccessible from behind, a different technique is called for. Drill several small holes through the metal inside the area – particularly in the deeper section. Then bolt long self-tapping screws into the holes, just sufficiently for them to gain a good purchase in the metal. Now the dent can be pulled out by pulling on the protruding heads of the bolts with a pair of pliers.

The next stage of the repair is the removal of the paint from the damaged area, and from an inch or so of the surrounding 'sound' bodywork. This is accomplished most easily by using a wire brush or abrasive pad on a power drill, although it can be done just as effectively by hand, using sheets of abrasive paper. To complete the preparation for filling, score the surface of the bare metal with a screwdriver or the tang of a file, or alternatively, drill small holes in the affected area. This will provide a good 'key' for the filler paste.

To complete the repair, see the Section on filling and respraying.

Rust holes or gashes

Remove all paint from the affected area, and from an inch or so of the surrounding 'sound' bodywork, using an abrasive pad or a wire brush on a power drill. If these are not available, a few sheets of abrasive paper will do the job most effectively. With the paint removed, you will be able to judge the severity of the corrosion, and therefore decide whether to renew the whole panel (if this is possible) or to repair the affected area. New body panels are not as expensive as most people think, and it is often quicker and more satisfactory to fit a new panel than to attempt to repair large areas of corrosion.

Remove all fittings from the affected area, except those which will act as a guide to the original shape of the damaged bodywork (eg, headlight shells, etc). Then, using tin snips or a hacksaw blade, remove all loose metal and any other metal badly affected by corrosion. Hammer the edges of the hole inwards, to create a slight depression for the filler paste.

Wire-brush the affected area to remove the powdery rust from the surface of the remaining metal. Paint the affected area with rust-inhibiting paint; if the back of the rusted area is accessible, treat this also.

Before filling can take place, it will be necessary to block the hole in some way. This can be achieved with aluminium or plastic mesh, or aluminium tape.

Aluminium or plastic mesh, or glass-fibre matting, is probably the best material to use for a large hole. Cut a piece to the approximate size and shape of the hole to be filled, then position it in the hole so that its edges are below the level of the surrounding bodywork. It can be retained in position by several blobs of filler paste around its periphery.

Aluminium tape should be used for small or very narrow holes. Pull a piece off the roll, trim it to the approximate size and shape required, then pull off the backing paper (if used) and stick the tape over the hole; it can be overlapped if the thickness of one piece is insufficient. Burnish down the edges of the tape with the handle of a screwdriver or similar, to ensure that the tape is securely attached to the metal underneath.

Filling and respraying

Before using this Section, see the Sections on dent, deep scratch, rust holes and gash repairs.

Many types of bodyfiller are available, but generally speaking, those proprietary kits which contain a tin of filler paste and a tube of resin hardener are best for this type of repair which can be used directly from the tube. A wide, flexible plastic or nylon applicator will be found invaluable for imparting a smooth and well-contoured finish to the surface of the filler.

Mix up a little filler on a clean piece of card or board – measure the hardener carefully (follow the maker's instructions on the pack), otherwise the filler will set too rapidly or too slowly. Using the applicator, apply the filler paste to the prepared area; draw the applicator across the surface of the filler to achieve the correct contour and to level the surface. When a contour that approximates to the correct one is achieved, stop working the paste – if you carry on too long, the paste will become sticky and begin to 'pick-up' on the applicator. Continue to add thin layers of filler paste at 20-minute intervals, until the level of the filler is just proud of the surrounding bodywork

Once the filler has hardened, the excess can be removed using a metal plane or file. From then on, progressively-finer grades of abrasive paper should be used, starting with a 40-grade production paper, and finishing with a 400-grade wet-and-dry paper. Always wrap the abrasive paper around a flat rubber, cork, or wooden block – otherwise the surface of the filler will not be completely flat. During the smoothing of the filler surface, the wet-and-dry paper should be periodically rinsed in water. This will ensure that a very smooth finish is imparted to the filler at the final stage.

At this stage, the 'dent' should be surrounded by a ring of bare metal, which in turn should be encircled by the finely 'feathered' edge of the good paintwork. Rinse the repair area with clean water, until all the dust produced by the rubbing-down operation has gone.

Spray the whole area with a light coat of primer – this will show up any imperfections in the surface of the filler. Repair these imperfections with fresh filler paste or bodystopper, and again smooth the surface with abrasive paper. If bodystopper is used, it can be mixed with cellulose thinners, to form a thin paste which is ideal for filling small holes. Repeat this spray-and-repair procedure until you are satisfied that the surface of the filler, and the feathered edge of the paintwork, are perfect. Clean the repair area with clean water, and allow to dry fully.

The repair area is now ready for final spraying. Paint spraying must be carried out in a warm, dry, windless and dust-free atmosphere. This condition can be created artificially if you have access to a large indoor working area, but if you are forced to work in the open, you will have to pick your day very carefully. If you are working indoors, dousing the floor in the work area with water will help to settle the dust which would otherwise be in the atmosphere. If the repair area is confined to one body panel, mask off the surrounding panels; this will help to minimise the effects of a slight mismatch in paint colours. Bodywork fittings (e.g. chrome strips, door handles etc) will also need to be masked off. Use genuine masking tape, and several thickness of newspaper, for the masking operations.

Before starting to spray, agitate the aerosol can thoroughly, then spray a test area (an old tin, or similar) until the technique is mastered. Cover the repair area with a thick coat of primer; the thickness should be built up using several thin layers of paint, rather than one thick one. Using 400 grade wet-and-dry paper, rub down the surface of the primer until it is smooth. While doing this, the work area should be thoroughly doused with water, and the wet-and-dry paper periodically rinsed in water. Allow to dry before spraying on more paint.

Spray on the top coat, again building up the thickness by using several thin layers of paint. Start spraying at one edge of the repair area, and then, using a side-to-side motion, work until the whole repair area and about 2 inches of the surrounding original paintwork is covered. Remove all masking material 10 to 15 minutes after spraying on the final coat of paint.

Allow the new paint at least two weeks to harden, then, using a paintwork renovator or a very fine cutting paste, blend the edges of the paint into the existing paintwork. Finally, apply wax polish.

Plastic components

With the use of more and more plastic body components by the vehicle manufacturers (e.g. bumpers, spoilers, and in some cases major body panels), rectification of more serious damage to such items has become a matter of either entrusting repair work to a specialist in this field, or renewing complete components. Repair of such damage by the DIY owner is not feasible, owing to the cost of the equipment and materials required for effecting such repairs. The basic technique involves making a groove along the line of the crack in the plastic, using a rotary burr in a power drill. The damaged part is then welded back together, using a hot air gun to heat up and fuse a plastic filler rod into the groove. Any excess plastic is then removed, and the area rubbed down to a smooth finish. It is important that a filler rod of the correct plastic is used, as body components can be made of a variety of different types (e.g. polycarbonate, ABS, polypropylene).

Damage of a less serious nature (abrasions, minor cracks etc) can be repaired by the DIY owner using a two-part epoxy filler repair material which can be used directly from the tube. Once mixed in equal proportions, this is used in similar fashion to the bodywork filler used on metal panels. The filler is usually cured in twenty to thirty minutes, ready for sanding and painting.

If the owner is renewing a complete component himself, or if he has repaired it with epoxy filler, he will be left with the problem of finding a suitable paint for finishing which is compatible with the type of plastic used. At one time, the use of a universal paint was not possible, owing to the complex range of plastics met with in body component applications. Standard paints, generally speaking, will not bond to plastic or rubber satisfactorily, but professional matched paints, to match any plastic or rubber finish, can be obtained from some dealers. However, it is now possible to obtain a plastic body parts finishing kit which consists of a pre-primer treatment, a primer and coloured top coat. Full instructions are normally supplied with a kit, but basically the method of use is to first apply the pre-primer to the component concerned, and allow it to dry for up to 30 minutes. Then the primer is applied, and left to dry for about an hour before finally applying the special-coloured top coat. The result is a correctly coloured component, where the paint will flex with the plastic or rubber, a property that standard paint does not normally possess.

5 Major body damage – repair

Where serious damage has occurred, or large areas need renewal due to neglect, it means that complete new panels will need welding-in, and this is best left to professionals. If the damage is due to impact, it will also be necessary to check completely the alignment of the bodyshell, and

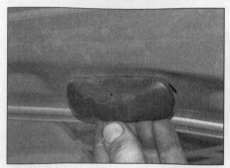

7.2a Pull the grommet from the underside of the bonnet . . .

7.5 Bonnet-to-hinge bolts (arrowed)

7.2b . . . the pull out the clip (arrowed) and disconnect the washer hose, then the wiring plug

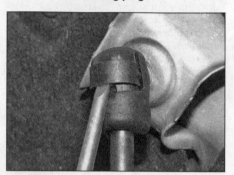

7.10 Lift the strut retaining spring at each end

this can only be carried out accurately by a VW dealer using special jigs. If the body is left misaligned, it is primarily dangerous, as the car will not handle properly, and secondly, uneven stresses will be imposed on the steering, suspension and possibly transmission, causing abnormal wear, or complete failure, particularly to such items as the tyres.

6 Door rattles –
tracing and rectification

1 Check first that the door is not loose at the hinges, and that the latch is holding the door firmly in position. Check also that the door lines up with the aperture in the body. If the door is out of alignment, adjust it with reference to Section 22.
2 If the latch is holding the door in the correct

position, but the latch still rattles, the lock mechanism is worn and should be renewed.
3 Other rattles from the door could be caused by wear in the window operating mechanism, interior lock mechanism, loose glass channels or loose wiring.

7 Bonnet and strut –
removal, refitting and adjustment

Bonnet

Removal

1 Fully open the bonnet, then place some cardboard or rags beneath the corners by the hinges to protect the bodywork.
2 Prise the grommets from the bonnet underside, and disconnect the windscreen washer tubes from the jets. Unplug the heated jet wiring

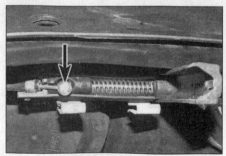

8.2 Pull the cable connection from the top of the headlight, prise open the cover, and disconnect the cable (arrowed)

8.3 The bonnet lock is secured by 2 nuts on the rear of the lock under the slam panel, and one bolt on the front (arrowed)

connectors (where applicable) and pull the hose/loom from the bonnet (see illustrations).
3 Prop the bonnet open using two stout lengths of wood, one positioned at each corner. Alternatively, enlist the help of an assistant to support the bonnet.
4 Disconnect the gas strut from the bonnet, with reference to the information given later in this Section.
5 Mark the location of the hinges with a pencil, then slacken the four hinge-to-bonnet retaining bolt (two each side) (see illustration).
6 Support the bonnet as the securing bolts are unscrewed, then withdraw the bonnet from the car.

Refitting and adjustment

7 Refitting is a reversal of removal. Ensure that the hinges are adjusted to their original positions. Close the bonnet very carefully initially; misalignment may cause the edges of the bonnet to damage the bodywork. If necessary, adjust the hinges to their original positions and check that the bonnet is level with the surrounding bodywork. If necessary, adjust the height of the bonnet front edge by bolting the rubber buffers in or out.
8 Check that the bonnet lock operates in a satisfactory manner. In particular, check that the safety catch holds the bonnet after the bonnet release cable has been pulled.

Strut

Removal

9 Prop the bonnet open using two stout lengths of wood, one positioned at each corner. Alternatively, enlist the help of an assistant to support the bonnet.
10 Slightly lift the retaining springs in the mountings at each end of the strut, using a suitable screwdriver (see illustration).
11 Pull the strut mounting from the pivot pin.

Refitting

12 Refitting is a reversal of removal.

8 Bonnet lock
and release cable –
removal and refitting

Bonnet lock

Removal

1 Remove the radiator grille as described in Section 9.
2 Unclip the coupling above the driver's side headlight, open the coupling and disconnect the bonnet release cable (see illustration).
3 Slacken the nuts and withdraw the 3 securing bolts and move the lock mechanism away from the slam panel (see illustration). Disconnect the wiring plug and bonnet release cable as the assembly is withdrawn.

Refitting

4 Reconnect the lock wiring plug and bonnet release cable.

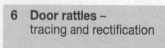

5 Position the lock mechanism on the slam panel, and tighten the retaining bolts to the specified torque.

6 Reconnect the cable as described in this Section, then refit the radiator grille. Check the action of the release cable/lock before closing the bonnet.

Cable

Removal

7 Pull the release handle to open the bonnet, then use a small, flat-bladed screwdriver to release the retaining clip, and remove the handle **(see illustrations)**.

8 Disconnect the cable from the handle.

9 Unclip the coupling above the driver's side headlight, open the coupling and disconnect the bonnet release cable **(see illustration 8.2)**.

10 Free the release cable from all its retaining clips in the engine compartment and wheel arch.

11 Attach a suitable length of strong cord to the end of the release cable at the release handle end, then carefully draw the cable through into the engine compartment.

12 Undo the cord from the cable, and leave the cord ends exposed in the engine compartment and footwell.

Refitting

13 Refit in the reverse order of removal. Tie the inner end of the cable to the exposed cord in the engine compartment, carefully pull the cable through to the release handle, then untie the cord.

14 When positioning the cable in the engine

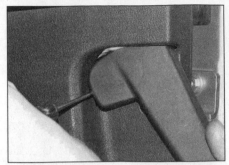

8.7a Insert a small screwdriver . . .

compartment and wheel arch, ensure that it is re-routed correctly to avoid kinks, sharp bends and chafing. Check for satisfactory operation of the cable and the lock before closing the bonnet. Ensure that the bonnet locks properly when closed, and also that the safety catch operates correctly when the bonnet release cable is actuated.

9 Bumpers and radiator grille – removal and refitting

Front bumper

Removal

1 Slacken the front roadwheel bolts, jack up the front of the vehicle and support it securely on axle stands (see *Jacking and vehicle support*). Remove the front roadwheels.

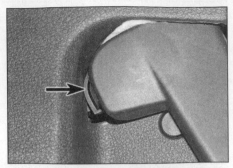

8.7b . . . then slide the retaining clip (arrowed) forwards and pull the handle inwards

2 Undo the fasteners each side securing the front lower section of the wheel arch liners **(see illustration)**.

3 Undo the 6 bolts at the top edge of the bumper **(see illustration)**.

4 Undo the bolts underneath securing the front section of the wheel arch liner each side **(see illustration)**.

5 Undo the 3 bolts underneath securing the lower rear edge of the bumper in the centre.

6 Pull back the wheel arch liners, then undo the 2 nuts and 1 bolt each side securing the lower section of the bumper **(see illustration)**.

7 With the help of an assistant, pull out the rear edges, then pull the front bumper forwards, and withdraw it from the car.

8 Disconnect any wiring plugs as the bumper is withdrawn. On models with headlight washers, depress the release clip and disconnect the washer hose as the bumper is withdrawn.

Refitting

9 Refitting is a reversal of removal. On completion, check for satisfactory operation of the accessory components as applicable.

Rear bumper

Removal – Saloon models

10 Remove the body-mounted tail lights as described in Chapter 12, then undo the 2 bolts each side in the tail light apertures **(see illustration)**.

11 Undo the 4 bolts in the wheel arch area each side, then prise up the centre pin and lever out the expansion rivet **(see illustrations 9.15a and 9.15b)**.

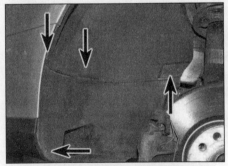

9.2 Undo the fasteners (arrowed) each side securing the lower wheel arch liner

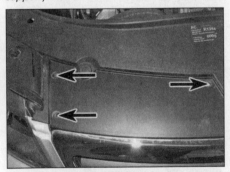

9.3 The top edge of the bumper is secured by 3 bolts (arrowed) each side

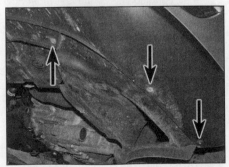

9.4 Undo the 3 bolts (arrowed) each side securing the bumper to the wheel arch liner

9.6 The bumper is secured by 2 nuts and 1 bolt each side (arrowed)

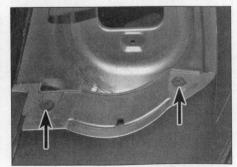

9.10 Undo the bolts in the tail light apertures (arrowed)

9.14 With the rear lights removed, undo the bolts (arrowed)

9.15a Undo the 4 bolts (arrowed) . . .

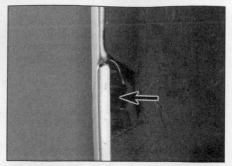

9.15b . . . the prise out the centre pin (arrowed) and lever out the expansion rivet

9.16a Remove the 2 bolts in the centre (arrowed) . . .

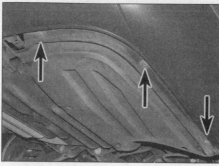

9.16b . . . and the bolts securing the panel under the right-hand side (arrowed)

12 From under the bumper, undo the 2 securing bolts in the centre, and the 3 bolts on the right-hand side (see illustrations 9.16a and 9.16b).

13 With the help of an assistant, pull the bumper rearwards and withdraw it from the rear of the car. Disconnect any wiring plugs as the bumper is withdrawn.

Removal – Estate models

14 Remove the body-mounted tail lights as described in Chapter 12, then undo the 2 bolts each side in the tail light apertures (see illustration).

15 Undo the 4 bolts each side in the wheel arch area, then prise up the centre pin, and lever out the plastic expansion rivet each side (see illustrations).

16 From under the bumper, undo the 2 securing bolts in the centre, and the bolts securing

the panel on the right-hand side (see illustrations).

17 With the help of an assistant, pull the bumper rearwards and remove it from the vehicle. Disconnect the parking aid sensors wiring plugs (where fitted) as the bumper is withdrawn.

Refitting

18 Refit in the reverse order of removal. Loosely fit all retaining bolts and bolts before fully-tightening them.

Radiator grille

19 Open the bonnet, then undo the 8 bolts at the top edge of the grille (see illustration).
20 Undo the 2 bolts at the lower edge of the grille, and manoeuvre it from place (see illustration).
21 Refitting is a reversal of removal.

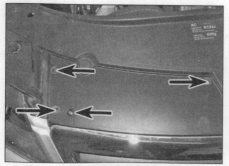

9.19 The top of the radiator grille is secured by 4 bolts each side (arrowed)

9.20 Radiator grille bolts (arrowed)

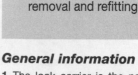

10 Lock carrier – removal and refitting

General information

1 The lock carrier is the name given to the section of bodywork that is mounted across the front of the engine compartment. A number of major components, including the bonnet lock mechanism, front bumper, radiator, automatic transmission fluid cooler and front light clusters are mounted on the lock carrier. The construction of the VW Passat bodywork is such that the lock carrier and its associated components can be removed without being extensively dismantled. In addition, the lock carrier can be moved forward several centimetres to a 'Service position' without having to disconnect the various hoses, pipes and wiring harnesses that serve the components mounted on it. In this position, access to components at the front of the engine compartment is greatly improved.

Removal

2 Set the lock carrier in the 'Service position' as described later in this Section.
3 Disconnect the wiring plugs from the rear of the right-hand headlight unit.
4 Disconnect the wiring from the crash sensor (where fitted) from the driver's side of the radiator, and release the wiring harness from its retaining clips.
5 Remove the intercooler as described in Chapter 4A.
6 The air conditioning condenser must now be removed from the lock carrier and secured to a suitable point at the front of the engine compartment using cable ties or wire (see illustration).

⚠️ **Warning: Do not disconnect the refrigerant pipes from the condenser (refer to the precautions in Chapter 3 regarding the dangers of air conditioning system refrigerant).**
Caution: Do not allow the condenser to hang by its refrigerant pipes, as the strain may cause them to fracture.
7 Enlist the help of an assistant to support the lock carrier during this final stage. Unscrew and remove the front impact absorber 10 mm

10.6 Use cable-ties to suspend the condenser from the engine cover mountings (arrowed – shown with the lock carrier removed for clarity)

10.10 Prise out the clips (arrowed) and disconnect the air pipe each side of the base of the intercooler

threaded rods then withdraw the lock carrier from the front of the vehicle.

Refitting

8 Refit in the reverse order of removal. Check the operation of the front lights, and the bonnet lock and safety catch, on completion. Refill and bleed the cooling system as described in Chapter 1, and have the headlights checked for correct beam alignment.

Setting the Service position

Note: *To carry out this procedure, it will necessary to fabricate two service tools, using two 10 mm diameter 300 mm lengths of threaded rod and a selection of hex nuts.*

9 Refer to Section 9 and remove the front bumper, then undo the fasteners and remove the engine undershield.
10 Release the clamps and disconnect the air pipes from the base of the intercooler **(see illustration)**.
11 Unscrew and remove bolts beneath each headlight at the side **(see illustration)**.
12 Unclip the foam packing on the bumper bar, then insert a length of 10 mm threaded rod into the upper, outer threaded hole each side/ above the impact absorbers **(see illustration)**. At the other end of the rods position a locknut and washer to limit the forward movement of the lock carrier.
13 Unscrew and remove the 2 bolts

securing the lock carrier to the top of the front wing on each side of the vehicle **(see illustration)**.
14 Unclip the bonnet release cable from the top of the right-hand headlight housing, then prise open the cable junction and disconnect the cable **(see illustration 8.2)**
15 Disconnect the bonnet release catch wiring plug, unclip the wiring loom from the right-hand side of the radiator, then disconnect the wiring plug from the left-hand headlight **(see illustration)**.
16 Prise up the cover from the intake hood at the lock carrier, and lift the intake tube from the hood **(see illustrations)**.
17 With the help of an assistant, carefully

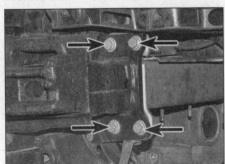

10.11 Undo the bolts (arrowed) each side under the headlights

10.12 Insert a 10 mm threaded rod (arrowed) into the upper, outer hole each side

10.13 Undo the 2 bolts each side (arrowed) securing the lock carrier to the front wing

10.15 Disconnect the bonnet release catch wiring plug (arrowed)

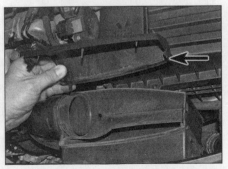

10.16a Release the clip (arrowed), prise up the intake hood cover . . .

10.16b . . . and lift the tube from the intake hood

10.17 Pull the lock carrier forwards approximately 10 cm

draw the lock carrier forwards approximately 10 cm **(see illustration)**.

18 The lock carrier can be refitted by following the removal procedure in reverse. Ensure that all fixings are tightened to the correct torque wrench setting, where specified. On completion, have the headlights checked for correct beam alignment.

11 Wheel arch liners – removal and refitting

Removal

1 Loosen the relevant wheel bolts, then raise the front or rear of the car and support on axle stands (see *Jacking and vehicle support*). Remove the relevant roadwheel.

2 The liner is secured by various fasteners.

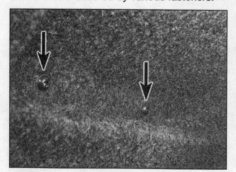

12.3a Undo the bolts (arrowed) in the hand grip recess

12.7 Undo the boot lid hinge Torx bolts

3 Undo and remove the liner securing bolts (see illustration 9.15a).

4 Lower the liner out of position, and manoeuvre it out from under the wing.

Refitting

5 Refitting is a reversal of removal. Renew any fasteners which were broken on removal.

12 Boot lid – removal and refitting

Removal

1 Raise the boot lid, then remove warning triangle from its holder (where fitted).

2 Undo the retaining bolt and detach the warning triangle holder (where fitted) from the boot lid.

3 Undo the trim retaining bolts from the hand grip recess, then carefully pull away the trim **(see illustrations)**. If necessary, use a flat, blunt tool to prise the clips from the boot lid.

4 Unplug the wiring connectors from the lock, switch and light units, then release the wiring loom from any clips. The wiring loom is routed through the boot lid hinge.

5 Mark the relationship between the boot lid and the hinges by drawing around the outside of each hinge with a marker pen.

6 Place cloths or pieces of cardboard over the surfaces of the rear wings, to prevent damage during removal.

7 Enlist the aid of an assistant to support the boot lid, then unscrew and remove the

12.3b Use a flat, blunt tool to release the trim clips

13.3 Boot lid retaining nuts (arrowed)

hinge-to-boot lid retaining bolts **(see illustration)**, and lift the lid clear.

Refitting

8 Refit in the reverse order of removal. Check the lid for correct alignment, and if necessary loosen off the hinge bolts to adjust, then retighten them; there should be an even gap between the outside edge of the boot lid and the surrounding bodywork.

13 Boot lid lock components – removal and refitting

1 Remove the trim from inside the boot lid, as described in Section 12.

Lock unit

Removal

2 Disconnect the lock wiring plug.

3 Mark the fitted position of the lock with a marker pen, then unscrew the retaining nuts and withdraw the lock unit from the boot lid **(see illustration)**.

Refitting

4 Refit in the reverse order of removal.

Handle

Removal

5 Disconnect the wiring plug from the handle.

6 Undo the 3 retaining bolts and remove the handle from the boot lid **(see illustration)**.

Refitting

7 Refitting is a reversal of removal.

14 Tailgate (Estate models) – removal and refitting

Removal

1 Open the tailgate and remove the warning triangle.

2 Unscrew the 4 lower trim panel securing bolts – 2 are located in the handle recesses, and 2 at the centre, lower edge of the trim **(see illustrations)**.

3 Carefully prise the lower section of the

13.6 Boot lid handle retaining bolts (arrowed)

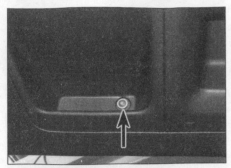

14.2a Undo the bolt (arrowed) in the handle recess each side . . .

14.2b . . . and the 2 bolts at the centre of the panel (arrowed)

14.3a Pull the trim panel away from the tailgate . . .

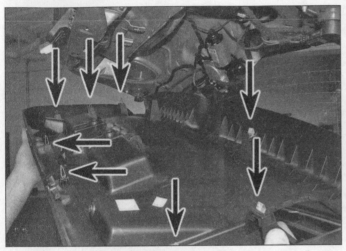

14.3b . . . to release the various spring clips (arrowed)

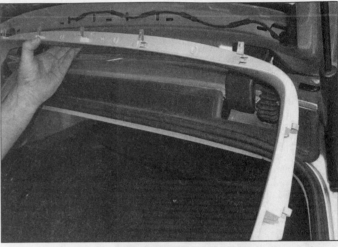

14.4 Pull the upper tailgate trim inwards to release the spring clips

trim panel from the tailgate using just enough force to overcome the spring clips **(see illustrations)**. Disconnect any wiring plugs as the panel is withdrawn.

4 Unclip the upper section of the trim panel from the tailgate rear window aperture **(see illustration)**. The trim panel is held by 2 clips each side, and 5 clips along its top edge.

5 Disconnect the wiring from the tailgate components (lock switch, wiper motor, number plate light units and demister element, etc) at the connectors. Note the routing and attachment locations of the wires, then release the rubber boot and pull the wiring through the aperture.

6 Disconnect the hose for the rear screen washer jet.

7 Prise off the plastic covers, then mark the relationship between the tailgate and its hinges using a felt tip pen **(see illustration)**.

8 Enlist the aid of an assistant to help support the tailgate, then detach the tailgate struts with reference to Section 15.

9 Unscrew and remove the tailgate-to-hinge securing bolts, and lift the tailgate clear of the vehicle.

Refitting

10 Refit in the reverse order of removal. Check that the tailgate is correctly aligned before fully-tightening the tailgate hinge bolts.

11 The fit and closing tension of the tailgate can be adjusted by altering the positions of the rubber buffers at the upper and lower edges of the tailgate.

15 Boot lid/tailgate support strut(s) – removal and refitting

Removal

1 On Saloon models, remove the rear seat belt inertia reel as described in Section 33.

14.7 Prise off the plastic covers

2 On all models, disconnect the strut(s) at the upper and lower balljoints by lifting (not removing) the spring clips, and prising the joint free **(see illustration)**.

3 If a strut is defective in operation, it must be renewed. Do not attempt to dismantle and repair the strut. Note that the struts are filled with pressurised gas, and so should not be punctured or disposed of by incineration.

Refitting

4 Refit in the reverse order of removal. Ensure that the strut is securely engaged with the balljoints.

15.2 Prise out the strut spring clip

16 Tailgate lock, cylinder and handle (Estate models) – removal and refitting

1 Remove the trim from inside the tailgate, as described in Section 14.

Lock unit

2 Disconnect the wiring plug from the lock unit.
3 Mark the fitted position of the lock with a marker pen, then unscrew the retaining bolts and withdraw the lock unit from the tailgate (see illustration).
4 Refit in the reverse order of removal.

Handle

Up to VIN 3C-8E108000/3C-8P064070

5 Disconnect the handle wiring plug. Undo the 4 retaining nuts, and remove the handle.
6 Refitting is a reversal of removal.

From VIN 3C-8E108001/3C-8P064071

7 Undo the 2 nuts and remove the cover from the tailgate (see illustration).
8 Disconnect the lock wiring plug, then undo the 2 nuts, squeeze together the sides of the retaining clip and remove the cover cap (see illustrations).
9 Withdraw the handle assembly from the tailgate.
10 Refitting is a reversal of removal.

17 Door trim panel – removal and refitting

Front door

Driver's door

1 Using a blunt, flat-bladed tool, carefully prise up the handle recess from the door trim. Where applicable, disconnect any wiring plugs as the trim is removed (see illustration).
2 Undo the 3 Torx bolts exposed in the handle recess aperture (see illustration).

Passenger's door

3 Using a blunt, flat-bladed tool, carefully prise out the pull handle cover (see illustration).

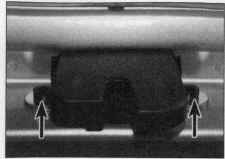

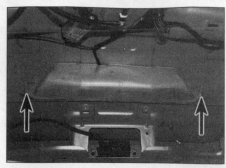

16.3 Tailgate lock retaining bolts (arrowed)

16.7 Undo the nuts (arrowed) and remove the handle cover

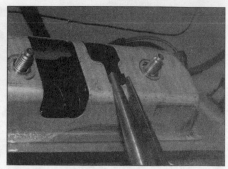

16.8a Undo the 2 nuts (arrowed) . . .

16.8b . . . then release the clip and remove the handle

4 Undo the 2 bolts in the handle recess (see illustration).

Both doors

5 Undo the 2 Torx bolts at the base of the door trim in the centre (see illustration).

6 Pull the trim away from the door frame at the lower, front and rear edges, releasing the retaining clips, then lift the trim panel up squarely (see illustration). Be prepared for some of the clips to break as the trim is removed.

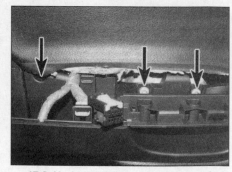

17.1 Prise up the handle recess/switch panel and disconnect any wiring plugs

17.2 Undo the 3 Torx bolts (arrowed)

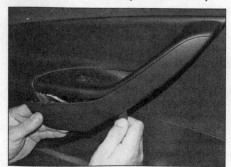

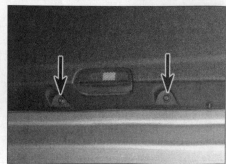

17.3 Prise the cover from the passenger's door pull handle

17.4 Remove the 2 Torx bolts securing the passenger's door trim panel (arrowed)

17.5 Undo the bolts in the centre of the door trim panel lower edge (arrowed)

17.6 Use a blunt, flat-bladed tool to release the trim panel retaining clips

17.7 Unhook the release handle operating cable (arrowed)

7 Unhook the operating cable from the rear of the interior handle as it becomes accessible **(see illustration)**.

8 Note their fitted positions, and disconnect the various wiring plugs as the panel is withdrawn.

9 Refit in the reverse order of removal, noting the following point:
  a) *Ensure that the wiring and connections are secure and correctly routed, clear of the window regulator and latch/lock components.*
  b) *Renew any damage retaining clips.*

Rear door

10 On models with manual windows, pull the spring collar rearwards and slide the window handle from the shaft **(see illustrations)**. Note the fitted position of the handle for refitting.

11 Using a blunt, flat-bladed tool, carefully prise out the pull handle cover **(see illustration)**.

12 Undo the 2 bolts in the handle recess **(see illustration)**.

13 Undo the bolt at the base of the door trim in the centre **(see illustration)**.

14 Pull the trim away from the door frame at the lower, front and rear edges, releasing the retaining clips, then lift the trim panel up squarely. Be prepared for some of the clips to break as the trim is removed.

15 Unhook the operating cable from the rear of the interior handle as it becomes accessible **(see illustration 17.7)**.

16 Note their fitted positions, and disconnect the various wiring plugs as the panel is withdrawn.

17 Check the door trim for any missing or broken clips, and renew where necessary.

18 Refit in the reverse order of removal, noting the following point:
  a) *Ensure that the wiring and connections*

are secure and correctly routed, clear of the window regulator and latch/lock components.
  b) *The window winder handle (where fitted) should be positioned at approximately ± 5° to the horizontal pointing forwards with the window closed.*

18 Central locking system – general

Refer to the information given in Chapter 12.

19 Door lock – removal and refitting

Removal

1 Refer to Section 21 and remove the window regulator assembly.

2 Disconnect the lock wiring plug **(see illustration)**.

3 Use a punch to remove the 3 clips, then detach the lock and bracket from the regulator panel **(see illustration)**. Punch the clips out from the inner side of the panel.

4 If required, the interior handle cable and/or exterior handle cable can be detached by rotating the outer cable fitting and pulling it from the bracket, then disconnecting the inner cable fitting **(see illustrations)**.

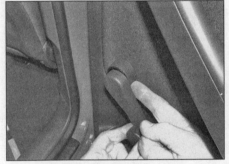

17.10a Press the spacer/clip . . .

17.10b . . . and slide the handle from the splines

17.11 Prise the rear door handle cover from place

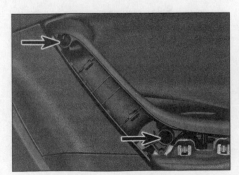

17.12 Undo the 2 bolts in the handle recess (arrowed)

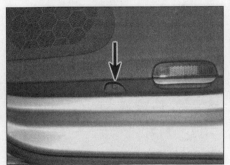

17.13 Remove the bolt (arrowed) at the lower edge of the rear door trim panel

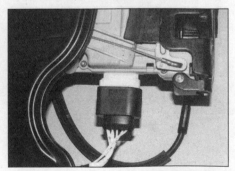

19.2 Disconnect the door lock wiring plug

19.3 Use a punch to remove the 3 lock bracket clips (arrowed)

Refitting

5 Refitting is a reversal of the removal procedure. Check that the door striker enters the lock centrally when the door is closed, and if necessary adjust the position of the striker.

---

20 Door handles and lock cylinder – removal and refitting

Exterior handles

Removal

1 Remove the lock cylinder/housing as described in this Section.
2 Pull the handle rearwards slightly, then outwards from the door at an angle of 90° **(see illustration)**.

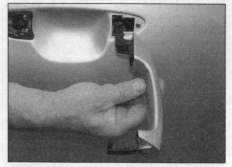

20.2 Pull the outer handle rearwards slightly, then outwards

20.7a Completely undo the lower bolt (arrowed) . . .

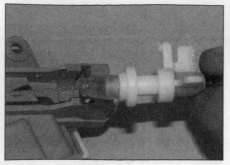

19.4a Rotate the cable outer fitting to release it . . .

Refitting

3 Position the front edge of the handle into the lock bracket in the door, then insert the rear edge and push it forwards slightly. **Note:** *The door handle should remain in the 'open' position. Any attempt to close the handle will result in damage to the lock bracket.*
4 Refit the lock cylinder/housing as described in this Section.

Lock cylinder/housing

Removal

5 Slide the emergency key from the remote control, then insert the key into the opening on the underside of the lock cylinder housing cap **(see illustration)**.
6 Gently pull the key outwards, prise the lower edge of the cap from place, then slide the cap upwards **(see illustration)**.
7 Remove the caps from the door edge, completely unscrew the lower bolt, then pull

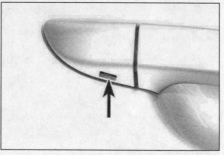

20.5 Insert the emergency key into the slot on the underside of the lock cylinder housing cap (arrowed) . . .

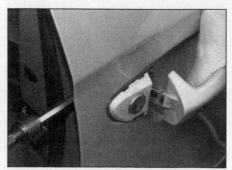

20.7b . . . slacken the upper bolt whilst pulling out the exterior handle . . .

19.4b . . . then disconnect the inner cable fitting

out the exterior handle and undo the upper retaining bolt until the lock cylinder/housing can removed from the door **(see illustrations)**. **Note:** *The door handle should remain in the 'open' position. Any attempt to close the handle will result in damage to the lock bracket.*

Refitting

8 Insert the lock cylinder/housing into the aperture, and gradually tighten the upper retaining bolt. The handle will automatically be drawn into place.
9 Removal of the lock cylinder is described within the handle removal procedure described previously.

Interior handles
Removal

10 With reference to Section 17 remove the door trim panel.
11 Disconnect the wiring from the central locking switch (where fitted).

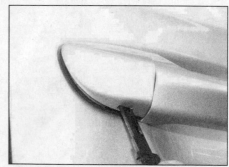

20.6 . . . then gently pull the key outwards to release the cap

20.7c . . . and remove the lock cylinder housing

20.12a Undo the interior release handle retaining bolt (arrowed) . . .

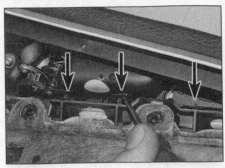

20.12b . . . then release the retaining clips (arrowed)

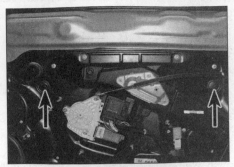

21.2a Prise out the plastic caps (arrowed) . . .

21.2b . . . and align the window clamping Torx bolts (arrowed)

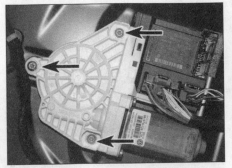

21.2c Undo the 3 bolts (arrowed) and pull the electric window motor from the shaft

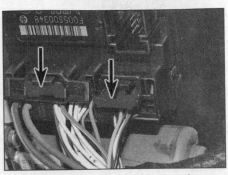

21.2d Slide out the locking catches (arrowed) and disconnect the wiring plug

12 Undo the retaining bolt, depress the retaining clips and remove the interior door handle from the panel **(see illustrations)**.

Refitting

13 Refitting is a reversal of removal.

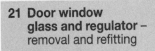

21 Door window glass and regulator – removal and refitting

Window glass – front door

1 Lower the door window approximately 135 mm, then remove the door trim as described in Section 17.
2 Lever out the plastic caps, then align the window so the clamping bolts are visible. **Note:** *If the glass cannot be aligned because of a fault with the motor, undo the 3 bolts and slide the motor from the regulator shaft. Disconnect the wiring plug as the motor is withdrawn (see illustrations).*
3 Slacken the clamping bolts by rotating the Torx heads *clockwise*, then lift the rear edge of the window glass and swing it forwards from the door **(see illustration)**.
4 Refitting is a reversal of removal, noting the following points:
  a) *Slide the glass into position, but only finger-tighten the retaining bolts anti-clockwise. Then pull the glass rearwards into the guide, and securely tighten the bolts.*
  b) *After refitting the door trim, re-initialise the electric window positions as described in Chapter 5, Section 3.*

Window glass – rear door

Estate models

5 Lower the window completely, then press the 'down' switch again. Carefully prise up

21.3 Lift the rear edge of the window and swing it forwards

21.6 Pull the rubber channels from the window front trim panel (arrowed)

the window exterior weather seal between the door and window **(see illustration)**.
6 Pull the rubber window channel and seal from the front and rear of the window front trim panel **(see illustration)**.

21.5 Carefully prise up the exterior weather seal

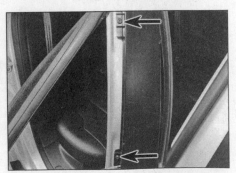

21.7 Undo the bolts (arrowed) and remove the trim panel

21.9a Remove the plastic cap . . .

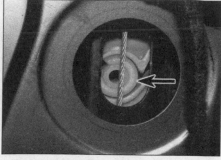

21.9b . . . and align the window so the spreader pin/plug (arrowed) is visible

21.10 Remove the spreader pin with a 5 mm bolt . . .

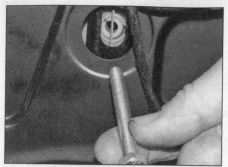

21.11 . . . and the spreader plug with an 8 mm bolt

21.13a Press-in the spreader pin . . .

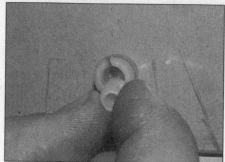

21.13b . . . until it's flush with the spreader plug

7 Undo the 2 retaining bolts, and pull the trim panel from place (see illustration).

All models

8 Remove the door inner trim panel as described in Section 17.

21.19a Lever the clip upwards . . .

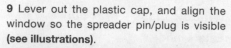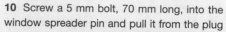

21.19b . . . pull back the rubber sleeve, and swing the locking catch (arrowed) downwards

9 Lever out the plastic cap, and align the window so the spreader pin/plug is visible (see illustrations).

10 Screw a 5 mm bolt, 70 mm long, into the window spreader pin and pull it from the plug

(see illustration). Discard the pin – a new one must be fitted.

11 Screw an 8 mm bolt, 80 mm long, into the spreader plug and pull the plug from the window clamp/regulator (see illustration). Discard the plug – a new one must be fitted.

12 Pull the rear of the window glass upwards and manoeuvre it from the door.

13 Fit the new spreader plug into the window fitting, then push the new spreader pin into place until it's flush with the plug (see illustrations).

14 Lower the window into place, then gently push the window down to engage it with the regulator.

15 The remainder of refitting is a reversal of removal. On models with electric rear windows, initialise the window positions as described in Chapter 5, Section 3.

Regulator

16 Remove the relevant door trim as described in Section 17. The regulator is integral with the carrier panel.

17 Remove the exterior door handle as described in Section 20.

18 Release the door window glass from the regulator as described previously in this Section.

19 Release the clip, pull the rubber wiring sleeve from the door pillar, then swing the locking catch downwards and disconnect the wiring plug (see illustrations). Prise the other end of the rubber sleeve from the door.

20 Disconnect the exterior mirror wiring plug, and the electric window motor wiring plug.

21 Release the clip at the front securing the wiring loom to the inside of the carrier panel.

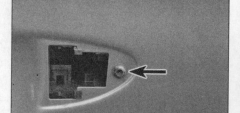

21.22 Remove the handle bracket bolt (arrowed)

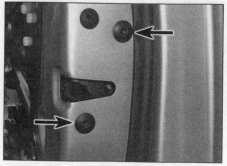

21.23 Undo the multi-spline bolts securing the door lock (arrowed)

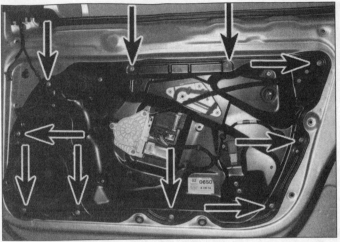

21.24 Undo the bolts (arrowed) around the carrier panel

22.2 Prise off the plastic cap (arrowed)

22 Undo the bolt securing the handle bracket to the outside of the door (see illustration).

23 Undo the 2 multi-spline bolts securing the door lock to the end of the door frame (see illustration).

24 Remove the bolts around the circumference of the carrier panel (see illustration).

25 Gently lift the carrier panel upwards, then guide the lower edge of the regulator assembly from the door, and lower the complete assembly downwards and forwards from place. Guide the wiring loom out with the panel. Note: *Take great care when guiding the lock assembly from the door. The plastic mounting bracket is easily damaged.*

26 Refitting is a reversal of removal.

22 Doors – removal and refitting

Note: *The doors are heavy – the help of an assistant is essential.*

Removal

Front doors

1 Release the clip and pull the wiring loom rubber sleeve from the door pillar. Swing the locking catch downwards and disconnect the wiring plug (see illustrations 21.19a and 21.19b).

2 Prise off the plastic caps, undo the bolts securing the 2 halves of the upper and lower door hinges, and lift the door upwards from place (see illustration).

Rear doors

3 On Saloon models, the procedure is identical to that described for front doors.

4 On Estate models, proceed as described in Paragraph 1, then undo the nut securing the 2 halves of the upper hinge, and then remove the lower bolt from the lower hinge.

5 Remove the door.

6 Clean the bolt threads with a wire brush,

and the nut threads with a tap, and treat them with thread-locking fluid when refitting the door.

Refitting

7 Refitting is a reversal of the removal procedure. On completion, shut the door and check it for closure and alignment. Check the depth at which the striker enters the lock. If adjustment is required, slacken the securing bolts and reposition the striker plate.

23 Windscreen, rear window glass and rear side window glass – general information

The windscreen, rear window glass and rear side window glass are directly bonded to the metalwork. Their removal and refitting requires the use of special tools not readily available to the home mechanic. This work should therefore be left to a VW dealer, or a specialist glass renewal company.

24 Sunroof – general

1 A sliding/tilting sunroof is fitted to some models. When fitted correctly, the roof panel in the fully closed position should be level with, or no more than 1.0 mm lower than, the roof panel at the leading edge. The rear edge must be level with, or no more than 1.0 mm higher than, the roof panel at the rear.

2 Removal and refitting, and adjustments to the roof panel, are best entrusted to a VW dealer or specialist, as specialised tools are required.

3 The sunroof panel motor can be removed and refitted as described in Chapter 12. If the motor malfunctions when the roof panel is in the open position, it can be wound shut manually; refer to Chapter 12 or the Owners Handbook supplied with the vehicle.

4 If the sunroof water drain hoses become blocked, they may be cleared by probing them with a length of suitable cable (an old speedometer drive cable is ideal). The front drain tubes terminate just below the A-pillars, between the pillar and the door – cleaning is carried out from the sunroof end. The rear drain tubes terminate in front of the rear wheel arch. Cleaning is carried out from the bottom end of the hose (remove the wheel arch liner as described in this Chapter).

25 Door mirror components – removal and refitting

Mirror housing

1 Remove the mirror as described in this Section.

2 Using a blunt, flat-bladed tool, carefully prise between the mirror housing and the indicator repeater light to release the 2 housing clips (see illustration).

3 Carefully prise the mirror housing upwards to release the guides, and remove it. Take great care not to damage the paintwork.

4 Refitting is a reversal of removal, ensuring the retaining clips fully engage with the mirror adjustment unit.

25.2 Release the housing clips (arrowed)

25.5 Prise the top of the mirror rearwards to release the clips

Mirror

 Warning: Wear gloves and eye protection when carrying out this operation, particularly if the mirror glass is broken.

5 Press in the bottom of the mirror, then insert a flat-bladed blunt tool behind the mirror, and carefully prise the upper part of the mirror from the retaining clips **(see illustration)**.

6 Disconnect the heater element wiring plugs as the mirror is withdrawn.

7 To refit, reconnect the wiring plugs, and press firmly at the centre of the mirror glass to engage the retaining clip. On completion, check the operation of the mirror adjustment mechanism using the adjustment knob/ buttons.

Complete assembly

8 Remove the door inner trim panel as described in Section 17.

26.1a Undo the bolt (arrowed) at the front of the console each side . . .

26.2b Note the arrow on the insulation panel (arrowed)

25.10 Pull the triangular trim from the door

9 Release the mirror wiring loom from any retaining clips, and disconnect the wiring plug.

10 Carefully prise the triangular trim from the top, front of the door **(see illustration)**.

11 Undo the 3 retaining bolts and withdraw the mirror from the door. Guide the wiring loom through as the mirror is withdrawn.

12 Refitting the mirror is a reversal of the removal procedure. Check the operation of the mirror adjustment on completion.

26 Centre console – removal and refitting

Removal

1 Prise out the plastic caps (where fitted) at the front of the console on each side, undo the retaining bolts, then pull the panels

26.1b . . . then pull the panel downwards and rearwards. Note the hook at the front of the panel (arrowed)

26.4 Prise up the selector lever surround

downwards from the top section of the console, then rearwards to remove them **(see illustrations)**.

Manual transmission models

2 Ensure the ignition is switched off, then open the front ashtray/storage tray, and use a blunt, flat-bladed tool to prise up the gear lever gaiter from the surround trim **(see illustrations)**. Pull the gaiter up around the gear lever knob.

3 Lift the gear lever insulation panel from around the lever. Note the arrow on the insulation panel indicating direction of travel.

Automatic transmission models

4 Using a blunt, flat-bladed tool, prise up the selector lever surround trim, and position it to one side **(see illustration)**.

All models

5 Pull the gear/selector lever surround panel from the console **(see illustration)**. Disconnect any wiring plugs as the panel is withdrawn.

6 Pull out the ashtray/storage tray insert, then undo the 2 retaining bolts and pull the ashtray/ storage tray from place **(see illustration)**. Disconnect any wiring plugs as the tray is withdrawn.

7 Carefully prise the infotainment unit surround trim from place **(see illustration)**.

8 Remove the heating/ventilation/air conditioning control panel as described in Chapter 3.

Models without a centre armrest

9 Remove the lining mat from the rear of the console, then undo the 2 nuts revealed.

26.2a Starting at the front edge, prise up the gear lever gaiter

26.5 Pull up the gear/selector lever surround panel

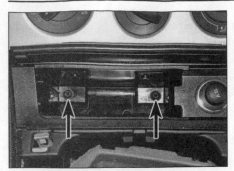

26.6 Lift out the ashtray/storage tray and undo the 2 bolts (arrowed)

26.7 Prise the infotainment surround trim from place

26.10a Prise the trim from the rear panel . . .

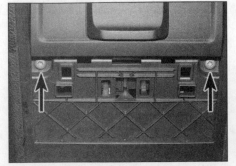

26.10b . . . and undo the 2 bolts (arrowed)

26.11a Slide up the vent panel . . .

26.11b . . . and undo the nuts (arrowed)

Models with a centre armrest

10 Carefully prise out the trim from the lower part of the rear panel or open the storage tray as applicable, then undo the 2 bolts revealed (see illustrations).

11 Pull up the vent panel from the rear of the console, then undo the 2 nuts revealed (see illustrations). Disconnect any wiring plugs as the panel is withdrawn.

12 Prise out the plastic caps and undo the bolt each side at the rear of the console (where fitted) (see illustration).

All models

13 Disconnect the wiring plug at the rear of the console (see illustration).

14 Undo the 2 bolts at the front upper edge of the console (see illustration).

15 Undo the 2 bolts each side at the centre of the console (see illustration).

16 Raise the rear of the console and disengage the locating lugs at the front upper edge. Manoeuvre the console from place, disconnecting any wiring plugs as the console is withdrawn (see illustration).

Refitting

17 Refitting is a reversal of the removal procedure.

26.12 Prise out the caps and undo the bolts

26.13 Disconnect the aux/iPod input wiring plug at the rear of the console

26.14 Undo the bolts at the front in the air conditioning/heater control panel aperture (arrowed) . . .

26.15 . . . and side of the console (arrowed)

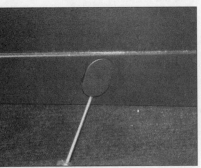

26.16 Lift the rear of the console, and disengage the lugs at the front

27.6 Insert a screwdriver into the slot and prise the panel from each end of the facia

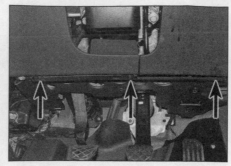

27.9a Panel retaining bolts (arrowed)

27.9b Release the clips and detach the diagnostic plug from the panel

27.10 Carefully prise away the trim below the centre vents . . .

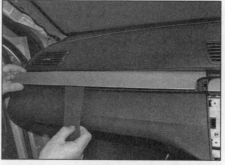

27.11 . . . and the trim on the passenger's side

27.12 Use the same method to remove the instrument panel surround trim

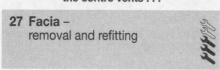

27 Facia –
removal and refitting

Removal

1 Disconnect the battery negative lead (refer to Chapter 5).

2 Remove the centre console as described in Section 26.

3 Remove the sunlight photo sensor as described in Chapter 3 (where applicable).

4 Remove the steering wheel as described in Chapter 10.

5 Remove the steering column switch unit as described in Chapter 12.

6 Carefully prise off the trim panels from each end of the facia **(see illustration)**.

7 Remove the A-pillar centre and lower trim panels as described in Section 31.

8 Remove the glovebox as described in Section 28.

9 Undo the 3 bolts and remove the panel above the pedals. Unclip and detach the diagnostic socket as the panel is withdrawn **(see illustrations)**.

10 Using a blunt, flat-bladed tool, carefully prise out the trim from the centre of the facia below the centre vents **(see illustration)**.

11 Carefully prise away the decorative trim strip on the passenger's side above the glovebox aperture **(see illustration)**.

12 Carefully prise the instrument panel surround trim from place **(see illustration)**.

13 Remove the infotainment unit as described in Chapter 12.

14 On models with storage compartments next the hazard switch, undo the 2 bolts and pull the centre storage cluster unit from the facia **(see illustration)**. Disconnect any wiring plugs as the unit is withdrawn.

15 On models without a storage compartment next to the hazard switch, carefully prise the trim surround around the hazard switch from place, then undo the 2 bolts and remove the dummy cover from place. Disconnect any wiring plugs as the unit is withdrawn.

16 On all models, remove the main light switch as described in Chapter 12.

17 The driver's side lower facia panel is secured by 2 bolts at the end, 3 bolts at the upper edge, 1 bolt at the inner edge, and 1 bolt in the light switch aperture. Undo the bolts and remove the panel **(see illustrations)**. Disconnect the wiring plugs as the panel is withdrawn.

18 Undo the 2 retaining bolts and remove the instrument cluster **(see illustration)**. Note that as the cluster is withdrawn, the wiring plug is automatically disconnected.

19 Disconnect the wiring plugs for the passenger's side airbag, and the temperature

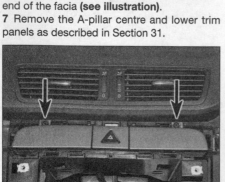

27.14 Undo the bolts (arrowed) and pull the storage unit and hazard warning switch rearwards

27.17a The driver's side panel is secured by 2 bolts (arrowed) at the end . . .

27.17b . . . 3 at the upper edge (arrowed) . . .

27.17c ... 1 bolt at the inner edge (arrowed) ...

27.17d ... and a bolt in the light switch aperture (arrowed)

27.17e Manoeuvre the panel rearwards a little, and disconnect the wiring plugs

sensors fitted to the left, and right-hand side vent ducts (where applicable).

20 The facia is now secured by 1 bolt in the instrument cluster aperture, 2 bolts and a nut at each end, and 4 bolts in the centre

section. Undo the bolts/nut, and with the help of an assistant, pull the facia panel rearwards to release the retaining clips (see illustrations). Manoeuvre the facia from the cabin.

Refitting

21 Refitting is a reversal of the removal process. Ensure that the heater control cables and all wiring harnesses are correctly routed and clipped in position.

27.18 The instrument panel is secured by 2 bolts (arrowed)

27.20a Undo the bolt in the instrument cluster aperture (arrowed) ...

27.20b ... 2 bolts (arrowed) ...

27.20c ... and a nut (arrowed) at the driver's end

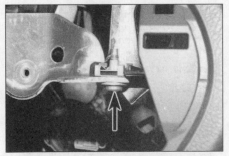

27.20d At the passenger's end, 1 bolt (arrowed) is accessed from the end of the facia ...

27.20e ... 1 from underneath (arrowed) ...

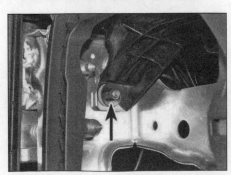

27.20f ... and the nut (arrowed) from the end

27.20g The facia is now secured by 2 bolts in the centre (arrowed) ...

27.20h ... and 1 each side at the lower edge (arrowed)

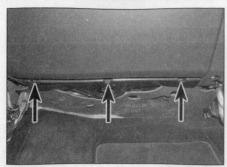

28.1a Undo the 3 bolts at the lower edge of the glovebox (arrowed) . . .

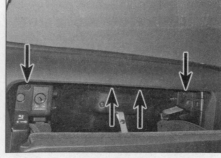

28.1b . . . and 4 at the upper edge (arrowed)

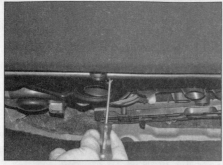

28.2a Insert a screwdriver through the hole in the centre of the glovebox lower edge . . .

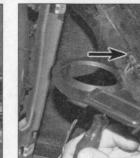

28.2b . . . to release the clip (arrowed)

28 Glovebox – removal and refitting

Removal

1 The glovebox is secured by 3 bolts at its lower edge, and 4 at its upper edge (see illustrations).
2 Use a screwdriver to release the clip and pull the glovebox from the facia (see illustrations). Ensure the multimedia/CD autochanger carrier is lowered from the roof of the glovebox.
3 Note their fitted positions and disconnect the wiring plugs/air duct as the glovebox is withdrawn.

Refitting

4 Refit in the reverse order of removal.

29.3 Prise apart the two halves of the trim

29 Interior mirror – removal and refitting

⚠ Warning: Use extreme care whilst attempting this procedure; the windscreen is easily cracked.

Basic mirror with rigid base

Removal

1 Twist the mirror 90° anti-clockwise, and remove it from the mounting plate.

Refitting

2 To refit, position the support arm at 90° to the vertical, then carefully turn it clockwise to the point where the lock spring is felt to engage.

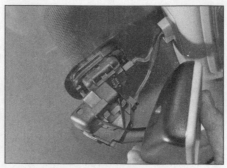

29.4 Slide the mirror down from the mounting

Mirror with rain sensor

Removal

3 Carefully prise apart the 2 halves of the trim around the mirror mounting base (see illustration).
4 Slide the mirror down the windscreen from the mounting. Disconnect the wiring plugs as the mirror assembly is withdrawn (see illustration).

Refitting

5 Refitting is a reversal of removal.

Mirror mounting plate

6 Renewal of the mirror mounting plate should be entrusted to a VW dealer or specialist, due to the use of dangerous chemicals used in the bonding process.

30 Seats – removal and refitting

Front seat

⚠ Warning: Both front seats are equipped with side airbags. Prior to disconnecting the airbag wiring plug, it is essential you are electrostatically discharged by touching a door lock or vehicle body briefly.

Removal

1 Move the seat forwards to the extent of its travel.
2 Undo the bolt at the rear of each seat rail securing the seat to the vehicle body (see illustration).
3 Move the seat fully rearwards.
4 Disconnect the battery negative cable (see Chapter 5).
5 Undo the bolt at the front of the each seat rail.
6 Lift up the cover in the floor then unplug the airbag wiring plug (see warning above), and where fitted, disconnect the wiring plugs for the seat heating and motor systems, and remove the seat from the vehicle (see illustrations). Note: Whilst the seat is removed from the vehicle, VW insist that the side airbag should still be earthed. This can be achieved with a VW adapter/loom (VAS 6229) plugged into

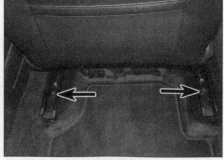

30.2 Undo the multi-spline bolts (arrowed) at the rear of the front seat rails

30.6a Lift up the carpet/cover and disconnect the seats wiring plugs

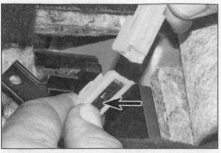

30.6b Slide back the black locking catch (arrowed) and disconnect the seat airbag wiring plug

30.14 Rear seat bench bolts (arrowed) – Estate models

the connector on the seat and the connector to the airbag module. In the absence of the VW adapter/loom, connect a cable from the yellow connector under the seat to a good chassis earth point. Due to the risk of injury or component failure, no further dismantling of the seats is recommended.

Refitting

7 Refit the seat in the reverse order of removal. **Note:** After refitting the seat(s), the airbag warning light on the dash may signal a fault. Take the vehicle to a VW dealer or suitably-equipped specialist to have the self-diagnosis system interrogated and the fault code erased.

Rear seat bench

Saloon models

8 On models with rear seat side airbags, disconnect the battery negative cable (see Chapter 5).
9 On models with an integrated child seat, swing the seat upwards, pull the foot insert from the mountings, then undo the 2 bolts and remove the child seat(s).
10 On all models, grasp the front lower edge of the seat and pull it upwards, to release the retaining pins from their plastic sockets.
11 Push the seat cushion rearwards firmly to detach the retainers, then pull the sides of the seat upwards out of the guide plate. Disconnect any wiring plugs as the seat is removed.
12 Refit the seat bench in the reverse order of removal, using new seat plastic sockets if the old ones are damaged.

Estate models

13 Fold the left- and right-hand side seat benches forwards, and disconnect any wiring plugs.
14 Each seat bench is secured by 2 bolts. Undo the bolts and remove the seat bench(es) **(see illustration)**.
15 Refitting is a reversal of removal.

Rear seat backrest

Backrest with integral seat belt

16 On Saloon models, remove the rear seat bench as previously described.
17 On Estate models, fold the seat benches forwards.

18 On all models, undo the bolt securing the centre seat belt anchorage to the vehicle body.
19 Undo the retaining bolt, lift out the clamp and remove the backrest, disengaging the backrest from the locating pin **(see illustrations)**. Disconnect any wiring plugs as the backrest is withdrawn.
20 Refit the seat backrest in the reverse order of removal.

Backrest without integral seat belt

21 Undo the bolt and lift the clamp from the centre seat backrest mounting **(see illustration 30.19a)**.
22 Lift the backrest from the centre mounting, disengaging it from the locating pin **(see illustration 30.19b)**. Disconnect any wiring plugs as the backrest is withdrawn.
23 Refit the seat backrest in the reverse order of removal.

---

31 Interior trim – removal and refitting

Interior trim panels

1 The interior trim panels are secured using either bolts or various types of trim fasteners, usually studs or clips.
2 Check that there are no other panels overlapping the one to be removed; usually there is a sequence that has to be followed, and this will only become obvious on close inspection.

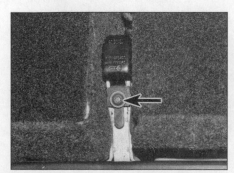

30.19a Undo the bolt (arrowed) and lift out the clamp

3 Remove all obvious fasteners, such as bolts. If the panel will not come free, it is held by hidden clips or fasteners. These are usually situated around the edge of the panel and can be prised up to release them; note, however that they can break quite easily so new ones should be available. The best way of releasing such clips without the correct type of tool is to use a large flat-bladed screwdriver. Note in many cases that the adjacent sealing strip must be prised back to release a panel.
4 When removing a panel, **never** use excessive force or the panel may be damaged; always check carefully that all fasteners or other relevant components have been removed or released before attempting to withdraw a panel.
5 Refitting is the reverse of the removal procedure; secure the fasteners by pressing them firmly into place and ensure that all disturbed components are correctly secured to prevent rattles.

Carpets

6 The passenger compartment floor carpet is in one piece and is secured at its edges by bolts or clips, usually the same fasteners used to secure the various adjoining trim panels.
7 Carpet removal and refitting is reasonably straightforward but very time-consuming because all adjoining trim panels must be removed first, as must components such as the seats, the centre console and seat belt lower anchorages.

Headlining

8 The headlining is clipped to the roof and

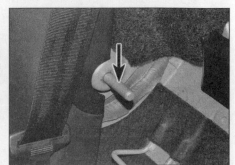

30.19b Disengage the seat backrest from the locating pin (arrowed)

31.13 Prise out the clip at the top of the trim (arrowed)

31.14 Pull the parcel shelf upwards to release the various clips (arrowed)

31.17 Prise out the airbag label at the top of the A-pillar trim, and undo the bolt revealed

can be withdrawn only once all fittings such as the grab handles, sunvisors, sunroof (if fitted), windscreen and rear quarter windows and related trim panels have been removed and the door, tailgate and sunroof aperture sealing strips (as applicable) have been prised clear.

9 Note that headlining removal requires considerable skill and experience if it is to be carried out without damage and is therefore best entrusted to an expert.

Parcel shelf (Saloon models)

10 On models with side airbags, disconnect the battery negative lead as described in Chapter 5.

11 Remove the rear seat backrest – see Section 30, then remove the C-pillar trim panels as described in this Section.

12 Undo the nut and pull the side padding upwards from the mountings. Disconnect any wiring plugs as the padding is withdrawn.

13 Prise out the clip at the top, then pull the wheel arch trim from the clips on each side **(see illustration)**.

14 Pull the parcel shelf upwards from the mountings **(see illustration)**.

15 Prise out the seat belt surround trim from the shelf each side, and guide the seat belt though the openings. Pull the parcel shelf forwards, and manoeuvre it from the cabin.

16 Refitting is a reversal of removal.

A-pillar trim

Upper section

17 Prise out the airbag label at the rear of the pillar trim, then undo the bolt in the label aperture **(see illustration)**.

18 Pull the A-pillar trim from place, releasing the 3 push-on clips, then pull it to the rear to release it from the facia panel. Manoeuvre the trim from the cabin.

19 Refitting is a reversal of removal, ensuring

the lug at the front edge of the trim engages correctly **(see illustration)**.

Middle section

20 Pull the trim panel rearwards to release the retaining clips **(see illustration)**.

21 Refitting is a reversal of removal.

Lower section

22 Remove the A-pillar middle section trim as previously described.

23 On the driver's side, remove the bonnet release lever, then prise off the cap, undo the centre bolt, remove the scrivet, then undo the fastener at the front of the trim **(see illustrations)**.

24 On both sides, lift the sill trim where it overlaps the pillar trim, then pull the pillar trim inwards to release the clips **(see illustration)**.

25 Disengage the trim from the door weatherstrip, and pull the trim rearwards.

26 Refitting is a reversal of removal.

31.19 Ensure the lug at the base of the A-pillar trim engages correctly with the facia

31.20 Pull the A-pillar trim middle section rearwards to release the clips

31.23a Prise off the cap, undo the bolt . . .

31.23b . . . then prise out the scrivet

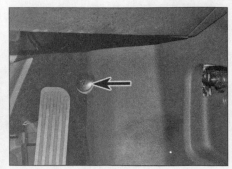

31.23c Undo the fastener (arrowed) at the front of the trim

31.24 Lift the sill trim where it overlaps the pillar trim

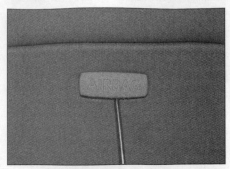

31.27 Prise out the airbag label at the top of the B-pillar trim

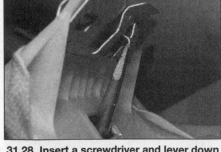

31.28 Insert a screwdriver and lever down the retaining clip (shown with the trim removed for clarity)

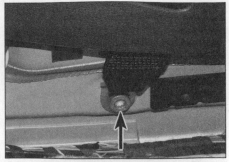

31.30 Seat belt lower anchorage bolt (arrowed)

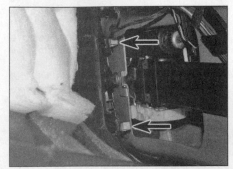

31.34 Pull the lower pillar trim inwards to release the spring clips at its base (arrowed)

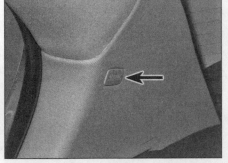

31.37 Prise out the airbag emblem (arrowed)

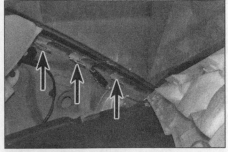

31.38 Refit the steel clips (arrowed) to the vehicle's C-pillar prior to refitting the trim panel

B-pillar trim

Upper section

27 Move the front seat fully forwards, then prise out the airbag emblem from the top of the pillar trim (see illustration).
28 Insert a flat-bladed screwdriver into the emblem aperture, and lever down the retaining clip (see illustration).
29 Pull the top of the pillar trim inwards.
30 If the trim is to be completely removed, pull the front sill trim upwards to release the clips, fold down the carpet and undo the seat belt lower anchorage bolt (see illustration). Feed the seat belt through the slot in the pillar trim.
31 Refitting is a reversal of removal, ensuring the seat belt height adjuster mechanism aligns correctly with the inside of the trim.

Lower section

32 Remove the upper section of the B-pillar trim as previously described.

33 Pull the sill trim panel upwards to release the retaining clips where it overlaps the pillar trim.
34 Pull the trim panel from the door weatherstrips, then pull the panel inwards to release the retaining clips (see illustration). Disconnect any wiring plugs as the panel is withdrawn.
35 Refitting is a reversal of removal.

C-pillar trim

Saloon models

36 On models with a rear sunblind, prise out sunblind trim strip from the C-pillar trim.
37 On all models, prise out the airbag emblem at the top of the trim, and undo the Torx bolt in the aperture (see illustration).
38 Release the pillar trim from the door rubber weatherstrip, and pull the trim inwards to release it from the retaining clips (see illustration).
39 Refitting is a reversal of removal.

Estate models

40 Prise out the airbag emblem at the top of the pillar trim, and undo the bolt in the aperture (see illustration).
41 Release the pillar trim from the door rubber weatherstrip, and pull the rear edge of the trim rearwards to release it from the retaining clips, then inwards (see illustration).
42 Refitting is a reversal of removal.

D-pillar trim

43 On models with rear side airbags, disconnect the battery negative lead as described in Chapter 5.
44 Remove the luggage compartment side trim panel as described in this Section.
45 Prise down the rear roof trim panel adjacent to the D-pillar trim (see illustration).
46 Pull the pillar trim inwards, then forwards to release the retaining clips (see illustration).
47 Refitting is a reversal of removal.

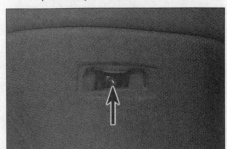

31.40 Prise out the airbag label at the top of the C-pillar trim and remove the bolt revealed (arrowed)

31.41 Pull the rear edge of the pillar trim rearwards, then inwards to release the clips

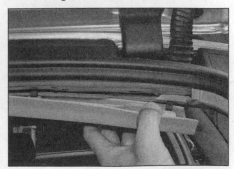

31.45 Pull the rear roof panel trim downwards

31.46 Pull the D-pillar trim inwards then forwards to release the clips

31.49 Pull the boot sill trim upwards to release the clips

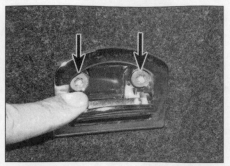

31.51 Load securing ring Torx bolts (arrowed)

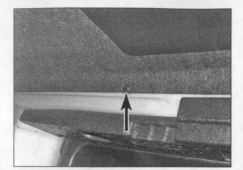

31.52 Remove the bolt (arrowed) at the lower edge of the trim

Luggage compartment side trim

Saloon models

48 Take out the luggage compartment floor covering.

31.54a Remove the 3 expansion rivets at the top edge of the trim (arrowed) . . .

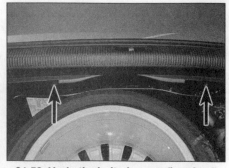

31.54c Release push-on clips at the rear edge (arrowed)

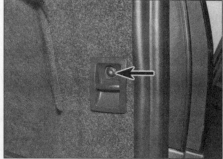

31.53 Remove the storage hook retaining bolt (arrowed)

49 Pull the rear sill trim upwards from its retaining clips (see illustration).
50 Remove the rear seat bench and backrest as described in Section 30.
51 Undo the 2 retaining bolts and remove the load securing ring (see illustration).

31.54b . . . and one at the rear (arrowed)

31.58 Undo the bolts (arrowed) and pull the tailgate sill trim upwards

52 Undo the bolt at the lower edge of the side trim (see illustration).
53 Undo the retaining bolt and remove the hook at the rear of the side trim (see illustration).
54 Prise out the centre pins, and lever out the 4 plastic expansion rivets (3 at the upper edge, and 1 at the rear) securing the side trim to the vehicle body. Release the push-on clips at the rear edge and manoeuvre the trim from place (see illustrations). Disconnect any wiring plugs as the trim is withdrawn.
55 Refitting is a reversal of removal.

Estate models

56 On models with rear side airbags, disconnect the battery as described in Chapter 5.
57 Undo the 2 bolts, remove the luggage compartment floor covering and the tool box lid.
58 Undo the 2 bolts and pull the tailgate sill trim upwards to release its retaining clips (see illustration).
59 Remove the rear seats as described in Section 30, then remove the rear seat side padding. The padding is secured by 1 nut at its base, then pull the padding upwards to release the clips (see illustrations). Disconnect any wiring plugs as the padding is withdrawn.
60 Pull the trim panel at the front, top of the wheel arch inwards to release the mountings (see illustration).
61 Undo the bolts and remove the load securing rings from the side panels.
62 Undo the bolt and remove the bag holder bracket.
63 Unscrew the centre pin, and prise out the

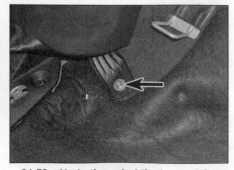

31.59a Undo the nut at the base of the side padding . . .

expansion rivet from the front, upper edge of the side trim **(see illustration)**.
64 Pull the side trim inwards to release the mounting clips. Guide the seat belt through the opening as the trim is withdrawn. Disconnect any wiring plugs as the trim is withdrawn.
65 Refitting is a reversal of removal. Ensure the upper clips are in place on the inner wing before refitting the panel **(see illustration)**.

Driver's side lower facia panel

66 Undo the 3 bolts and remove the panel above the pedals. Unclip and detach the diagnostic socket as the panel is withdrawn **(see illustrations 27.9a and 27.9b)**.
67 Prise the panel from the driver's end of the facia **(see illustration 27.6)**.
68 Remove the main light switch as described in Chapter 12.
69 Prise away the trim strip beneath the facia centre vents **(see illustration 27.10)**.
70 Carefully prise the instrument panel trim panel rearwards **(see illustration 27.12)**
71 The driver's side lower facia panel is secured by 2 bolts at the end, 3 bolts at the upper edge, 1 bolt at the inner edge, and 1 bolt in the light switch aperture. Undo the bolts and remove the panel **(see illustrations 27.17a to 27.17e)**. Disconnect the wiring plugs as the panel is withdrawn.
72 Refitting is a reversal of removal.

32 Seat belt tensioning mechanism – general information

All models are fitted with seat belt pretensioners that are integrated into the airbag control system. The system is designed to instantaneously take up any slack in the seat belt in the case of a direct or oblique frontal impact, therefore reducing the possibility of injury to the occupants. Each front seat inertia reel is fitted with its own tensioner, which is triggered by a frontal impact above a predetermined force. Lesser impacts and impacts to the rear of the vehicle will not trigger the system.

When the system is triggered, the explosive gas in the tensioner mechanism retracts and locks the seat belt. This prevents the seat belt moving and keeps the occupant firmly in position in the seat. Once the tensioner has been triggered, the seat belt will be permanently locked and the assembly must be renewed, together with the impact sensors.

Always disconnect the battery negative lead (see Chapter 5) before working on the pretensioners.

Note the following warnings before contemplating any work on the front seat belts.

 Warning:
• **Do not expose the tensioner mechanism to temperatures in excess of 100°C.**
• **If the tensioner mechanism is dropped, it**

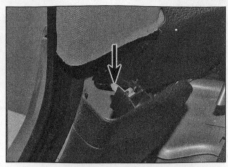
31.60 Pull the trim at the top of the wheel arch inwards to release the clip (arrowed)

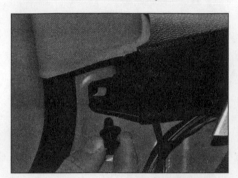
31.59b . . . then pull the padding upwards to release the clips

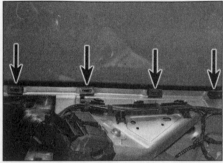

31.63 Unscrew the centre pin, and prise out the plastic expansion rivet (arrowed)

31.65 Ensure the steel clips are in place on the wing (arrowed)

must be renewed, even it has suffered no apparent damage.
• **Do not allow any solvents to come into contact with the tensioner mechanism.**
• **Do not attempt to open the tensioner mechanism as it contains explosive gas.**
• **Tensioners must be discharged before they are disposed of, but this task should be entrusted to an VW dealer.**

33 Seat belts – general, removal and refitting

Note: *Refer to the warnings in Section 32 before working on the front seat belts.*

General

1 Periodically check the belts for fraying or other damage. If evident, renew the belt.
2 If the belts become dirty, wipe them with

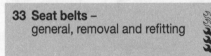
33.10a Undo the seat belt inertia reel bolt (arrowed)

a damp cloth, using a little liquid detergent only.
3 Check the tightness of the anchor bolts, and if they are ever disconnected, make quite sure that the original sequence of fitting of washers, bushes, and anchor plate is retained.
4 Access to the front belt height adjuster and inertia reel units can be made by removing the trim from the B-pillar on the side concerned.
5 The rear seat belt anchorages can be checked by removing the rear seat bench. Access to the rear seat inertia reel units is made by removing the rear seat backrest, parcel shelf and luggage area side trim.
6 The torque wrench settings for the seat belt anchor bolts and other attachments are given in the Specifications at the start of this Chapter.
7 Never modify the seat belts, or alter the attachments to the body, in any way.

Front seat belt

8 Disconnect the battery negative lead as described in Chapter 5.
9 Remove the upper and lower B-pillar trims as described in Section 31.
10 Undo the inertia reel mounting bolt and manoeuvre the reel from the pillar. Disconnect the pretensioners wiring plug by opening the locking element, depressing the clip and disconnecting the plug **(see illustrations)**.
11 Undo the bolt at the upper seat belt anchorage point **(see illustration)**.
12 Undo the 2 bolts and remove the seat belt guide from the B-pillar **(see illustration)**.
13 To remove the seat belt stalk, remove the

33.10b Pull open the locking element, depress the clip and pull the plug apart

33.11 Seat belt upper anchorage bolt

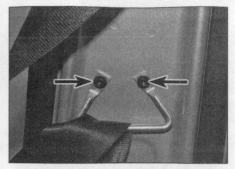

33.12 Seat belt guide bolts (arrowed)

relevant front seat as described in Section 30, then undo the bolt on the underside of the seat, and remove the stalk. Disconnect the wiring as the stalk is withdrawn **(see illustration)**.

14 Refitting is a reversal of removal, ensuring all fasteners are tightened to their specified torque where given.

Rear side seat belt

Saloon models

15 Remove the luggage compartment side trim panels, and parcel shelf as described in Section 31.
16 On models with pretensioners, disconnect the wiring plug, and undo the bolt securing the pretensioner to the vehicle body. Undo the lower seat belt anchorage point/relay bracket bolt.
17 Undo the retaining bolt and remove the

inertia reel, along with the seat belt **(see illustration)**.
18 Refitting is a reversal of removal, ensuring all fasteners are tightened to their specified torque where given.

Estate models

19 Remove the rear seats as described in Section 30, and the luggage compartment side panel trims as described in Section 31. On models with pretensioners, disconnect the wiring plug, and undo the bolt securing the pretensioner to the vehicle body.
20 Undo the lower seat belt anchorage point/ relay bracket bolt and remove the belt **(see illustration)**.
21 Undo the 2 bolts and remove the seat belt guide (where fitted).
22 Undo the retaining bolt, and remove the inertia reel along with the seat belt **(see illustration)**.

23 Refitting is a reversal of removal, ensuring all fasteners are tightened to their specified torque where given.

Rear centre seat belt

Note: *This procedure requires dexterity and patience.*
24 The centre rear seat belt reel is attached to the rear seat backrest. Remove the backrest as described in Section 30. Depress the release buttons on the guide collars, and remove the headrests from the backrest.
25 Undo the 2 bolts and remove the backrest stop bracket **(see illustration)**.
26 Open the ski hatch, undo the 2 retaining bolts and remove the armrest assembly **(see illustration)**.
27 Use a screwdriver to release the clip on each side, and remove the plastic cover from the seat back release button and the seat belt

33.13 Seat belt stalk bolt (arrowed)

33.17 Rear seat belt inertia reel bolt (arrowed) – Saloon models

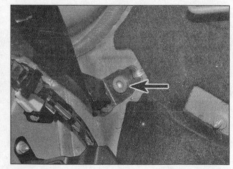

33.20 Rear side seat belt lower anchorage bolt (arrowed)

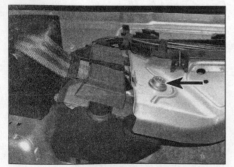

33.22 Undo the bolt (arrowed) and remove the rear side seat belt inertia reel

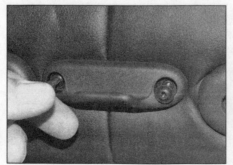

33.25 Undo the stop bracket bolts

33.26 The armrest/ski hatch assembly is secured by 2 bolts (arrowed)

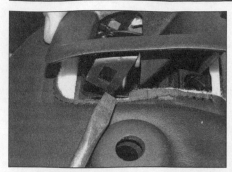

33.27a Press in the clip each side of the seat backrest release button cover . . .

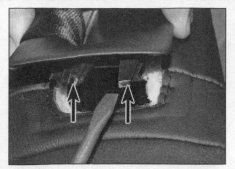

33.27b . . . and the seat belt guide (arrowed)

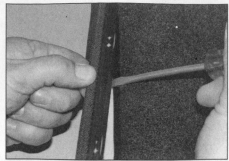

33.28a Unclip the seat cover beading . . .

guide **(see illustrations)**. Note that damage to the covers is quite likely during the removal procedure.

28 Unclip the seat cover beading from the top, and outside edge of the seat frame, then unclip it from the upper section of the inner edge. Take care not to mark the seat covering **(see illustrations)**.

29 Carefully ease the seat cover and padding over the headrest guide tubes, then to aid refitting, squeeze together the clips at the base of the tubes and remove them **(see illustrations)**.

30 Fold down the covering and padding, then undo the retaining nut and remove the inertia reel **(see illustration)**.

31 Refitting is a reversal of removal, ensuring all fasteners are tightened to their specified torque where given.

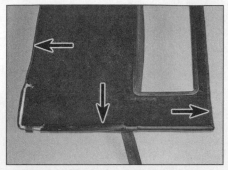

33.28b . . . from the outside edge, top, and the upper section of the inner edge (arrowed)

33.29a Ease the seat cover and padding over the headrest guide tubes

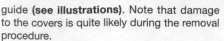

34 Sunvisors –
removal and refitting

Removal

1 Remove the relevant upper A-pillar trim panel as described in Section 31.

2 Remove the front interior light assembly as described in Chapter 12.

3 Remove the grab handles as described in Section 35.

4 Swing the sunvisor out of its retaining clip. Prise off the plastic cover to expose the clip retaining bolt. Undo the bolt and remove the retaining clip **(see illustration)**.

5 To remove the sunvisor/hinge, prise out the plastic cap, undo the retaining bolt and support the sunvisor to prevent any strain on the wiring **(see illustration)**.

6 Gently pull the headlining down a little, then slide the wiring plug from the retaining clip in the headlining, feed it through the sunvisor mounting hole, and disconnect the wiring plug. **Note:** *Don't pull the wiring plug through the mounting hole too far, or the wiring may be damaged.*

Refitting

7 Refitting is a reversal of removal.

33.29b Squeeze together the clips and remove the guide tubes

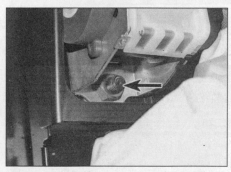

33.30 Seat belt inertia reel bolt (arrowed)

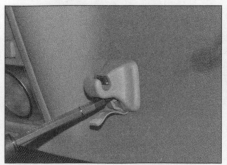

34.4 Prise out the cap and undo the sunvisor clip bolt

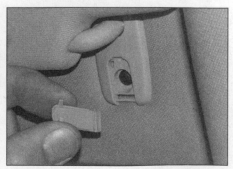

34.5 Prise out the cap and undo the sunvisor hinge bolt

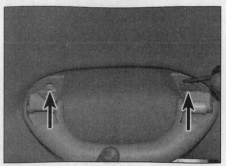

35.1 Prise open the caps and undo the grab handle bolts (arrowed)

35 Grab handles –
removal and refitting

Removal

1 Hold down the grab handle, and prise out the plastic caps. Undo the retaining bolts and remove the handles **(see illustration)**.

Refitting

2 Refitting is a reversal of removal.

Chapter 12
Body electrical systems

Contents

Degrees of difficulty

Easy, suitable for novice with little experience	Fairly easy, suitable for beginner with some experience	Fairly difficult, suitable for competent DIY mechanic	Difficult, suitable for experienced DIY mechanic	Very difficult, suitable for expert DIY or professional

Specifications

System type ... 12 volt, negative earth

Bulbs	Power rating (watts)
Direction indicators	H21
Direction indicator side repeaters	LEDs
Door entry lights	5 capless
Foglight:	
Front	55 H11
Rear	21
Footwell lights	5 capless
Headlights:	
Halogen:	
Dipped	55 H7
Main	55 H7
Gas discharge:	
Dipped/main	35 D1S
Cornering light	55 H7
Interior lights:	
Front	10 festoon
Rear	5 capless
Luggage compartment light	10 festoon
Number plate light:	
Bolted light unit	5 festoon
Clipped light unit	5 capless
Reading lights	5 capless
Reversing light	21
Sidelights	5 capless
Stop-lights (body-mounted and high-level)	LEDs
Vanity lights	5 festoon
Tail light (tailgate/boot lid mounted)	21

Torque wrench settings

	Nm	lbf ft
Airbag control unit nuts	7	5
Crash sensor bolts	9	7
Driver's airbag-to-steering wheel bolts	7	5
Head airbag retaining bolts	4	3
Passenger airbag unit nuts/bolts	9	7
Rear window wiper arm nut	12	9
Windscreen wiper arm nuts	20	15
Windscreen wiper linkage bolts	8	6

1 General information and precautions

⚠ **Warning: Before carrying out any work on the electrical system, read through the precautions given in 'Safety first!' at the beginning of this manual, and in Chapter 5.**

1 The electrical system is of 12 volt negative earth type. Power for the lights and all electrical accessories is supplied by a lead-acid type battery which is charged by the alternator.

2 This Chapter covers repair and service procedures for the various electrical components not associated with the engine. Information on the battery, alternator and starter motor can be found in Chapter 5.

3 It should be noted that prior to working on any component in the electrical system, the battery negative terminal should first be disconnected to prevent the possibility of electrical short-circuits and/or fires.

2 Electrical fault finding – general information

Note: *Refer to the precautions given in 'Safety first!' and in Chapter 5A before starting work. The following tests relate to testing of the main electrical circuits, and should not be used to test delicate electronic circuits (such as anti-lock braking systems), particularly where an electronic control module is used.*

Caution: The VW Passat electrical system is extremely complex. Many of the ECMs are connected via a Databus system, where they are able to share information from the various sensors, and communicate with each other. For instance, as the automatic gearbox approaches a gear ratio shift point, it signals the engine management ECM via the Databus. As the gearchange is made by the transmission ECM, the engine management ECM retards the ignition timing, momentarily reducing engine output, to ensure a smoother transition from one gear ratio to the next. Due to the design of the Databus system, it is not advisable to backprobe the ECMs with a multimeter in the traditional manner. Instead, the electrical systems are equipped with a sophisticated self-diagnosis system, which can interrogate the various ECMs to reveal stored fault

codes, and help pin-point faults. In order to access the self-diagnosis system, specialist test equipment (fault code reader/scanner) is required.

General

1 Typically, electrical circuit consists of an electrical component, any switches, relays, motors, fuses, fusible links or circuit breakers related to that component, and the wiring and connectors which link the component to both the battery and the chassis. To help to pin-point a problem in an electrical circuit, wiring diagrams are included at the end of this Chapter.

2 Have a good look at the appropriate wiring diagram, before attempting to diagnose an electrical fault, to obtain a complete understanding of the components included in the particular circuit concerned. The possible sources of a fault can be narrowed down by noting if other components related to the circuit are operating properly. If several components or circuits fail at one time, the problem is likely to be related to a shared fuse or earth connection.

3 An electrical problem will usually stem from simple cause, such as loose or corroded connections, a faulty earth connection, a blown fuse, a melted fusible link, or a faulty relay (refer to Section 3 for details of testing relays). Visually inspect the condition of all fuses, wires and connections in a problem circuit before testing the components. Use the wiring diagrams to determine which terminal connections will need to be checked in order to pin-point the trouble-spot.

4 The basic tools required for electrical fault finding include a circuit tester or voltmeter (a 12 volt bulb with a set of test leads can also be used for certain tests); a self-powered test light (sometimes known as a continuity tester); an ohmmeter (to measure resistance); a battery and set of test leads; and a jumper wire, preferably with a circuit breaker or fuse incorporated, which can be used to bypass suspect wires or electrical components. Before attempting to locate a problem with test instruments, use the wiring diagram to determine where to make the connections.

5 Sometimes, an intermittent wiring fault (usually caused to a poor or dirty connection, or damaged wiring insulation) can be pin-pointed by performing a wiggle test on the wiring. This involves wiggling the wiring by hand to see if the fault occurs as the wiring is moved. It should be possible to narrow down the source of the fault to a particular section

of wiring. This method of testing can be used in conjunction with any of the tests described in the following sub-Sections.

6 Apart from problems due to poor connections, two basic types of fault can occur in an electrical circuit: open-circuit, or short-circuit.

7 Largely, open-circuit faults are caused by a break somewhere in the circuit, which prevents current from flowing. An open-circuit fault will prevent a component from working, but will not cause the relevant circuit fuse to blow.

8 Low resistance or short-circuit faults are caused by a 'short'; a failure point which allows the current flowing in the circuit to 'escape' along an alternative route, somewhere in the circuit. This typically occurs when a positive supply wire touches either an earth wire, or an earthed component such as the bodyshell. Such faults are normally caused by a breakdown in wiring insulation, A short circuit fault will normally cause the relevant circuit fuse to blow.

9 Fuses are designed to protect a circuit from being overloaded. A blown fuse indicates that there may be problem in that particular circuit and it is important to identify and rectify the problem before renewing the fuse. Always renew a blown fuse with one of the correct current rating; fitting a fuse of a different rating may cause an overloaded circuit to overheat and even catch fire.

Finding an open-circuit

10 One of the most straightforward ways of finding an open-circuit fault is by using a circuit test meter or voltmeter. Connect one lead of the meter to either the negative battery terminal or a known good earth. Connect the other lead to a connector in the circuit being tested, preferably nearest to the battery or fuse. Switch on the circuit, bearing in mind that some circuits are live only when the ignition switch is moved to a particular position. If voltage is present (indicated either by the tester bulb lighting or a voltmeter reading, as applicable), this means that the section of the circuit between the relevant connector and the battery is problem-free. Continue to check the remainder of the circuit in the same fashion. When a point is reached at which no voltage is present, the problem must lie between that point and the previous test point with voltage. Most problems can be traced to a broken, corroded or loose connection.

 Warning: Under no circumstances may live measuring instruments such as ohmmeters, voltmeters or

2.14a The main earth strap connection is on the left-hand side chassis member in the engine compartment under the air cleaner (arrowed)

2.14b Others are on the rear wheel arch (arrowed) . . .

a bulb and test leads be used to test any of the airbag circuitry. Any testing of these components must be left to a VW dealer or specialist, as there is a danger of activating the system if the correct procedures are not followed.

Finding a short-circuit

11 Loading the circuit during testing will produce false results and may damage your test equipment, so all electrical loads must be disconnected from the circuit before it can be checked for short circuits. Loads are the components which draw current from a circuit, such as bulbs, motors, heating elements, etc.

12 Keep both the ignition and the circuit under test switched off, then remove the relevant fuse from the circuit, and connect a circuit test meter or voltmeter to the fuse connections.

13 Switch on the circuit, bearing in mind that some circuits are live only when the ignition switch is moved to a particular position. If voltage is present (indicated either by the tester bulb lighting or a voltmeter reading, as applicable), this means that there is a short-circuit. If no voltage is present, but the fuse still blows with the load(s) connected, this indicates an internal fault in the load(s).

Finding an earth fault

14 The battery negative terminal is connected to 'earth': the metal of the engine/transmission and the car body – and most systems are wired so that they only receive a positive feed, the current returning through the metal of the car body. This means that the component mounting and the body form part of that circuit. Loose or corroded mountings can therefore cause a range of electrical faults, ranging from total failure of a circuit, to a puzzling partial fault. In particular, lights may shine dimly (especially when another circuit sharing the same earth point is in operation), motors (eg, wiper motors or the radiator auxiliary cooling fan motor) may run slowly, and the operation of one circuit may have an apparently unrelated effect on another.

Note that on many vehicles, earth straps are used between certain components, such as the engine/transmission and the body, usually where there is no metal-to-metal contact between components due to flexible rubber mountings, etc **(see illustrations)**.

15 To check whether a component is properly earthed, disconnect the battery and connect one lead of an ohmmeter to a known good earth point. Connect the other lead to the wire or earth connection being tested. The resistance reading should be zero; if not, check the connection as follows.

16 If an earth connection is thought to be faulty, dismantle the connection and clean back to bare metal both the bodyshell and the wire terminal or the component earth connection mating surface. Be careful to remove all traces of dirt and corrosion, then use a knife to trim away any paint, so that a clean metal-to-metal joint is made. On reassembly, tighten the joint fasteners securely; if a wire terminal is being refitted, use serrated washers between the terminal and the bodyshell to ensure a clean and secure connection. When the connection is remade, prevent the onset of corrosion in the future by applying a coat of petroleum jelly or silicone-based grease or by spraying on (at regular intervals) a proprietary ignition sealer or a water dispersant lubricant.

2.14c . . . under the centre console (arrowed) . . .

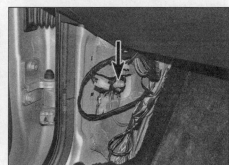

2.14d . . . behind the left- and right-hand footwell panels (arrowed) . . .

2.14e . . . on the facia crossmember support brackets each side (arrowed) . . .

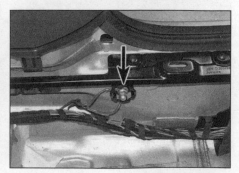

2.14f . . . on the inner side of each sill (arrowed)

3.2a Prise open the cover panel at the driver's end of the facia to access the main fusebox

3.2b Slide forward the catches . . .

3.2c . . . and lift the lid from the engine compartment fusebox

3.10 The relays are located behind the driver's side of the facia

3 Fuses and relays – general information

Main fuses

1 The fuses are located on a single panel at the right-hand end of the facia on RHD models, at the left-hand end on LHD models, and in the engine compartment adjacent to the battery.

2 Access to the fuses is gained by pulling open the cover panel on the facia, or unclipping the fusebox cover in the engine compartment (see illustrations).

3 Each fuse is numbered; the fuses ratings and circuits they protect are listed on the rear face of the cover panel. A list of fuses is given with the wiring diagrams.

4 To remove a fuse, first switch off the circuit

4.2a Open the flap, insert a screwdriver into the slot on each side . . .

concerned (or the ignition), then pull the fuse out of its terminals. The wire within the fuse should be visible; if the fuse is blown the wire will have a break in it, which will be visible through the plastic casing.

5 Always renew a fuse with one of an identical rating; never use a fuse with a different rating from the original or substitute anything else. Never renew a fuse more than once without tracing the source of the trouble. The fuse rating is stamped on top of the fuse; note that the fuses are also colour-coded for easy recognition.

6 If a new fuse blows immediately, find the cause before renewing it again; a short to earth as a result of faulty insulation is most likely. Where a fuse protects more than one circuit, try to isolate the defect by switching on each circuit in turn (if possible) until the fuse blows again. Always carry a supply of spare fuses of each relevant rating on the vehicle, a spare of

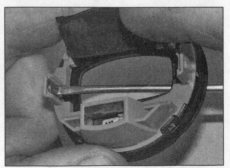

4.2b . . . to release the retaining clips

each rating should be clipped into the base of the fusebox.

Fusible links

7 On all models, a fusible link is located on the front of the fusebox in the engine compartment (see illustration 3.2c). A melted link indicates a serious wiring fault – renewing the link should not be attempted without first diagnosing the cause of the problem.

8 Prior to renewing the link, first disconnect the battery negative cable (see Chapter 5). Unclip the cover to gain access to the metal link. Slacken the retaining bolts/nuts, then slide the link out of position.

9 Fit the new link (noting the information given in paragraphs 5 and 6) then tighten its retaining bolts securely and clip the cover into position.

Relays

10 The main relays are located behind a panel on the driver's side of the facia. The facia relays are mounted on common base, which is accessed by removing the driver's side lower facia panel as described in Chapter 11 (see illustration).

11 The relays are of sealed construction, and cannot be repaired if faulty. The relays are of the plug-in type, and may be removed by pulling directly from their terminals. In some cases, it will be necessary to prise the two plastic clips outwards before removing the relay.

12 If a circuit or system controlled by a relay develops a fault and the relay is suspect, operate the system; if the relay is functioning, it should be possible to hear it click as it is energised. If this is the case, the fault lies with the components or wiring of the system. If the relay is not being energised, then either the relay is not receiving a main supply or a switching voltage, or the relay itself is faulty. Testing is by the substitution of a known good unit, but be careful; while some relays are identical in appearance and in operation, others look similar but perform different functions.

13 To renew a relay, first ensure that the ignition switch is off. The relay can then simply be pulled out from the socket and the new relay pressed in.

4 Ignition switch/ steering column lock – removal and refitting

Ignition switch

Removal

1 Remove the driver's side lower facia panel as described in Chapter 11.

2 Press down the opening flap, then use 2 small screwdrivers to depress the retaining clip on each side, and pull the switch trim from place (see illustrations).

3 Undo the retaining bolt, release the retaining clip on each side, and remove the switch from the panel (see illustrations).

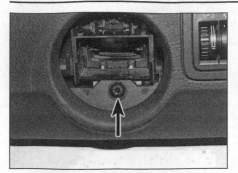

4.3a Undo the bolt (arrowed) . . .

4.3b . . . and release the clip on each side

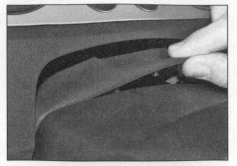

5.2a Unclip the gap cover

Refitting

4 Refitting is a reversal of removal.

Steering column lock

5 The steering column lock is integral with the steering column. Removal of the column is described in Chapter 10.

> **5 Steering column switch assembly – removal and refitting**

Electronic steering control unit

1 Remove the steering wheel as described in Chapter 10.
2 Release the gap cover, then unclip and remove the upper shroud from the steering column **(see illustrations)**.
3 Undo the two upper bolts and single lower

5.2b Prise the upper shroud from the lower shroud

bolt and remove the lower shroud from the steering column **(see illustrations)**. As the shroud is being removed, release it from the height and reach adjustment handle.
4 Undo the retaining bolt at the rear of the control unit **(see illustration)**.

5.2c Note how the lug (arrowed) engages with the slot (arrowed)

5 Note their fitted positions and disconnect the wiring plugs from the control unit **(see illustration)**.
6 Release the retaining clips each side of the unit, then pull it downwards from the column switch assembly **(see illustrations)**.

5.3a Undo the upper bolts (arrowed) . . .

5.3b . . . and the lower bolt (arrowed)

5.4 Steering control unit retaining bolt (arrowed)

5.5 Disconnect the wiring plugs from each side, and rear of the control unit

5.6a Release the clips (arrowed) each side . . .

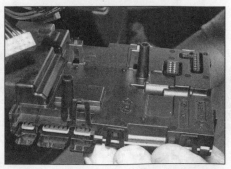

5.6b . . . and lower the control unit from the column

5.9 Lift the locking tabs and pull the contact unit from the column

5.10 The black strips (arrowed) must be visible in the window

5.14 Release the clips (arrowed) and pull the sensor segment from the switch unit

5.17 Column switch unit multi-spline retaining bolts (arrowed)

7 Refitting is a reversal of removal. If a new unit has been fitted, it must be 'coded' using dedicated diagnostic equipment. Entrust this task to a VW dealer or suitably-equipped specialist.

Airbag contact unit

8 Remove the electronic steering column control unit as previously described in this Section.
9 Lift the locking tabs slightly and pull the contract assembly from the column (see illustration). Note: *Do not allow the contact unit to rotate as it's withdrawn.*
10 Ensure the contact unit is in the 'central position'. This is indicated by the coloured strip (black), or roller (yellow), being located in the 'sight' window (see illustration).
11 Fit the assembly over the end of the column, until the clips engage.

12 The remainder of refitting is a reversal of removal.

Steering angle sensor segment

13 Remove the airbag contact unit as previously described in this Section.
14 Release the 2 clips and pull the segment rearwards from the column switch unit (see illustration).
15 Refitting is a reversal of removal.

Column switch unit

16 Remove the steering angle sensor segment as previously described in this Section.
17 Undo the 2 retaining bolts and slide the switch unit from the column (see illustration). No further dismantling of the switch unit is recommended. If faulty, the complete unit must be renewed.
18 Refitting is a reversal of removal.

6 Switches – removal and refitting

Facia-mounted light switch

1 With the light switch in position O, press the switch centre inwards and turn it slightly to the right. Hold this position and pull the switch from the facia (see illustration).
2 As the switch is withdrawn from the facia, disconnect the wiring plug.
3 To refit, reconnect the wiring plug.
4 Hold the switch and press the rotary part inwards and slightly to the right.
5 Insert the switch into the dash, turn the rotary part to position O and release. Check the switch for correct operation.

Glovebox light switch

6 Remove the glovebox as described in Chapter 11.
7 Prise out the actuating arm pin, rotate the switch body/arm clockwise and detach it from the glovebox (see illustration).
8 Refitting is a reversal of removal.

Door mirror adjuster

9 Using a blunt, flat-bladed tool, carefully prise up the mirror switch panel from the armrest (see illustration 6.26).
10 Detach the wiring connector, then carefully release the retaining clips and remove the switch downwards from the panel (see illustration).
11 Refit in the reverse order of removal.

Sunroof control

12 Remove the interior light assembly as described in Section 8.
13 Disconnect the sunroof switch wiring plug, then release the 3 retaining clips and remove the switch.
14 Refit in the reverse order of removal.

Central locking switch

15 Remove the interior door handle as described in Chapter 11.
16 Release the retaining clips, then press the switch from the panel (see illustration).
17 Refitting is a reversal of removal.

6.1 In position O, press the switch in, rotate it clockwise, and pull it from the facia

6.7 Rotate the switch body/arm clockwise

6.10 Use a screwdriver to release mirror adjuster clips

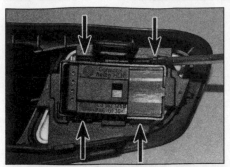

6.16 Release the clips (arrowed) and press the central locking switch from the panel

6.23 Push the handbrake switch from the panel

6.26 Prise up the switch panel from the door trim

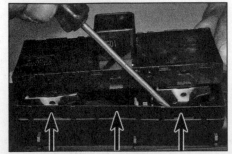

6.28 Release the 3 clips (arrowed) each side and pull the window switch block from the panel

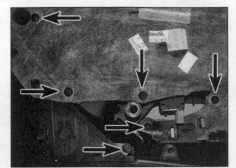

6.32 Front interior door handle assembly retaining bolts (arrowed)

6.33 The passenger's window switch is secured by 2 clips (arrowed) each side

Interior monitoring switch/ vehicle inclination sensor

18 The monitoring switch and inclination sensor form one component. Carefully prise the switch/sensor from the driver's side B-pillar trim.
19 Disconnect the switch/sensor wiring plug.
20 Refitting is a reversal of removal.

Courtesy light switches

21 The courtesy light are controlled by microswitches incorporated into the door locks. The switches are not available separately. If defective, the door lock assembly must be renewed (see Chapter 11).

Handbrake switch

22 Using a blunt, flat-bladed tool, prise the panel from the driver's end of the facia.
23 Reach through the end of the facia and push the handbrake switch from place **(see illustration)**.
24 Detach the wiring connector from the switch.
25 Refit in the reverse order of removal.

Window switches

Driver's door switch panel

26 Using a blunt, flat-bladed tool, carefully prise up the switch panel from the door trim **(see illustration)**.
27 Unclip and disconnect the wiring plug from the underside of the panel.
28 Release the 3 retaining clips each side and remove the switch assembly from the panel **(see illustration)**.

29 Refitting is a reversal of removal.

Passenger's side switch

30 Remove the door trim panel as described in Chapter 11.
31 Disconnect the wiring plug from the underside of the switch.
32 Undo the 6 bolts and detach the interior pull handle assembly from the door trim panel **(see illustration)**.
33 Release the retaining clips and remove the switch **(see illustration)**.
34 Refitting is a reversal of removal.

Rear door switch

35 Remove the door trim panel as described in Chapter 11.
36 Working on the inside for the door trim panel, undo the 6 retaining bolts and detach the interior release handle assembly from the panel **(see illustration)**.

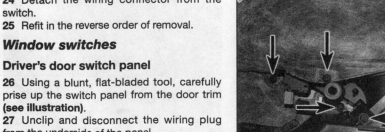

6.36 Rear interior door handle assembly retaining bolts (arrowed)

37 Release the retaining clips and push the switch downwards from the panel **(see illustration)**.
38 Refitting is a reversal of removal.

Stop-light switch

39 Refer to Chapter 9.

Steering column switch

40 Refer to Section 5.

Headlight control

41 Remove the light switch as described in paragraphs 1 and 2 of this Section.
42 Reach through the light switch aperture, and upwards from the storage compartment aperture, then push the headlight range control switch from the panel. Disconnect the wiring plug as the switch is withdrawn **(see illustration)**.
43 Refit in the reverse order of removal.

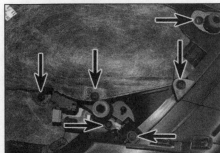

6.37 The rear window switch is secured by 2 clips (arrowed) each side

6.42 Push the light control switch from the panel

6.44 Prise away the trim panel below the vents

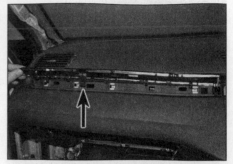

6.45 Prise the trim panel rearwards. Note the retaining bolt location (arrowed)

6.46 Carefully prise away the instrument panel trim

6.47 Switch mounting panel bolts (arrowed)

6.48 Pull the switch surround trim from place

Hazard warning switch

44 Carefully prise away the trim panel beneath the facia centre vents (see illustration).

45 Remove the glovebox as described in Chapter 11, then undo the bolt on the underside, and carefully prise the trim strip above the glovebox aperture rearwards (see illustration).

46 Prise the instrument panel trim rearwards (see illustration).

47 Undo the 2 bolts and pull the switch mounting panel from the facia. Disconnect the wiring plug(s) as the panel is withdrawn (see illustration).

48 Prise the hazard switch surround trim panel from place (see illustration).

49 Release the clips and remove the switch from the panel (see illustration).

50 Refitting is a reversal of removal.

ESP/parking aid/rear roller blind/tyre pressure monitor/ auto-hold switches

51 Using a blunt, flat-bladed tool, carefully prise the panel beneath the switches upwards from the centre console. Take great care not to damage the surrounding area.

52 Disconnect the wiring plugs from the switches.

53 Release the retaining clips and remove the relevant switch (see illustration).

54 Refitting is the reversal of removal.

Seat heating switches

55 The front seat heating switches are integral with the heating/air conditioning control panel, and cannot be renewed

separately. Removal of the panel is described in Chapter 3.

56 To remove the rear seat switches, carefully prise rearwards the panel beneath the switches.

57 Undo the 2 retaining bolts, then pull the console rear panel rearwards at its base, then upwards to detach it from the console.

58 Disconnect the switch wiring plugs, then unclip the relevant switch from the panel.

59 Refitting is a reversal of removal.

Boot lid/tailgate/ fuel filler flap release switch

60 Remove the interior door trim panel as described in Chapter 11.

61 Disconnect the wiring plug, then release the clips and remove the switch (see illustration).

62 Refitting is a reversal of removal.

6.49 Release the clip above and below the switch

6.53 Depress the clips (arrowed) and remove the switch

6.61 The switch is secured by 2 clips at the top, and 2 at the bottom

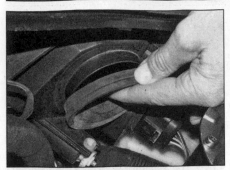

7.1 Pull the plastic cover from the rear of the headlight

7.2 Rotate the bulbholder (arrowed) anti-clockwise

7.4 The lug on the flange must align with the control on the bulbholder (arrowed)

7 Exterior light bulbs – renewal

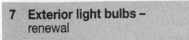

Note: *Whenever a bulb is renewed, note the following points:*
a) *Remember that if the light has just been in use, the bulb may be extremely hot.*
b) ***Do not*** *touch the bulb glass with the fingers, as the small deposits can cause the bulb to cloud over.*
c) *Always check the bulb contacts and holder, ensuring that there is clean metal-to-metal contact. Clean off any corrosion or dirt before fitting a new bulb.*
d) *Wherever bayonet-type bulbs are fitted, ensure that the live contacts bear firmly against the bulb contact.*
e) *Always ensure that the new bulb is of the correct rating and that it is completely clean before fitting it.*

Halogen headlights

Note: *This section does not cover bulb renewal on models fitted with gas discharge headlights; refer to Section 10 for renewal details.*
1 Release the plastic cover from the rear of the headlight **(see illustration)**.

Hella headlights

2 Rotate the bulbholder anti-clockwise and pull it from the reflector as far as the wiring allows **(see illustration)**.
3 Pull the bulb from the holder. If the bulb is to be refitted, do not touch the glass with the

fingers. If the glass is accidentally touched, clean it with methylated spirit.
4 Press the new bulb into the holder, so the lug on the bulb flange is aligned with the control on the bulbholder **(see illustration)**.
5 Position the bulb and holder in the reflector, then rotate it clockwise to the stop.
6 Check the seal is intact, then refit the plastic cover to the rear of the headlight.

Valeo headlights

7 To remove the main beam bulb, push the top of the bulb/connector upwards until the retaining clip releases. To remove the dipped beam, rotate the bulbholder anti-clockwise and pull it from the reflector **(see illustrations)**.
8 Disconnect the wiring plug/bulbholder **(see illustration)**. If the bulb is to be refitted, do not touch the glass with the fingers. If the glass is accidentally touched, clean it with methylated spirit.

7.7a Push the main beam bulb connector upwards until the clip releases

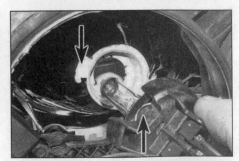

7.7b Rotate the dipped beam bulbholder anti-clockwise and pull it from the reflector

9 When refitting the main beam, align the lug on the bulb with the cut-out in the reflector, then push the bulb into place. When fully fitted, an audible click will be heard **(see illustration)**. When refitting the dipped beam, push the bulb into the bulbholder then position the bulbholder in the reflector and rotate it clockwise. Note that the bulbholder will only fit one way around **(see illustration)**.
10 Reconnect the wiring plug to the bulb, and refit the plastic cover on the back of the headlight.

Sidelight

Note: *This section does not cover sidelight bulb renewal on models fitted with gas discharge headlights; refer to Section 10 for renewal details.*
11 Remove the plastic cover from the rear of the headlight **(see illustration)**.

7.8 Pull the bulb from the bulbholder/wiring plug

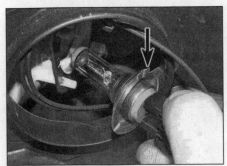

7.9a The lug (arrowed) at the top of the main beam bulb must be at the top

7.9b The lug (arrowed) on the dipped beam reflector must align with the cut-out in the bulbholder (arrowed)

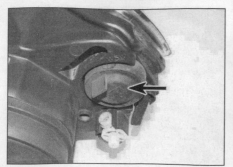

7.11 Remove the plastic cover (arrowed) to access the sidelight bulb

7.12 Pull the sidelight bulbholder from the headlight

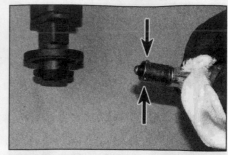

7.20 The indicator bulb is of the halogen type – don't touch it with bare fingers. Note the offset bayonet pins (arrowed)

12 Pull the bulbholder from the headlight **(see illustration)**.

13 Pull the wedge-type bulb directly from the bulbholder.

14 Fit the new bulb using a reversal of the removal procedure.

Front foglight

15 Remove the foglight as described in Section 9.

16 Rotate the bulb and holder assembly anti-clockwise and remove it. Note that the bulb is integral with the holder.

17 Refitting is a reversal of removal.

Direction indicator

18 Remove the direction indicator as described in Section 9.

19 Rotate the bulbholder anti-clockwise and pull it from place.

20 Depress and twist the bulb to remove it from the bulbholder **(see illustration)**.

21 Fit the new bulb using a reversal of the removal procedure.

Direction indicator side repeater

22 The bulb is integral with the side repeater. If defective, the complete repeater assembly must be renewed as described in Section 9.

Rear lights

Tailgate/boot lid mounted

23 Open the boot lid/tailgate and prise open the access flap from the boot lid/tailgate trim panel **(see illustrations)**.

24 Rotate the bulbholder and remove it from the light unit **(see illustration)**.

25 Press and twist the relevant bulb anti-clockwise, and withdraw it from the bulbholder **(see illustration)**.

26 Fit the new bulb using a reversal of the removal procedure.

Body-mounted

27 Light Emitting Diodes (LEDs) are soldered to a printed circuit board to provide illumination for the body-mounted rear lights light. It is not possible to renew them. Where an LED is not functioning, the complete light unit must be renewed as described in Section 9.

Number plate light

28 Remove the number plate light unit as described in Section 9.

29 Prise out the lens and remove the festoon-type bulb from its holder, or rotate the bulbholder anti-clockwise, and pull the capless bulb from place as applicable **(see illustration)**.

30 Fit the new bulb using a reversal of the removal procedure.

High-level stop-light

31 Light Emitting Diodes (LEDs) are soldered to a printed circuit board to provide illumination for the high-level stop light. It is not possible to renew them. Where an LED is not functioning, the complete stop-light unit must be renewed as described in Section 9.

8 Interior light bulbs – renewal
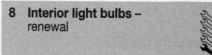

Note: *Whenever a bulb is renewed, note the following points:*

7.23a Prise open the rear light access flap from the trim panel – Saloon models

7.23b Prise open the rear light access flap from the trim panel – Estate models

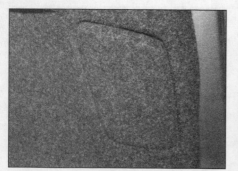

7.24 Rotate the bulbholder anti-clockwise (left-hand side) or clockwise (right-hand side)

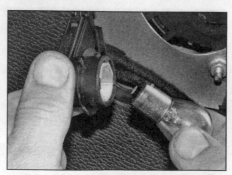

7.25 Depress and twist the bulb to remove it from the light unit

7.29 Pull the festoon bulb from the contacts

8.1 Lever down the panel at the rear of the light unit

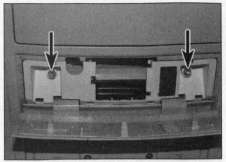

8.2a Undo the 2 bolts (arrowed) . . .

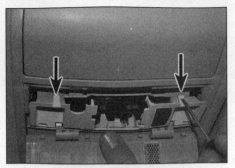

8.2b . . . release the clips (arrowed) and lower the light unit

a) *Remember that if the light has just been in use, the bulb may be extremely hot.*

b) *Always check the bulb contacts and holder, ensuring that there is clean metal-to-metal contact between the bulb and its live and earth. Clean off any corrosion or dirt before fitting a new bulb.*

c) *Wherever bayonet-type bulbs are fitted, ensure that the live contact(s) bear firmly against the bulb contact.*

d) *Always ensure that the new bulb is of the correct rating and that it is completely clean before fitting it.*

Front interior/reading lights

1 Carefully lever down the trim panel at the rear of the interior light unit **(see illustration)**.
2 Undo the 2 bolts, release the 2 clips and lower the light unit from place **(see illustrations)**. Disconnect the wiring plugs as the unit is removed.
3 Fit the new bulb using a reversal of the removal procedure.

Reading lights

4 Rotate the relevant bulbholder anti-clockwise and remove it **(see illustration)**.
5 Pull the capless bulb from the holder.
6 Fit the new bulb using a reversal of the removal procedure.

Interior lights

7 Release the contacts and pull the festoon bulb from place.
8 Fit the new bulb using a reversal of the removal procedure.

Rear interior/reading lights

9 Using a blunt, flat-bladed tool, carefully prise the lens/cover from the light unit **(see illustration)**.
10 Pull the relevant capless bulb from the holder **(see illustration)**.
11 Fit the new bulb using a reversal of the removal procedure.

Glovebox light

12 Insert a flat-bladed screwdriver behind the end of the lens, and prise free the light lens/unit.
13 Unclip the heat shield, and pull the capless bulb from its holder.
14 Fit the new bulb using a reversal of the removal procedure.

Sunvisor/vanity mirror light

15 Prise the light unit from the headlining, starting at the outside edge **(see illustration)**.
16 Prise the festoon bulb from the contacts.
17 Fit the new bulb using a reversal of the removal procedure.

Instrument panel bulbs

18 On all models covered by this Manual, it is not possible to renew the instrument panel bulbs individually as they are of LED design and soldered to a printed circuit board. Where an LED is not functioning, the complete instrument panel must be renewed.

Luggage compartment light

19 Insert a flat-bladed screwdriver behind the end of the lens, and prise free the light lens/unit.
20 Pull the festoon bulb from the contacts.

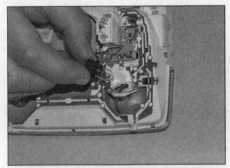

8.4 Rotate the bulbholder anti-clockwise to remove it

8.10 Pull the capless bulb(s) from the holder(s)

21 Fit the new bulb using a reversal of the removal procedure.

Switch illumination

22 Switch illumination bulbs are usually built into the switch itself, and cannot be renewed separately. Refer to Section 6 and remove the switch – bulb renewal should then be self-evident, if it is possible; otherwise, renew the switch.

Heater/air conditioning control panel illumination

23 The control panel is illuminated by non-renewable LEDs. If defective, the control panel may need to be renewed.

Door courtesy light

24 Using a screwdriver, carefully prise the light lens from place.

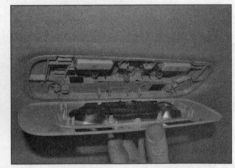

8.9 Prise the lens/cover from the rear light unit

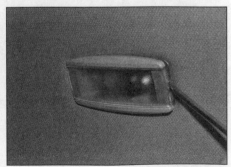

8.15 Insert a small screwdriver into the slot and prise the vanity light from the headlining

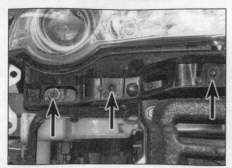

9.2 Undo the 3 bolts (arrowed) and remove the guide beneath the headlight

9.4a Undo the bolt at the outer edge, and the one at the inner edge . . .

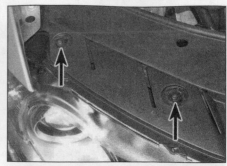

9.4b . . . then the two at the top (arrowed)

25 Pull the capless bulb from the holder.
26 Fit the new bulb using a reversal of the removal procedure.

Footwell light

27 Insert a flat-bladed screwdriver behind the end of the lens, and prise free the light lens/unit.
28 Unclip the heat shield, and pull the capless bulb from its holder.
29 Fit the new bulb using a reversal of the removal procedure.

9 Exterior light units – removal, refitting and beam adjustment

Headlight unit

Caution: On models equipped with gas
discharge headlights, disconnect the battery negative lead, as described in Chapter 5, prior to working on the headlights.

1 Remove the front bumper as described in Chapter 11.
2 Undo the 3 bolts and remove the guide from under the headlight **(see illustration)**.
3 Reach behind the headlight, depress the retaining clip and disconnect the wiring plug.
4 Undo the 2 bolts at the top of the headlight, then one underneath at the outer edge, and the one at the inside edge **(see illustrations)**. Take care not to damage the vehicle paintwork as the headlight is removed.
5 Refitting is a reversal of the removal procedure. On completion check for satisfactory operation, and have the headlight beam adjustment checked as soon as possible.

Front foglight

6 Undo the retaining bolt, release the

retaining clip at the top edge, and pull the foglight surround grille from place **(see illustration 9.9a)**.
7 Undo the 3 mounting bolts and pull the foglight forwards. Disconnect the wiring plug as the unit is withdrawn.
8 Refitting is a reversal of removal, but have the foglight beam setting checked at the earliest opportunity. An approximate adjustment can be made by positioning the car 10 metres in front of a wall marked with the centre point of the foglight lens. Turn the adjustment bolt as required. Note that only height adjustment is possible – there is no lateral adjustment.

Direction indicator

9 Undo the retaining bolt, release the retaining clip at the top edge, and pull the grille beneath the direction indicator from place **(see illustrations)**.
10 Undo the retaining bolt on the underside of the indicator light unit, and pull it from the bumper **(see illustrations)**. Disconnect the wiring as the light unit is withdrawn.
11 Refitting is a reversal of removal.

Direction indicator side repeater

12 Remove the door mirror glass and housing as described in Chapter 11.
13 Release the 2 clips and remove the mirror housing trim **(see illustration)**.
14 Undo the 2 bolts securing repeater housing **(see illustration)**. Disconnect the wiring plug as the assembly is lowered.
15 If required, release the clip and detach

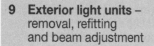

9.9a Undo the bolt (arrowed) . . .

9.10a Undo the bolt (arrowed) . . .

9.9b . . . and release the clip (arrowed) securing the grille beneath the direction indicator

9.10b . . . and pull the direction indicator from the bumper

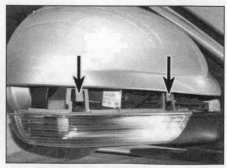

9.13 Prise between the repeater and the housing, and release the clips (arrowed)

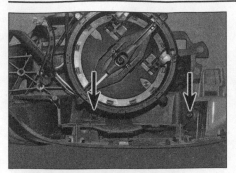

9.14 Undo the repeater retaining bolts (arrowed)

9.15 Repeater trim clip (arrowed)

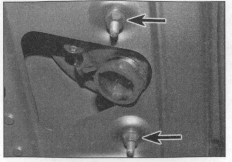

9.19a Undo the light mounting nuts (arrowed) – Saloon models

9.19b Undo the light mounting nuts (arrowed) – Estate models

9.21 Prise open the access flap

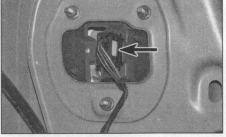

9.22 Slide forwards the connector locking catch (arrowed)

the repeater housing from the trim (see illustration).
16 Refitting is a reversal of removal.

Boot lid/tailgate mounted lights

17 Open the boot lid/tailgate and prise open the cover from the trim panel (see illustration 7.23a and 7.23b).
18 Disconnect the wiring plug from the light unit.
19 Undo the nuts and remove the light unit (see illustrations).
20 Refitting is a reversal of removal, but tighten the upper mounting nut first, and ensure that the seal is correctly positioned.

Body-mounted rear lights

Saloon models

21 Prise open the access flap in the luggage compartment (see illustration).
22 Pull forwards the locking catch, and disconnect the wiring plug from the rear of the light unit (see illustration).
23 Undo the 3 retaining nuts and remove the light unit.
24 Refitting is a reversal of removal.

Estate models

25 Starting at the edge of the rear light, carefully unclip the trim between the tailgate aperture and the light unit (see illustration).
26 Undo the retaining nut, then gently prise the front, outer edge of the rear light outwards to release the inner retaining clips (see illustrations).
27 Pull the light unit rearwards, release the catch disconnect the wiring plug (see illustration).

28 Refitting is a reversal of removal.

Number plate light

29 On bolted-type lights, undo the 2 bolts, insert a flat-bladed screwdriver into the slot at

the end of the lens, and carefully lever the light unit from place. Disconnect the wiring plug as the unit is withdrawn.
30 On clipped-type lights, insert a screwdriver and push the light to the right to compress the

9.25 Unclip the trim between the light unit and the tailgate aperture

9.26a Undo the retaining nut . . .

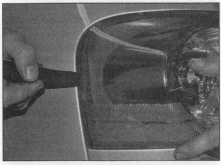

9.26b . . . then prise the edge of the light unit outwards a little, and pull it rearwards

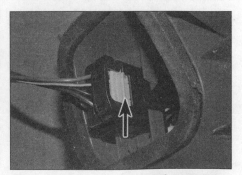

9.27 Pull the catch (arrowed) rearwards and disconnect the wiring plug

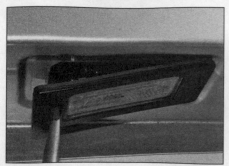

9.30 Push the number plate light to compress the clip and pull it from place

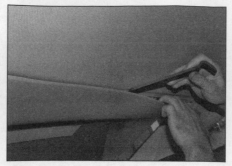

9.32 Carefully prise down the trim at the rear of the headlining

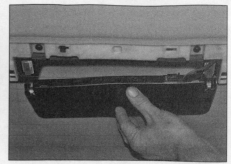

9.33 Slide the light unit rearwards to remove it

clip, then pull the light unit from place **(see illustration)**. Disconnect the wiring plug as the light is withdrawn.

31 Refitting is a reversal of removal.

High-level stop-light

Saloon models

32 Carefully prise down the headlining trim under the stop-light **(see illustration)**.

33 Slide the high-level stop-light rearwards from the guide rails **(see illustration)**. Disconnect the wiring plug as the unit is withdrawn.

34 Refitting is a reversal of removal. Ensure the spring clips are correctly positioned *under* the guide slots in the light unit.

Estate models

35 Carefully insert a blunt, flat-bladed tool between the upper edge of the high-level stop-light and the roof spoiler, then prise the light unit downwards to release the upper retaining clips **(see illustration)**.

36 Pull the light unit rearwards and disconnect the wiring plug.

37 Refitting is a reversal of removal.

Headlight beam adjustment

Note: *This section does not cover models fitted with gas discharge headlights; refer to Section 10 for details.*

Note: *On models with automatic (self-levelling) headlights, adjustment is only possible using dedicated VW diagnostic equipment. Entrust this task to a VW dealer or suitably-equipped specialist.*

38 Accurate adjustment of the headlight beam is only possible using optical beam

9.35 Carefully prise the high-level stop-light from the spoiler – Estate models

setting equipment, and this work should therefore be carried out by a VW dealer or suitably-equipped workshop. Tyre pressures must correct, the car must be loaded with the driver (or equivalent of 75 kg), and the fuel tank should be at least 90% full. If the fuel tank is only half-full, an additional weight of 30 kg must be positioned in the luggage compartment.

39 For reference, the headlights can be adjusted using the adjuster bolts, accessible via the top of each light unit **(see illustration)**.

40 Some models are equipped with an electrically-operated headlight beam adjustment system which is controlled through the switch in the facia. On these models, ensure that the switch is set to the basic O position before adjusting the headlight aim.

---

10 Gas discharge headlight system – component removal, refitting and beam adjustment

General information

1 Gas discharge headlights were available as an optional extra on all models covered in this Manual. The headlights are fitted with bulbs that produce light by means of an electric arc, rather than by heating a metal filament as in conventional halogen bulbs. The arc is generated by a control circuit which operates at voltages of above 28 000 volts. A single gas discharge bulb is fitted. In order to simulate dipped and main beams, the angle of the bulb in

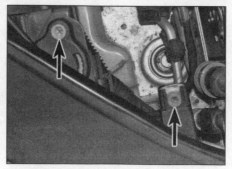

9.39 Headlight beam adjustment bolts (arrowed)

relation to the reflector is altered by a solenoid, which is integral with the headlight, and cannot be renewed separately. The intensity of the emitted light means that the headlight beam has to be controlled dynamically to avoid dazzling other road users. An electronic control module monitors the vehicle's pitch and overall ride height by sensors mounted on the front and rear suspension and adjusts the beam range accordingly, using the range control motors built into the headlight units. Additionally, gas discharge headlights fitted to the Passat range are equipped with 'cornering' lights. These are traditional halogen bulbs fitted to the inner side of each headlight. On models with dynamic cornering lights, these are swivelled in relation to the steering wheel position, by means of electric motors integral with the headlights.

⚠ *Warning: The discharge bulb starter circuitry operates at extremely high voltages. To avoid the risk of electric shock, ensure that the battery negative cable is disconnected before working on the headlight units (see Chapter 5), then additionally switch the dipped beam on and off to discharge any residual voltage.*

Bulb renewal

Gas discharge bulb

Caution: The bulb is under gas pressure of at least 7 bar, therefore it is recommended that protective glasses are worn during this procedure.

2 Remove the headlight unit as described in Section 9.

3 Release the retaining clip, then pull the cap/power output module from the rear of the headlight. Disconnect the wiring plugs as the cap/module is withdrawn.

4 Disconnect the wiring plug, then release the retaining clip and pull the bulb from the reflector. Note how the lugs on the bulb engage with the slots in the reflector. If the bulb is to be refitted, do not touch the glass with the fingers. If the glass is accidentally touched, clean it with methylated spirit.

5 Fit the new bulb using a reversal of the removal procedure.

Cornering light bulb

6 Prise apart the retaining clips and remove the plastic cap from the rear of the headlight.

7 Push the top of the bulb/connector downwards until the retaining clip releases.
8 Manoeuvre the bulb from the reflector and disconnect the wiring plug. If the bulb is to be refitted, do not touch the glass with the fingers. If the glass is accidentally touched, clean it with methylated spirit.
9 Fit the new bulb using a reversal of the removal procedure.

Sidelight

10 Prise apart the retaining clips and remove the plastic cap from the rear of the headlight.
11 Grip the bulbholder and pull it from the reflector.
12 Pull the wedge-type bulb directly from the bulbholder.
13 Fit the new bulb using a reversal of the removal procedure.

Cornering light and range control unit

14 Remove the passenger's glovebox as described in Chapter 11.
15 Disconnect the wiring plug from the control unit, then undo the 2 retaining bolts, and remove the control unit.
16 Refitting is a reversal of removal. Note that if a new control unit has been fitted, it must be coded, and basic setting of the headlight carried out, using VW diagnostic equipment. Entrust this task to a VW dealer or suitably-equipped specialist.

Bulb control unit

17 Remove the headlight as described in Section 9.
18 Undo the 6 bolts and detach the control unit from the base of the headlight housing. Disconnect the wiring plugs as the unit is withdrawn.
19 Refitting is a reversal of removal.

Power output module

20 Remove the headlight unit as described in Section 9.
21 Undo the 4 retaining bolts and remove the power output module from the rear of the headlight.
22 Disconnect the wiring plugs as the module is withdrawn.
23 Refitting is a reversal of removal. Note that if a new module has been fitted, it must be coded, and basic setting of the headlight carried out using VW diagnostic equipment. Entrust this task to a VW dealer or suitably-equipped specialist.

Ride height sensor

24 The removal and refitting the ride height sensors is described in Chapter 10.

Beam adjustment

25 The headlight range is controlled dynamically by an electronic control module which monitors the ride height of the vehicle by sensors fitted to the front and rear suspension. Beam adjustment can only be carried out using VW test equipment.

11.3 Instrument panel retaining bolts (arrowed)

11 Instrument panel – removal and refitting

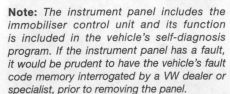

Note: *The instrument panel includes the immobiliser control unit and its function is included in the vehicle's self-diagnosis program. If the instrument panel has a fault, it would be prudent to have the vehicle's fault code memory interrogated by a VW dealer or specialist, prior to removing the panel.*
Note: *If the instrument panel is being substituted with a new or exchange unit, the assistance of a VW dealer or specialist is required to initialise/adapt the various instrument panel functions.*
1 Fully extend the steering column, and move it to its lowest position.
2 Remove the driver's side lower facia panel as described in Chapter 11.

3 Undo the 2 bolts securing the instrument panel at its lower edge **(see illustration)**.
4 Pull the instrument panel rearwards. As the panel is withdrawn, the wiring connectors will be automatically unplugged.
5 Refitting is a reversal of removal, but see the note at the beginning of this section.

12 Windscreen wiper components – removal and refitting

Wiper blades

1 Refer to *Weekly checks*.

Wiper arms

Removal

2 Switch on the ignition and turn it off again, then within 10 seconds briefly press the wiper control switch downwards and release it. This will cause the wipers to move to the 'Service' position.
3 Before removing an arm, mark its parked position on the glass with a strip of adhesive tape. Prise off the cover and unscrew the spindle nut **(see illustrations)**. Note that on Estate models with a tailgate wiper, prise apart the two cover sides slightly and pull the cover from place. Pull out the washer jet and undo the spindle nut **(see illustrations)**. Remove the washer and ease the arm from the spindle by rocking it slowly from side-to-side. If necessary, use a small two-legged puller to remove the arm.

12.3a Prise up the rubber cover (arrowed)

12.3b If necessary, use a puller to release the wiper arm

12.3c Prise apart the sides and pivot up the cover

12.3d Pull the washer jet (arrowed) from the spindle

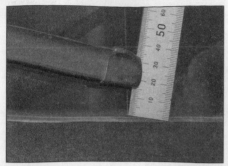

12.4 The end of the wiper blade should be 14 mm above the plenum chamber cover

12.6 Pull up the rubber seal, and slide the clips forwards (arrowed)

12.7 Starting in the middle pull the plenum chamber cover up from the base of the windscreen

12.9a Undo the wiper linkage bolts/nut (arrowed) . . .

12.9b . . . and manoeuvre the assembly from place

12.10 Prise the linkage arm from the ball stud (arrowed)

Refitting

4 Refitting is a reversal of removal, but before tightening the spindle nuts, position the wiper blades as marked before removal. If the

12.11 Mark the position of the crank and undo the nut (arrowed)

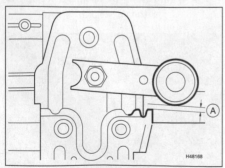

12.13 The distance (A) between the crank arm and the retaining plate should be 2.7 mm for Bosch motors, or 6.4 mm for Mitsuba motors

position of the blades has been lost, or the windscreen renewed, position the blades so that the ends of the blades are 14 mm above the plenum chamber cover **(see illustration)**.

Wiper motor

Removal

5 Remove the wiper arms as described previously.

6 Pull up the rubber seal at the front edge of the plenum chamber cover **(see illustration)**.

7 Pull the 4 cover retaining clips forwards, then pull the plenum chamber cover upwards from the base of the windscreen, starting in the middle **(see illustration)**.

8 Disconnect the motor wiring plug.

9 Undo the retaining nut and bolts, then manoeuvre the assembly from place **(see illustrations)**.

10 Using a screwdriver, carefully prise the linkage arm from the balljoint stud **(see illustration)**.

11 Undo the nut and detach the crank arm from the wiper motor **(see illustration)**.

12 To separate the motor from the linkage, undo the three retaining bolts and remove the motor.

Refitting

13 When refitting, with the motor/linkage back in place, refit the crank arm so the distance between the stop on the retaining plate and the motor crank arm is 2.7 mm on Bosch motors, or 6.4 mm on Mitsuba motors, and tighten the retaining nut securely **(see illustration)**. The remainder of refitting is a reversal of removal.

13 Washer system – general

1 All models are fitted with a windscreen washer system. Estate models also have a tailgate washer, and some models are fitted with headlight washers.

2 The fluid reservoir for the windscreen/headlight washer is located behind the left- hand side of the front bumper. The windscreen washer fluid pump is attached to the side of the reservoir body, and the level sensor is attached to the underside of the reservoir behind the headlight **(see illustration)**. Where headlight washers are fitted, a lift cylinder/accumulator is located in the supply tube, behind the front bumper. Access to the reservoir is achieved by removing the right-hand headlight (Section 9) and placing the lock carrier in the 'Service position' (Chapter 11).

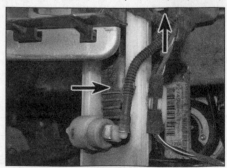

13.2 Washer pump and level sensor (arrowed)

In order to access the pump, only the bumper need be removed (Chapter 11).

3 The tailgate washer is fed by the same reservoir and pump, operating in the reverse direction.

4 Access to the headlight washer lift cylinders is by removal of the front bumper (Chapter 11). No dismantling of the lift cylinders is recommended. If defective, the complete assembly must be renewed.

5 The reservoir fluid level must be regularly topped-up with windscreen washer fluid containing an antifreeze agent, but not cooling system antifreeze – see *Weekly checks*.

6 The supply hoses are attached by rubber couplings to their various connections, and if required, can be detached by simply pulling them free from the appropriate connector.

7 The windscreen washer jets can be adjusted by using a screwdriver to rotate the adjuster bolt on the jet – clockwise for lower, anti-clockwise for higher. To remove a washer jet, open the bonnet, push the jet upwards, then pull the lower edge forwards **(see illustrations)**.

8 Pull off the hose, disconnect the wiring plug (where applicable), and remove the jet.

9 To remove the rear washer jet, pull open the plastic cover over the wiper spindle, and pull the jet from place **(see illustration)**.

10 The headlight washer jets are best adjusted using the VW tool, and should therefore be entrusted to a VW garage to set.

14 Tailgate wiper motor – removal and refitting

1 Make sure the tailgate wiper is switched off and in its rest position, then remove the tailgate trim panel as described in Chapter 11.

2 Remove the wiper arm and blade as described in Section 12.

3 Detach the wiring connector from the wiper motor, then disconnect the washer jet hose.

4 Undo the 3 wiper motor mounting nuts and remove the wiper motor from the tailgate **(see illustration)**. Check the condition of the spindle rubber grommet in the tailgate, and if necessary, renew it.

5 Refit in the reverse order of removal. Refit the wiper arm and blade so that the arm is parked correctly.

15 Horns – removal and refitting

1 The horns are located at the front end of the vehicle. Raise the front end of the vehicle and support it securely on axle stands (see *(Jacking and vehicle support)*. Undo the fasteners and remove the engine undershield **(see illustration)**.

2 Disconnect the horn wiring plug, undo the mounting bolt and remove the horn from the vehicle **(see illustration)**.

13.7a Washer jet adjustment bolt (arrowed)

13.9 Pull the tailgate washer jet from the spindle

3 Refit in the reverse order of removal. Check for satisfactory operation on completion.

16 Sunroof motor – removal and refitting

Closing sunroof manually

1 If the motor malfunctions when the roof panel is in the open position, it can be wound shut manually. To do this, unclip the lens from the overhead interior light by inserting a screwdriver into the lens recesses.

2 Release the crank tool from the inside of the fusebox cover, then insert it into the hexagonal socket adjacent to the interior light bulb. The tool can then be turned to close the sunroof as required.

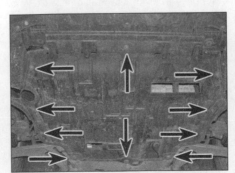
15.1 Undo the fasteners (arrowed) and remove the undershield

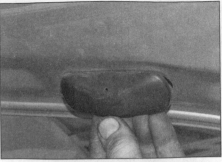
13.7b Pull the lower edge of the jet forwards

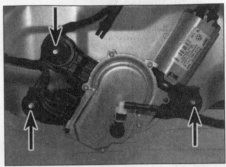
14.4 Tailgate wiper motor retaining nuts (arrowed)

Motor

3 Ensure the sunroof is fully closed, then turn off the ignition, remove the key, and open the door. Don't close the door, or turn the ignition on until the motor is refitted, or its preselection switch recognition will fail, and the sunroof will not operate correctly. If this is unavoidable, it will be necessary to carry out the adjustment procedure as described later in this Section. Remove the front interior light unit as described in Section 8.

4 Undo the 3 retaining bolts and lower the motor from place. Disconnect the wiring plug as the motor is withdrawn. Discard the bolts – new ones must be fitted.

5 Refitting is a reversal of removal.

Drive position adjustment

6 With the motor removed but the wiring plug

15.2 Disconnect the horn wiring plug (arrowed)

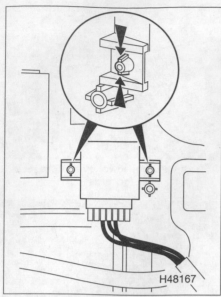

18.5 Squeeze together the sides of the parking aid control unit fasteners

reconnected, select 'open sunroof' with the control switch.
7 Now select 'close sunroof' using the control switch.
8 Now select 'tilt sunroof' using the control switch.
9 Again, select 'close sunroof' using the control switch.
10 If a white dot is visible in the motor drive aperture, the motor is now in the correct position for refitment.

17 Central locking system – general information

1 All models are equipped with a central door locking system, which automatically locks all doors and the tailgate/boot lid in unison with the manual locking of the driver's front door. The system is operated electronically with motors/switches incorporated into the door lock assemblies. The system is controlled by an electronic control unit located behind the passenger's glovebox.
2 The control unit is equipped with a self-

diagnosis capability. Should the system develop a fault, have the control unit interrogated by a VW dealer or suitably-equipped specialist. Once the fault has been established, refer to the relevant Section of Chapter 11 to renew a door lock or tailgate/boot lid lock as applicable.

18 Parking aid components – general, removal and refitting

General information

1 The parking aid system is available on all models. Four ultrasound sensors located in the bumpers measure the distance to the closest object behind or in front the car, and inform the driver using acoustic signals from a buzzer located under the rear luggage compartment trim. The nearer the object, the more frequent the acoustic signals.
2 The system includes a control unit and self-diagnosis program, and therefore, in the event of a fault, the vehicle should be taken to a VW dealer or suitably-equipped specialist.

Control unit

3 On vehicles up to 03/2008, the control unit is located behind the right-hand trim in the rear luggage compartment. Remove the luggage compartment side panel trim as described in Chapter 11.
4 On vehicles from 04/2008, the control unit is located above the main fusebox on the driver's side of the facia. Remove the driver's side lower facia panel as described in Chapter 11.
5 Disconnect the control unit wiring plugs, then squeeze together the side of the fasteners and remove the control unit (see illustration).
6 Refitting is a reversal of removal.

Range/distance sensor

Front sensors

7 Remove the front direction indicator (Section 9) and the radiator grille (Chapter 11).
8 Disconnect the sensor wiring plug, then push the retaining clips apart, and pull the sensor from position.
9 Refitting is a reversal of removal. Press the sensor firmly into position until the retaining clips engage.

Rear sensors

10 Remove the rear bumper as described in Chapter 11, then press the retaining clips outwards. Now press out the sensor inwards from the outside of the bumper.
11 Disconnect the wiring and remove the sensor.
12 Refitting is a reversal of removal. Press the sensor firmly into position until the retaining clips engage.

Warning buzzer

Rear buzzer

13 On Saloon models, the rear warning buzzer is located beneath the rear shelf. Remove the parcel shelf as described in Chapter 11. Prise up the centre pin, lever out the plastic expansion rivets, lift the buzzer from position, and disconnect the wiring plug.
14 On Estate models, the warning buzzer is located behind the right-hand rear luggage compartment trim. Remove the trim as described in Chapter 11, then prise up the centre pins, lever out the plastic expansion rivets, and lift the buzzer from position. Disconnect the wiring plug.
15 Refitting is a reversal of removal.

Front buzzer

16 Remove the driver's side lower facia panel as described in Chapter 11.
17 Disconnect the wiring plug, then prise up the centre pins, lever out the plastic expansion rivets, and remove the buzzer.
18 Refitting is a reversal of removal.

19 Infotainment unit and autochanger – removal and refitting

Note: This Section applies only to standard-fit audio equipment.

Removal

Radio/CD/navigation unit

1 Carefully prise the infotainment unit surround trim from place using a blunt, flat-bladed tool (see illustration). Disconnect any wiring plugs as the trim is removed.
2 Undo the 4 retaining bolts (see illustration).
3 Withdraw the infotainment unit from the mounting case, then disconnect the wiring plugs as the unit is withdrawn.

Autochanger

4 Open the passenger's glovebox, and insert the special VW tools into the slots in the front face of the autochanger (see illustration).
5 Pull the autochanger from position, then disconnect the wiring plugs.

Multimedia control unit

6 Amongst other functions, the Multimedia control unit provides an audio input (AUX-IN), a USB input, and an iPod connection interface. To remove the control unit, open the passenger's glovebox, and insert VW removal

19.1 Carefully prise the surround trim from place

19.2 Infotainment unit retaining bolts (arrowed)

tools (T10057) into the slots at the lower edge of the unit, and pull the unit from place **(see illustration)**.

7 Disconnect the wiring plugs as the unit is withdrawn.

Refitting

Radio/CD/navigation unit

8 Refitting is a reversal of removal. If the radio is of the security code type, it will be necessary to enter the code number before using the radio.

Autochanger

9 Reconnect the wiring plugs, and push the unit fully into position, until the retaining clips engage.

Multimedia control unit

10 Refitting is a reversal of removal.

20 Audio amplifier –
removal and refitting

1 The audio amplifier (where fitted) is located under the driver's seat, either slide the seat fully back, or to improve access, remove the seat as described in Chapter 11.
2 Unclip the amplifier cover, and pull it forwards.
3 Undo the 2 bolts and remove the amplifier. Disconnect the wiring plugs as the amplifier is withdrawn.
4 Refitting is a reversal of removal.

21 Speakers –
removal and refitting

1 The audio system speakers are fitted in the front and rear door trim panels, the facia panel, under the rear parcel shelf (Saloon models), and behind the luggage compartment side trim panel (Estate models). Separate mid-range and high frequency tweeters are fitted in the front and rear door trim panels.

Door speakers

Low frequency speaker

2 To remove a door-mounted speaker, remove the appropriate door trim as described in Chapter 11.
3 Drill out the 6 rivets, and remove the speaker. Disconnect the speaker wiring plugs as the speaker is withdrawn **(see illustration)**.
4 Refit in the reverse order of removal.

Front door high frequency speaker

5 Remove the door trim as described in Chapter 11.
6 Starting at the rear edge, carefully prise the speaker trim panel from the door trim. Disconnect the wiring plug as the panel is withdrawn. According to VW, the speaker is only available complete with the trim panel.
7 Refit in the reverse order of removal.

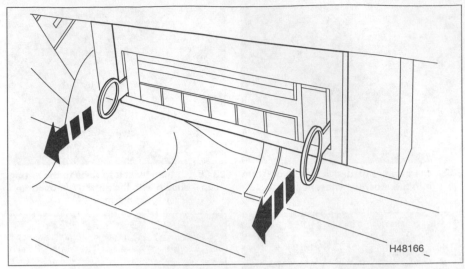

19.4 Insert the tools and pull the autochanger from position

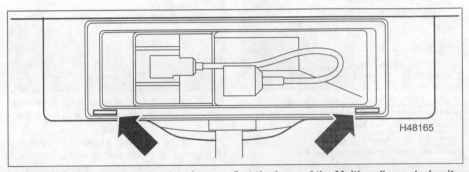

19.6 Insert the tools into the slots (arrowed) at the base of the Multimedia control unit

Rear door high frequency speaker

8 Remove the door interior release handle as described in Chapter 11.
9 Disconnect the wiring plug, then release the 2 retaining clips and detach the speaker/trim from the handle **(see illustration)**.
10 Refit in the reverse order of removal.

22 Airbag system –
general information and precautions

 Warning: Before carrying out any operations on the airbag system, disconnect the battery negative

terminal (see Chapter 5), then wait at least 5 minutes for any residual electric energy to dissipate before proceeding. When operations are complete, make sure no one is inside the vehicle when the battery is reconnected.

• *Note that the airbag(s) must not be subjected to temperatures in excess of 90°C. When the airbag is removed, ensure that it is stored with the pad uppermost to prevent possible inflation.*

• *Do not allow any solvents or cleaning agents to contact the airbag assemblies. They must be cleaned using only a damp cloth.*

• *The airbags and control unit are both*

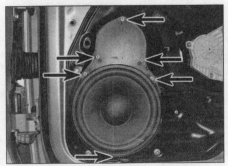

21.3 Drill out the speaker retaining rivets (arrowed)

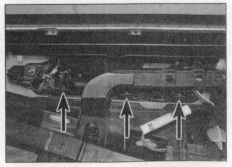

21.9 Release the clips (arrowed) and detach the speaker/trim from the handle

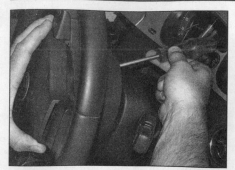

23.3a Insert a flat-bladed screwdriver 8 mm into the steering wheel boss . . .

23.3b . . . then twist it to release the airbag clip – shown with the airbag removed for clarity

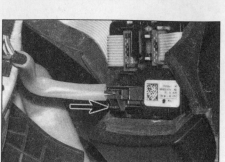

23.6a Lift the retaining clip (arrowed) and disconnect the plug from the steering wheel

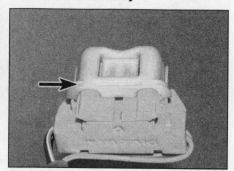

23.6b Slide up the locking catch (arrowed) and disconnect the wiring plug from the airbag

sensitive to impact. If either is dropped or damaged they should be renewed.

• Disconnect the airbag control unit wiring plug prior to using arc-welding equipment on the vehicle.

Both a driver's and passenger's airbag were fitted as standard equipment to models in the VW Passat range. The driver's airbag is fitted to the centre of the steering wheel. The passenger's airbag is fitted to the upper surface of the facia, above the glovebox. The airbag system comprises the airbag unit(s) (complete with gas generators), an impact sensor, the control unit and a warning light in the instrument panel. Seat-mounted side airbags, overhead curtain airbags and rear side airbags are also fitted on certain models, and seat belt tensioners are incorporated in the front seat belt reels and rear seat belt anchors.

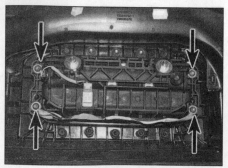

23.11 Passenger's airbag retaining bolts (arrowed)

The airbag system is triggered in the event of a direct or offset frontal impact above a predetermined force. The airbag is inflated within milliseconds, and forms a safety cushion between the driver and the steering wheel or the passenger and the facia. This prevents contact between the upper body and the steering wheel, column and facia, and therefore greatly reduces the risk of injury. The airbag then deflates almost immediately through vents in the side of the airbag.

Every time the ignition is switched on, the airbag control unit performs a self-test. The self-test takes approximately 3 seconds, and during this time the airbag warning light on the facia is illuminated. After the self-test has been completed, the warning light should go out. If the warning light fails to come on, remains illuminated after the initial 3-second period, or comes on at any time when the vehicle is being driven, there is a fault in the airbag system. The vehicle should then be taken to a VW dealer or specialist for examination at the earliest possible opportunity.

23 Airbag system components – removal and refitting

Note: *Refer to the warnings in Section 22 before carrying out the following operations.*

Driver's airbag

1 Switch the ignition on.

2 Set the steering wheel to straight-ahead, then turn it 90° to the left or right. Release the steering column adjustment lever, and pull the wheel out and down as far as possible.

3 Locate the access hole in the reverse side of the steering wheel. Insert a flat-bladed screwdriver approximately 8 mm, and turn the screwdriver clockwise (top surface towards the left-hand side) to release the fastener **(see illustrations)**. Turn the airbag 180° and release the second fastener on the opposite side.

4 Turn the wheel 90° to the straight ahead position, and turn off the ignition.

5 Disconnect the battery negative lead as described in Chapter 5.

6 Temporarily touch the striker plate of the front door to discharge any electrostatic electricity, then carefully lift the airbag assembly away from the steering wheel, release the locking device and disconnect the wiring connector(s) **(see illustrations)**. Note that the airbag must not be knocked or dropped, and should be stored the correct way up with its padded surface uppermost.

7 On refitting, reconnect the wiring connectors and locate the airbag unit in the steering wheel, making sure the wire does not become trapped, and the connectors audibly engage (click). Switch on the ignition, **then** reconnect the battery negative lead (see Chapter 5). Ensure no-one is in the vehicle when the battery is reconnected.

Passenger airbag

8 Disconnect the battery negative lead as described in Chapter 5.

9 Remove the passenger's glovebox as described in Chapter 11.

10 Release the locking catch, then disconnect the airbag wiring plug.

11 Undo the 4 retaining bolts **(see illustration)**, and manoeuvre the airbag from place.

12 Refitting is a reversal of removal. Apply a little thread-locking compound to the bolts. Ensure that the wiring connector is securely reconnected. Ensure that no-one is inside the vehicle. Switch on the ignition, then reconnect the battery negative lead as described in Chapter 5.

Airbag wiring contact unit

13 Removal and refitting the contact unit is described in Section 5.

Airbag control unit

14 Disconnect the battery negative lead as described in Chapter 5.

15 Refer to Chapter 11 and remove the centre console.

16 Release the locking device and disconnect the wiring plug for the control unit **(see illustration)**.

17 Undo the retaining nuts and remove the control unit.

18 Refitting is a reversal of removal. If a new control unit has been fitted, it must be coded using VW diagnostic equipment. Entrust this

23.16 The airbag control unit is located under the heater housing

23.27 Release the locking catch (arrowed) and disconnect the crash sensor wiring plug

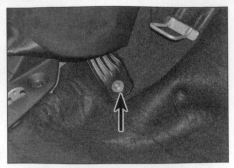

23.30 Undo the nut (arrowed) at the base of the side padding

task to a VW dealer or suitably-equipped specialist.

Side airbags

19 The side airbags are incorporated into the side of the front and rear seats. Removal of the units requires the seat upholstery to be removed. This is a specialist task, which we recommend should be entrusted to a VW dealer or specialist.

Head airbags

20 The head airbags run from the rear of the passenger cabin to the front A-pillars on each side. Removal of the airbags requires the headlining to be lowered. This is a specialist task, and should be entrusted to a VW dealer or upholstery specialist.

Rear side airbags

21 The side airbags are incorporated into the side padding adjacent to the rear seat backrests. Removal of the units is a specialist task, which we recommend should be entrusted to a VW dealer or specialist.

Crash sensors

22 Disconnect the battery negative lead as described in Chapter 5.

Front sensors

23 The front sensors (where fitted) are located either side of the radiator fan assembly on the lock carrier/crossmember. Release the retaining tab and disconnect the sensor wiring plug.
24 Undo the 2 bolts and remove the sensor.
25 Refitting is a reversal of removal, noting the following points:
a) Turn the ignition on, ensure no-one is in the vehicle, then reconnect the battery negative lead (see Chapter 5).
b) It is possible that when the battery is reconnected, the airbag warning light may indicate that a fault has been stored. Have the fault erased, and see if it re-occurs – consult a VW dealer or specialist.

Front side sensors

26 Remove the door inner trim panel as described in Chapter 11.
27 The crash sensors may be fitted on the inside, or outside of the window regulator/

carrier assembly. On models with the sensor on the outside, remove the window regulator/ carrier assembly as described in Chapter 11. Release the locking catch and disconnect the wiring plug from the sensor (see illustration).
28 Drill out the rivets securing the sensor to the regulator/carrier assembly. Note that the sensor must be handled carefully. Do not refit a sensor that has been dropped or knocked.
29 Refitting is a reversal of removal, noting the following points:
a) Turn the ignition on, ensure no-one is in the vehicle, then reconnect the battery negative lead (see Chapter 5).
b) It is possible that when the battery is reconnected, the airbag warning light may indicate that a fault has been stored. Have the fault erased, and see if it re-occurs – consult a VW dealer or specialist.

Rear side sensors

30 Remove the rear seat as described in Chapter 11. Remove the rear seat side padding. The padding is secured by 1 nut at its base, then pull the padding upwards to release the clips (see illustration). Disconnect any wiring plugs as the padding is withdrawn.
31 Pull the trim panel at the front, top of the wheel arch inwards to release the mountings (see illustration).
32 Release the locking tab and disconnect the sensor wiring plug (see illustration).
33 Undo the bolt and remove the sensor. Note that the sensor must be handled carefully. Do not refit a sensor that has been dropped or knocked.

23.31 Pull the panel inwards to release the upper clip (arrowed)

34 Refitting is a reversal of removal, noting the following points:
a) Turn the ignition on, ensure no-one is in the vehicle, then reconnect the battery negative lead (see Chapter 5).
b) It is possible that when the battery is reconnected, the airbag warning light may indicate that a fault has been stored. Have the fault erased, and see if it re-occurs – consult a VW dealer or specialist.

24 Anti-theft alarm system – general information

An anti-theft alarm and immobiliser system is fitted as standard equipment. Should the system become faulty, the vehicle should be taken to a VW dealer or specialist for examination. They will have access to a special diagnostic tester which will quickly trace any fault present in the system.

25 Convenience system electronic control module – removal and refitting

Removal

1 The convenience system electronic control module (ECM) is responsible for the operation of the central locking, boot/ tailgate release, fuel filler flap release,

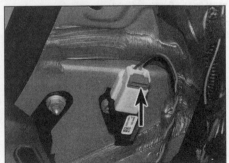

23.32 Pull up the locking tab (arrowed) and disconnect the sensor wiring plug

25.2 Convenience system control module nuts (arrowed)

25.3 Disconnect the ECM wiring plugs

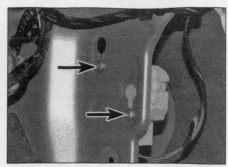

26.3 Fuel filler flap locking motor bolts (arrowed)

anti-theft alarm, immobiliser, entry and start authorisation and tyre pressure monitoring. The ECM is located in front of the passenger's glovebox. Ensure the ignition is switched off, then remove the glovebox as described in Chapter 11.

2 Undo the 2 retaining nuts and remove the bracket, complete with the ECM **(see illustration)**.

3 Disconnect the wiring plugs **(see illustration)**. Note that the plugs are different, and can only be fitted in one position.

4 If required, slide across the locking catch and detach the ECM from the bracket.

Refitting

5 Refitting is a reversal of removal. If a new ECM is being fitted, it will be necessary for the unit to be initialised prior to use by means of dedicated test equipment. Consult your local VW dealer or suitably-equipped specialist.

26 Fuel filler flap locking motor – removal and refitting

1 Remove the right-hand side luggage compartment side trim panel (see Chapter 11).

2 Disconnect the motor wiring plug.

3 Undo the 2 bolts and pull the motor and actuating rod rearwards **(see illustration)**.

4 Manoeuvre the motor into position, reconnect the wiring plug and tighten the retaining bolts securely.

5 Refit the luggage compartment trim panel.

27 On-board power supply control unit – removal and refitting

1 The on-board power supply control unit is responsible for supply power to the lighting

system, washer/wiper system, horns and accessory circuits. The control unit receives signals via a databus network from the lighting switch, hazard warning switch, steering column switch module, and the instrument panel module. The control unit is integral with the relay carrier and cannot be renewed individually. The control unit is located behind the driver's side of the facia. Release the fasteners and remove the trim panel above the pedals. Unclip the diagnostic plug as the panel is withdrawn.

2 Ensure the ignition is switched off, then slide across the locking bars, and disconnect the wiring plugs from the control unit and relay carrier.

3 Release the 2 clips, undo the 2 bolts and lower the control unit/carrier from place.

4 Refitting is a reversal of removal, noting that if a new unit is fitted, it may need to be adapted/initialised using VW diagnostic equipment. Entrust this task to a VW dealer or suitably-equipped specialist.

VW Passat wiring diagrams

Diagram 1

WARNING: This vehicle is fitted with a supplemental restraint system (SRS) consisting of a combination of driver (and passenger) airbag(s), side impact protection airbags and seatbelt pre-tensioners. The use of electrical test equipment on any SRS wiring systems may cause the seatbelt pre-tensioners to abruptly retract and airbags to explosively deploy, resulting in potentially severe personal injury. Extreme care should be taken to correctly identify any circuits to be tested to avoid choosing any of the SRS wiring in error.
For further information see airbag system precautions in body electrical systems chapter.
Note: The SRS wiring harness can normally be identified by yellow and/or orange harness or harness connectors.

Key to symbols

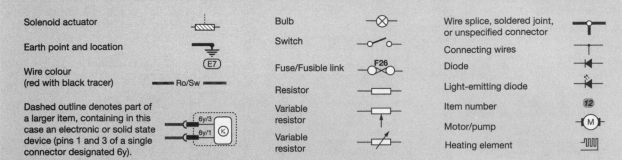

| Solenoid actuator |
| Earth point and location |
| Wire colour (red with black tracer) — Ro/Sw — |
| Dashed outline denotes part of a larger item, containing in this case an electronic or solid state device (pins 1 and 3 of a single connector designated 6y). |

| Bulb |
| Switch |
| Fuse/Fusible link F26 |
| Resistor |
| Variable resistor |
| Variable resistor |

| Wire splice, soldered joint, or unspecified connector |
| Connecting wires |
| Diode |
| Light-emitting diode |
| Item number 12 |
| Motor/pump |
| Heating element |

Earth locations

E1   LH engine compartment
E2   LH 'A' pillar
E3   On engine/gearbox
E4   Engine bay, front of RH longitudinal member
E5   Engine bay, front of LH longitudinal member
E6   RH luggage compartment
E7   On transmission tunnel
E8   On bulkhead
E9   RH luggage compartment
E10 LH luggage compartment
E11 Centre front of roof
E12 LH 'B' pillar
E13 LH 'B' pillar
E14 LH 'B' pillar
E15 On bulkhead
E16 Engine bay, front of LH longitudinal member
E17 Engine bay, front of LH longitudinal member
E18 On centre of rear lid

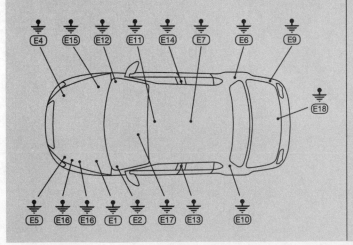

Typical battery fusebox 4

(low specification models)

FA1	150A	Alternator
FA2	80A	Power steering
FA3	80A	Radiator cooling fan
FA4	60A	Front seat adjustment, supply to fuses
FA5	80A	Front seat adjustment, supply to fuses
FA6	100A	Supply to fuses
FA7	60A	Auxiliary heater
FA8	40A	ABS

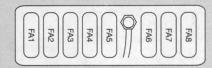

Typical battery fusebox 4

(high specification models)

FA1	150A	Alternator
FA2	80A	Power steering
FA3	80A	Radiator cooling fan
FA4	60A	Front seat adjustment, supply to fuses
FA5	80A	Front seat adjustment, supply to fuses
FA6	100A	Supply to fuses
FA7	40A	ABS

H47108

VW Passat wiring diagrams

Diagram 2

Typical engine fusebox 5

(up to April 2005)

FB1	5A	Automatic transmission	FB31	30A	Wiper motor control unit
FB2	30A	ABS	FB32	-	Spare
FB3	20A	Convenience system control unit	FB33	-	Spare
FB4	5A	On-board supply control unit	FB34	-	Spare
FB5	20A	Horn	FB35	-	Spare
FB6	-	Spare	FB36	-	Spare
FB7	-	Spare	FB37	-	Spare
FB8	-	Spare	FB38	10A	Engine management
FB9	-	Spare	FB39	15A	Engine management
FB10	-	Spare	FB40	15A	Engine management
FB11	-	Spare	FB41	-	Spare
FB12	-	Spare	FB42	-	Spare
FB13	-	Spare	FB43	-	Spare
FB14	-	Spare	FB44	-	Spare
FB15	-	Spare	FB45	-	Spare
FB16	10A	Steering column control unit	FB46	-	Spare
FB17	5A	Instrument cluster	FB47	40A	On-board supply control unit,
FB18	30A	Amplifier			LH main/dip headlight, LH tail
FB19	15A	Audio system, navigation			light (outer light ring), RH side &
FB20	5A	Aerial control unit, telephone			tail light (inner light ring)
FB21	-	Spare	FB48	40A	On-board supply control unit,
FB22	-	Spare			RH main/dip headlight, RH tail
FB23	10A	Terminal 15 supply relay,			light (outer light ring), LH side &
		engine management control unit			tail light (inner light ring)
FB24	10A	Data bus diagnostic interface	FB49	50A	On-board supply control unit
FB25	-	Spare	FB50	60A	Second battery charging relay
FB26	10A	Terminal 30 supply relay	FB51	-	Spare
FB27	10A	Engine management	FB52	60A	Heated windscreen
FB28	30A	Engine management	FB53	50A	On-board supply control unit
FB29	10A	Engine management	FB54	50A	Engine management
FB30	20A	Auxiliary heater control unit			

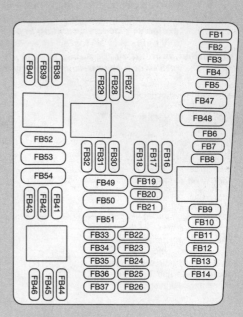

Typical engine fusebox 5

(From May 2005)

FB1	7.5A	Multimedia	FB21	20A	Auxiliary heater
FB2	30A	ABS	FB22	30A	Wiper motor control unit
FB3	20A	Horn, on-board supply control unit	FB23	10A	Engine management
FB4	20A	Convenience system control unit	FB24	10A	Engine management
FB5	5A	Battery monitor control unit	FB25	40A	On-board supply control unit,
FB6	5A	Automatic transmission			RH main/dip headlight, RH tail
FB7	15A	Audio system, navigation			light (outer light ring), LH side &
FB8	-	Spare			tail light (inner light ring)
FB9	5A	Steering column control unit	FB26	40A	On-board supply control unit,
FB10	20A	Engine management			LH main/dip headlight, LH tail
FB11	5A	Instrument cluster			light (outer light ring), RH side &
FB12	5A	Aerial control unit, telephone			tail light (inner light ring)
FB13	10A	Engine management	FB27	60A	Heated windscreen
FB14	30A	Engine management	FB28	40A	Engine management
FB15	10A	Data bus diagnostic interface	FB29	50A	On-board supply control unit,
FB16	10A	Engine management			'x' contact relief relay
FB17	10A	Engine management	FB30	50A	On-board supply control unit
FB18	10A	Engine management			
FB19	30A	Amplifier			
FB20	15A	Engine management			

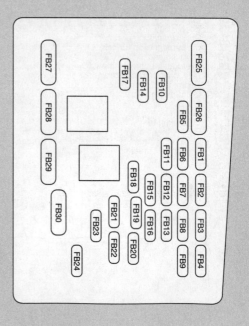

VW Passat wiring diagrams

Diagram 3

Typical LH dashboard fusebox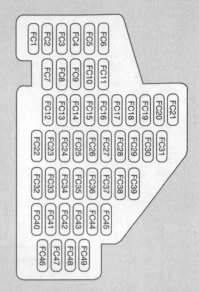

FC1	10A	Roller blind
FC2	5A	TCS/ESP/ABS, electronic handbrake
FC3	5A	Light switch, stop light switch, oil level & temp., power steering
FC4	5A	Electronic damping, trailer control unit, headlight levelling, diagnostic connector
FC5	10A	Switch illumination regulator, headlight levelling
FC6	10A	All wheel drive control unit
FC7	5A	Instrument cluster, data bus diagnostic interface
FC8	10A	Headlight levelling
FC9	10A	Airbags
FC10	10A	Engine management
FC11	-	Spare
FC12	10A	Front door control units
FC13	10A	Light switch, tiptronic, diagnostic connector
FC14	10A	Alarm
FC15	10A	On-board supply control unit, front interior light
FC16	10A	Electronic ignition lock, column lock control unit
FC17	5A	Electronic parking brake, ABS
FC18	10A	Crankcase breather heater
FC19	7.5A	Cruise control, parking aid, lane departure
FC20	-	Spare
FC21	10A	Heated seats, air conditioning, interior mirror
FC22	20A	Electronic parking brake
FC23	15A	Trailer control unit
FC24	20A	Electronic parking brake
FC25	20A	Trailer control unit
FC26	15A	Electronic damping
FC27	15A	Engine management

FC28	10A	Rear door control units, convenience system control unit
FC29	25A	Heated rear seats
FC30	20A	Sunroof
FC31	-	Spare
FC32	30A	Heated rear window
FC33	30A	Headlight washer
FC34	25A	Heated front seats
FC35	30A	Rear door control units
FC36	15A	Seat adjustment
FC37	10A	Air conditioning
FC38	40A	Air conditioning
FC39	5A	Multifunction switch, automatic transmission, reversing light switch
FC40	15A	Washer pump, rear wiper motor
FC41	20A	Front & rear cigar lighter
FC42	15A	12v socket
FC43	20A	Auxiliary heater
FC44	30A	Front door control units
FC45	20A	Auxiliary heater
FC46	-	Spare
FC47	10A	Telephone
FC48	5A	Instrument cluster
FC49	-	Spare

Typical RH dashboard fusebox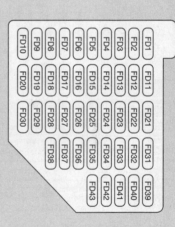

FD1	5A	Compass
FD2	5A	Electronic parking brake
FD3	5A	Compass, ABS
FD4	5A	Cruise control
FD5	10A	RH headlight
FD6	5A	Tiptronic
FD7	5A	Headlight levelling
FD8	5A	Oil level & temp. sensor
FD9	10A	Airbags
FD10	5A	Engine management
FD11	-	Spare
FD12	10A	Front passenger & rear RH door control units
FD13	10A	Parking aid
FD14	5A	Reversing camera
FD15	5A	Air conditioning
FD16	5A	Tiptronic
FD17	5A	Electronic handbrake, ABS
FD18	-	Spare
FD19	-	Spare
FD20	-	Spare
FD21	-	Spare
FD22	-	Spare
FD23	30A	Rear door control units

FD24	30A	Power latching LH rear door
FD25	30A	Power latching RH rear door
FD26	-	Spare
FD27	25A	Heated rear seats
FD28	15A	Engine management
FD29	30A	Front door control units
FD30	20A	Electronic handbrake, convenience system control unit
FD31	20A	Electronic fuel pump
FD32	-	Spare
FD33	20A	12v socket
FD34	15A	Engine management
FD35	20A	Front & rear cigar lighter
FD36	-	Spare
FD37	-	Spare
FD38	15A	12v socket
FD39	10A	Heated seats, air conditioning, washer jet heating
FD40	-	Spare
FD41	-	Spare
FD42	-	Spare
FD43	-	Spare
FD44	-	Spare

H47110

Colour codes

Ws	White	**Or**	Orange
Bl	Blue	**Ro**	Red
Gr	Grey	**Rs**	Pink
Ge	Yellow	**Gn**	Green
Br	Brown	**Li**	Purple
Sw	Black		

* Low specification models
** High specification models

Key to items

1 Battery
2 Starter motor
3 Alternator
4 Battery fusebox
5 Engine fusebox
6 On-board power supply control unit
   a = terminal 15 supply relay
   b = horn relay
   c = 'x' contact relief relay
7 Starter relay

8 High tone horn
9 Low tone horn
10 Steering column control unit
11 Steering wheel clock springs
12 Horn switch
13 Engine cooling fan 1
14 Engine cooling fan 2
15 LH dashboard fusebox
16 RH dashboard fusebox
17 12v socket 1

18 12v socket 2
19 Blocking diode
20 Front cigar lighter
21 Rear cigar lighter

Diagram 4

H47111

Typical starting & charging

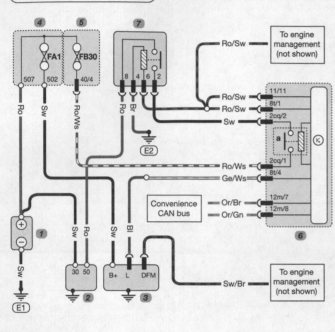

Typical engine cooling fan

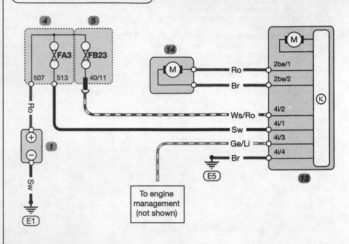

Typical horn

Typical cigar lighter & accessory socket

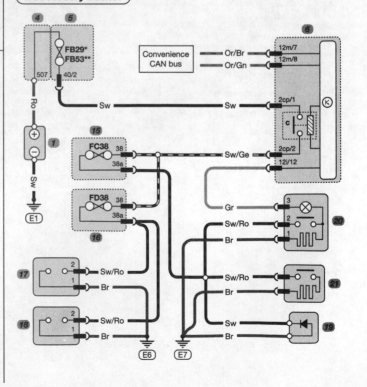

Colour codes

Ws	White	Or	Orange
Bl	Blue	Ro	Red
Gr	Grey	Rs	Pink
Ge	Yellow	Gn	Green
Br	Brown	Li	Purple
Sw	Black		

Key to items

1 Battery
4 Battery fusebox
5 Engine fusebox
6 On-board power supply control unit
  a = terminal 15 supply relay
  c = 'x' contact relief relay
10 Steering column control unit
15 LH dashboard fusebox
23 Stop light switch
24 Reversing light switch
25 High level stop light
26 LH reversing light
27 RH reversing light
28 LH rear light unit
  a = stop light
  b = tail light
29 RH rear light unit
  a = stop light
  b = tail light
30 Number plate light
31 LH headlight unit
  a = sidelight
  b = main beam
  c = dip beam
32 RH headlight unit
  a = sidelight
  b = main beam
  c = dip beam
33 Light switch
  a = off/auto/side/headlight
  b = control unit
  c = switch illumination
34 Diagnostic connector
35 Combination switch
  a = headlight dip/flash switch

Diagram 5

H47112

Typical stop & reversing lights

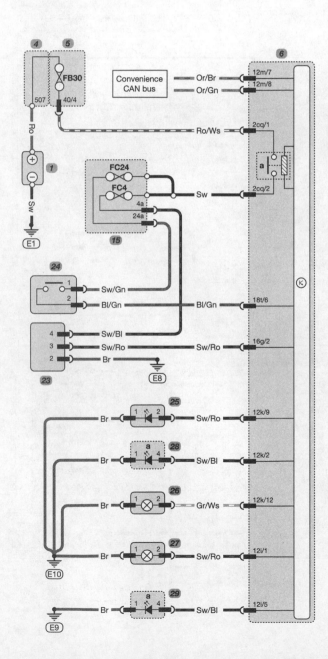

Typical headlights, side, tail & number plate lights

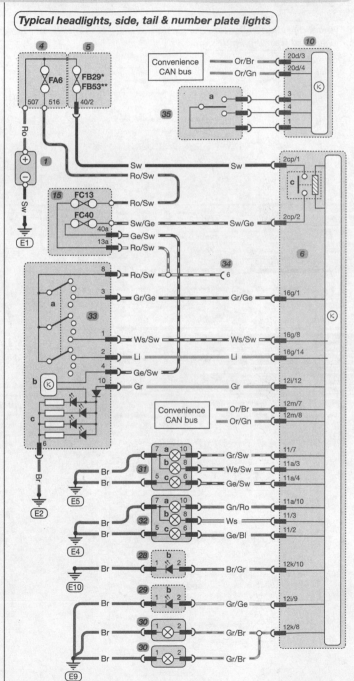

Colour codes

Ws	White	**Or**	Orange
Bl	Blue	**Ro**	Red
Gr	Grey	**Rs**	Pink
Ge	Yellow	**Gn**	Green
Br	Brown	**Li**	Purple
Sw	Black		

Key to items

1 Battery
4 Battery fusebox
5 Engine fusebox
6 On-board power supply control unit
  a = terminal 15 supply relay
  c = 'x' contact relief relay
10 Steering column control unit
15 LH dashboard fusebox
28 LH rear light unit
  c = direction indicator
29 RH rear light unit
  c = direction indicator

31 LH headlight unit
  d = headlight levelling
32 RH headlight unit
  d = headlight levelling
33 Light switch
  b = control unit
  c = switch illumination
  d = front foglight switch
  e = rear foglight switch
35 Combination switch
  b = direction indication switch
38 Hazard warning switch

39 LH front direction indicator
40 RH front direction indicator
41 Driver's door control unit
42 Passenger's door control unit
43 Driver's mirror assembly
  a = indicator side repeater
44 Passenger's mirror assembly
  a = indicator side repeater
45 LH front foglight
46 RH front foglight
47 Rear foglight
48 Headlight levelling/interior dimmer switch

Diagram 6

H47113

Typical direction indicators & hazard warning lights

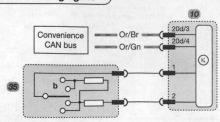

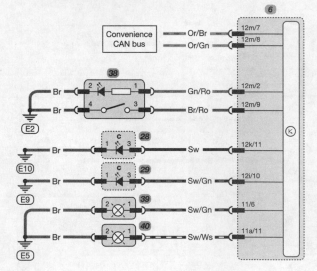

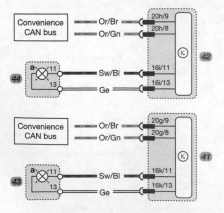

Typical front/rear foglights

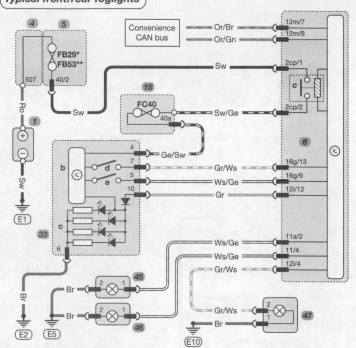

Typical headlight levelling

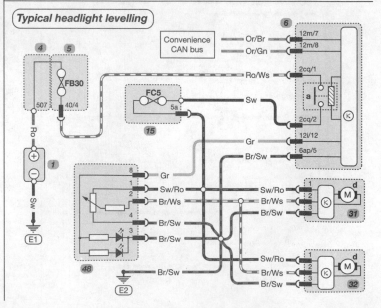

Colour codes

Ws	White	**Or**	Orange
Bl	Blue	**Ro**	Red
Gr	Grey	**Rs**	Pink
Ge	Yellow	**Gn**	Green
Br	Brown	**Li**	Purple
Sw	Black		

Key to items

1 Battery
4 Battery fusebox
5 Engine fusebox
6 On-board power supply control unit
  a = terminal 15 supply relay
  c = 'x' contact relief relay
15 LH dashboard fusebox
16 RH dashboard fusebox
34 Diagnostic connector
50 Front wiper motor
51 Rain/light sensor
52 Rear wiper motor
53 Front washer pump (saloon)
54 Front/rear washer pump (estate)
55 Data bus diagnostic interface
56 Oil level/temperature sender
57 Fuel gauge sender unit/fuel pump

58 Front LH pad wear sensor
59 Oil pressure switch
60 Low brake fluid level sensor
61 Low washer fluid level sensor
62 Low coolant level sensor
63 Ambient air temperature sensor
64 Instrument cluster
  a = trailer coupling warning light
  b = electronic handbrake warning light
  c = low washer fluid warning light
  d = coolant temp/level warning light
  e = coolant temp gauge
  f = warning buzzer
  g = LH indicator warning light
  h = RH indicator warning light
  i = brake system warning light
  j = bulb failure warning light

k = main beam warning light
l = alternator warning light
m = sidelight warning light
n = rear foglight warning light
o = oil pressure warning light
p = cruise control warning light
q = low fuel warning light
r = glow plug warning light
s = oil level warning light
t = engine man warning light
u = tachometer
v = speedometer
w = fuel gauge
x = ABS warning light
y = WSP/TCS warning light

Diagram 7

H47114

Typical wash/wipe

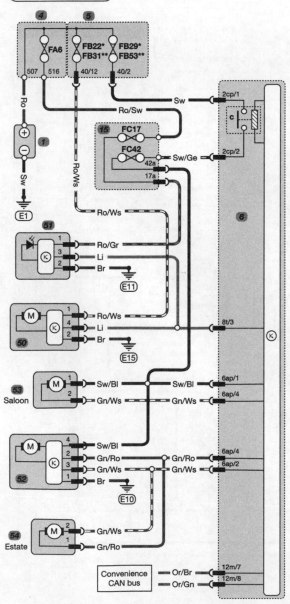

Typical instrument cluster

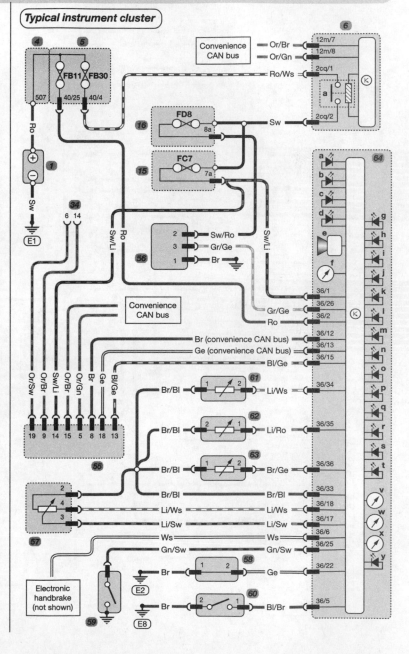

Colour codes

Ws	White	**Or**	Orange
Bl	Blue	**Ro**	Red
Gr	Grey	**Rs**	Pink
Ge	Yellow	**Gn**	Green
Br	Brown	**Li**	Purple
Sw	Black		

Key to items

6 On-board power supply control unit
  d = terminal 30 relay
41 Driver's door control unit
42 Passenger's door control unit
43 Driver's mirror assembly
  b = entry light
44 Passenger's mirror assembly
  b = entry light
48 Headlight levelling/interior dimming switch
67 Convenience system control unit
68 Driver's front entry light
69 Passenger's front entry light
70 LH rear entry light
71 RH rear entry light

72 Driver's vanity mirror light
73 Driver's vanity mirror light switch
74 Passenger's vanity mirror light
75 Passenger's vanity mirror light switch
76 Front interior light assembly
  a = interior light
  b = LH reading light
  c = RH reading light
  d = illumination
77 Rear interior light assembly
  a = interior light
  b = LH reading light
  c = RH reading light
78 Storage compartment light

79 Luggage compartment light
80 Rear lid locking motor/
  luggage compartment light switch
81 Glovebox light
82 Glovebox light switch
83 LH rear footwell light
84 RH rear footwell light

Diagram 8

H47115

Typical interior lighting

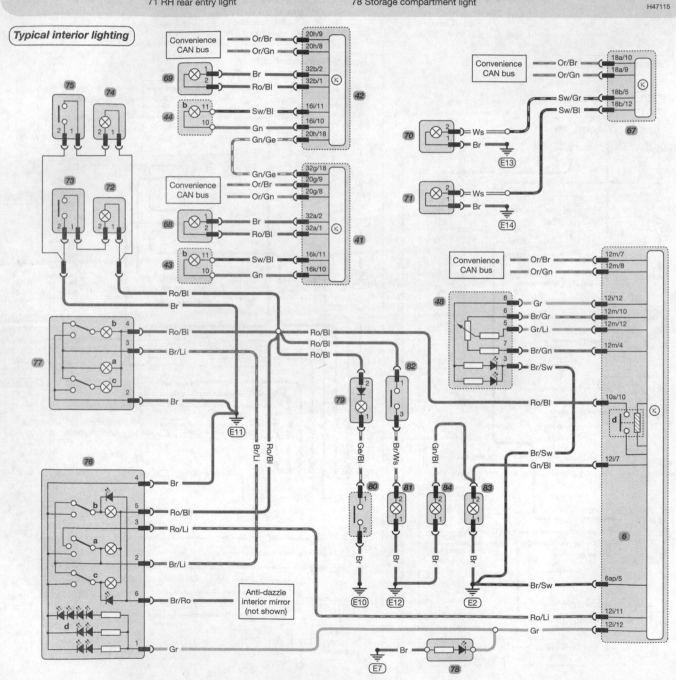

Colour codes

Ws	White	Or	Orange
Bl	Blue	Ro	Red
Gr	Grey	Rs	Pink
Ge	Yellow	Gn	Green
Br	Brown	Li	Purple
Sw	Black		

Key to items

1 Battery
4 Battery fusebox
5 Engine fusebox
6 On-board power supply control unit
   a = terminal 15 supply relay
   c = 'x' contact relief relay
   e = heated rear window relay
15 LH dashboard fusebox
16 RH dashboard fusebox
87 Heated rear window
88 Filter (saloon only)

89 Air conditioning control unit
   a = heater blower switch
   b = heated rear window warning light
   c = air conditioning switch
   d = heated rear window switch
   e = driver's heated seat switch
   f = passenger's heated seat switch
   g = recirculation warning light
   h = recirculation switch
   i = temperature selector
90 Compressor clutch

91 High pressure sensor
92 Recirculation flap motor
93 Centre vent temperature sensor
94 Footwell vent temperature sensor
95 Evaporator temperature sensor
96 Temperature flap control motor
97 Heater blower resistors
98 Heater blower motor

Diagram 9

H47116

Typical air conditioning & heated rear window

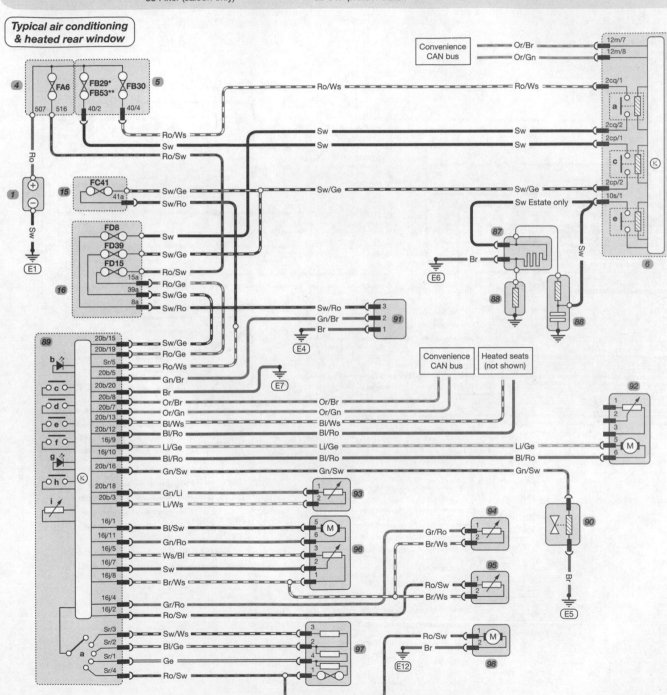

Colour codes

Ws	White	Or	Orange
Bl	Blue	Ro	Red
Gr	Grey	Rs	Pink
Ge	Yellow	Gn	Green
Br	Brown	Li	Purple
Sw	Black		

Key to items

1 Battery
4 Battery fusebox
15 LH dashboard fusebox
16 RH dashboard fusebox
41 Driver's door control unit
42 Passenger's door control unit
43 Driver's mirror assembly
  c = heated mirror element
  d = mirror fold motor
  e = vertical adjustment motor
  f = horizontal adjustment motor
  g = anti-dazzle mirror

44 Passenger's mirror assembly
  c = heated mirror element
  d = mirror fold motor
  e = vertical adjustment motor
  f = horizontal adjustment motor
  g = anti-dazzle mirror
100 Mirror adjustment switch
  a = mirror fold switch
  b = change over switch
  c = adhustment switch
  d = mirror heater switch
  e = switch illumination

Diagram 10

H47117

Typical electric mirrors

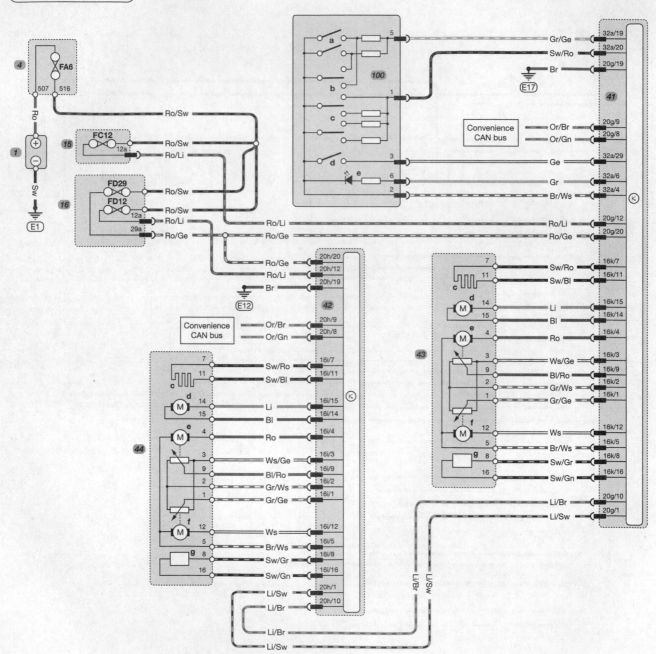

Colour codes

Ws	White	Or	Orange
Bl	Blue	Ro	Red
Gr	Grey	Rs	Pink
Ge	Yellow	Gn	Green
Br	Brown	Li	Purple
Sw	Black		

Key to items

1 Battery
4 Battery fusebox
15 LH dashboard fusebox
16 RH dashboard fusebox
41 Driver's door control unit
42 Passenger's door control unit
67 Convenience system control unit
105 Driver's side interior locking switch
106 Passenger's side interior locking switch
107 Rear lid/fuel tank flap release switch

108 Deadlock function warning light
109 Driver's door lock assembly
  a = deadlock
  b = lock motor
  c = door switch
  d = lock switch
110 Passenger's door lock assembly
  (as above)
111 LH rear door lock motor
  (as above)

112 RH rear door lock motor
  (as above)
113 Rear lock unit
  a = luggage compartment light
    switch
  b = lock motor
  c = lock switch
114 Tank flap motor
115 Central locking antenna

Diagram 11

H47118

Typical central locking

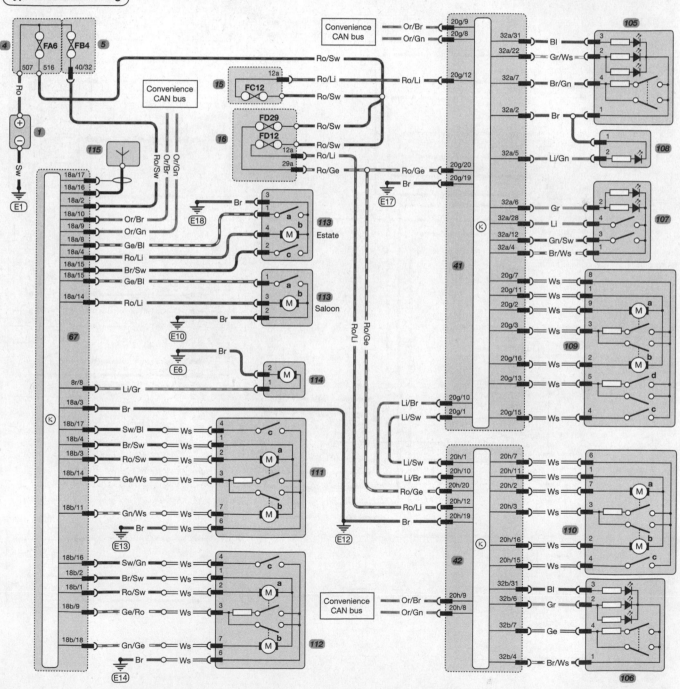

Colour codes

Ws	White	Or	Orange
Bl	Blue	Ro	Red
Gr	Grey	Rs	Pink
Ge	Yellow	Gn	Green
Br	Brown	Li	Purple
Sw	Black		

Key to items

1 Battery
4 Battery fusebox
15 LH dashboard fusebox
16 RH dashboard fusebox
41 Driver's door control unit
42 Passenger's door control unit
118 LH rear door control unit
119 RH rear door control unit

120 Driver's door window switch
   a = RH front window
   b = LH front window
   c = RH rear window
   d = LH rear window
   e = switch illumination
   f = child lock
121 Passenger's window switch

122 LH rear window switch
123 RH rear window switch

Diagram 12

H47119

Typical electric windows

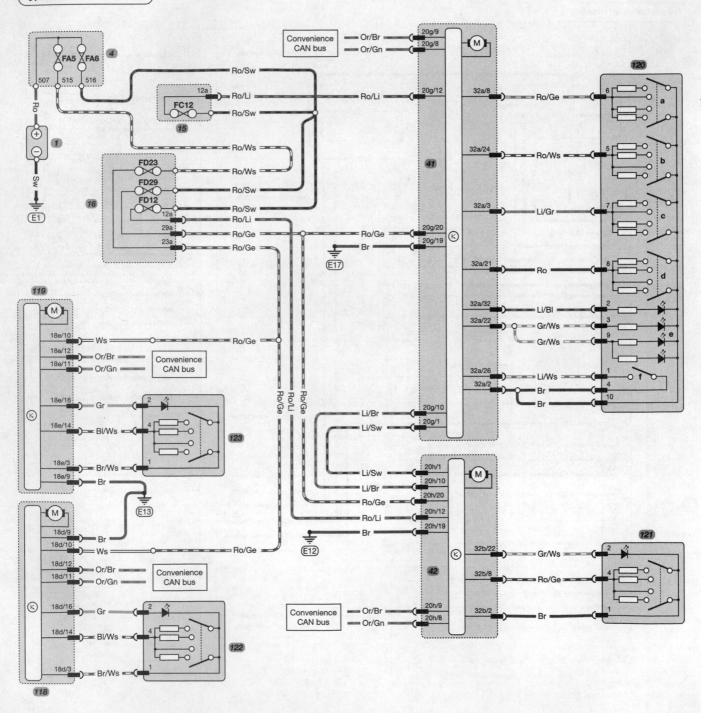

Dimensions and weights

Note: *All figures are approximate, and may vary according to model. Refer to manufacturer's data for exact figures.*

Dimensions
Overall length	4765 mm
Overall width (including mirrors)	1820 mm
Overall height (unladen, including roof rails)	1472 mm
Turning circle	11.4 m

Weights
Kerb weight	1422 to 1479 kg
Maximum towing weight:	
Trailer without brakes	740 to 750 kg
Trailer with brakes	1500 to 2000 kg
Maximum roof rack load	100 kg

Fuel economy

Although depreciation is still the biggest part of the cost of motoring for most car owners, the cost of fuel is more immediately noticeable. These pages give some tips on how to get the best fuel economy.

Working it out

Manufacturer's figures

Car manufacturers are required by law to provide fuel consumption information on all new vehicles sold. These 'official' figures are obtained by simulating various driving conditions on a rolling road or a test track. Real life conditions are different, so the fuel consumption actually achieved may not bear much resemblance to the quoted figures.

How to calculate it

Many cars now have trip computers which will

display fuel consumption, both instantaneous and average. Refer to the owner's handbook for details of how to use these.

To calculate consumption yourself (and maybe to check that the trip computer is accurate), proceed as follows.

1. Fill up with fuel and note the mileage, or zero the trip recorder.
2. Drive as usual until you need to fill up again.
3. Note the amount of fuel required to refill the tank, and the mileage covered since the previous fill-up.
4. Divide the mileage by the amount of fuel used to obtain the consumption figure.

For example:

Mileage at first fill-up (a) = 27,903
Mileage at second fill-up (b) = 28,346
Mileage covered (b - a) = 443
Fuel required at second fill-up = 48.6 litres

The half-completed changeover to metric units in the UK means that we buy our fuel in litres, measure distances in miles and talk about fuel consumption in miles per gallon. There are two ways round this: the first is to convert the litres to gallons before doing the calculation (by dividing by 4.546, or see Table 1). So in the example:

48.6 litres ÷ 4.546 = 10.69 gallons
443 miles ÷ 10.69 gallons = 41.4 mpg

The second way is to calculate the consumption in miles per litre, then multiply that figure by 4.546 (or see Table 2).

So in the example, fuel consumption is:

443 miles ÷ 48.6 litres = 9.1 mpl
9.1 mpl x 4.546 = 41.4 mpg

The rest of Europe expresses fuel consumption in litres of fuel required to travel 100 km (l/100 km). For interest, the conversions are given in Table 3. In practice it doesn't matter what units you use, provided you know what your normal consumption is and can spot if it's getting better or worse.

Table 1: conversion of litres to Imperial gallons

litres	1	2	3	4	5	10	20	30	40	50	60	70
gallons	0.22	0.44	0.66	0.88	1.10	2.24	4.49	6.73	8.98	11.22	13.47	15.71

Table 2: conversion of miles per litre to miles per gallon

miles per litre	5	6	7	8	9	10	11	12	13	14
miles per gallon	23	27	32	36	41	46	50	55	59	64

Table 3: conversion of litres per 100 km to miles per gallon

litres per 100 km	4	4.5	5	5.5	6	6.5	7	8	9	10
miles per gallon	71	63	56	51	47	43	40	35	31	28

Maintenance

A well-maintained car uses less fuel and creates less pollution. In particular:

Filters

Change air and fuel filters at the specified intervals.

Oil

Use a good quality oil of the lowest viscosity specified by the vehicle manufacturer (see *Lubricants and fluids*). Check the level often and be careful not to overfill.

Spark plugs

When applicable, renew at the specified intervals.

Tyres

Check tyre pressures regularly. Under-inflated tyres have an increased rolling resistance. It is generally safe to use the higher pressures specified for full load conditions even when not fully laden, but keep an eye on the centre band of tread for signs of wear due to over-inflation.

When buying new tyres, consider the 'fuel saving' models which most manufacturers include in their ranges.

Driving style

Acceleration

Acceleration uses more fuel than driving at a steady speed. The best technique with modern cars is to accelerate reasonably briskly to the desired speed, changing up through the gears as soon as possible without making the engine labour.

Air conditioning

Air conditioning absorbs quite a bit of energy from the engine – typically 3 kW (4 hp) or so. The effect on fuel consumption is at its worst in slow traffic. Switch it off when not required.

Anticipation

Drive smoothly and try to read the traffic flow so as to avoid unnecessary acceleration and braking.

Automatic transmission

When accelerating in an automatic, avoid depressing the throttle so far as to make the transmission hold onto lower gears at higher speeds. Don't use the 'Sport' setting, if applicable.

When stationary with the engine running, select 'N' or 'P'. When moving, keep your left foot away from the brake.

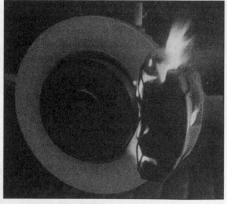

Braking

Braking converts the car's energy of motion into heat – essentially, it is wasted. Obviously some braking is always going to be necessary, but with good anticipation it is surprising how much can be avoided, especially on routes that you know well.

Carshare

Consider sharing lifts to work or to the shops. Even once a week will make a difference.

Electrical loads

Electricity is 'fuel' too; the alternator which charges the battery does so by converting some of the engine's energy of motion into electrical energy. The more electrical accessories are in use, the greater the load on the alternator. Switch off big consumers like the heated rear window when not required.

Freewheeling

Freewheeling (coasting) in neutral with the engine switched off is dangerous. The effort required to operate power-assisted brakes and steering increases when the engine is not running, with a potential lack of control in emergency situations.

In any case, modern fuel injection systems automatically cut off the engine's fuel supply on the overrun (moving and in gear, but with the accelerator pedal released).

Gadgets

Bolt-on devices claiming to save fuel have been around for nearly as long as the motor car itself. Those which worked were rapidly adopted as standard equipment by the vehicle manufacturers. Others worked only in certain situations, or saved fuel only at the expense of unacceptable effects on performance, driveability or the life of engine components.

The most effective fuel saving gadget is the driver's right foot.

Journey planning

Combine (eg) a trip to the supermarket with a visit to the recycling centre and the DIY store, rather than making separate journeys.

When possible choose a travelling time outside rush hours.

Load

The more heavily a car is laden, the greater the energy required to accelerate it to a given speed. Remove heavy items which you don't need to carry.

One load which is often overlooked is the contents of the fuel tank. A tankful of fuel (55 litres / 12 gallons) weighs 45 kg (100 lb) or so. Just half filling it may be worthwhile.

Lost?

At the risk of stating the obvious, if you're going somewhere new, have details of the route to hand. There's not much point in achieving record mpg if you also go miles out of your way.

Parking

If possible, carry out any reversing or turning manoeuvres when you arrive at a parking space so that you can drive straight out when you leave. Manoeuvering when the engine is cold uses a lot more fuel.

Driving around looking for free on-street parking may cost more in fuel than buying a car park ticket.

Premium fuel

Most major oil companies (and some supermarkets) have premium grades of fuel which are several pence a litre dearer than the standard grades. Reports vary, but the consensus seems to be that if these fuels improve economy at all, they do not do so by enough to justify their extra cost.

Roof rack

When loading a roof rack, try to produce a wedge shape with the narrow end at the front. Any cover should be securely fastened – if it flaps it's creating turbulence and absorbing energy.

Remove roof racks and boxes when not in use – they increase air resistance and can create a surprising amount of noise.

Short journeys

The engine is at its least efficient, and wear is highest, during the first few miles after a cold start. Consider walking, cycling or using public transport.

Speed

The engine is at its most efficient when running at a steady speed and load at the rpm where it develops maximum torque. (You can find this figure in the car's handbook.) For most cars this corresponds to between 55 and 65 mph in top gear.

Above the optimum cruising speed, fuel consumption starts to rise quite sharply. A car travelling at 80 mph will typically be using 30% more fuel than at 60 mph.

Supermarket fuel

It may be cheap but is it any good? In the UK all supermarket fuel must meet the relevant British Standard. The major oil companies will say that their branded fuels have better additive packages which may stop carbon and other deposits building up. A reasonable compromise might be to use one tank of branded fuel to three or four from the supermarket.

Switch off when stationary

Switch off the engine if you look like being stationary for more than 30 seconds or so. This is good for the environment as well as for your pocket. Be aware though that frequent restarts are hard on the battery and the starter motor.

Windows

Driving with the windows open increases air turbulence around the vehicle. Closing the windows promotes smooth airflow and

reduced resistance. The faster you go, the more significant this is.

And finally . . .

Driving techniques associated with good fuel economy tend to involve moderate acceleration and low top speeds. Be considerate to the needs of other road users who may need to make brisker progress; even if you do not agree with them this is not an excuse to be obstructive.

Safety must always take precedence over economy, whether it is a question of accelerating hard to complete an overtaking manoeuvre, killing your speed when confronted with a potential hazard or switching the lights on when it starts to get dark.

Conversion factors

Length (distance)

Inches (in)	x 25.4	= Millimetres (mm)	x 0.0394	= Inches (in)
Feet (ft)	x 0.305	= Metres (m)	x 3.281	= Feet (ft)
Miles	x 1.609	= Kilometres (km)	x 0.621	= Miles

Volume (capacity)

Cubic inches (cu in; in³)	x 16.387	= Cubic centimetres (cc; cm³)	x 0.061	= Cubic inches (cu in; in³)
Imperial pints (Imp pt)	x 0.568	= Litres (l)	x 1.76	= Imperial pints (Imp pt)
Imperial quarts (Imp qt)	x 1.137	= Litres (l)	x 0.88	= Imperial quarts (Imp qt)
Imperial quarts (Imp qt)	x 1.201	= US quarts (US qt)	x 0.833	= Imperial quarts (Imp qt)
US quarts (US qt)	x 0.946	= Litres (l)	x 1.057	= US quarts (US qt)
Imperial gallons (Imp gal)	x 4.546	= Litres (l)	x 0.22	= Imperial gallons (Imp gal)
Imperial gallons (Imp gal)	x 1.201	= US gallons (US gal)	x 0.833	= Imperial gallons (Imp gal)
US gallons (US gal)	x 3.785	= Litres (l)	x 0.264	= US gallons (US gal)

Mass (weight)

Ounces (oz)	x 28.35	= Grams (g)	x 0.035	= Ounces (oz)
Pounds (lb)	x 0.454	= Kilograms (kg)	x 2.205	= Pounds (lb)

Force

Ounces-force (ozf; oz)	x 0.278	= Newtons (N)	x 3.6	= Ounces-force (ozf; oz)
Pounds-force (lbf; lb)	x 4.448	= Newtons (N)	x 0.225	= Pounds-force (lbf; lb)
Newtons (N)	x 0.1	= Kilograms-force (kgf; kg)	x 9.81	= Newtons (N)

Pressure

Pounds-force per square inch (psi; lbf/in²; lb/in²)	x 0.070	= Kilograms-force per square centimetre (kgf/cm²; kg/cm²)	x 14.223	= Pounds-force per square inch (psi; lbf/in²; lb/in²)
Pounds-force per square inch (psi; lbf/in²; lb/in²)	x 0.068	= Atmospheres (atm)	x 14.696	= Pounds-force per square inch (psi; lbf/in²; lb/in²)
Pounds-force per square inch (psi; lbf/in²; lb/in²)	x 0.069	= Bars	x 14.5	= Pounds-force per square inch (psi; lbf/in²; lb/in²)
Pounds-force per square inch (psi; lbf/in²; lb/in²)	x 6.895	= Kilopascals (kPa)	x 0.145	= Pounds-force per square inch (psi; lbf/in²; lb/in²)
Kilopascals (kPa)	x 0.01	= Kilograms-force per square centimetre (kgf/cm²; kg/cm²)	x 98.1	= Kilopascals (kPa)
Millibar (mbar)	x 100	= Pascals (Pa)	x 0.01	= Millibar (mbar)
Millibar (mbar)	x 0.0145	= Pounds-force per square inch (psi; lbf/in²; lb/in²)	x 68.947	= Millibar (mbar)
Millibar (mbar)	x 0.75	= Millimetres of mercury (mmHg)	x 1.333	= Millibar (mbar)
Millibar (mbar)	x 0.401	= Inches of water (inH₂O)	x 2.491	= Millibar (mbar)
Millimetres of mercury (mmHg)	x 0.535	= Inches of water (inH₂O)	x 1.868	= Millimetres of mercury (mmHg)
Inches of water (inH₂O)	x 0.036	= Pounds-force per square inch (psi; lbf/in²; lb/in²)	x 27.68	= Inches of water (inH₂O)

Torque (moment of force)

Pounds-force inches (lbf in; lb in)	x 1.152	= Kilograms-force centimetre (kgf cm; kg cm)	x 0.868	= Pounds-force inches (lbf in; lb in)
Pounds-force inches (lbf in; lb in)	x 0.113	= Newton metres (Nm)	x 8.85	= Pounds-force inches (lbf in; lb in)
Pounds-force inches (lbf in; lb in)	x 0.083	= Pounds-force feet (lbf ft; lb ft)	x 12	= Pounds-force inches (lbf in; lb in)
Pounds-force feet (lbf ft; lb ft)	x 0.138	= Kilograms-force metres (kgf m; kg m)	x 7.233	= Pounds-force feet (lbf ft; lb ft)
Pounds-force feet (lbf ft; lb ft)	x 1.356	= Newton metres (Nm)	x 0.738	= Pounds-force feet (lbf ft; lb ft)
Newton metres (Nm)	x 0.102	= Kilograms-force metres (kgf m; kg m)	x 9.804	= Newton metres (Nm)

Power

Horsepower (hp)	x 745.7	= Watts (W)	x 0.0013	= Horsepower (hp)

Velocity (speed)

Miles per hour (miles/hr; mph)	x 1.609	= Kilometres per hour (km/hr; kph)	x 0.621	= Miles per hour (miles/hr; mph)

Fuel consumption*

Miles per gallon, Imperial (mpg)	x 0.354	= Kilometres per litre (km/l)	x 2.825	= Miles per gallon, Imperial (mpg)
Miles per gallon, US (mpg)	x 0.425	= Kilometres per litre (km/l)	x 2.352	= Miles per gallon, US (mpg)

Temperature

Degrees Fahrenheit = (°C x 1.8) + 32

Degrees Celsius (Degrees Centigrade; °C) = (°F - 32) x 0.56

It is common practice to convert from miles per gallon (mpg) to litres/100 kilometres (l/100km), where mpg x l/100 km = 282

Spare parts are available from many sources, including maker's appointed garages, accessory shops, and motor factors. To be sure of obtaining the correct parts, it will sometimes be necessary to quote the vehicle identification number. If possible, it can also be useful to take the old parts along for positive identification. Items such as starter motors and alternators may be available under a service exchange scheme – any parts returned should be clean.

Our advice regarding spare parts is as follows.

Officially appointed garages

This is the best source of parts which are peculiar to your car, and which are not otherwise generally available (eg, badges, interior trim, certain body panels, etc). It is also the only place at which you should buy parts if the car is still under warranty.

Accessory shops

These are very good places to buy materials and components needed for the maintenance of your car (oil, air and fuel filters, light bulbs, drivebelts, greases, brake pads, touch-up paint, etc). Components of this nature sold by a reputable shop are usually of the same standard as those used by the car manufacturer.

Besides components, these shops also sell tools and general accessories, usually have convenient opening hours, charge lower prices, and can often be found close to home. Some accessory shops have parts counters where components needed for almost any repair job can be purchased or ordered.

Motor factors

Good factors will stock all the more important components which wear out comparatively quickly, and can sometimes supply individual components needed for the overhaul of a larger assembly (eg, brake seals and hydraulic parts, bearing shells, pistons, valves). They may also handle work such as cylinder block reboring, crankshaft regrinding, etc.

Engine reconditioners

These specialise in engine overhaul and can also supply components. It is recommended that the establishment is a member of the Federation of Engine Re-Manufacturers, or a similar society.

Tyre and exhaust specialists

These outlets may be independent, or members of a local or national chain. They frequently offer competitive prices when compared with a main dealer or local garage, but it will pay to obtain several quotes before making a decision. When researching prices, also ask what extras may be added – for instance fitting a new valve, balancing the wheel and tyre disposal all both commonly charged on top of the price of a new tyre.

Other sources

Beware of parts or materials obtained from market stalls, car boot sales, on-line auctions or similar outlets. Such items are not invariably sub-standard, but there is little chance of compensation if they do prove unsatisfactory. In the case of safety-critical components such as brake pads, there is the risk not only of financial loss, but also of an accident causing injury or death.

Second-hand components or assemblies obtained from a car breaker can be a good buy in some circumstances, but this sort of purchase is best made by the experienced DIY mechanic.

Jacking and vehicle support

The jack supplied with the vehicle tool kit should only be used for changing the road-wheels – see *Wheel changing* at the front of this manual. When carrying out any other kind of work, raise the vehicle using a hydraulic trolley jack, and always supplement the jack with axle stands positioned under the vehicle jacking points.

When using a trolley jack or axle stands, always position the jack head or axle stand head under, or adjacent to one of the relevant wheel changing jacking points under the sills **(see illustration)**. Use a block of wood between the jack or axle stand and the sill.

Do not attempt to jack the vehicle under the front crossmember, the sump, or any of the suspension components.

The jack supplied with the vehicle locates in the jacking points on the underside of the sills – see *Wheel changing* at the front of this manual. Ensure that the jack head is correctly engaged before attempting to raise the vehicle.

Never work under, around, or near a raised vehicle, unless it is adequately supported in at least two places.

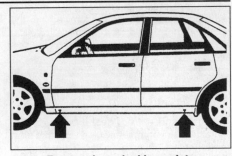

Front and rear jacking points

Audio unit anti-theft system – precaution

The audio unit fitted as standard equipment by VW may be equipped with a built-in security code to deter thieves. If the power source to the unit is cut, the anti-theft system will activate. Even if the power source is immediately reconnected, the unit will not function until the correct security code has been entered. Therefore, if you do not know the correct security code for the unit, do not disconnect the battery negative lead, or remove the unit from the vehicle.

Whenever servicing, repair or overhaul work is carried out on the car or its components, observe the following procedures and instructions. This will assist in carrying out the operation efficiently and to a professional standard of workmanship.

Joint mating faces and gaskets

When separating components at their mating faces, never insert screwdrivers or similar implements into the joint between the faces in order to prise them apart. This can cause severe damage which results in oil leaks, coolant leaks, etc upon reassembly. Separation is usually achieved by tapping along the joint with a soft-faced hammer in order to break the seal. However, note that this method may not be suitable where dowels are used for component location.

Where a gasket is used between the mating faces of two components, a new one must be fitted on reassembly; fit it dry unless otherwise stated in the repair procedure. Make sure that the mating faces are clean and dry, with all traces of old gasket removed. When cleaning a joint face, use a tool which is unlikely to score or damage the face, and remove any burrs or nicks with an oilstone or fine file.

Make sure that tapped holes are cleaned with a pipe cleaner, and keep them free of jointing compound, if this is being used, unless specifically instructed otherwise.

Ensure that all orifices, channels or pipes are clear, and blow through them, preferably using compressed air.

Oil seals

Oil seals can be removed by levering them out with a wide flat-bladed screwdriver or similar implement. Alternatively, a number of self-tapping screws may be screwed into the seal, and these used as a purchase for pliers or some similar device in order to pull the seal free.

Whenever an oil seal is removed from its working location, either individually or as part of an assembly, it should be renewed.

The very fine sealing lip of the seal is easily damaged, and will not seal if the surface it contacts is not completely clean and free from scratches, nicks or grooves. If the original sealing surface of the component cannot be restored, and the manufacturer has not made provision for slight relocation of the seal relative to the sealing surface, the component should be renewed.

Protect the lips of the seal from any surface which may damage them in the course of fitting. Use tape or a conical sleeve where possible. Where indicated, lubricate the seal lips with oil before fitting and, on dual-lipped seals, fill the space between the lips with grease.

Unless otherwise stated, oil seals must be fitted with their sealing lips toward the lubricant to be sealed.

Use a tubular drift or block of wood of the appropriate size to install the seal and, if the seal housing is shouldered, drive the seal down to the shoulder. If the seal housing is unshouldered, the seal should be fitted with its face flush with the housing top face (unless otherwise instructed).

Screw threads and fastenings

Seized nuts, bolts and screws are quite a common occurrence where corrosion has set in, and the use of penetrating oil or releasing fluid will often overcome this problem if the offending item is soaked for a while before attempting to release it. The use of an impact driver may also provide a means of releasing such stubborn fastening devices, when used in conjunction with the appropriate screwdriver bit or socket. If none of these methods works, it may be necessary to resort to the careful application of heat, or the use of a hacksaw or nut splitter device. Before resorting to extreme methods, check that you are not dealing with a left-hand thread!

Studs are usually removed by locking two nuts together on the threaded part, and then using a spanner on the lower nut to unscrew the stud. Studs or bolts which have broken off below the surface of the component in which they are mounted can sometimes be removed using a stud extractor.

Always ensure that a blind tapped hole is completely free from oil, grease, water or other fluid before installing the bolt or stud. Failure to do this could cause the housing to crack due to the hydraulic action of the bolt or stud as it is screwed in.

For some screw fastenings, notably cylinder head bolts or nuts, torque wrench settings are no longer specified for the latter stages of tightening, "angle-tightening" being called up instead. Typically, a fairly low torque wrench setting will be applied to the bolts/nuts in the correct sequence, followed by one or more stages of tightening through specified angles.

When checking or retightening a nut or bolt to a specified torque setting, slacken the nut or bolt by a quarter of a turn, and then retighten to the specified setting. However, this should not be attempted where angular tightening has been used.

Locknuts, locktabs and washers

Any fastening which will rotate against a component or housing during tightening should always have a washer between it and the relevant component or housing.

Spring or split washers should always be renewed when they are used to lock a critical component such as a big-end bearing retaining bolt or nut. Locktabs which are folded over to retain a nut or bolt should always be renewed.

Self-locking nuts can be re-used in non-critical areas, providing resistance can be felt when the locking portion passes over the bolt or stud thread. However, it should be noted that self-locking stiffnuts tend to lose their effectiveness after long periods of use, and should then be renewed as a matter of course.

Split pins must always be replaced with new ones of the correct size for the hole.

When thread-locking compound is found on the threads of a fastener which is to be re-used, it should be cleaned off with a wire brush and solvent, and fresh compound applied on reassembly.

Special tools

Some repair procedures in this manual entail the use of special tools such as a press, two or three-legged pullers, spring compressors, etc. Wherever possible, suitable readily-available alternatives to the manufacturer's special tools are described, and are shown in use. In some instances, where no alternative is possible, it has been necessary to resort to the use of a manufacturer's tool, and this has been done for reasons of safety as well as the efficient completion of the repair operation. Unless you are highly-skilled and have a thorough understanding of the procedures described, never attempt to bypass the use of any special tool when the procedure described specifies its use. Not only is there a very great risk of personal injury, but expensive damage could be caused to the components involved.

Environmental considerations

When disposing of used engine oil, brake fluid, antifreeze, etc, give due consideration to any detrimental environmental effects. Do not, for instance, pour any of the above liquids down drains into the general sewage system, or onto the ground to soak away. Many local council refuse tips provide a facility for waste oil disposal, as do some garages. You can find your nearest disposal point by calling the Environment Agency on 08708 506 506 or by visiting www.oilbankline.org.uk.

Note: It is illegal and anti-social to dump oil down the drain. To find the location of your local oil recycling bank, call 08708 506 506 or visit www.oilbankline.org.uk.

Modifications are a continuing and unpublicised process in vehicle manufacture, quite apart from major model changes. Spare parts manuals and lists are compiled upon a numerical basis, the individual vehicle identification numbers being essential to correct identification of the component concerned.

When ordering spare parts, always give as much information as possible. Quote the car model, year of manufacture, body and engine numbers as appropriate.

The *vehicle identification plate* is situated at the base of the passenger's side door pillar **(see illustration)**. The *vehicle identification number* is also repeated in the form of plate visible through the windscreen on the passenger's side, on the right-hand side of the engine compartment, under the rear seat, and on the driver's side sill **(see illustrations)**.

The *engine number* is stamped on the front, left-hand side of the cylinder block. The *engine code* can also be found on the vehicle data sticker in the luggage compartment adjacent to the spare wheel, and on a sticker on the toothed belt or valve cover.

Other identification numbers or codes are stamped on major items such as the gearbox, etc. These numbers are also printed on the *vehicle data sticker* located in the luggage compartment adjacent to the spare wheel **(see illustration)**.

Vehicle identification plate at the base of the passenger's side door pillar

Vehicle identification number visible through the windscreen on the passenger's side

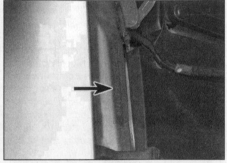

VIN stamped into the inner wing in the engine compartment (arrowed)

VIN stamped into the driver's side sill (arrowed)

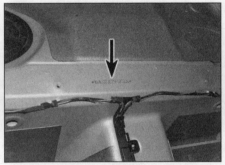

VIN stamped into the body under the rear seat (arrowed)

The vehicle data sticker is located in the luggage compartment (arrowed)

Introduction

A selection of good tools is a fundamental requirement for anyone contemplating the maintenance and repair of a motor vehicle. For the owner who does not possess any, their purchase will prove a considerable expense, offsetting some of the savings made by doing-it-yourself. However, provided that the tools purchased meet the relevant national safety standards and are of good quality, they will last for many years and prove an extremely worthwhile investment.

To help the average owner to decide which tools are needed to carry out the various tasks detailed in this manual, we have compiled three lists of tools under the following headings: *Maintenance and minor repair, Repair and overhaul*, and *Special*. Newcomers to practical mechanics should start off with the *Maintenance and minor repair* tool kit, and confine themselves to the simpler jobs around the vehicle. Then, as confidence and experience grow, more difficult tasks can be undertaken, with extra tools being purchased as, and when, they are needed. In this way, a *Maintenance and minor repair* tool kit can be built up into a *Repair and overhaul* tool kit over a considerable period of time, without any major cash outlays. The experienced do-it-yourselfer will have a tool kit good enough for most repair and overhaul procedures, and will add tools from the *Special* category when it is felt that the expense is justified by the amount of use to which these tools will be put.

Maintenance and minor repair tool kit

The tools given in this list should be considered as a minimum requirement if routine maintenance, servicing and minor repair operations are to be undertaken. We recommend the purchase of combination spanners (ring one end, open-ended the other); although more expensive than open-ended ones, they do give the advantages of both types of spanner.

☐ *Combination spanners:*
  Metric - 8 to 19 mm inclusive
☐ *Adjustable spanner - 35 mm jaw (approx.)*
☐ *Spark plug spanner (with rubber insert) - petrol models*
☐ *Spark plug gap adjustment tool - petrol models*
☐ *Set of feeler gauges*
☐ *Brake bleed nipple spanner*
☐ *Screwdrivers:*
  Flat blade - 100 mm long x 6 mm dia
  Cross blade - 100 mm long x 6 mm dia
  Torx - various sizes (not all vehicles)
☐ *Combination pliers*
☐ *Hacksaw (junior)*
☐ *Tyre pump*
☐ *Tyre pressure gauge*
☐ *Oil can*
☐ *Oil filter removal tool (if applicable)*
☐ *Fine emery cloth*
☐ *Wire brush (small)*
☐ *Funnel (medium size)*
☐ *Sump drain plug key (not all vehicles)*

Repair and overhaul tool kit

These tools are virtually essential for anyone undertaking any major repairs to a motor vehicle, and are additional to those given in the *Maintenance and minor repair* list. Included in this list is a comprehensive set of sockets. Although these are expensive, they will be found invaluable as they are so versatile - particularly if various drives are included in the set. We recommend the half-inch square-drive type, as this can be used with most proprietary torque wrenches.

The tools in this list will sometimes need to be supplemented by tools from the *Special* list:

☐ *Sockets to cover range in previous list (including Torx sockets)*
☐ *Reversible ratchet drive (for use with sockets)*
☐ *Extension piece, 250 mm (for use with sockets)*
☐ *Universal joint (for use with sockets)*
☐ *Flexible handle or sliding T "breaker bar" (for use with sockets)*
☐ *Torque wrench (for use with sockets)*
☐ *Self-locking grips*
☐ *Ball pein hammer*
☐ *Soft-faced mallet (plastic or rubber)*
☐ *Screwdrivers:*
  Flat blade - long & sturdy, short (chubby), and narrow (electrician's) types
  Cross blade – long & sturdy, and short (chubby) types
☐ *Pliers:*
  Long-nosed
  Side cutters (electrician's)
  Circlip (internal and external)
☐ *Cold chisel - 25 mm*
☐ *Scriber*
☐ *Scraper*
☐ *Centre-punch*
☐ *Pin punch*
☐ *Hacksaw*
☐ *Brake hose clamp*
☐ *Brake/clutch bleeding kit*
☐ *Selection of twist drills*
☐ *Steel rule/straight-edge*
☐ *Allen keys (inc. splined/Torx type)*
☐ *Selection of files*
☐ *Wire brush*
☐ *Axle stands*
☐ *Jack (strong trolley or hydraulic type)*
☐ *Light with extension lead*
☐ *Universal electrical multi-meter*

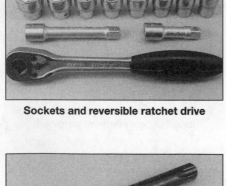
Sockets and reversible ratchet drive

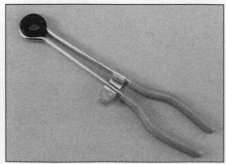
Brake bleeding kit

Torx key, socket and bit

Hose clamp

Angular-tightening gauge

Special tools

The tools in this list are those which are not used regularly, are expensive to buy, or which need to be used in accordance with their manufacturers' instructions. Unless relatively difficult mechanical jobs are undertaken frequently, it will not be economic to buy many of these tools. Where this is the case, you could consider clubbing together with friends (or joining a motorists' club) to make a joint purchase, or borrowing the tools against a deposit from a local garage or tool hire specialist.

The following list contains only those tools and instruments freely available to the public, and not those special tools produced by the vehicle manufacturer specifically for its dealer network. You will find occasional references to these manufacturers' special tools in the text of this manual. Generally, an alternative method of doing the job without the vehicle manufacturers' special tool is given. However, sometimes there is no alternative to using them. Where this is the case and the relevant tool cannot be bought or borrowed, you will have to entrust the work to a dealer.

☐ Angular-tightening gauge
☐ Valve spring compressor
☐ Valve grinding tool
☐ Piston ring compressor
☐ Piston ring removal/installation tool
☐ Cylinder bore hone
☐ Balljoint separator
☐ Coil spring compressors (where applicable)
☐ Two/three-legged hub and bearing puller
☐ Impact screwdriver
☐ Micrometer and/or vernier calipers
☐ Dial gauge
☐ Tachometer
☐ Fault code reader
☐ Cylinder compression gauge
☐ Hand-operated vacuum pump and gauge
☐ Clutch plate alignment set
☐ Brake shoe steady spring cup removal tool
☐ Bush and bearing removal/installation set
☐ Stud extractors
☐ Tap and die set
☐ Lifting tackle

Buying tools

Reputable motor accessory shops and superstores often offer excellent quality tools at discount prices, so it pays to shop around.

Remember, you don't have to buy the most expensive items on the shelf, but it is always advisable to steer clear of the very cheap tools. Beware of 'bargains' offered on market stalls, on-line or at car boot sales. There are plenty of good tools around at reasonable prices, but always aim to purchase items which meet the relevant national safety standards. If in doubt, ask the proprietor or manager of the shop for advice before making a purchase.

Care and maintenance of tools

Having purchased a reasonable tool kit, it is necessary to keep the tools in a clean and serviceable condition. After use, always wipe off any dirt, grease and metal particles using a clean, dry cloth, before putting the tools away. Never leave them lying around after they have been used. A simple tool rack on the garage or workshop wall for items such as screwdrivers and pliers is a good idea. Store all normal spanners and sockets in a metal box. Any measuring instruments, gauges, meters, etc, must be carefully stored where they cannot be damaged or become rusty.

Take a little care when tools are used. Hammer heads inevitably become marked, and screwdrivers lose the keen edge on their blades from time to time. A little timely attention with emery cloth or a file will soon restore items like this to a good finish.

Working facilities

Not to be forgotten when discussing tools is the workshop itself. If anything more than routine maintenance is to be carried out, a suitable working area becomes essential.

It is appreciated that many an owner-mechanic is forced by circumstances to remove an engine or similar item without the benefit of a garage or workshop. Having done this, any repairs should always be done under the cover of a roof.

Wherever possible, any dismantling should be done on a clean, flat workbench or table at a suitable working height.

Any workbench needs a vice; one with a jaw opening of 100 mm is suitable for most jobs. As mentioned previously, some clean dry storage space is also required for tools, as well as for any lubricants, cleaning fluids, touch-up paints etc, which become necessary.

Another item which may be required, and which has a much more general usage, is an electric drill with a chuck capacity of at least 8 mm. This, together with a good range of twist drills, is virtually essential for fitting accessories.

Last, but not least, always keep a supply of old newspapers and clean, lint-free rags available, and try to keep any working area as clean as possible.

Micrometers

Dial test indicator ("dial gauge")

Oil filter removal tool (strap wrench type)

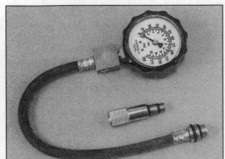
Compression tester

Fault code reader

This is a guide to getting your vehicle through the MOT test. Obviously it will not be possible to examine the vehicle to the same standard as the professional MOT tester. However, working through the following checks will enable you to identify any problem areas before submitting the vehicle for the test.

It has only been possible to summarise the test requirements here, based on the regulations in force at the time of printing. Test standards are becoming increasingly stringent, although there are some exemptions for older vehicles.

An assistant will be needed to help carry out some of these checks.

The checks have been sub-divided into four categories, as follows:

1 Checks carried out **FROM THE DRIVER'S SEAT**

2 Checks carried out **WITH THE VEHICLE ON THE GROUND**

3 Checks carried out **WITH THE VEHICLE RAISED AND THE WHEELS FREE TO TURN**

4 Checks carried out on **YOUR VEHICLE'S EXHAUST EMISSION SYSTEM**

---

1 Checks carried out **FROM THE DRIVER'S SEAT**

Handbrake

☐ Test the operation of the handbrake. Excessive travel (too many clicks) indicates incorrect brake or cable adjustment.
☐ Check that the handbrake cannot be released by tapping the lever sideways. Check the security of the lever mountings.

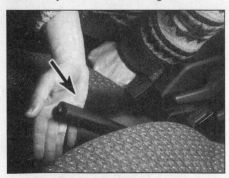

Footbrake

☐ Depress the brake pedal and check that it does not creep down to the floor, indicating a master cylinder fault. Release the pedal, wait a few seconds, then depress it again. If the pedal travels nearly to the floor before firm resistance is felt, brake adjustment or repair is necessary. If the pedal feels spongy, there is air in the hydraulic system which must be removed by bleeding.

☐ Check that the brake pedal is secure and in good condition. Check also for signs of fluid leaks on the pedal, floor or carpets, which would indicate failed seals in the brake master cylinder.
☐ Check the servo unit (when applicable) by operating the brake pedal several times, then keeping the pedal depressed and starting the engine. As the engine starts, the pedal will move down slightly. If not, the vacuum hose or the servo itself may be faulty.

Steering wheel and column

☐ Examine the steering wheel for fractures or looseness of the hub, spokes or rim.
☐ Move the steering wheel from side to side and then up and down. Check that the steering wheel is not loose on the column, indicating wear or a loose retaining nut. Continue moving the steering wheel as before, but also turn it slightly from left to right.
☐ Check that the steering wheel is not loose on the column, and that there is no abnormal

movement of the steering wheel, indicating wear in the column support bearings or couplings.

Windscreen, mirrors and sunvisor

☐ The windscreen must be free of cracks or other significant damage within the driver's field of view. (Small stone chips are acceptable.) Rear view mirrors must be secure, intact, and capable of being adjusted.

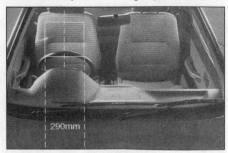

290mm

☐ The driver's sunvisor must be capable of being stored in the "up" position.

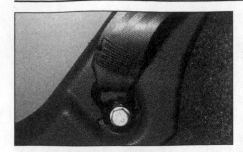

Seat belts and seats

Note: *The following checks are applicable to all seat belts, front and rear.*

☐ Examine the webbing of all the belts (including rear belts if fitted) for cuts, serious fraying or deterioration. Fasten and unfasten each belt to check the buckles. If applicable, check the retracting mechanism. Check the security of all seat belt mountings accessible from inside the vehicle.

☐ Seat belts with pre-tensioners, once activated, have a "flag" or similar showing on the seat belt stalk. This, in itself, is not a reason for test failure.

☐ The front seats themselves must be securely attached and the backrests must lock in the upright position.

Doors

☐ Both front doors must be able to be opened and closed from outside and inside, and must latch securely when closed.

2 Checks carried out WITH THE VEHICLE ON THE GROUND

Vehicle identification

☐ Number plates must be in good condition, secure and legible, with letters and numbers correctly spaced – spacing at (**A**) should be at least twice that at (**B**).

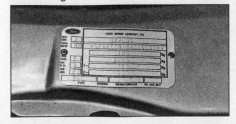

☐ The VIN plate and/or homologation plate must be legible.

Electrical equipment

☐ Switch on the ignition and check the operation of the horn.

☐ Check the windscreen washers and wipers, examining the wiper blades; renew damaged or perished blades. Also check the operation of the stop-lights.

☐ Check the operation of the sidelights and number plate lights. The lenses and reflectors must be secure, clean and undamaged.

☐ Check the operation and alignment of the headlights. The headlight reflectors must not be tarnished and the lenses must be undamaged.

☐ Switch on the ignition and check the operation of the direction indicators (including the instrument panel tell-tale) and the hazard warning lights. Operation of the sidelights and stop-lights must not affect the indicators - if it does, the cause is usually a bad earth at the rear light cluster.

☐ Check the operation of the rear foglight(s), including the warning light on the instrument panel or in the switch.

☐ The ABS warning light must illuminate in accordance with the manufacturers' design. For most vehicles, the ABS warning light should illuminate when the ignition is switched on, and (if the system is operating properly) extinguish after a few seconds. Refer to the owner's handbook.

Footbrake

☐ Examine the master cylinder, brake pipes and servo unit for leaks, loose mountings, corrosion or other damage.

☐ The fluid reservoir must be secure and the fluid level must be between the upper (**A**) and lower (**B**) markings.

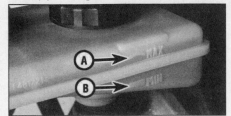

☐ Inspect both front brake flexible hoses for cracks or deterioration of the rubber. Turn the steering from lock to lock, and ensure that the hoses do not contact the wheel, tyre, or any part of the steering or suspension mechanism. With the brake pedal firmly depressed, check the hoses for bulges or leaks under pressure.

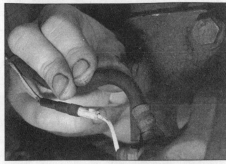

Steering and suspension

☐ Have your assistant turn the steering wheel from side to side slightly, up to the point where the steering gear just begins to transmit this movement to the roadwheels. Check for excessive free play between the steering wheel and the steering gear, indicating wear or insecurity of the steering column joints, the column-to-steering gear coupling, or the steering gear itself.

☐ Have your assistant turn the steering wheel more vigorously in each direction, so that the roadwheels just begin to turn. As this is done, examine all the steering joints, linkages, fittings and attachments. Renew any component that shows signs of wear or damage. On vehicles with power steering, check the security and condition of the steering pump, drivebelt and hoses.

☐ Check that the vehicle is standing level, and at approximately the correct ride height.

Shock absorbers

☐ Depress each corner of the vehicle in turn, then release it. The vehicle should rise and then settle in its normal position. If the vehicle continues to rise and fall, the shock absorber is defective. A shock absorber which has seized will also cause the vehicle to fail.

Exhaust system

☐ Start the engine. With your assistant holding a rag over the tailpipe, check the entire system for leaks. Repair or renew leaking sections.

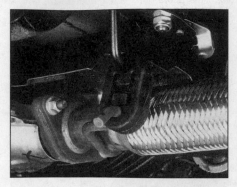

3 Checks carried out
WITH THE VEHICLE RAISED AND THE WHEELS FREE TO TURN

Jack up the front and rear of the vehicle, and securely support it on axle stands. Position the stands clear of the suspension assemblies. Ensure that the wheels are clear of the ground and that the steering can be turned from lock to lock.

Steering mechanism

☐ Have your assistant turn the steering from lock to lock. Check that the steering turns smoothly, and that no part of the steering mechanism, including a wheel or tyre, fouls any brake hose or pipe or any part of the body structure.
☐ Examine the steering rack rubber gaiters for damage or insecurity of the retaining clips. If power steering is fitted, check for signs of damage or leakage of the fluid hoses, pipes or connections. Also check for excessive stiffness or binding of the steering, a missing split pin or locking device, or severe corrosion of the body structure within 30 cm of any steering component attachment point.

Front and rear suspension and wheel bearings

☐ Starting at the front right-hand side, grasp the roadwheel at the 3 o'clock and 9 o'clock positions and rock gently but firmly. Check for free play or insecurity at the wheel bearings, suspension balljoints, or suspension mountings, pivots and attachments.
☐ Now grasp the wheel at the 12 o'clock and 6 o'clock positions and repeat the previous inspection. Spin the wheel, and check for roughness or tightness of the front wheel bearing.

☐ If excess free play is suspected at a component pivot point, this can be confirmed by using a large screwdriver or similar tool and levering between the mounting and the component attachment. This will confirm whether the wear is in the pivot bush, its retaining bolt, or in the mounting itself (the bolt holes can often become elongated).

☐ Carry out all the above checks at the other front wheel, and then at both rear wheels.

Springs and shock absorbers

☐ Examine the suspension struts (when applicable) for serious fluid leakage, corrosion, or damage to the casing. Also check the security of the mounting points.
☐ If coil springs are fitted, check that the spring ends locate in their seats, and that the spring is not corroded, cracked or broken.
☐ If leaf springs are fitted, check that all leaves are intact, that the axle is securely attached to each spring, and that there is no deterioration of the spring eye mountings, bushes, and shackles.

☐ The same general checks apply to vehicles fitted with other suspension types, such as torsion bars, hydraulic displacer units, etc. Ensure that all mountings and attachments are secure, that there are no signs of excessive wear, corrosion or damage, and (on hydraulic types) that there are no fluid leaks or damaged pipes.
☐ Inspect the shock absorbers for signs of serious fluid leakage. Check for wear of the mounting bushes or attachments, or damage to the body of the unit.

Driveshafts (fwd vehicles only)

☐ Rotate each front wheel in turn and inspect the constant velocity joint gaiters for splits or damage. Also check that each driveshaft is straight and undamaged.

Braking system

☐ If possible without dismantling, check brake pad wear and disc condition. Ensure that the friction lining material has not worn excessively, (A) and that the discs are not fractured, pitted, scored or badly worn (B).

☐ Examine all the rigid brake pipes underneath the vehicle, and the flexible hose(s) at the rear. Look for corrosion, chafing or insecurity of the pipes, and for signs of bulging under pressure, chafing, splits or deterioration of the flexible hoses.
☐ Look for signs of fluid leaks at the brake calipers or on the brake backplates. Repair or renew leaking components.
☐ Slowly spin each wheel, while your assistant depresses and releases the footbrake. Ensure that each brake is operating and does not bind when the pedal is released.

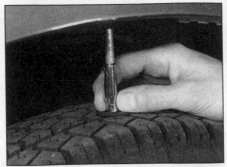

□ Examine the handbrake mechanism, checking for frayed or broken cables, excessive corrosion, or wear or insecurity of the linkage. Check that the mechanism works on each relevant wheel, and releases fully, without binding.

□ It is not possible to test brake efficiency without special equipment, but a road test can be carried out later to check that the vehicle pulls up in a straight line.

Fuel and exhaust systems

□ Inspect the fuel tank (including the filler cap), fuel pipes, hoses and unions. All components must be secure and free from leaks.

□ Examine the exhaust system over its entire length, checking for any damaged, broken or missing mountings, security of the retaining clamps and rust or corrosion.

Wheels and tyres

□ Examine the sidewalls and tread area of each tyre in turn. Check for cuts, tears, lumps, bulges, separation of the tread, and exposure of the ply or cord due to wear or damage. Check that the tyre bead is correctly seated on the wheel rim, that the valve is sound and properly seated, and that the wheel is not distorted or damaged.

□ Check that the tyres are of the correct size for the vehicle, that they are of the same size

and type on each axle, and that the pressures are correct.

□ Check the tyre tread depth. The legal minimum at the time of writing is 1.6 mm over at least three-quarters of the tread width. Abnormal tread wear may indicate incorrect front wheel alignment.

Body corrosion

□ Check the condition of the entire vehicle structure for signs of corrosion in load-bearing areas. (These include chassis box sections, side sills, cross-members, pillars, and all suspension, steering, braking system and seat belt mountings and anchorages.) Any corrosion which has seriously reduced the thickness of a load-bearing area is likely to cause the vehicle to fail. In this case professional repairs are likely to be needed.

□ Damage or corrosion which causes sharp or otherwise dangerous edges to be exposed will also cause the vehicle to fail.

4 Checks carried out on YOUR VEHICLE'S EXHAUST EMISSION SYSTEM

Petrol models

□ The engine should be warmed up, and running well (ignition system in good order, air filter element clean, etc).

□ Before testing, run the engine at around 2500 rpm for 20 seconds. Let the engine drop to idle, and watch for smoke from the exhaust. If the idle speed is too high, or if dense blue or black smoke emerges for more than 5 seconds, the vehicle will fail. Typically, blue smoke signifies oil burning (engine wear); black smoke means unburnt fuel (dirty air cleaner element, or other fuel system fault).

□ An exhaust gas analyser for measuring carbon monoxide (CO) and hydrocarbons (HC) is now needed. If one cannot be hired or borrowed, have a local garage perform the check.

CO emissions (mixture)

□ The MOT tester has access to the CO limits for all vehicles. The CO level is measured at idle speed, and at 'fast idle' (2500 to 3000 rpm). The following limits are given as a general guide:

At idle speed – Less than 0.5% CO
At 'fast idle' – Less than 0.3% CO
Lambda reading – 0.97 to 1.03

□ If the CO level is too high, this may point to poor maintenance, a fuel injection system problem, faulty lambda (oxygen) sensor or catalytic converter. Try an injector cleaning treatment, and check the vehicle's ECU for fault codes.

HC emissions

□ The MOT tester has access to HC limits for all vehicles. The HC level is measured at 'fast idle' (2500 to 3000 rpm). The following limits are given as a general guide:

At 'fast idle' – Less then 200 ppm

□ Excessive HC emissions are typically caused by oil being burnt (worn engine), or by a blocked crankcase ventilation system ('breather'). If the engine oil is old and thin, an oil change may help. If the engine is running badly, check the vehicle's ECU for fault codes.

Diesel models

□ The only emission test for diesel engines is measuring exhaust smoke density, using a calibrated smoke meter. The test involves accelerating the engine at least 3 times to its maximum unloaded speed.

Note: *On engines with a timing belt, it is VITAL that the belt is in good condition before the test is carried out.*

□ With the engine warmed up, it is first purged by running at around 2500 rpm for 20 seconds. A governor check is then carried out, by slowly accelerating the engine to its maximum speed. After this, the smoke meter is connected, and the engine is accelerated quickly to maximum speed three times. If the smoke density is less than the limits given below, the vehicle will pass:

Non-turbo vehicles: 2.5m-1
Turbocharged vehicles: 3.0m-1

□ If excess smoke is produced, try fitting a new air cleaner element, or using an injector cleaning treatment. If the engine is running badly, where applicable, check the vehicle's ECU for fault codes. Also check the vehicle's EGR system, where applicable. At high mileages, the injectors may require professional attention.

Engine

☐ Engine fails to rotate when attempting to start
☐ Engine rotates, but will not start
☐ Engine difficult to start when cold
☐ Engine difficult to start when hot
☐ Starter motor noisy or excessively-rough in engagement
☐ Engine starts, but stops immediately
☐ Engine idles erratically
☐ Engine misfires at idle speed
☐ Engine misfires throughout the driving speed range
☐ Engine hesitates on acceleration
☐ Engine stalls
☐ Engine lacks power
☐ Engine backfires
☐ Oil pressure warning light illuminated with engine running
☐ Engine runs-on after switching off
☐ Engine noises

Cooling system

☐ Overheating
☐ Overcooling
☐ External coolant leakage
☐ Internal coolant leakage
☐ Corrosion

Fuel and exhaust systems

☐ Excessive fuel consumption
☐ Fuel leakage and/or fuel odour
☐ Excessive noise or fumes from exhaust system

Clutch

☐ Pedal travels to floor – no pressure or very little resistance
☐ Clutch fails to disengage (unable to select gears)
☐ Clutch slips (engine speed increases, with no increase in vehicle speed)
☐ Judder as clutch is engaged
☐ Noise when depressing or releasing clutch pedal

Manual transmission

☐ Noisy in neutral with engine running
☐ Noisy in one particular gear
☐ Difficulty engaging gears
☐ Jumps out of gear
☐ Vibration
☐ Lubricant leaks

Automatic transmission (DSG)

☐ Fluid leakage
☐ General gear selection problems
☐ Transmission will not downshift (kickdown) with accelerator pedal fully depressed
☐ Engine will not start in any gear, or starts in gears other than Park or Neutral
☐ Transmission slips, shifts roughly, is noisy, or has no drive in forward or reverse gears

Driveshafts

☐ Vibration when accelerating or decelerating
☐ Clicking or knocking noise on turns (at slow speed on full-lock)

Braking system

☐ Vehicle pulls to one side under braking
☐ Noise (grinding or high-pitched squeal) when brakes applied
☐ Excessive brake pedal travel
☐ Brake pedal feels spongy when depressed
☐ Excessive brake pedal effort required to stop vehicle
☐ Judder felt through brake pedal or steering wheel when braking
☐ Pedal pulsates when braking hard
☐ Brakes binding
☐ Rear wheels locking under normal braking

Steering and suspension

☐ Vehicle pulls to one side
☐ Wheel wobble and vibration
☐ Excessive pitching and/or rolling around corners, or during braking
☐ Wandering or general instability
☐ Excessively-stiff steering
☐ Excessive play in steering
☐ Lack of power assistance
☐ Tyre wear excessive

Electrical system

☐ Battery will not hold a charge for more than a few days
☐ Ignition/no-charge warning light remains illuminated with engine running
☐ Ignition/no-charge warning light fails to come on
☐ Lights inoperative
☐ Instrument readings inaccurate or erratic
☐ Horn inoperative, or unsatisfactory in operation
☐ Windscreen/tailgate wipers inoperative, or unsatisfactory in operation
☐ Windscreen washers inoperative, or unsatisfactory in operation
☐ Electric windows inoperative, or unsatisfactory in operation

Introduction

The vehicle owner who does his or her own maintenance according to the recommended service schedules should not have to use this section of the manual very often. Modern component reliability is such that, provided those items subject to wear or deterioration are inspected or renewed at the specified intervals, sudden failure is comparatively rare. Faults do not usually just happen as a result of sudden failure, but develop over a period of time. Major mechanical failures in particular are usually preceded by characteristic symptoms over hundreds or even thousands of miles. Those components which do occasionally fail without warning are often small and easily carried in the vehicle.

With any fault-finding, the first step is to decide where to begin investigations. Sometimes this is obvious, but on other occasions, a little detective work will be necessary. The owner who makes half a dozen haphazard adjustments or renewals may be successful in curing a fault (or its symptoms), but will be none the wiser if the fault recurs, and ultimately may have spent more time and money than was necessary. A calm and logical approach will be found to be more satisfactory in the long run. Always take into account any warning signs or abnormalities that may have been noticed in the period preceding the fault – power loss, high or low gauge readings, unusual smells, etc – and remember that failure of components such as fuses or spark plugs may only be pointers to some underlying fault.

The pages which follow provide an easy-reference guide to the more common problems which may occur during the operation of the vehicle. These problems and their possible causes are grouped under headings denoting various components or systems, such as Engine, Cooling system, etc. The general Chapter which deals with the problem is also shown in brackets; refer to the relevant part of that Chapter for system-specific information. Whatever the fault, certain basic principles apply. These are as follows:

Verify the fault. This is simply a matter of being sure that you know what the symptoms are before starting work. This is particularly important if you are investigating a fault for someone else, who may not have described it very accurately.

Don't overlook the obvious. For example, if the vehicle won't start, is there fuel in the tank? (Don't take anyone else's word on this particular point, and don't trust the fuel gauge either!) If an electrical fault is indicated, look for loose or broken wires before digging out the test gear.

Cure the disease, not the symptom. Substituting a flat battery with a fully-charged one will get you off the hard shoulder, but if the underlying cause is not attended to, the new battery will go the same way. Similarly, changing oil-fouled spark plugs for a new set will get you moving again, but remember that the reason for the fouling (if it wasn't simply an incorrect grade of plug) will have to be established and corrected.

Don't take anything for granted. Particularly, don't forget that a new component may itself be defective (especially if its been rattling around in the boot for months), and don't leave components out of a fault diagnosis sequence just because they are new or recently-fitted. When you do finally diagnose a difficult fault, you'll probably realise that all the evidence was there from the start.

Diesel fault diagnosis

The majority of starting problems on small diesel engines are electrical in origin. The mechanic who is familiar with petrol engines but less so with diesel may be inclined to view the diesel's injectors and pump in the same light as the spark plugs and distributor, but this is generally a mistake.

When investigating complaints of difficult starting for someone else, make sure that the correct starting procedure is understood and is being followed. Some drivers are unaware of the significance of the preheating warning light – many modern engines are sufficiently forgiving for this not to matter in mild weather, but with the onset of winter, problems begin. Glow plugs in particular are often neglected – just one faulty plug will make cold-weather starting very difficult.

As a rule of thumb, if the engine is difficult to start but runs well when it has finally got going, the problem is electrical (battery, starter motor or preheating system). If poor performance is combined with difficult starting, the problem is likely to be in the fuel system. The low-pressure (supply) side of the fuel system should be checked before suspecting the injectors and high-pressure pump. The most common fuel supply problem is air getting into the system, and any pipe from the fuel tank forwards must be scrutinised if air leakage is suspected.

Engine

Engine fails to rotate when attempting to start

☐ Battery terminal connections loose or corroded (see *Weekly checks*).
☐ Battery discharged or faulty (Chapter 5).
☐ Broken, loose or disconnected wiring in the starting circuit (Chapter 5).
☐ Defective starter solenoid or switch (Chapter 5).
☐ Defective starter motor (Chapter 5).
☐ Starter pinion or flywheel/driveplate ring gear teeth loose or broken (Chapter 2 and 5).
☐ Engine earth strap broken or disconnected (Chapter 5 or 12).

Engine rotates, but will not start

☐ Fuel tank empty.
☐ Battery discharged (engine rotates slowly) (Chapter 5).
☐ Battery terminal connections loose or corroded (see *Weekly checks*).
☐ Preheating system faulty (Chapter 5).
☐ Air in fuel system (Chapter 4).
☐ Major mechanical failure (e.g. timing belt) (Chapter 2).

Engine difficult to start when cold

☐ Battery discharged (Chapter 5).
☐ Battery terminal connections loose or corroded (see *Weekly checks*).
☐ Preheating system faulty (Chapter 5).
☐ Low cylinder compressions (Chapter 2).

Engine difficult to start when hot

☐ Air filter element dirty or clogged (Chapter 1).
☐ Low cylinder compressions (Chapter 2).

Starter motor noisy or excessively-rough in engagement

☐ Starter pinion or flywheel ring gear teeth loose or broken (Chapter 2 and 5).
☐ Starter motor mounting bolts loose or missing (Chapter 5).
☐ Starter motor internal components worn or damaged (Chapter 5).

Engine starts, but stops immediately

☐ Air in fuel system (Chapter 4).

Engine idles erratically

☐ Air filter element clogged (Chapter 1).
☐ Uneven or low cylinder compressions (Chapter 2).
☐ Camshaft lobes worn (Chapter 2).
☐ Timing belt incorrectly fitted (Chapter 2).
☐ Faulty injector(s) (Chapter 4).

Engine misfires at idle speed

☐ Faulty injector – diesel models (Chapter 4).
☐ Air in fuel system (Chapter 4).
☐ Uneven or low cylinder compressions (Chapter 2).
☐ Disconnected, leaking, or perished crankcase ventilation hoses (Chapter 4).

Engine misfires throughout the driving speed range

☐ Fuel filter choked (Chapter 1).
☐ Fuel tank vent blocked, or fuel pipes restricted (Chapter 4).
☐ Faulty injector(s) (Chapter 4).
☐ Uneven or low cylinder compressions (Chapter 2).

Engine hesitates on acceleration

☐ Faulty mass airflow sensor (Chapter 4).
☐ Faulty injector(s) (Chapter 4C.

Engine stalls

☐ Fuel filter choked (Chapter 1).
☐ Fuel pump faulty, or delivery pressure low –(Chapter 4).
☐ Fuel tank vent blocked, or fuel pipes restricted (Chapter 4).
☐ Air in fuel system (Chapter 4).
☐ Faulty injector(s) (Chapter 4).

Engine lacks power

☐ Timing belt incorrectly fitted or tensioned (Chapter 2).
☐ Fuel filter choked (Chapter 1).
☐ Fuel pump faulty, or delivery pressure low (Chapter 4).
☐ Uneven or low cylinder compressions (Chapter 2).
☐ Faulty injector(s) (Chapter 4).
☐ Brakes binding (Chapters 1 and 9).
☐ Clutch slipping (Chapter 6).
☐ Air filter element clogged (Chapter 1).

Engine (continued)

Engine backfires

- ☐ Timing belt incorrectly fitted or tensioned (Chapter 2).

Oil pressure warning light illuminated with engine running

- ☐ Low oil level, or incorrect oil grade (*Weekly checks*).
- ☐ Faulty oil pressure switch (Chapter 2).
- ☐ Worn engine bearings and/or oil pump (Chapter 2).
- ☐ High engine operating temperature (Chapter 3).
- ☐ Oil pressure relief valve defective (Chapter 2).
- ☐ Oil pick-up strainer clogged (Chapter 2).

Engine runs-on after switching off

- ☐ Excessive carbon build-up in engine (Chapter 2).
- ☐ High engine operating temperature (Chapter 3).
- ☐ Faulty stop solenoid (Chapter 4).

Engine noises

Pre-ignition (pinking) or knocking during acceleration or under load

- ☐ Excessive carbon build-up in engine (Chapter 2).

Whistling or wheezing noises

- ☐ Leaking exhaust manifold gasket or pipe-to-manifold joint (Chapter 4).
- ☐ Leaking vacuum hose (Chapters 4 and 9).
- ☐ Blowing cylinder head gasket (Chapter 2).

Tapping or rattling noises

- ☐ Worn valve gear or camshaft (Chapter 2).
- ☐ Ancillary component fault (coolant pump, alternator, etc) (Chapters 3, 5, etc).

Knocking or thumping noises

- ☐ Worn big-end bearings (regular heavy knocking, perhaps less under load) (Chapter 2).
- ☐ Worn main bearings (rumbling and knocking, perhaps worsening under load) (Chapter 2).
- ☐ Piston slap (most noticeable when cold) (Chapter 2).
- ☐ Ancillary component fault (coolant pump, alternator, etc) (Chapters 3, 5, etc).

Cooling system

Overheating

- ☐ Insufficient coolant in system (*Weekly checks*).
- ☐ Thermostat faulty (Chapter 3).
- ☐ Radiator core blocked, or grille restricted (Chapter 3).
- ☐ Electric cooling fan or thermostatic switch faulty (Chapter 3).
- ☐ Inaccurate temperature gauge sender unit (Chapter 3).
- ☐ Airlock in cooling system.
- ☐ Expansion tank pressure cap faulty (Chapter 3).

Overcooling

- ☐ Thermostat faulty (Chapter 3).
- ☐ Inaccurate temperature gauge sender unit (Chapter 3).

External coolant leakage

- ☐ Deteriorated or damaged hoses or hose clips (Chapter 1).
- ☐ Radiator core or heater matrix leaking (Chapter 3).
- ☐ Pressure cap faulty (Chapter 3).
- ☐ Coolant pump internal seal leaking (Chapter 3).
- ☐ Coolant pump-to-housing seal leaking (Chapter 3).
- ☐ Boiling due to overheating (Chapter 3).
- ☐ Core plug leaking (Chapter 2).

Internal coolant leakage

- ☐ Leaking cylinder head gasket (Chapter 2).
- ☐ Cracked cylinder head or cylinder block (Chapter 2).

Corrosion

- ☐ Infrequent draining and flushing (Chapter 1).
- ☐ Incorrect coolant mixture or inappropriate coolant type (see *Weekly checks*).

Fuel and exhaust systems

Excessive fuel consumption

- ☐ Air filter element dirty or clogged (Chapter 1).
- ☐ Faulty injector(s) (Chapter 4).
- ☐ Faulty brake calipers (Chapter 9).
- ☐ Tyres under-inflated (see *Weekly checks*).

Fuel leakage and/or fuel odour

- ☐ Damaged fuel tank, pipes or connections (Chapter 4).

Excessive noise or fumes from exhaust system

- ☐ Leaking exhaust system or manifold joints (Chapters 1 and 4).
- ☐ Leaking, corroded or damaged silencers or pipe (Chapters 1 and 4).
- ☐ Broken mountings causing body or suspension contact (Chapter 1).

Clutch

Pedal travels to floor – no pressure or very little resistance

- ☐ Faulty master or slave cylinder (Chapter 6).
- ☐ Faulty hydraulic release system (Chapter 6).
- ☐ Broken clutch release bearing or arm (Chapter 6).
- ☐ Broken diaphragm spring in clutch pressure plate (Chapter 6).

Clutch fails to disengage (unable to select gears)

- ☐ Faulty master or slave cylinder (Chapter 6).
- ☐ Faulty hydraulic release system (Chapter 6).
- ☐ Clutch disc sticking on gearbox input shaft splines (Chapter 6).
- ☐ Clutch disc sticking to flywheel or pressure plate (Chapter 6).
- ☐ Faulty pressure plate assembly (Chapter 6).
- ☐ Clutch release mechanism worn or incorrectly assembled (Chapter 6).

Clutch slips (engine speed increases, with no increase in vehicle speed)

- ☐ Faulty hydraulic release system (Chapter 6).

- ☐ Clutch disc linings excessively worn (Chapter 6).
- ☐ Clutch disc linings contaminated with oil or grease (Chapter 6).
- ☐ Faulty pressure plate or weak diaphragm spring (Chapter 6).

Judder as clutch is engaged

- ☐ Clutch disc linings contaminated with oil or grease (Chapter 6).
- ☐ Clutch disc linings excessively worn (Chapter 6).
- ☐ Faulty or distorted pressure plate or diaphragm spring (Chapter 6).
- ☐ Worn or loose engine or gearbox mountings (Chapter 2).
- ☐ Clutch disc hub or gearbox input shaft splines worn (Chapter 6).

Noise when depressing or releasing clutch pedal

- ☐ Worn clutch release bearing (Chapter 6).
- ☐ Worn or dry clutch pedal pivot (Chapter 6).
- ☐ Faulty pressure plate assembly (Chapter 6).
- ☐ Pressure plate diaphragm spring broken (Chapter 6).
- ☐ Broken clutch friction plate cushioning springs (Chapter 6).

Manual transmission

Noisy in neutral with engine running

- ☐ Input shaft bearings worn (noise apparent with clutch pedal released, but not when depressed) (Chapter 7A).*
- ☐ Clutch release bearing worn (noise apparent with clutch pedal depressed, possibly less when released) (Chapter 6).

Noisy in one particular gear

- ☐ Worn, damaged or chipped gear teeth (Chapter 7A).*

Difficulty engaging gears

- ☐ Clutch fault (Chapter 6).
- ☐ Worn or damaged gear linkage (Chapter 7A).
- ☐ Worn synchroniser units (Chapter 7A).*

Jumps out of gear

- ☐ Worn or damaged gear linkage (Chapter 7A).

- ☐ Worn synchroniser units (Chapter 7A).*
- ☐ Worn selector forks (Chapter 7A).*

Vibration

- ☐ Lack of oil (Chapter 1).
- ☐ Worn bearings (Chapter 7A).*

Lubricant leaks

- ☐ Leaking oil seal (Chapter 7A).
- ☐ Leaking housing joint (Chapter 7A).*
- ☐ Leaking input shaft oil seal (Chapter 7A).

Although the corrective action necessary to remedy the symptoms described is beyond the scope of the home mechanic, the above information should be helpful in isolating the cause of the condition, so that the owner can communicate clearly with a professional mechanic.

Automatic transmission (DSG)

Note: *Due to the complexity of the DSG transmission, it is difficult for the home mechanic to properly diagnose and service this unit. For problems other than the following, the vehicle should be taken to a dealer service department or automatic transmission specialist. Do not be too hasty in removing the transmission if a fault is suspected, as most of the testing is carried out with the unit still fitted.*

Fluid leakage

- ☐ Automatic transmission fluid is usually dark in colour. Fluid leaks should not be confused with engine oil, which can easily be blown onto the transmission by airflow.
- ☐ To determine the source of a leak, first remove all built-up dirt and grime from the transmission housing and surrounding areas using a degreasing agent, or by steam-cleaning. Drive the vehicle at low speed, so airflow will not blow the leak far from its source. Raise and support the vehicle, and determine where the leak is coming from.

General gear selection problems

- ☐ Chapter 7 deals with checking and adjusting the selector mechanism on automatic transmissions. The following are common problems which may be caused by a poorly-adjusted mechanism:
  - a) *Engine starting in gears other than Park or Neutral.*
  - b) *Indicator panel indicating a gear other than the one actually being used.*

- c) *Vehicle moves when in Park or Neutral.*
- d) *Poor gear shift quality or erratic gear changes.*
- ☐ Refer to Chapter 7B for the selector mechanism adjustment procedure.

Transmission will not downshift (kickdown) with accelerator pedal fully depressed

- ☐ Low transmission fluid level (Chapter 1).
- ☐ Incorrect selector mechanism adjustment (Chapter 7B).

Engine will not start in any gear, or starts in gears other than Park or Neutral

- ☐ Incorrect selector mechanism adjustment (Chapter 7B).

Transmission slips, shifts roughly, is noisy, or has no drive in forward or reverse gears

- ☐ There are many probable causes for the above problems, but unless there is a very obvious reason (such as a loose or corroded wiring plug connection on or near the transmission), the car should be taken to a franchise dealer or specialist for the fault to be diagnosed. The transmission control unit incorporates a self-diagnosis facility, and any fault codes can quickly be read and interpreted by a dealer with the proper diagnostic equipment.

Driveshafts

Vibration when accelerating or decelerating

- ☐ Worn inner constant velocity joint (Chapter 8).
- ☐ Bent or distorted driveshaft (Chapter 8).

Clicking or knocking noise on turns (at slow speed on full-lock)

- ☐ Worn outer constant velocity joint (Chapter 8).
- ☐ Lack of constant velocity joint lubricant, possibly due to damaged gaiter (Chapter 8).

Braking system

Note: *Before assuming that a brake problem exists, make sure that the tyres are in good condition and correctly inflated, that the front wheel alignment is correct, and that the vehicle is not loaded with weight in an unequal manner. Apart from checking the condition of all pipe and hose connections, any faults occurring on the anti-lock braking system should be referred to a VW dealer for diagnosis.*

Vehicle pulls to one side under braking

- ☐ Worn, defective, damaged or contaminated front or rear brake pads on one side (Chapters 1 and 9).
- ☐ Seized or partially-seized front or rear brake caliper (Chapter 9).
- ☐ A mixture of brake pad lining materials fitted between sides (Chapter 9).
- ☐ Brake caliper mounting bolts loose (Chapter 9).
- ☐ Worn or damaged steering or suspension components (Chapters 1 and 10).

Noise (grinding or high-pitched squeal) when brakes applied

- ☐ Brake pad friction lining material worn down to metal backing (Chapters 1 and 9).
- ☐ Excessive corrosion of brake disc – may be apparent after the vehicle has been standing for some time (Chapters 1 and 9).
- ☐ Foreign object (stone chipping, etc) trapped between brake disc and shield (Chapters 1 and 9).

Excessive brake pedal travel

- ☐ Faulty master cylinder (Chapter 9).
- ☐ Air in hydraulic system (Chapter 9).
- ☐ Faulty vacuum servo unit (Chapter 9).
- ☐ Faulty vacuum pump (Chapter 9).

Brake pedal feels spongy when depressed

- ☐ Air in hydraulic system (Chapter 9).
- ☐ Deteriorated flexible rubber brake hoses (Chapters 1 and 9).
- ☐ Master cylinder mountings loose (Chapter 9).
- ☐ Faulty master cylinder (Chapter 9).

Excessive brake pedal effort required to stop vehicle

- ☐ Faulty vacuum servo unit (Chapter 9).
- ☐ Disconnected, damaged or insecure brake servo vacuum hose (Chapters 1 and 9).
- ☐ Faulty vacuum pump (Chapter 9).
- ☐ Primary or secondary hydraulic circuit failure (Chapter 9).
- ☐ Seized brake caliper (Chapter 9).
- ☐ Brake pads incorrectly fitted (Chapter 9).
- ☐ Incorrect grade of brake pads fitted (Chapter 9).
- ☐ Brake pads contaminated (Chapter 9).

Judder felt through brake pedal or steering wheel when braking

- ☐ Excessive run-out or distortion of brake disc(s) (Chapter 9).
- ☐ Brake pad linings worn (Chapters 1 and 9).
- ☐ Brake caliper mounting bolts loose (Chapter 9).
- ☐ Wear in suspension or steering components or mountings (Chapters 1 and 10).

Pedal pulsates when braking hard

- ☐ Normal feature of ABS – no fault

Brakes binding

- ☐ Seized brake caliper piston(s) (Chapter 9).
- ☐ Faulty master cylinder (Chapter 9).

Rear wheels locking under normal braking

- ☐ Rear brake pad linings contaminated (Chapters 1 and 9).
- ☐ Rear brake discs warped (Chapters 1 and 9).

Steering and suspension

Note: *Before diagnosing suspension or steering faults, be sure that the trouble is not due to incorrect tyre pressures, mixtures of tyre types, or binding brakes.*

Vehicle pulls to one side

- [ ] Defective tyre (see *Weekly checks*).
- [ ] Excessive wear in suspension or steering components (Chapters 1 and 10).
- [ ] Incorrect front wheel alignment (Chapter 10).
- [ ] Accident damage to steering or suspension components (Chapters 1 and 10).

Wheel wobble and vibration

- [ ] Front roadwheels out of balance (vibration felt mainly through the steering wheel) (Chapter 10).
- [ ] Rear roadwheels out of balance (vibration felt throughout the vehicle) (Chapter 10).
- [ ] Roadwheels damaged or distorted (Chapter 10).
- [ ] Faulty or damaged tyre (*Weekly checks*).
- [ ] Worn steering or suspension joints, bushes or components (Chapters 1 and 10).
- [ ] Wheel bolts loose (Chapter 1 and 10).

Excessive pitching and/or rolling around corners, or during braking

- [ ] Defective shock absorbers (Chapters 1 and 10).
- [ ] Broken or weak coil spring and/or suspension component (Chapters 1 and 10).
- [ ] Worn or damaged anti-roll bar or mountings (Chapter 10).

Wandering or general instability

- [ ] Incorrect front wheel alignment (Chapter 10).
- [ ] Worn steering or suspension joints, bushes or components (Chapters 1 and 10).
- [ ] Roadwheels out of balance (Chapter 10).
- [ ] Faulty or damaged tyre (*Weekly checks*).
- [ ] Wheel bolts loose (Chapter 10).
- [ ] Defective shock absorbers (Chapters 1 and 10).

Excessively-stiff steering

- [ ] Seized track rod end balljoint or suspension balljoint (Chapters 1 and 10).
- [ ] Broken or incorrectly adjusted auxiliary drivebelt (Chapter 1).
- [ ] Incorrect front wheel alignment (Chapter 10).
- [ ] Steering gear damaged (Chapter 10).

Excessive play in steering

- [ ] Worn steering column universal joint(s) (Chapter 10).
- [ ] Worn steering track rod end balljoints (Chapters 1 and 10).
- [ ] Worn steering gear (Chapter 10).
- [ ] Worn steering or suspension joints, bushes or components (Chapters 1 and 10).

Lack of power assistance

- [ ] Faulty steering gear (Chapter 10).

Tyre wear excessive

Tyres worn on inside or outside edges

- [ ] Incorrect camber or castor angles (Chapter 10).
- [ ] Worn steering or suspension joints, bushes or components (Chapters 1 and 10).
- [ ] Excessively-hard cornering.
- [ ] Accident damage.

Tyre treads exhibit feathered edges

- [ ] Incorrect toe setting (Chapter 10).

Tyres worn in centre of tread

- [ ] Tyres over-inflated (*Weekly checks*).

Tyres worn on inside and outside edges

- [ ] Tyres under-inflated (*Weekly checks*).
- [ ] Worn shock absorbers (Chapter 10).

Tyres worn unevenly

- [ ] Tyres/wheels out of balance (*Weekly checks*).
- [ ] Excessive wheel or tyre run-out (Chapter 10).
- [ ] Worn shock absorbers (Chapters 1 and 10).
- [ ] Faulty tyre (*Weekly checks*).

Electrical system

Note: *For problems associated with the starting system, refer to the faults listed under Engine earlier in this Section.*

Battery will not hold a charge more than a few days

- [ ] Battery defective internally (Chapter 5).
- [ ] Battery electrolyte level low – where applicable (*Weekly checks*).
- [ ] Battery terminal connections loose or corroded (*Weekly checks*).
- [ ] Auxiliary drivebelt worn – or incorrectly adjusted, where applicable (Chapter 1).
- [ ] Alternator not charging at correct output (Chapter 5).
- [ ] Alternator or voltage regulator faulty (Chapter 5).
- [ ] Short-circuit causing continual battery drain (Chapters 5 and 12).

Ignition/no-charge warning light remains illuminated with engine running

- [ ] Auxiliary drivebelt broken, worn, or incorrectly adjusted (Chapter 1).
- [ ] Internal fault in alternator or voltage regulator (Chapter 5).
- [ ] Broken, disconnected, or loose wiring in charging circuit (Chapter 5).

Ignition/no-charge warning light fails to come on

- [ ] Broken, disconnected, or loose wiring in warning light circuit (Chapter 12).
- [ ] Alternator faulty (Chapter 5).

Electrical system (continued)

Lights inoperative

- [ ] Bulb blown (Chapter 12).
- [ ] Corrosion of bulb or bulbholder contacts (Chapter 12).
- [ ] Blown fuse (Chapter 12).
- [ ] Faulty relay (Chapter 12).
- [ ] Broken, loose, or disconnected wiring (Chapter 12).
- [ ] Faulty switch (Chapter 12).

Instrument readings inaccurate or erratic

Fuel or temperature gauges give no reading

- [ ] Faulty gauge sender unit (Chapters 3 and 4).
- [ ] Wiring open-circuit (Chapter 12).
- [ ] Faulty gauge (Chapter 12).

Fuel or temperature gauges give continuous maximum reading

- [ ] Faulty gauge sender unit (Chapters 3 and 4).
- [ ] Wiring short-circuit (Chapter 12).
- [ ] Faulty gauge (Chapter 12).

Horn inoperative, or unsatisfactory in operation

Horn operates all the time

- [ ] Horn contacts permanently bridged or horn push stuck down (Chapter 12).

Horn fails to operate

- [ ] Blown fuse (Chapter 12).
- [ ] Cable or cable connections loose, broken or disconnected (Chapter 12).
- [ ] Faulty horn (Chapter 12).

Horn emits intermittent or unsatisfactory sound

- [ ] Cable connections loose (Chapter 12).
- [ ] Horn mountings loose (Chapter 12).
- [ ] Faulty horn (Chapter 12).

Windscreen/tailgate wipers inoperative, or unsatisfactory in operation

Wipers fail to operate, or operate very slowly

- [ ] Wiper blades stuck to screen, or linkage seized or binding (*Weekly checks* and Chapter 12).
- [ ] Blown fuse (Chapter 12).
- [ ] Cable or cable connections loose, broken or disconnected (Chapter 12).
- [ ] Faulty relay (Chapter 12).
- [ ] Faulty wiper motor (Chapter 12).

Wiper blades sweep over too large or too small an area of the glass

- [ ] Wiper arms incorrectly positioned on spindles (Chapter 12).
- [ ] Excessive wear of wiper linkage (Chapter 12).
- [ ] Wiper motor or linkage mountings loose or insecure (Chapter 12).

Wiper blades fail to clean the glass effectively

- [ ] Wiper blade rubbers worn or perished (*Weekly checks*).
- [ ] Wiper arm tension springs broken, or arm pivots seized (Chapter 12).
- [ ] Insufficient windscreen washer additive to adequately remove road film (*Weekly checks*).

Windscreen washers inoperative, or unsatisfactory in operation

One or more washer jets inoperative

- [ ] Blocked washer jet (Chapter 12).
- [ ] Disconnected, kinked or restricted fluid hose (Chapter 12).
- [ ] Insufficient fluid in washer reservoir (*Weekly checks*).

Washer pump fails to operate

- [ ] Broken or disconnected wiring or connections (Chapter 12).
- [ ] Blown fuse (Chapter 12).
- [ ] Faulty washer switch (Chapter 12).
- [ ] Faulty washer pump (Chapter 12).

Electric windows inoperative, or unsatisfactory in operation

Window glass will only move in one direction

- [ ] Faulty switch (Chapter 12).

Window glass slow to move

- [ ] Regulator seized or damaged, or in need of lubrication (Chapter 11).
- [ ] Door internal components or trim fouling regulator (Chapter 11).
- [ ] Faulty motor (Chapter 11).

Window glass fails to move

- [ ] Blown fuse (Chapter 12).
- [ ] Faulty relay (Chapter 12).
- [ ] Broken or disconnected wiring or connections (Chapter 12).
- [ ] Faulty motor (Chapter 12).

Central locking system inoperative, or unsatisfactory in operation

Complete system failure

- [ ] Blown fuse (Chapter 12).
- [ ] Faulty relay (Chapter 12).
- [ ] Broken or disconnected wiring or connections (Chapter 12).

Latch locks but will not unlock, or unlocks but will not lock

- [ ] Faulty switch (Chapter 12).
- [ ] Broken or disconnected latch operating rods or levers (Chapter 11).
- [ ] Faulty relay (Chapter 12).

One lock fails to operate

- [ ] Broken or disconnected wiring or connections (Chapter 12).
- [ ] Faulty motor (Chapter 11).
- [ ] Broken, binding or disconnected lock operating rods or levers (Chapter 11).
- [ ] Fault in door lock (Chapter 11).

Note: *References throughout this index are in the form* **"Chapter number"** • **"Page number"**. *So, for example, 2C•15 refers to page 15 of Chapter 2C.*

Note: *References throughout this index are in the form* **"Chapter number"** • **"Page number"**. *So, for example, 2C•15 refers to page 15 of Chapter 2C.*

Note: *References throughout this index are in the form* "Chapter number" • "Page number". *So, for example, 2C•15 refers to page 15 of Chapter 2C.*

Note: *References throughout this index are in the form* "**Chapter number**" • "**Page number**". *So, for example, 2C•15 refers to page 15 of Chapter 2C.*

Note: *References throughout this index are in the form* "**Chapter number**" • "**Page number**". *So, for example, 2C•15 refers to page 15 of Chapter 2C.*

Haynes Manuals – The Complete UK Car List

Title	Book No.
ALFA ROMEO Alfasud/Sprint (74 - 88) up to F *	0292
Alfa Romeo Alfetta (73 - 87) up to E *	0531
AUDI 80, 90 & Coupe Petrol (79 - Nov 88) up to F	0605
Audi 80, 90 & Coupe Petrol (Oct 86 - 90) D to H	1491
Audi 100 & 200 Petrol (Oct 82 - 90) up to H	0907
Audi 100 & A6 Petrol & Diesel (May 91 - May 97) H to P	3504
Audi A3 Petrol & Diesel (96 - May 03) P to 03	4253
Audi A4 Petrol & Diesel (95 - 00) M to X	3575
Audi A4 Petrol & Diesel (01 - 04) X to 54	4609
AUSTIN A35 & A40 (56 - 67) up to F *	0118
Austin/MG/Rover Maestro 1.3 & 1.6 Petrol (83 - 95) up to M	0922
Austin/MG Metro (80 - May 90) up to G	0718
Austin/Rover Montego 1.3 & 1.6 Petrol (84 - 94) A to L	1066
Austin/MG/Rover Montego 2.0 Petrol (84 - 95) A to M	1067
Mini (59 - 69) up to H *	0527
Mini (69 - 01) up to X	0646
Austin/Rover 2.0 litre Diesel Engine (86 - 93) C to L	1857
Austin Healey 100/6 & 3000 (56 - 68) up to G *	0049
BEDFORD CF Petrol (69 - 87) up to E	0163
Bedford/Vauxhall Rascal & Suzuki Supercarry (86 - Oct 94) C to M	3015
BMW 316, 320 & 320i (4-cyl) (75 - Feb 83) up to Y *	0276
BMW 320, 320i, 323i & 325i (6-cyl) (Oct 77 - Sept 87) up to E	0815
BMW 3- & 5-Series Petrol (81 - 91) up to J	1948
BMW 3-Series Petrol (Apr 91 - 99) H to V	3210
BMW 3-Series Petrol (Sept 98 - 03) S to 53	4067
BMW 520i & 525e (Oct 81 - June 88) up to E	1560
BMW 525, 528 & 528i (73 - Sept 81) up to X *	0632
BMW 5-Series 6-cyl Petrol (April 96 - Aug 03) N to 03	4151
BMW 1500, 1502, 1600, 1602, 2000 & 2002 (59 - 77) up to S *	0240
CHRYSLER PT Cruiser Petrol (00 - 03) W to 53	4058
CITROËN 2CV, Ami & Dyane (67 - 90) up to H	0196
Citroën AX Petrol & Diesel (87 - 97) D to P	3014
Citroën Berlingo & Peugeot Partner Petrol & Diesel (96 - 05) P to 55	4281
Citroën BX Petrol (83 - 94) A to L	0908
Citroën C15 Van Petrol & Diesel (89 - Oct 98) F to S	3509
Citroën C3 Petrol & Diesel (02 - 05) 51 to 05	4197
Citroen C5 Petrol & Diesel (01-08) Y to 08	4745
Citroën CX Petrol (75 - 88) up to F	0528
Citroën Saxo Petrol & Diesel (96 - 04) N to 54	3506
Citroën Visa Petrol (79 - 88) up to F	0620
Citroën Xantia Petrol & Diesel (93 - 01) K to Y	3082
Citroën XM Petrol & Diesel (89 - 00) G to X	3451
Citroën Xsara Petrol & Diesel (97 - Sept 00) R to W	3751
Citroën Xsara Picasso Petrol & Diesel (00 - 02) W to 52	3944
Citroen Xsara Picasso (03-08)	4784
Citroën ZX Diesel (91 - 98) J to S	1922
Citroën ZX Petrol (91 - 98) H to S	1881
Citroën 1.7 & 1.9 litre Diesel Engine (84 - 96) A to N	1379
FIAT 126 (73 - 87) up to E *	0305
Fiat 500 (57 - 73) up to M *	0090
Fiat Bravo & Brava Petrol (95 - 00) N to W	3572
Fiat Cinquecento (93 - 98) K to R	3501
Fiat Panda (81 - 95) up to M	0793
Fiat Punto Petrol & Diesel (94 - Oct 99) L to V	3251
Fiat Punto Petrol (Oct 99 - July 03) V to 03	4066
Fiat Punto Petrol (03-07) 03 to 07	4746
Fiat Regata Petrol (84 - 88) A to F	1167
Fiat Tipo Petrol (88 - 91) E to J	1625
Fiat Uno Petrol (83 - 95) up to M	0923
Fiat X1/9 (74 - 89) up to G *	0273
FORD Anglia (59 - 68) up to G *	0001

Title	Book No.
Ford Capri II (& III) 1.6 & 2.0 (74 - 87) up to E *	0283
Ford Capri II (& III) 2.8 & 3.0 V6 (74 - 87) up to E	1309
Ford Cortina Mk I & Corsair 1500 ('62 - '66) up to D*	0214
Ford Cortina Mk III 1300 & 1600 (70 - 76) up to P	*0070
Ford Escort Mk I 1100 & 1300 (68 - 74) up to N *	0171
Ford Escort Mk I Mexico, RS 1600 & RS 2000 (70 - 74) up to N *	0139
Ford Escort Mk II Mexico, RS 1800 & RS 2000 (75 - 80) up to W *	0735
Ford Escort (75 - Aug 80) up to V *	0280
Ford Escort Petrol (Sept 80 - Sept 90) up to H	0686
Ford Escort & Orion Petrol (Sept 90 - 00) H to X	1737
Ford Escort & Orion Diesel (Sept 90 - 00) H to X	4081
Ford Fiesta (76 - Aug 83) up to Y	0334
Ford Fiesta Petrol (Aug 83 - Feb 89) A to F	1030
Ford Fiesta Petrol (Feb 89 - Oct 95) F to N	1595
Ford Fiesta Petrol & Diesel (Oct 95 - Mar 02) N to 02	3397
Ford Fiesta Petrol & Diesel (Apr 02 - 07) 02 to 57	4170
Ford Focus Petrol & Diesel (98 - 01) S to Y	3759
Ford Focus Petrol & Diesel (Oct 01 - 05) 51 to 05	4167
Ford Galaxy Petrol & Diesel (95 - Aug 00) M to W	3984
Ford Granada Petrol (Sept 77 - Feb 85) up to B *	0481
Ford Granada & Scorpio Petrol (Mar 85 - 94) B to M	1245
Ford Ka (96 - 02) P to 52	3570
Ford Mondeo Petrol (93 - Sept 00) K to X	1923
Ford Mondeo Petrol & Diesel (Oct 00 - Jul 03) X to 03	3990
Ford Mondeo Petrol & Diesel (July 03 - 07) 03 to 56	4619
Ford Mondeo Diesel (93 - 96) L to N	3465
Ford Orion Petrol (83 - Sept 90) up to H	1009
Ford Sierra 4-cyl Petrol (82 - 93) up to K	0903
Ford Sierra V6 Petrol (82 - 91) up to J	0904
Ford Transit Petrol (Mk 2) (78 - Jan 86) up to C	0719
Ford Transit Petrol (Mk 3) (Feb 86 - 89) C to G	1468
Ford Transit Diesel (Feb 86 - 99) C to T	3019
Ford Transit Diesel (00-06)	4775
Ford 1.6 & 1.8 litre Diesel Engine (84 - 96) A to N	1172
Ford 2.1, 2.3 & 2.5 litre Diesel Engine (77 - 90) up to H	1606
FREIGHT ROVER Sherpa Petrol (74 - 87) up to E	0463
HILLMAN Avenger (70 - 82) up to Y	0037
Hillman Imp (63 - 76) up to R *	0022
HONDA Civic (Feb 84 - Oct 87) A to E	1226
Honda Civic (Nov 91 - 96) J to N	3199
Honda Civic Petrol (Mar 95 - 00) M to X	4050
Honda Civic Petrol & Diesel (01 - 05) X to 55	4611
Honda CR-V Petrol & Diesel (01-06)	4747
Honda Jazz (01 - Feb 08) 51 - 57	4735
HYUNDAI Pony (85 - 94) C to M	3398
JAGUAR E Type (61 - 72) up to L *	0140
Jaguar MkI & II, 240 & 340 (55 - 69) up to H *	0098
Jaguar XJ6, XJ & Sovereign; Daimler Sovereign (68 - Oct 86) up to D	0242
Jaguar XJ6 & Sovereign (Oct 86 - Sept 94) D to M	3261
Jaguar XJ12, XJS & Sovereign; Daimler Double Six (72 - 88) up to F	0478
JEEP Cherokee Petrol (93 - 96) K to N	1943
LADA 1200, 1300, 1500 & 1600 (74 - 91) up to J	0413
Lada Samara (87 - 91) D to J	1610
LAND ROVER 90, 110 & Defender Diesel (83 - 07) up to 56	3017
Land Rover Discovery Petrol & Diesel (89 - 98) G to S	3016
Land Rover Discovery Diesel (Nov 98 - Jul 04) S to 04	4606
Land Rover Freelander Petrol & Diesel (97 - Sept 03) R to 53	3929
Land Rover Freelander Petrol & Diesel (Oct 03 - Oct 06) 53 to 56	4623

Title	Book No.
Land Rover Series IIA & III Diesel (58 - 85) up to C	0529
Land Rover Series II, IIA & III 4-cyl Petrol (58 - 85) up to C	0314
MAZDA 323 (Mar 81 - Oct 89) up to G	1608
Mazda 323 (Oct 89 - 98) G to R	3455
Mazda 626 (May 83 - Sept 87) up to E	0929
Mazda B1600, B1800 & B2000 Pick-up Petrol (72 - 88) up to F	0267
Mazda RX-7 (79 - 85) up to C *	0460
MERCEDES-BENZ 190, 190E & 190D Petrol & Diesel (83 - 93) A to L	3450
Mercedes-Benz 200D, 240D, 240TD, 300D & 300TD 123 Series Diesel (Oct 76 - 85)	1114
Mercedes-Benz 250 & 280 (68 - 72) up to L *	0346
Mercedes-Benz 250 & 280 123 Series Petrol (Oct 76 - 84) up to B *	0677
Mercedes-Benz 124 Series Petrol & Diesel (85 - Aug 93) C to K	3253
Mercedes-Benz A-Class Petrol & Diesel (98-04) S to 54	4748
Mercedes-Benz C-Class Petrol & Diesel (93 - Aug 00) L to W	3511
Mercedes-Benz C-Class (00-06)	4780
MGA (55 - 62) *	0475
MGB (62 - 80) up to W	0111
MG Midget & Austin-Healey Sprite (58 - 80) up to W *	0265
MINI Petrol (July 01 - 05) Y to 05	4273
MITSUBISHI Shogun & L200 Pick-Ups Petrol (83 - 94) up to M	1944
MORRIS Ital 1.3 (80 - 84) up to B	0705
Morris Minor 1000 (56 - 71) up to K	0024
NISSAN Almera Petrol (95 - Feb 00) N to V	4053
Nissan Almera & Tino Petrol (Feb 00 - 07) V to 56	4612
Nissan Bluebird (May 84 - Mar 86) A to C	1223
Nissan Bluebird Petrol (Mar 86 - 90) C to H	1473
Nissan Cherry (Sept 82 - 86) up to D	1031
Nissan Micra (83 - Jan 93) up to K	0931
Nissan Micra (93 - 02) K to 52	3254
Nissan Micra Petrol (03-07) 52 to 57	4734
Nissan Primera Petrol (90 - Aug 99) H to T	1851
Nissan Stanza (82 - 86) up to D	0824
Nissan Sunny Petrol (May 82 - Oct 86) up to D	0895
Nissan Sunny Petrol (Oct 86 - Mar 91) D to H	1378
Nissan Sunny Petrol (Apr 91 - 95) H to N	3219
OPEL Ascona & Manta (B Series) (Sept 75 - 88) up to F *	0316
Opel Ascona Petrol (81 - 88)	3215
Opel Astra Petrol (Oct 91 - Feb 98)	3156
Opel Corsa Petrol (83 - Mar 93)	3160
Opel Corsa Petrol (Mar 93 - 97)	3159
Opel Kadett Petrol (Nov 79 - Oct 84) up to B	0634
Opel Kadett Petrol (Oct 84 - Oct 91)	3196
Opel Omega & Senator Petrol (Nov 86 - 94)	3157
Opel Rekord Petrol (Feb 78 - Oct 86) up to D	0543
Opel Vectra Petrol (Oct 88 - Oct 95)	3158
PEUGEOT 106 Petrol & Diesel (91 - 04) J to 53	1882
Peugeot 205 Petrol (83 - 97) A to P	0932
Peugeot 206 Petrol & Diesel (98 - 01) S to X	3757
Peugeot 206 Petrol & Diesel (02 - 06) 51 to 06	4613
Peugeot 306 Petrol & Diesel (93 - 02) K to 02	3073
Peugeot 307 Petrol & Diesel (01 - 04) Y to 54	4147
Peugeot 309 Petrol (86 - 93) C to K	1266
Peugeot 405 Petrol (88 - 97) E to P	1559
Peugeot 405 Diesel (88 - 97) E to P	3198
Peugeot 406 Petrol & Diesel (96 - Mar 99) N to T	3394
Peugeot 406 Petrol & Diesel (Mar 99 - 02) T to 52	3982

* Classic reprint

* Classic reprint

Preserving Our Motoring Heritage

< The Model J Duesenberg Derham Tourster. Only eight of these magnificent cars were ever built – this is the only example to be found outside the United States of America

Almost every car you've ever loved, loathed or desired is gathered under one roof at the Haynes Motor Museum. Over 300 immaculately presented cars and motorbikes represent every aspect of our motoring heritage, from elegant reminders of bygone days, such as the superb Model J Duesenberg to curiosities like the bug-eyed BMW Isetta. There are also many old friends and flames. Perhaps you remember the 1959 Ford Popular that you did your courting in? The magnificent 'Red Collection' is a spectacle of classic sports cars including AC, Alfa Romeo, Austin Healey, Ferrari, Lamborghini, Maserati, MG, Riley, Porsche and Triumph.

A Perfect Day Out

Each and every vehicle at the Haynes Motor Museum has played its part in the history and culture of Motoring. Today, they make a wonderful spectacle and a great day out for all the family. Bring the kids, bring Mum and Dad, but above all bring your camera to capture those golden memories for ever. You will also find an impressive array of motoring memorabilia, a comfortable 70 seat video cinema and one of the most extensive transport book shops in Britain. The Pit Stop Cafe serves everything from a cup of tea to wholesome, home-made meals or, if you prefer, you can enjoy the large picnic area nestled in the beautiful rural surroundings of Somerset.

John Haynes O.B.E., Founder and Chairman of the museum at the wheel of a Haynes Light 12. >

< *Graham Hill's Lola Cosworth Formula 1 car next to a 1934 Riley Sports.*

The Museum is situated on the A359 Yeovil to Frome road at Sparkford, just off the A303 in Somerset. It is about 40 miles south of Bristol, and 25 minutes drive from the M5 intersection at Taunton.
Open 9.30am - 5.30pm (10.00am - 4.00pm Winter) 7 days a week, *except Christmas Day, Boxing Day and New Years Day*
Special rates available for schools, coach parties and outings Charitable Trust No. 292048